BABE in the WOODS

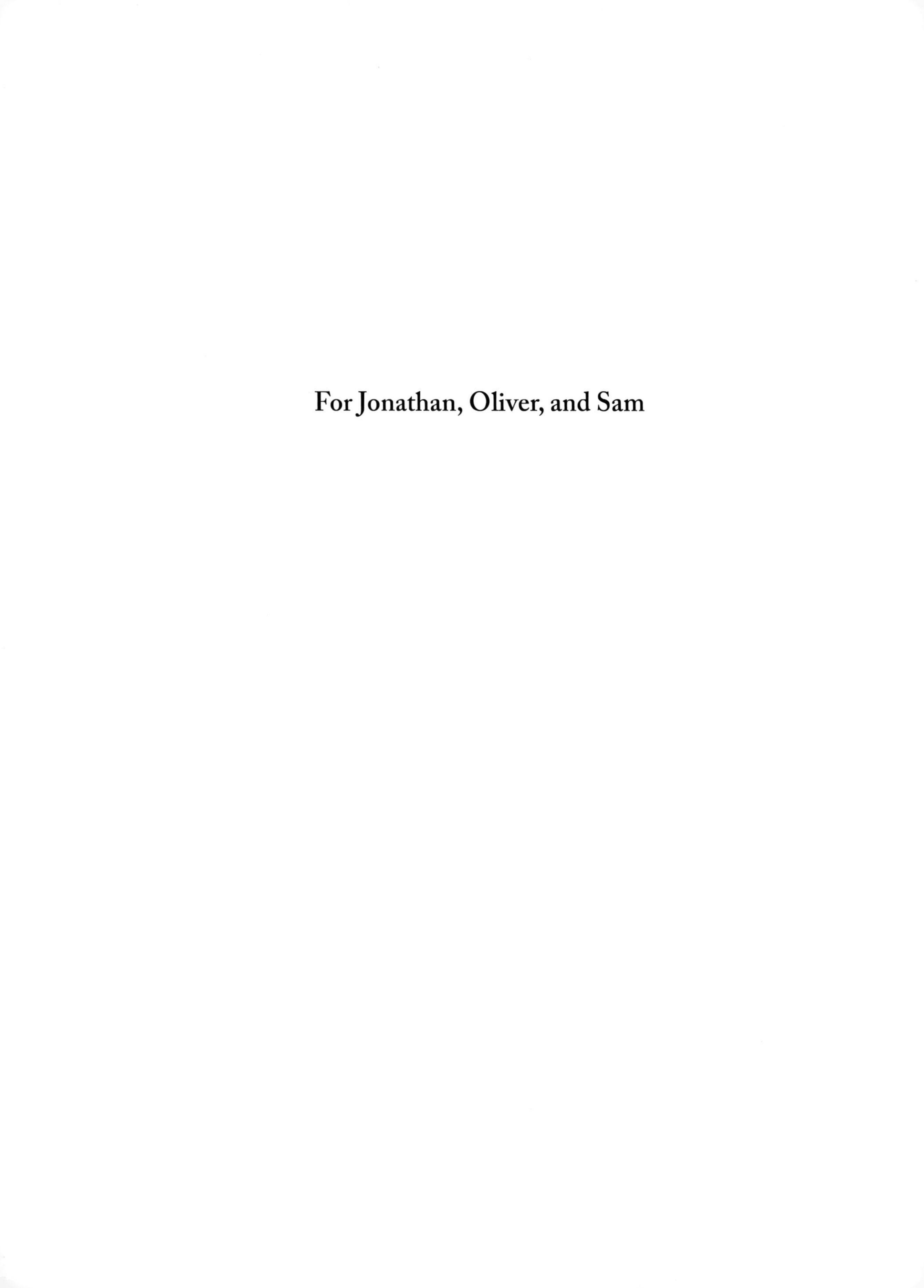

For Jonathan, Oliver, and Sam

Babe in the Woods

or the Art of Getting Lost

Julie Heffernan

ALGONQUIN BOOKS OF CHAPEL HILL 2024

Published by
Algonquin Books of Chapel Hill
Post Office Box 2225
Chapel Hill, North Carolina 27515-2225

an imprint of Workman Publishing
a division of Hachette Book Group, Inc.
1290 Avenue of the Americas
New York, NY 10104

Printed in Thailand.

CIP data for this title is available from the Library of Congress.

ISBN 978-1-64375-559-5 (PB)
ISBN 978-1-64375-560-1 (E-book)

10 9 8 7 6 5 4 3 2 1
First Edition

BABE in the WOODS

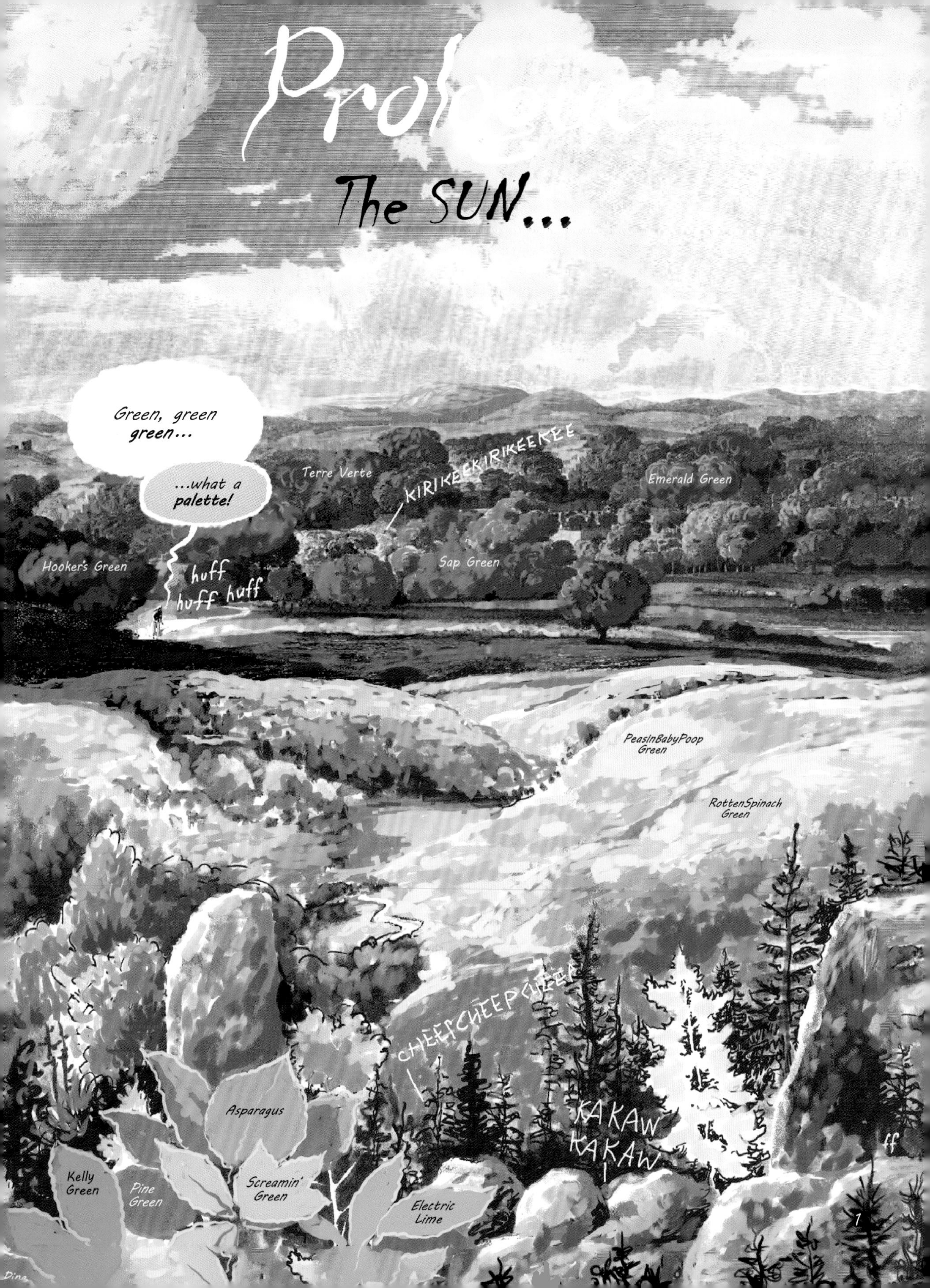

Prol

The SUN...

Green, green **green...**

...what a **palette!**

Terre Verte

KIRIKEEKIRIKEEKEE

Emerald Green

Hooker's Green

huff huff huff

Sap Green

PeasInBabyPoop Green

RottenSpinach Green

CHEEPCHEEPCHEEP

KAKAW KAKAW

ff

Asparagus

Kelly Green

Pine Green

Screamin' Green

Electric Lime

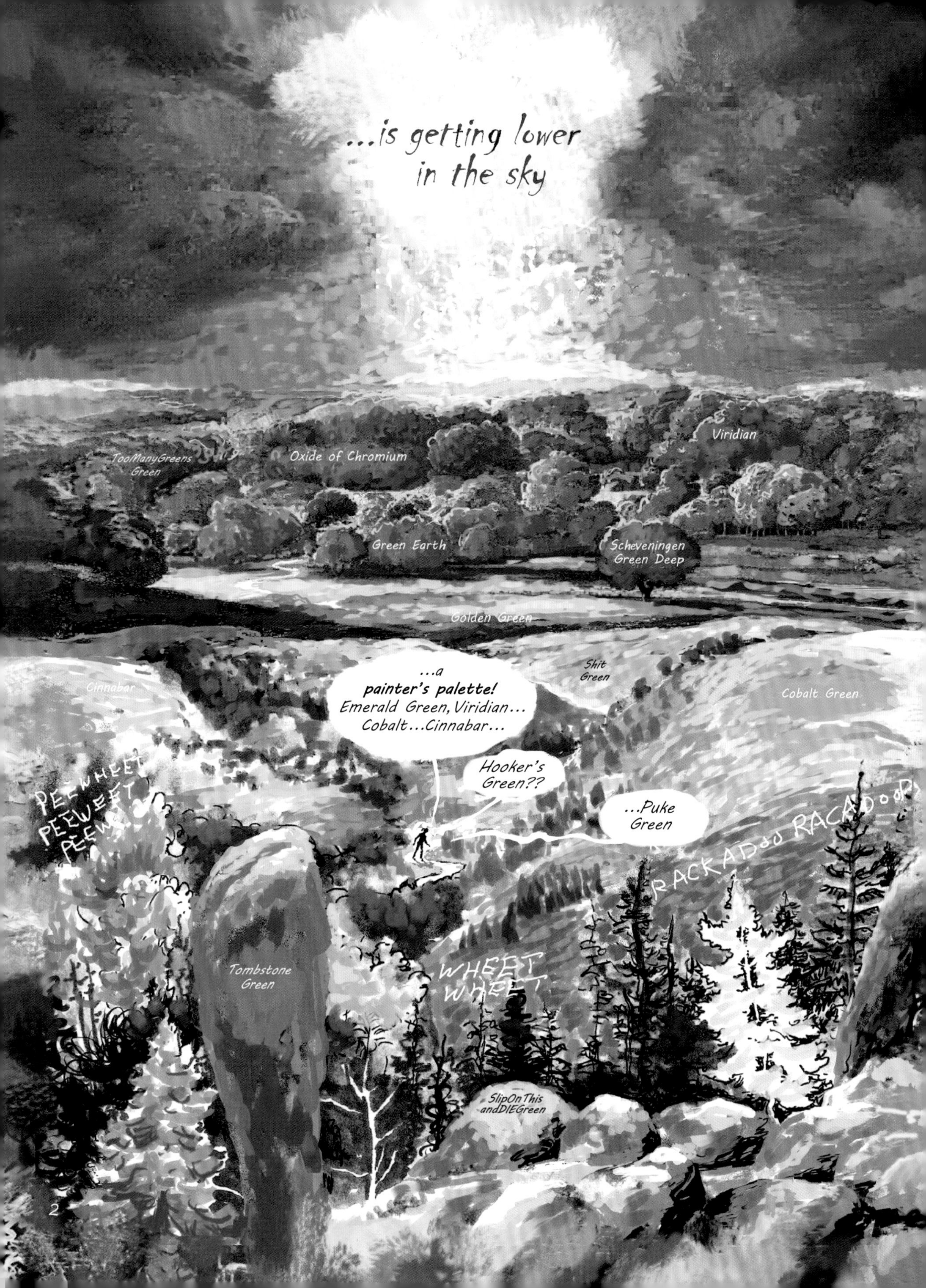
...is getting lower in the sky
TooManyGreens Green
Oxide of Chromium
Viridian
Green Earth
Scheveningen Green Deep
Golden Green
Cinnabar
Shit Green
Cobalt Green
...a **painter's palette!** Emerald Green, Viridian... Cobalt...Cinnabar...
Hooker's Green??
...Puke Green
PEEWHEET PEEWEET PEEW
RACKADOO RACKADOO RACKADOO
WHEET WHEET
Tombstone Green
SlipOn This andDIEGreen

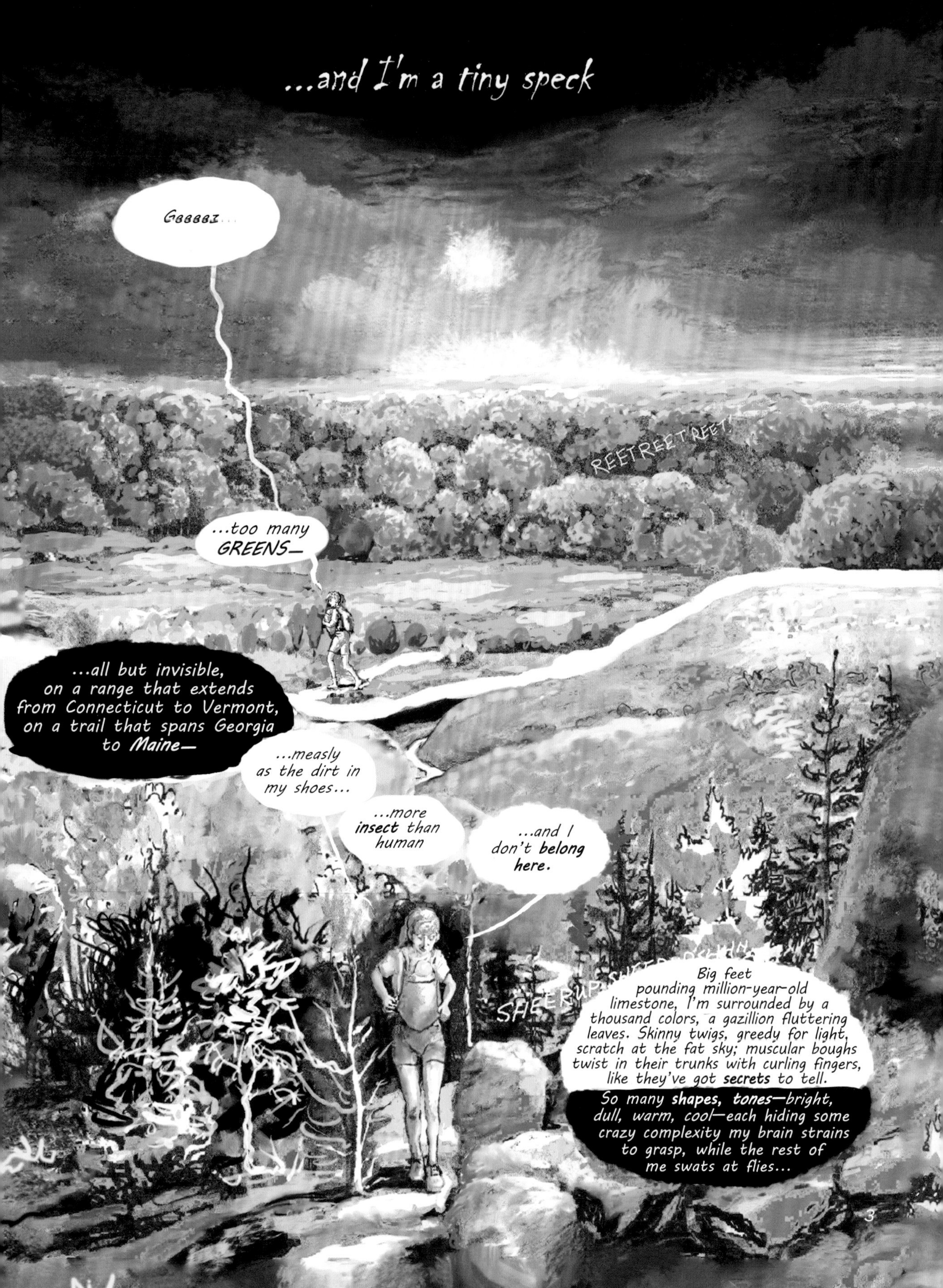
...and I'm a tiny speck
Gbbbbz...
REETREETREET!
...too many GREENS—
...all but invisible, on a range that extends from Connecticut to Vermont, on a trail that spans Georgia to Maine—
...measly as the dirt in my shoes...
...more insect than human
...and I don't belong here.
SHEERUP
Big feet pounding million-year-old limestone, I'm surrounded by a thousand colors, a gazillion fluttering leaves. Skinny twigs, greedy for light, scratch at the fat sky; muscular boughs twist in their trunks with curling fingers, like they've got secrets to tell.
So many shapes, tones—bright, dull, warm, cool—each hiding some crazy complexity my brain strains to grasp, while the rest of me swats at flies...

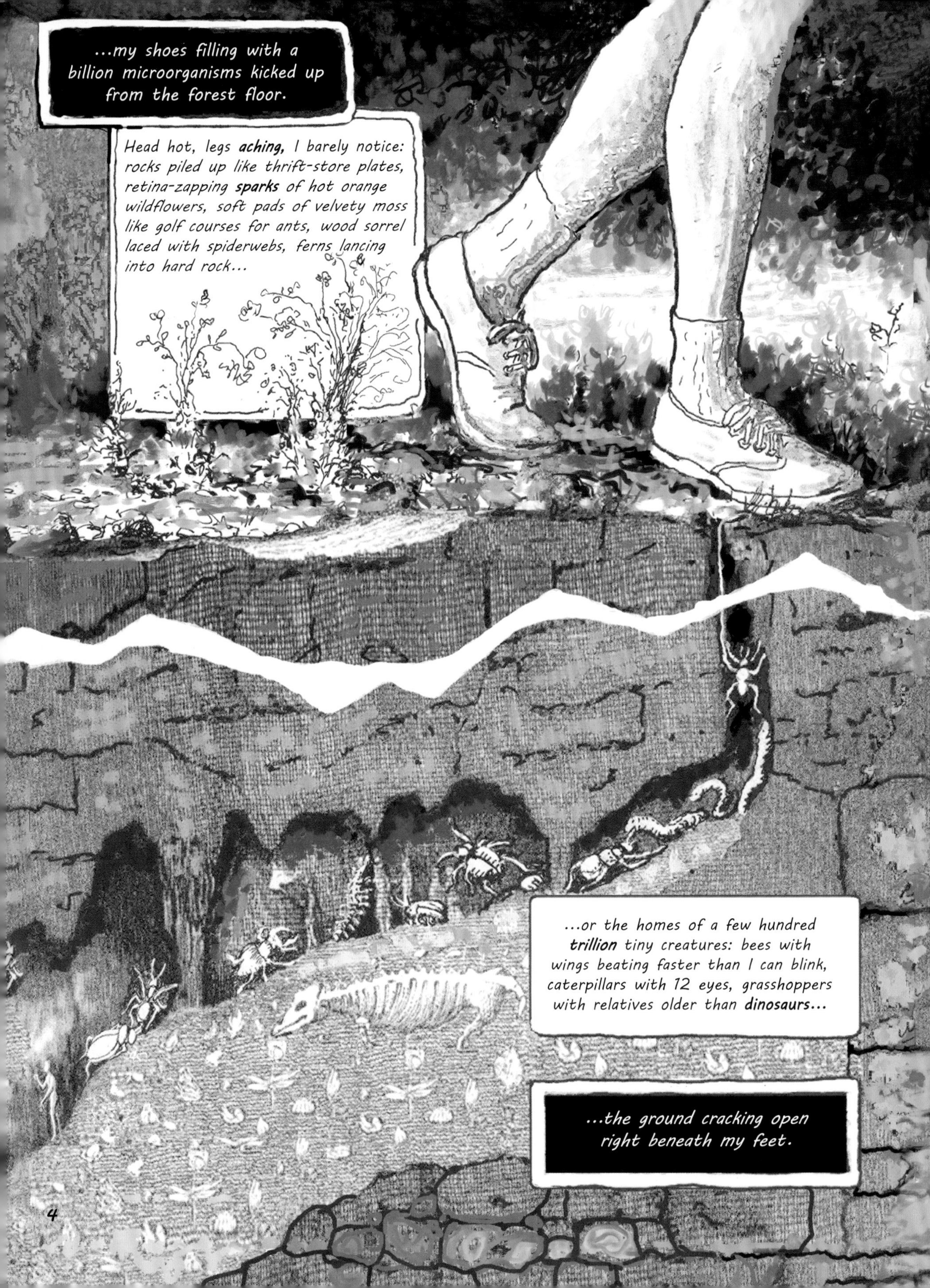
...my shoes filling with a billion microorganisms kicked up from the forest floor.
Head hot, legs **aching,** I barely notice: rocks piled up like thrift-store plates, retina-zapping **sparks** of hot orange wildflowers, soft pads of velvety moss like golf courses for ants, wood sorrel laced with spiderwebs, ferns lancing into hard rock...
...or the homes of a few hundred **trillion** tiny creatures: bees with wings beating faster than I can blink, caterpillars with 12 eyes, grasshoppers with relatives older than **dinosaurs**...
...the ground cracking open right beneath my feet.

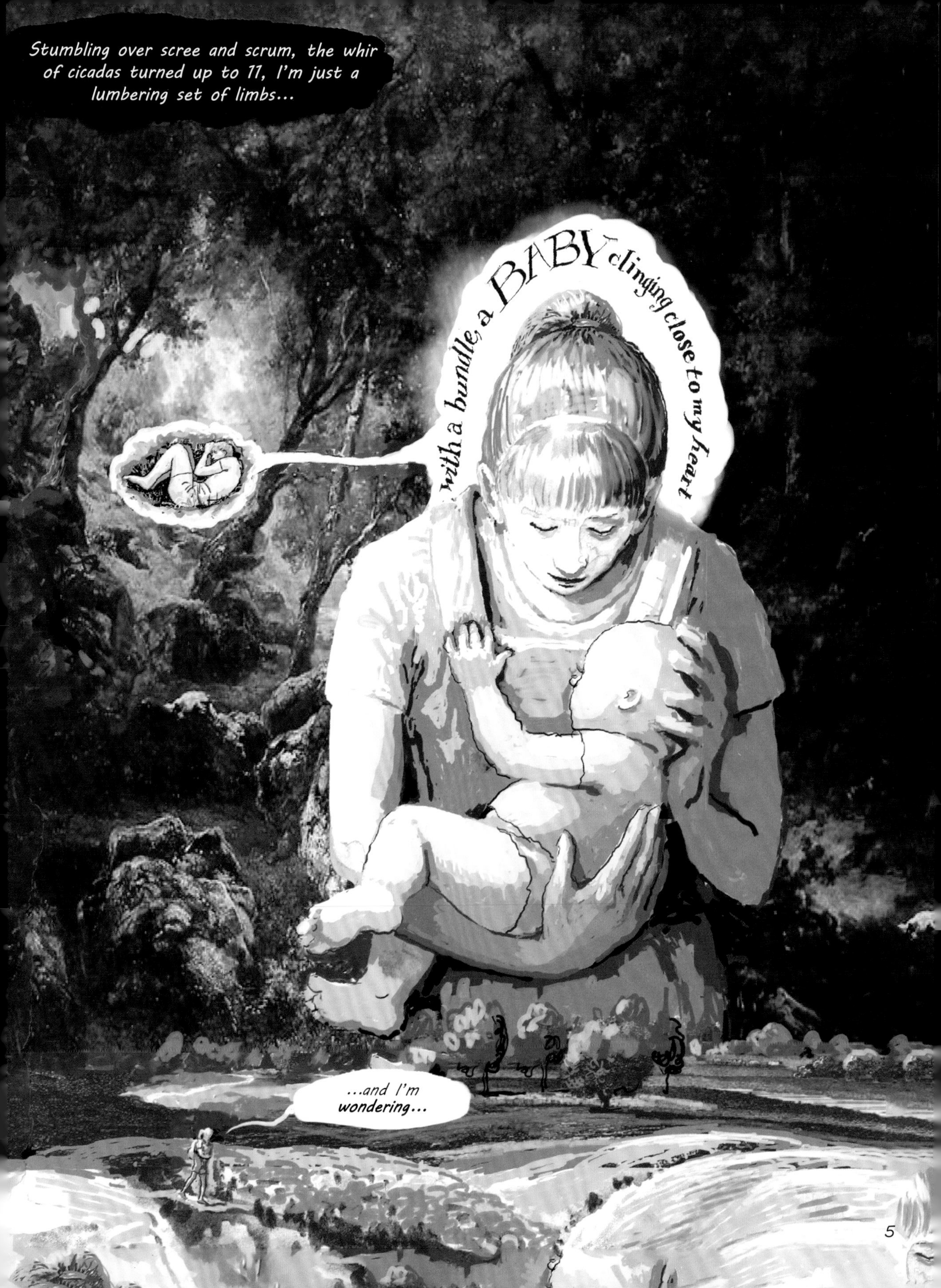
Stumbling over scree and scrum, the whir of cicadas turned up to 11, I'm just a lumbering set of limbs...
with a bundle, a BABY clinging close to my heart
...and I'm wondering...

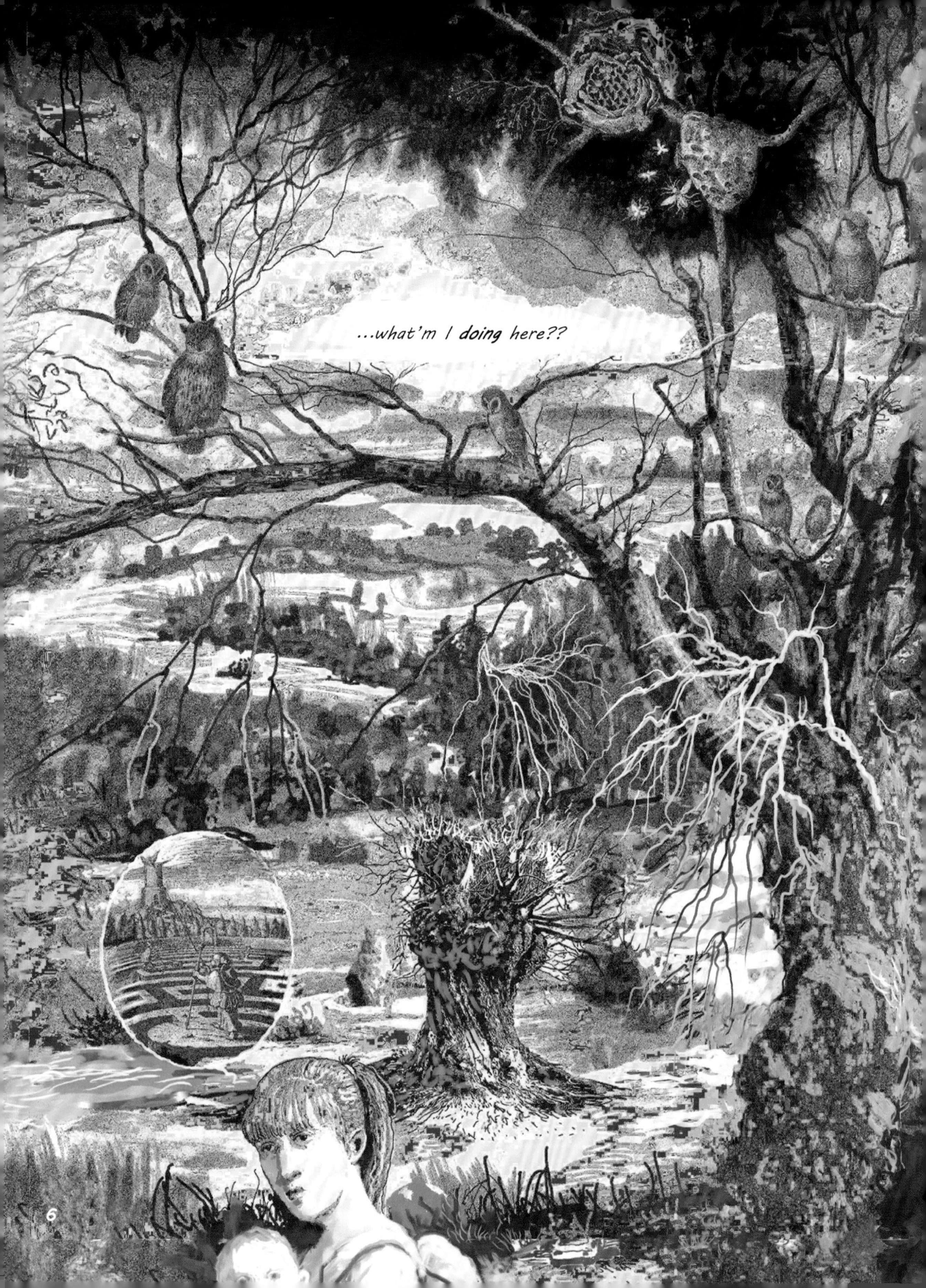
...what'm I *doing* here??

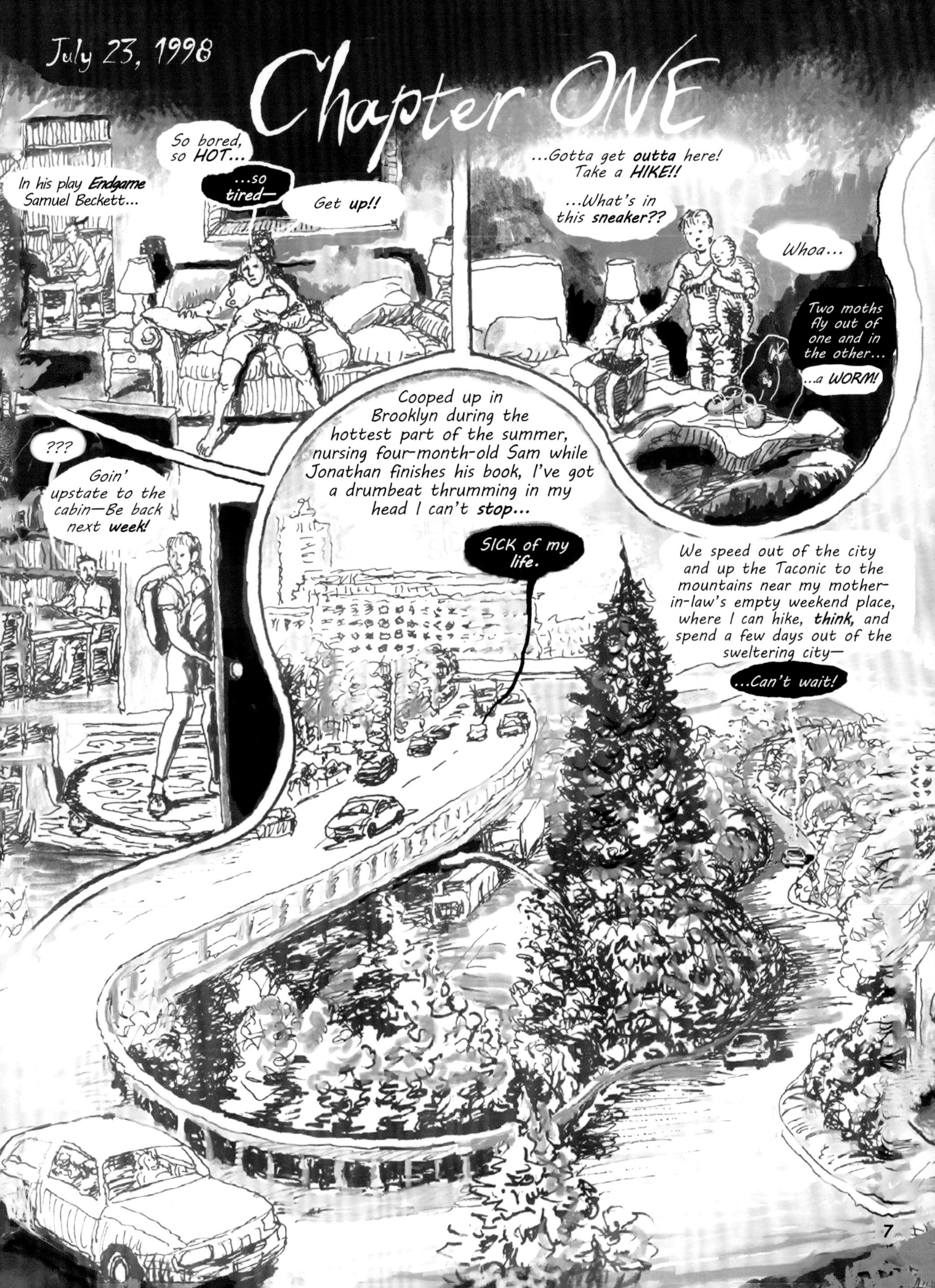
July 23, 1998
Chapter ONE
In his play Endgame Samuel Beckett...
So bored, so HOT...
...so tired—
Get up!!
...Gotta get outta here! Take a HIKE!!
...What's in this sneaker??
Whoa...
Two moths fly out of one and in the other...
...a WORM!
???
Goin' upstate to the cabin—Be back next week!
Cooped up in Brooklyn during the hottest part of the summer, nursing four-month-old Sam while Jonathan finishes his book, I've got a drumbeat thrumming in my head I can't stop...
SICK of my life.
We speed out of the city and up the Taconic to the mountains near my mother-in-law's empty weekend place, where I can hike, think, and spend a few days out of the sweltering city—
...Can't wait!

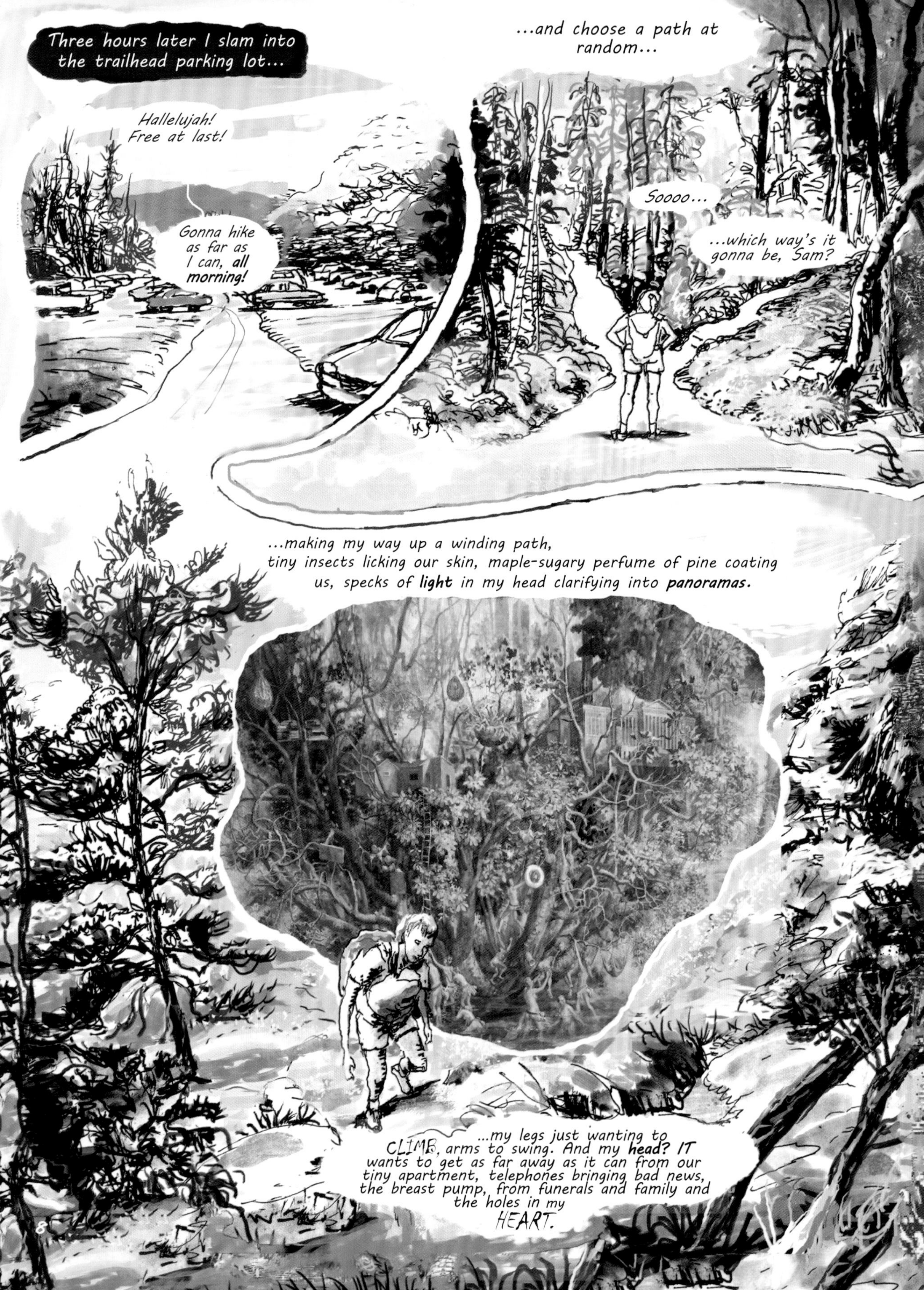
Three hours later I slam into the trailhead parking lot...
Hallelujah! Free at last!
Gonna hike as far as I can, all morning!
...and choose a path at random...
Soooo...
...which way's it gonna be, Sam?
...making my way up a winding path, tiny insects licking our skin, maple-sugary perfume of pine coating us, specks of light in my head clarifying into panoramas.
...my legs just wanting to CLIMB, arms to swing. And my head? IT wants to get as far away as it can from our tiny apartment, telephones bringing bad news, the breast pump, from funerals and family and the holes in my HEART.

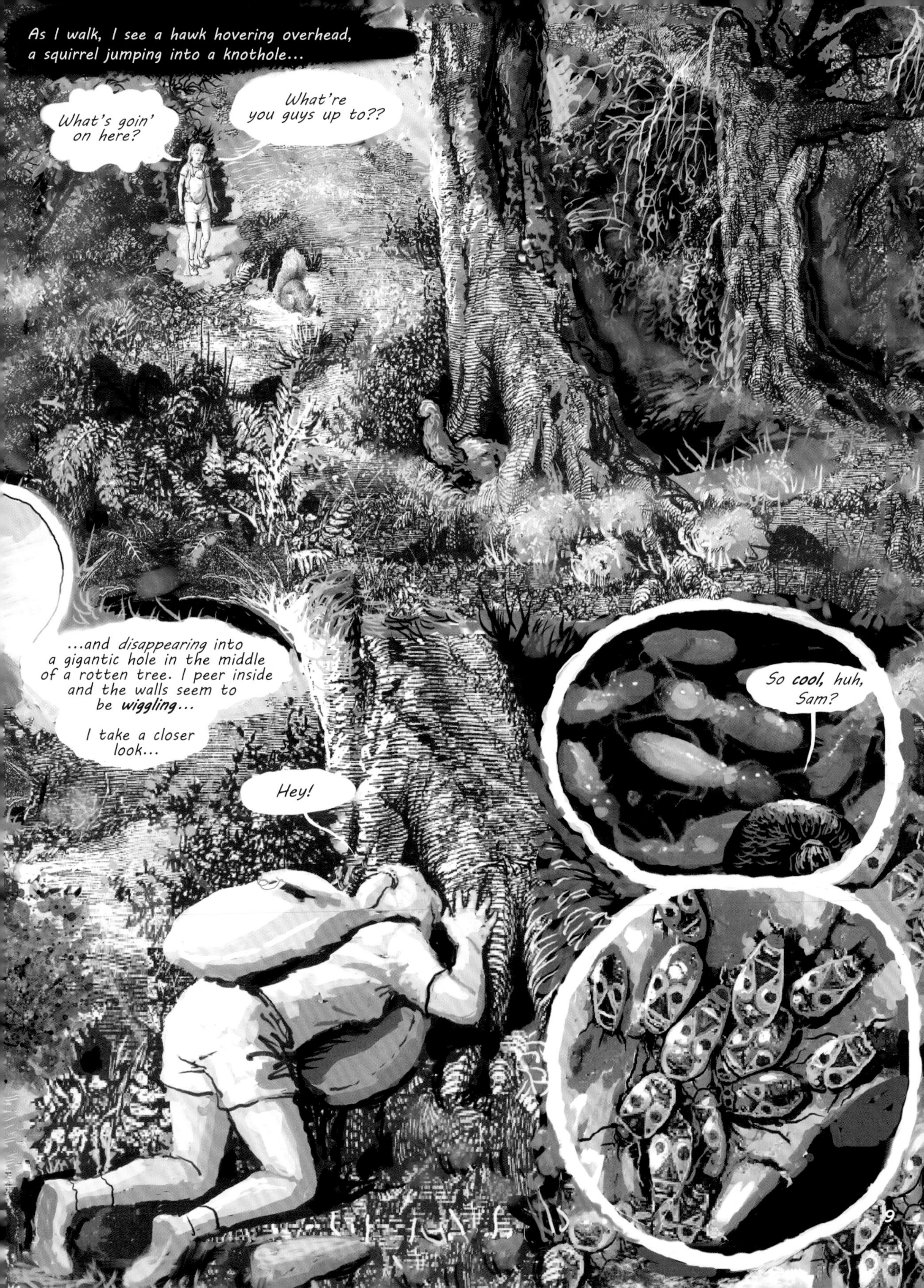
As I walk, I see a hawk hovering overhead, a squirrel jumping into a knothole...
What's goin' on here?
What're you guys up to??
...and disappearing into a gigantic hole in the middle of a rotten tree. I peer inside and the walls seem to be **wiggling**...
I take a closer look...
Hey!
So **cool**, huh, Sam?

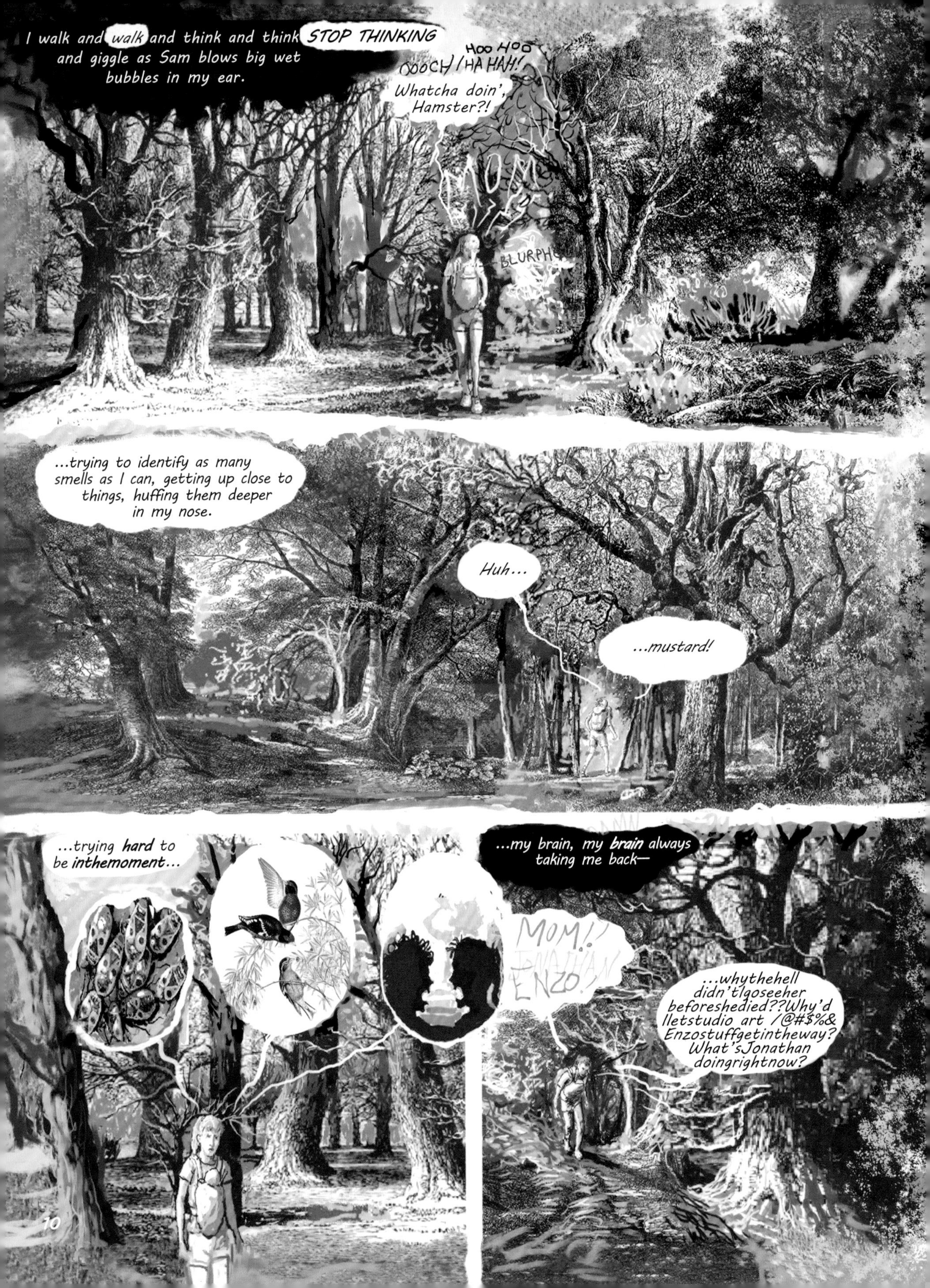

I walk and walk and think and think STOP THINKING and giggle as Sam blows big wet bubbles in my ear.

HOO HOO OOOCH / HA HAH!

Whatcha doin', Hamster?!

MOM

BLURPH

...trying to identify as many smells as I can, getting up close to things, huffing them deeper in my nose.

Huh...

...mustard!

...trying **hard** to be ***inthemoment***...

...my brain, my **brain** always taking me back—

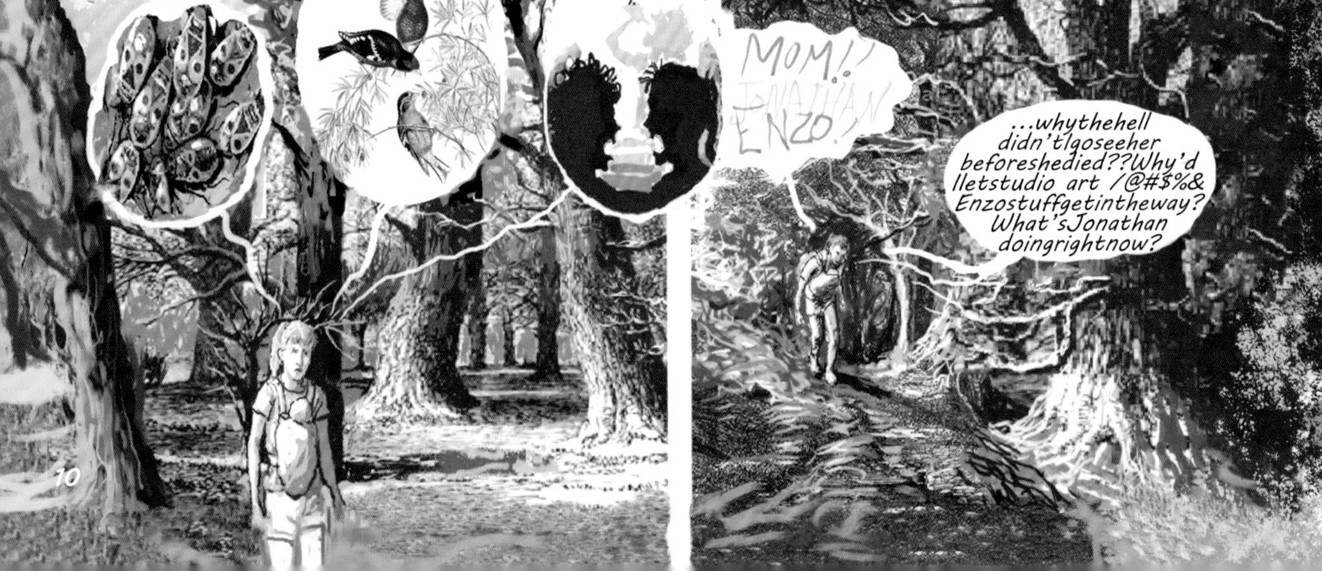

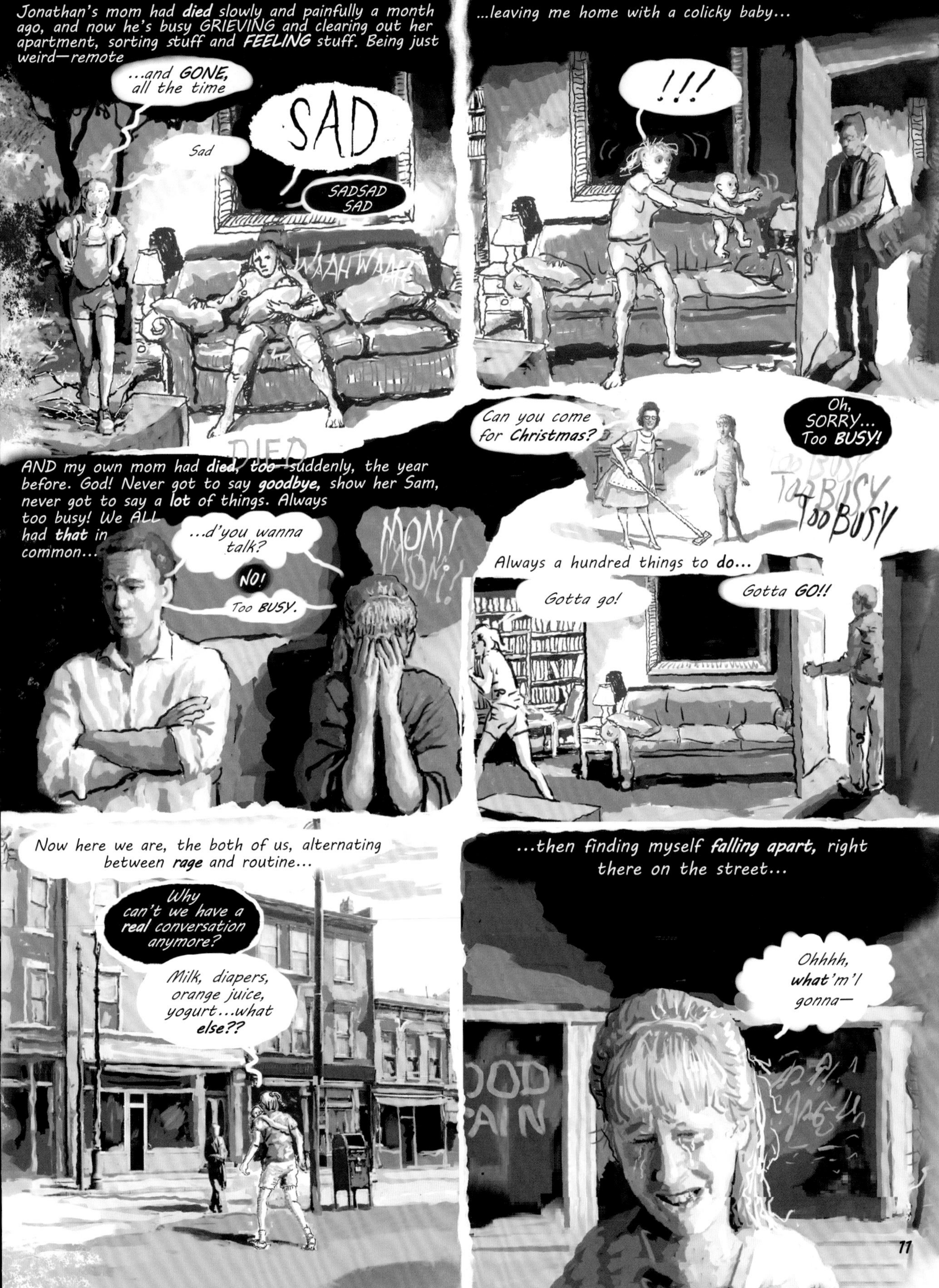
Jonathan's mom had died slowly and painfully a month ago, and now he's busy GRIEVING and clearing out her apartment, sorting stuff and FEELING stuff. Being just weird—remote
...and GONE, all the time
Sad
SAD
SADSAD SAD
WAAH WAAH
...leaving me home with a colicky baby...
!!!
DIED
AND my own mom had died, too—suddenly, the year before. God! Never got to say goodbye, show her Sam, never got to say a lot of things. Always too busy! We ALL had that in common...
Can you come for Christmas?
Oh, SORRY... Too BUSY!
TOO BUSY
TOO BUSY
TOO BUSY
...d'you wanna talk?
NO!
Too BUSY.
MOM! MOM!
Always a hundred things to do...
Gotta go!
Gotta GO!!
Now here we are, the both of us, alternating between rage and routine...
Why can't we have a real conversation anymore?
Milk, diapers, orange juice, yogurt...what else??
...then finding myself falling apart, right there on the street...
Ohhhh, what'm'I gonna—
OOD
AIN

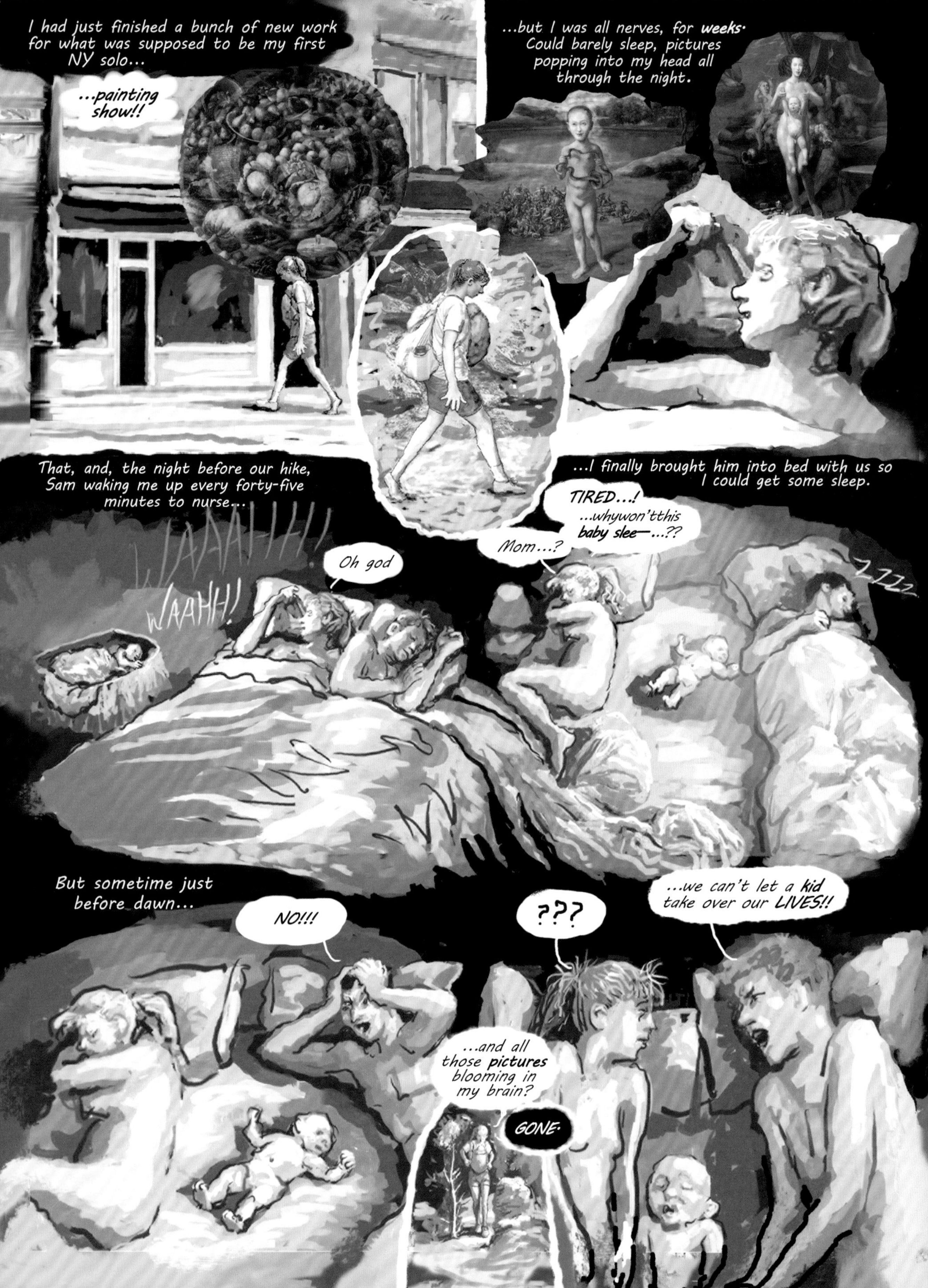
I had just finished a bunch of new work for what was supposed to be my first NY solo...
...painting show!!
...but I was all nerves, for weeks. Could barely sleep, pictures popping into my head all through the night.
That, and, the night before our hike, Sam waking me up every forty-five minutes to nurse...
...I finally brought him into bed with us so I could get some sleep.
WAAAHHH!
WAAHH!
Oh god
Mom...?
TIRED...!
...whywon'tthis baby slee—...??
ZZZz
But sometime just before dawn...
NO!!!
???
...we can't let a kid take over our LIVES!!
...and all those pictures blooming in my brain?
GONE.

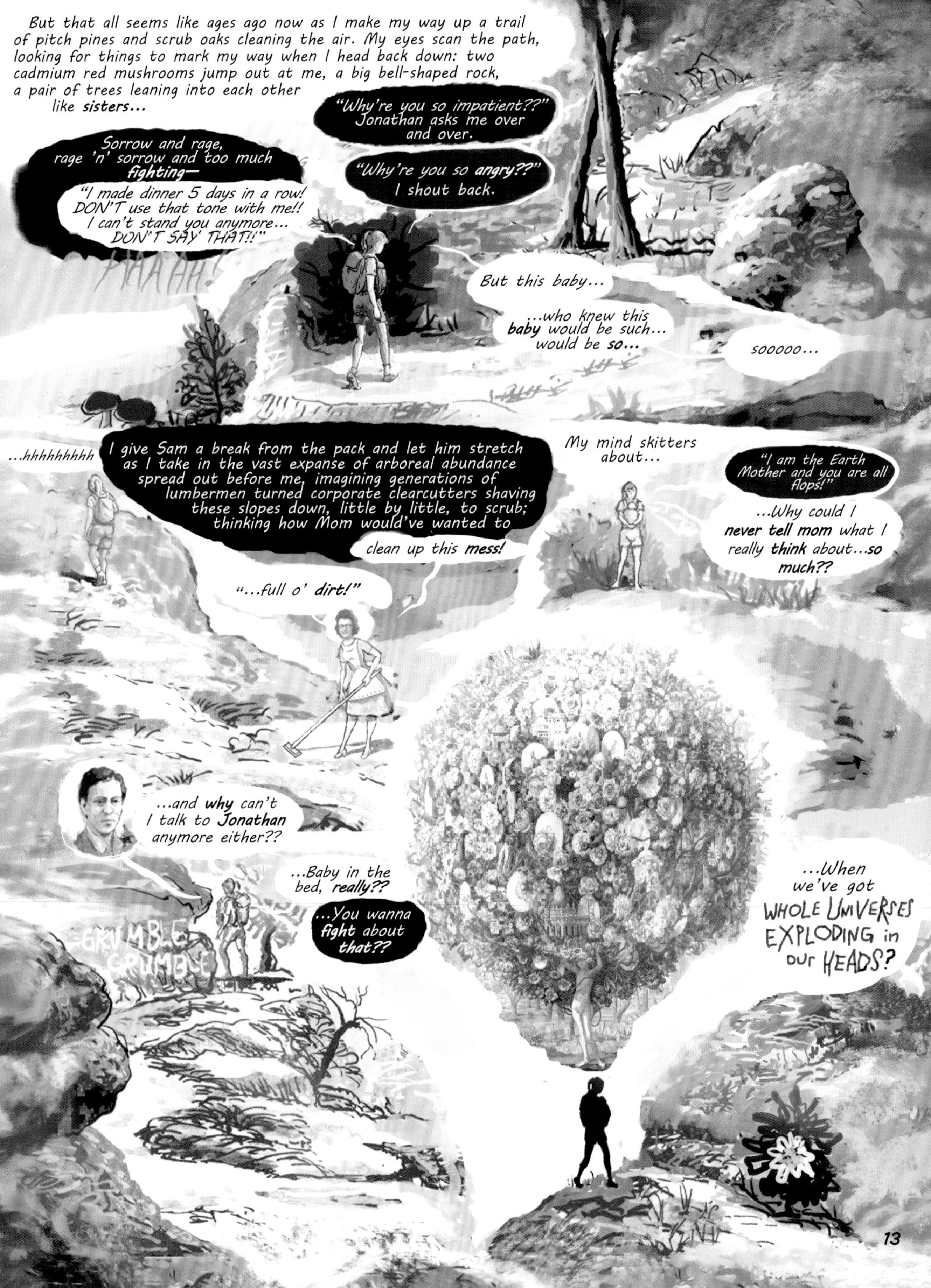

But that all seems like ages ago now as I make my way up a trail of pitch pines and scrub oaks cleaning the air. My eyes scan the path, looking for things to mark my way when I head back down: two cadmium red mushrooms jump out at me, a big bell-shaped rock, a pair of trees leaning into each other like sisters...
"Why're you so impatient??" Jonathan asks me over and over.
Sorrow and rage, rage 'n' sorrow and too much fighting—
"Why're you so angry??" I shout back.
"I made dinner 5 days in a row! DON'T use that tone with me!! I can't stand you anymore... DON'T SAY THAT!!"
But this baby...
...who knew this baby would be such... would be so...
sooooo...
...hhhhhhhhh
I give Sam a break from the pack and let him stretch as I take in the vast expanse of arboreal abundance spread out before me, imagining generations of lumbermen turned corporate clearcutters shaving these slopes down, little by little, to scrub; thinking how Mom would've wanted to
clean up this mess!
"...full o' dirt!"
My mind skitters about...
"I am the Earth Mother and you are all flops!"
...Why could I never tell mom what I really think about...so much??
...and why can't I talk to Jonathan anymore either??
...Baby in the bed, really??
...You wanna fight about that??
GRUMBLE GRUMBLE
...When we've got WHOLE UNIVERSES EXPLODING in our HEADS?

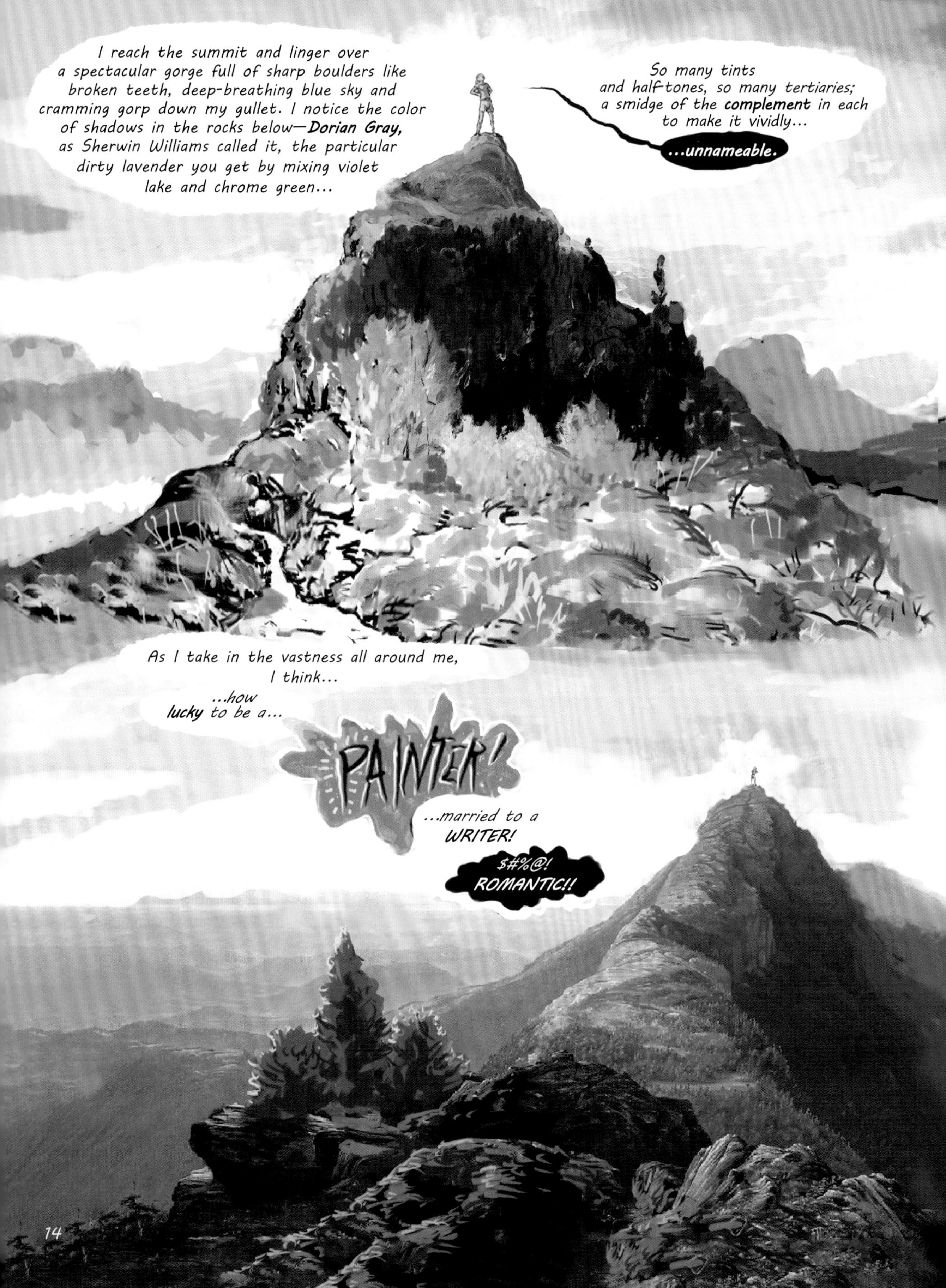
I reach the summit and linger over a spectacular gorge full of sharp boulders like broken teeth, deep-breathing blue sky and cramming gorp down my gullet. I notice the color of shadows in the rocks below—Dorian Gray, as Sherwin Williams called it, the particular dirty lavender you get by mixing violet lake and chrome green...
So many tints and half-tones, so many tertiaries; a smidge of the complement in each to make it vividly...
...unnameable.
As I take in the vastness all around me, I think...
...how lucky to be a...
PAINTER!
...married to a WRITER!
$#%@! ROMANTIC!!

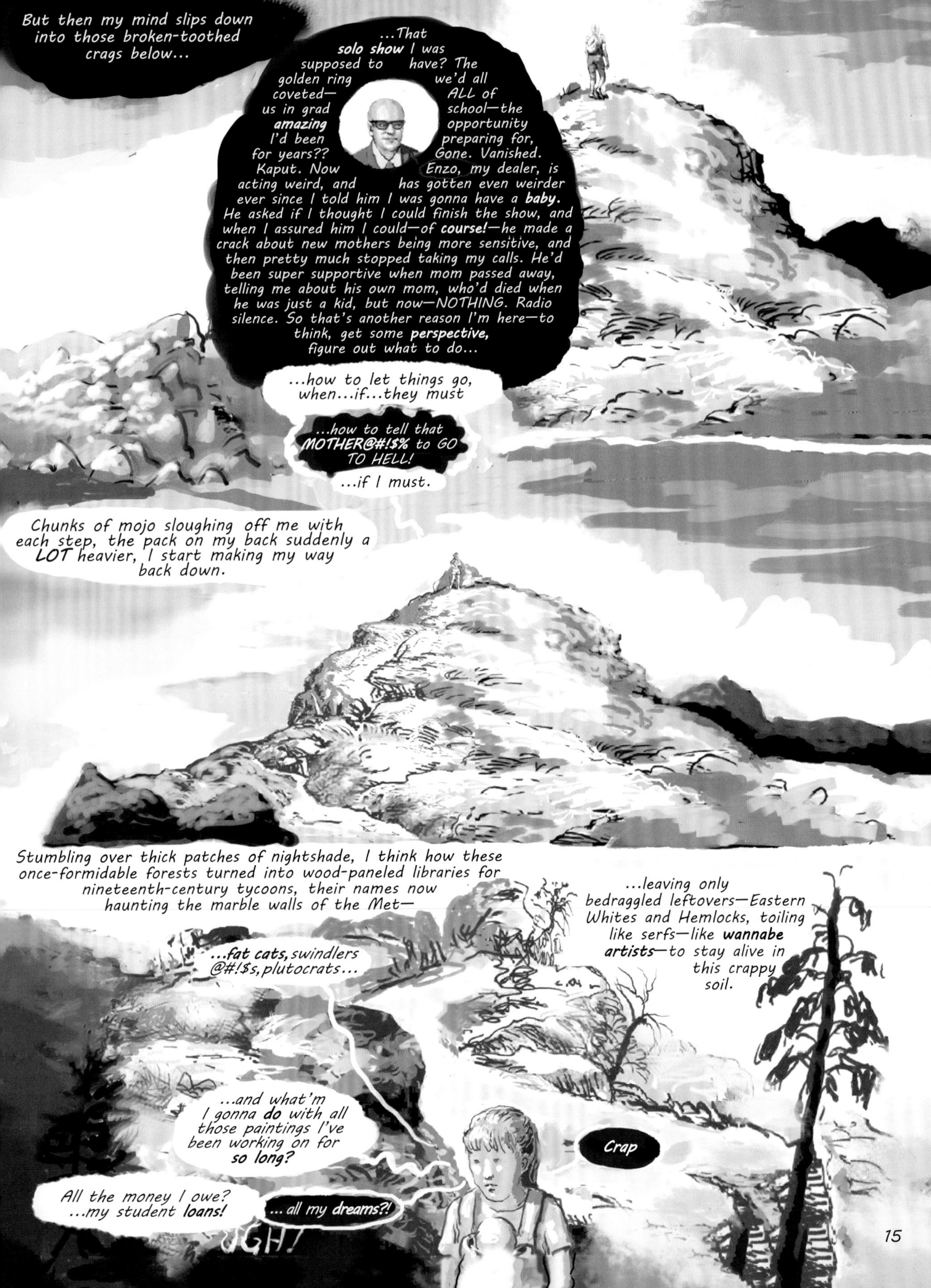

But then my mind slips down into those broken-toothed crags below...
...That solo show I was supposed to have? The golden ring we'd all coveted—ALL of us in grad school—the amazing opportunity I'd been preparing for, for years?? Gone. Vanished. Kaput. Now Enzo, my dealer, is acting weird, and has gotten even weirder ever since I told him I was gonna have a baby. He asked if I thought I could finish the show, and when I assured him I could—of course!—he made a crack about new mothers being more sensitive, and then pretty much stopped taking my calls. He'd been super supportive when mom passed away, telling me about his own mom, who'd died when he was just a kid, but now—NOTHING. Radio silence. So that's another reason I'm here—to think, get some perspective, figure out what to do...
...how to let things go, when...if...they must
...how to tell that MOTHER@#!$% to GO TO HELL!
...if I must.
Chunks of mojo sloughing off me with each step, the pack on my back suddenly a LOT heavier, I start making my way back down.
Stumbling over thick patches of nightshade, I think how these once-formidable forests turned into wood-paneled libraries for nineteenth-century tycoons, their names now haunting the marble walls of the Met—
...fat cats, swindlers @#!$s, plutocrats...
...leaving only bedraggled leftovers—Eastern Whites and Hemlocks, toiling like serfs—like wannabe artists—to stay alive in this crappy soil.
...and what'm I gonna do with all those paintings I've been working on for so long?
Crap
All the money I owe? ...my student loans!
... all my dreams?!

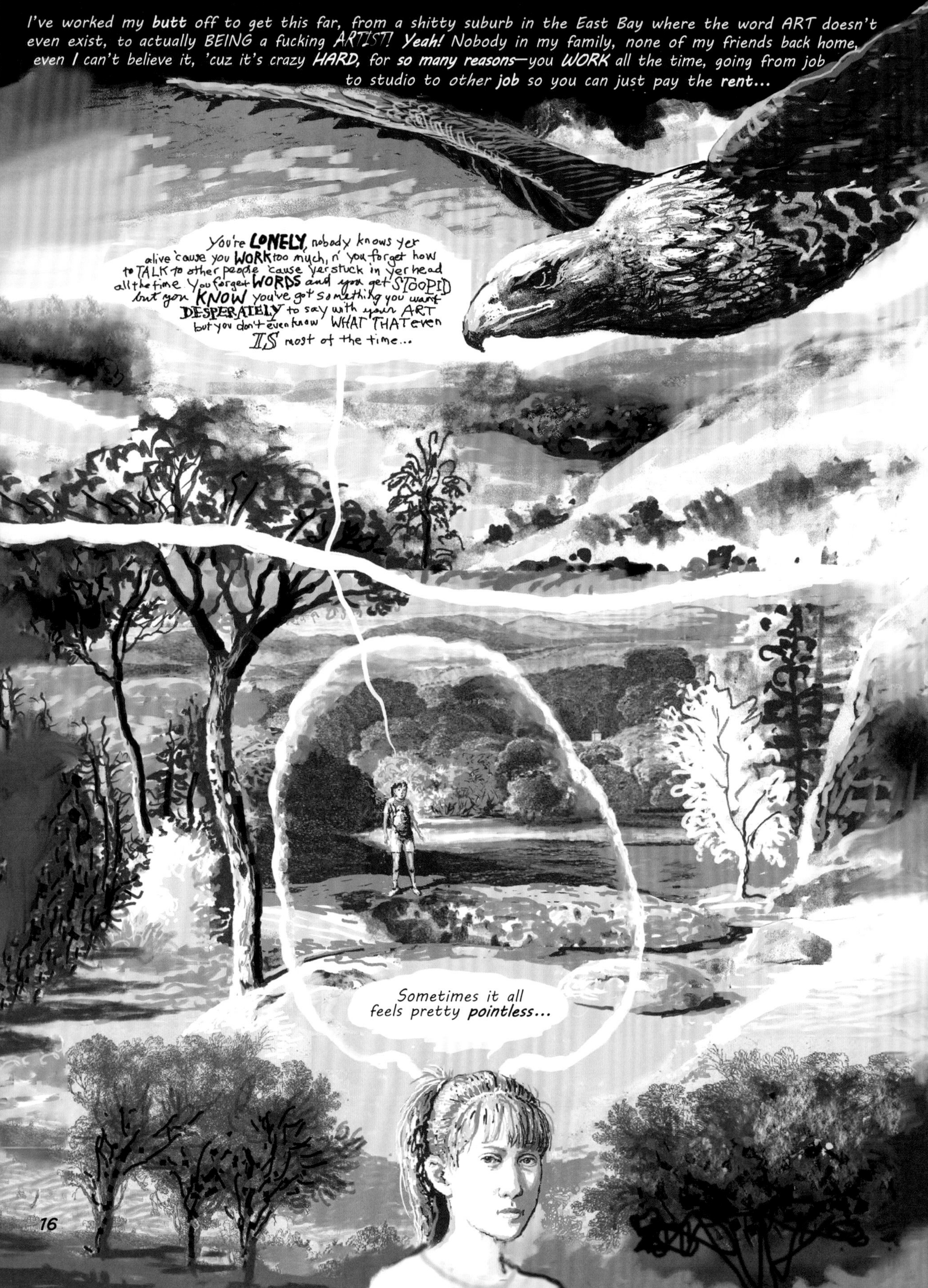
I've worked my butt off to get this far, from a shitty suburb in the East Bay where the word ART doesn't even exist, to actually BEING a fucking ARTIST! Yeah! Nobody in my family, none of my friends back home, even I can't believe it, 'cuz it's crazy HARD, for so many reasons—you WORK all the time, going from job to studio to other job so you can just pay the rent...
You're LONELY, nobody knows yer alive 'cause you WORK too much, n' you forget how to TALK to other people 'cause yer stuck in yer head all the time. You forget WORDS and you get STOOPID but you KNOW you've got something you want DESPERATELY to say with your ART but you don't even know WHAT THAT even IS most of the time...
Sometimes it all feels pretty pointless...

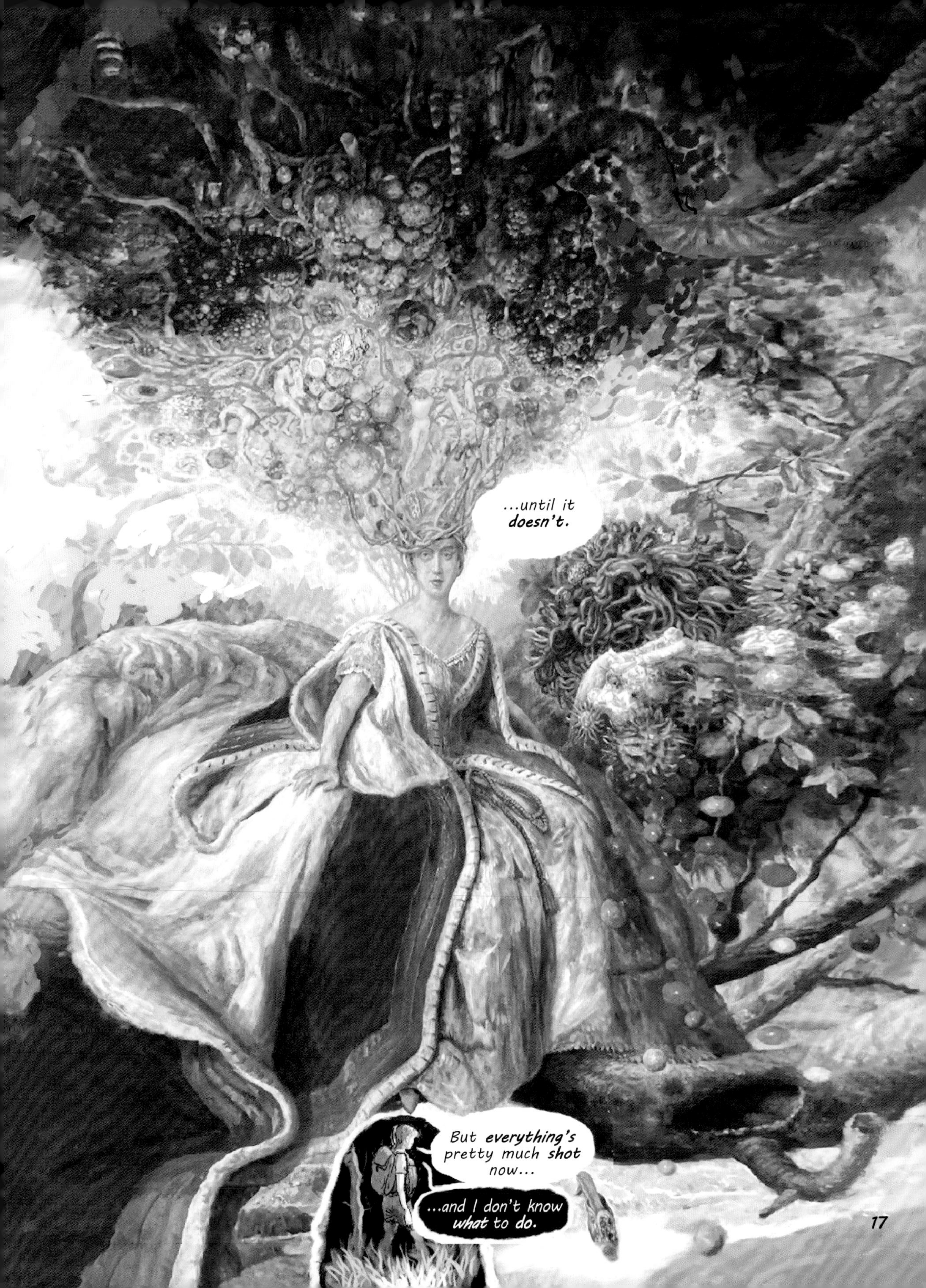
...until it doesn't.
But everything's pretty much shot now...
...and I don't know what to do.

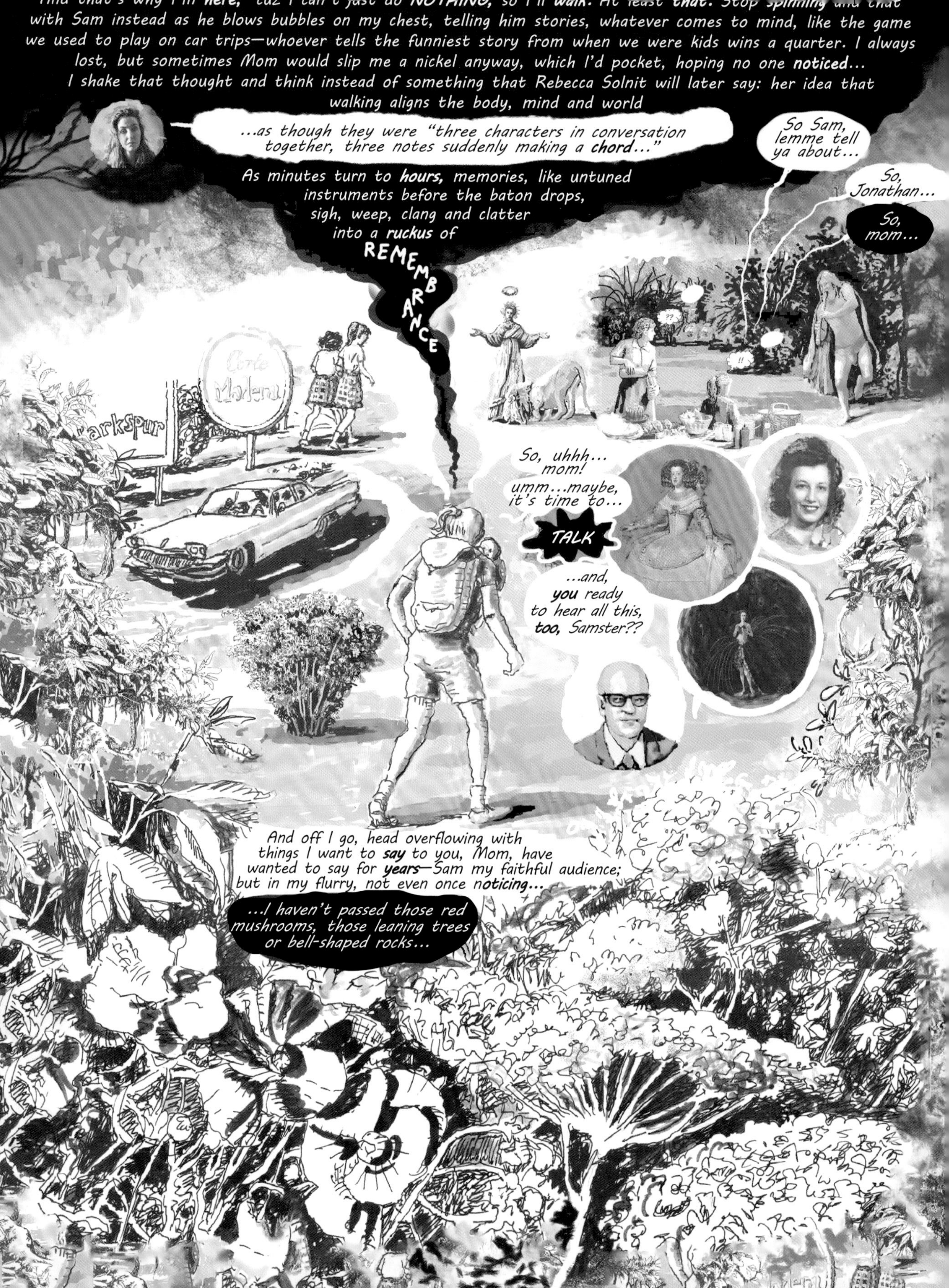

And that's why I'm here, 'cuz I can't just do NOTHING, so I'll walk. At least that. Stop spinning and chat with Sam instead as he blows bubbles on my chest, telling him stories, whatever comes to mind, like the game we used to play on car trips—whoever tells the funniest story from when we were kids wins a quarter. I always lost, but sometimes Mom would slip me a nickel anyway, which I'd pocket, hoping no one noticed...
I shake that thought and think instead of something that Rebecca Solnit will later say: her idea that walking aligns the body, mind and world
...as though they were "three characters in conversation together, three notes suddenly making a chord..."
As minutes turn to hours, memories, like untuned instruments before the baton drops, sigh, weep, clang and clatter into a ruckus of
REMEMBRANCE
So Sam, lemme tell ya about...
So, Jonathan...
So, mom...
So, uhhh... mom! umm...maybe, it's time to...
TALK
...and, you ready to hear all this, too, Samster??
And off I go, head overflowing with things I want to say to you, Mom, have wanted to say for years—Sam my faithful audience; but in my flurry, not even once noticing...
...I haven't passed those red mushrooms, those leaning trees or bell-shaped rocks...

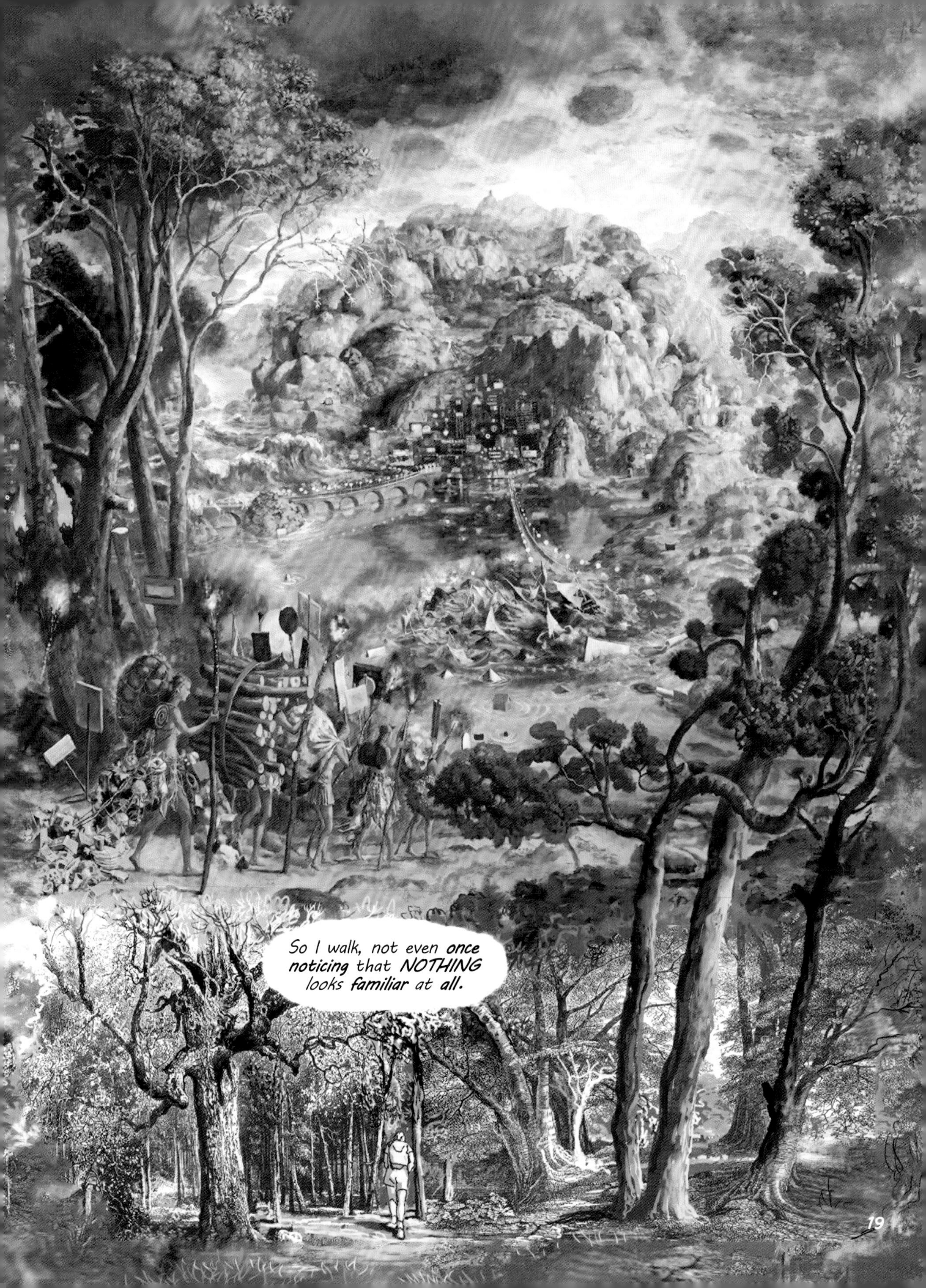
So I walk, not even once noticing that NOTHING looks familiar at all.

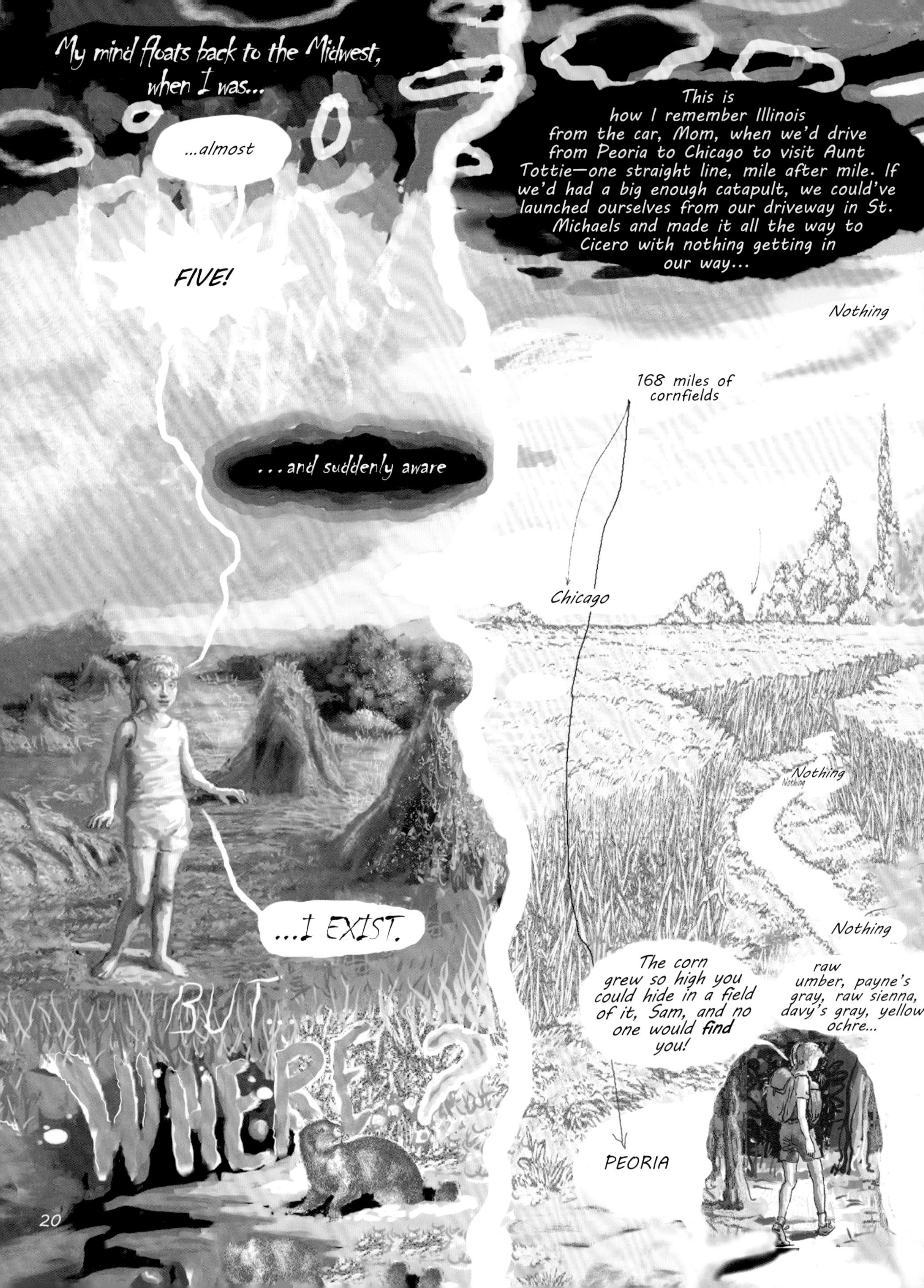

My mind floats back to the Midwest, when I was...
...almost
FIVE!
...and suddenly aware
...I EXIST.
BUT... WHERE?
This is how I remember Illinois from the car, Mom, when we'd drive from Peoria to Chicago to visit Aunt Tottie—one straight line, mile after mile. If we'd had a big enough catapult, we could've launched ourselves from our driveway in St. Michaels and made it all the way to Cicero with nothing getting in our way...
Nothing
168 miles of cornfields
Chicago
Nothing
Nothing
The corn grew so high you could hide in a field of it, Sam, and no one would **find** you!
raw umber, payne's gray, raw sienna, davy's gray, yellow ochre...
PEORIA

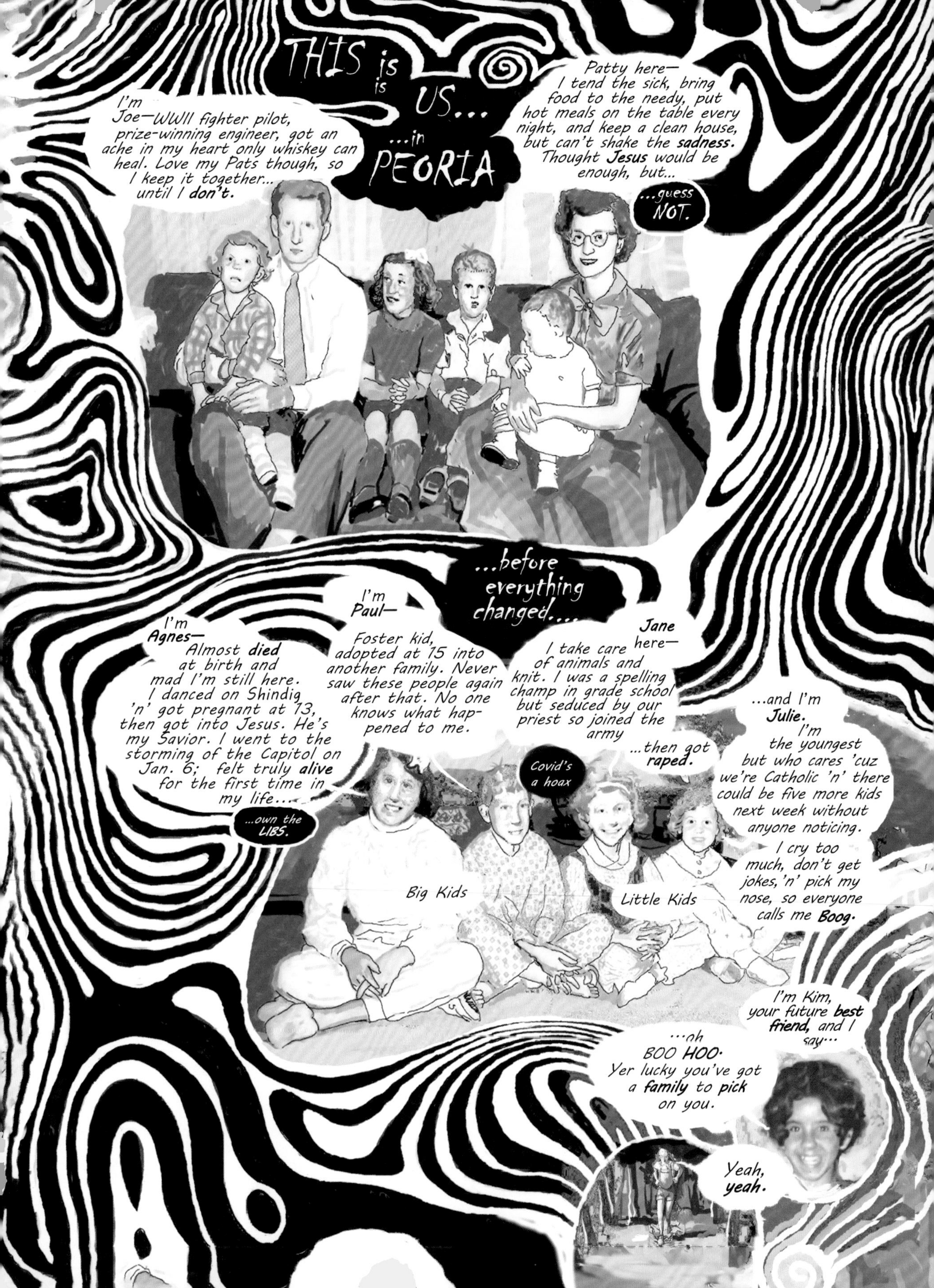
THIS is US... ...in PEORIA
I'm Joe—WWII fighter pilot, prize-winning engineer, got an ache in my heart only whiskey can heal. Love my Pats though, so I keep it together... until I **don't**.
Patty here— I tend the sick, bring food to the needy, put hot meals on the table every night, and keep a clean house, but can't shake the **sadness**. Thought **Jesus** would be enough, but...
...guess NOT.
...before everything changed....
I'm **Agnes**— Almost **died** at birth and mad I'm still here. I danced on Shindig 'n' got pregnant at 13, then got into Jesus. He's my Savior. I went to the storming of the Capitol on Jan. 6; felt truly **alive** for the first time in my life...
...own the LIBS.
I'm **Paul**— Foster kid, adopted at 15 into another family. Never saw these people again after that. No one knows what happened to me.
Covid's a hoax
Jane here— I take care of animals and knit. I was a spelling champ in grade school but seduced by our priest so joined the army
...then got **raped**.
...and I'm **Julie**. I'm the youngest but who cares 'cuz we're Catholic 'n' there could be five more kids next week without anyone noticing.
I cry too much, don't get jokes, 'n' pick my nose, so everyone calls me **Boog**.
Big Kids
Little Kids
I'm Kim, your future **best friend**, and I say...
...oh BOO HOO. Yer lucky you've got a **family** to **pick** on you.
Yeah, **yeah**.

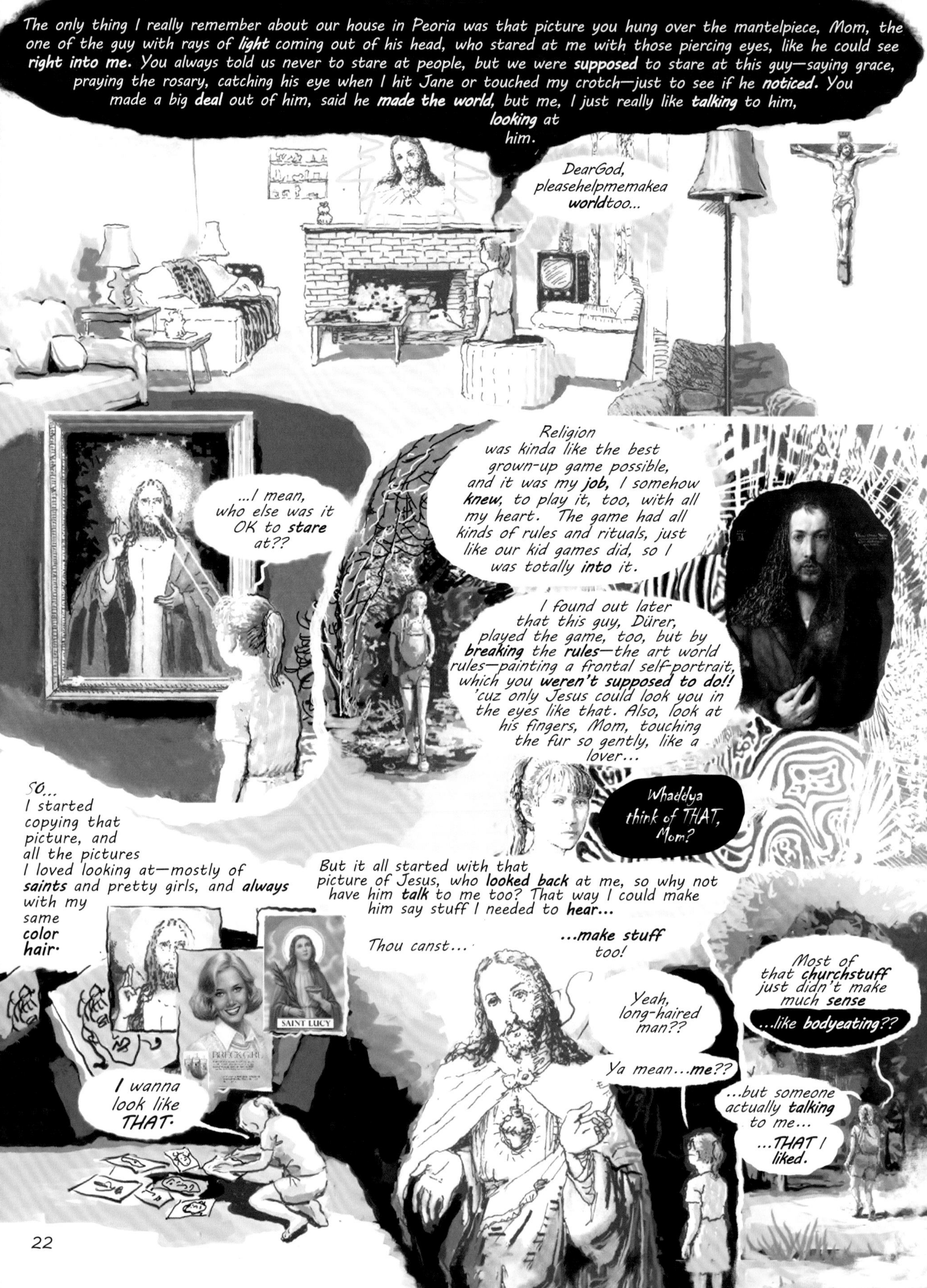

The only thing I really remember about our house in Peoria was that picture you hung over the mantelpiece, Mom, the one of the guy with rays of light coming out of his head, who stared at me with those piercing eyes, like he could see right into me. You always told us never to stare at people, but we were supposed to stare at this guy—saying grace, praying the rosary, catching his eye when I hit Jane or touched my crotch—just to see if he noticed. You made a big deal out of him, said he made the world, but me, I just really like talking to him, looking at him.
DearGod, pleasehelpmemakea worldtoo...
...I mean, who else was it OK to stare at??
Religion was kinda like the best grown-up game possible, and it was my job, I somehow knew, to play it, too, with all my heart. The game had all kinds of rules and rituals, just like our kid games did, so I was totally into it.
I found out later that this guy, Dürer, played the game, too, but by breaking the rules—the art world rules—painting a frontal self-portrait, which you weren't supposed to do!! 'cuz only Jesus could look you in the eyes like that. Also, look at his fingers, Mom, touching the fur so gently, like a lover...
Whaddya think of THAT, Mom?
SO... I started copying that picture, and all the pictures I loved looking at—mostly of saints and pretty girls, and always with my same color hair.
But it all started with that picture of Jesus, who looked back at me, so why not have him talk to me too? That way I could make him say stuff I needed to hear...
Thou canst...
...make stuff too!
SAINT LUCY
BRECK GIRL
I wanna look like THAT.
Yeah, long-haired man??
Ya mean...me??
Most of that churchstuff just didn't make much sense
...like bodyeating??
...but someone actually talking to me...
...THAT I liked.

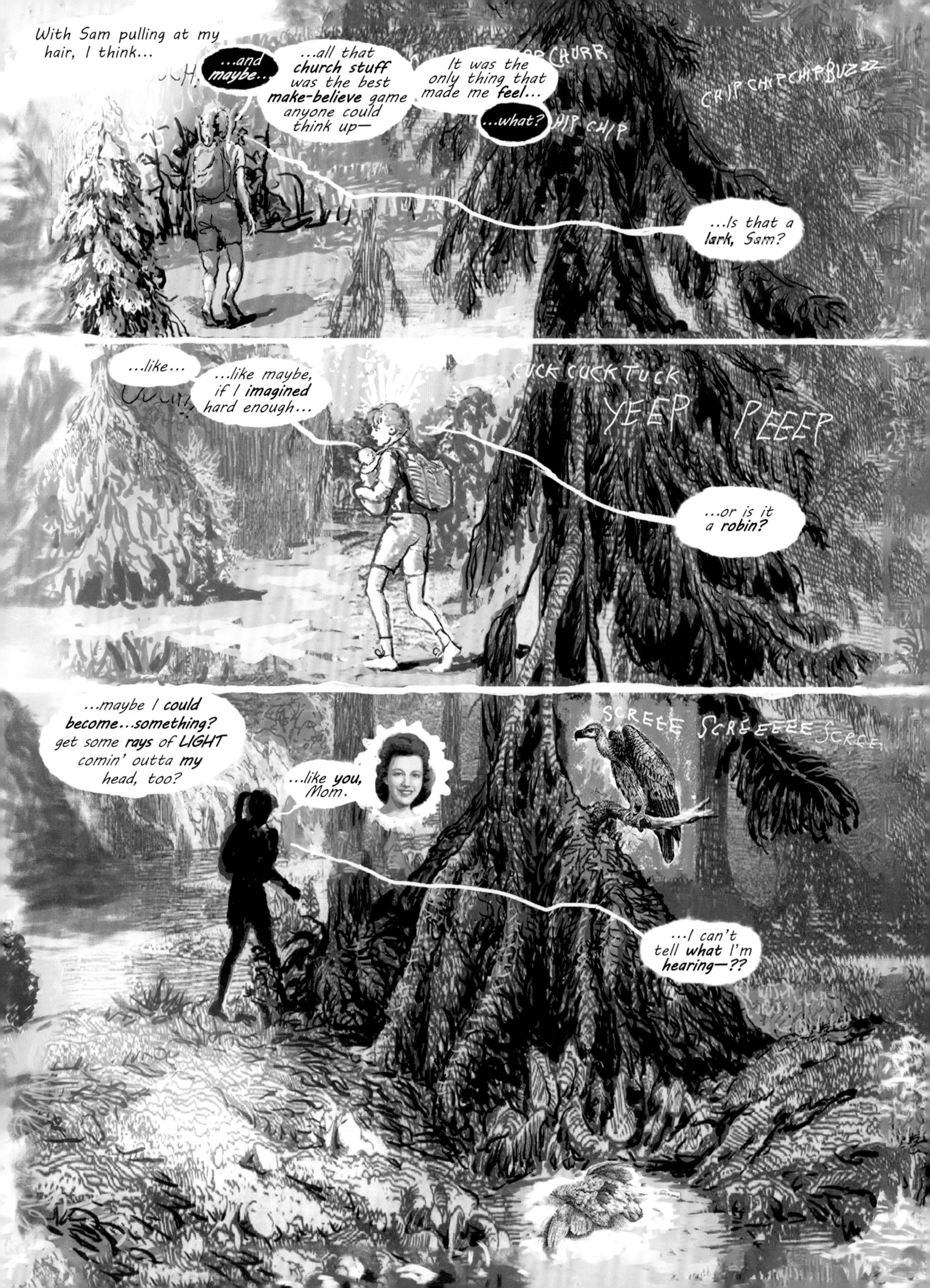

With Sam pulling at my hair, I think...
...and maybe...
...all that church stuff was the best make-believe game anyone could think up—
It was the only thing that made me feel...
...what?
CHURR
CHIP CHIP CHIP BUZZ
CHIP CHIP
...Is that a lark, Sam?
...like...
...like maybe, if I imagined hard enough...
CUCK CUCK TUCK
YEEP
PEEEP
...or is it a robin?
...maybe I could become...something? get some rays of LIGHT comin' outta my head, too?
...like you, Mom.
SCREEE
...I can't tell what I'm hearing—??

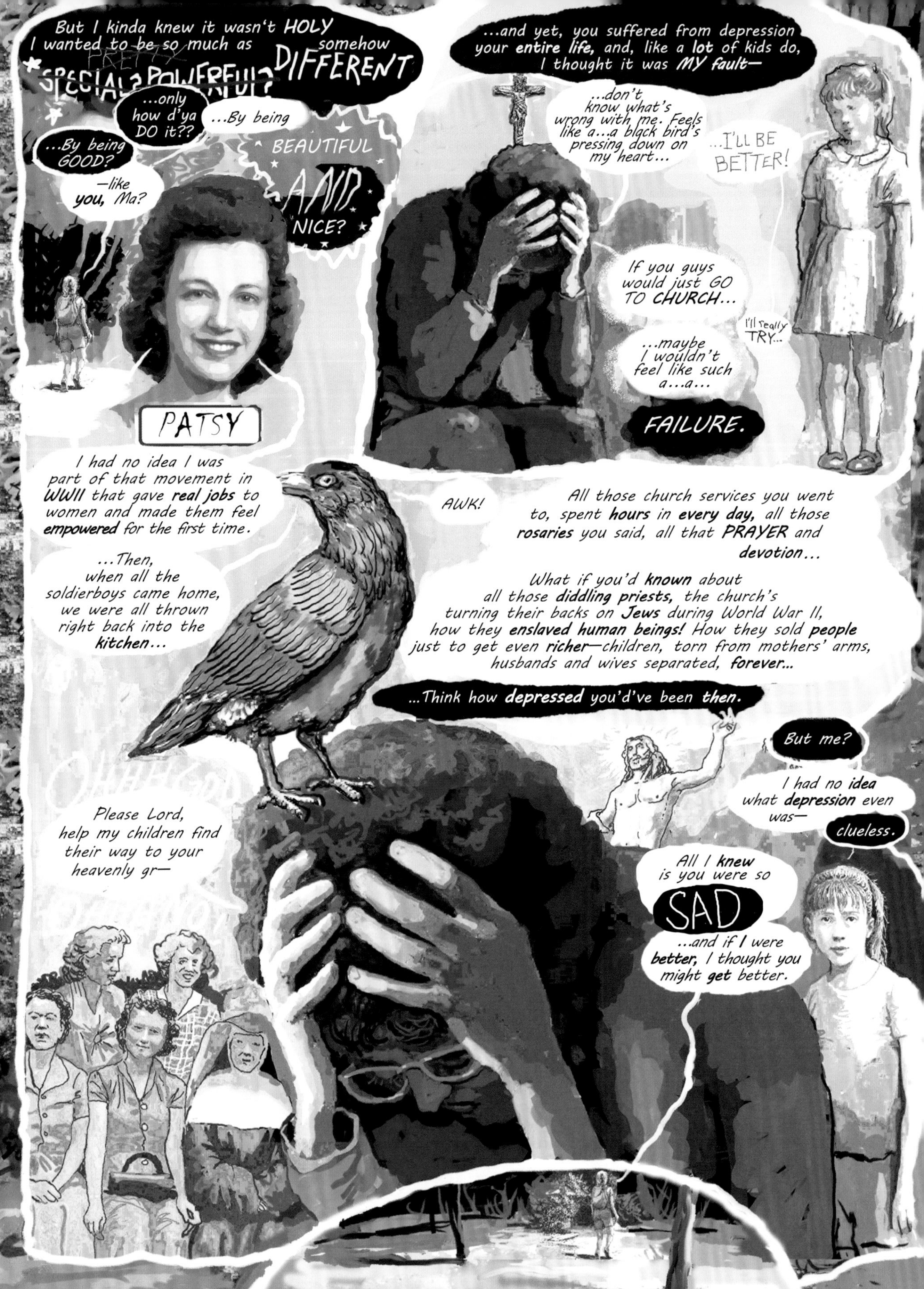

But I kinda knew it wasn't HOLY I wanted to be so much as
PRETTY
SPECIAL? POWERFUL?
somehow DIFFERENT
...only how d'ya DO it??
...By being GOOD?
—like you, Ma?
...By being
BEAUTIFUL
AND
NICE?
PATSY
...and yet, you suffered from depression your entire life, and, like a lot of kids do, I thought it was MY fault—
...don't know what's wrong with me. Feels like a...a black bird's pressing down on my heart...
...I'LL BE BETTER!
If you guys would just GO TO CHURCH...
...maybe I wouldn't feel like such a...a...
FAILURE.
I'll really TRY...
I had no idea I was part of that movement in WWII that gave real jobs to women and made them feel empowered for the first time.
...Then, when all the soldierboys came home, we were all thrown right back into the kitchen...
AWK!
All those church services you went to, spent hours in every day, all those rosaries you said, all that PRAYER and devotion...
What if you'd known about all those diddling priests, the church's turning their backs on Jews during World War II, how they enslaved human beings! How they sold people just to get even richer—children, torn from mothers' arms, husbands and wives separated, forever...
...Think how depressed you'd've been then.
Please Lord, help my children find their way to your heavenly gr—
But me?
I had no idea what depression even was—
clueless.
All I knew is you were so
SAD
...and if I were better, I thought you might get better.

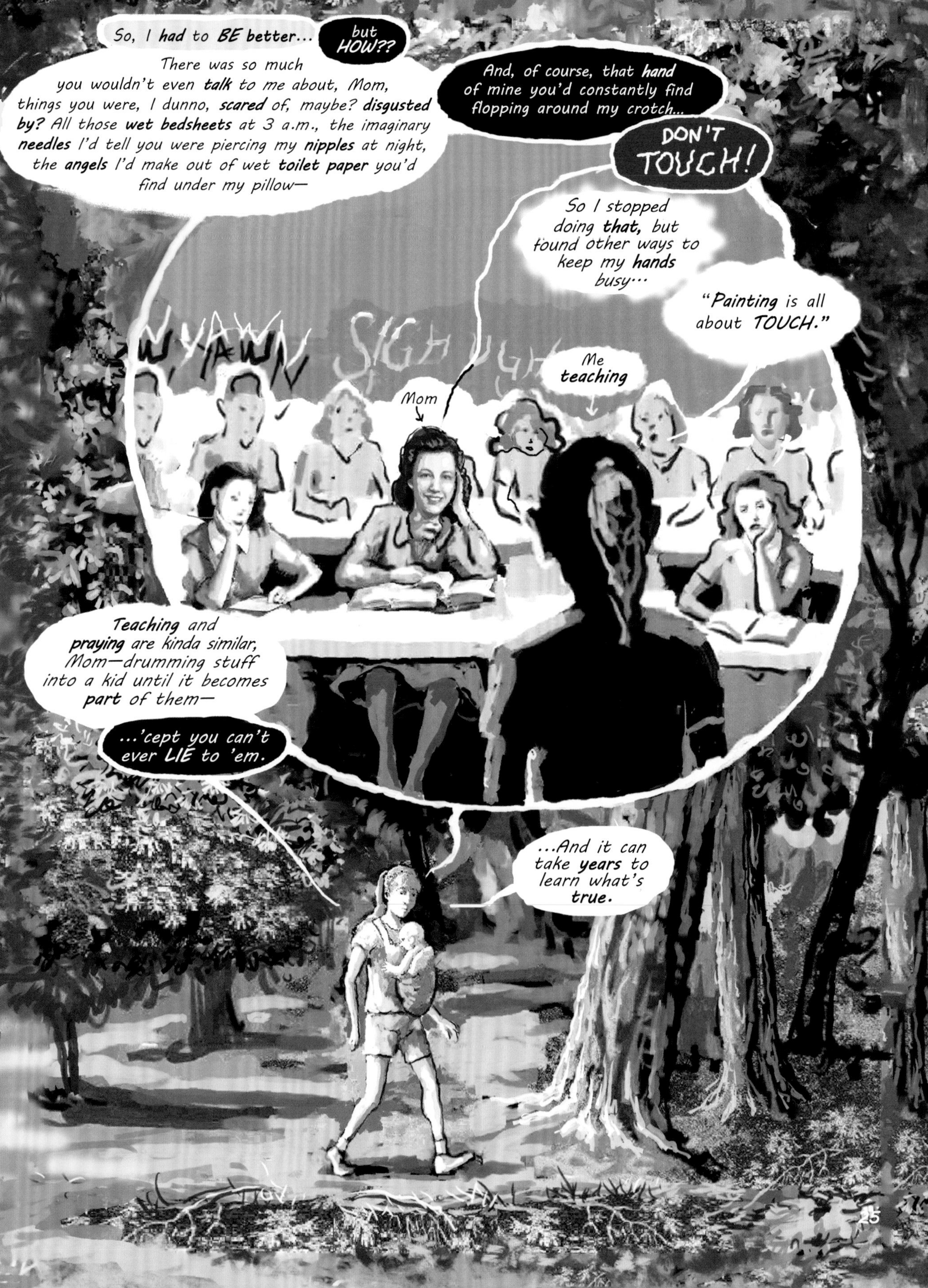
So, I had to BE better...
but HOW??
There was so much you wouldn't even talk to me about, Mom, things you were, I dunno, scared of, maybe? disgusted by? All those wet bedsheets at 3 a.m., the imaginary needles I'd tell you were piercing my nipples at night, the angels I'd make out of wet toilet paper you'd find under my pillow—
And, of course, that hand of mine you'd constantly find flopping around my crotch...
DON'T TOUCH!
So I stopped doing that, but found other ways to keep my hands busy...
"Painting is all about TOUCH."
YAWN YAWN
SIGH UGH
Me teaching
Mom
Teaching and praying are kinda similar, Mom—drumming stuff into a kid until it becomes part of them—
...'cept you can't ever LIE to 'em.
...And it can take years to learn what's true.

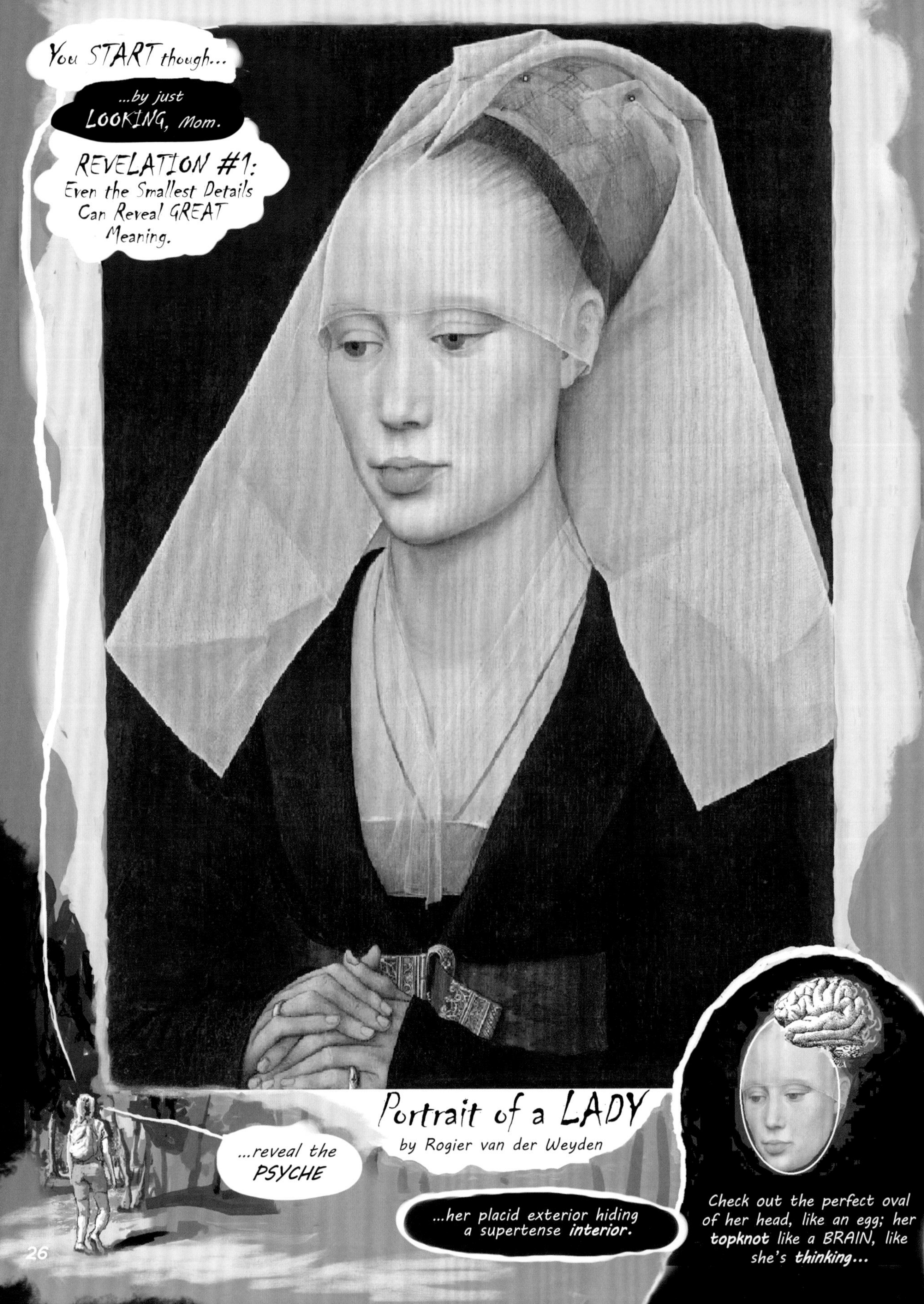
You START though...
...by just LOOKING, Mom.
REVELATION #1: Even the Smallest Details Can Reveal GREAT Meaning.
...reveal the PSYCHE
Portrait of a LADY
by Rogier van der Weyden
...her placid exterior hiding a supertense interior.
Check out the perfect oval of her head, like an egg; her topknot like a BRAIN, like she's thinking...

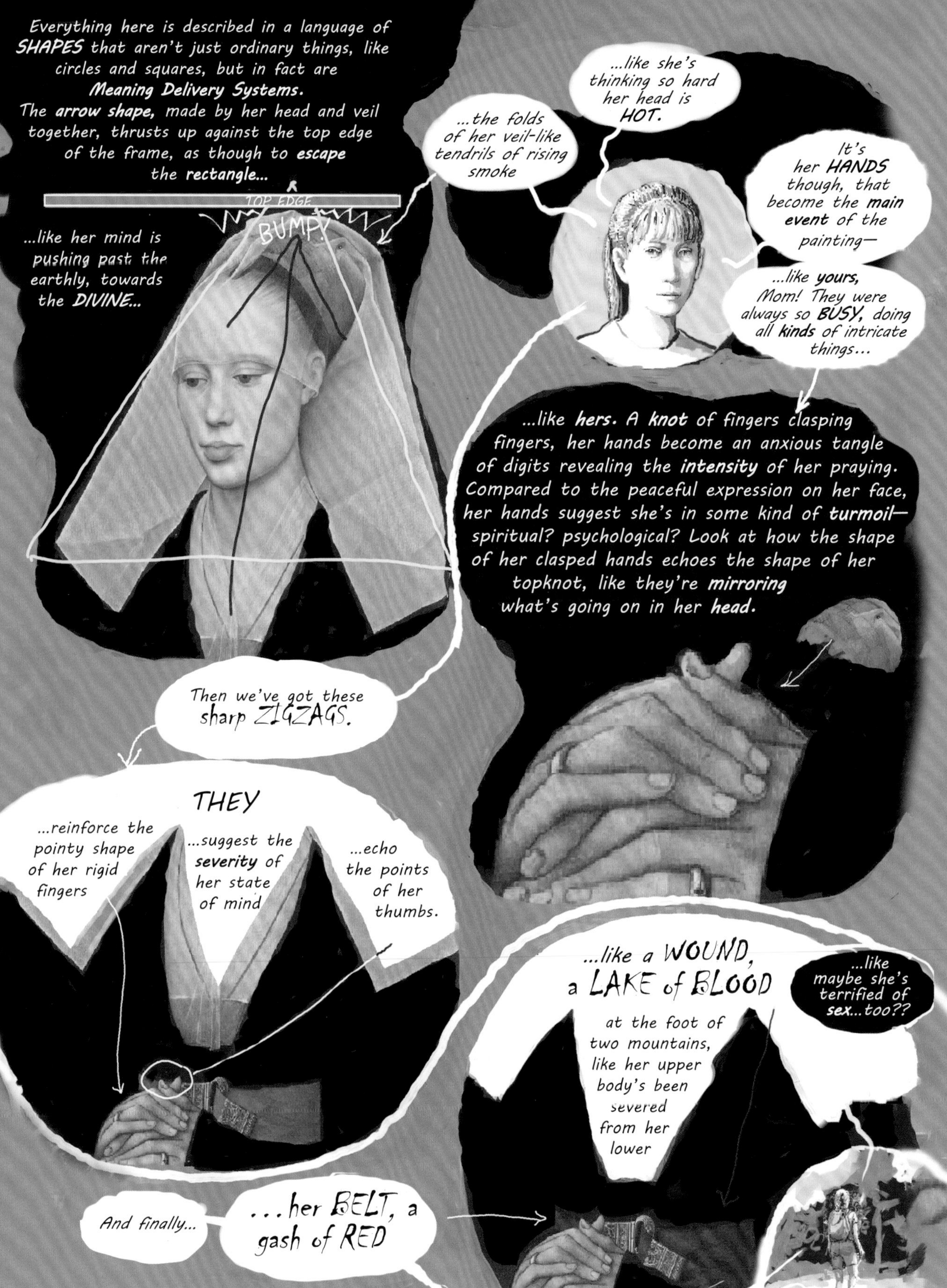

Everything here is described in a language of SHAPES that aren't just ordinary things, like circles and squares, but in fact are Meaning Delivery Systems. The arrow shape, made by her head and veil together, thrusts up against the top edge of the frame, as though to escape the rectangle...
TOP EDGE
BUMP!
...like her mind is pushing past the earthly, towards the DIVINE...
...the folds of her veil-like tendrils of rising smoke
...like she's thinking so hard her head is HOT.
It's her HANDS though, that become the main event of the painting—
...like yours, Mom! They were always so BUSY, doing all kinds of intricate things...
...like hers. A knot of fingers clasping fingers, her hands become an anxious tangle of digits revealing the intensity of her praying. Compared to the peaceful expression on her face, her hands suggest she's in some kind of turmoil—spiritual? psychological? Look at how the shape of her clasped hands echoes the shape of her topknot, like they're mirroring what's going on in her head.
Then we've got these sharp ZIGZAGS.
THEY
...reinforce the pointy shape of her rigid fingers
...suggest the severity of her state of mind
...echo the points of her thumbs.
And finally...
...her BELT, a gash of RED
...like a WOUND, a LAKE of BLOOD
at the foot of two mountains, like her upper body's been severed from her lower
...like maybe she's terrified of sex...too??

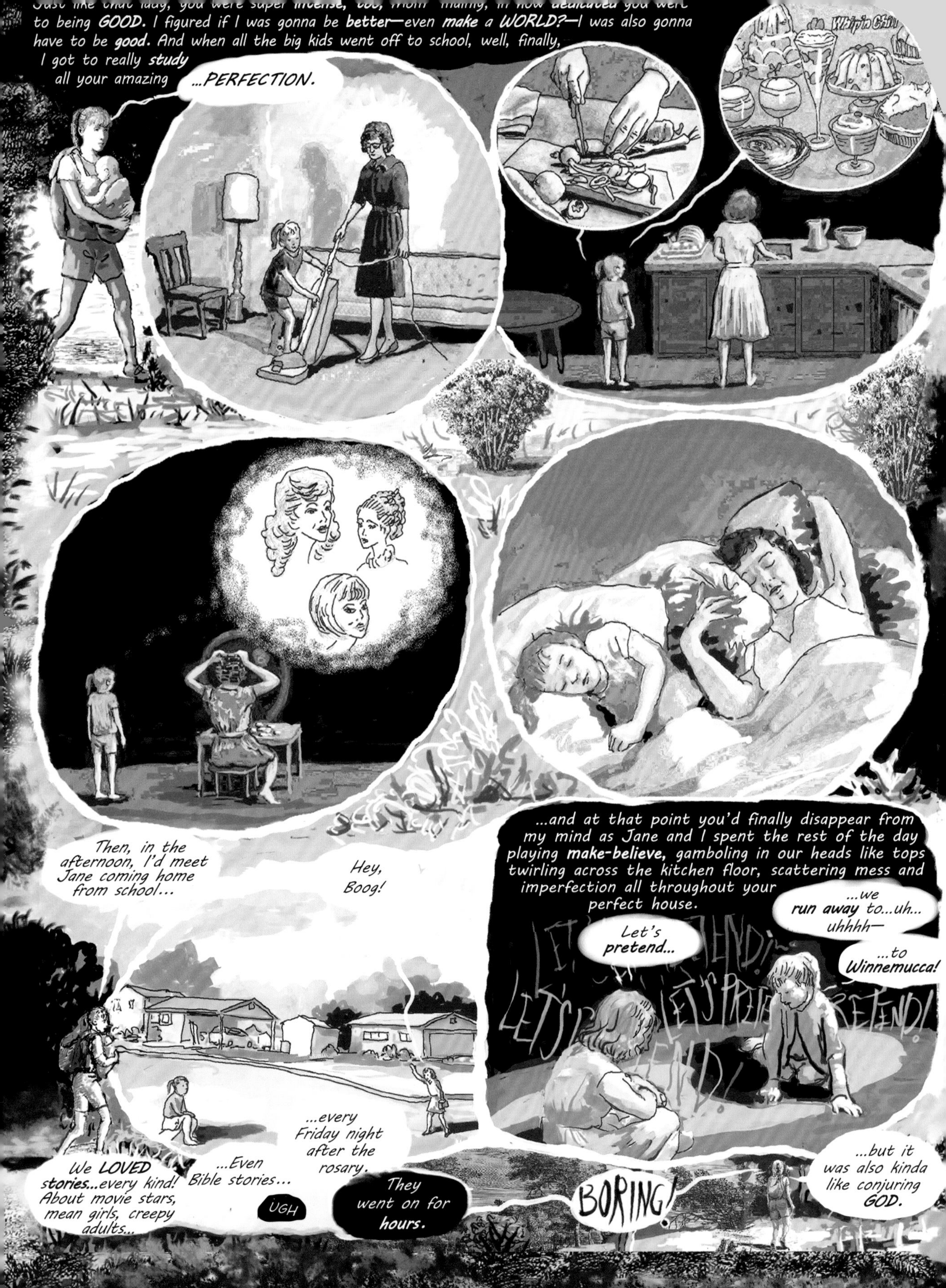

to being **GOOD.** I figured if I was gonna be **better**—even **make** a **WORLD?**—I was also gonna have to be **good.** And when all the big kids went off to school, well, finally, I got to really **study** all your amazing
...PERFECTION.
Whip'n Chill
Then, in the afternoon, I'd meet Jane coming home from school...
Hey, Boog!
...and at that point you'd finally disappear from my mind as Jane and I spent the rest of the day playing **make-believe,** gamboling in our heads like tops twirling across the kitchen floor, scattering mess and imperfection all throughout your perfect house.
Let's **pretend...**
...we **run away** to...uh... uhhhh—
...to **Winnemucca!**
We **LOVED stories...**every kind! About movie stars, mean girls, creepy adults...
...Even Bible stories...
UGH
...every Friday night after the rosary.
They went on for **hours.**
BORING!
...but it was also kinda like conjuring **GOD.**

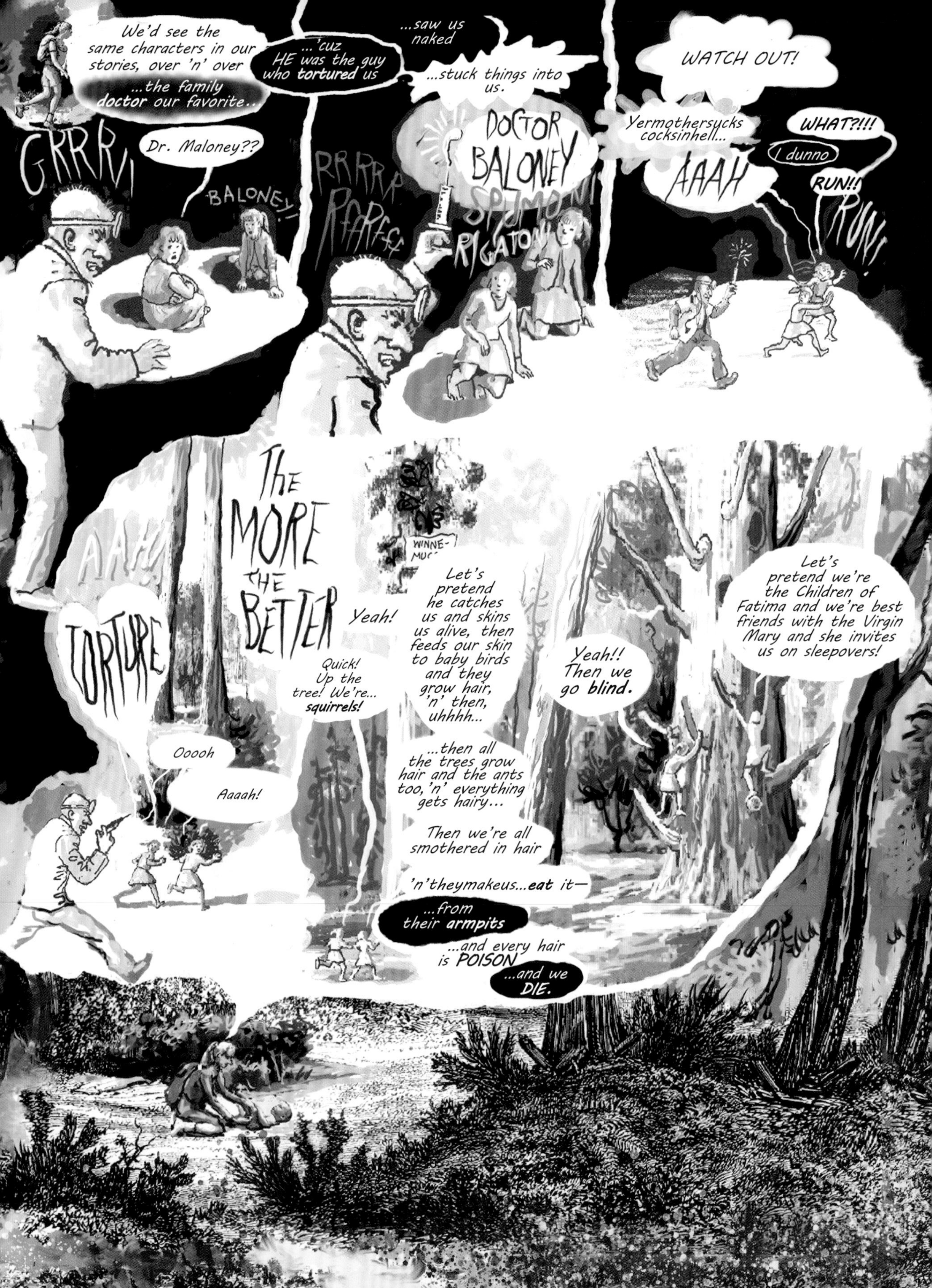

We'd see the same characters in our stories, over 'n' over
...the family doctor our favorite...
...'cuz HE was the guy who tortured us
...saw us naked
...stuck things into us.
WATCH OUT!
GRRRR!
Dr. Maloney??
BALONEY!
RRRRRR RRRRR
DOCTOR BALONEY
SPUMONI
RIGATONI
Yermothersucks cocksinhell...
AAAH
WHAT?!!!
I dunno
RUN!!
RUN!
AAH!
The MORE the BETTER
TORTURE
WINNE-MUC
Yeah!
Quick! Up the tree! We're... squirrels!
Let's pretend he catches us and skins us alive, then feeds our skin to baby birds and they grow hair, 'n' then, uhhhh...
...then all the trees grow hair and the ants too, 'n' everything gets hairy...
Then we're all smothered in hair
'n'theymakeus...eat it—
...from their armpits
...and every hair is POISON
...and we DIE.
Yeah!! Then we go blind.
Let's pretend we're the Children of Fatima and we're best friends with the Virgin Mary and she invites us on sleepovers!
Ooooh
Aaaah!

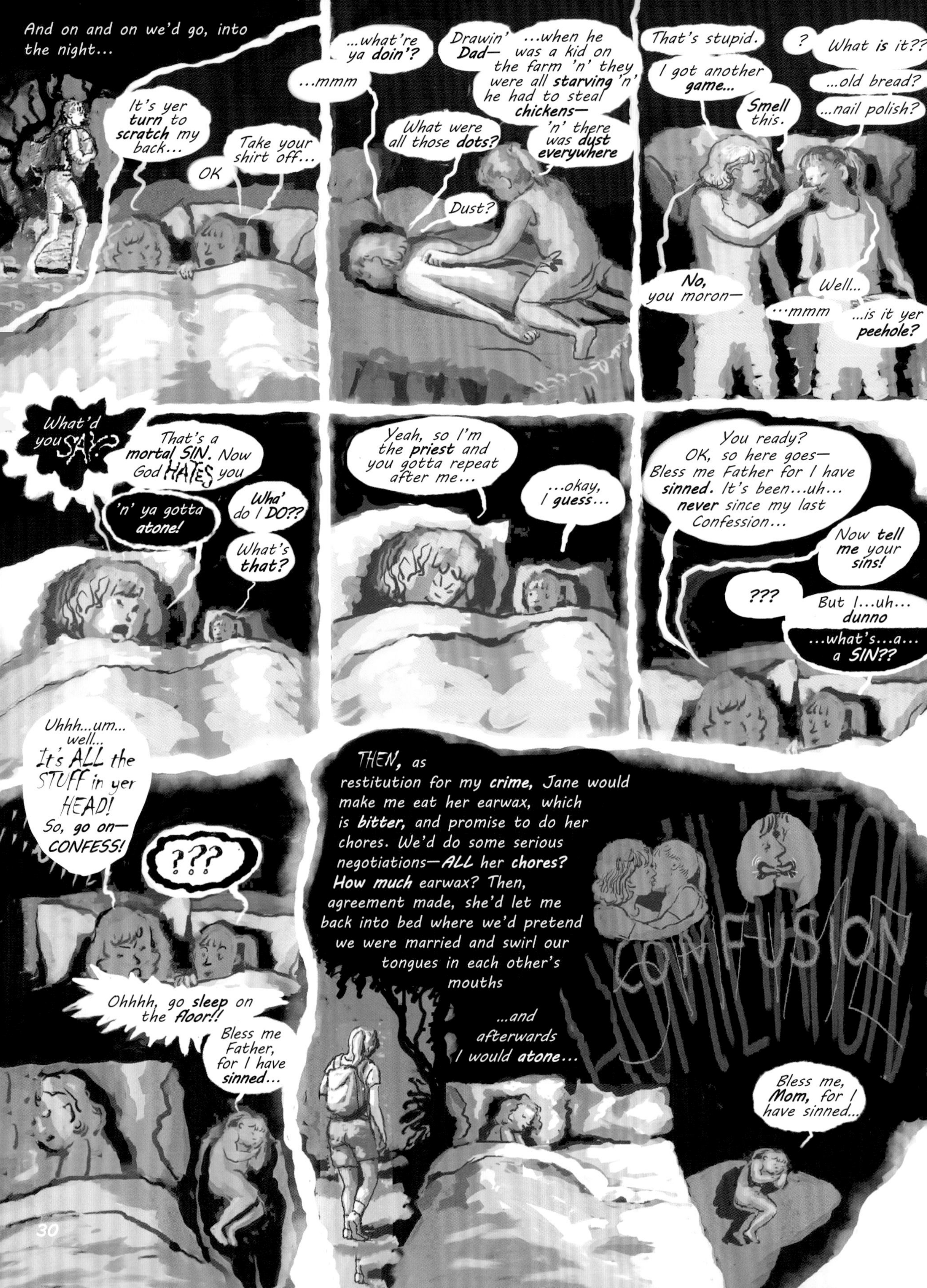

And on and on we'd go, into the night...
It's yer turn to scratch my back...
Take your shirt off...
OK
...what're ya doin'?
...mmm
Drawin' Dad—
...when he was a kid on the farm 'n' they were all starving 'n' he had to steal chickens—
'n' there was dust everywhere
What were all those dots?
Dust?
That's stupid.
I got another game...
Smell this.
?
What is it??
...old bread?
...nail polish?
No, you moron—
Well...
...mmm
...is it yer peehole?
What'd you SAY??
That's a mortal SIN. Now God HATES you
'n' ya gotta atone!
Wha' do I DO??
What's that?
Yeah, so I'm the priest and you gotta repeat after me...
...okay, I guess...
You ready? OK, so here goes— Bless me Father for I have sinned. It's been...uh... never since my last Confession...
Now tell me your sins!
???
But I...uh... dunno
...what's...a... a SIN??
Uhhh...um... well... It's ALL the STUFF in yer HEAD! So, go on— CONFESS!
???
Ohhhh, go sleep on the floor!!
Bless me Father, for I have sinned...
THEN, as restitution for my crime, Jane would make me eat her earwax, which is bitter, and promise to do her chores. We'd do some serious negotiations—ALL her chores? How much earwax? Then, agreement made, she'd let me back into bed where we'd pretend we were married and swirl our tongues in each other's mouths
...and afterwards I would atone...
CONFUSION
HUMILIATION
Bless me, Mom, for I have sinned...

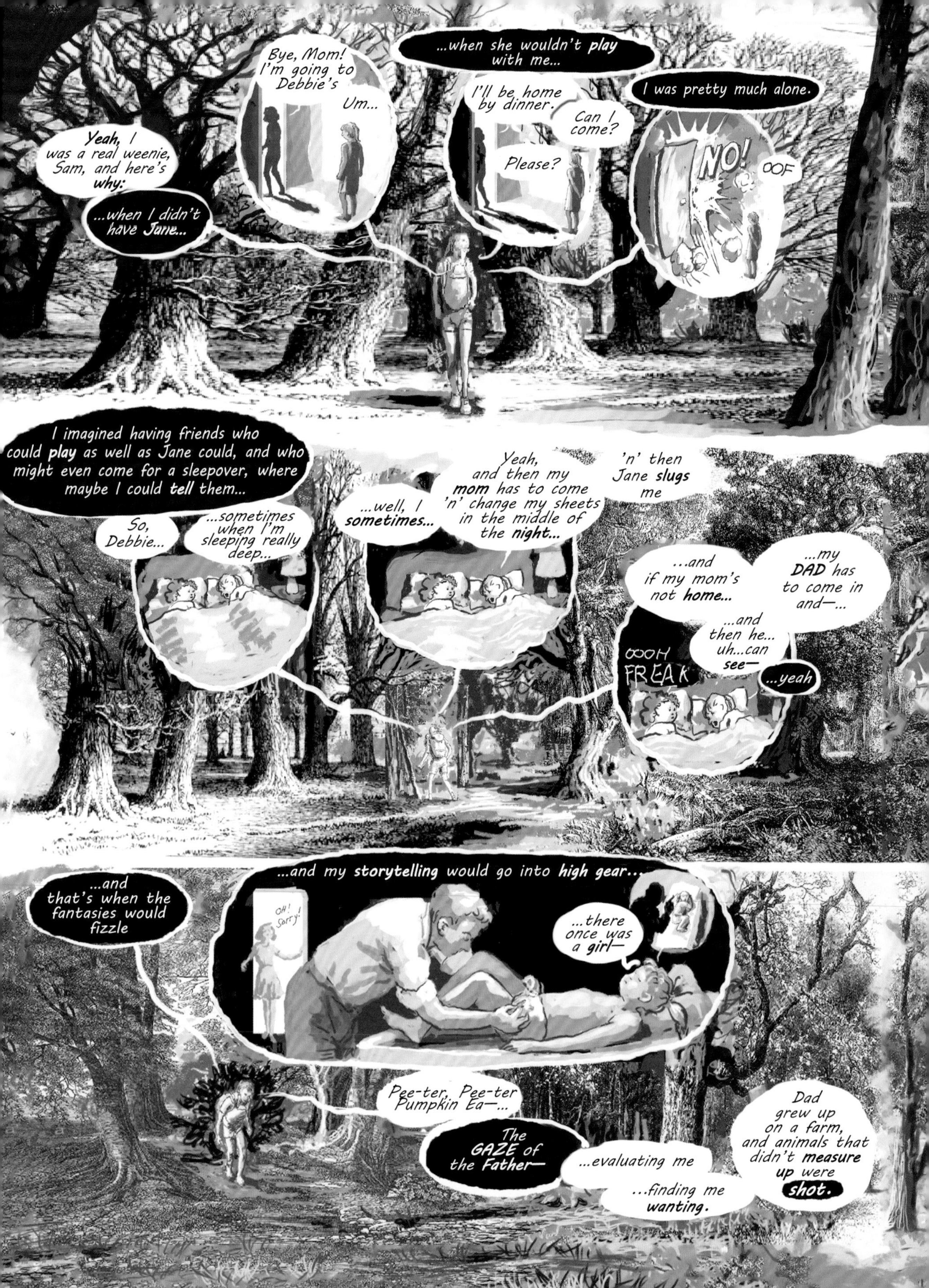
Yeah, I was a real weenie, Sam, and here's why:
...when I didn't have Jane...
Bye, Mom! I'm going to Debbie's
Um...
...when she wouldn't play with me...
I'll be home by dinner.
Can I come?
Please?
I was pretty much alone.
NO!
OOF
I imagined having friends who could play as well as Jane could, and who might even come for a sleepover, where maybe I could tell them...
So, Debbie...
...sometimes when I'm sleeping really deep...
...well, I sometimes...
Yeah, and then my mom has to come 'n' change my sheets in the middle of the night...
'n' then Jane slugs me
...and if my mom's not home...
...my DAD has to come in and—...
...and then he... uh...can see—
OOOH FREAK
...yeah
...and that's when the fantasies would fizzle
...and my storytelling would go into high gear...
OH! Sorry!
...there once was a girl—
Pee-ter, Pee-ter Pumpkin Ea—...
The GAZE of the Father—
...evaluating me
...finding me wanting.
Dad grew up on a farm, and animals that didn't measure up were shot.

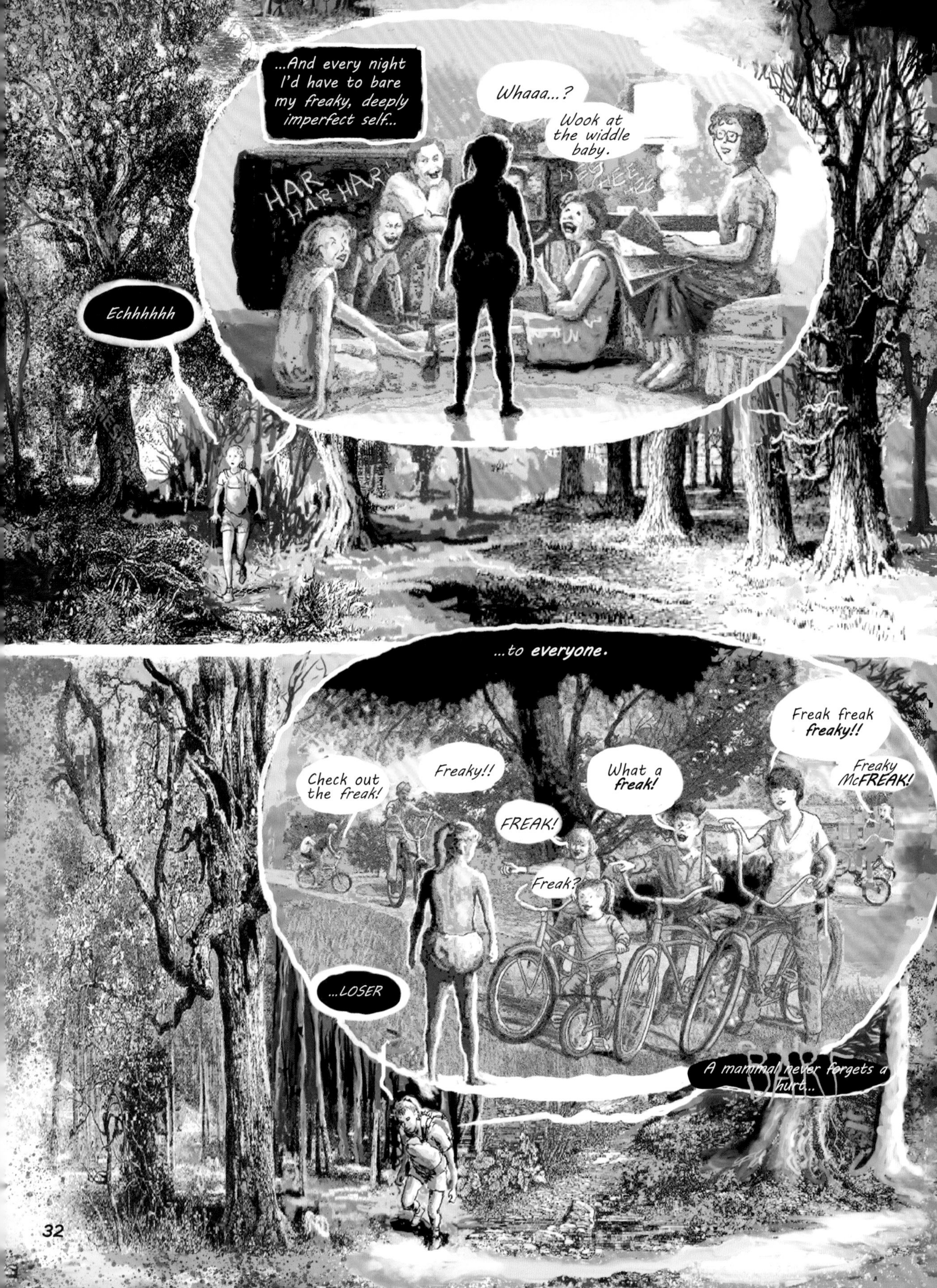
...And every night I'd have to bare my freaky, deeply imperfect self...
Whaaa...?
Wook at the widdle baby.
HAR HAR HAR
Echhhhhh
...to **everyone.**
Check out the freak!
Freaky!!
FREAK!
Freak?
What a **freak!**
Freak freak **freaky!!**
Freaky Mc**FREAK!**
...LOSER
A mammal never forgets a hurt...

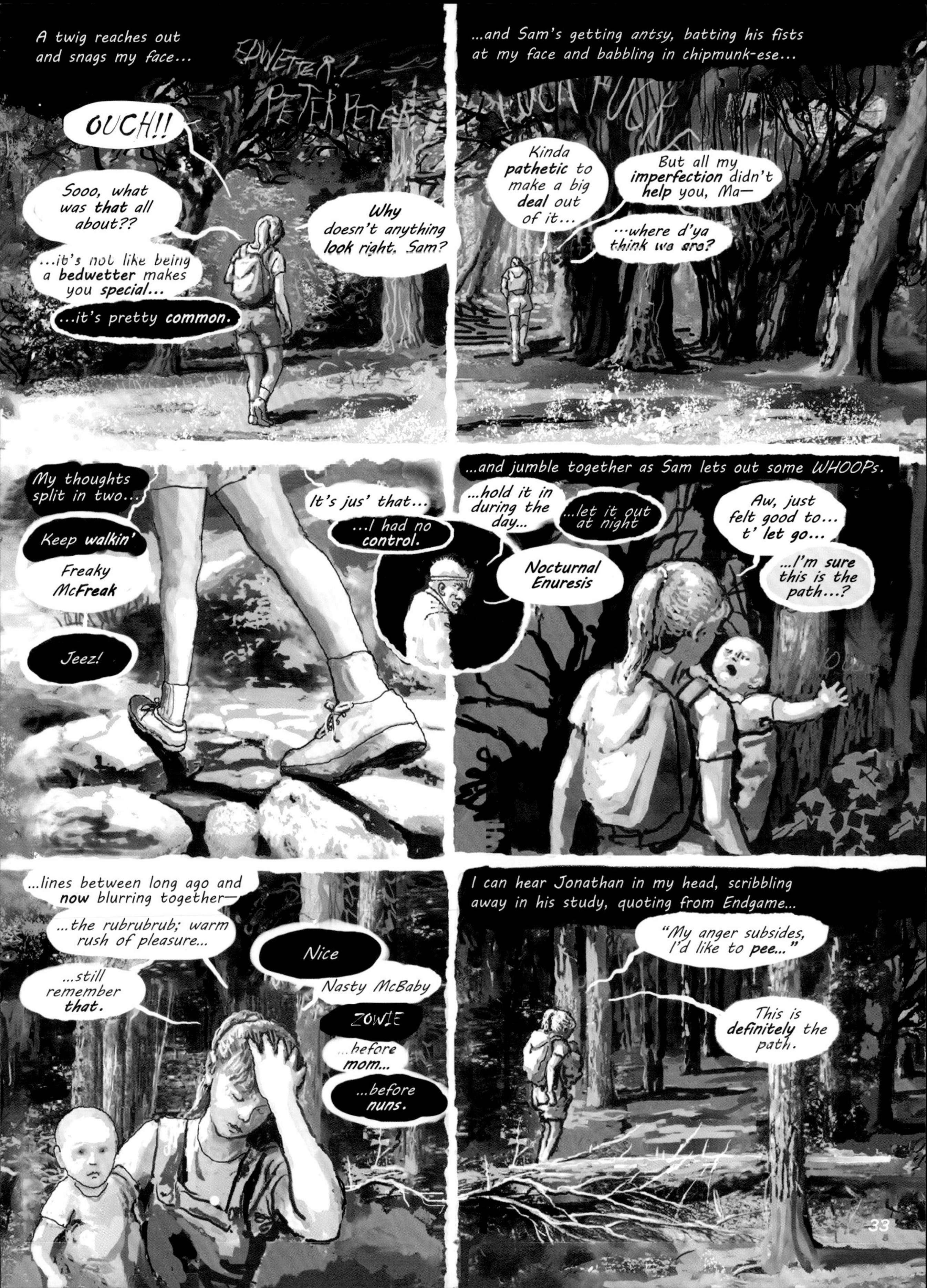

A twig reaches out and snags my face…

OUCH!!

Sooo, what was that all about??

…it's not like being a bedwetter makes you special…

…it's pretty common.

Why doesn't anything look right, Sam?

…and Sam's getting antsy, batting his fists at my face and babbling in chipmunk-ese…

Kinda pathetic to make a big deal out of it…

But all my imperfection didn't help you, Ma—

…where d'ya think we are?

My thoughts split in two…

Keep walkin'

Freaky McFreak

Jeez!

It's jus' that…

…I had no control.

…and jumble together as Sam lets out some WHOOPs.

…hold it in during the day…

…let it out at night

Nocturnal Enuresis

Aw, just felt good to… t' let go…

…I'm sure this is the path…?

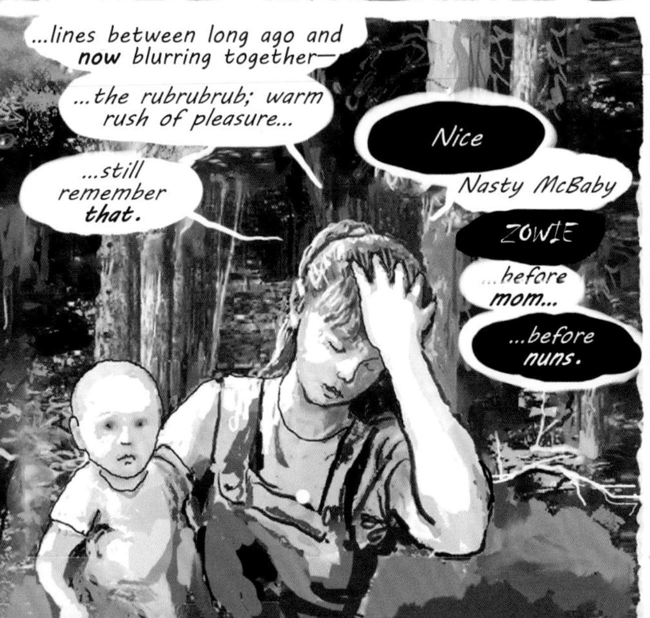

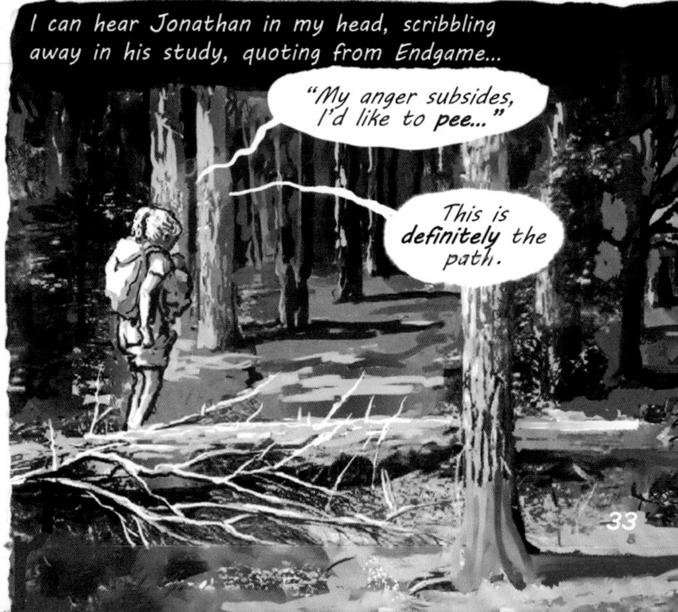

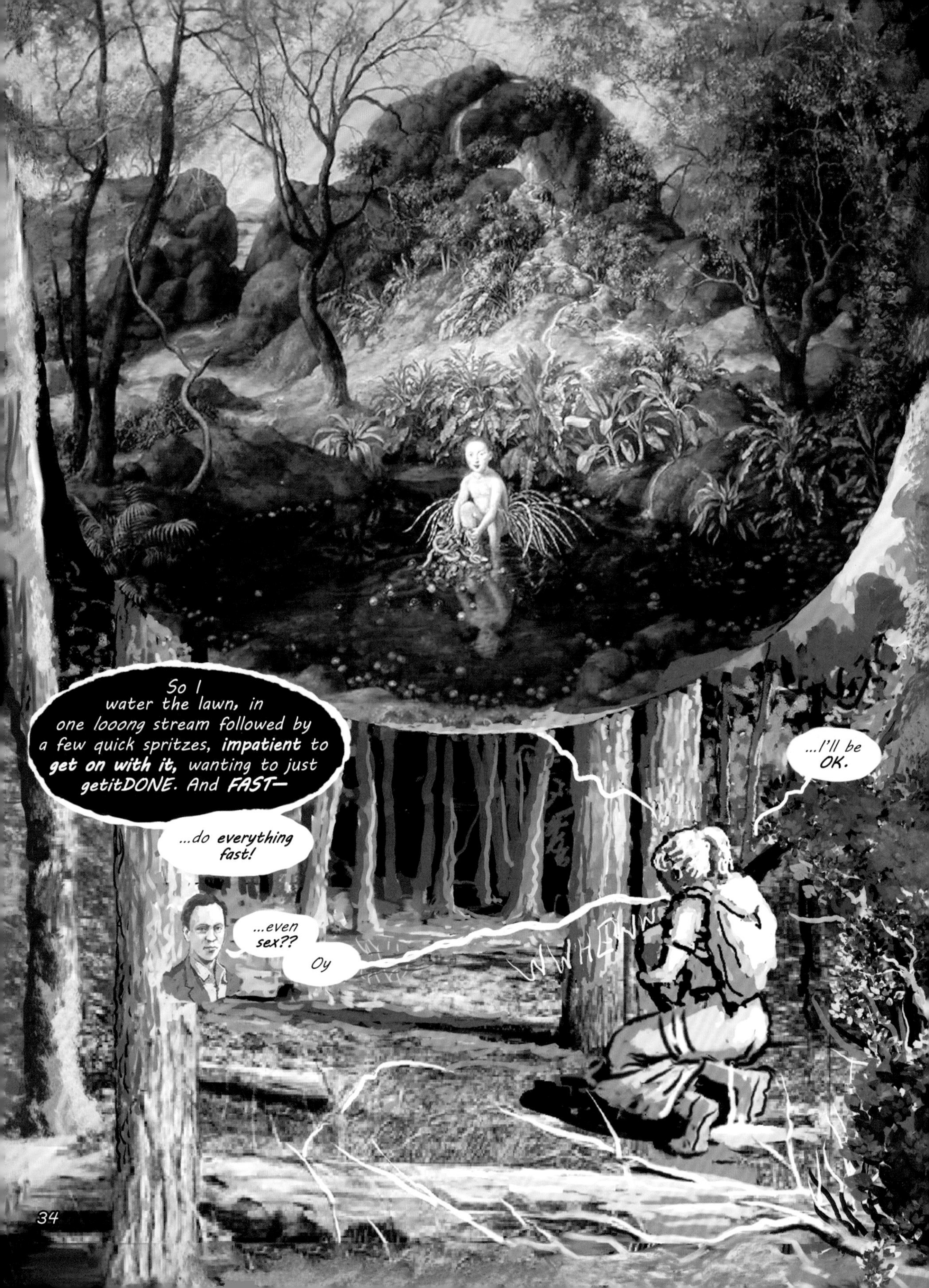
So I water the lawn, in one looong stream followed by a few quick spritzes, **impatient** to **get on with it,** wanting to just getitDONE. And **FAST—**
...I'll be **OK.**
...do **everything** fast!
...even **sex??**
Oy
WWHEWW

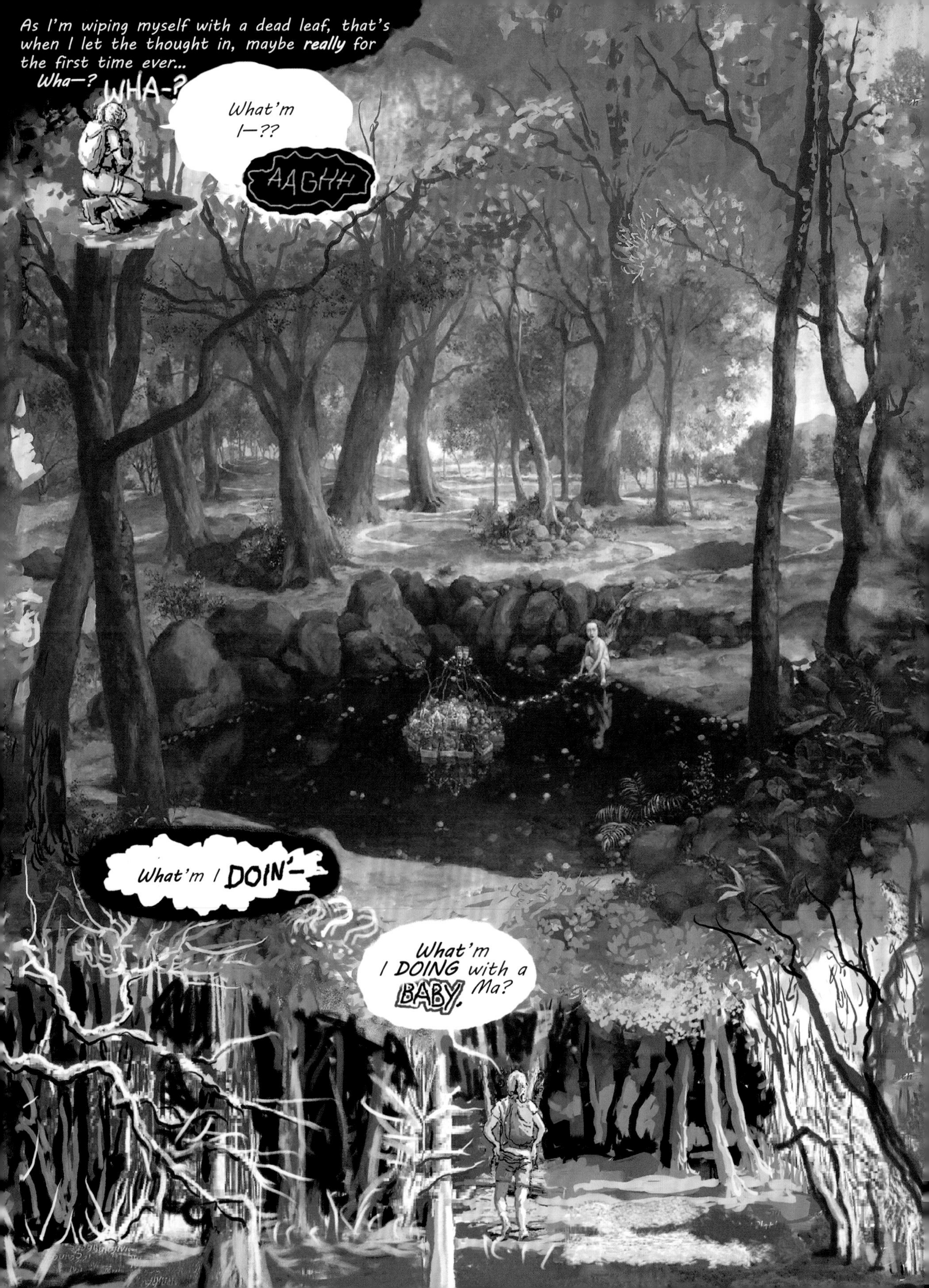
As I'm wiping myself with a dead leaf, that's when I let the thought in, maybe **really** for the first time ever...
Wha—?
WHA-?
What'm I—??
AAGHH
What'm I DOIN'-
What'm I DOING with a BABY, Ma?

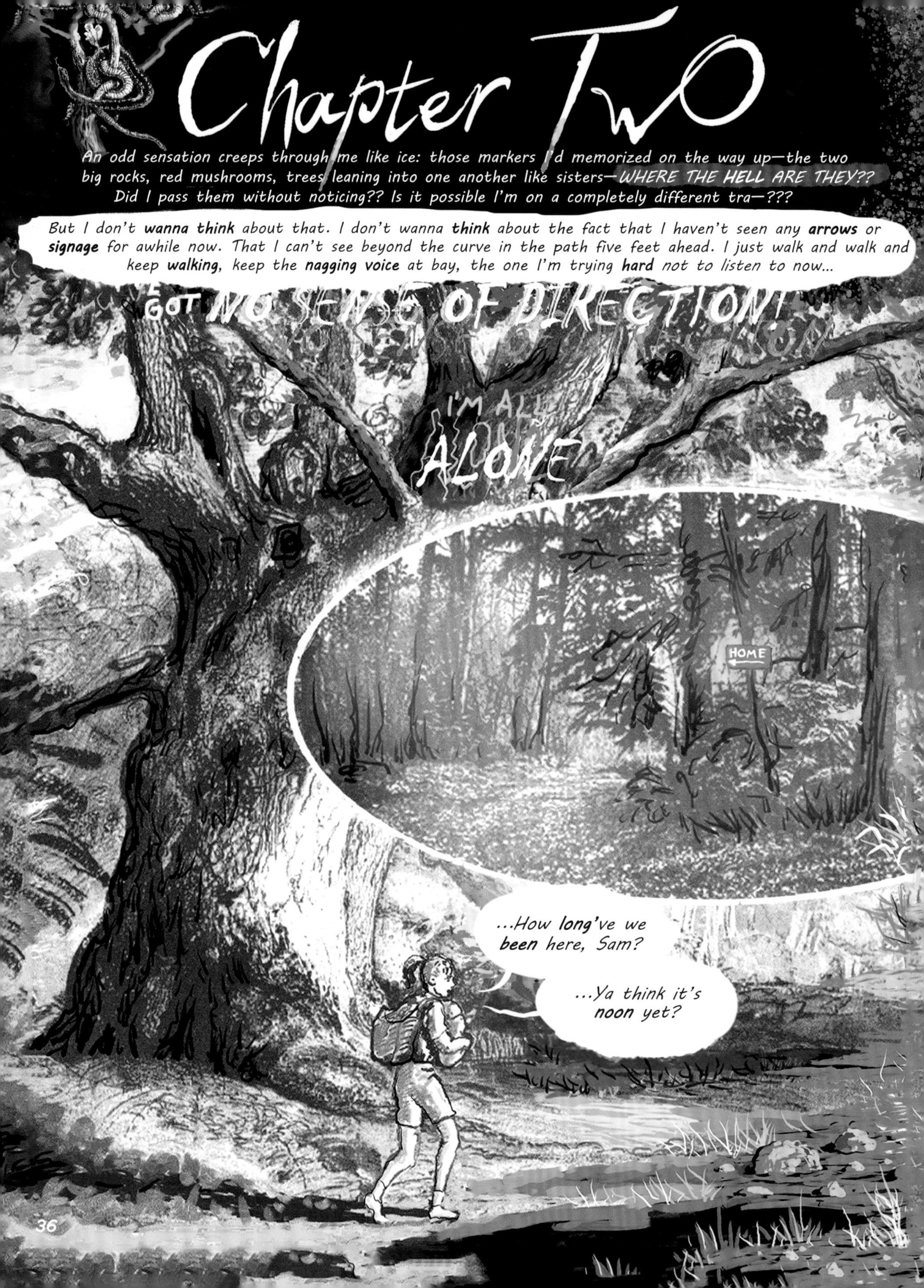
Chapter Two
An odd sensation creeps through me like ice: those markers I'd memorized on the way up—the two big rocks, red mushrooms, trees leaning into one another like sisters—WHERE THE HELL ARE THEY?? Did I pass them without noticing?? Is it possible I'm on a completely different tra—???
But I don't wanna think about that. I don't wanna think about the fact that I haven't seen any arrows or signage for awhile now. That I can't see beyond the curve in the path five feet ahead. I just walk and walk and keep walking, keep the nagging voice at bay, the one I'm trying hard not to listen to now...
GOT NO SENSE OF DIRECTION!
I'M ALL ALONE
HOME
...How long've we been here, Sam?
...Ya think it's noon yet?

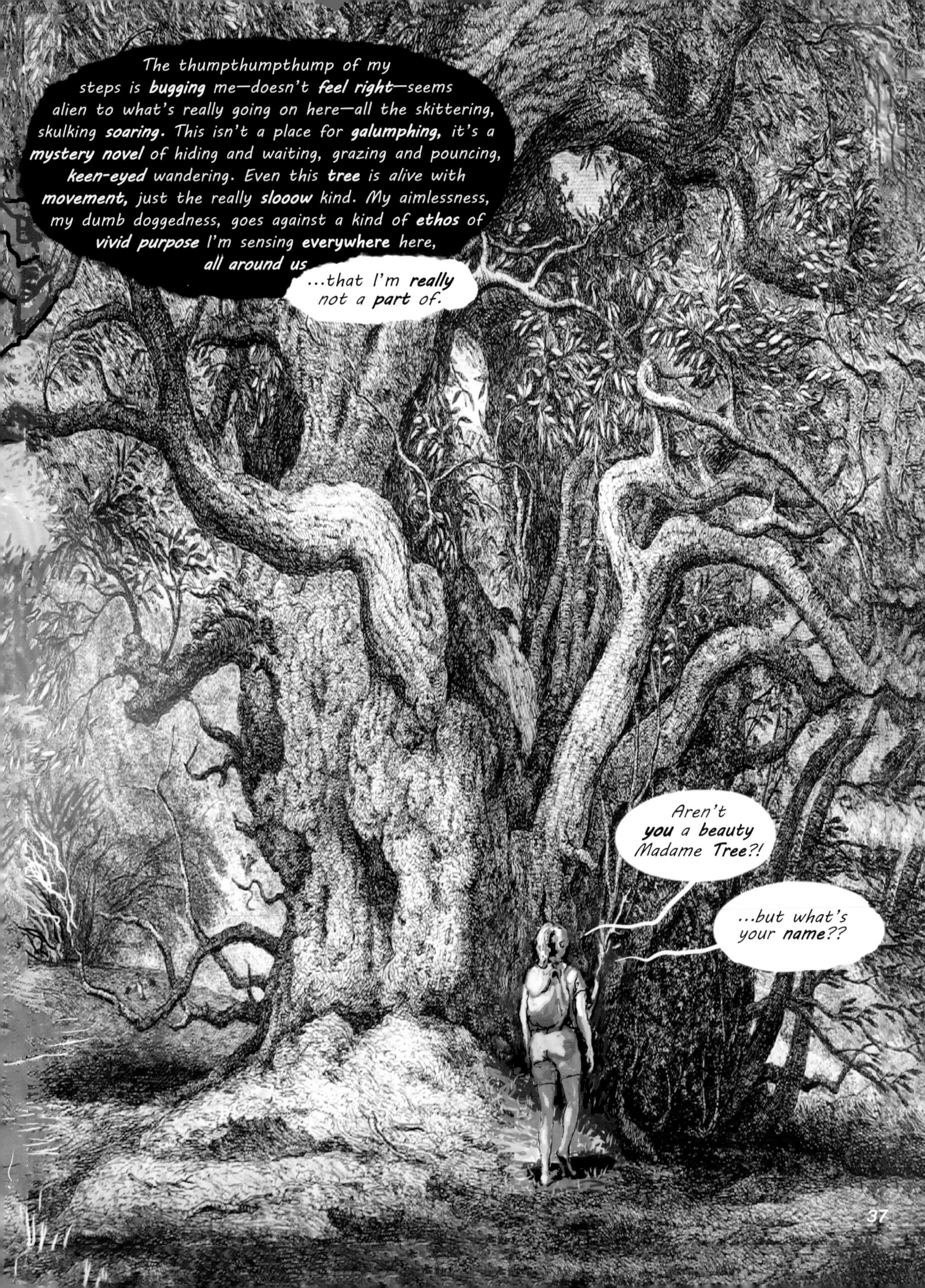
The thumpthumpthump of my steps is bugging me—doesn't feel right—seems alien to what's really going on here—all the skittering, skulking soaring. This isn't a place for galumphing, it's a mystery novel of hiding and waiting, grazing and pouncing, keen-eyed wandering. Even this tree is alive with movement, just the really slooow kind. My aimlessness, my dumb doggedness, goes against a kind of ethos of vivid purpose I'm sensing everywhere here, all around us
...that I'm really not a part of.
Aren't you a beauty Madame Tree?!
...but what's your name??

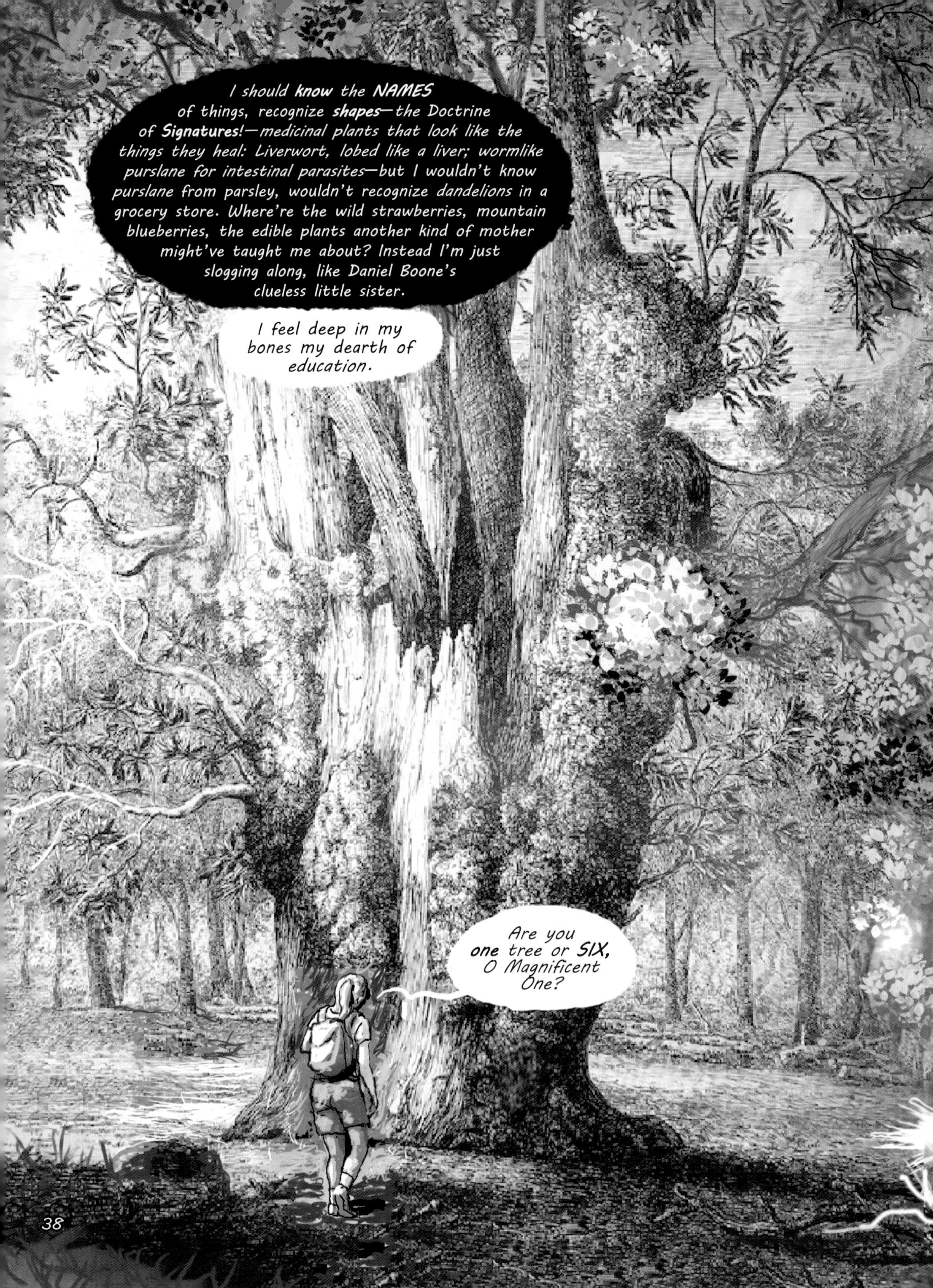
I should know the NAMES of things, recognize shapes—the Doctrine of Signatures!—medicinal plants that look like the things they heal: Liverwort, lobed like a liver; wormlike purslane for intestinal parasites—but I wouldn't know purslane from parsley, wouldn't recognize dandelions in a grocery store. Where're the wild strawberries, mountain blueberries, the edible plants another kind of mother might've taught me about? Instead I'm just slogging along, like Daniel Boone's clueless little sister.
I feel deep in my bones my dearth of education.
Are you one tree or SIX, O Magnificent One?

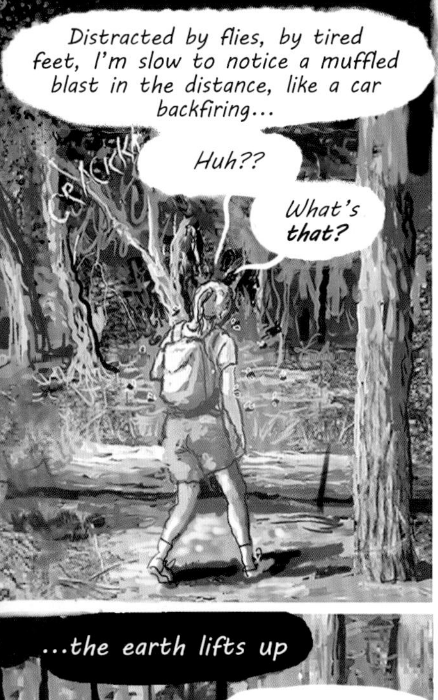
Distracted by flies, by tired feet, I'm slow to notice a muffled blast in the distance, like a car backfiring...
Huh??
What's **that?**

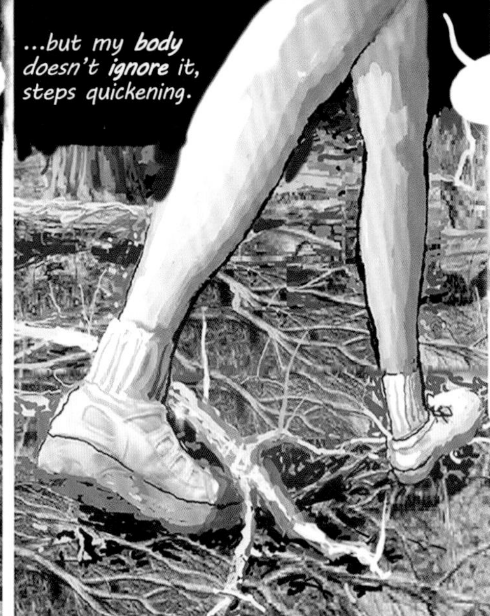
...but my **body** doesn't **ignore** it, steps quickening.

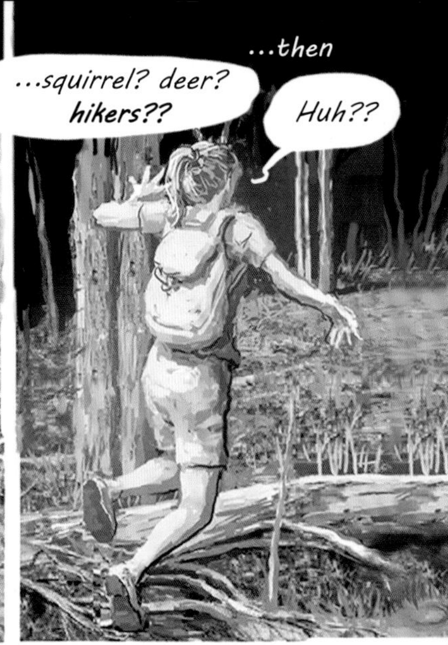
...squirrel? deer? **hikers??**
...then
Huh??

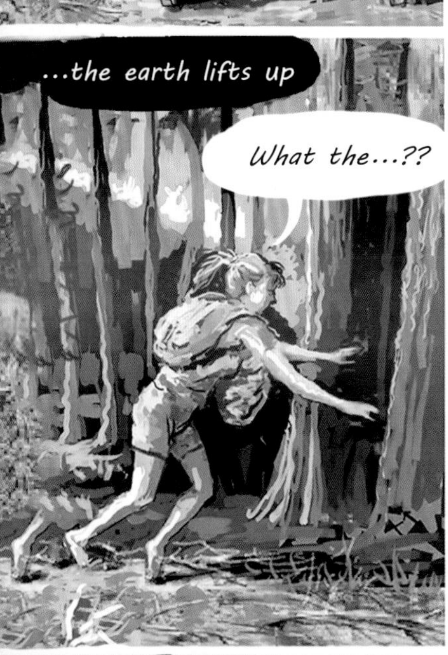
...the earth lifts up
What the...??

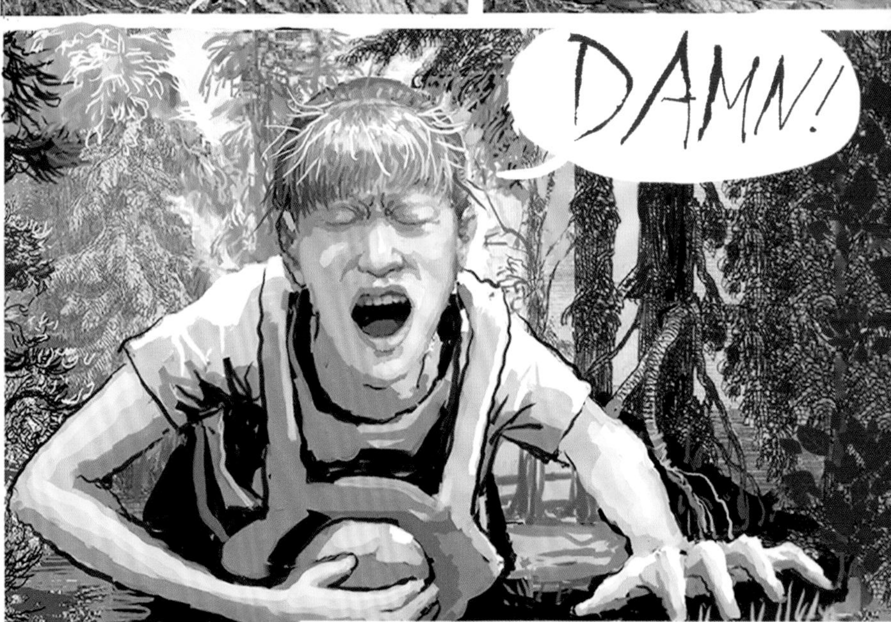
DAMN!

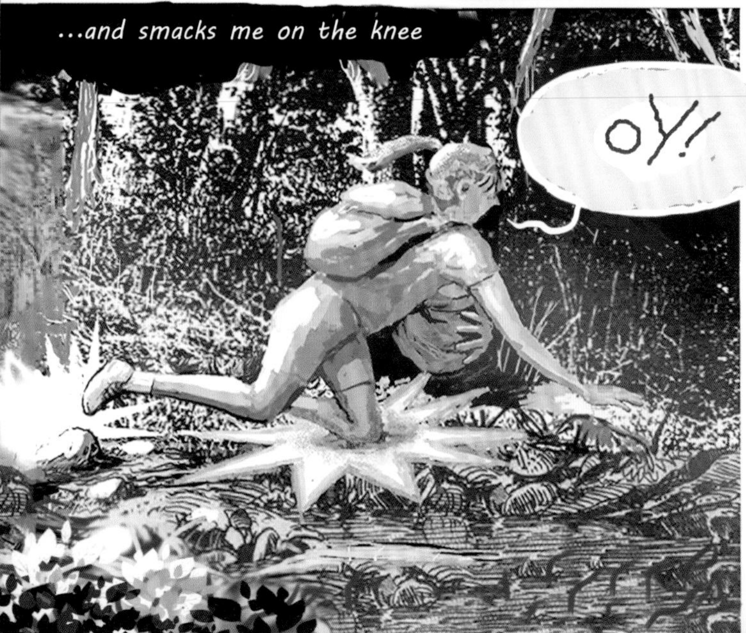
...and smacks me on the knee
OY!

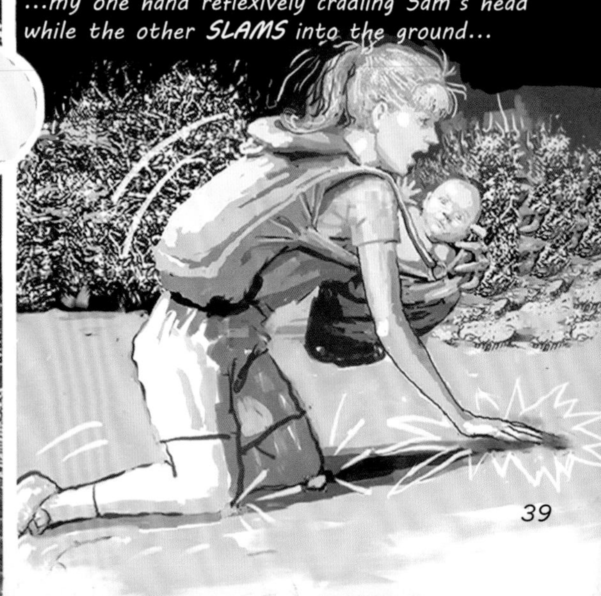
...my one hand reflexively cradling Sam's head while the other **SLAMS** into the ground...

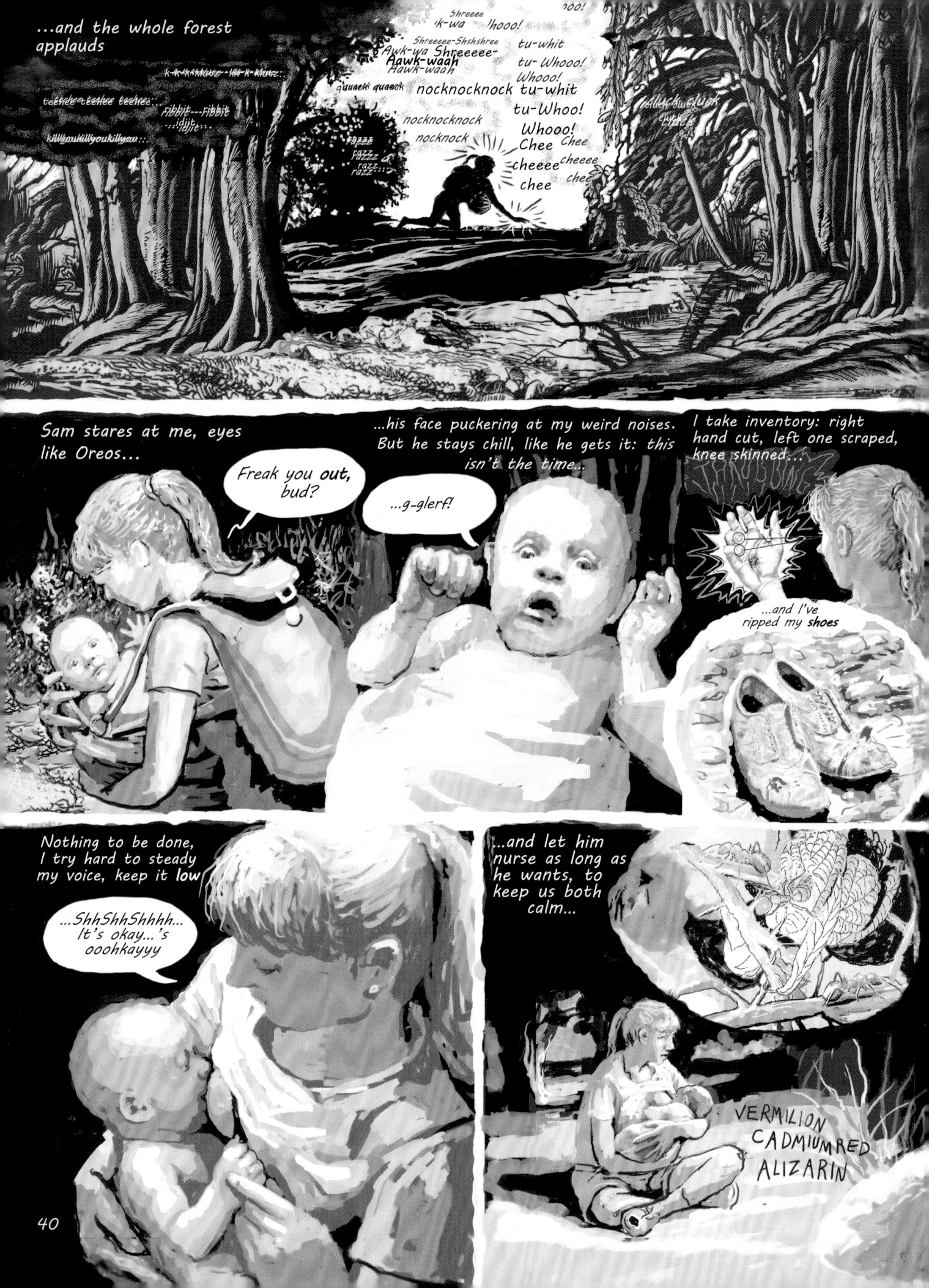

...and the whole forest applauds

Shreeee
Awk-wa Shreeeee-
Aawk-waah
Awk-waah
quaack quaack
nocknocknock tu-whit
tu-Whoo!
Whooo!
nocknocknock
nocknock
Chee Chee
cheeee cheeee
chee chee
tu-whit
tu-Whoo!
Whooo!
ribbit---ribbit
...idjit...
razz
razz
razz
razz
cluck cluck
cluck

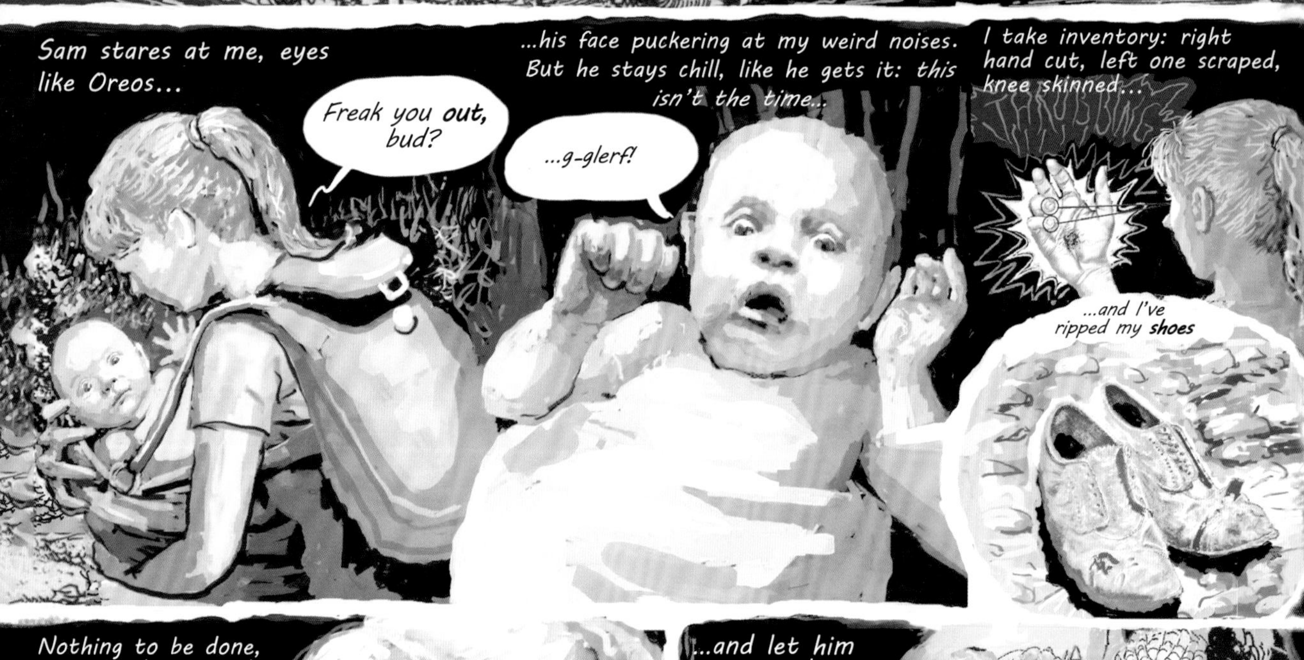

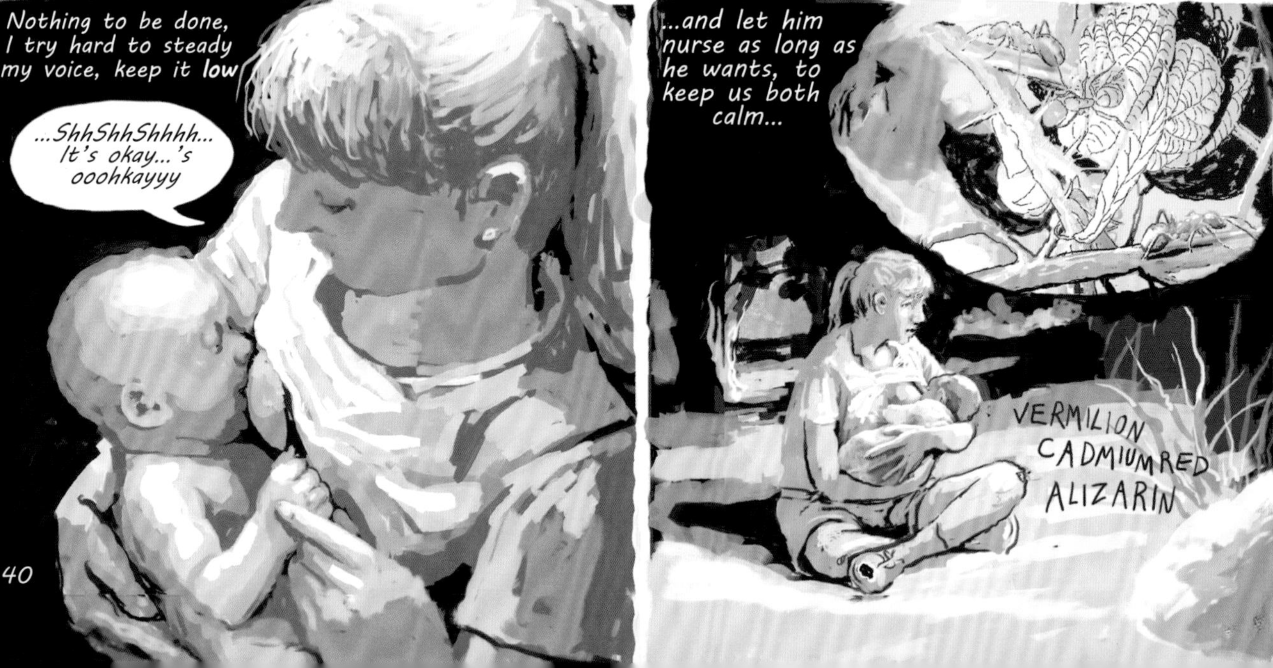

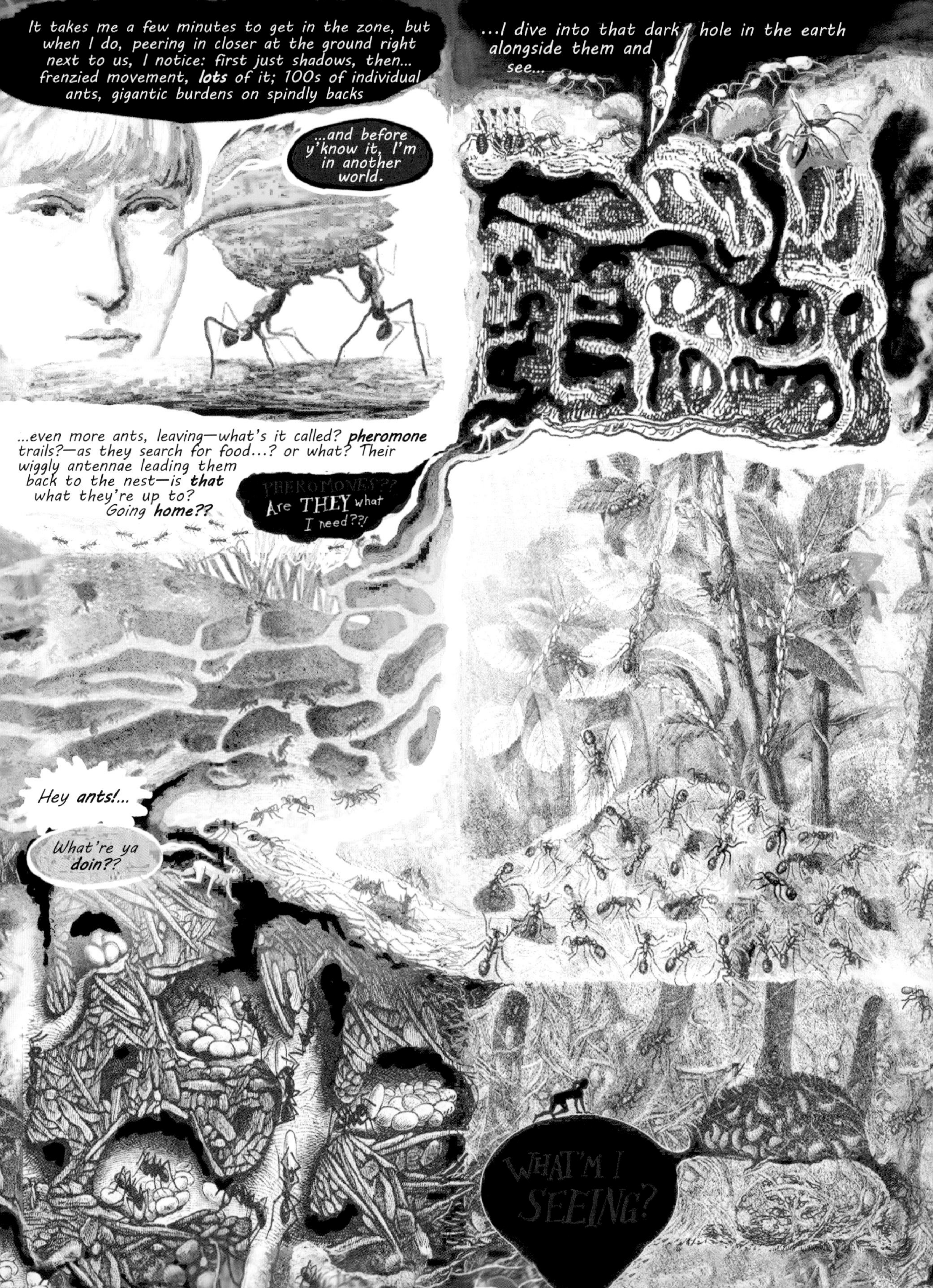
It takes me a few minutes to get in the zone, but when I do, peering in closer at the ground right next to us, I notice: first just shadows, then... frenzied movement, **lots** of it; 100s of individual ants, gigantic burdens on spindly backs
...and before y'know it, I'm in another world.
...I dive into that dark hole in the earth alongside them and see...
...even more ants, leaving—what's it called? **pheromone** trails?—as they search for food...? or what? Their wiggly antennae leading them back to the nest—is **that** what they're up to? Going **home??**
PHEROMONES?? Are THEY what I need??!
Hey **ants!...**
What're ya **doin??**
WHAT'M I SEEING?

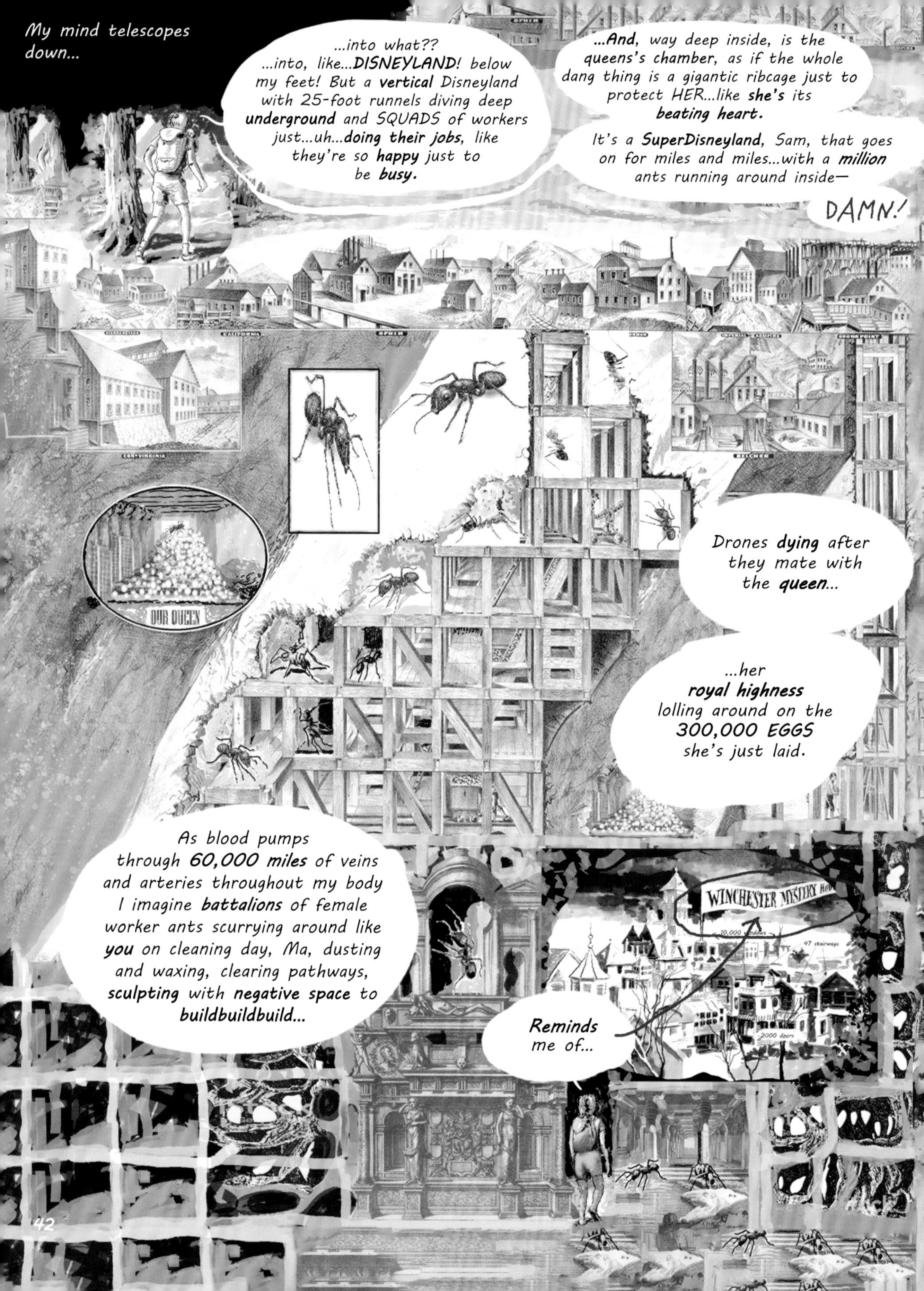
My mind telescopes down...
...into what?? ...into, like...DISNEYLAND! below my feet! But a vertical Disneyland with 25-foot runnels diving deep underground and SQUADS of workers just...uh...doing their jobs, like they're so happy just to be busy.
...And, way deep inside, is the queens's chamber, as if the whole dang thing is a gigantic ribcage just to protect HER...like she's its beating heart.
It's a SuperDisneyland, Sam, that goes on for miles and miles...with a million ants running around inside—
DAMN!
OPHIR
CALIFORNIA
CON. VIRGINIA
BELCHER
OUR QUEEN
Drones dying after they mate with the queen...
...her royal highness lolling around on the 300,000 EGGS she's just laid.
As blood pumps through 60,000 miles of veins and arteries throughout my body I imagine battalions of female worker ants scurrying around like you on cleaning day, Ma, dusting and waxing, clearing pathways, sculpting with negative space to buildbuildbuild...
WINCHESTER MYSTERY HO
97 stairways
2000 doors
Reminds me of...

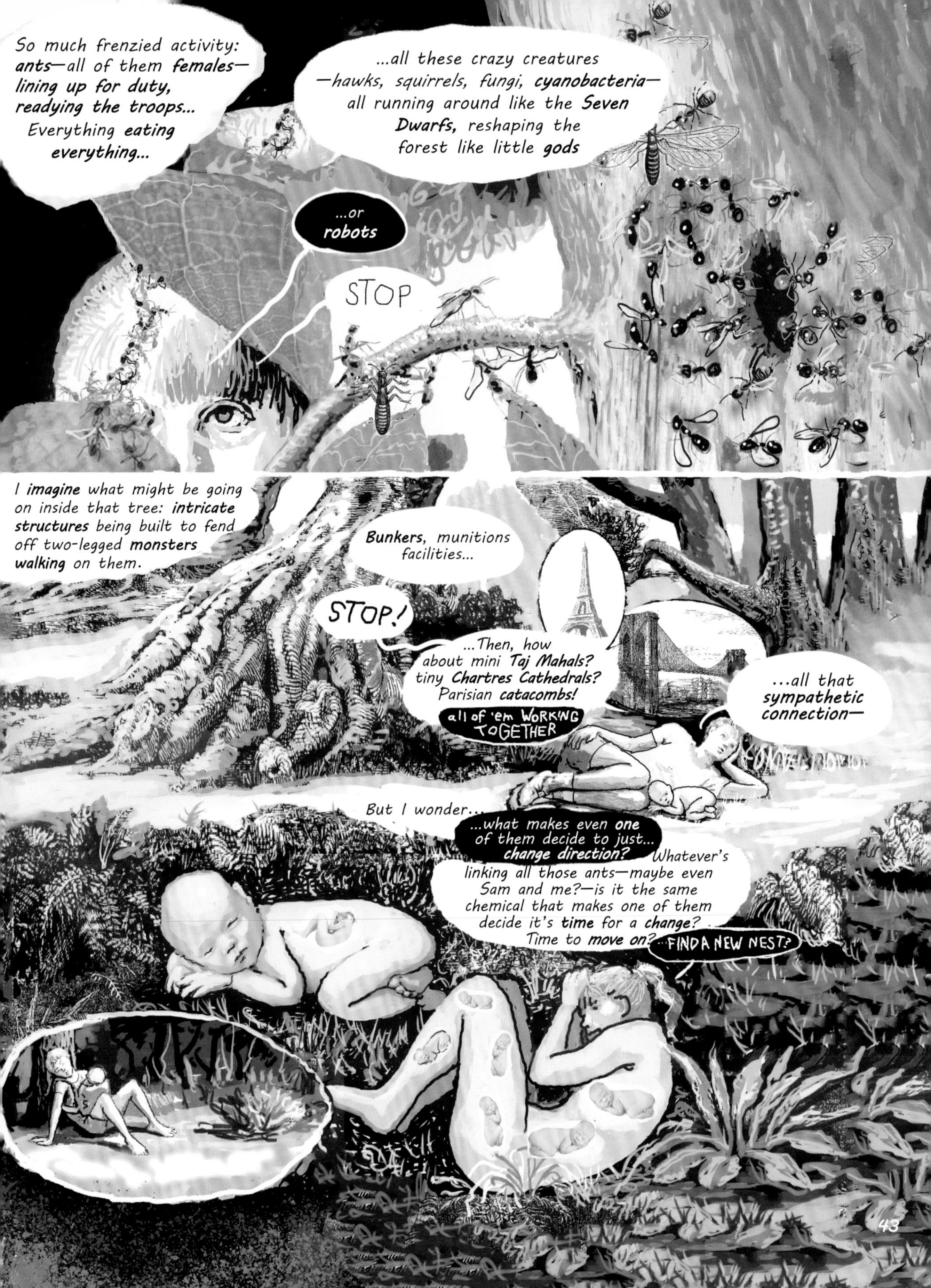

So much frenzied activity: ants—all of them females—lining up for duty, readying the troops... Everything eating everything...
...all these crazy creatures —hawks, squirrels, fungi, cyanobacteria— all running around like the Seven Dwarfs, reshaping the forest like little gods
...or robots
STOP
I imagine what might be going on inside that tree: intricate structures being built to fend off two-legged monsters walking on them.
Bunkers, munitions facilities...
STOP!
...Then, how about mini Taj Mahals? tiny Chartres Cathedrals? Parisian catacombs!
all of 'em WORKING TOGETHER
...all that sympathetic connection—
But I wonder...
...what makes even one of them decide to just... change direction?
Whatever's linking all those ants—maybe even Sam and me?—is it the same chemical that makes one of them decide it's time for a change? Time to move on?
...FIND A NEW NEST?

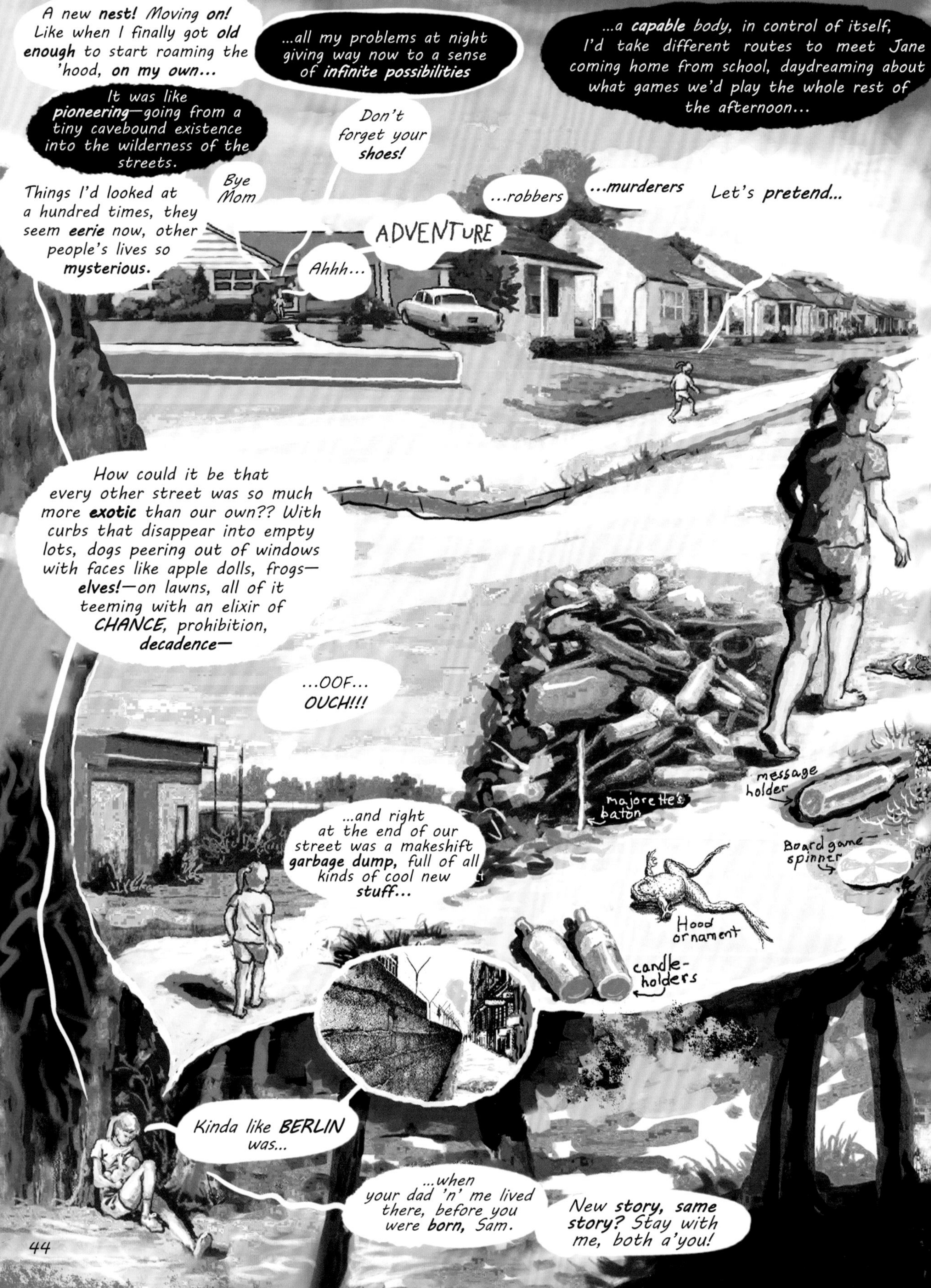

A new nest! Moving on! Like when I finally got old enough to start roaming the 'hood, on my own...
...all my problems at night giving way now to a sense of infinite possibilities
...a capable body, in control of itself, I'd take different routes to meet Jane coming home from school, daydreaming about what games we'd play the whole rest of the afternoon...
It was like pioneering—going from a tiny cavebound existence into the wilderness of the streets.
Don't forget your shoes!
Things I'd looked at a hundred times, they seem eerie now, other people's lives so mysterious.
Bye Mom
...robbers
...murderers
Let's pretend...
ADVENTURE
Ahhh...
How could it be that every other street was so much more exotic than our own?? With curbs that disappear into empty lots, dogs peering out of windows with faces like apple dolls, frogs—elves!—on lawns, all of it teeming with an elixir of CHANCE, prohibition, decadence—
...OOF... OUCH!!!
...and right at the end of our street was a makeshift garbage dump, full of all kinds of cool new stuff...
majorette's baton
message holder
Board game spinner
Hood ornament
candle-holders
Kinda like BERLIN was...
...when your dad 'n' me lived there, before you were born, Sam.
New story, same story? Stay with me, both a'you!

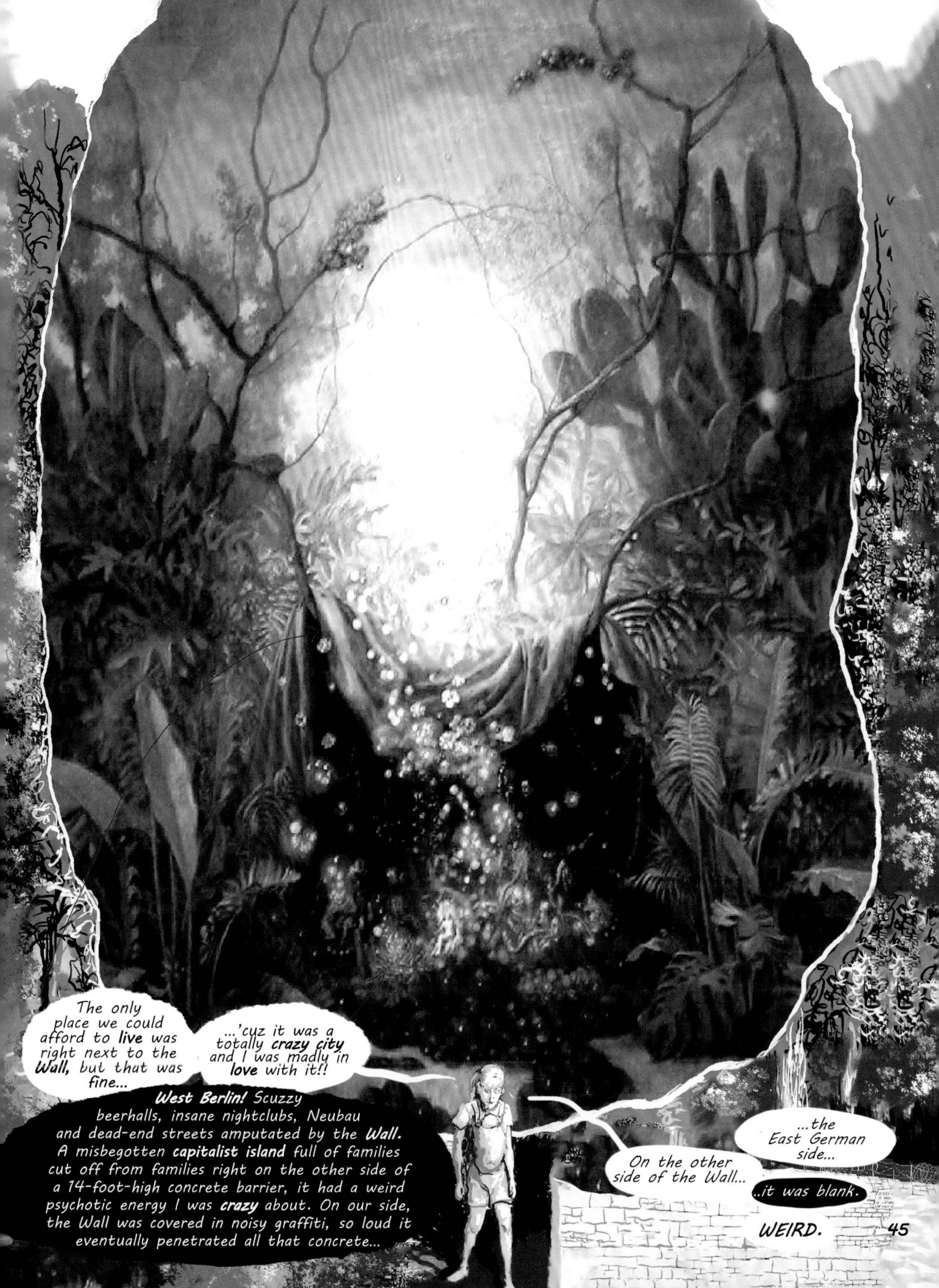
The only place we could afford to live was right next to the Wall, but that was fine...
...'cuz it was a totally crazy city and I was madly in love with it!!
West Berlin! Scuzzy beerhalls, insane nightclubs, Neubau and dead-end streets amputated by the Wall. A misbegotten capitalist island full of families cut off from families right on the other side of a 14-foot-high concrete barrier, it had a weird psychotic energy I was crazy about. On our side, the Wall was covered in noisy graffiti, so loud it eventually penetrated all that concrete...
On the other side of the Wall...
...the East German side...
..it was blank.
WEIRD.

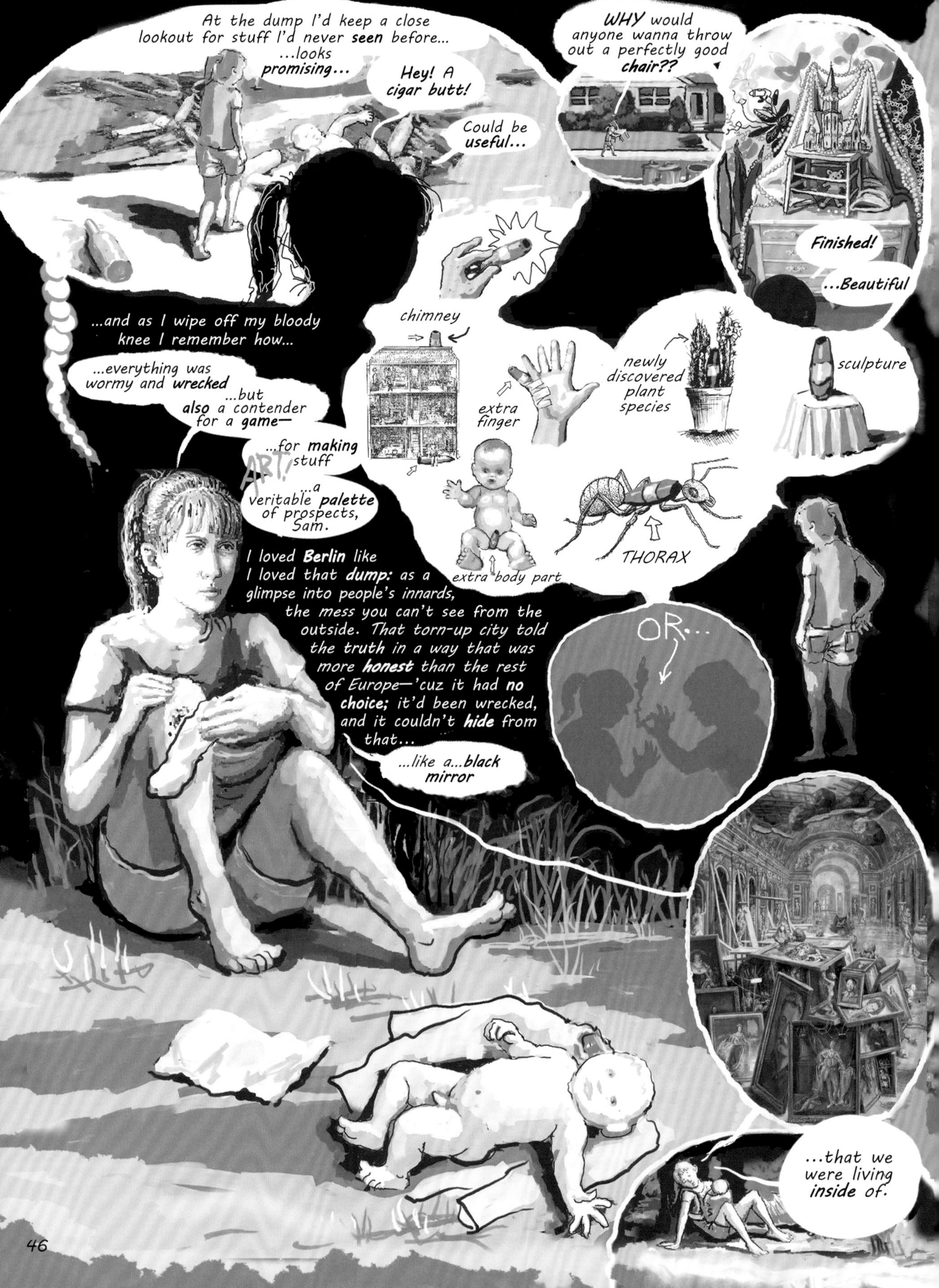
At the dump I'd keep a close lookout for stuff I'd never seen before...
...looks promising...
Hey! A cigar butt!
Could be useful...
WHY would anyone wanna throw out a perfectly good chair??
Finished!
...Beautiful
...and as I wipe off my bloody knee I remember how...
...everything was wormy and wrecked
...but also a contender for a game—
...for making stuff
ART!
...a veritable palette of prospects, Sam.
chimney
extra finger
newly discovered plant species
sculpture
extra body part
THORAX
OR...
I loved Berlin like I loved that dump: as a glimpse into people's innards, the mess you can't see from the outside. That torn-up city told the truth in a way that was more honest than the rest of Europe—'cuz it had no choice; it'd been wrecked, and it couldn't hide from that...
...like a...black mirror
...that we were living inside of.

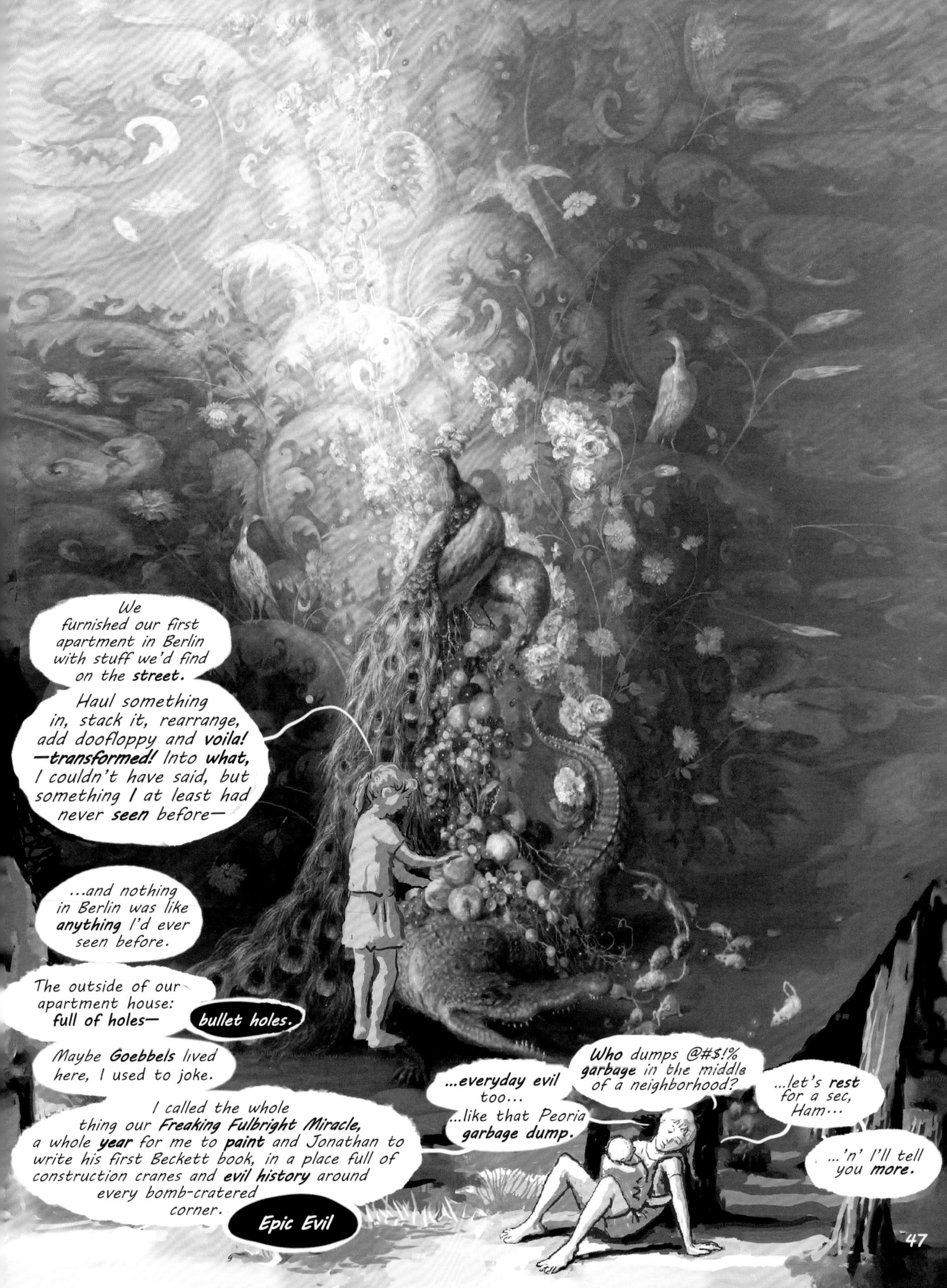
We furnished our first apartment in Berlin with stuff we'd find on the **street.**
Haul something in, stack it, rearrange, add doofloppy and **voila! —transformed!** Into **what,** I couldn't have said, but something **I** at least had never **seen** before—
...and nothing in Berlin was like **anything** I'd ever seen before.
The outside of our apartment house: **full of holes—**
bullet holes.
Maybe **Goebbels** lived here, I used to joke.
I called the whole thing our **Freaking Fulbright Miracle,** a whole **year** for me to **paint** and Jonathan to write his first Beckett book, in a place full of construction cranes and **evil history** around every bomb-cratered corner.
Epic Evil
...everyday evil too... ...like that Peoria **garbage dump.**
Who dumps @#$!% **garbage** in the middle of a neighborhood?
...let's **rest** for a sec, Ham...
...'n' I'll tell you **more.**

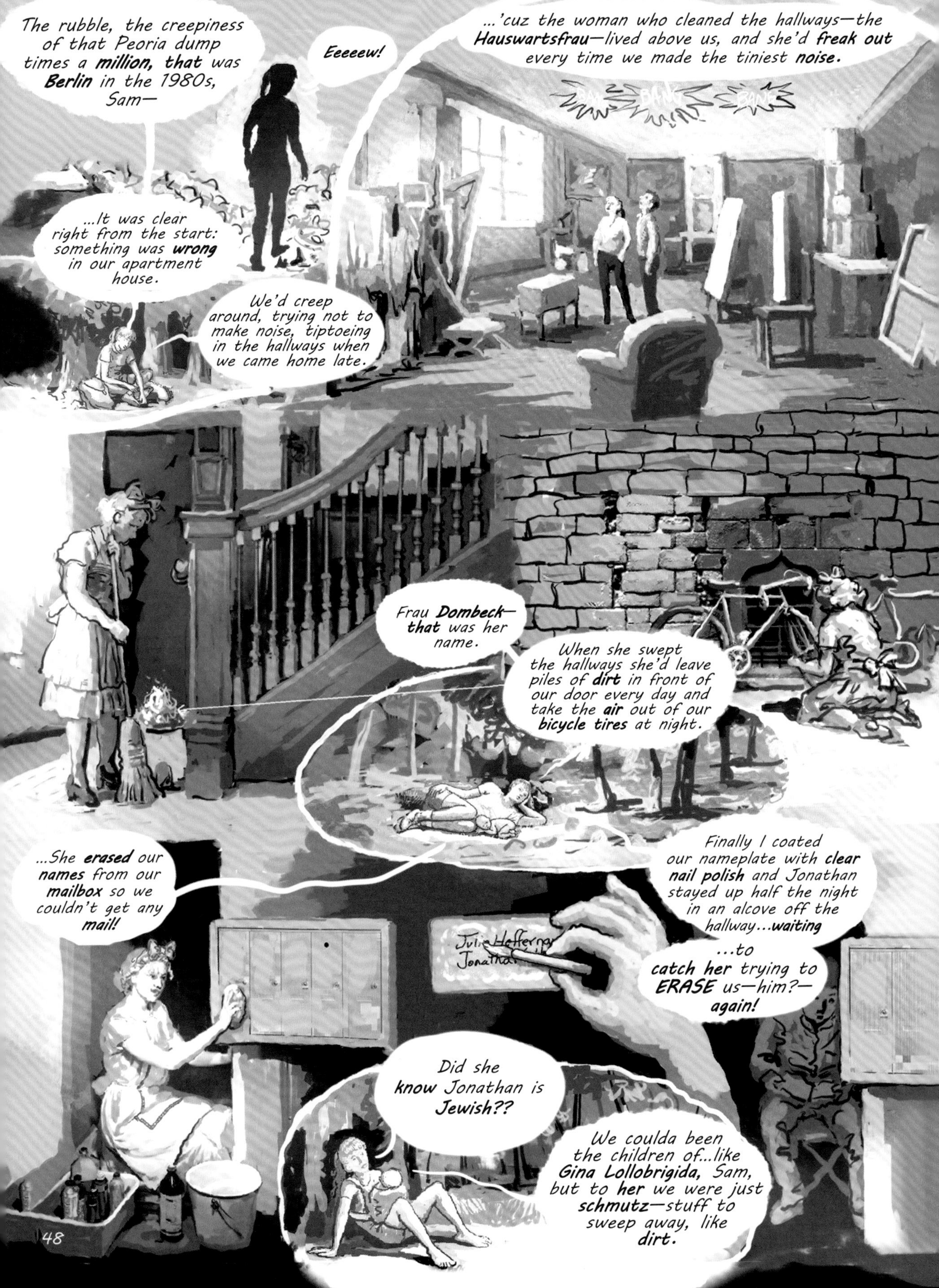
The rubble, the creepiness of that Peoria dump times a **million, that** was **Berlin** in the 1980s, Sam—
Eeeeew!
...'cuz the woman who cleaned the hallways—the **Hauswartsfrau**—lived above us, and she'd **freak out** every time we made the tiniest **noise.**
BANG BANG BANG
...It was clear right from the start: something was **wrong** in our apartment house.
We'd creep around, trying not to make noise, tiptoeing in the hallways when we came home late.
Frau **Dombeck—that** was her name.
When she swept the hallways she'd leave piles of **dirt** in front of our door every day and take the **air** out of our **bicycle tires** at night.
...She **erased** our **names** from our **mailbox** so we couldn't get any **mail!**
Finally I coated our nameplate with **clear nail polish** and Jonathan stayed up half the night in an alcove off the hallway...**waiting**
...to **catch her** trying to **ERASE** us—him?—**again!**
Did she **know** Jonathan is **Jewish??**
We coulda been the children of...like **Gina Lollobrigida,** Sam, but to **her** we were just **schmutz**—stuff to sweep away, like **dirt.**

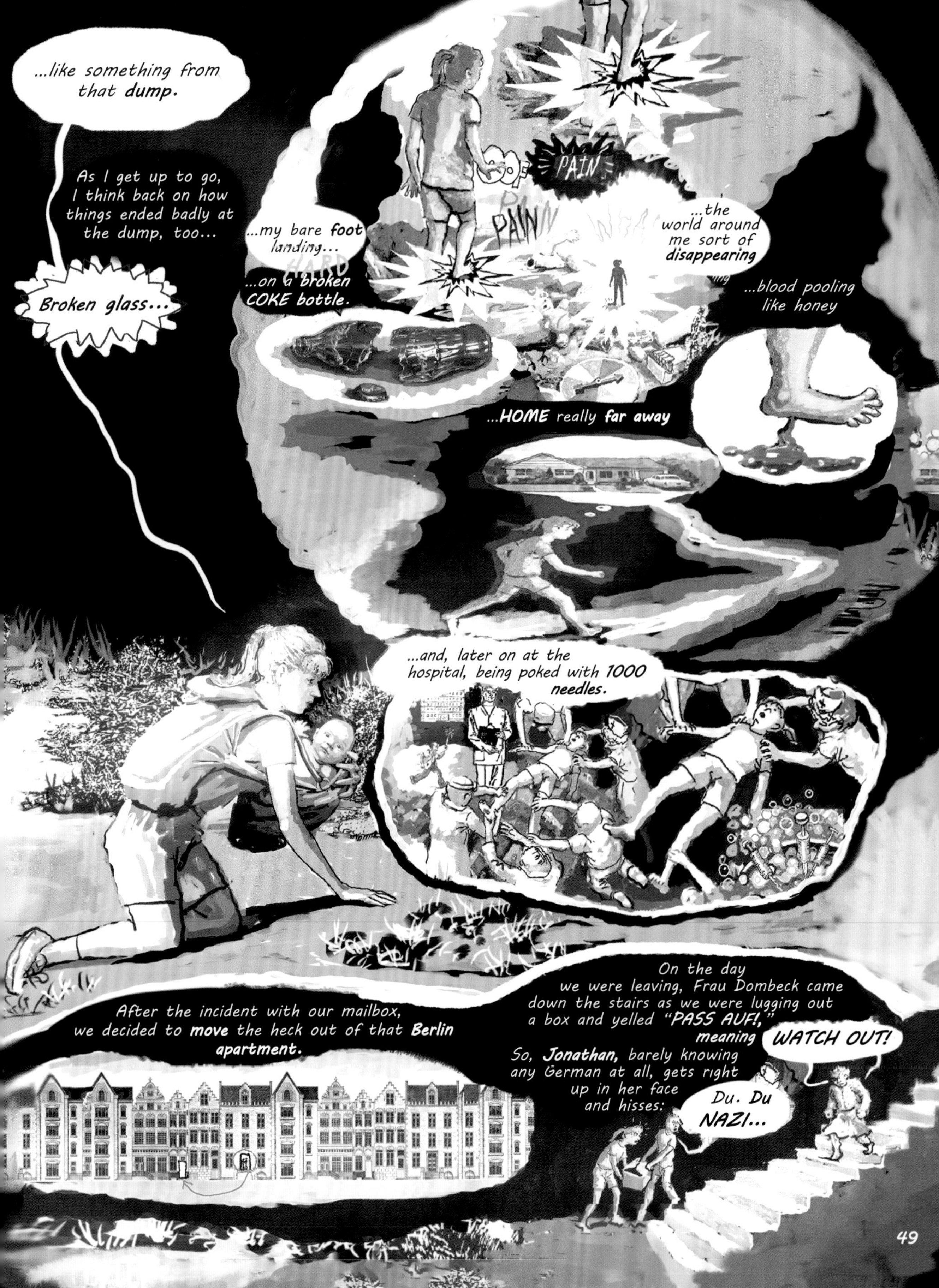
...like something from that dump.
As I get up to go, I think back on how things ended badly at the dump, too...
Broken glass...
...my bare foot landing...
HARD
PAIN
PAIN
...on a broken COKE bottle.
...the world around me sort of disappearing
...blood pooling like honey
...HOME really far away
...and, later on at the hospital, being poked with 1000 needles.
After the incident with our mailbox, we decided to move the heck out of that Berlin apartment.
On the day we were leaving, Frau Dombeck came down the stairs as we were lugging out a box and yelled "PASS AUF!," meaning
WATCH OUT!
So, Jonathan, barely knowing any German at all, gets right up in her face and hisses:
Du. Du NAZI...

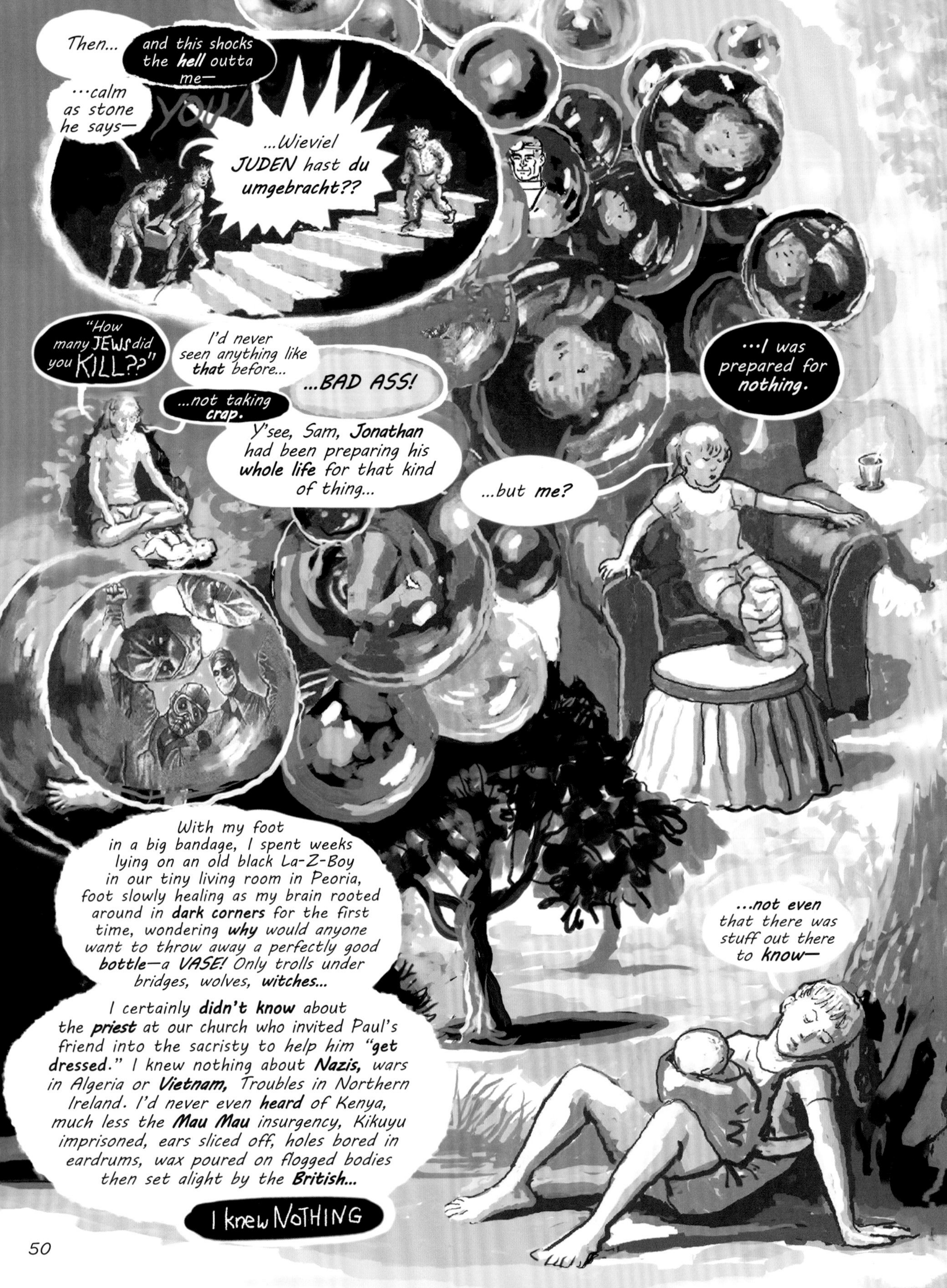
Then...
and this shocks the hell outta me—
...calm as stone he says—
YOU!
...Wieviel JUDEN hast du umgebracht??
"How many JEWS did you KILL??"
I'd never seen anything like that before...
...BAD ASS!
...not taking crap.
Y'see, Sam, Jonathan had been preparing his whole life for that kind of thing...
...but me?
...I was prepared for nothing.
With my foot in a big bandage, I spent weeks lying on an old black La-Z-Boy in our tiny living room in Peoria, foot slowly healing as my brain rooted around in dark corners for the first time, wondering why would anyone want to throw away a perfectly good bottle—a VASE! Only trolls under bridges, wolves, witches...
I certainly didn't know about the priest at our church who invited Paul's friend into the sacristy to help him "get dressed." I knew nothing about Nazis, wars in Algeria or Vietnam, Troubles in Northern Ireland. I'd never even heard of Kenya, much less the Mau Mau insurgency, Kikuyu imprisoned, ears sliced off, holes bored in eardrums, wax poured on flogged bodies then set alight by the British...
...not even that there was stuff out there to know—
I knew NOTHING

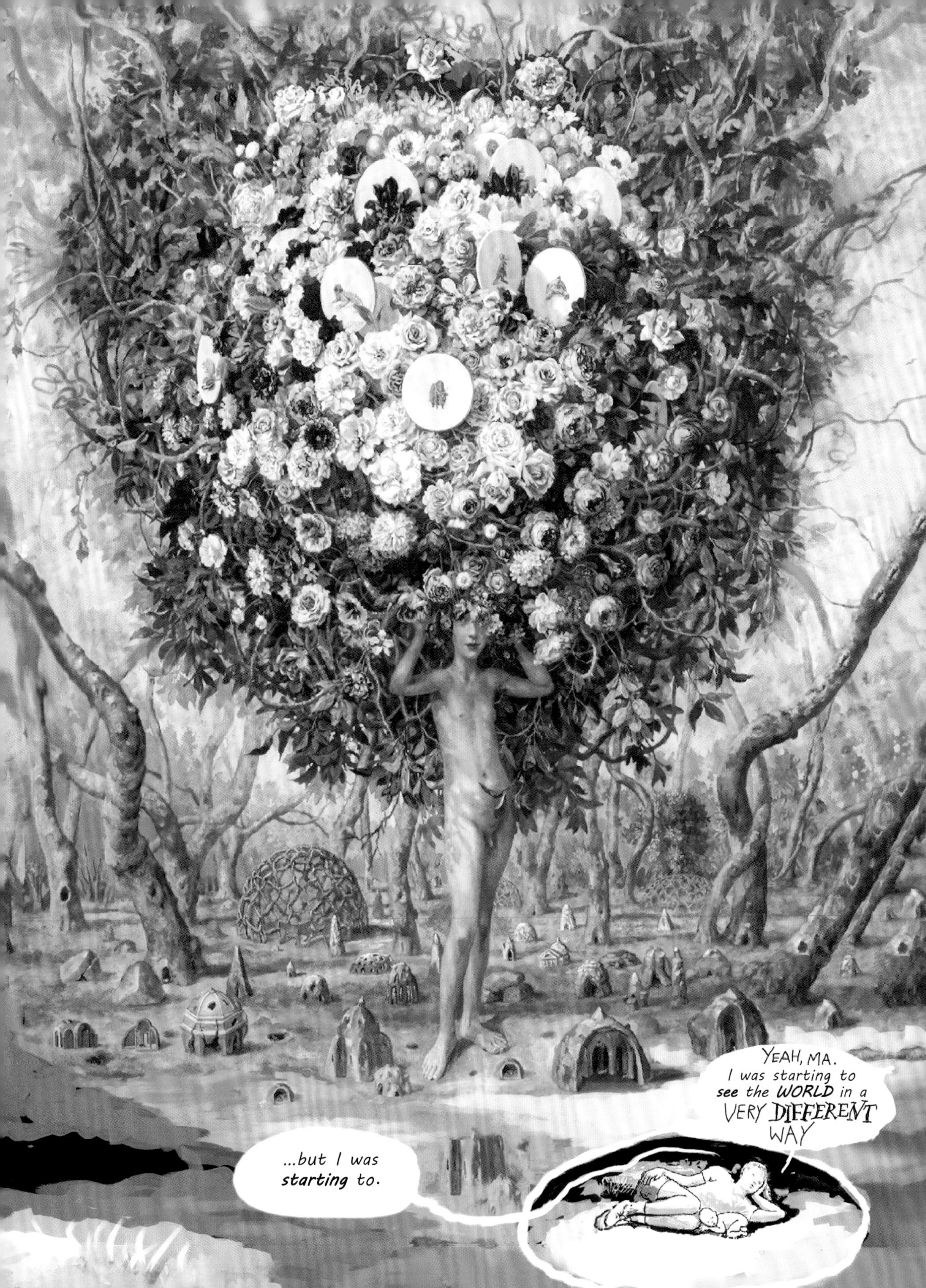
YEAH, MA. I was starting to see the WORLD in a VERY DIFFERENT WAY
...but I was starting to.

Chapter THREE

Under a twisty oak I find a bed of soft green moss I can't resist.

A chattering breeze **chides** me— I ignore it. All the little irksome sounds— I shut them **out**—settling deeper into the moss 'n' leaves, every muscle **sighing**...

...just a little rest

...been walking **all morning**

FIVE MINUTES!

Prob'ly only— what?—1:00? 2:00 at **most**?

...that pesky little voice inside me whispering—

WHAT'RE YOU DOING?

...to which I respond—

...leaveme**alone**—

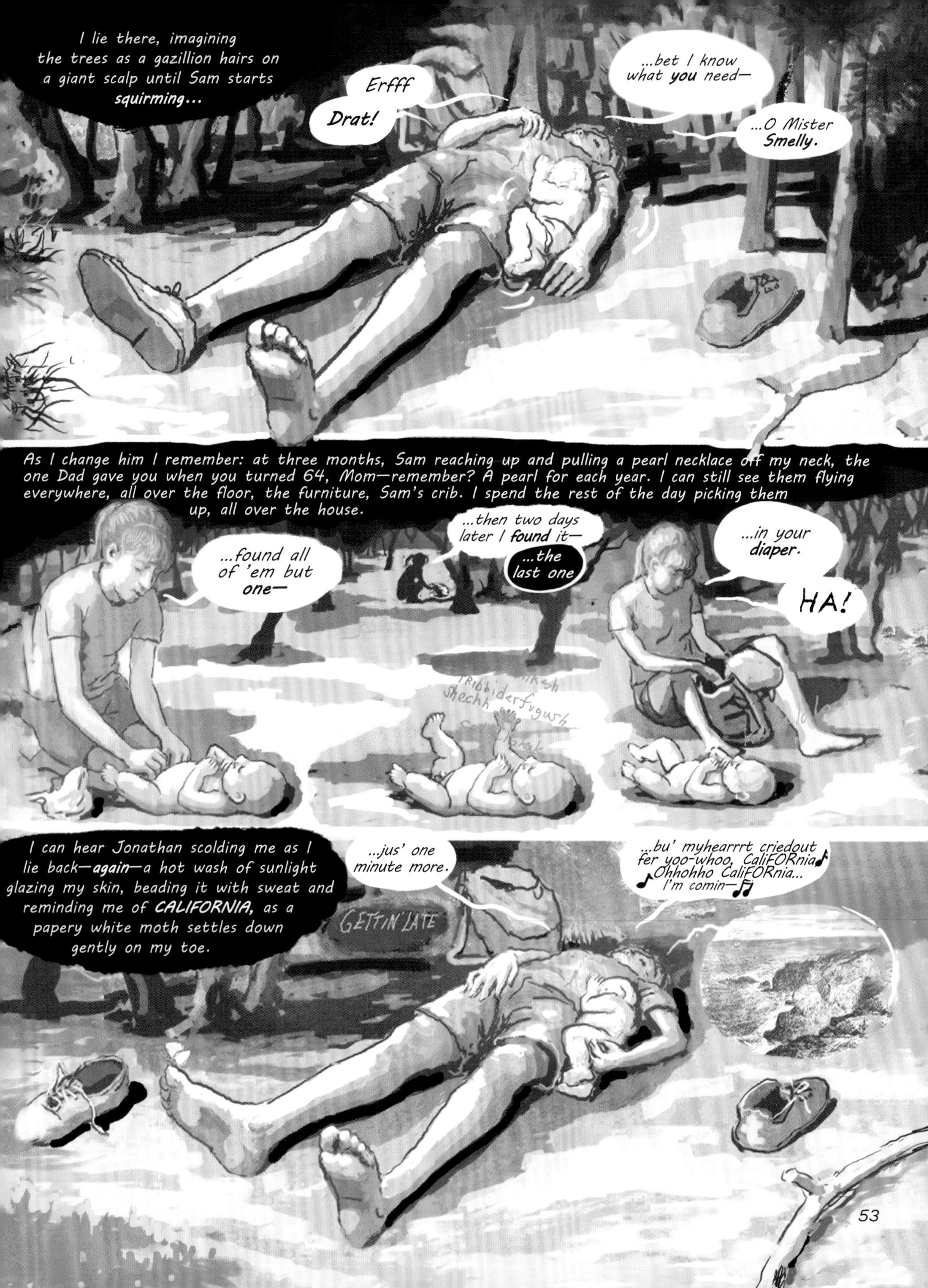
I lie there, imagining the trees as a gazillion hairs on a giant scalp until Sam starts **squirming...**
Erfff
Drat!
...bet I know what **you** need—
...O Mister **Smelly.**
As I change him I remember: at three months, Sam reaching up and pulling a pearl necklace off my neck, the one Dad gave you when you turned 64, Mom—remember? A pearl for each year. I can still see them flying everywhere, all over the floor, the furniture, Sam's crib. I spend the rest of the day picking them up, all over the house.
...found all of 'em but **one**—
...then two days later I **found** it—
...the last one
...in your **diaper.**
HA!
Shechh
Tribbiderfugush
I can hear Jonathan scolding me as I lie back—**again**—a hot wash of sunlight glazing my skin, beading it with sweat and reminding me of **CALIFORNIA,** as a papery white moth settles down gently on my toe.
...jus' one minute more.
GETTIN' LATE
...bu' myhearrrt criedout fer yoo-whoo, CaliFORnia♪ ♪Ohhohho CaliFORnia... I'm comin—♫
53

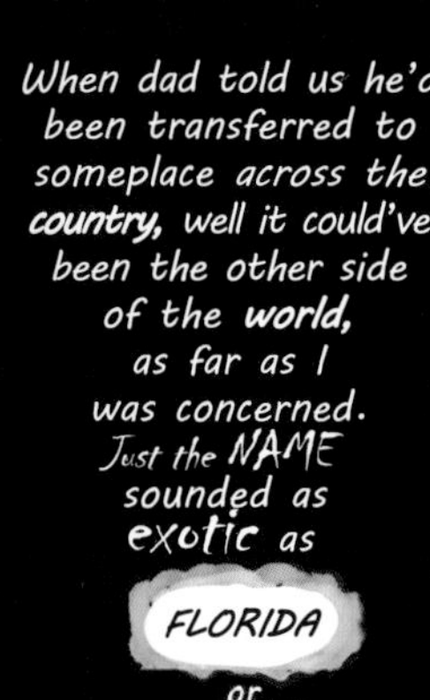

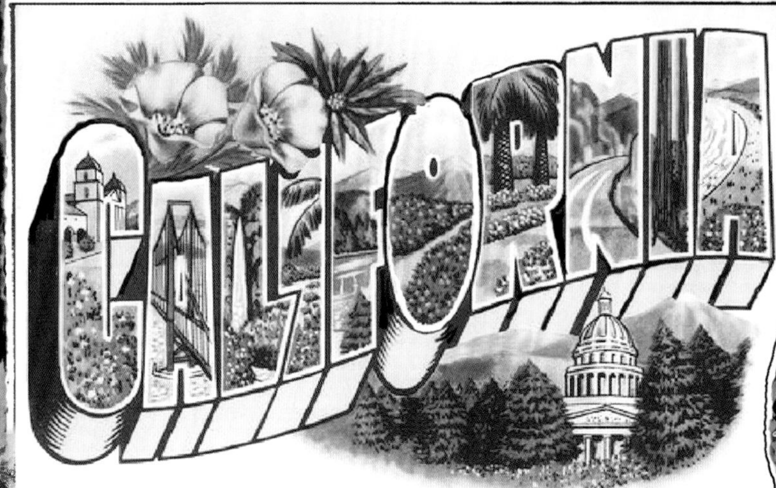

CAROL DODA

You guys **thought** you were **also** transferring your strict, midwestern, churchgoing values...

...little did **they know...**

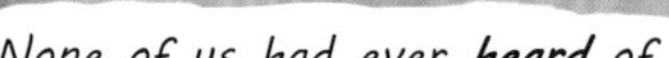

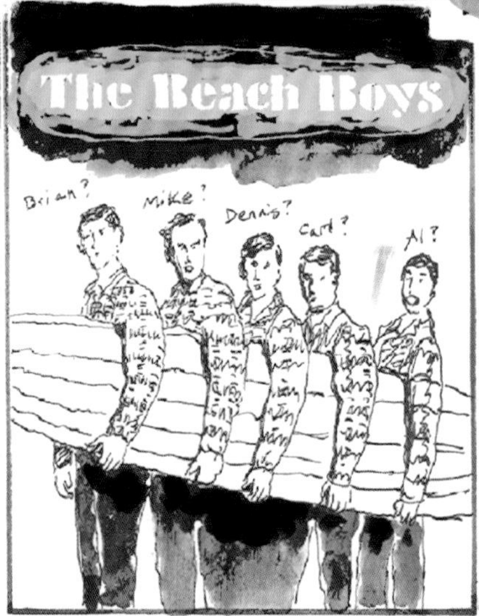

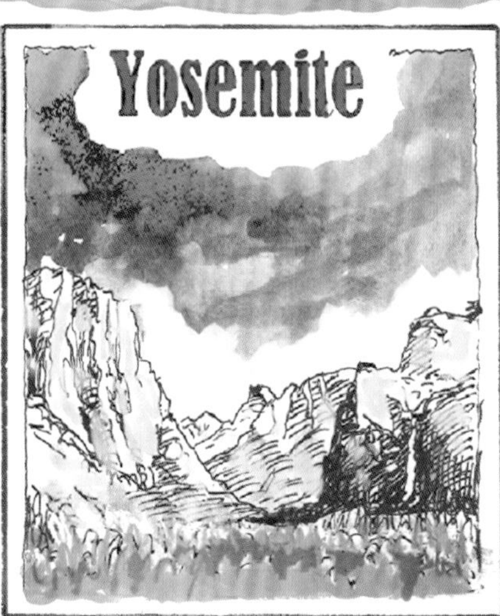

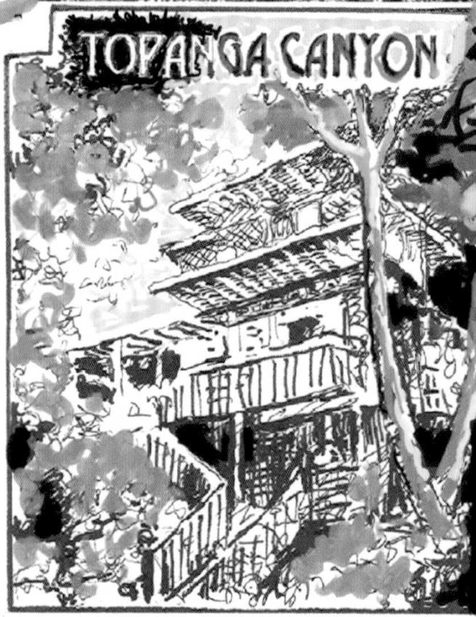

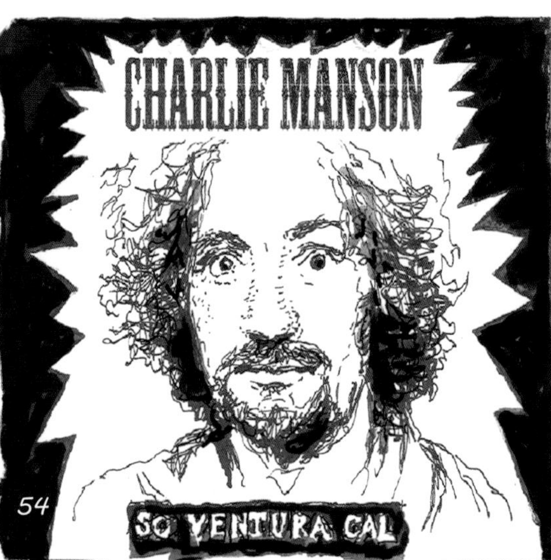

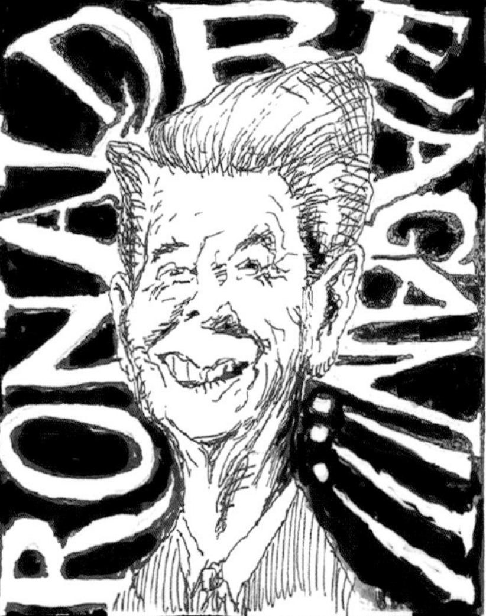

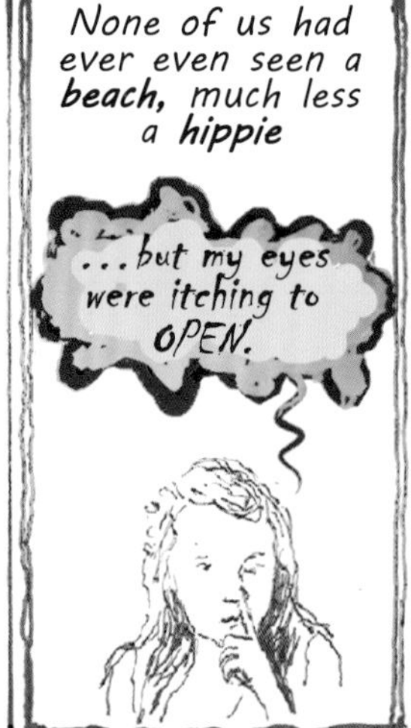

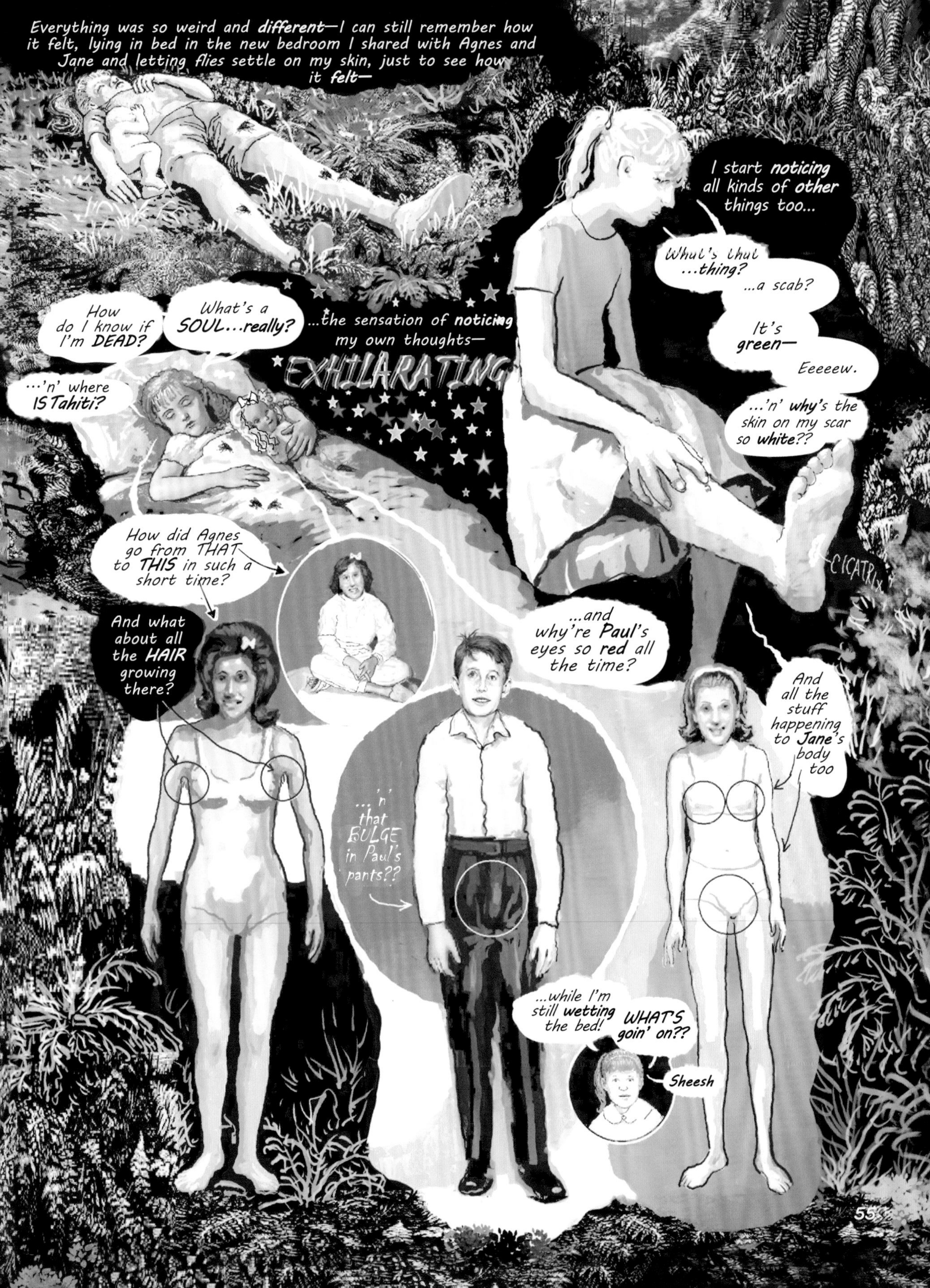

Everything was so weird and different—I can still remember how it felt, lying in bed in the new bedroom I shared with Agnes and Jane and letting flies settle on my skin, just to see how it felt—
I start noticing all kinds of other things too...
What's that ...thing? ...a scab?
It's green—
Eeeeew.
...'n' why's the skin on my scar so white??
CICATRIX
How do I know if I'm DEAD?
What's a SOUL...really?
...the sensation of noticing my own thoughts—
EXHILARATING
...'n' where IS Tahiti?
How did Agnes go from THAT to THIS in such a short time?
And what about all the HAIR growing there?
...and why're Paul's eyes so red all the time?
And all the stuff happening to Jane's body too
...'n' that BULGE in Paul's pants??
...while I'm still wetting the bed!
WHAT'S goin' on??
Sheesh

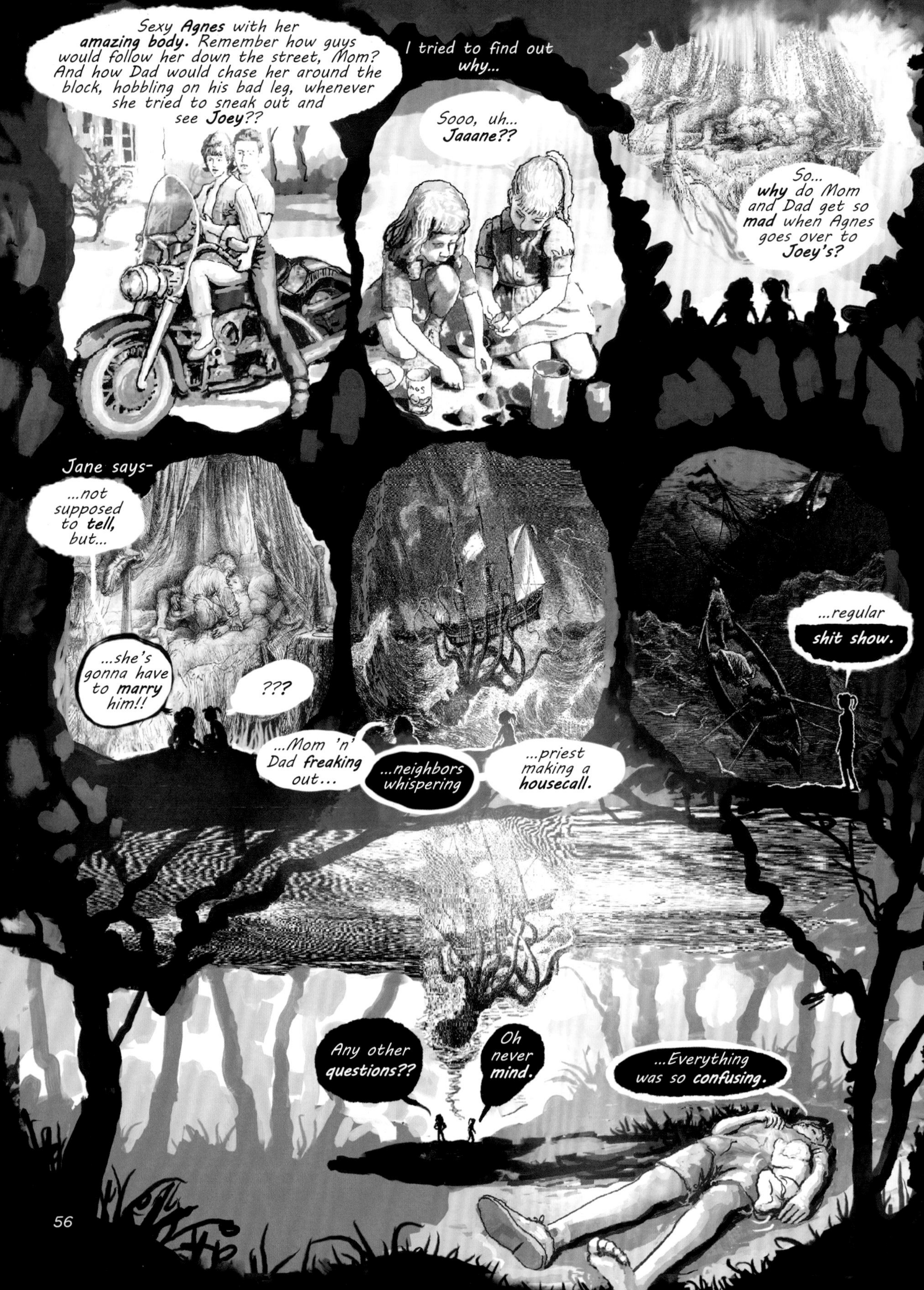
Sexy Agnes with her amazing body. Remember how guys would follow her down the street, Mom? And how Dad would chase her around the block, hobbling on his bad leg, whenever she tried to sneak out and see Joey??
I tried to find out why...
Sooo, uh... Jaaane??
So... why do Mom and Dad get so mad when Agnes goes over to Joey's?
Jane says-
...not supposed to tell, but...
...she's gonna have to marry him!!
???
...Mom 'n' Dad freaking out...
...neighbors whispering
...priest making a housecall.
...regular
shit show.
Any other questions??
Oh never mind.
...Everything was so confusing.

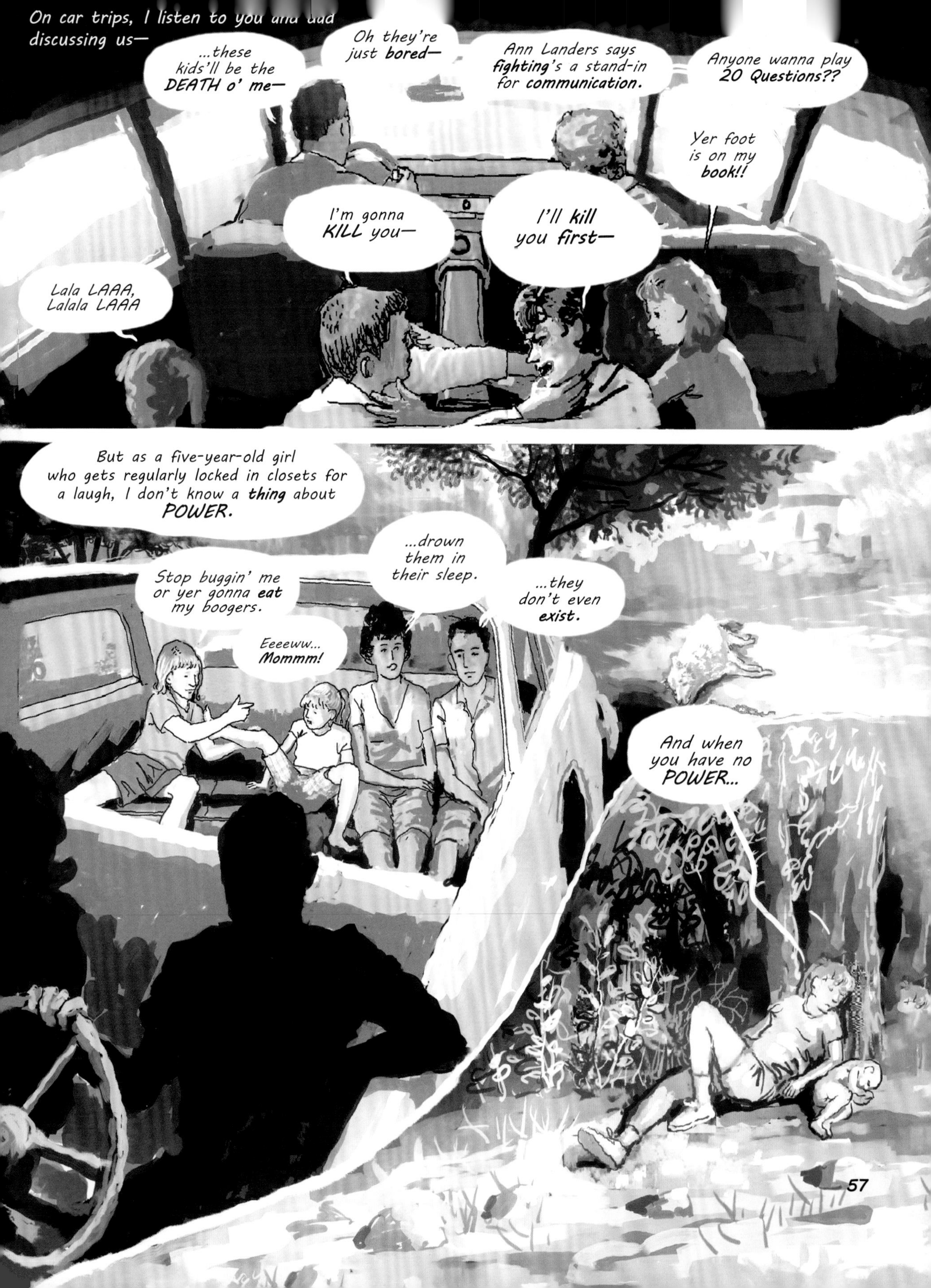
On car trips, I listen to you and dad discussing us—
...these kids'll be the DEATH o' me—
Oh they're just bored—
Ann Landers says fighting's a stand-in for communication.
Anyone wanna play 20 Questions??
Yer foot is on my book!!
I'm gonna KILL you—
I'll kill you first—
Lala LAAA, Lalala LAAA
But as a five-year-old girl who gets regularly locked in closets for a laugh, I don't know a thing about POWER.
Stop buggin' me or yer gonna eat my boogers.
Eeeeww... Mommm!
...drown them in their sleep.
...they don't even exist.
And when you have no POWER...

Massacre of the Innocents by Giotto

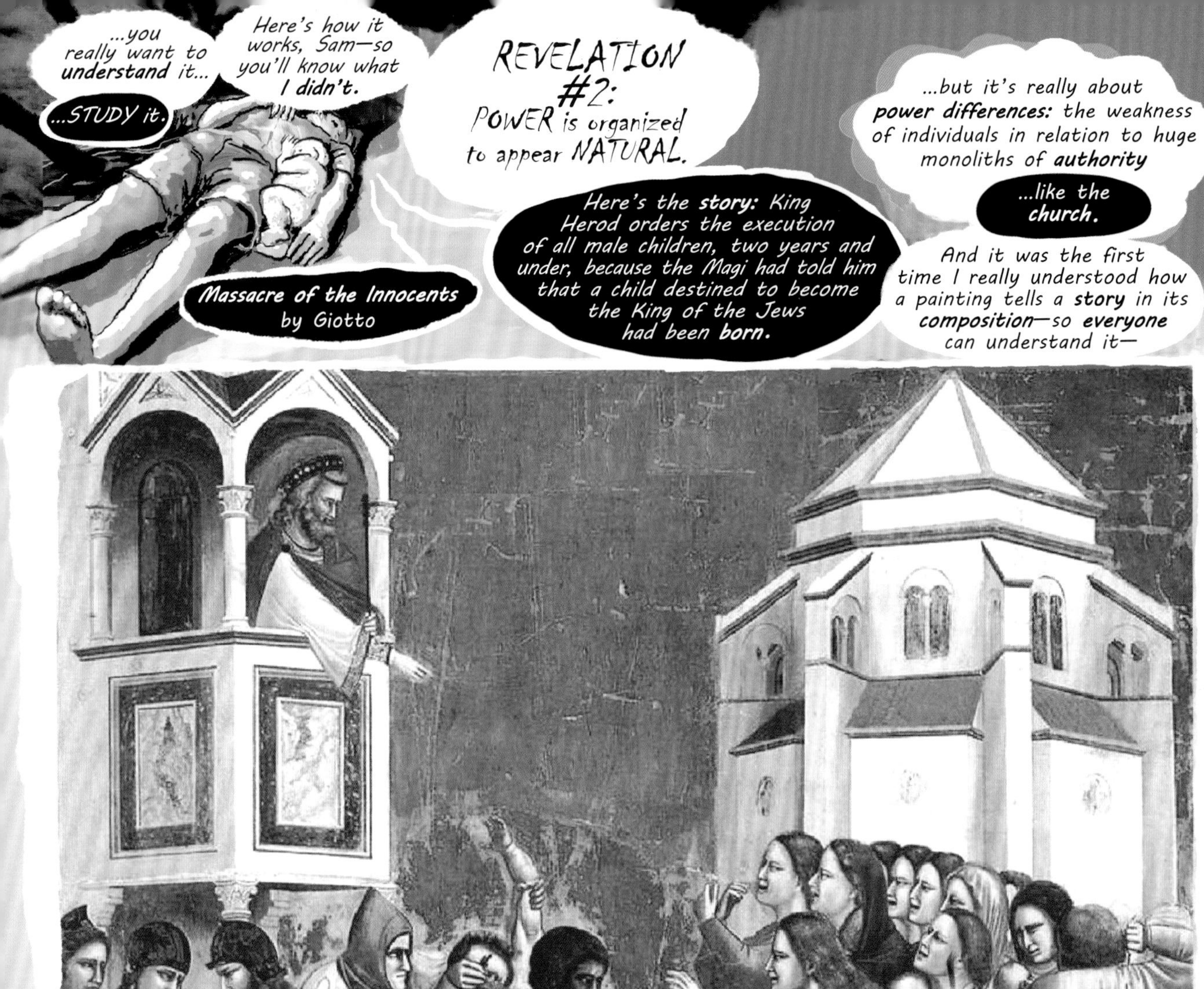

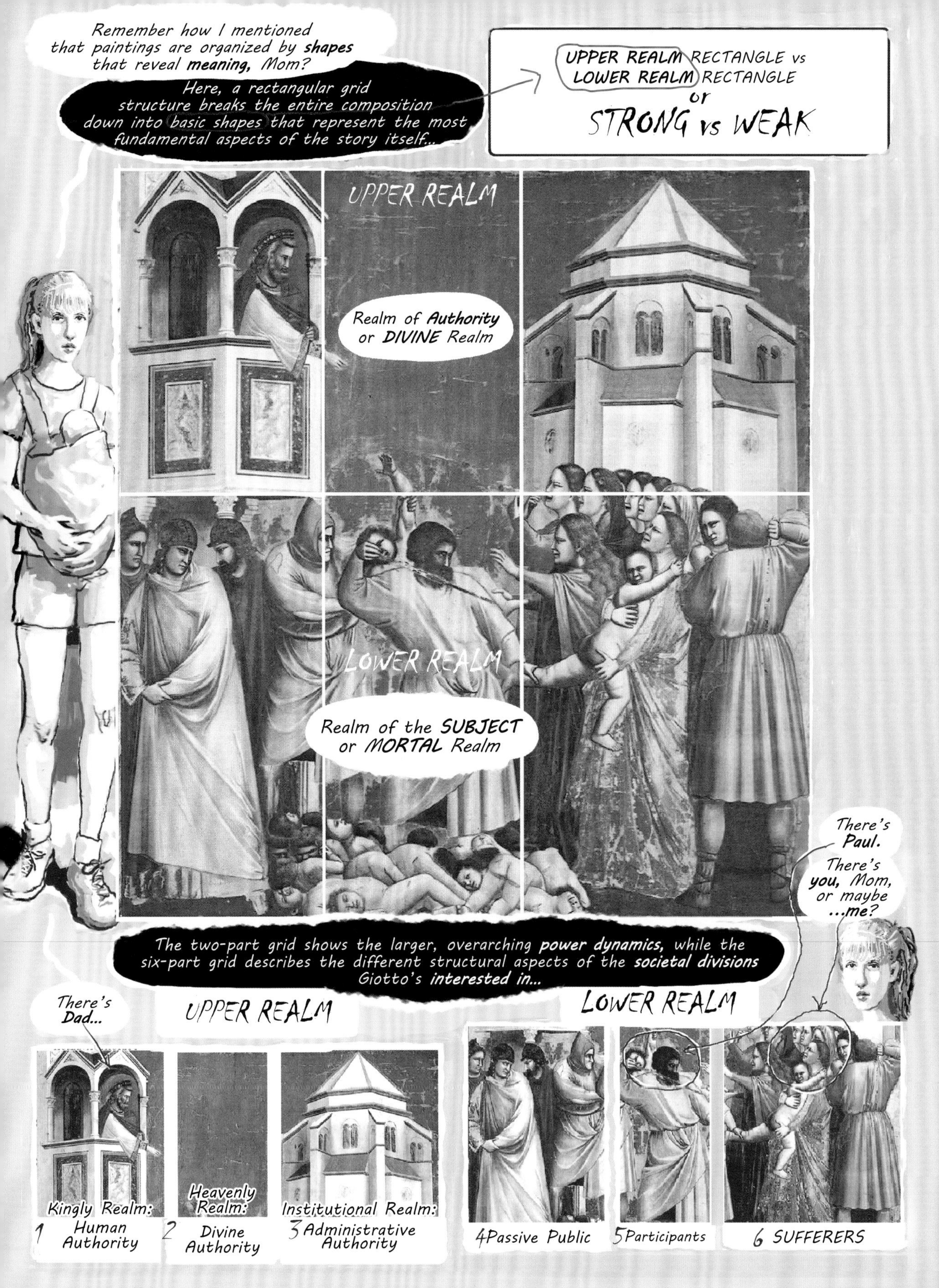

Remember how I mentioned that paintings are organized by **shapes** that reveal **meaning,** Mom?

Here, a rectangular grid structure breaks the entire composition down into basic shapes that represent the most fundamental aspects of the story itself...

UPPER REALM RECTANGLE vs
LOWER REALM RECTANGLE
or
STRONG vs WEAK

UPPER REALM

Realm of ***Authority*** or ***DIVINE*** Realm

LOWER REALM

Realm of the ***SUBJECT*** or ***MORTAL*** Realm

There's **Paul.**

There's **you,** Mom, or maybe **...me?**

The two-part grid shows the larger, overarching ***power dynamics,*** while the six-part grid describes the different structural aspects of the ***societal divisions*** Giotto's ***interested in...***

There's **Dad...**

UPPER REALM

LOWER REALM

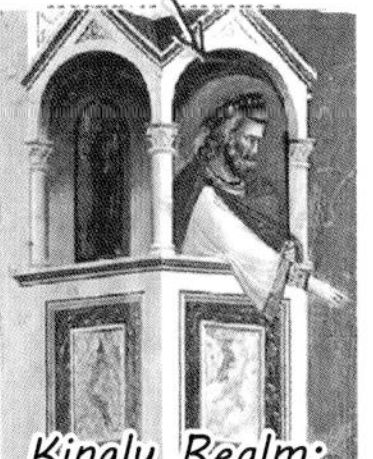

Kingly Realm:
1 Human Authority

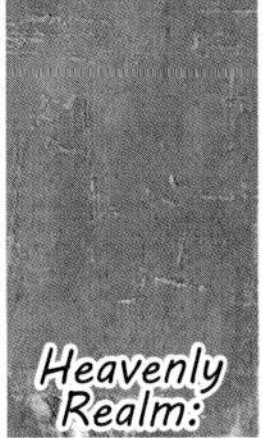

Heavenly Realm:
2 Divine Authority

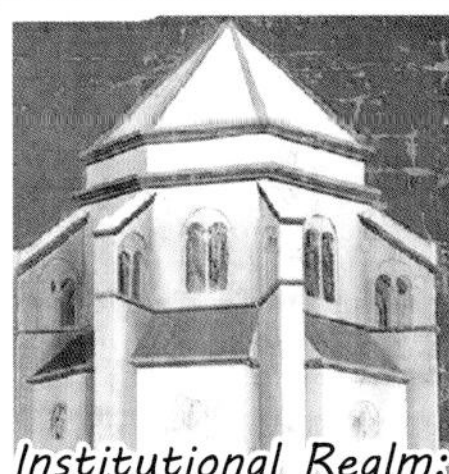

Institutional Realm:
3 Administrative Authority

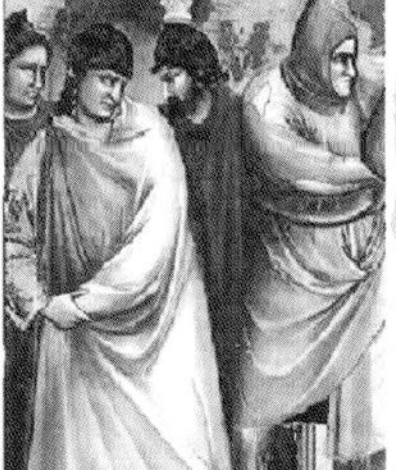

4 Passive Public

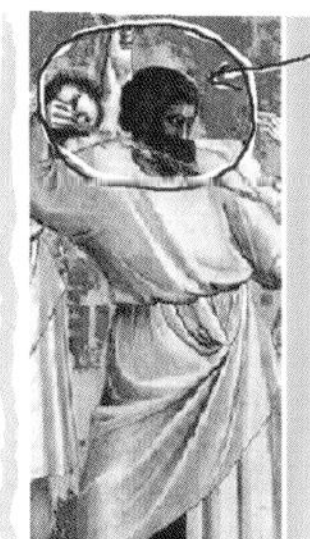

5 Participants

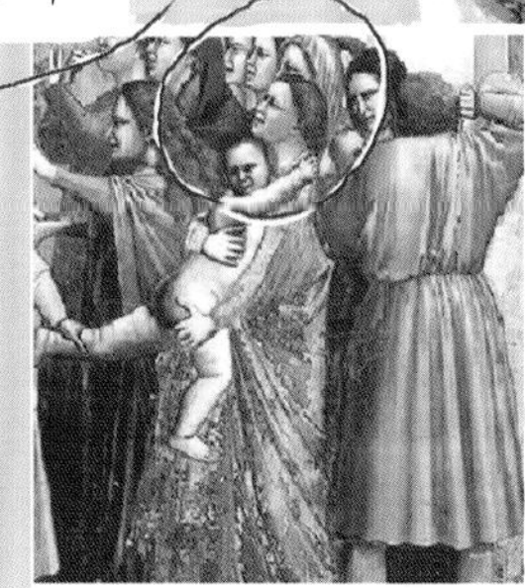

6 SUFFERERS

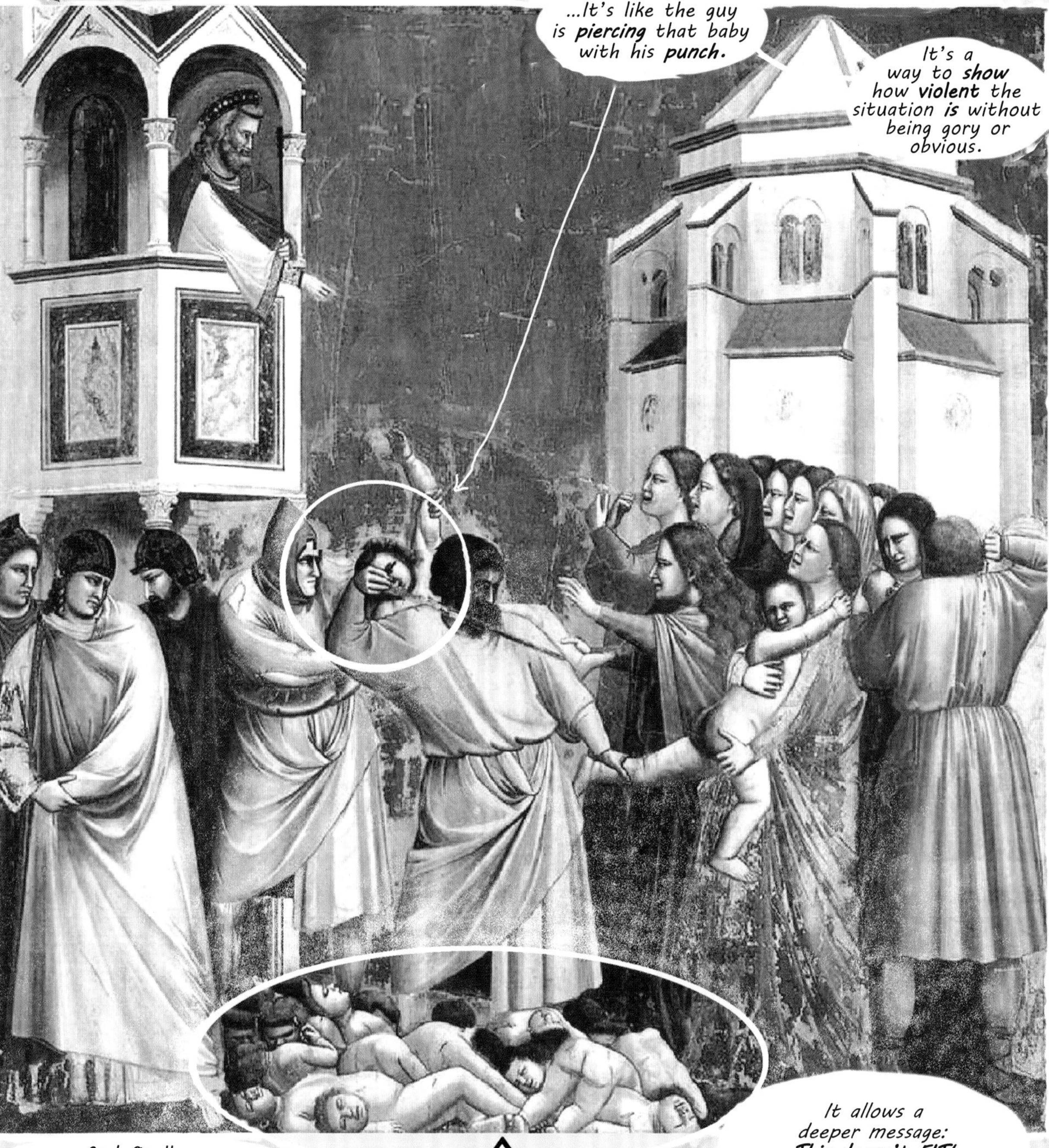

Also, there's CONFLATION of SPACE
That's when something behind changes the meaning of the thing in front of it—like the fist of the main soldier right in front of the baby's head behind it...
...It's like the guy is piercing that baby with his punch.
It's a way to show how violent the situation is without being gory or obvious.
And finally, the WILD CARD...
(that's the best part 'cuz it BREAKS the RULES)
...it's the pile of dead BABIES—
The WILD CARD DEFIES expectations—here, by deviating from the painting's strict grid structure—and upends the logic, opening up the painting to reveal new MEANINGS.
It's as though Giotto was giving the babies an actual burial at the bottom of the painting.
It allows a deeper message: This doesn't FIT! This defies LOGIC!!
Brilliant storytelling, right Sam?
Mom??
So wise.

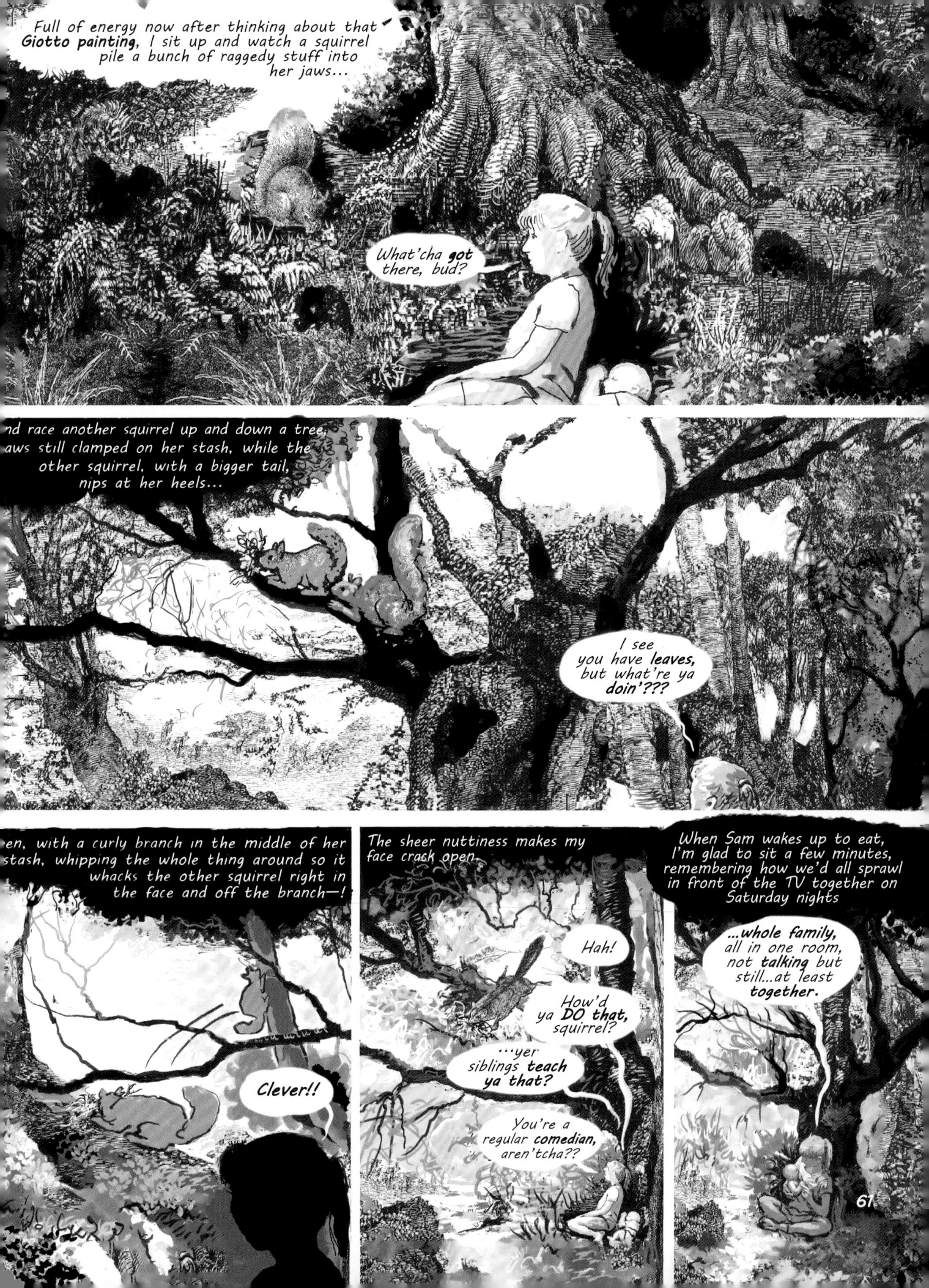

Full of energy now after thinking about that **Giotto painting**, I sit up and watch a squirrel pile a bunch of raggedy stuff into her jaws...

What'cha **got** there, bud?

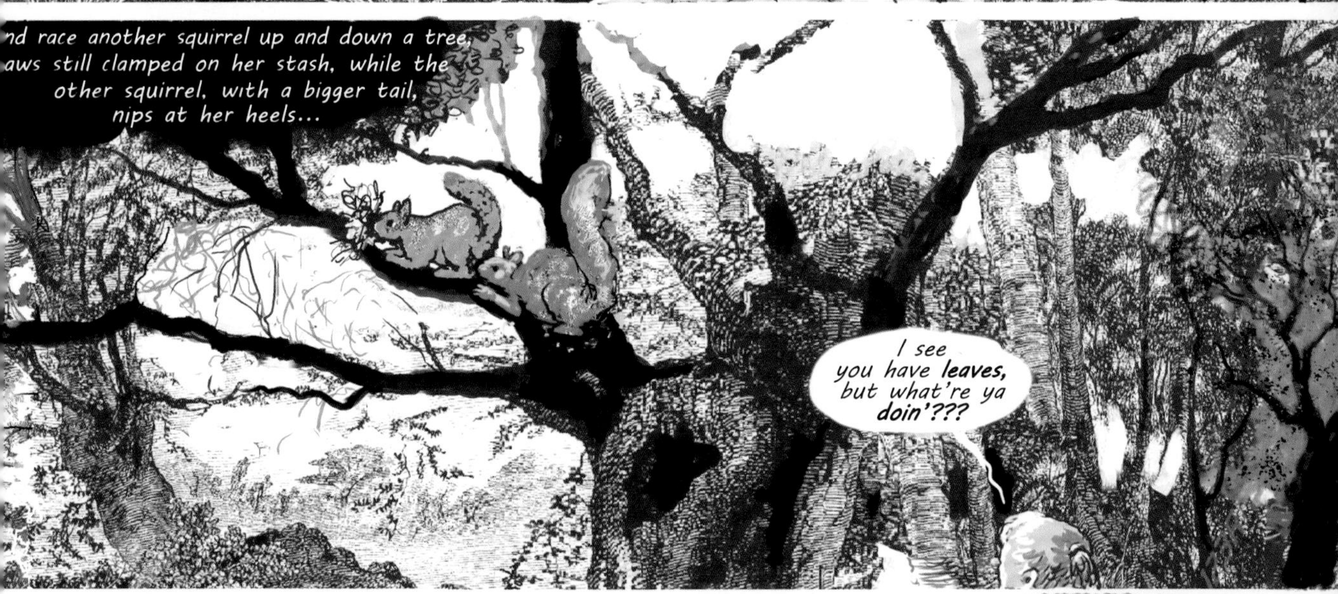

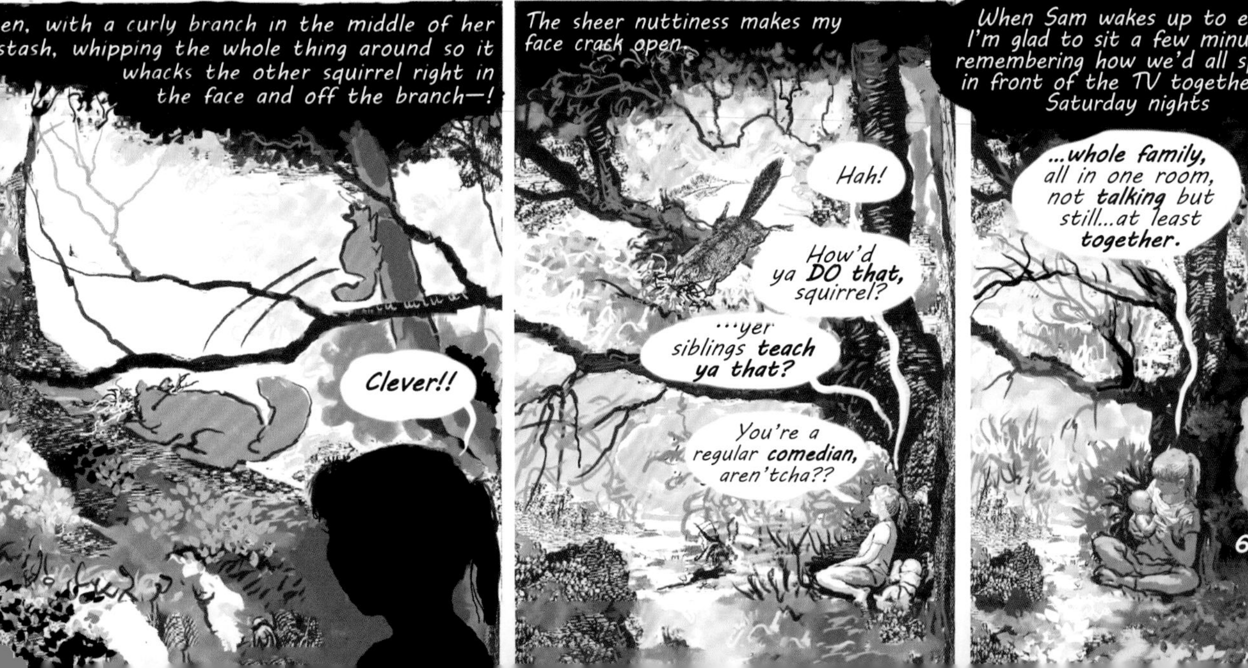

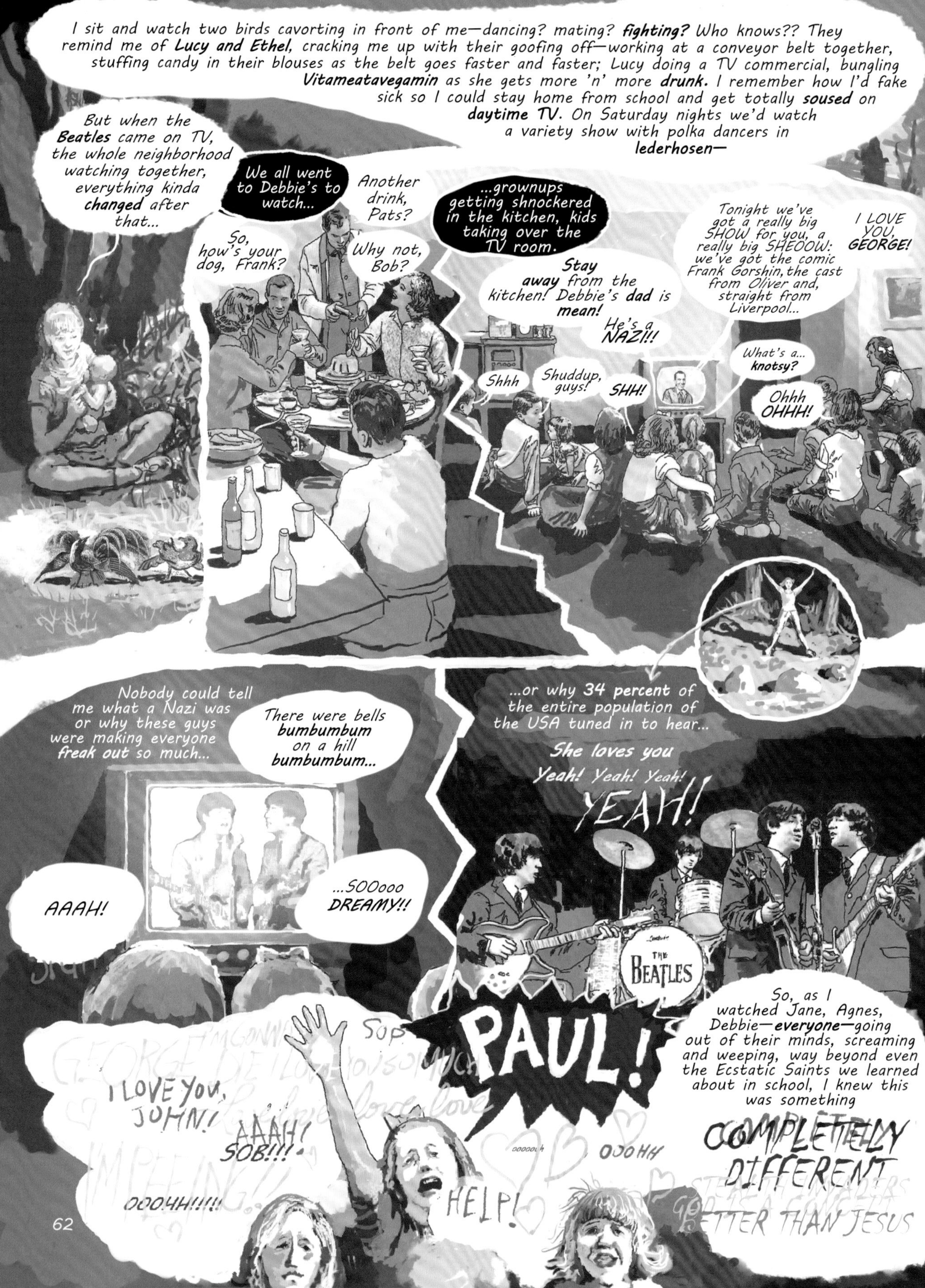

I sit and watch two birds cavorting in front of me—dancing? mating? **fighting?** Who knows?? They remind me of **Lucy and Ethel**, cracking me up with their goofing off—working at a conveyor belt together, stuffing candy in their blouses as the belt goes faster and faster; Lucy doing a TV commercial, bungling **Vitameatavegamin** as she gets more 'n' more **drunk.** I remember how I'd fake sick so I could stay home from school and get totally **soused** on **daytime TV**. On Saturday nights we'd watch a variety show with polka dancers in **lederhosen**—
But when the **Beatles** came on TV, the whole neighborhood watching together, everything kinda **changed** after that...
We all went to Debbie's to watch...
So, how's your dog, Frank?
Another drink, Pats?
Why not, Bob?
...grownups getting shnockered in the kitchen, kids taking over the TV room.
Stay away from the kitchen! Debbie's **dad** is **mean!**
He's a **NAZI!!!**
Tonight we've got a really big SHOW for you, a really big SHEOOW: we've got the comic Frank Gorshin, the cast from Oliver and, straight from Liverpool...
I LOVE YOU, **GEORGE!**
Shhh
Shuddup, guys!
SHH!
What's a... **knotsy?**
Ohhh **OHHH!**
Nobody could tell me what a Nazi was or why these guys were making everyone **freak out** so much...
There were bells **bumbumbum** on a hill **bumbumbum...**
...or why **34 percent** of the entire population of the USA tuned in to hear...
She loves you
Yeah! Yeah! Yeah!
YEAH!
AAAH!
...SOOooo **DREAMY!!**
THE BEATLES
PAUL!
So, as I watched Jane, Agnes, Debbie—**everyone**—going out of their minds, screaming and weeping, way beyond even the Ecstatic Saints we learned about in school, I knew this was something
COMPLETELY DIFFERENT
I LOVE YOU, JOHN!
AAAH! SOB!!!
OOOHH!!!!
HELP!
OOOHH
BETTER THAN JESUS

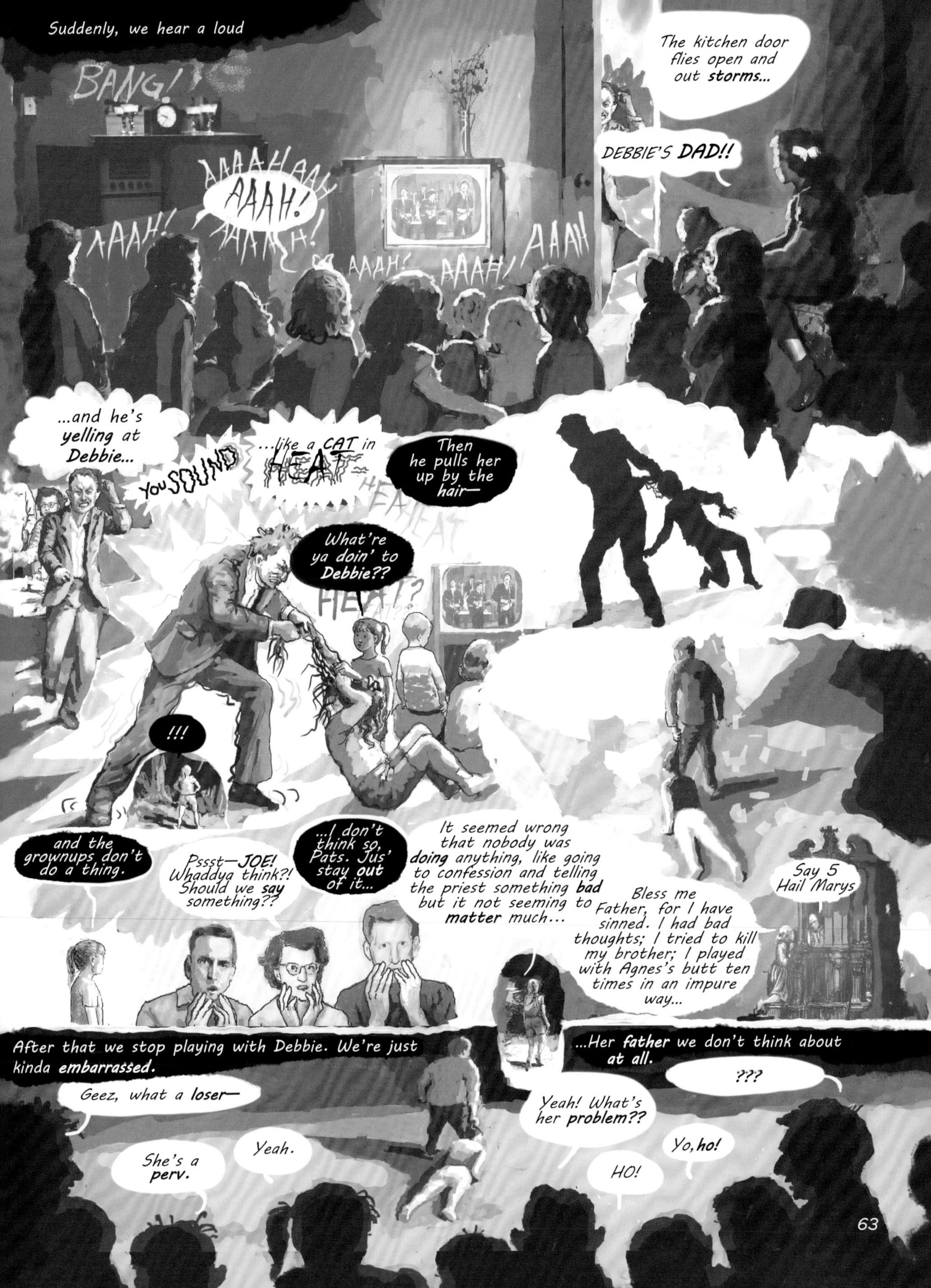

Suddenly, we hear a loud
BANG!
AAAH!
AAAH!
AAAH!
AAAH!
AAAH
The kitchen door flies open and out storms...
DEBBIE'S DAD!!
...and he's yelling at Debbie...
You SOUND
...like a CAT in HEAT
Then he pulls her up by the hair—
What're ya doin' to Debbie??
!!!
and the grownups don't do a thing.
Pssst—JOE! Whaddya think?! Should we say something??
...I don't think so, Pats. Jus' stay out of it...
It seemed wrong that nobody was doing anything, like going to confession and telling the priest something bad but it not seeming to matter much...
Bless me Father, for I have sinned. I had bad thoughts; I tried to kill my brother; I played with Agnes's butt ten times in an impure way...
Say 5 Hail Marys
After that we stop playing with Debbie. We're just kinda embarrassed.
...Her father we don't think about at all.
Geez, what a loser—
???
Yeah! What's her problem??
She's a perv.
Yeah.
Yo, ho!
HO!

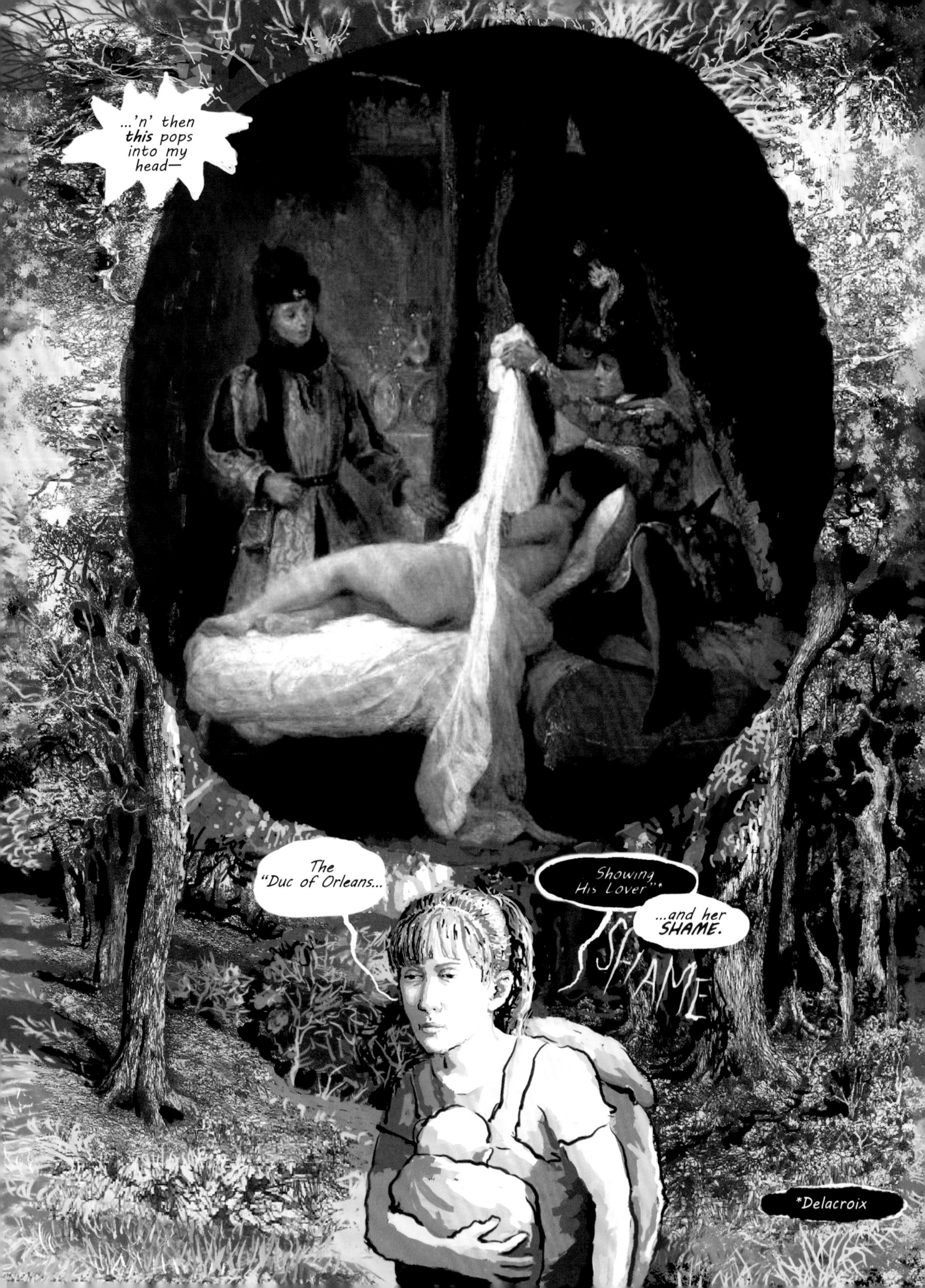
...'n' then **this** pops into my head—
The "Duc of Orleans...
Showing His Lover"*
...and her **SHAME.**
SHAME
*Delacroix

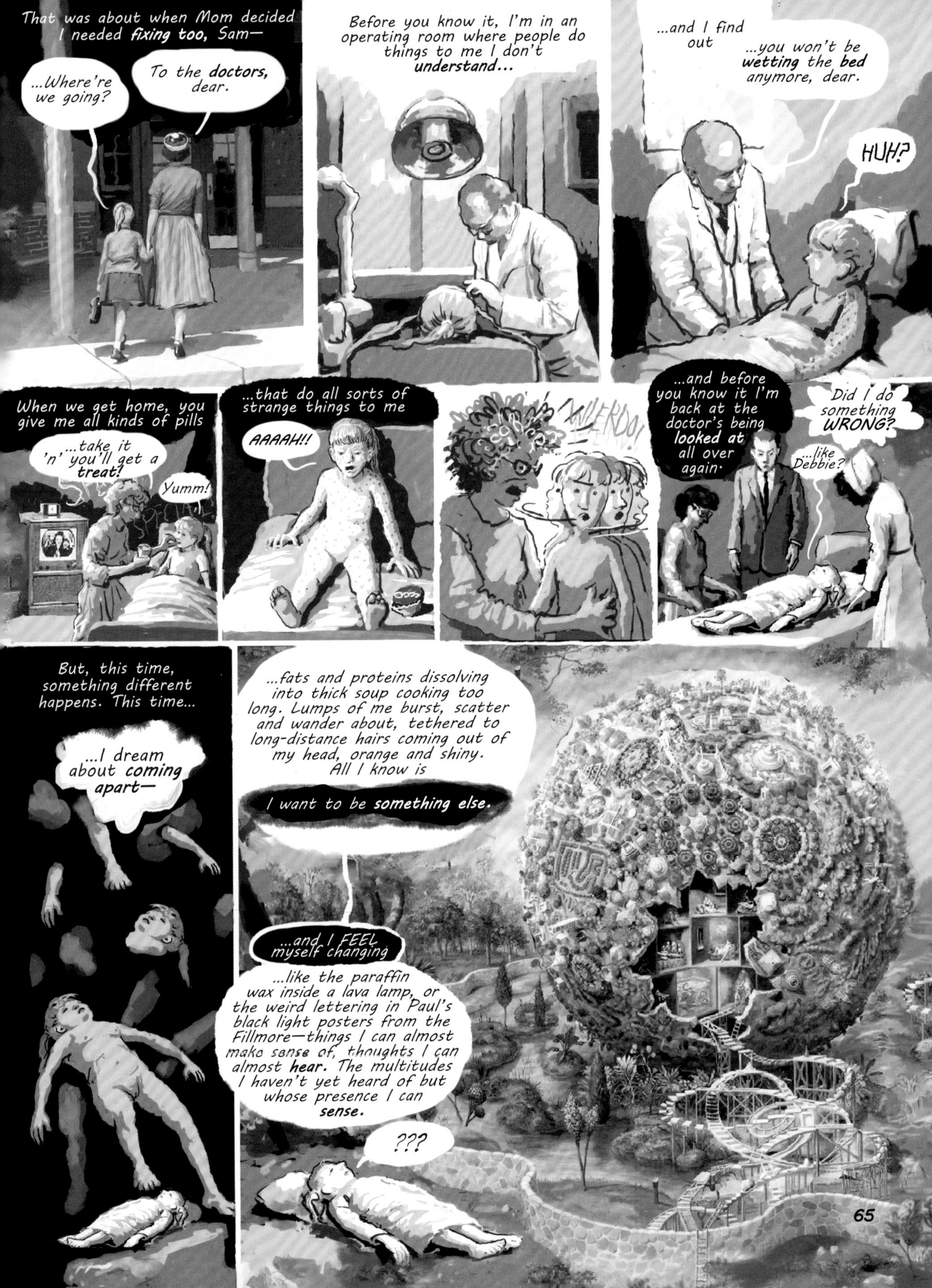
That was about when Mom decided I needed **fixing too,** Sam—
...Where're we going?
To the **doctors,** dear.
Before you know it, I'm in an operating room where people do things to me I don't **understand...**
...and I find out
...you won't be **wetting** the **bed** anymore, dear.
HUH?
When we get home, you give me all kinds of pills
...take it 'n' you'll get a **treat!**
Yumm!
...that do all sorts of strange things to me
AAAAH!!
...and before you know it I'm back at the doctor's being **looked at** all over again.
Did I do something **WRONG?**
...like Debbie?
But, this time, something different happens. This time...
...I dream about **coming apart**—
...fats and proteins dissolving into thick soup cooking too long. Lumps of me burst, scatter and wander about, tethered to long-distance hairs coming out of my head, orange and shiny. All I know is
I want to be **something else.**
...and I FEEL myself changing
...like the paraffin wax inside a lava lamp, or the weird lettering in Paul's black light posters from the Fillmore—things I can almost make sense of, thoughts I can almost **hear.** The multitudes I haven't yet heard of but whose presence I can **sense.**
???

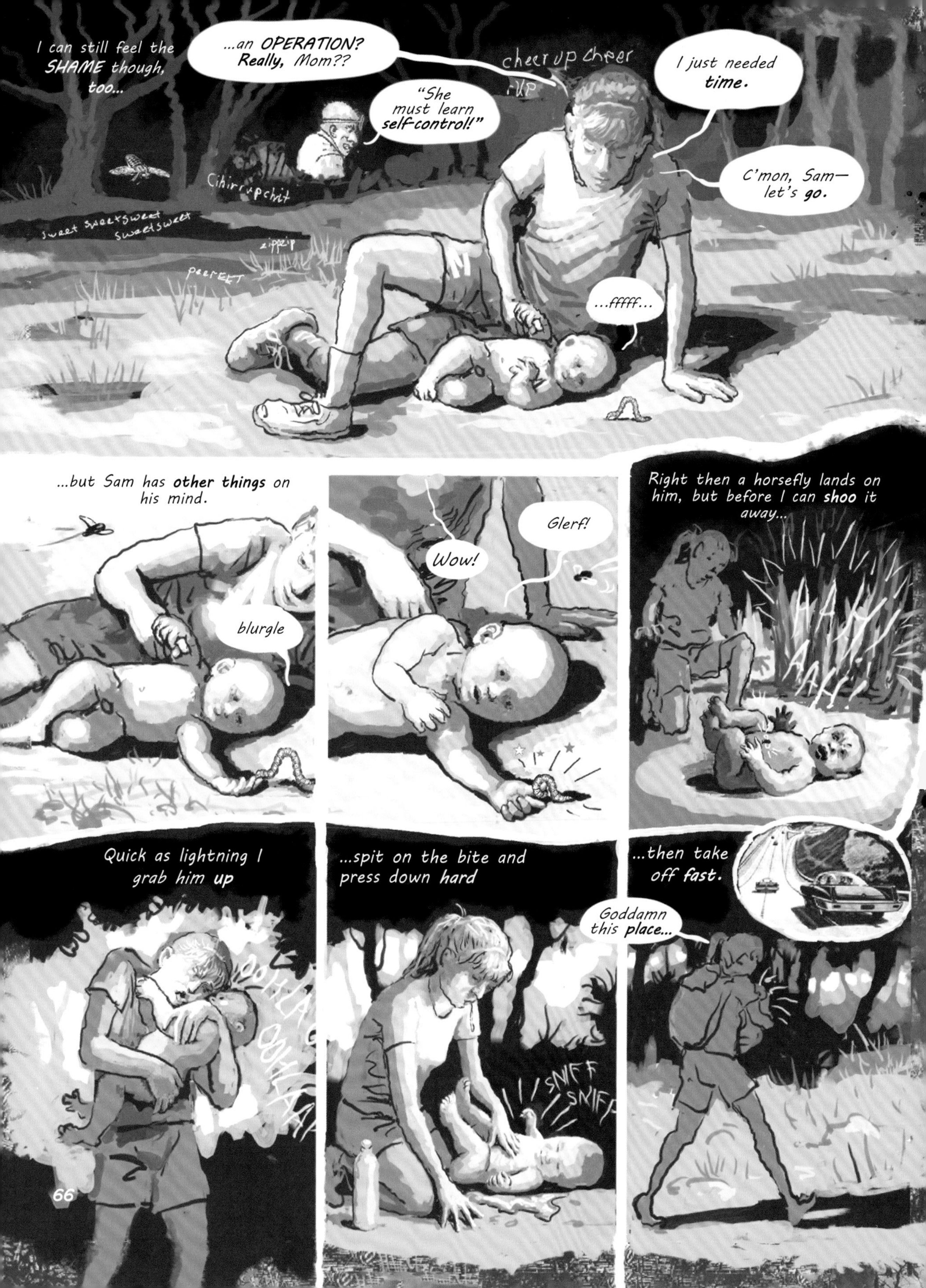

I can still feel the SHAME though, too...
...an OPERATION? Really, Mom??
"She must learn self-control!"
cheer up cheer up
I just needed time.
C'mon, Sam— let's go.
...fffff...
...but Sam has other things on his mind.
blurgle
Wow!
Glerf!
Right then a horsefly lands on him, but before I can shoo it away...
Quick as lightning I grab him up
...spit on the bite and press down hard
SNIFF SNIFF
...then take off fast.
Goddamn this place...

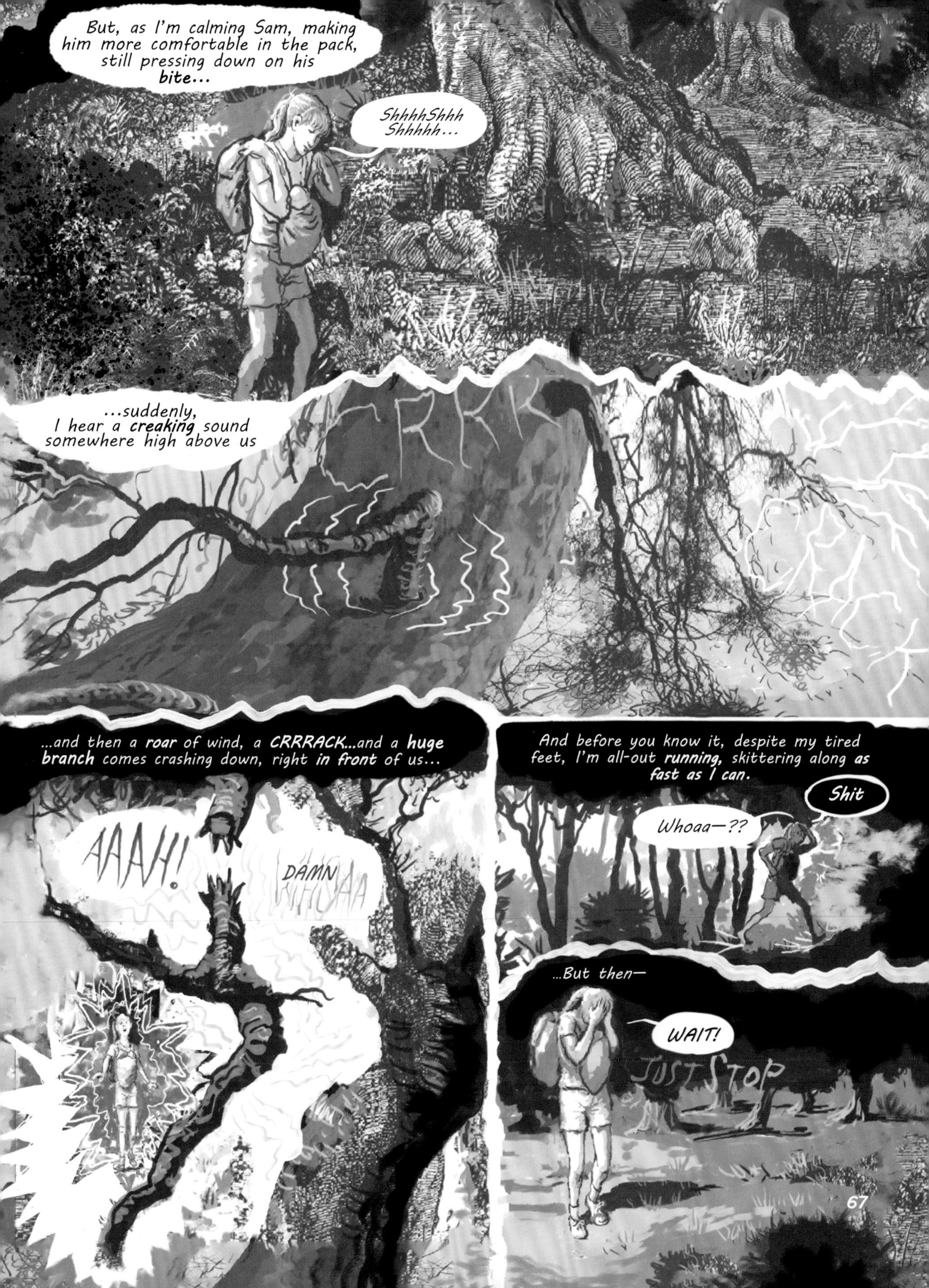
But, as I'm calming Sam, making him more comfortable in the pack, still pressing down on his **bite...**
ShhhhShhh Shhhhh...
...suddenly, I hear a **creaking** sound somewhere high above us
CRRK
CRACK
...and then a **roar** of wind, a **CRRRACK...**and a **huge branch** comes crashing down, right **in front** of us...
AAAH!
DAMN
WHOAA
And before you know it, despite my tired feet, I'm all-out **running,** skittering along **as fast as I can.**
Shit
Whoaa—??
...But then—
WAIT!
JUST STOP

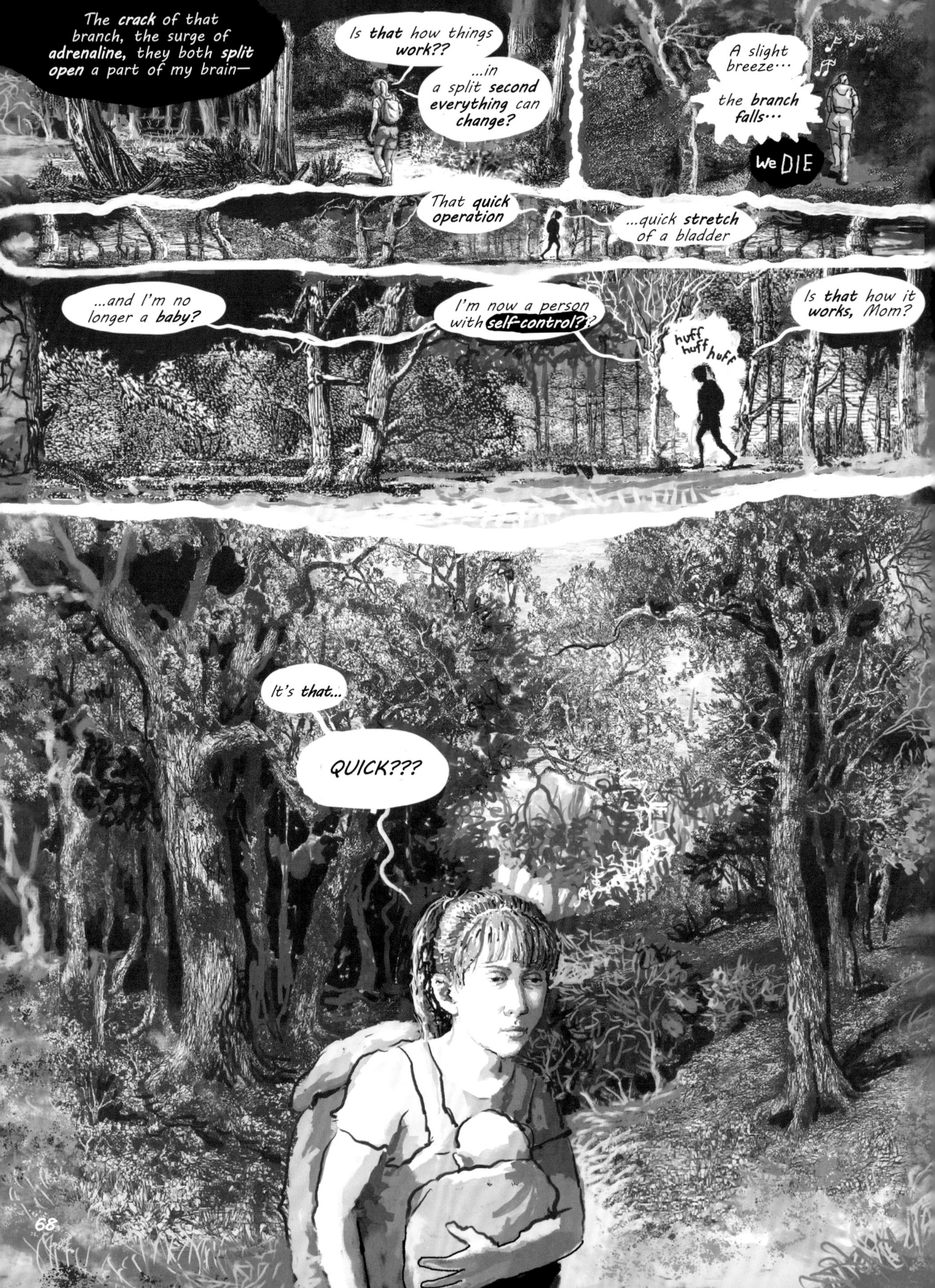
The crack of that branch, the surge of adrenaline, they both split open a part of my brain—
Is that how things work??
...in a split second everything can change?
A slight breeze···
the branch falls···
We DIE
That quick operation
...quick stretch of a bladder
...and I'm no longer a baby?
I'm now a person with self-control??
huff huff huff
Is that how it works, Mom?
It's that...
QUICK???

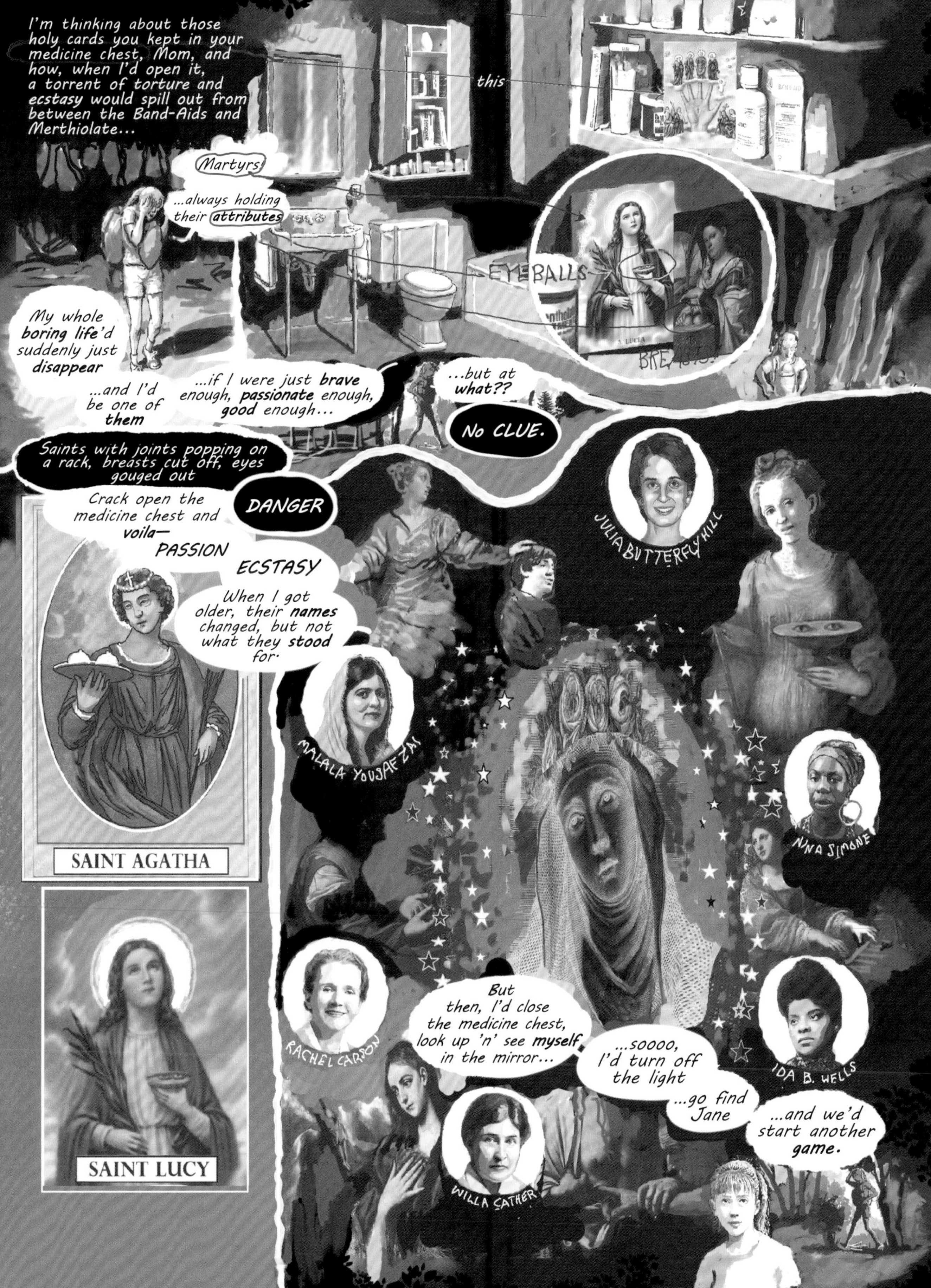

I'm thinking about those holy cards you kept in your medicine chest, Mom, and how, when I'd open it, a torrent of torture and ecstasy would spill out from between the Band-Aids and Merthiolate...
this
Martyrs
...always holding their attributes
EYEBALLS
S. LUCIA
BREASTS!
My whole boring life'd suddenly just disappear
...and I'd be one of them
...if I were just brave enough, passionate enough, good enough...
...but at what??
No CLUE.
Saints with joints popping on a rack, breasts cut off, eyes gouged out
Crack open the medicine chest and voila—
DANGER
PASSION
ECSTASY
When I got older, their names changed, but not what they stood for.
JULIA BUTTERFLY HILL
MALALA YOUSAFZAI
NINA SIMONE
SAINT AGATHA
SAINT LUCY
RACHEL CARSON
IDA B. WELLS
WILLA CATHER
But then, I'd close the medicine chest, look up 'n' see myself in the mirror...
...soooo, I'd turn off the light
...go find Jane
...and we'd start another game.

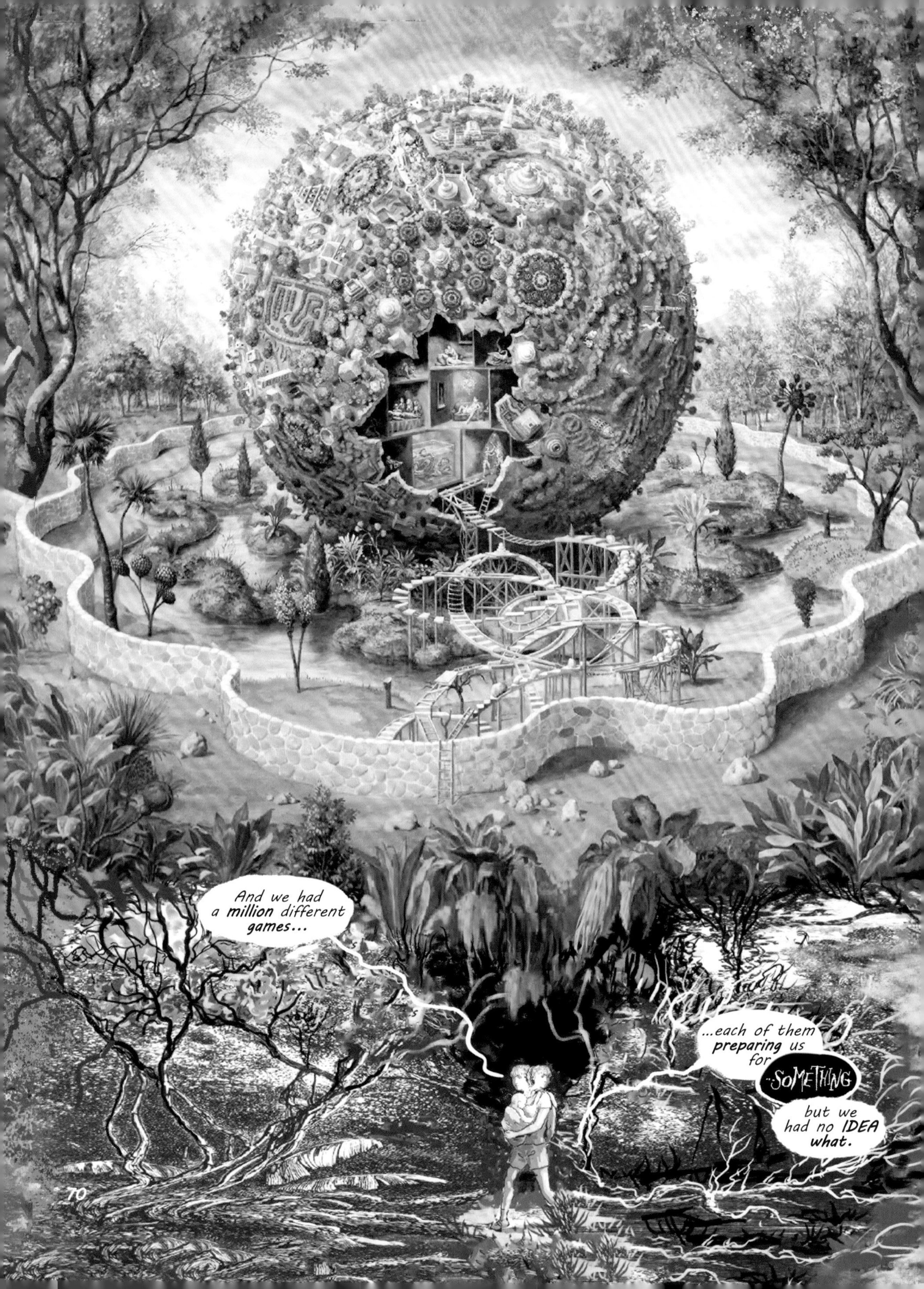
And we had a million different games...
...each of them preparing us for
...SOMETHING
but we had no IDEA what.

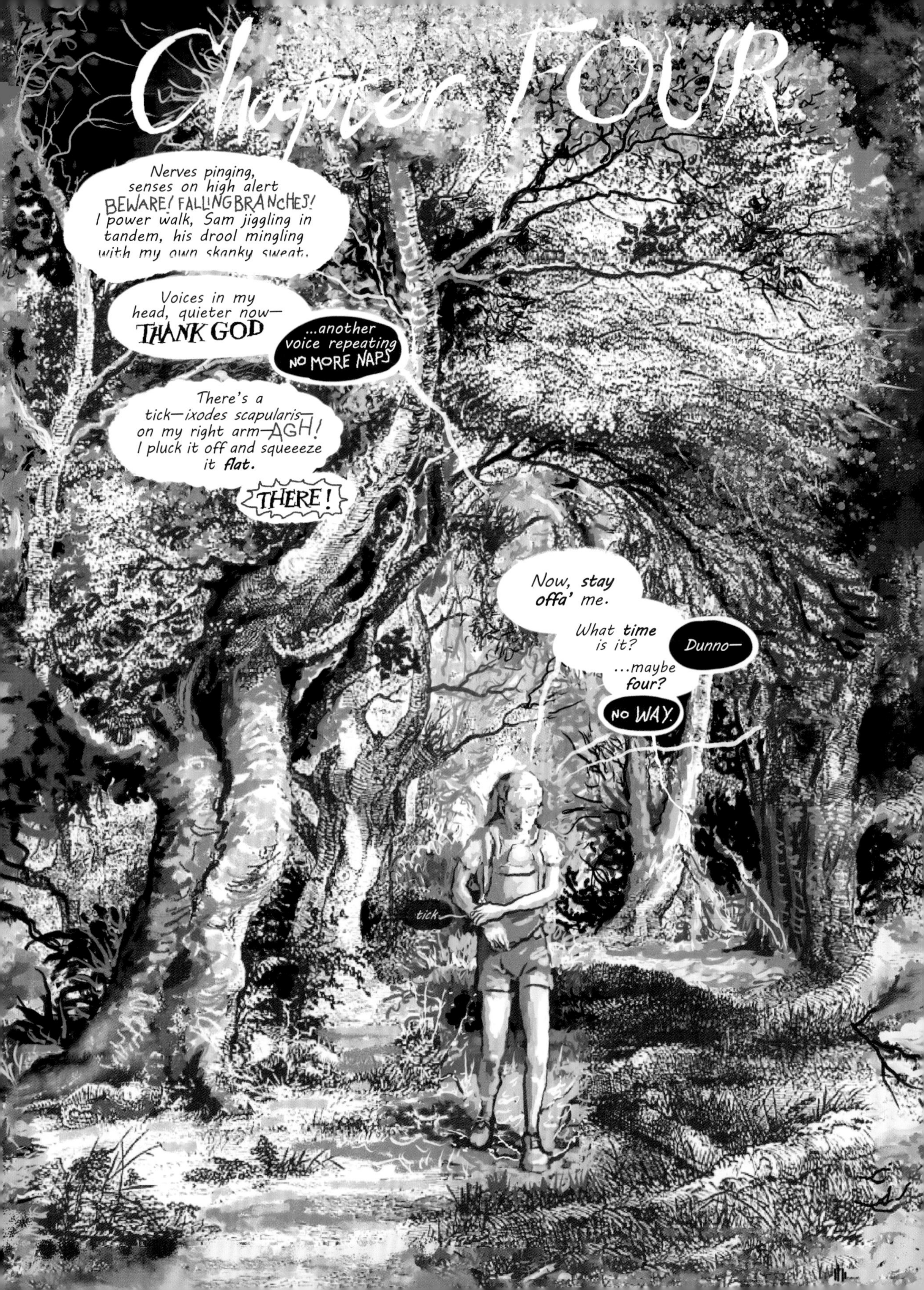
Chapter FOUR
Nerves pinging, senses on high alert BEWARE! FALLING BRANCHES! I power walk, Sam jiggling in tandem, his drool mingling with my own skanky sweat.
Voices in my head, quieter now—THANK GOD
...another voice repeating NO MORE NAPS
There's a tick—ixodes scapularis—on my right arm—AGH! I pluck it off and squeeeze it flat.
THERE!
Now, stay offa' me.
What time is it?
Dunno—
...maybe four?
NO WAY.
tick

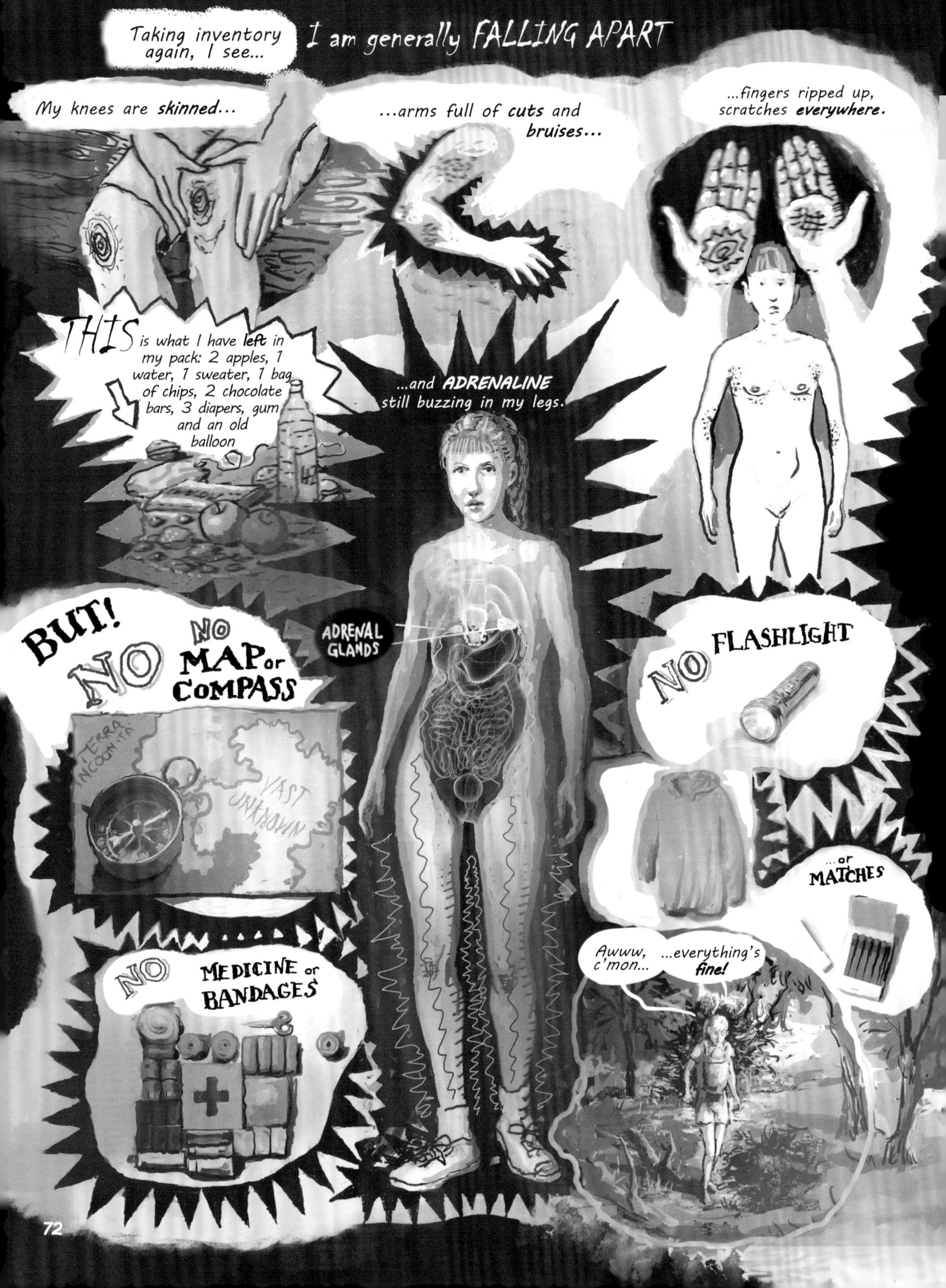

Taking inventory again, I see...
I am generally FALLING APART
My knees are **skinned**...
...arms full of **cuts** and **bruises**...
...fingers ripped up, scratches **everywhere**.
THIS is what I have **left** in my pack: 2 apples, 1 water, 1 sweater, 1 bag of chips, 2 chocolate bars, 3 diapers, gum and an old balloon
...and **ADRENALINE** still buzzing in my legs.
ADRENAL GLANDS
BUT! NO
NO MAP or COMPASS
TERRA INCOGNITA
VAST UNKNOWN
NO FLASHLIGHT
...or MATCHES
NO MEDICINE or BANDAGES
Awww, c'mon...
...everything's **fine!**

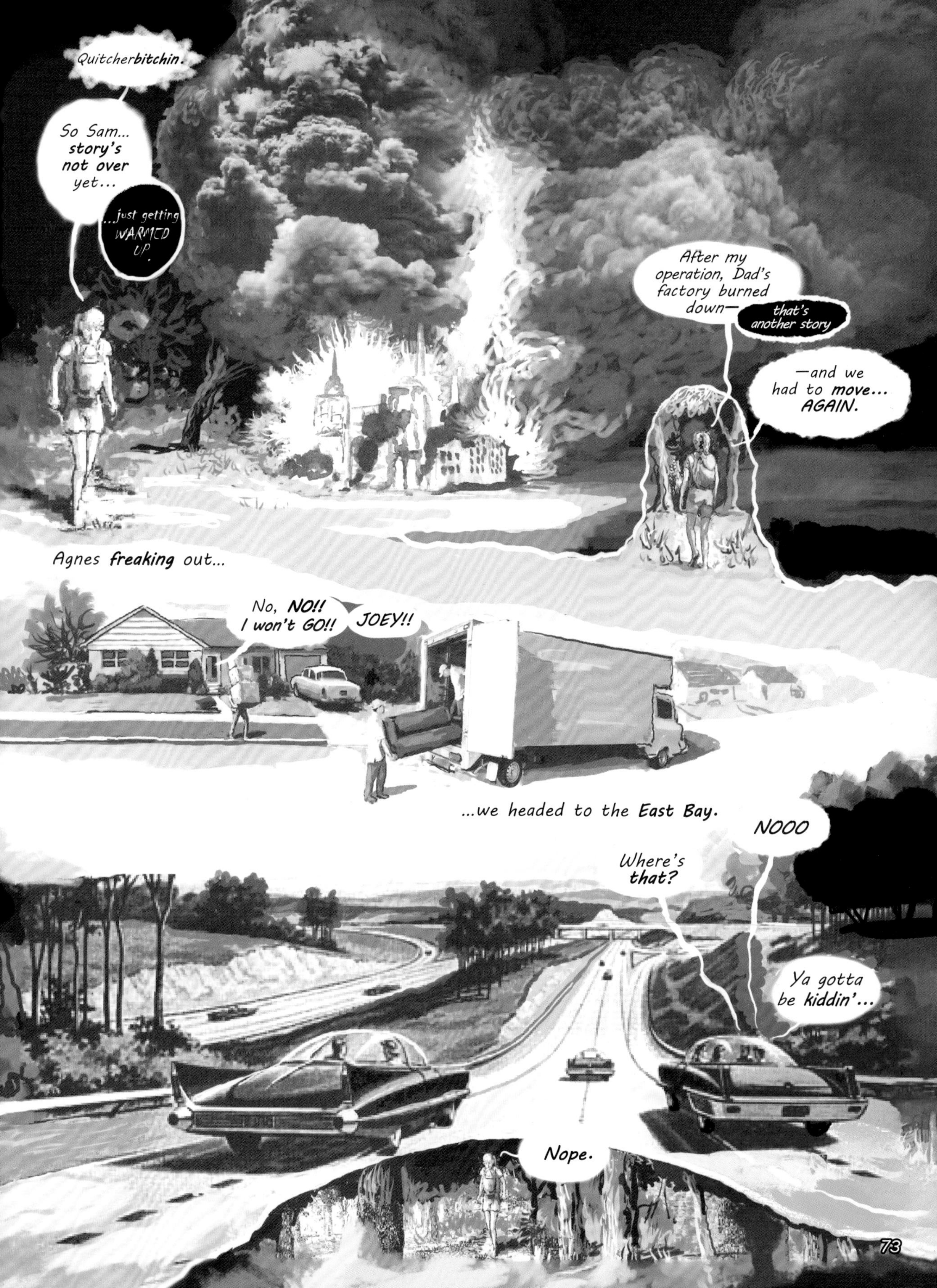
Quitcherbitchin.
So Sam... story's not over yet...
...just getting WARMED UP.
After my operation, Dad's factory burned down—
that's another story
—and we had to move... AGAIN.
Agnes freaking out...
No, NO!! I won't GO!!
JOEY!!
...we headed to the East Bay.
NOOO
Where's that?
Ya gotta be kiddin'...
Nope.

...To...

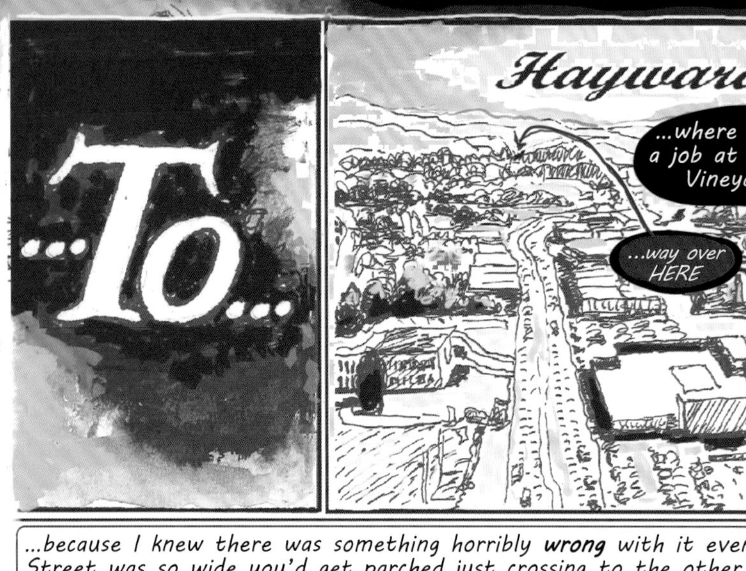

We called it

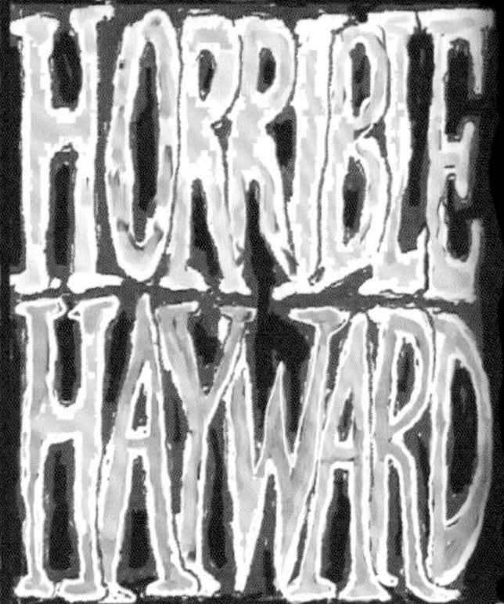

...because I knew there was something horribly **wrong** with it even though I was only eight years old. Medinah Street was so wide you'd get parched just crossing to the other side, and **all** the houses were always **shuttered,** even on Halloween. ***"What's everyone doing?"*** I'd ask Jane as we slunk around the neighborhood drinking Cherry Cokes. ***"Are they all* DEAD??"**

Cars would speed by so fast on their way to the shopping mall on the corner that one of our neighbors was ***killed*** by a passing Thunderbird when she stepped off the curb to cross the street—

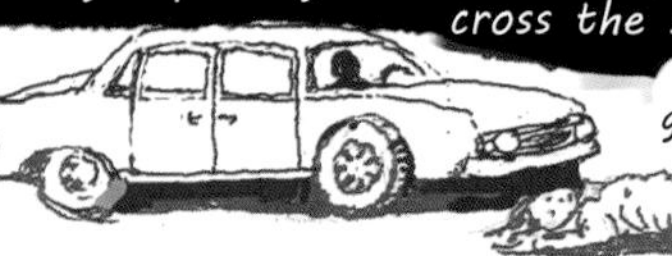

Was this place gonna ***kill me, too??***

Every day was the ***same...***

Whaddya wanna ***do?***

I dunno... ***DIE*** maybe?

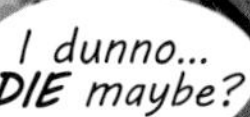

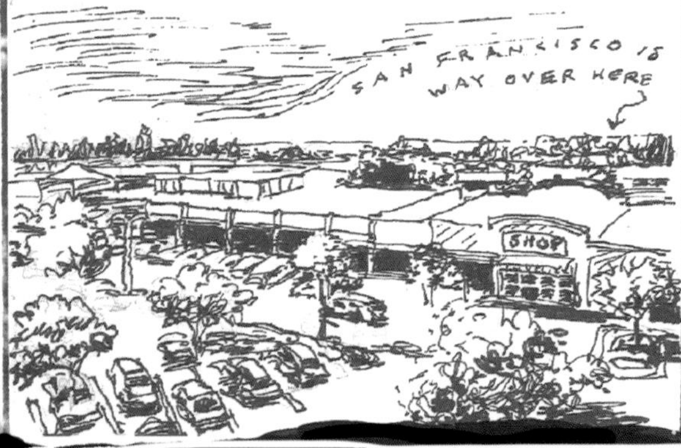

Jane and I would spend our days walking back and forth to Gourmet House, the restaurant up the street that offered chop suey from China and American cheese nachos from Mexico. We'd buy glazed donuts and eat them in a dark red booth smoking butts of cigarettes with lipstick marks that'd been left behind in the aluminum foil ashtrays.

*I knew there must be something **better** than **this...***

I would climb up on the roof at night and watch the moon rise over the glow of hazy light across the bay, and imagine living on a ***houseboat*** in Sausalito, breaking into ***mansions*** in Tiburon, getting ***kidnapped*** by boys at school and locked in their closets till I was a teenager...

Anything** but **this...

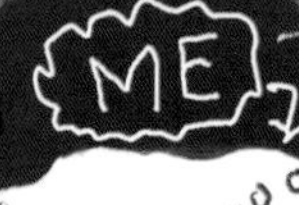

DEAD GRASS

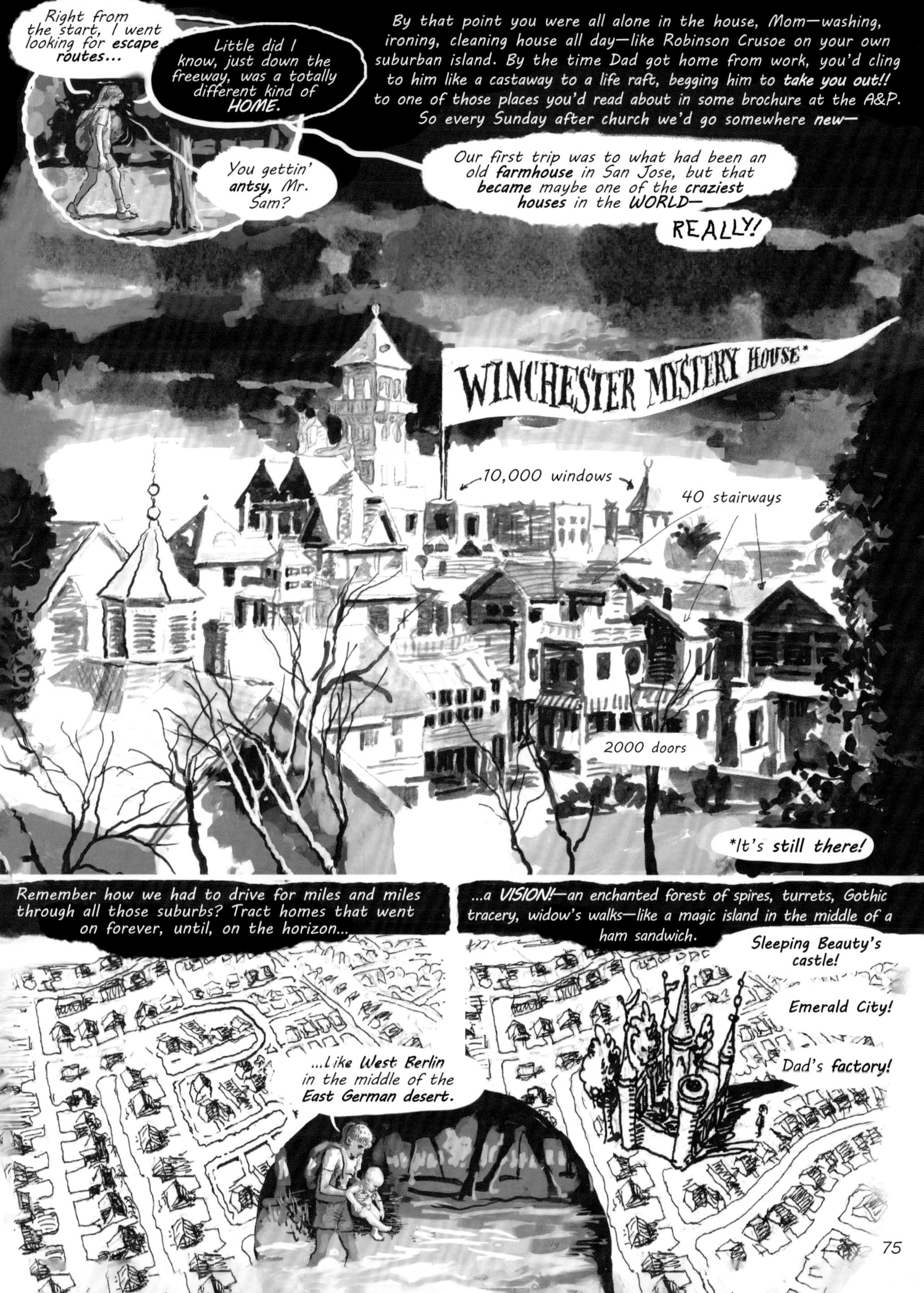
Right from the start, I went looking for escape routes...
Little did I know, just down the freeway, was a totally different kind of HOME.
By that point you were all alone in the house, Mom—washing, ironing, cleaning house all day—like Robinson Crusoe on your own suburban island. By the time Dad got home from work, you'd cling to him like a castaway to a life raft, begging him to take you out!! to one of those places you'd read about in some brochure at the A&P. So every Sunday after church we'd go somewhere new—
You gettin' antsy, Mr. Sam?
Our first trip was to what had been an old farmhouse in San Jose, but that became maybe one of the craziest houses in the WORLD—
REALLY!
WINCHESTER MYSTERY HOUSE*
10,000 windows
40 stairways
2000 doors
*It's still there!
Remember how we had to drive for miles and miles through all those suburbs? Tract homes that went on forever, until, on the horizon...
...a VISION!—an enchanted forest of spires, turrets, Gothic tracery, widow's walks—like a magic island in the middle of a ham sandwich.
Sleeping Beauty's castle!
Emerald City!
Dad's factory!
...Like West Berlin in the middle of the East German desert.

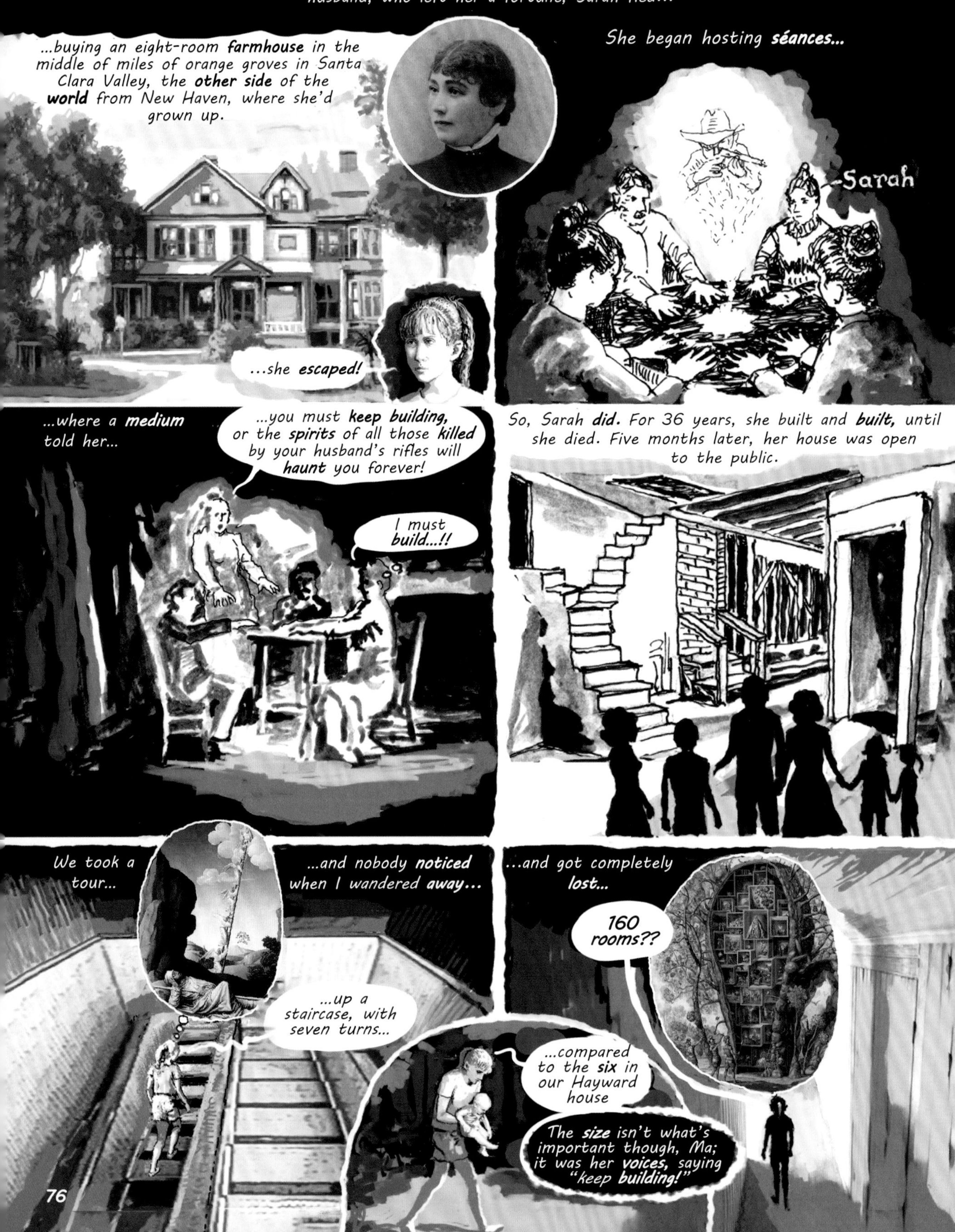
It was built by Sarah Lockwood Pardee Winchester, widow of the guy who'd brought us the Winchester
Repeating Rifle: the **Gun that Won the West.** Feeling cursed after losing her infant daughter and husband, who left her a fortune, Sarah fled...
...buying an eight-room **farmhouse** in the middle of miles of orange groves in Santa Clara Valley, the **other side** of the **world** from New Haven, where she'd grown up.
...she **escaped!**
She began hosting **séances...**
Sarah
...where a **medium** told her...
...you must **keep building,** or the **spirits** of all those **killed** by your husband's rifles will **haunt** you forever!
I must **build...!!**
So, Sarah **did.** For 36 years, she built and **built,** until she died. Five months later, her house was open to the public.
We took a tour...
...and nobody **noticed** when I wandered **away...**
...up a staircase, with seven turns...
...and got completely **lost...**
160 rooms??
...compared to the **six** in our Hayward house
The **size** isn't what's important though, Ma; it was her **voices,** saying "keep **building!**"

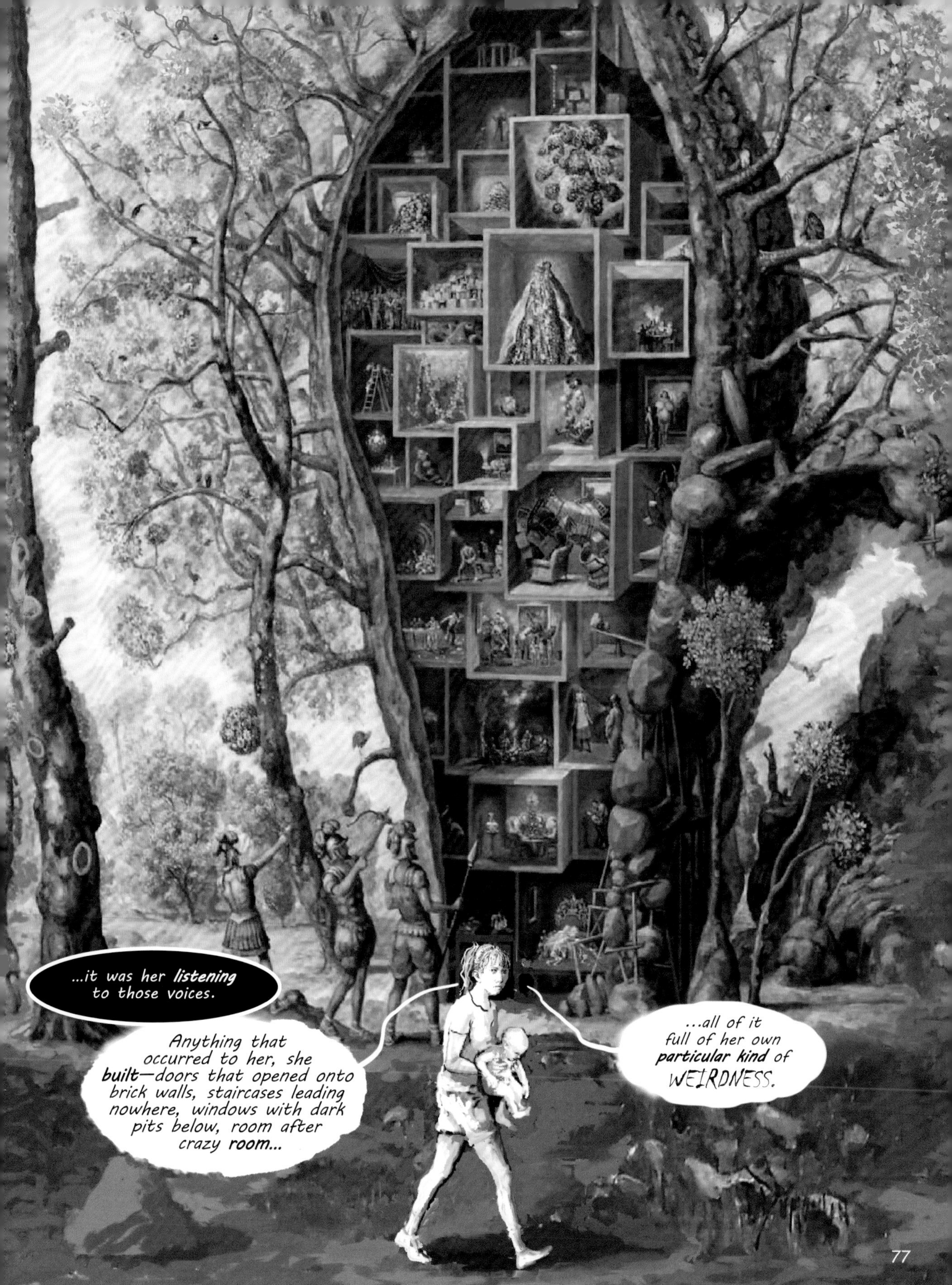

...it was her *listening* to those voices.
Anything that occurred to her, she **built**—doors that opened onto brick walls, staircases leading nowhere, windows with dark pits below, room after crazy **room...**
...all of it full of her own **particular kind** of WEIRDNESS.

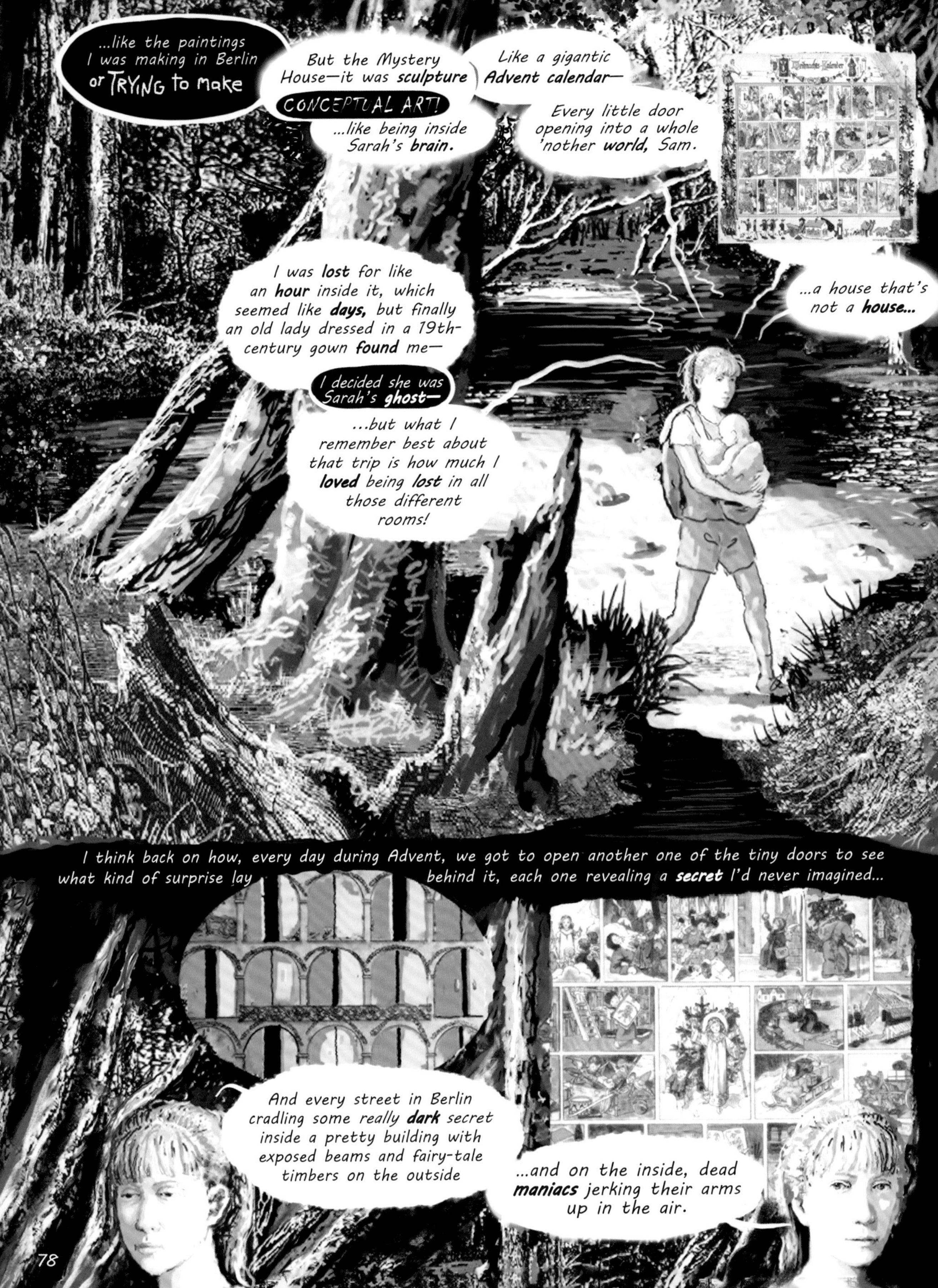
...like the paintings I was making in Berlin or TRYING to make
But the Mystery House—it was sculpture
CONCEPTUAL ART!
...like being inside Sarah's brain.
Like a gigantic Advent calendar—
Every little door opening into a whole 'nother world, Sam.
...a house that's not a house...
I was lost for like an hour inside it, which seemed like days, but finally an old lady dressed in a 19th-century gown found me—
I decided she was Sarah's ghost—
...but what I remember best about that trip is how much I loved being lost in all those different rooms!
I think back on how, every day during Advent, we got to open another one of the tiny doors to see what kind of surprise lay behind it, each one revealing a secret I'd never imagined...
And every street in Berlin cradling some really dark secret inside a pretty building with exposed beams and fairy-tale timbers on the outside
...and on the inside, dead maniacs jerking their arms up in the air.

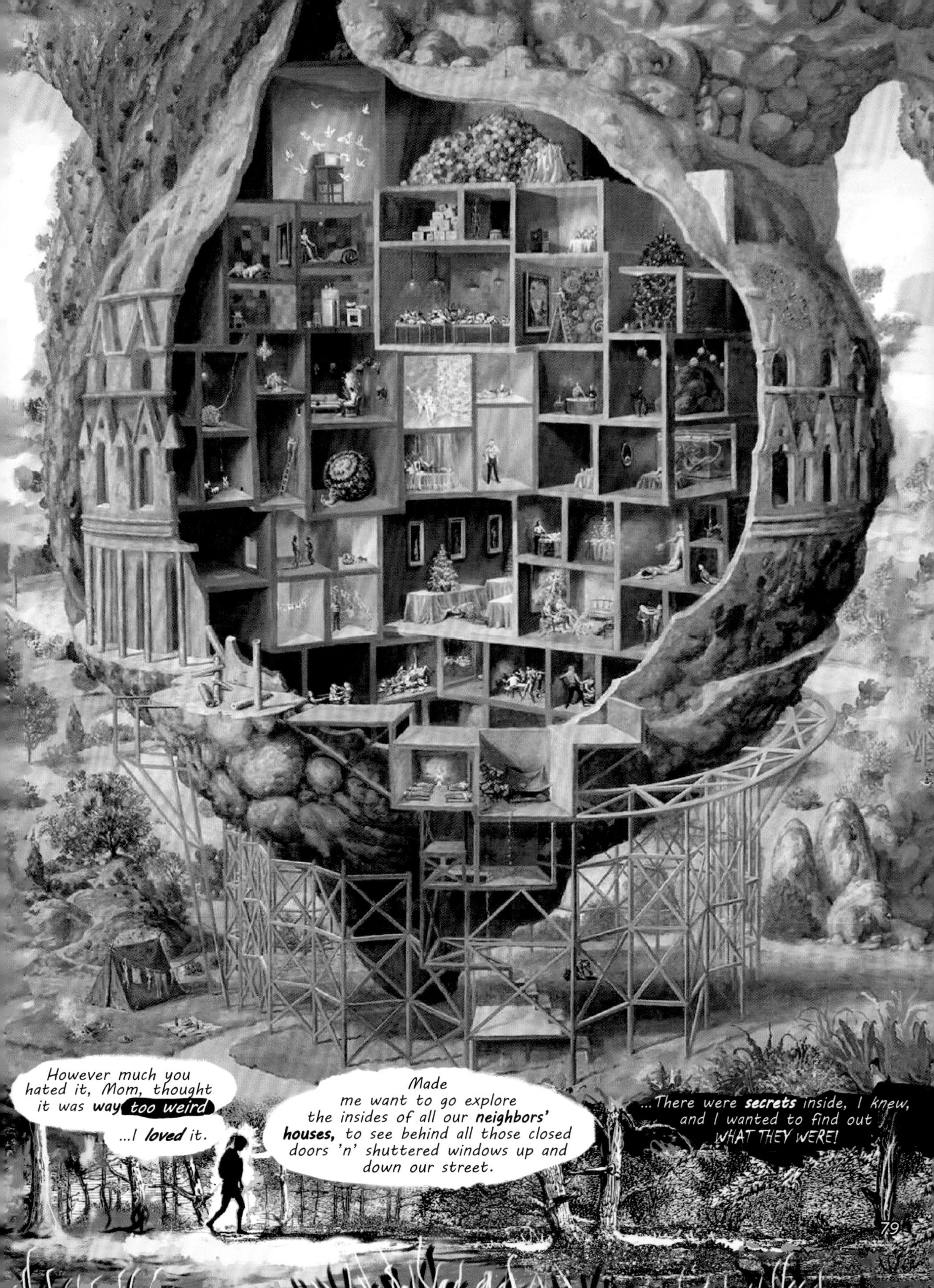
However much you hated it, Mom, thought it was way too weird
...I loved it.
Made me want to go explore the insides of all our neighbors' houses, to see behind all those closed doors 'n' shuttered windows up and down our street.
...There were secrets inside, I knew, and I wanted to find out WHAT THEY WERE!

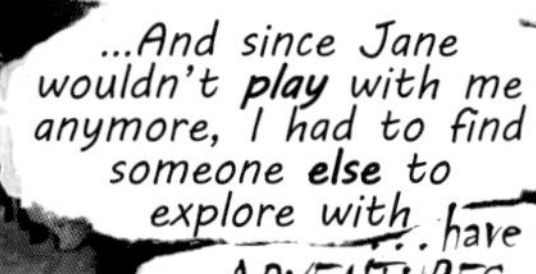

WANDERING...

Wandering through landscapes, and then later through **paintings,** that's what I **love,** Mom. The simple act of putting one foot in front of the other, making my way forward, and then up—and even **further up** and **up**—allowed me the vistas I needed for *wondering:* what's **beyond** this or that? Beyond the dullness of Hayward and the stunted nuns who taught us?? Beyond the hazy torpor of getting stoned and the urgent sussurations of horny boys? Beyond the climate of **NO** that was the Church and our house? Whatever else there might be out there, well, maybe I could find it simply by **moving**—forward, backward, up, down, I didn't care. Just keep *moving*—**get outta there.**

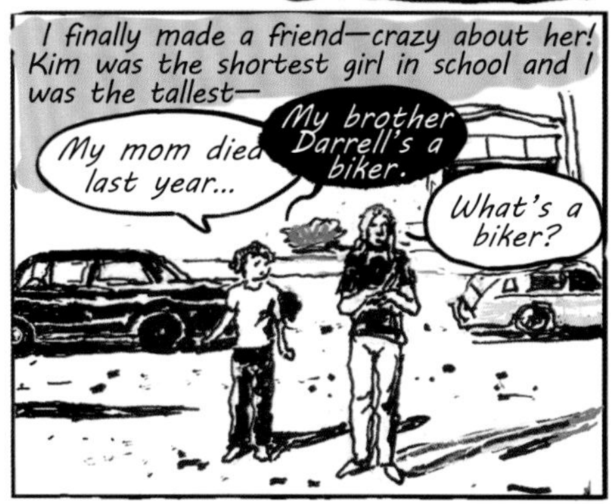

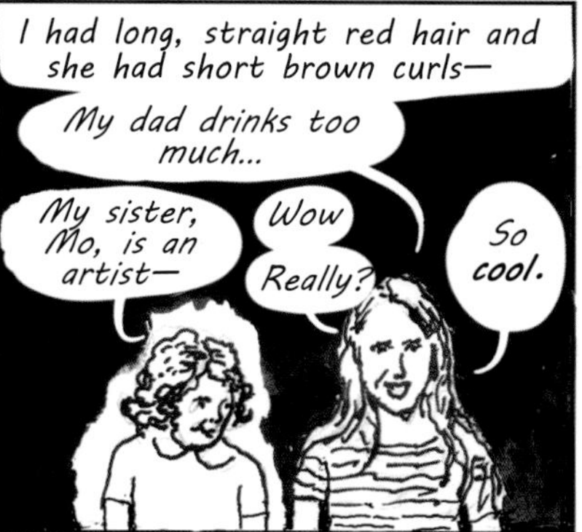

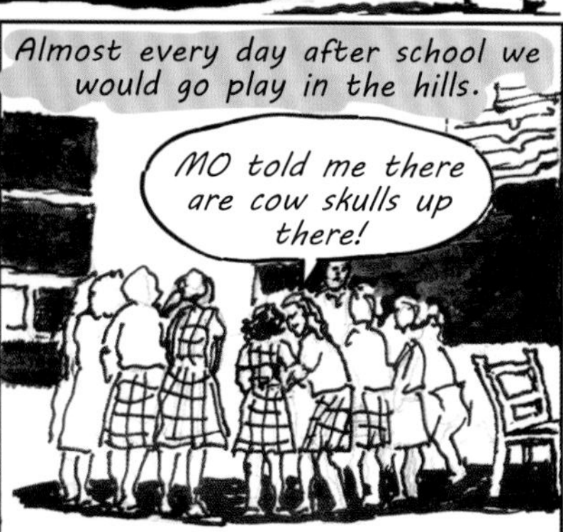

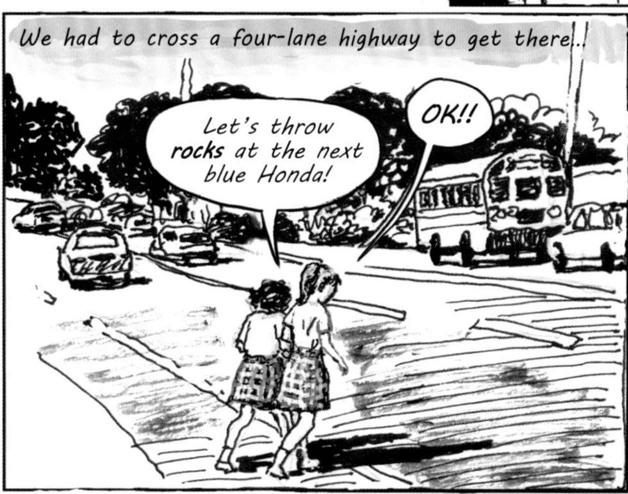

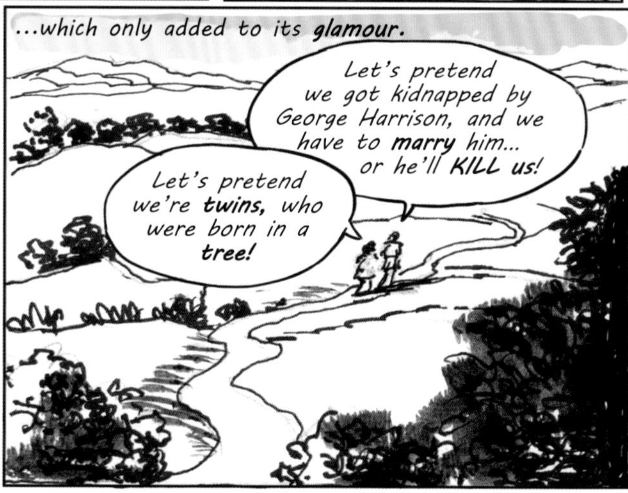

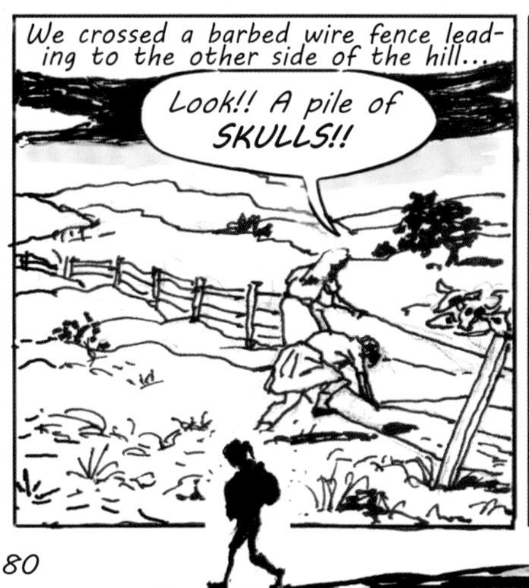

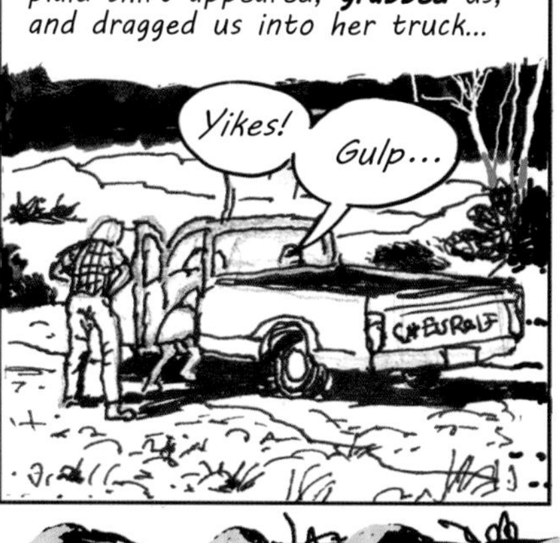

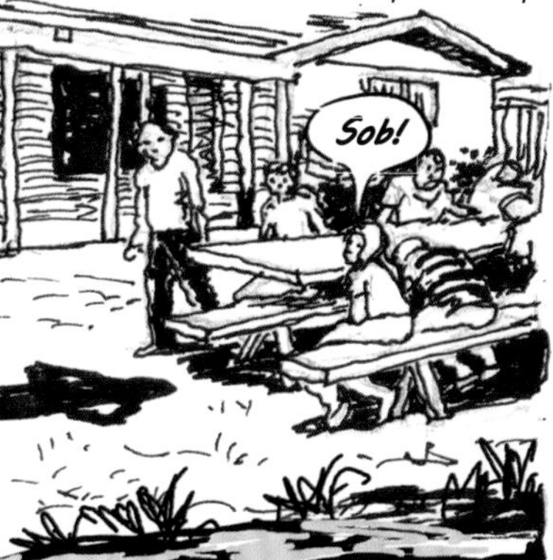

AND WONDERING

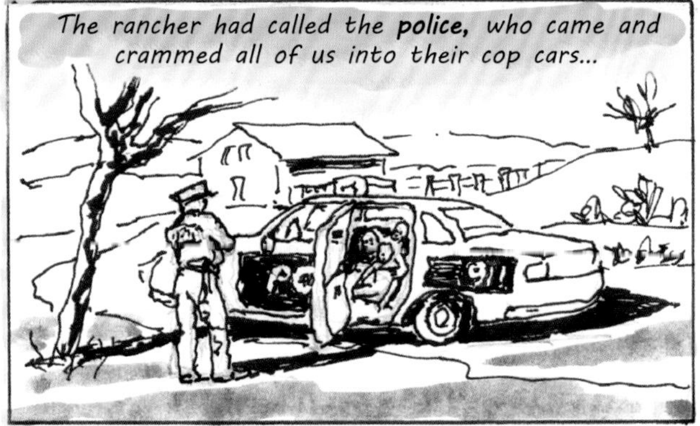

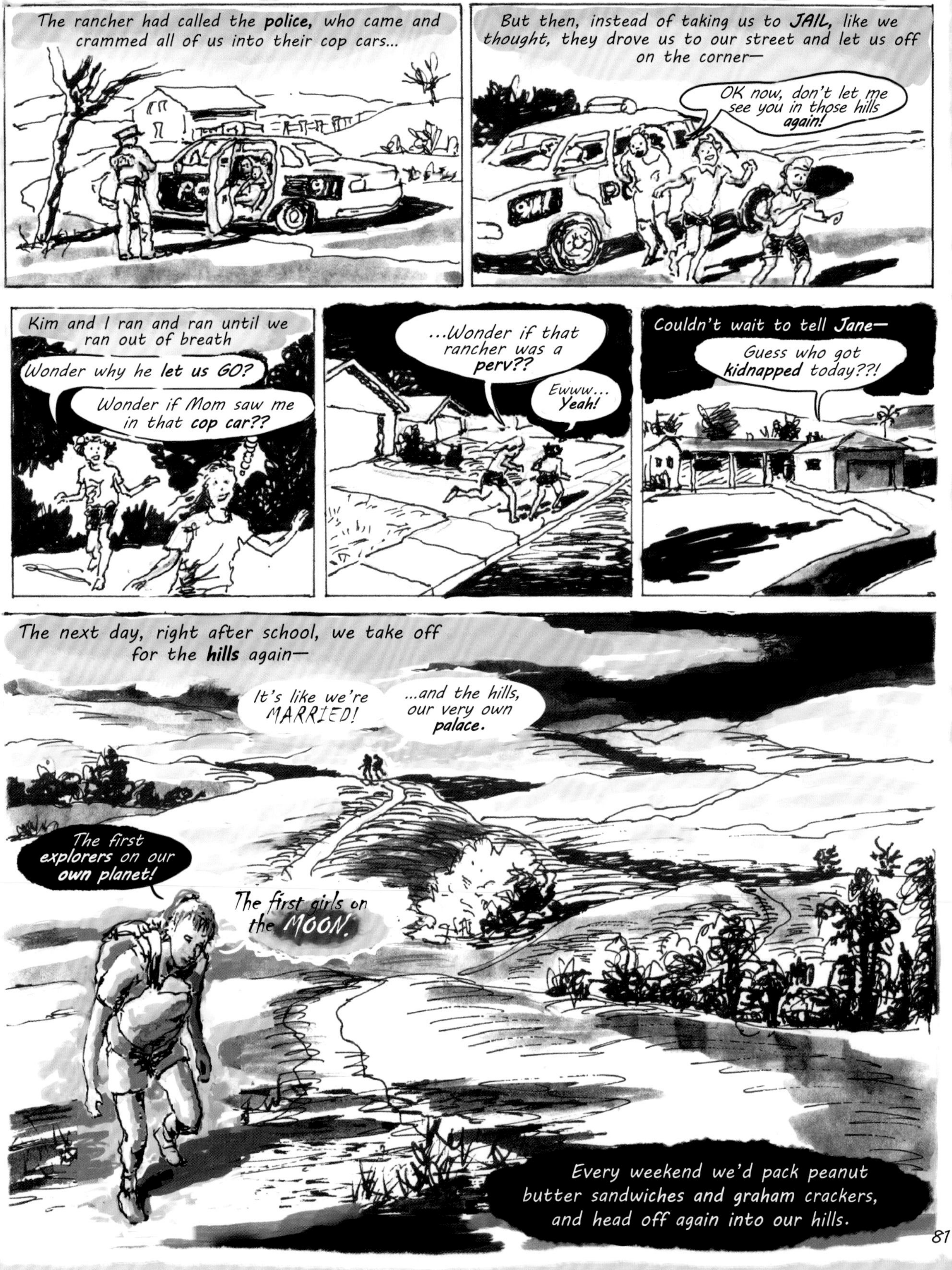

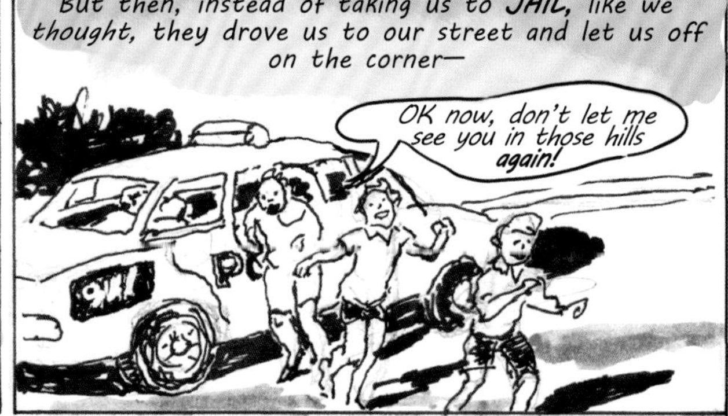

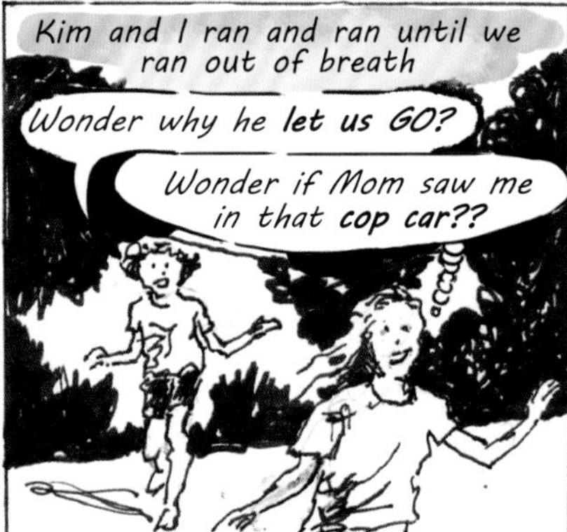

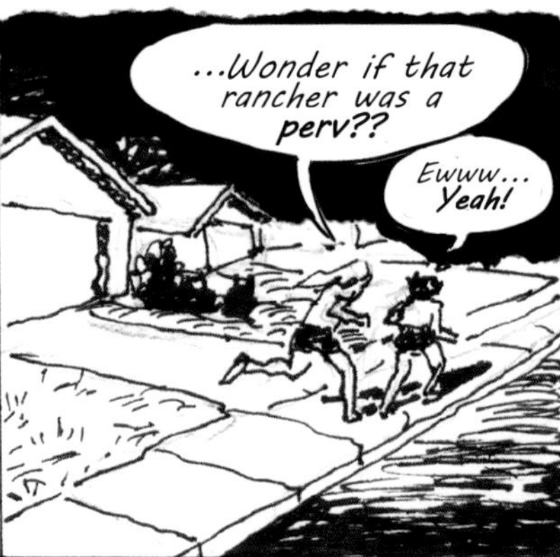

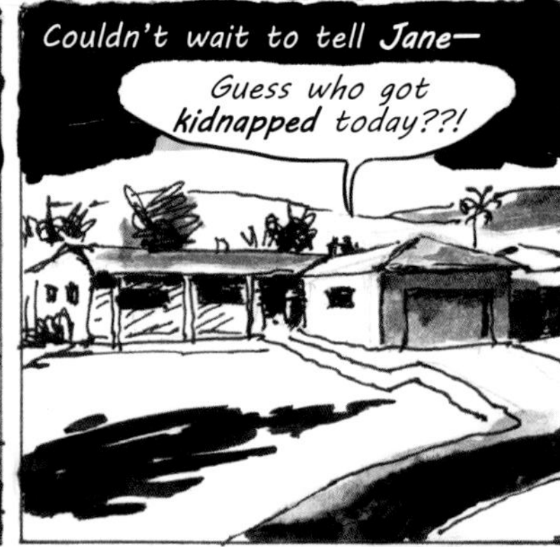

The next day, right after school, we take off for the **hills** again—

It's like we're MARRIED!

...and the hills, our very own **palace.**

The first **explorers** on our **own planet!**

The first girls on the MOON.

Every weekend we'd pack peanut butter sandwiches and graham crackers, and head off again into our hills.

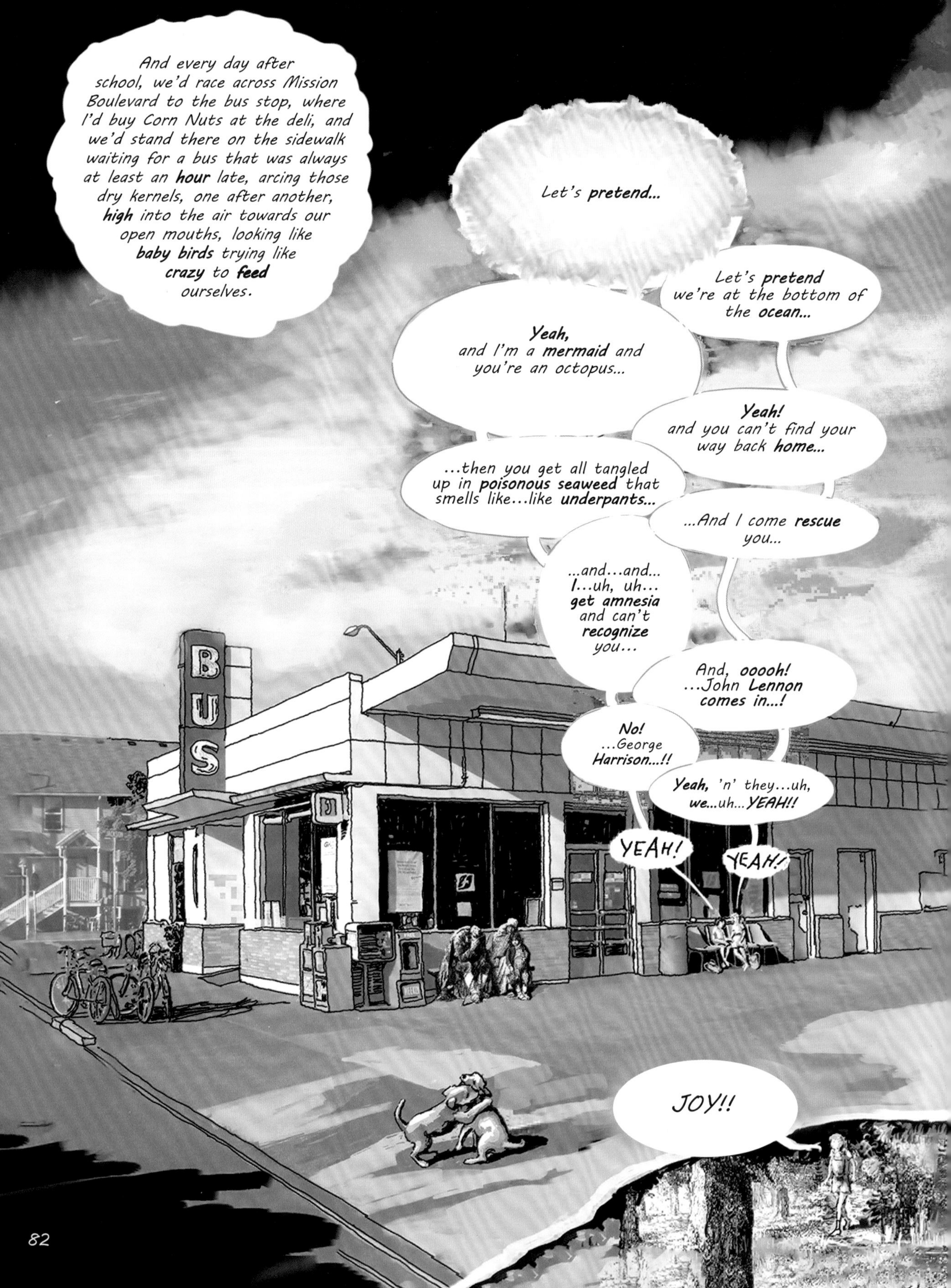
And every day after school, we'd race across Mission Boulevard to the bus stop, where I'd buy Corn Nuts at the deli, and we'd stand there on the sidewalk waiting for a bus that was always at least an **hour** late, arcing those dry kernels, one after another, **high** into the air towards our open mouths, looking like **baby birds** trying like **crazy** to **feed** ourselves.
Let's **pretend...**
Let's **pretend** we're at the bottom of the **ocean...**
Yeah, and I'm a **mermaid** and you're an octopus...
Yeah! and you can't find your way back **home...**
...then you get all tangled up in **poisonous seaweed** that smells like...like **underpants...**
...And I come **rescue** you...
...and...and... **I**...uh, uh... **get amnesia** and can't **recognize** you...
And, **ooooh!** ...John **Lennon** comes in...!
No! ...George **Harrison...!!**
Yeah, 'n' they...uh, **we**...uh... **YEAH!!**
YEAH!
YEAH!
BUS
JOY!!

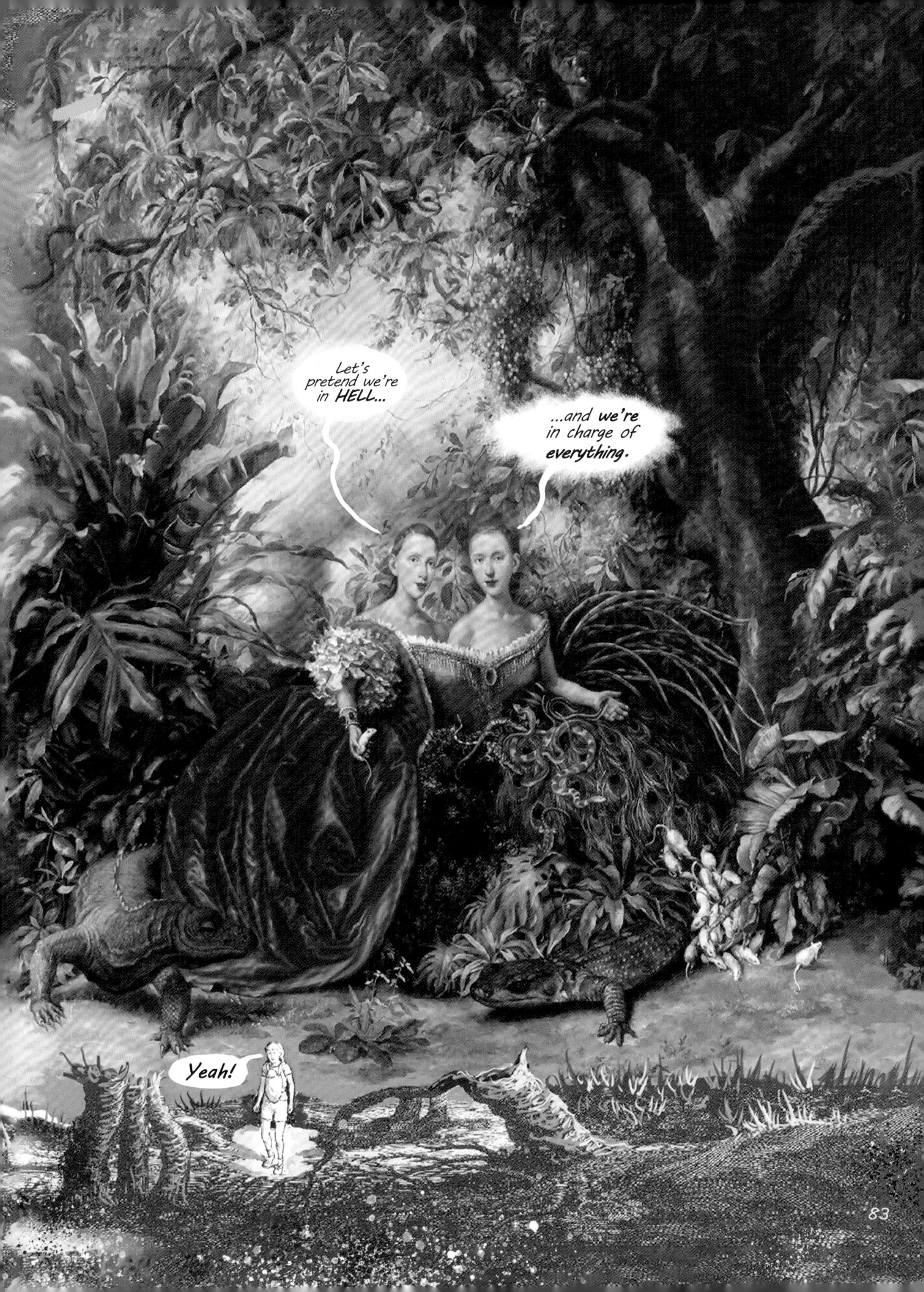
Let's pretend we're in HELL...
...and we're in charge of everything.
Yeah!

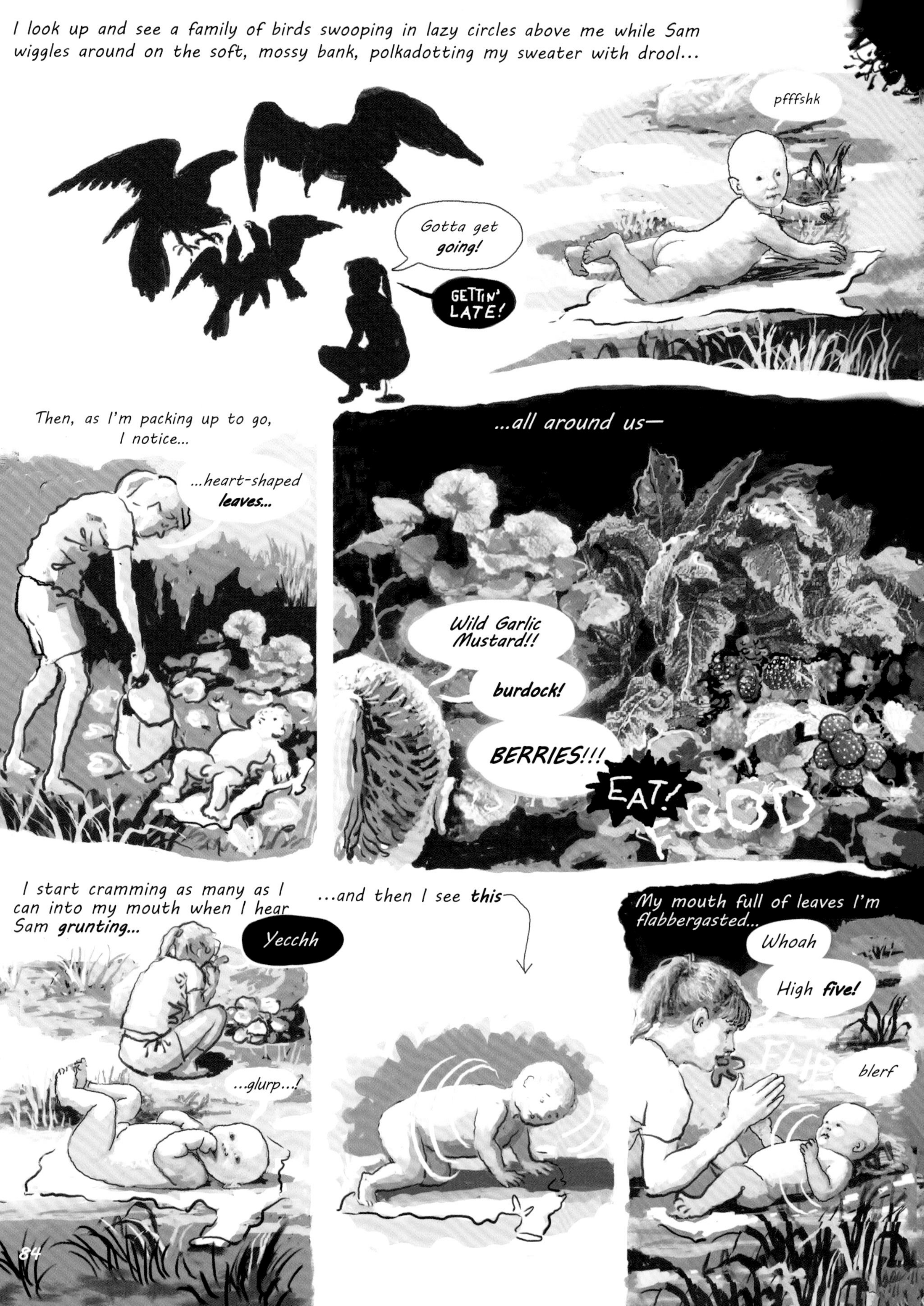
I look up and see a family of birds swooping in lazy circles above me while Sam wiggles around on the soft, mossy bank, polkadotting my sweater with drool...
pfffshk
Gotta get going!
GETTIN' LATE!
Then, as I'm packing up to go, I notice...
...heart-shaped leaves...
...all around us—
Wild Garlic Mustard!!
burdock!
BERRIES!!!
EAT!
FOOD
I start cramming as many as I can into my mouth when I hear Sam grunting...
Yecchh
...glurp...!
...and then I see this
My mouth full of leaves I'm flabbergasted...
Whoah
High five!
FLIP
blerf

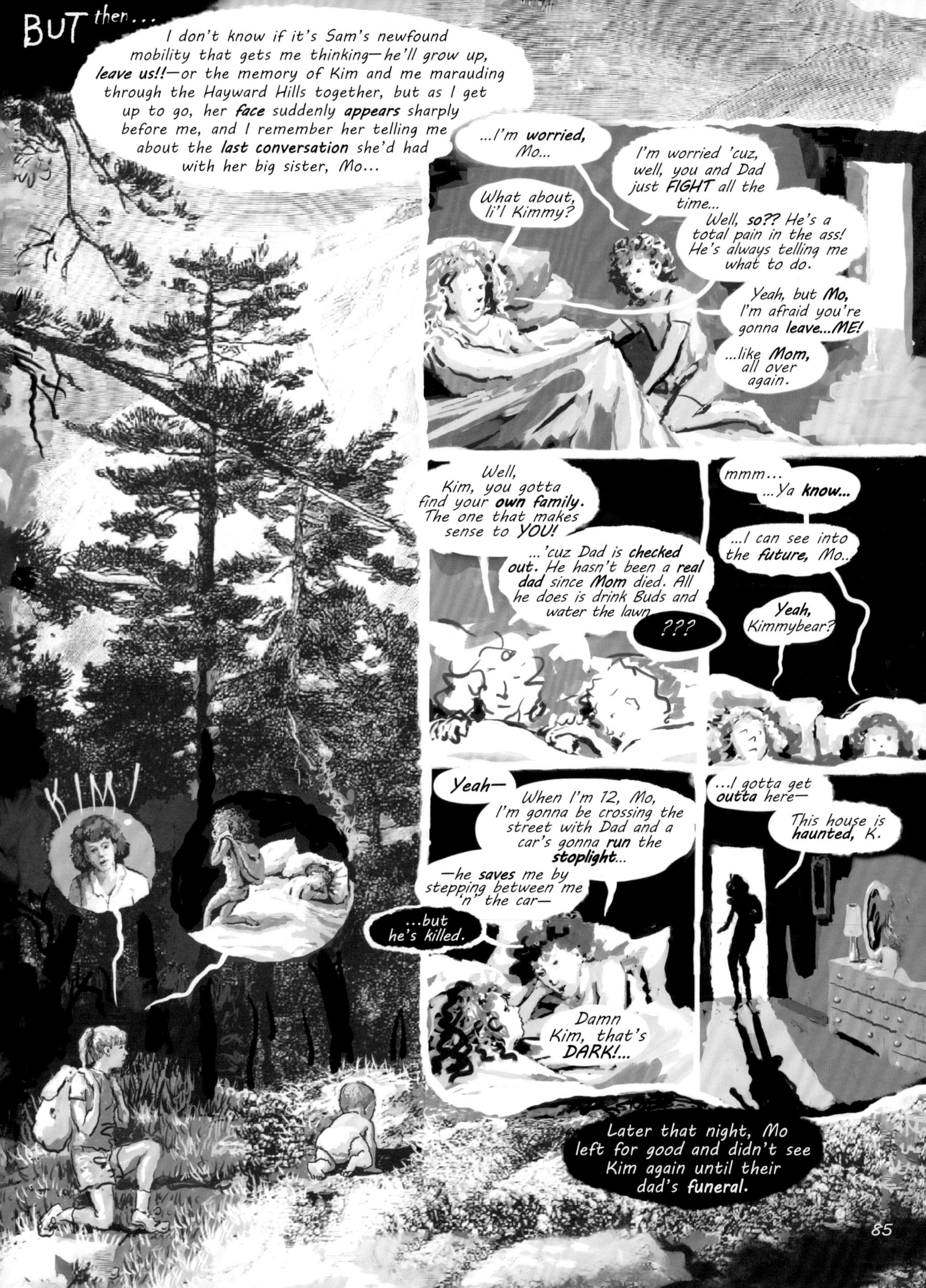
BUT then...
I don't know if it's Sam's newfound mobility that gets me thinking—he'll grow up, leave us!!—or the memory of Kim and me marauding through the Hayward Hills together, but as I get up to go, her face suddenly appears sharply before me, and I remember her telling me about the last conversation she'd had with her big sister, Mo...
...I'm worried, Mo...
What about, li'l Kimmy?
I'm worried 'cuz, well, you and Dad just FIGHT all the time...
Well, so?? He's a total pain in the ass! He's always telling me what to do.
Yeah, but Mo, I'm afraid you're gonna leave...ME!
...like Mom, all over again.
Well, Kim, you gotta find your own family. The one that makes sense to YOU!
...'cuz Dad is checked out. He hasn't been a real dad since Mom died. All he does is drink Buds and water the lawn.
???
mmm... ...Ya know...
...I can see into the future, Mo...
Yeah, Kimmybear?
Yeah—
When I'm 12, Mo, I'm gonna be crossing the street with Dad and a car's gonna run the stoplight...
—he saves me by stepping between me 'n' the car—
...but he's killed.
Damn Kim, that's DARK!...
...I gotta get outta here—
This house is haunted, K.
KIM!
Later that night, Mo left for good and didn't see Kim again until their dad's funeral.

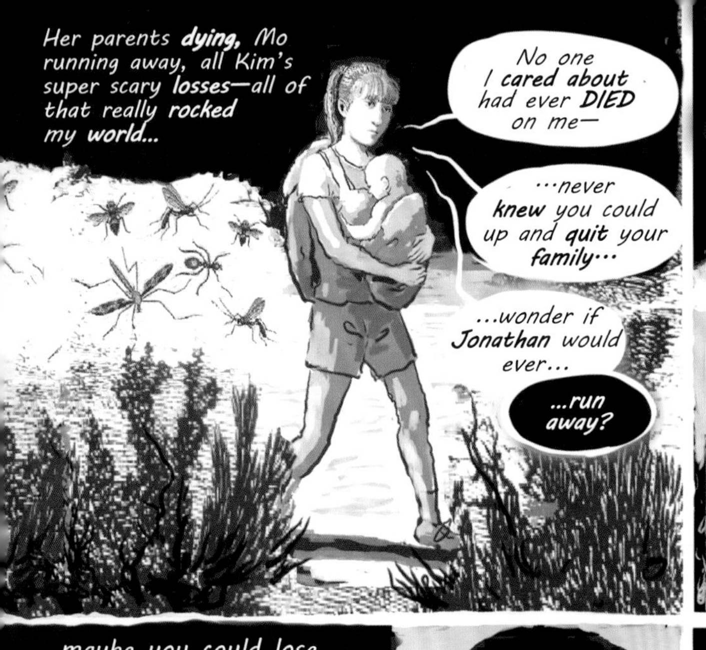
Her parents dying, Mo running away, all Kim's super scary losses—all of that really rocked my world...
No one I cared about had ever DIED on me—
...never knew you could up and quit your family...
...wonder if Jonathan would ever...
...run away?

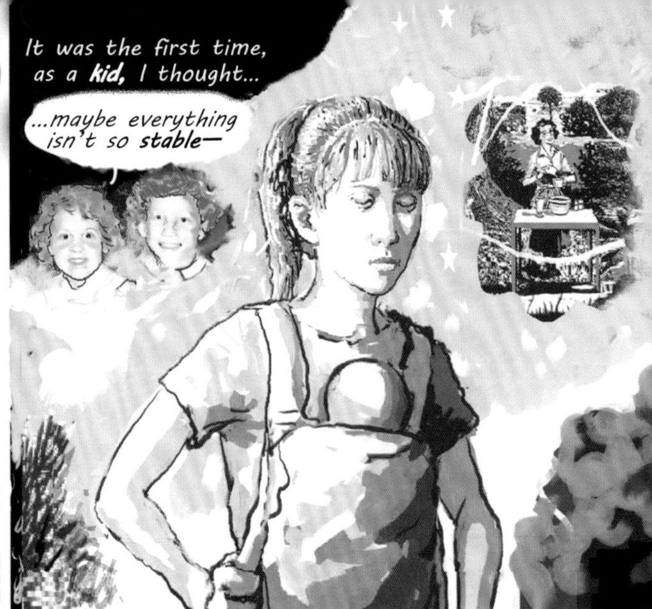
It was the first time, as a kid, I thought...
...maybe everything isn't so stable—

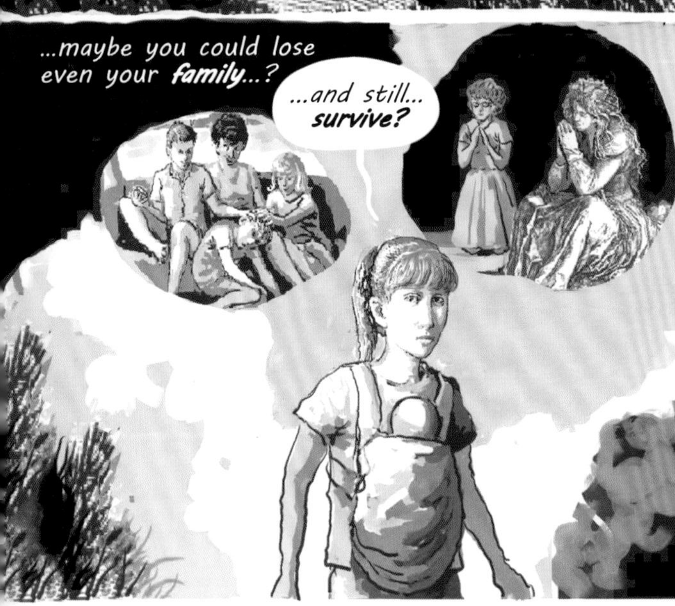
...maybe you could lose even your family...?
...and still... survive?

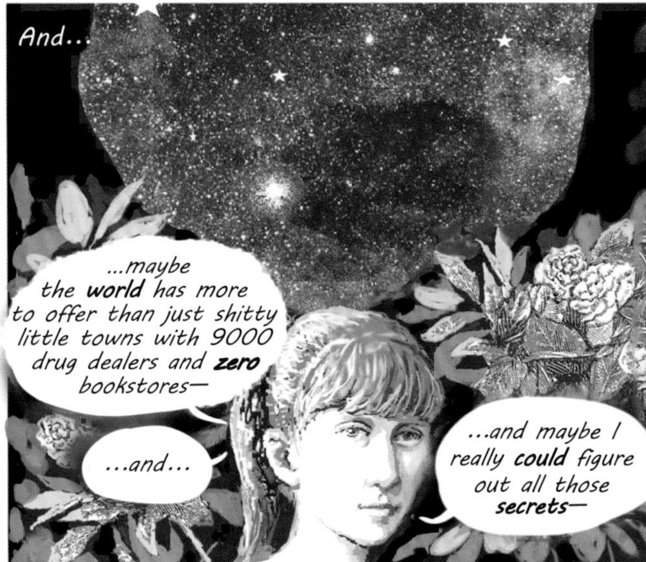
And...
...maybe the world has more to offer than just shitty little towns with 9000 drug dealers and zero bookstores—
...and...
...and maybe I really could figure out all those secrets—

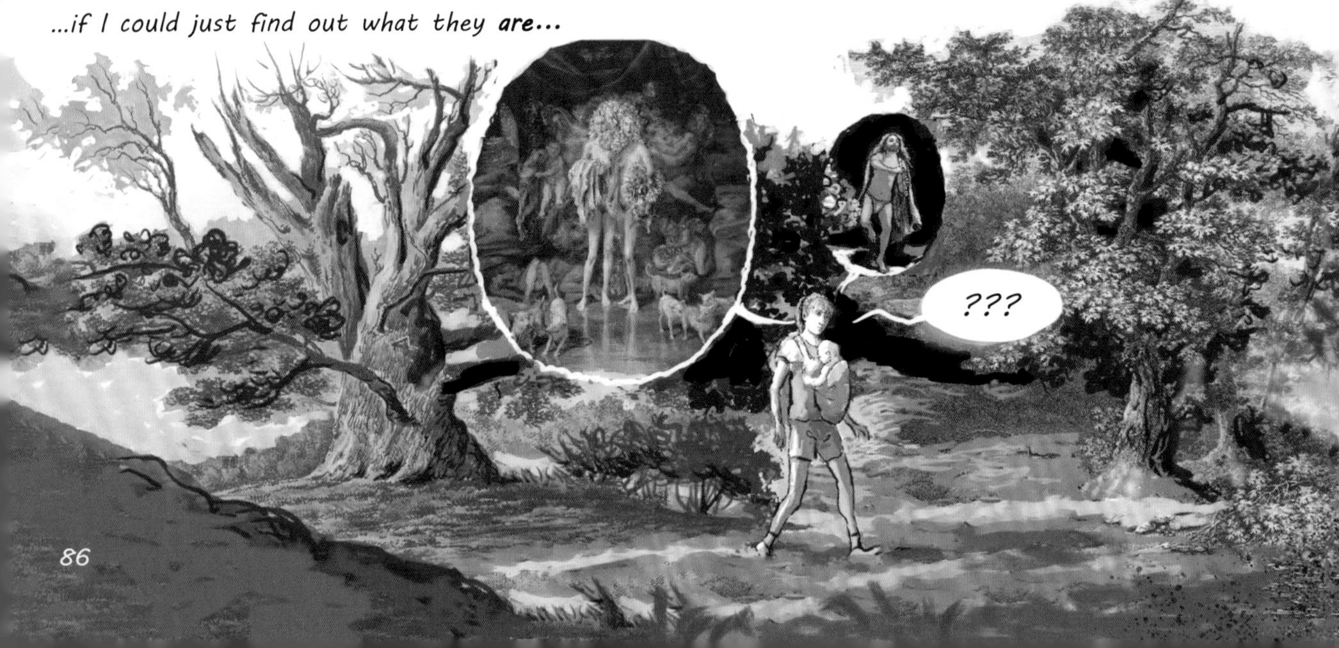
...if I could just find out what they are...
???

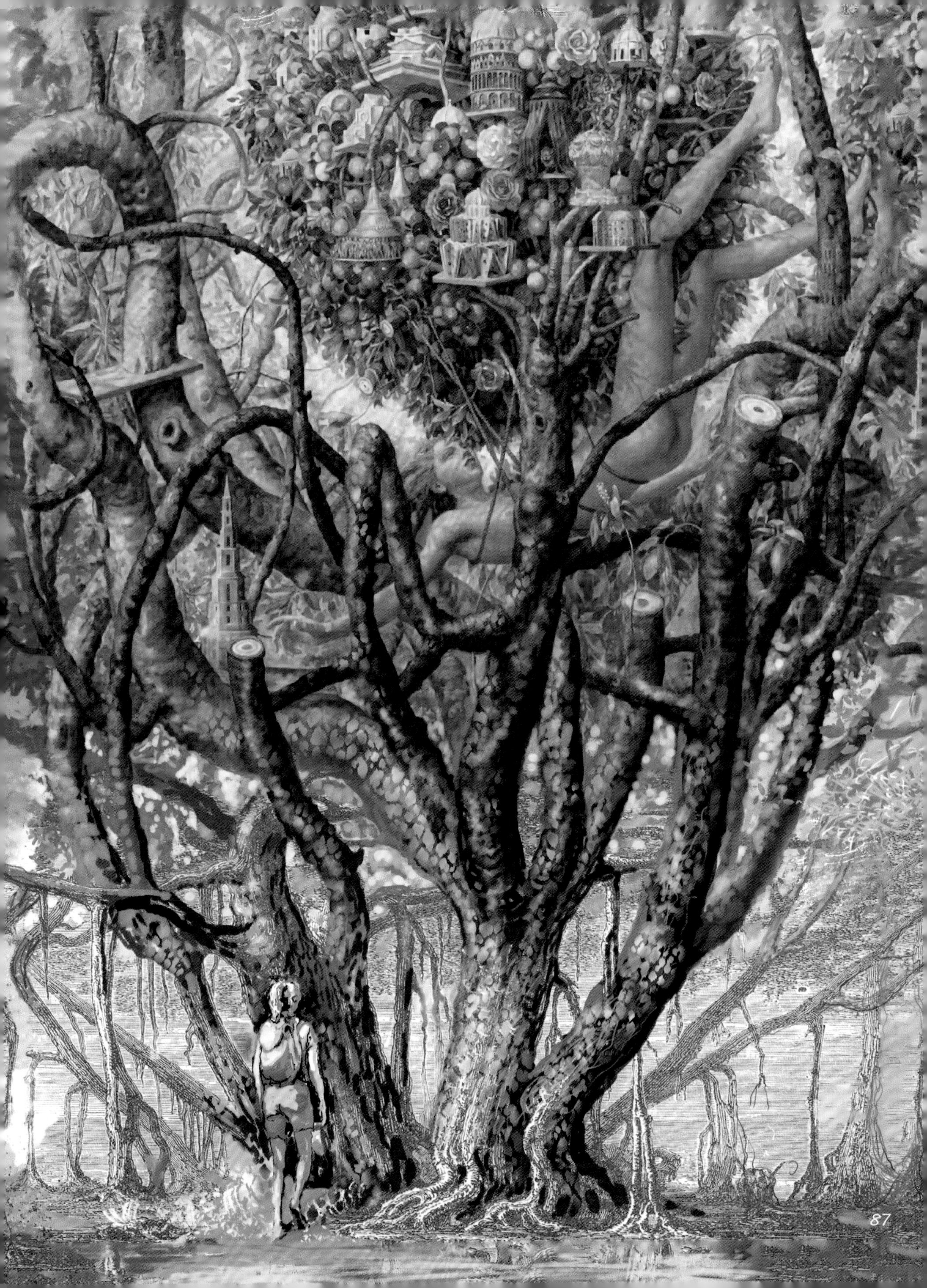

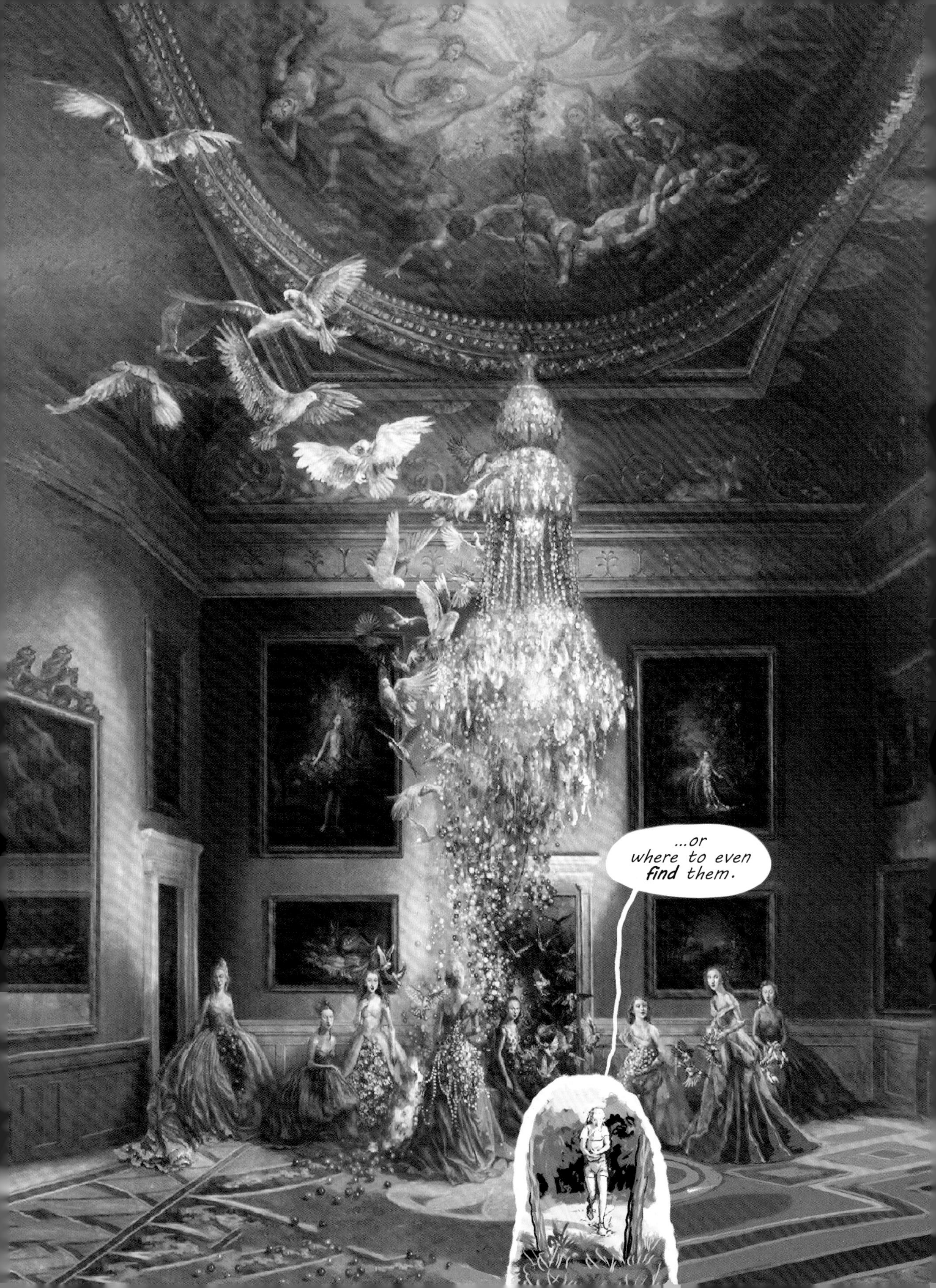
...or where to even find them.

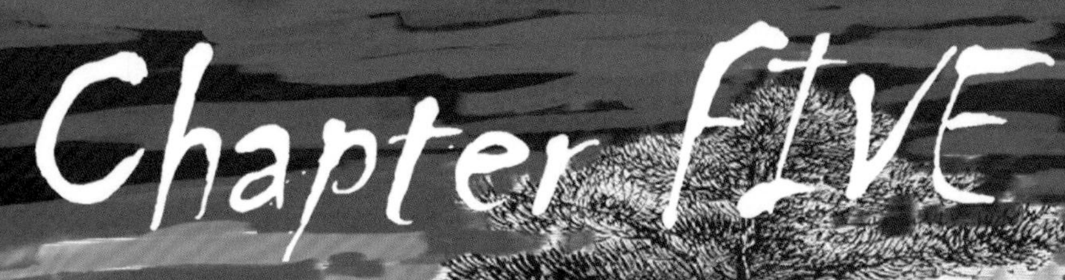

Ecchh

All those leaves and berries seem to have gone right through me— Feeling **worse!**

From the soreness of my feet I figure I've walked maybe...nine, **ten** miles by now? Not the **twenty** Jonathan and I did once in Yosemite, but **far enough**—

all day

...more like **five** miles...

...**six** at the **most.**

My TOES ache!!

And the cuts on my hands won't stop **throbbing.**

The sky's changing color, deepening into Prussian blue as the sun fades. Gnats wing about in lopsided circles, spelling out secret alphabets in the dusty light as mosquitoes feast on my **blood.**

...cerulean, manganese blue, cobalt, teal, phthalo blue, ultramarine, indanthrone blue...

SLAP

So, Mo **escaped...**

...she got outta **Hayward!**

Sarah Winchester got out of New Haven

...reimagined the whole **idea** of **home.**

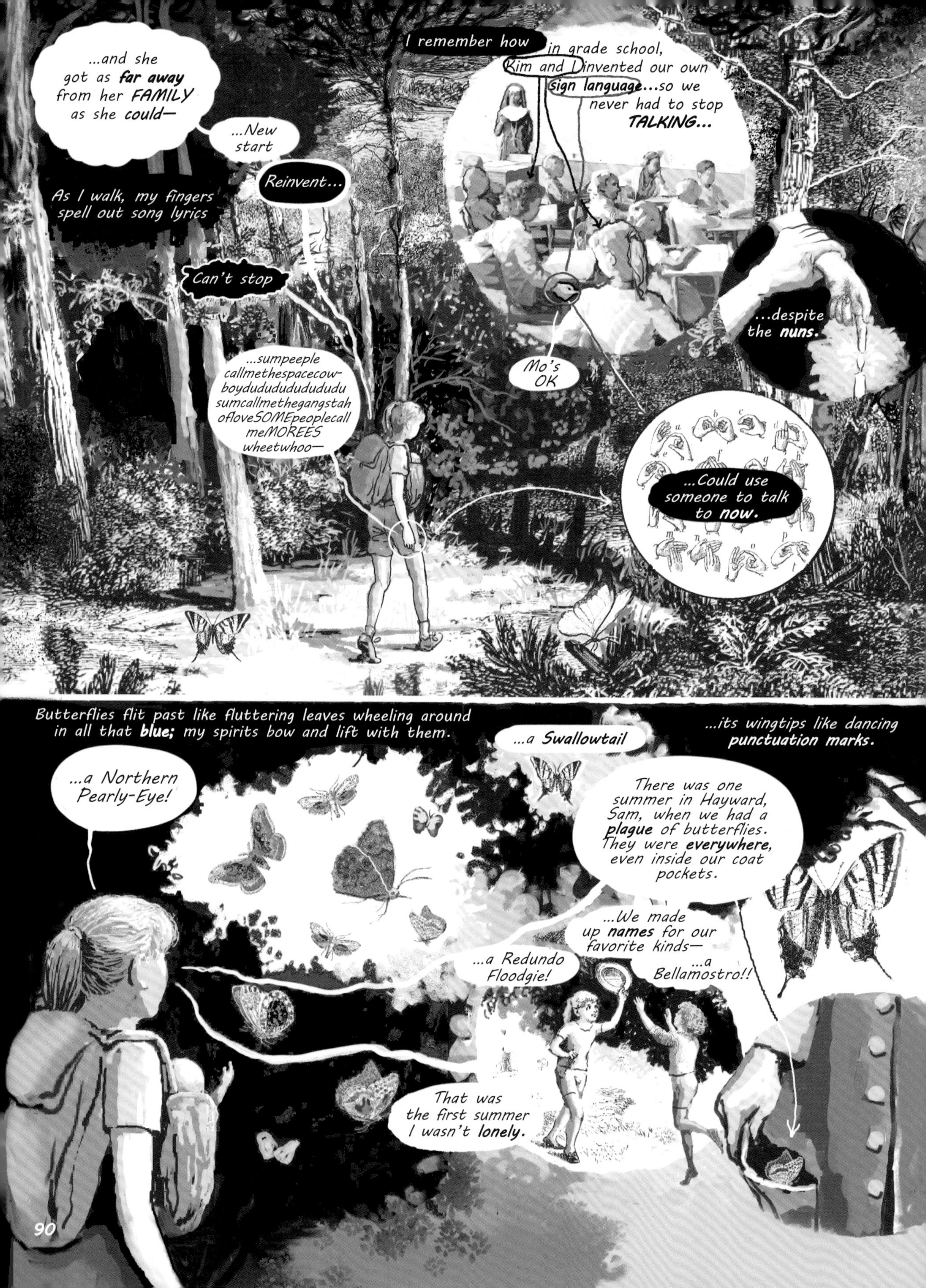

...and she got as far away from her FAMILY as she could—
...New start
Reinvent...
As I walk, my fingers spell out song lyrics
Can't stop
I remember how in grade school, Kim and I invented our own sign language...so we never had to stop TALKING...
...despite the nuns.
Mo's OK
...sumpeeple callmethespacecow-boydudududududu sumcallmethegangstah ofloveSOMEpeoplecall meMOREES wheetwhoo—
...Could use someone to talk to now.
Butterflies flit past like fluttering leaves wheeling around in all that blue; my spirits bow and lift with them.
...a Swallowtail
...its wingtips like dancing punctuation marks.
...a Northern Pearly-Eye!
There was one summer in Hayward, Sam, when we had a plague of butterflies. They were everywhere, even inside our coat pockets.
...We made up names for our favorite kinds—
...a Redundo Floodgie!
...a Bellamostro!!
That was the first summer I wasn't lonely.

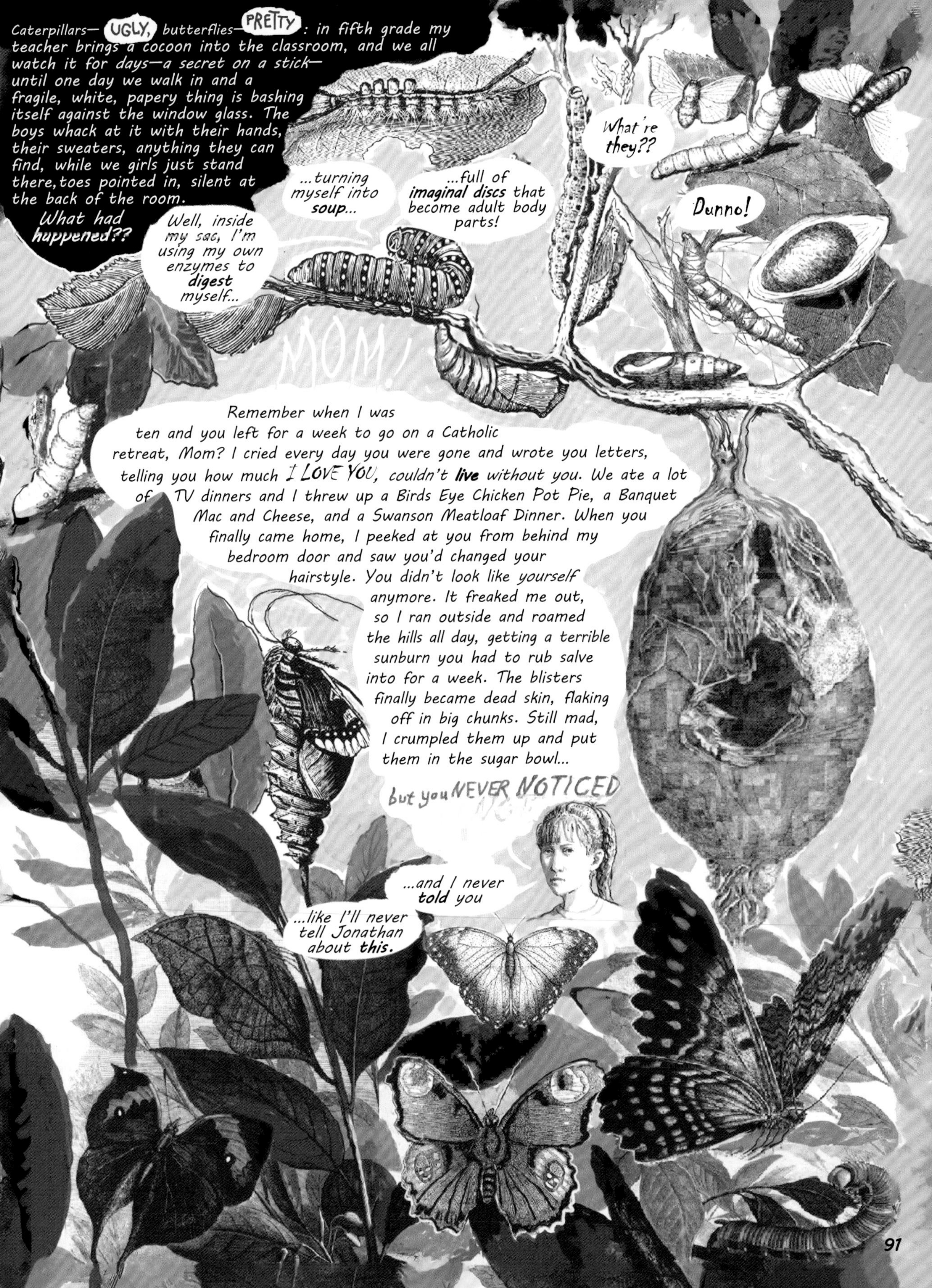

Caterpillars— UGLY, butterflies— PRETTY : in fifth grade my teacher brings a cocoon into the classroom, and we all watch it for days—a secret on a stick— until one day we walk in and a fragile, white, papery thing is bashing itself against the window glass. The boys whack at it with their hands, their sweaters, anything they can find, while we girls just stand there, toes pointed in, silent at the back of the room.
What had happened??
Well, inside my sac, I'm using my own enzymes to digest myself...
...turning myself into soup...
...full of imaginal discs that become adult body parts!
What're they??
Dunno!
MOM!
Remember when I was ten and you left for a week to go on a Catholic retreat, Mom? I cried every day you were gone and wrote you letters, telling you how much I LOVE YOU, couldn't live without you. We ate a lot of TV dinners and I threw up a Birds Eye Chicken Pot Pie, a Banquet Mac and Cheese, and a Swanson Meatloaf Dinner. When you finally came home, I peeked at you from behind my bedroom door and saw you'd changed your hairstyle. You didn't look like yourself anymore. It freaked me out, so I ran outside and roamed the hills all day, getting a terrible sunburn you had to rub salve into for a week. The blisters finally became dead skin, flaking off in big chunks. Still mad, I crumpled them up and put them in the sugar bowl...
but you NEVER NOTICED
...and I never told you
...like I'll never tell Jonathan about this.

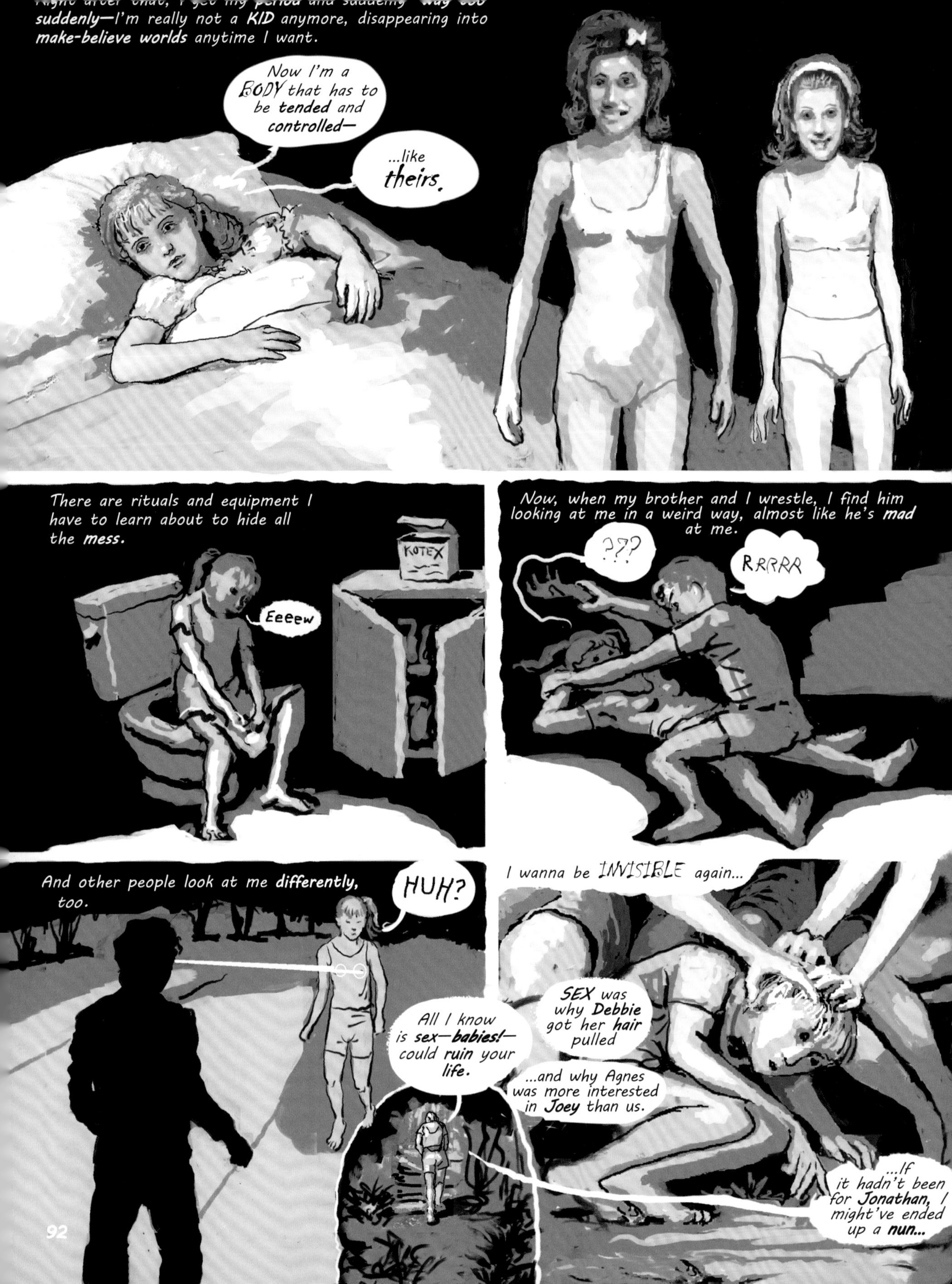
suddenly—I'm really not a KID anymore, disappearing into make-believe worlds anytime I want.
Now I'm a BODY that has to be tended and controlled—
...like theirs.
There are rituals and equipment I have to learn about to hide all the mess.
KOTEX
Eeeew
Now, when my brother and I wrestle, I find him looking at me in a weird way, almost like he's mad at me.
???
RRRRA
And other people look at me differently, too.
HUH?
I wanna be INVISIBLE again...
All I know is sex—babies!—could ruin your life.
SEX was why Debbie got her hair pulled
...and why Agnes was more interested in Joey than us.
...If it hadn't been for Jonathan, I might've ended up a nun...

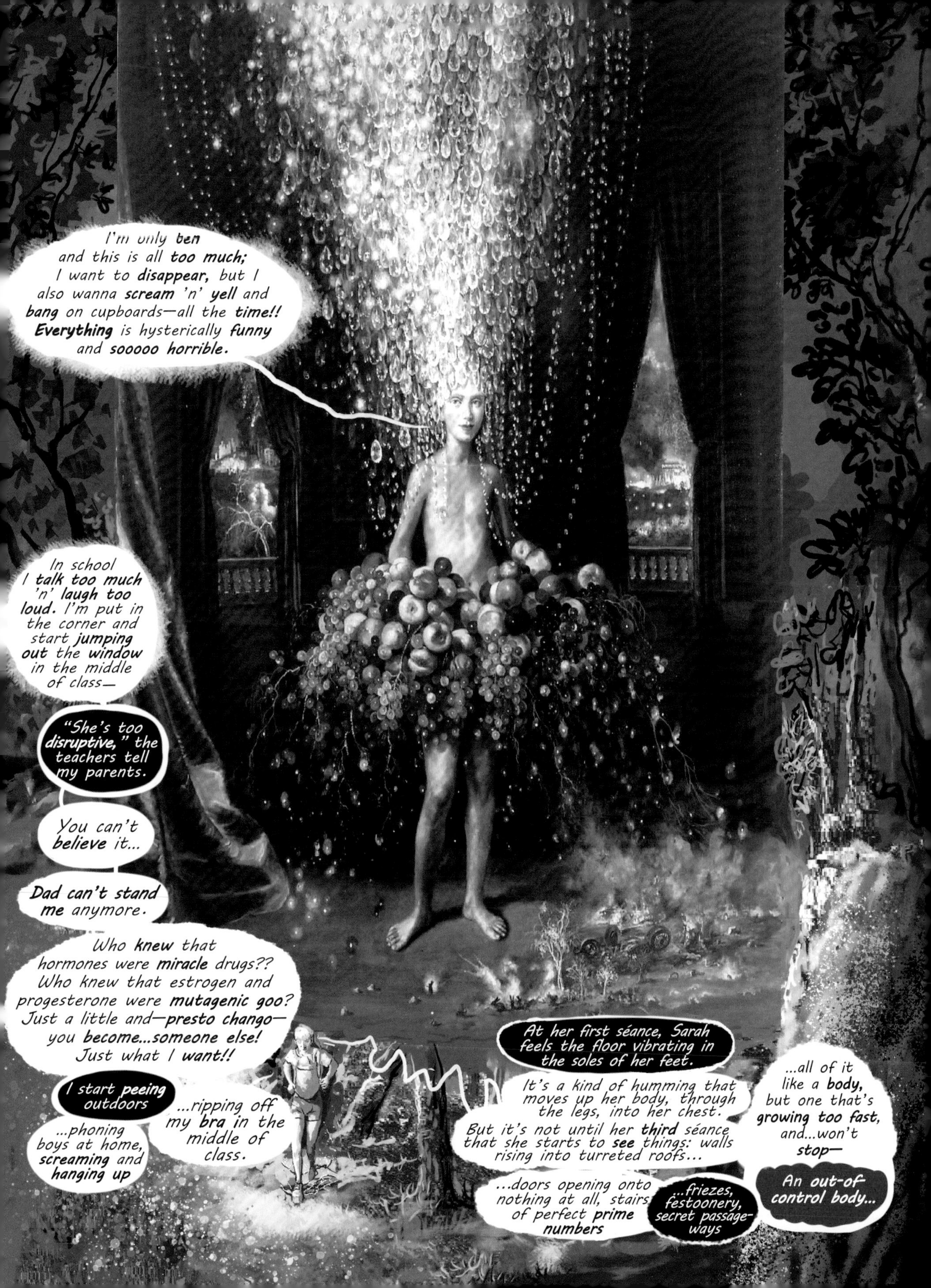

I'm only **ten** and this is all **too much;** I want to **disappear,** but I also wanna **scream** 'n' **yell** and **bang** on cupboards—all the **time!!** **Everything** is hysterically **funny** and **sooooo horrible.**

In school I **talk too much** 'n' **laugh too loud.** I'm put in the corner and start **jumping out** the **window** in the middle of class—

"She's too **disruptive,**" the teachers tell my parents.

You can't **believe** it...

Dad can't stand me anymore.

Who **knew** that hormones were **miracle** drugs?? Who knew that estrogen and progesterone were **mutagenic goo?** Just a little and—**presto chango**—you **become...someone else!** Just what I **want!!**

I start **peeing** outdoors

...phoning boys at home, **screaming** and **hanging up**

...ripping off my **bra** in the middle of class.

At her first séance, Sarah feels the floor vibrating in the soles of her feet.

It's a kind of humming that moves up her body, through the legs, into her chest.

But it's not until her **third** séance that she starts to **see** things: walls rising into turreted roofs...

...doors opening onto nothing at all, stairs of perfect **prime numbers**

...friezes, festoonery, secret passage-ways

...all of it like a **body,** but one that's **growing too fast,** and...won't **stop**—

An out-of-control body...

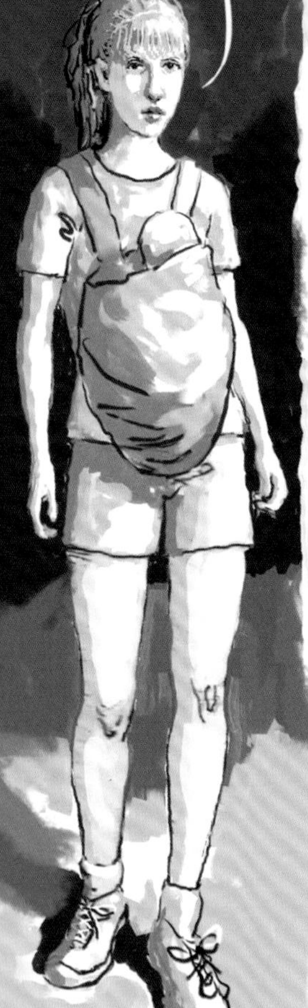

...like **MINE!**
BIZARRE
...something not to TALK about...
unseemly
It wanted to do things it had never wanted to DO before...
ESCAPE
...climb **Mount Everest...**
...disappear
...Voices whispering inside Sarah, first her mother's, her husband's, then the **medium's,** but when she knocks out her first wall...
...the voices really start making **sense**

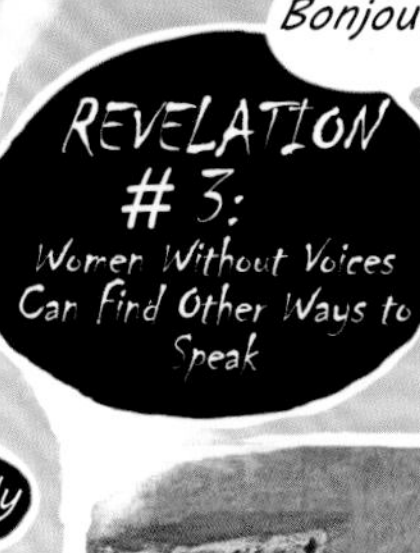

REVELATION #3:
Women Without Voices Can Find Other Ways to Speak
Bonjour!
Je suis Marthe—
LARGE YELLOW NUDE by Pierre Bonnard
and I'm here in my bathroom. This is where I go to watch the light spray across white tiles and dissolve into colors: amber, turquoise, rose...and Pierre **paints** it. Here, he shows me drying myself, but what's most **important** is that messy **reddish thing** in front of me, the only part of this painting with any **thick paint** on it, which is a **clue** to why it's **important!**
Did you **mind** him **painting** you all the time??
Pourquoi pas? This painting is a game changer, and I should know because it's about **me**—his **wife,** Marthe de Meligny. My **real name** is **Marie Boursin,** but it was only when we got **married,** 32 years after we met, that I told him my actual **name**—
...and that I was **8** years **older** than he'd thought!
Silly men! believe what they **want.**
I hated my seamstress job but **Pierre** gave me a way out
...and I gave **him** a new way to see **women.**

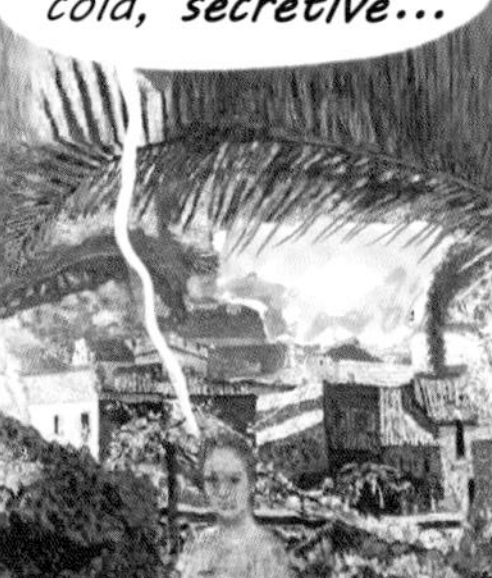

Pierre's family thinks I'm neurotic, cold, **secretive...**

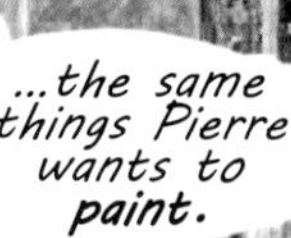

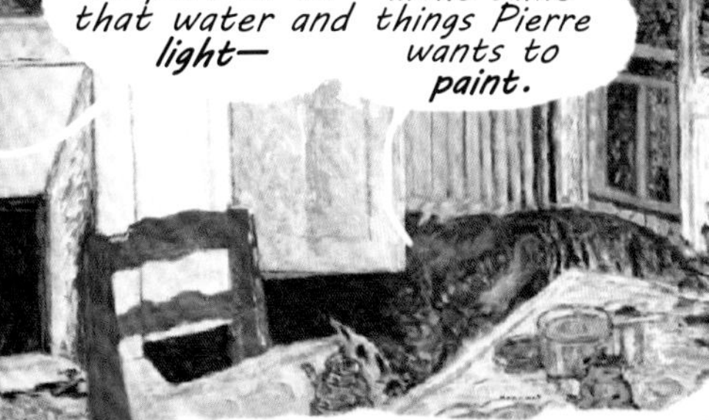

In truth, I just want to be part of all that water and **light**—
...the same things Pierre wants to **paint.**

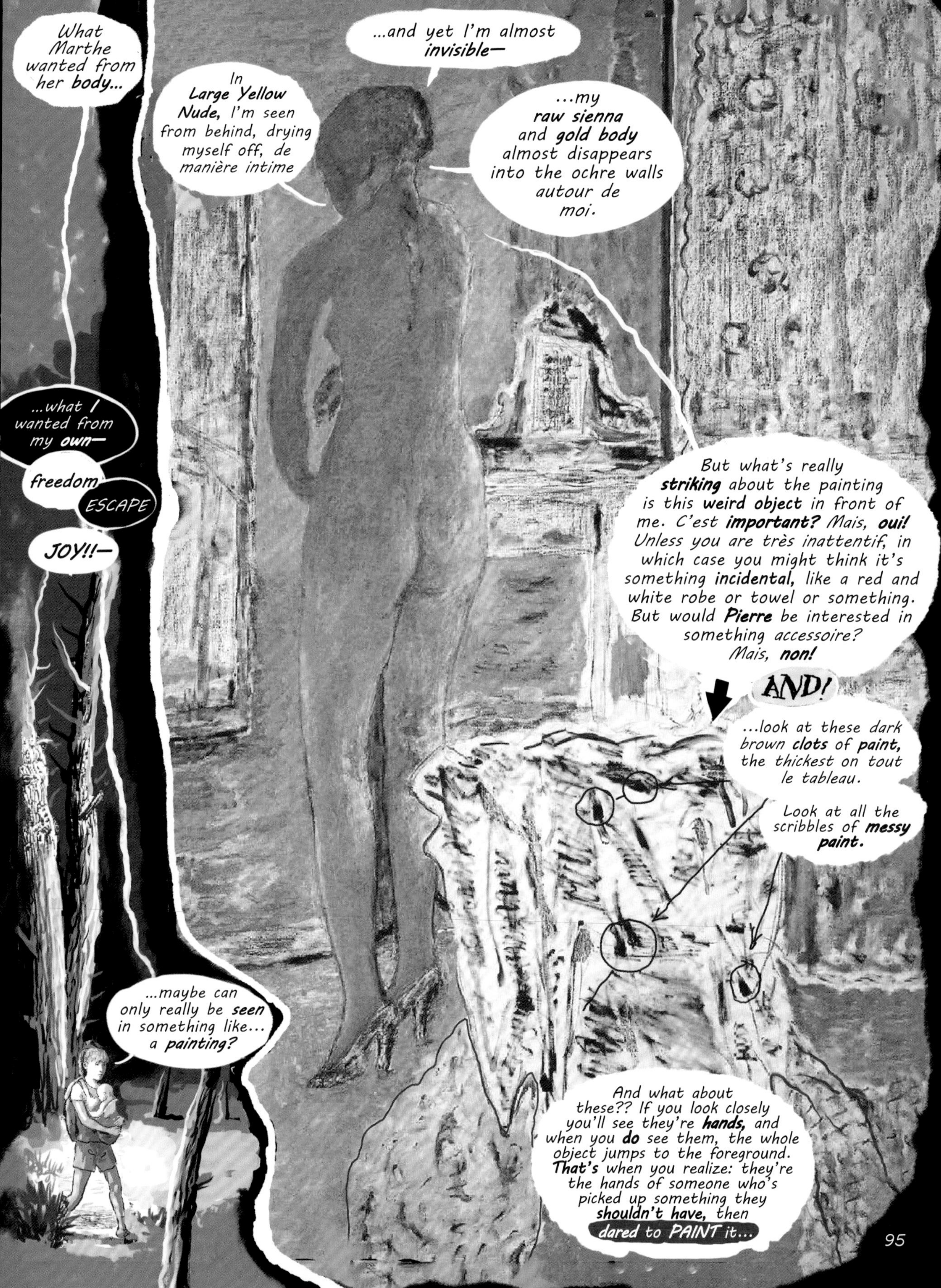
What Marthe wanted from her body...
...what I wanted from my own—
freedom
ESCAPE
JOY!!—
...maybe can only really be seen in something like... a painting?
In Large Yellow Nude, I'm seen from behind, drying myself off, de manière intime
...and yet I'm almost invisible—
...my raw sienna and gold body almost disappears into the ochre walls autour de moi.
But what's really striking about the painting is this weird object in front of me. C'est important? Mais, oui! Unless you are très inattentif, in which case you might think it's something incidental, like a red and white robe or towel or something. But would Pierre be interested in something accessoire? Mais, non!
AND!
...look at these dark brown clots of paint, the thickest on tout le tableau.
Look at all the scribbles of messy paint.
And what about these?? If you look closely you'll see they're hands, and when you do see them, the whole object jumps to the foreground. That's when you realize: they're the hands of someone who's picked up something they shouldn't have, then dared to PAINT it...

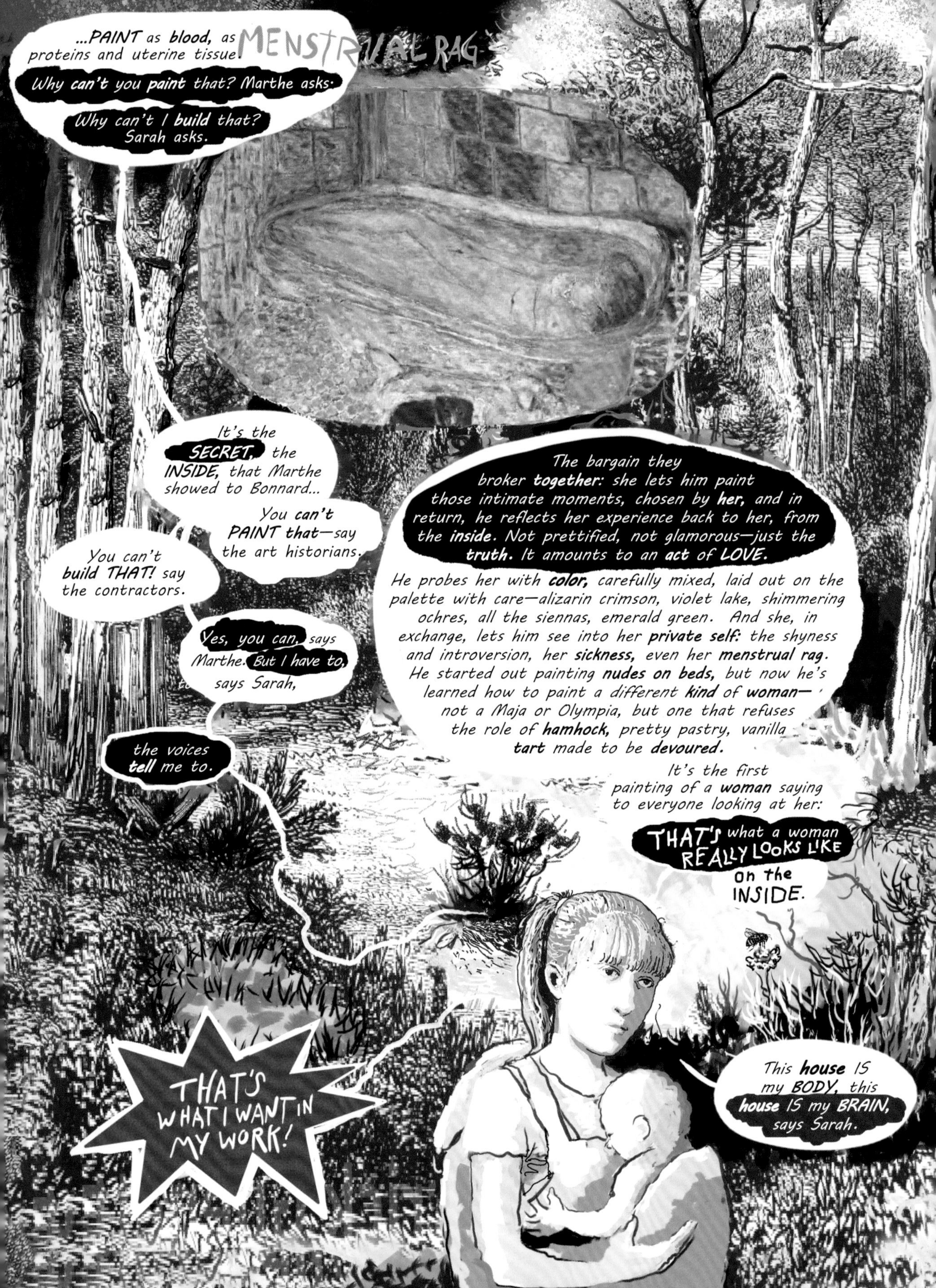
...PAINT as blood, as proteins and uterine tissue.
MENSTRUAL RAG
Why can't you paint that? Marthe asks.
Why can't I build that? Sarah asks.
It's the SECRET, the INSIDE, that Marthe showed to Bonnard...
You can't PAINT that—say the art historians.
You can't build THAT! say the contractors.
Yes, you can, says Marthe. But I have to, says Sarah,
the voices tell me to.
The bargain they broker together: she lets him paint those intimate moments, chosen by her, and in return, he reflects her experience back to her, from the inside. Not prettified, not glamorous—just the truth. It amounts to an act of LOVE.
He probes her with color, carefully mixed, laid out on the palette with care—alizarin crimson, violet lake, shimmering ochres, all the siennas, emerald green. And she, in exchange, lets him see into her private self: the shyness and introversion, her sickness, even her menstrual rag. He started out painting nudes on beds, but now he's learned how to paint a different kind of woman— not a Maja or Olympia, but one that refuses the role of hamhock, pretty pastry, vanilla tart made to be devoured.
It's the first painting of a woman saying to everyone looking at her:
THAT'S what a woman REALLY LOOKS LIKE on the INSIDE.
THAT'S WHAT I WANT IN MY WORK!
This house IS my BODY, this house IS my BRAIN, says Sarah.

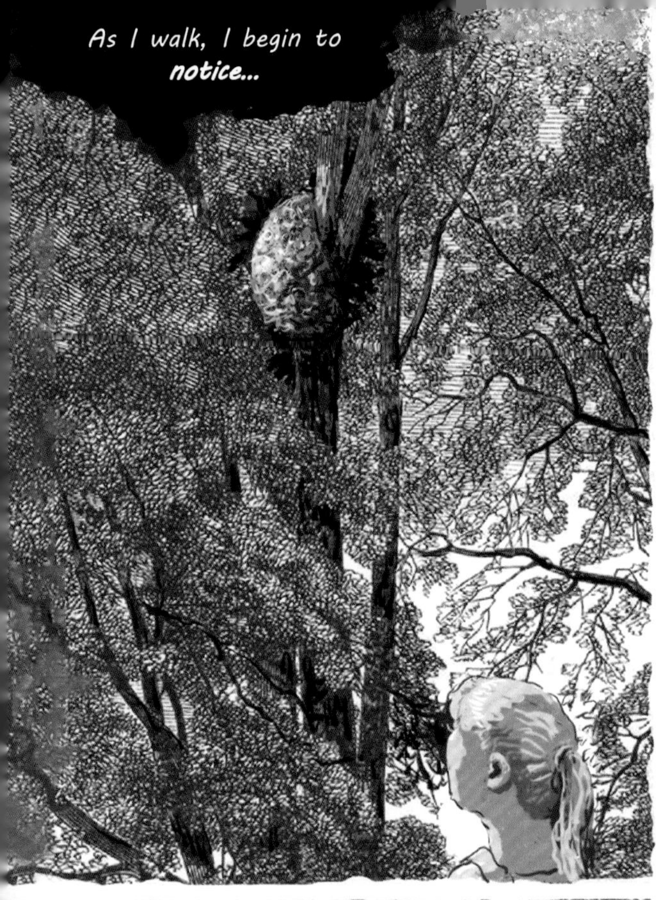
As I walk, I begin to **notice...**

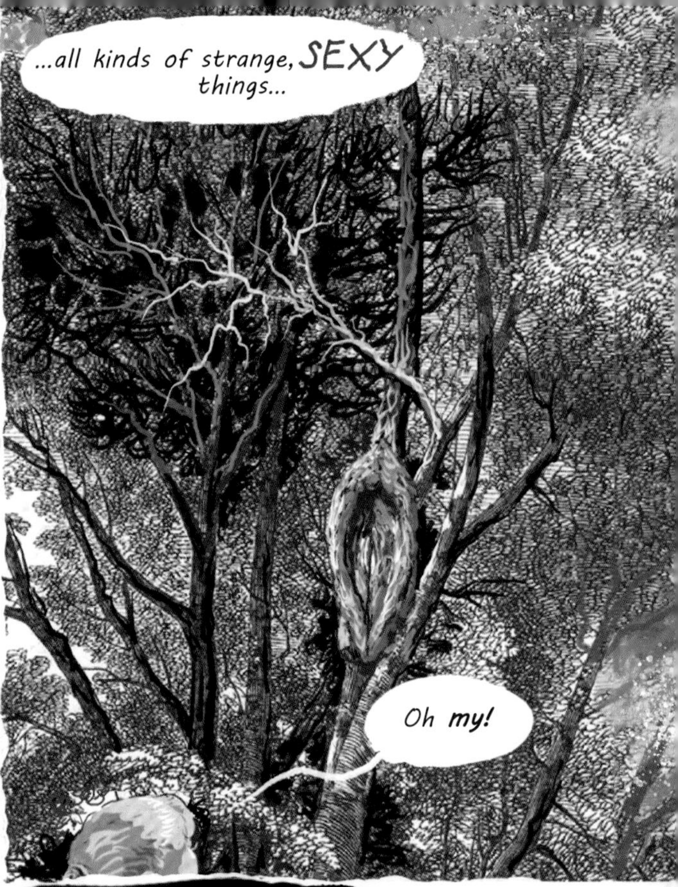
...all kinds of strange, SEXY things...
Oh **my!**

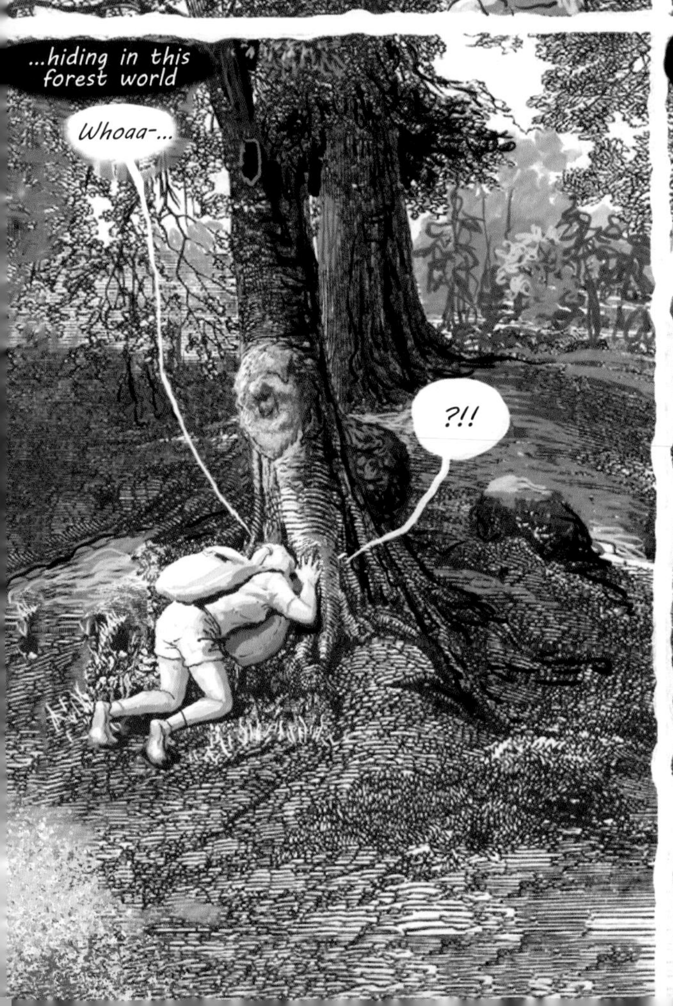
...hiding in this forest world
Whoaa-...
?!!

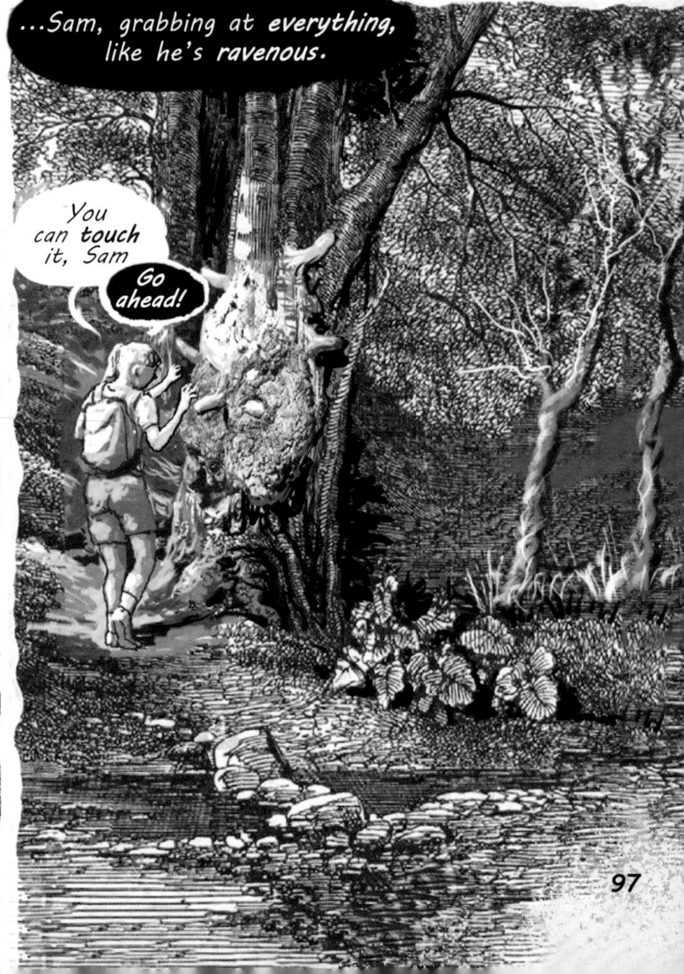
...Sam, grabbing at **everything,** like he's **ravenous.**
You can **touch** it, Sam
Go ahead!

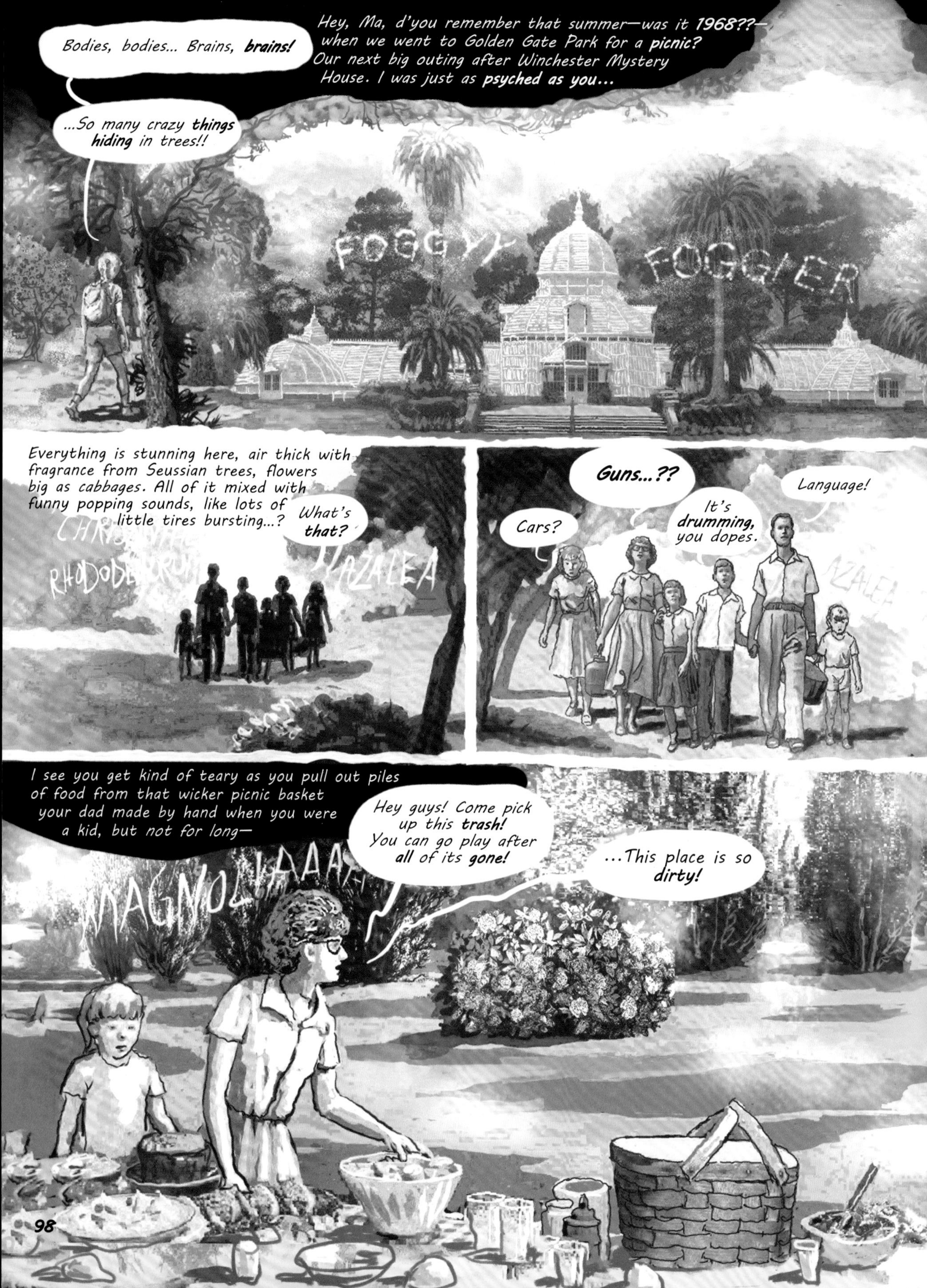
Hey, Ma, d'you remember that summer—was it 1968??—when we went to Golden Gate Park for a picnic? Our next big outing after Winchester Mystery House. I was just as psyched as you...
Bodies, bodies... Brains, brains!
...So many crazy things hiding in trees!!
FOGGY
FOGGIER
Everything is stunning here, air thick with fragrance from Seussian trees, flowers big as cabbages. All of it mixed with funny popping sounds, like lots of little tires bursting...?
What's that?
AZALEA
Guns...??
Cars?
It's drumming, you dopes.
Language!
AZALEA
I see you get kind of teary as you pull out piles of food from that wicker picnic basket your dad made by hand when you were a kid, but not for long—
Hey guys! Come pick up this trash! You can go play after all of its gone!
...This place is so dirty!

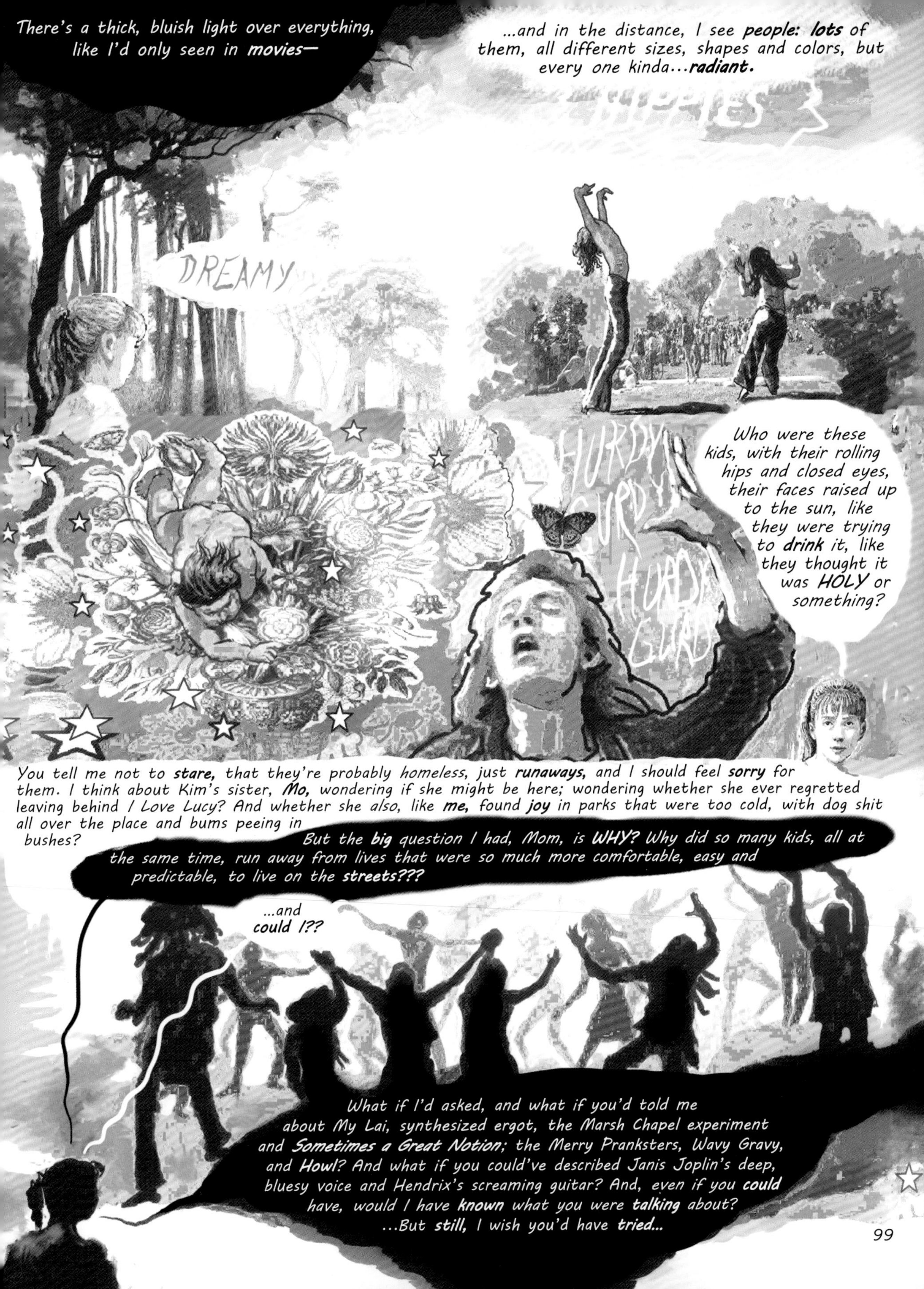
There's a thick, bluish light over everything, like I'd only seen in movies—
...and in the distance, I see people: lots of them, all different sizes, shapes and colors, but every one kinda...radiant.
HIPPIES
DREAMY
Who were these kids, with their rolling hips and closed eyes, their faces raised up to the sun, like they were trying to drink it, like they thought it was HOLY or something?
HURDY GURDY
HURDY GURDY
You tell me not to stare, that they're probably homeless, just runaways, and I should feel sorry for them. I think about Kim's sister, Mo, wondering if she might be here; wondering whether she ever regretted leaving behind I Love Lucy? And whether she also, like me, found joy in parks that were too cold, with dog shit all over the place and bums peeing in bushes?
But the big question I had, Mom, is WHY? Why did so many kids, all at the same time, run away from lives that were so much more comfortable, easy and predictable, to live on the streets???
...and could I??
What if I'd asked, and what if you'd told me about My Lai, synthesized ergot, the Marsh Chapel experiment and Sometimes a Great Notion; the Merry Pranksters, Wavy Gravy, and Howl? And what if you could've described Janis Joplin's deep, bluesy voice and Hendrix's screaming guitar? And, even if you could have, would I have known what you were talking about? ...But still, I wish you'd have tried...

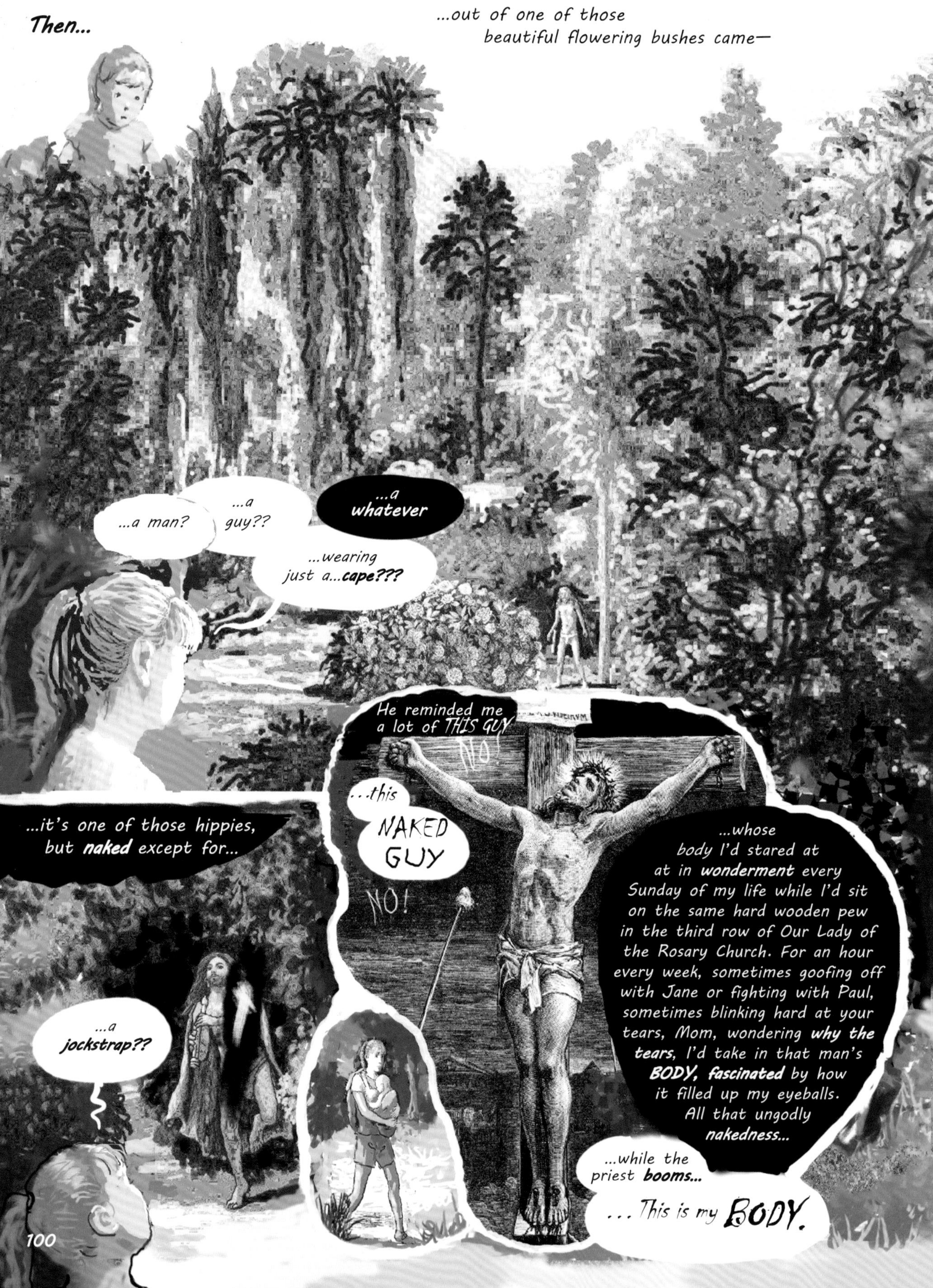
Then...
...out of one of those beautiful flowering bushes came—
...a man?
...a guy??
...a whatever
...wearing just a...cape???
...it's one of those hippies, but naked except for...
...a jockstrap??
He reminded me a lot of THIS GUY
NO!
...this NAKED GUY
NO!
...whose body I'd stared at at in wonderment every Sunday of my life while I'd sit on the same hard wooden pew in the third row of Our Lady of the Rosary Church. For an hour every week, sometimes goofing off with Jane or fighting with Paul, sometimes blinking hard at your tears, Mom, wondering why the tears, I'd take in that man's BODY, fascinated by how it filled up my eyeballs. All that ungodly nakedness...
...while the priest booms...
...This is my BODY.

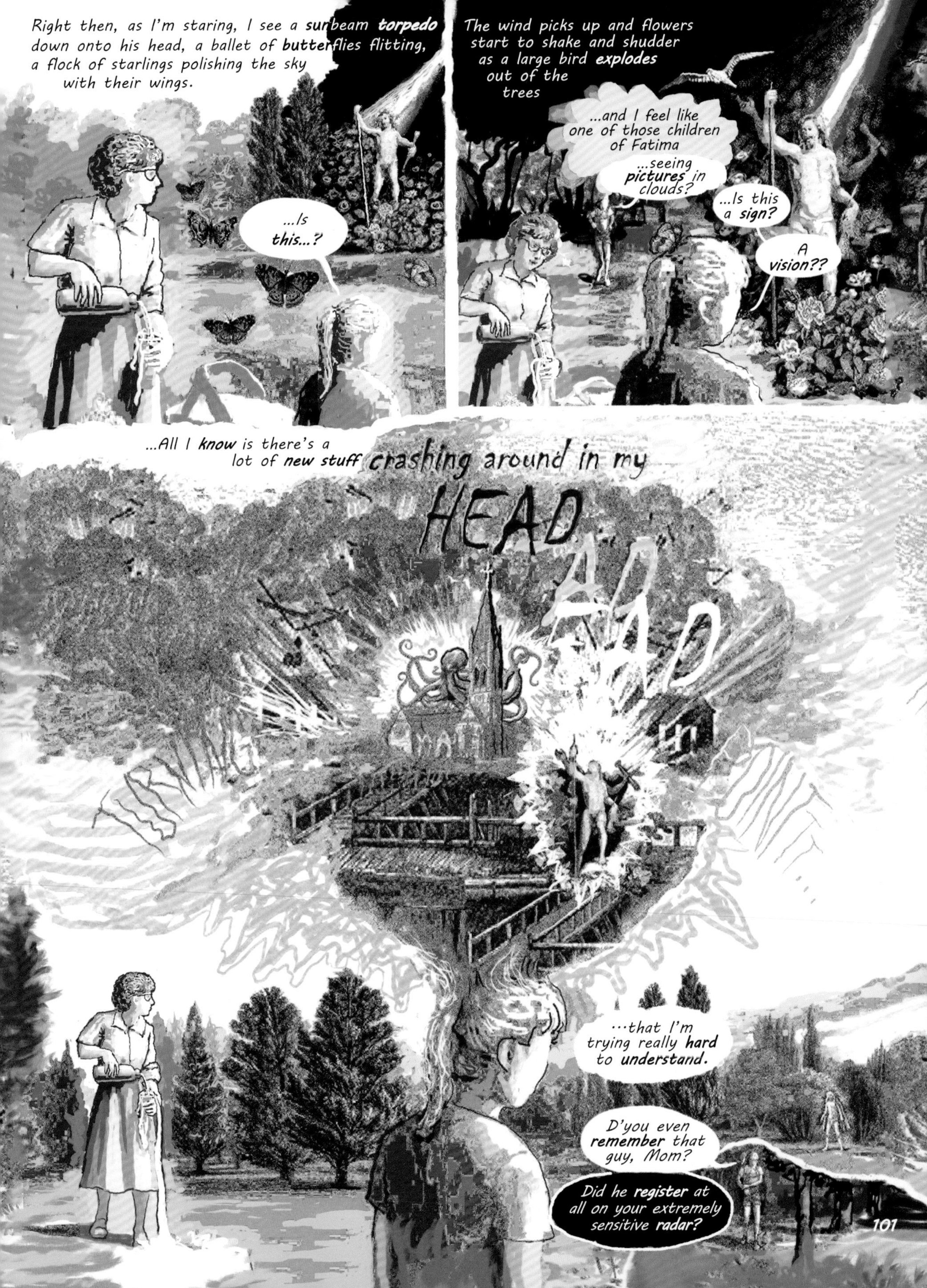
Right then, as I'm staring, I see a sunbeam torpedo down onto his head, a ballet of butterflies flitting, a flock of starlings polishing the sky with their wings.
...Is this...?
The wind picks up and flowers start to shake and shudder as a large bird explodes out of the trees
...and I feel like one of those children of Fatima
...seeing pictures in clouds?
...Is this a sign?
A vision??
...All I know is there's a lot of new stuff crashing around in my
HEAD
...that I'm trying really hard to understand.
D'you even remember that guy, Mom?
Did he register at all on your extremely sensitive radar?

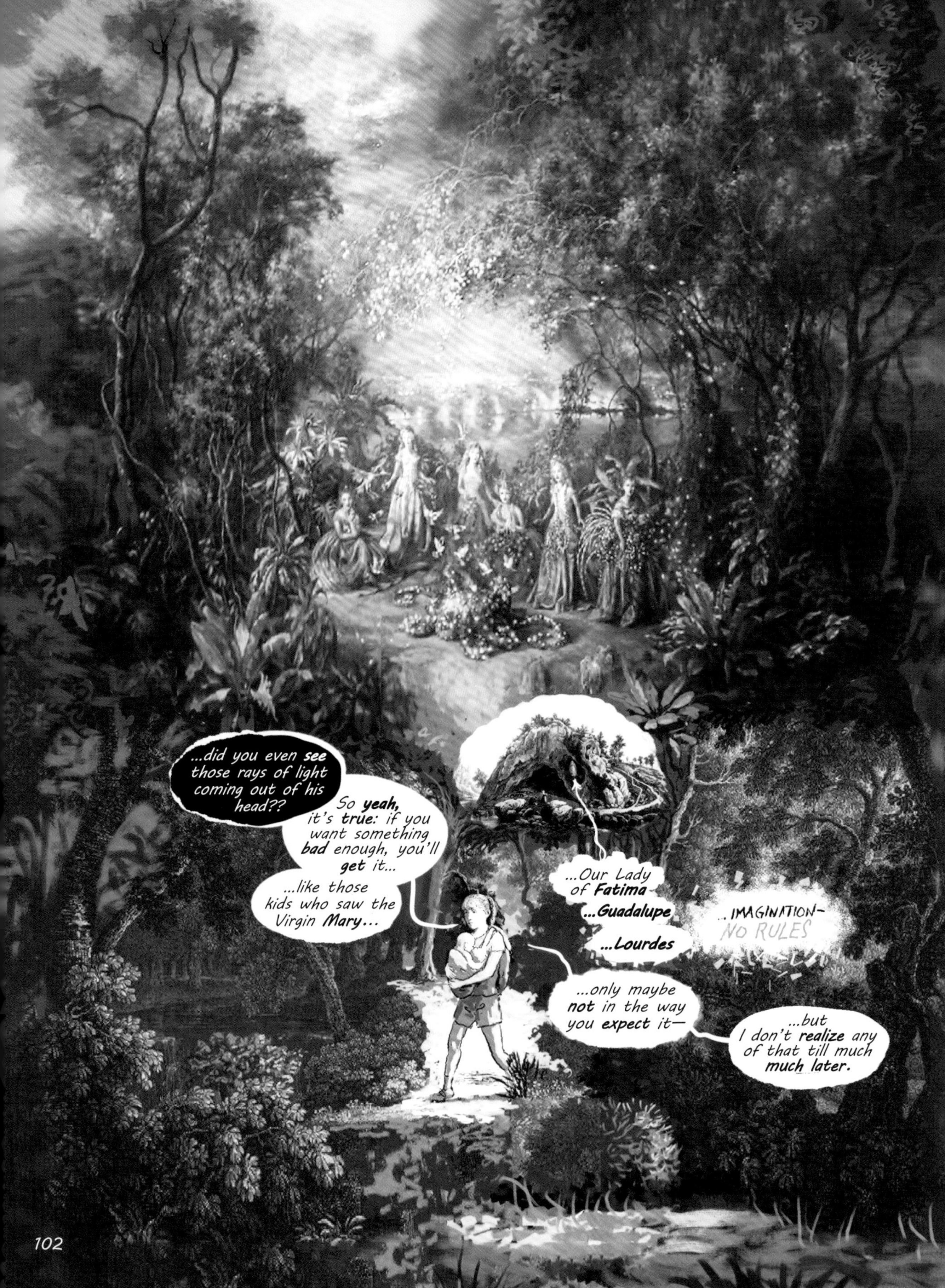
...did you even see those rays of light coming out of his head??
So yeah, it's true: if you want something bad enough, you'll get it...
...like those kids who saw the Virgin Mary...
...Our Lady of Fatima
...Guadalupe
...Lourdes
...IMAGINATION-
NO RULES
...only maybe not in the way you expect it—
...but I don't realize any of that till much much later.

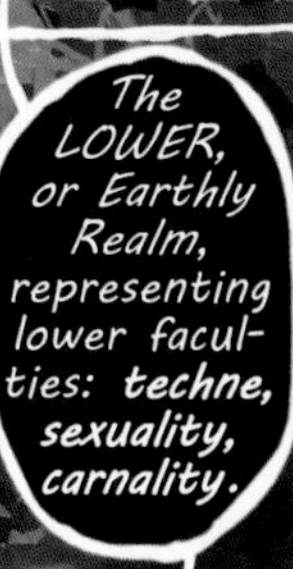
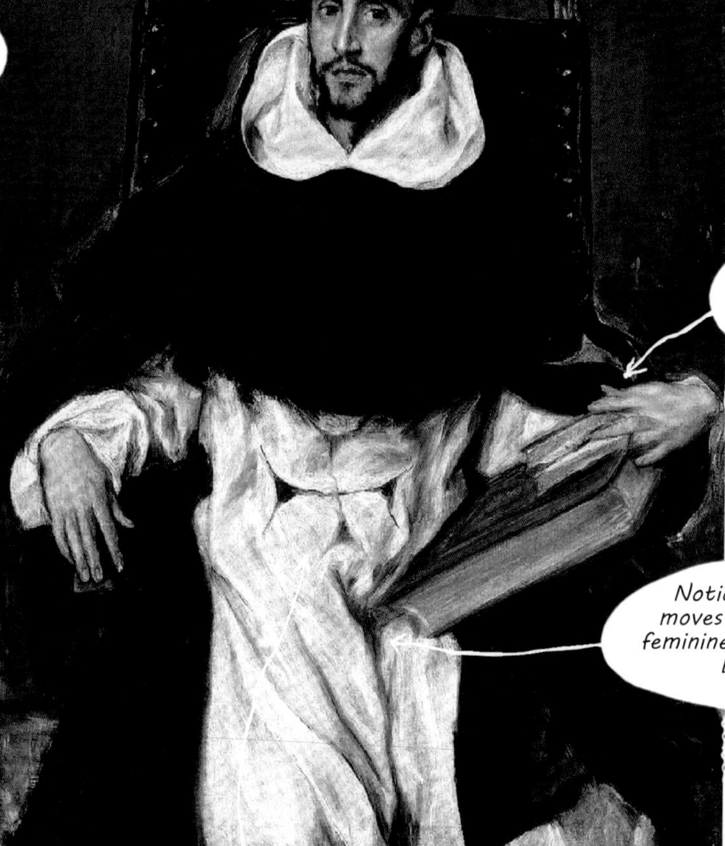

Portrait of Fray Hortensio Félix Paravicino by El Greco

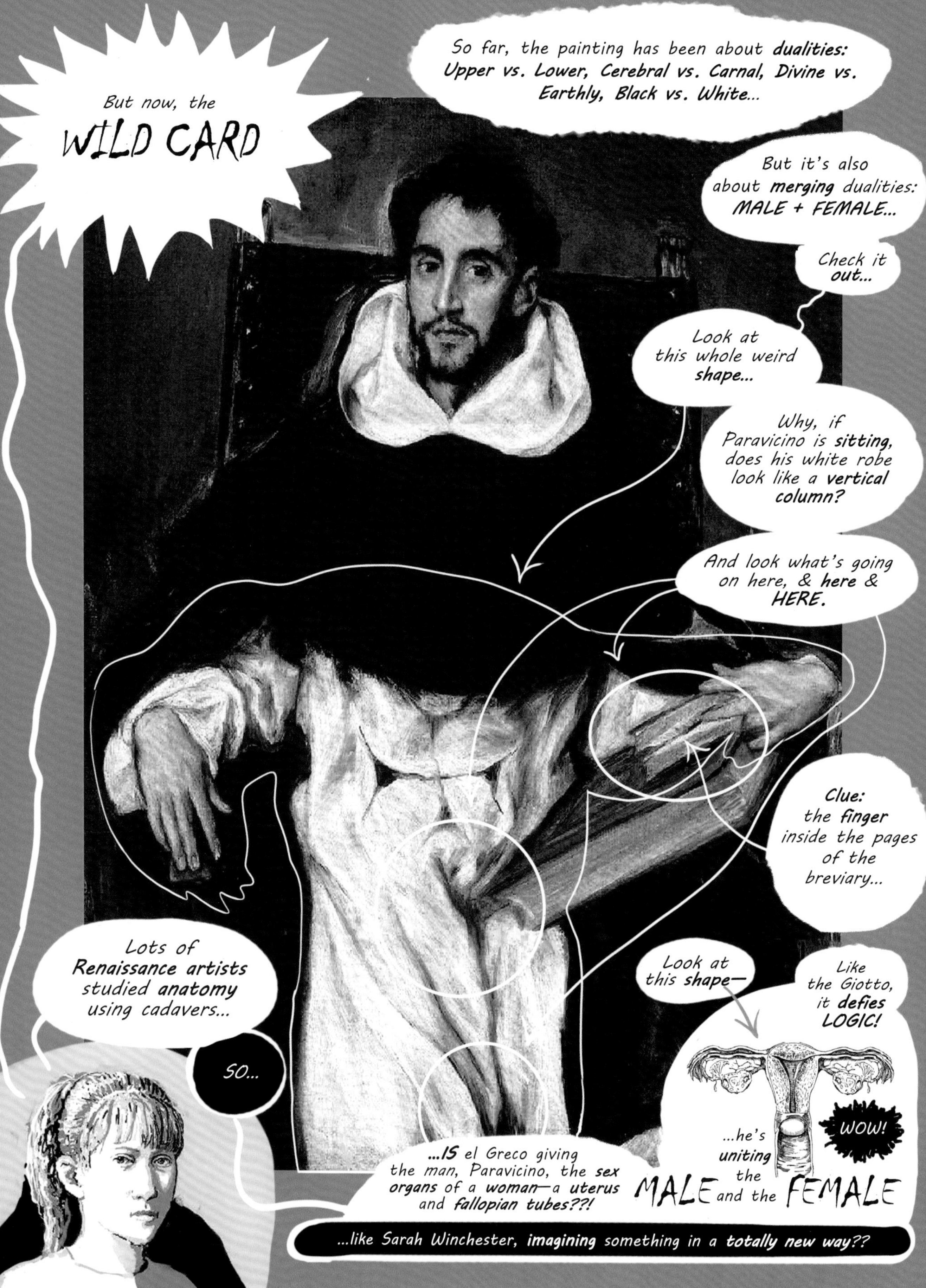
But now, the WILD CARD
So far, the painting has been about dualities: Upper vs. Lower, Cerebral vs. Carnal, Divine vs. Earthly, Black vs. White...
But it's also about merging dualities: MALE + FEMALE...
Check it out...
Look at this whole weird shape...
Why, if Paravicino is sitting, does his white robe look like a vertical column?
And look what's going on here, & here & HERE.
Clue: the finger inside the pages of the breviary...
Lots of Renaissance artists studied anatomy using cadavers...
SO...
...IS el Greco giving the man, Paravicino, the sex organs of a woman—a uterus and fallopian tubes??!
Look at this shape—
Like the Giotto, it defies LOGIC!
WOW!
...he's uniting the MALE and the FEMALE
...like Sarah Winchester, imagining something in a totally new way??

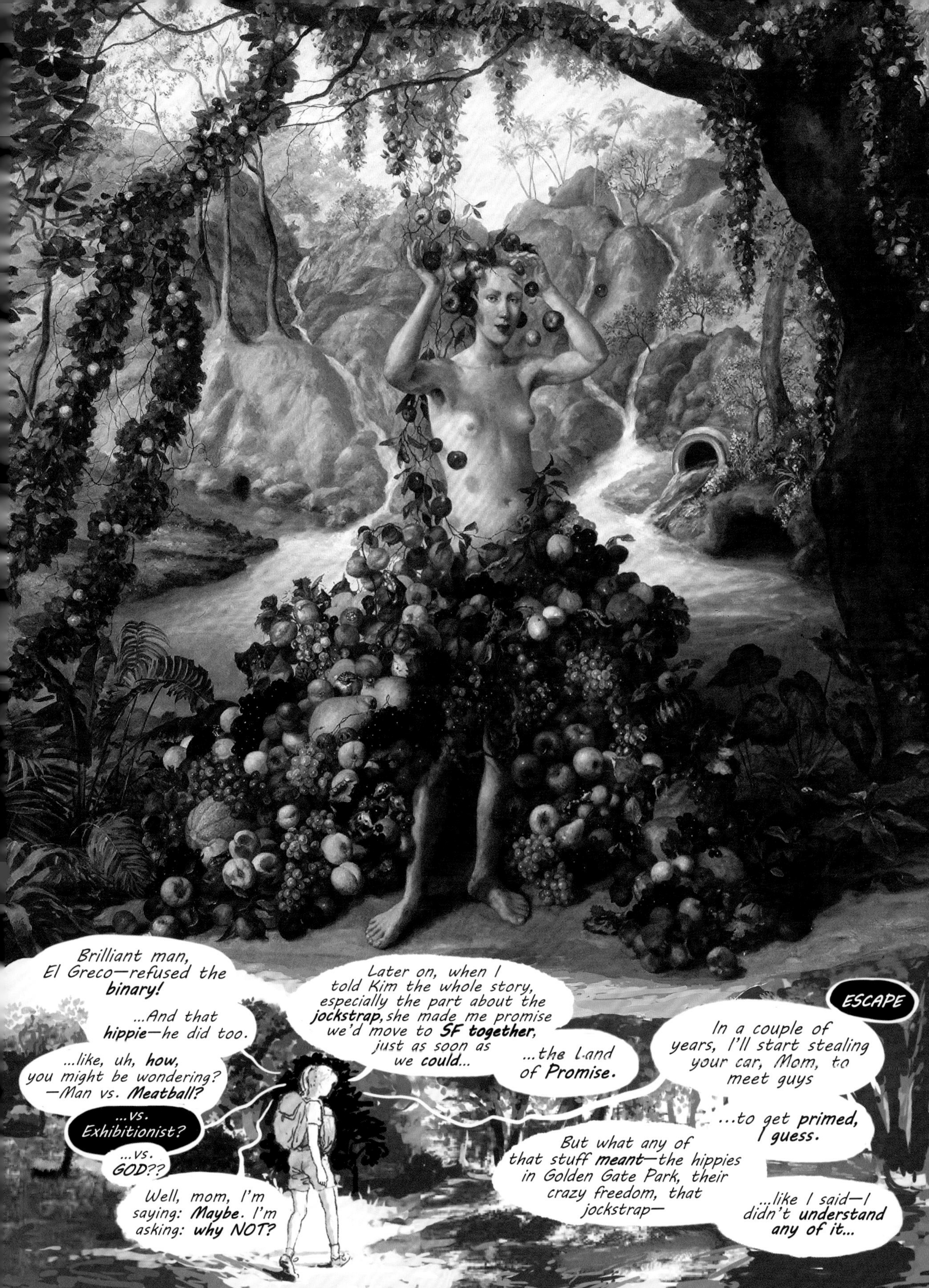
Brilliant man, El Greco—refused the **binary!**
...And that **hippie**—he did too.
...like, uh, **how**, you might be wondering? —Man vs. **Meatball?**
...vs. Exhibitionist?
...vs. **GOD??**
Well, mom, I'm saying: **Maybe**. I'm asking: **why NOT?**
Later on, when I told Kim the whole story, especially the part about the **jockstrap**, she made me promise we'd move to **SF together**, just as soon as we **could**...
...the Land of **Promise.**
ESCAPE
In a couple of years, I'll start stealing your car, Mom, to meet guys
...to get **primed**, I **guess.**
But what any of that stuff **meant**—the hippies in Golden Gate Park, their crazy freedom, that jockstrap—
...like I said—I didn't **understand any of it...**

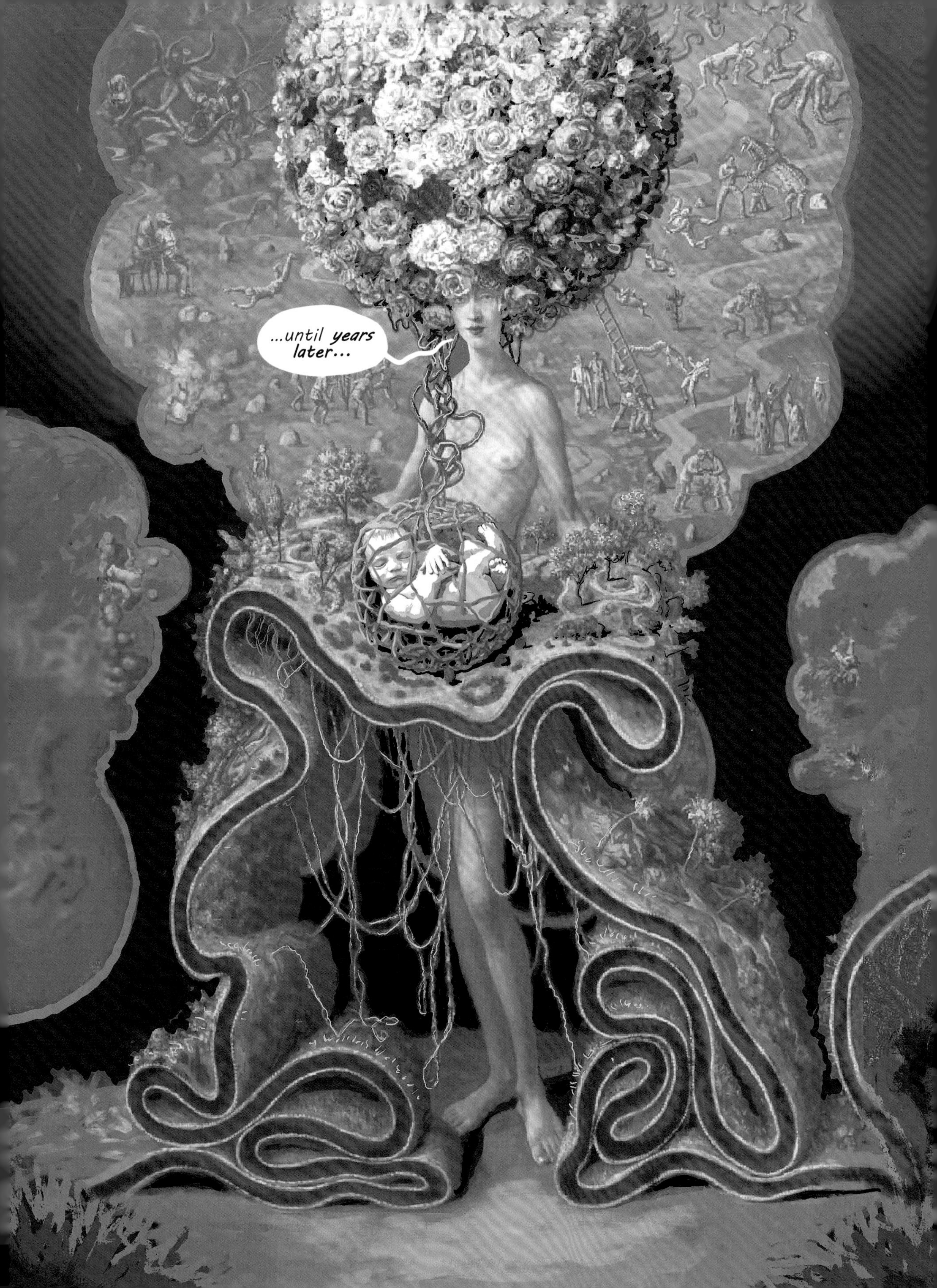
...until years later...

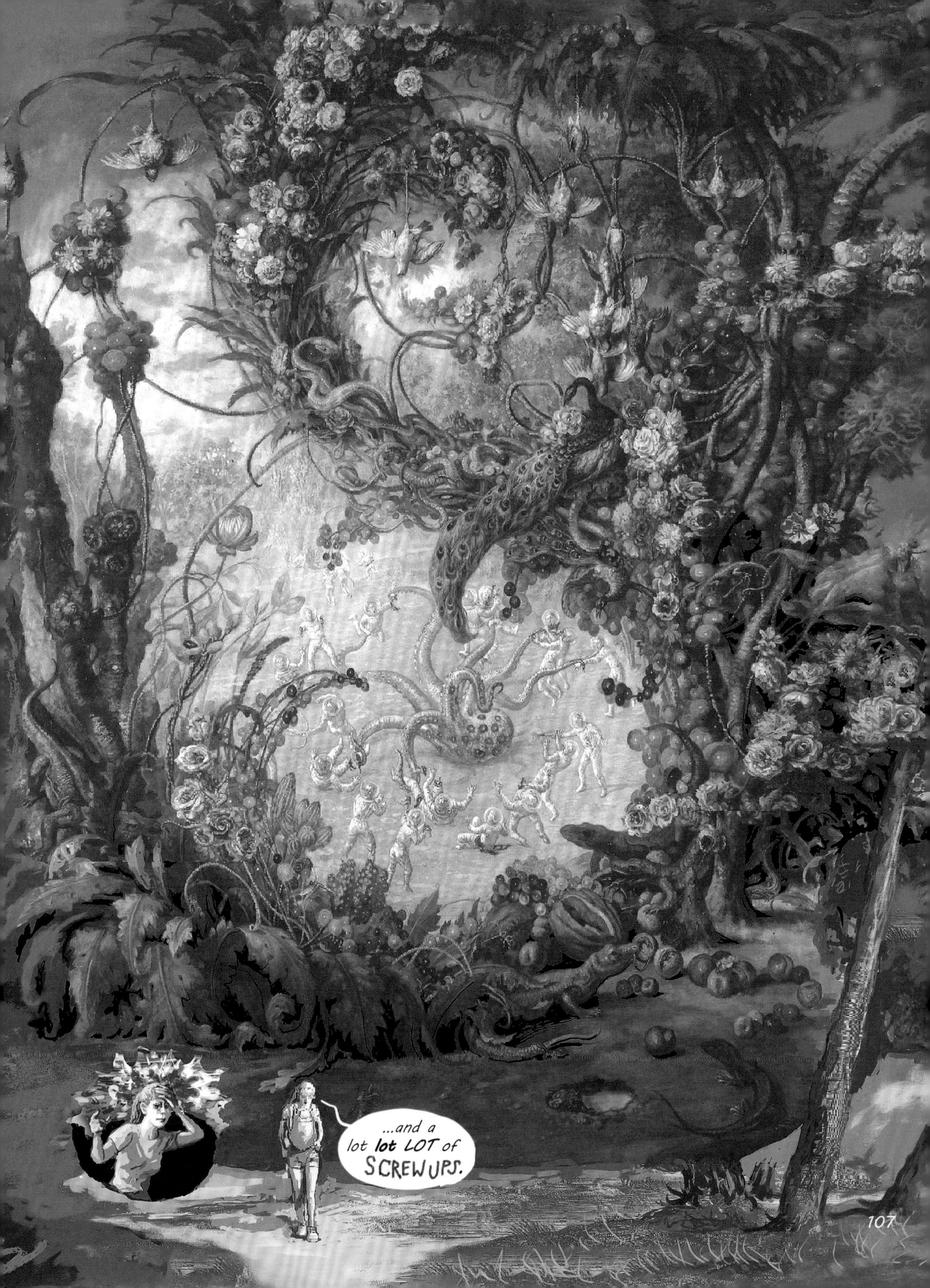
...and a lot lot LOT of SCREWUPS.

Chapter SIX

An hour later, I'm hurrying along a **lot** faster now, hopping over roots way **higher,** brambles more **tangled** than before, skirting a thicket of saplings whose tops have been lopped off, leaving just **stubs** behind.

There's a **chill** in the air, little fingers of mist stealing into my bones.

Aarghh

That **hippie...**

...just a **burnout**

...played a stupid flute.

Who cares???

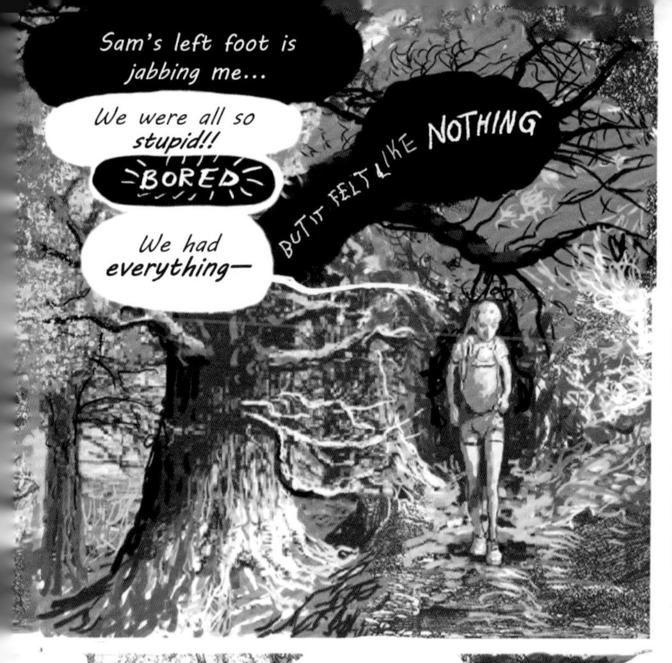

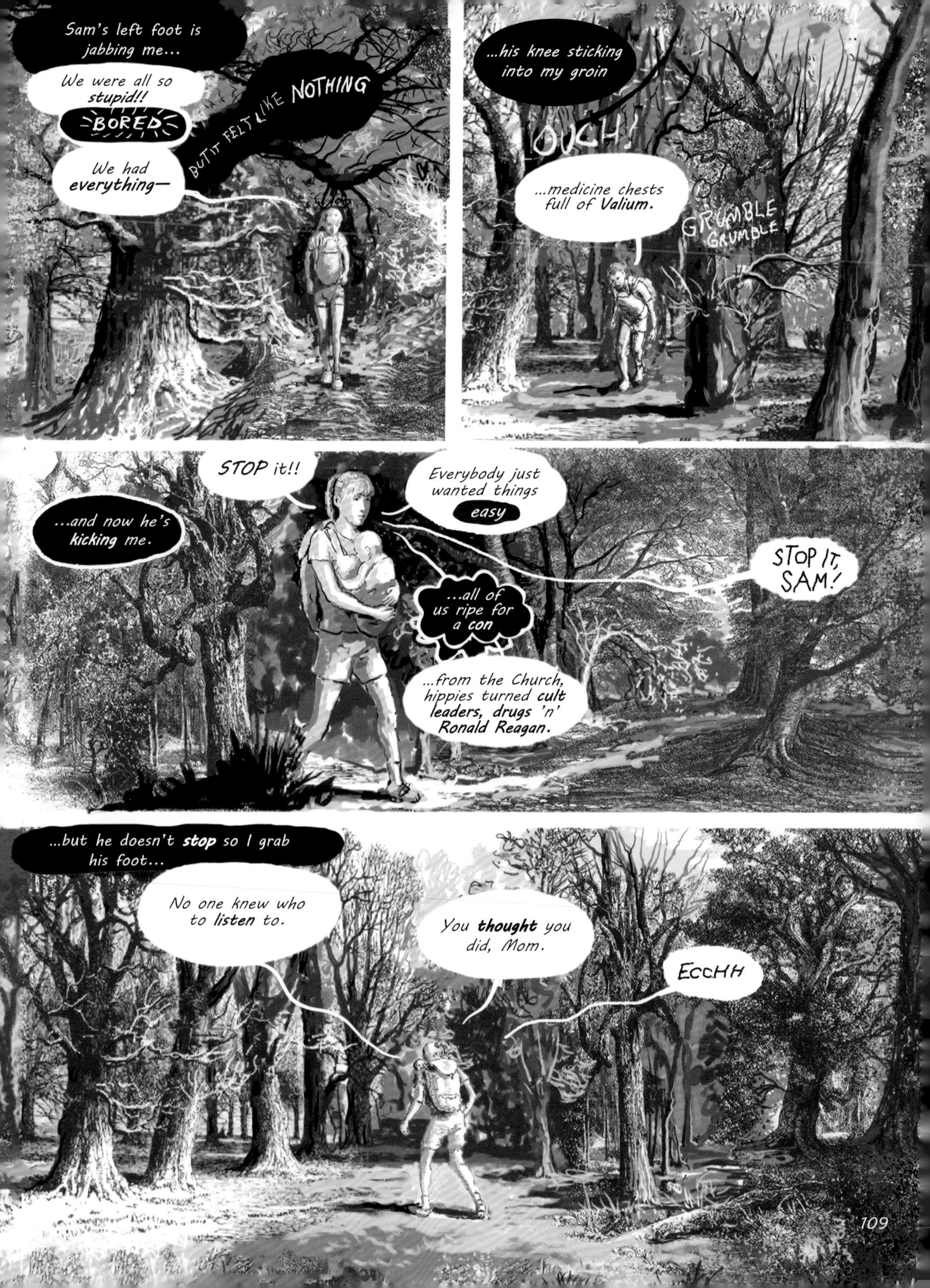

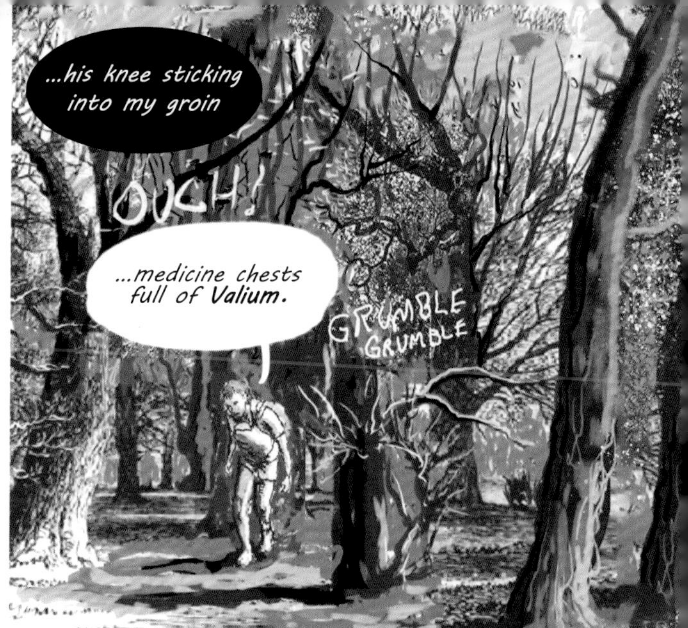

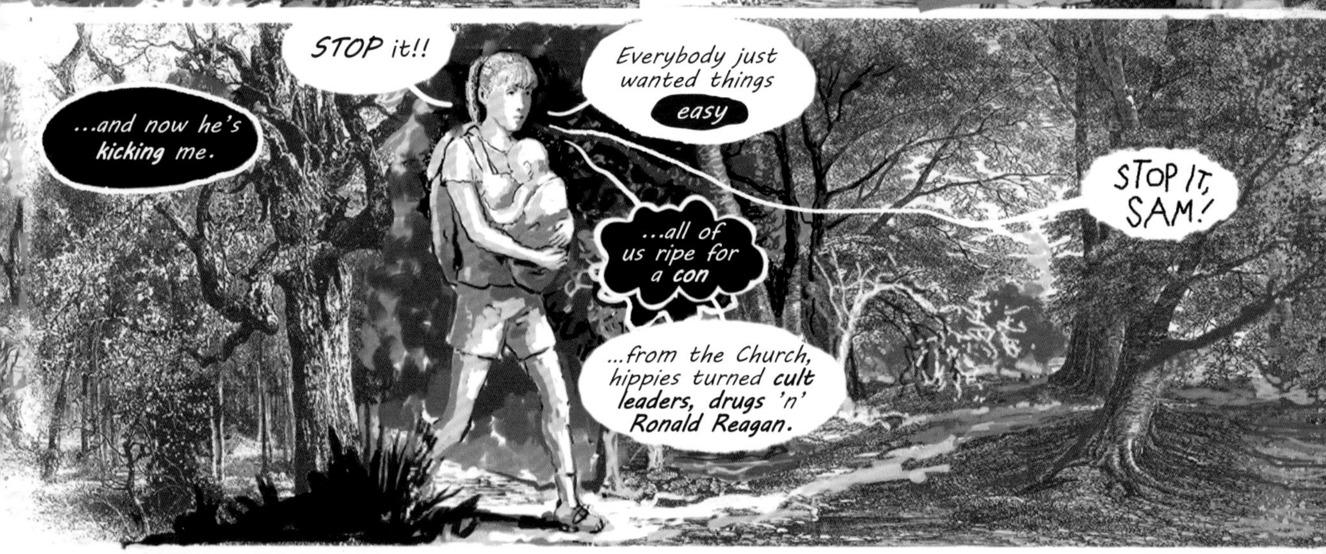

...but he doesn't **stop** so I grab his foot...

No one knew who to **listen** to.

You **thought** you did, Mom.

ECCHH

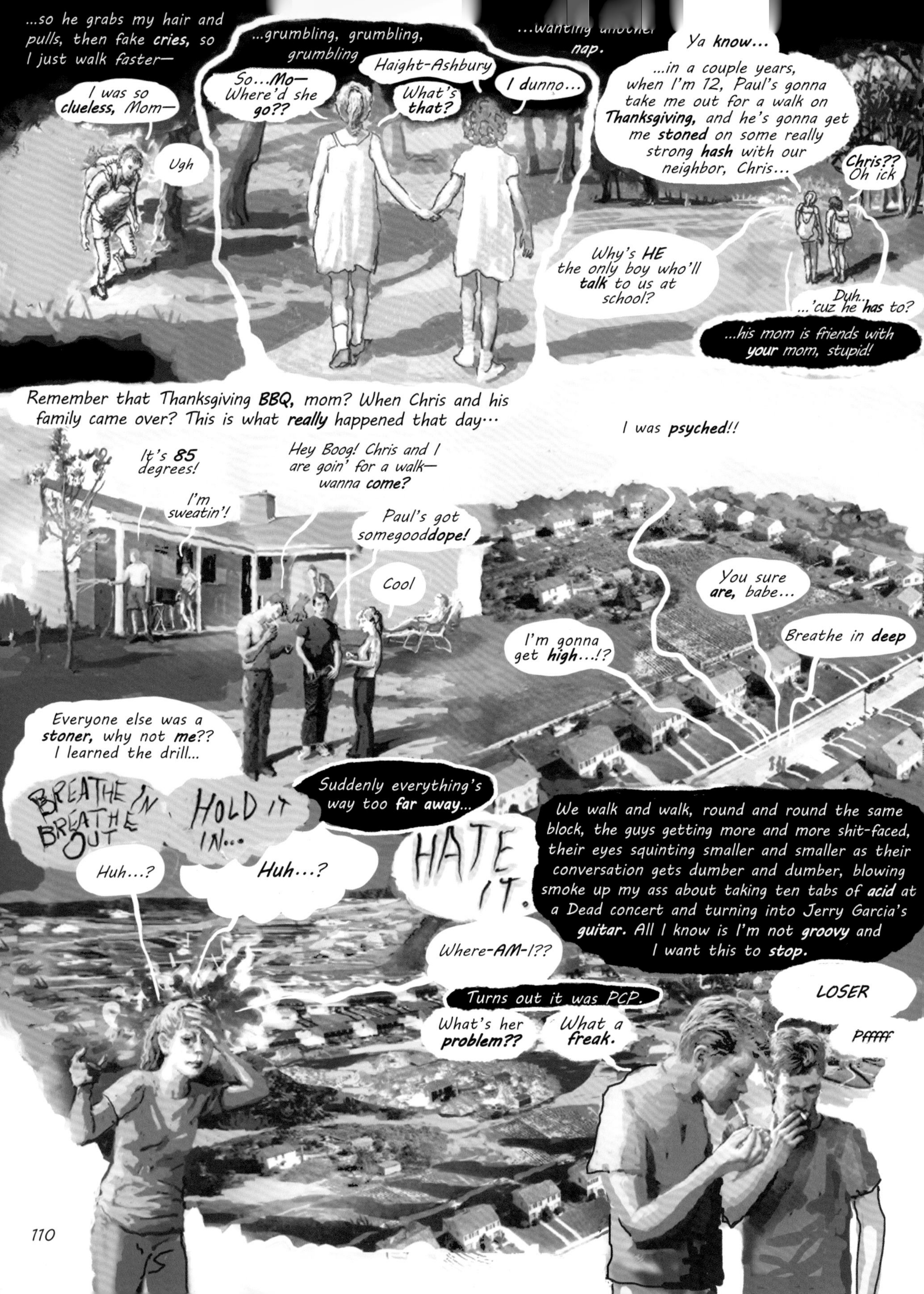
...so he grabs my hair and pulls, then fake cries, so I just walk faster—
I was so clueless, Mom—
Ugh
...grumbling, grumbling, grumbling
So...Mo— Where'd she go??
Haight-Ashbury
What's that?
I dunno...
nap.
Ya know...
...in a couple years, when I'm 12, Paul's gonna take me out for a walk on Thanksgiving, and he's gonna get me stoned on some really strong hash with our neighbor, Chris...
Chris?? Oh ick
Why's HE the only boy who'll talk to us at school?
Duh.. ...'cuz he has to?
...his mom is friends with your mom, stupid!
Remember that Thanksgiving BBQ, mom? When Chris and his family came over? This is what really happened that day...
It's 85 degrees!
I'm sweatin'!
Hey Boog! Chris and I are goin' for a walk— wanna come?
Paul's got somegooddope!
Cool
I was psyched!!
You sure are, babe...
I'm gonna get high...!?
Breathe in deep
Everyone else was a stoner, why not me?? I learned the drill...
BREATHE IN BREATHE OUT
HOLD IT IN...
Suddenly everything's way too far away...
Huh...?
Huh...?
HATE IT.
We walk and walk, round and round the same block, the guys getting more and more shit-faced, their eyes squinting smaller and smaller as their conversation gets dumber and dumber, blowing smoke up my ass about taking ten tabs of acid at a Dead concert and turning into Jerry Garcia's guitar. All I know is I'm not groovy and I want this to stop.
Where-AM-I??
Turns out it was PCP.
What's her problem??
What a freak.
LOSER
Pfffff

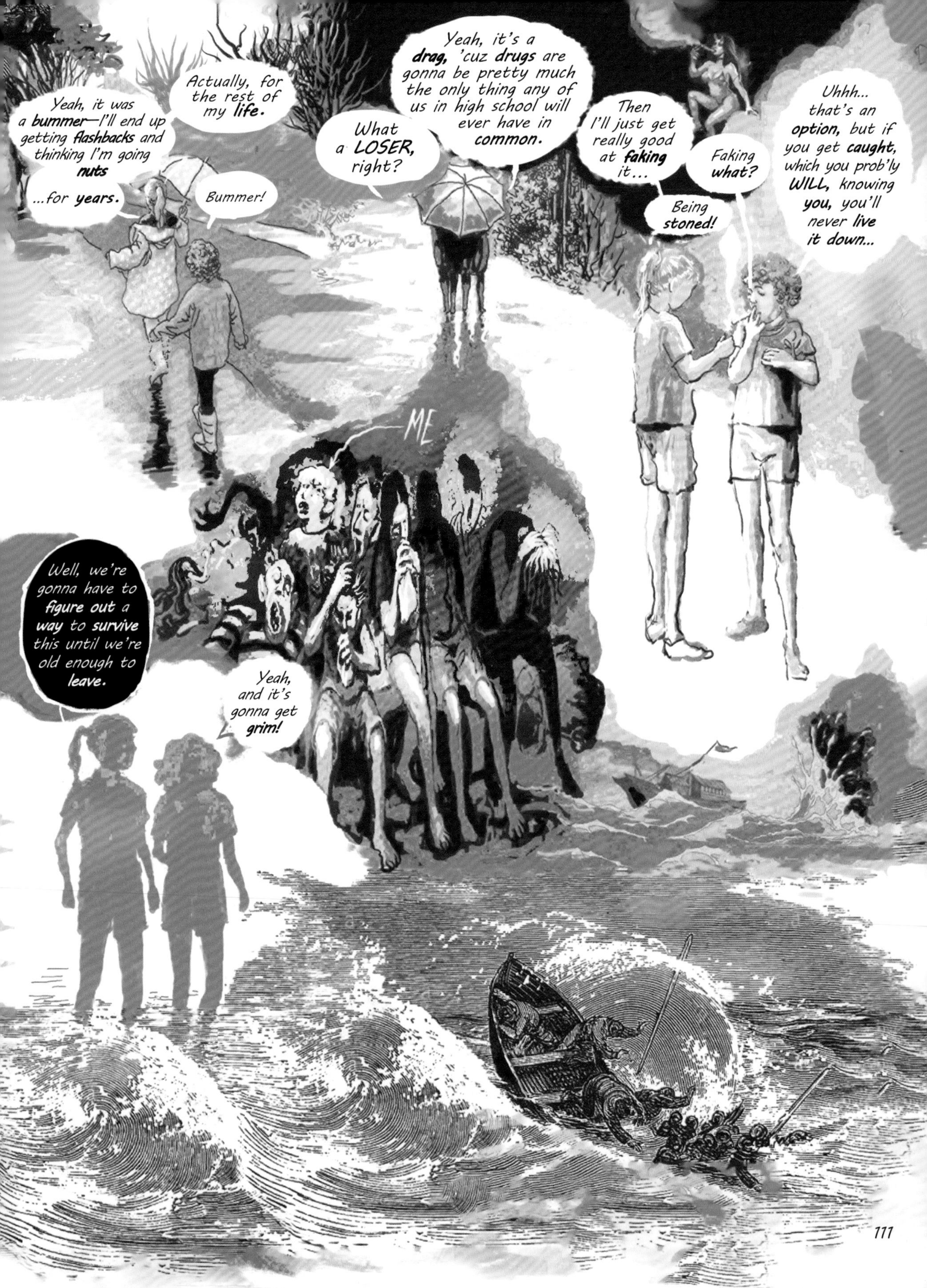
Yeah, it was a bummer—I'll end up getting flashbacks and thinking I'm going nuts
...for years.
Actually, for the rest of my life.
Bummer!
What a LOSER, right?
Yeah, it's a drag, 'cuz drugs are gonna be pretty much the only thing any of us in high school will ever have in common.
Then I'll just get really good at faking it...
Faking what?
Being stoned!
Uhhh... that's an option, but if you get caught, which you prob'ly WILL, knowing you, you'll never live it down...
ME
Well, we're gonna have to figure out a way to survive this until we're old enough to leave.
Yeah, and it's gonna get grim!

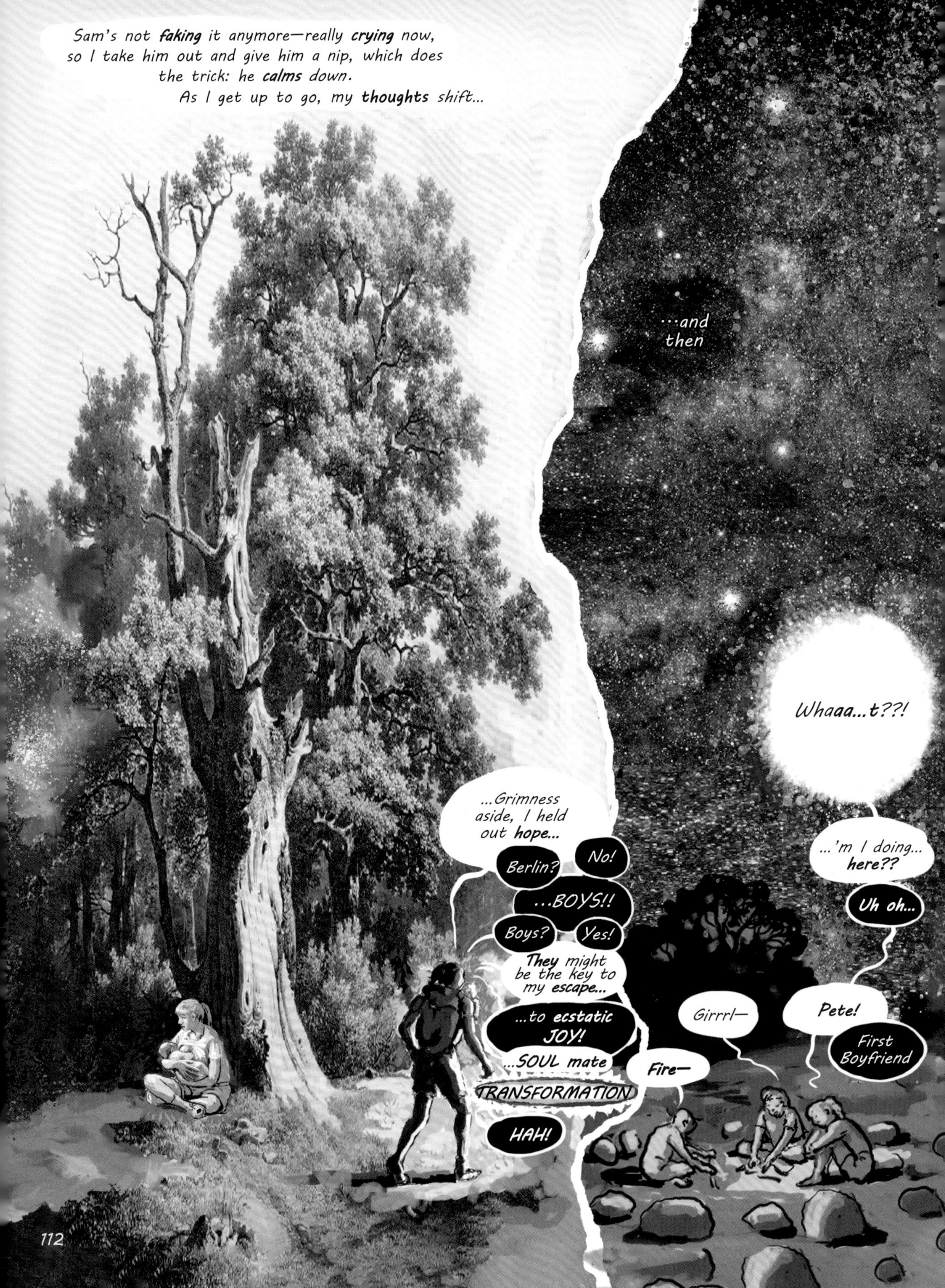
Sam's not **faking** it anymore—really **crying** now, so I take him out and give him a nip, which does the trick: he **calms** down.
As I get up to go, my **thoughts** shift...
...and then
Whaaa...t??!
...Grimness aside, I held out **hope**...
Berlin?
No!
...BOYS!!
Boys?
Yes!
They might be the key to my **escape**...
...to **ecstatic JOY!**
...SOUL mate
TRANSFORMATION
HAH!
Fire—
...'m I doing... **here??**
Uh oh...
Girrrl—
Pete!
First Boyfriend

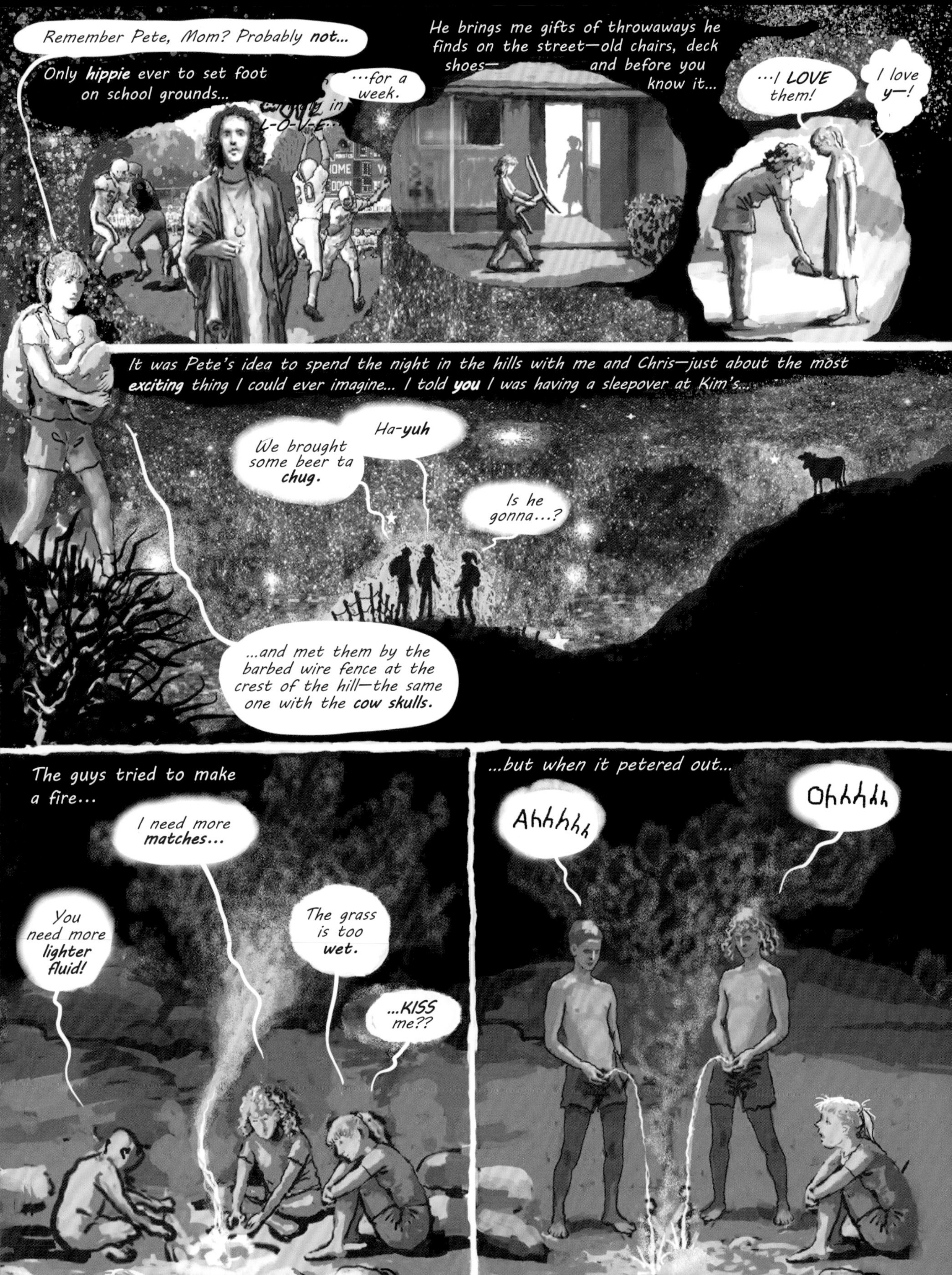
Remember Pete, Mom? Probably **not...**
Only **hippie** ever to set foot on school grounds...
in L-O-V-E...
...for a week.
He brings me gifts of throwaways he finds on the street—old chairs, deck shoes— and before you know it...
...I **LOVE** them!
I love y—!
It was Pete's idea to spend the night in the hills with me and Chris—just about the most **exciting** thing I could ever imagine... I told **you** I was having a sleepover at Kim's...
We brought some beer ta **chug.**
Ha-**yuh**
Is he gonna...?
...and met them by the barbed wire fence at the crest of the hill—the same one with the **cow skulls.**
The guys tried to make a fire...
I need more **matches...**
You need more **lighter fluid!**
The grass is too **wet.**
...**KISS** me??
...but when it petered out...
Ahhhhh
Ohhhhh

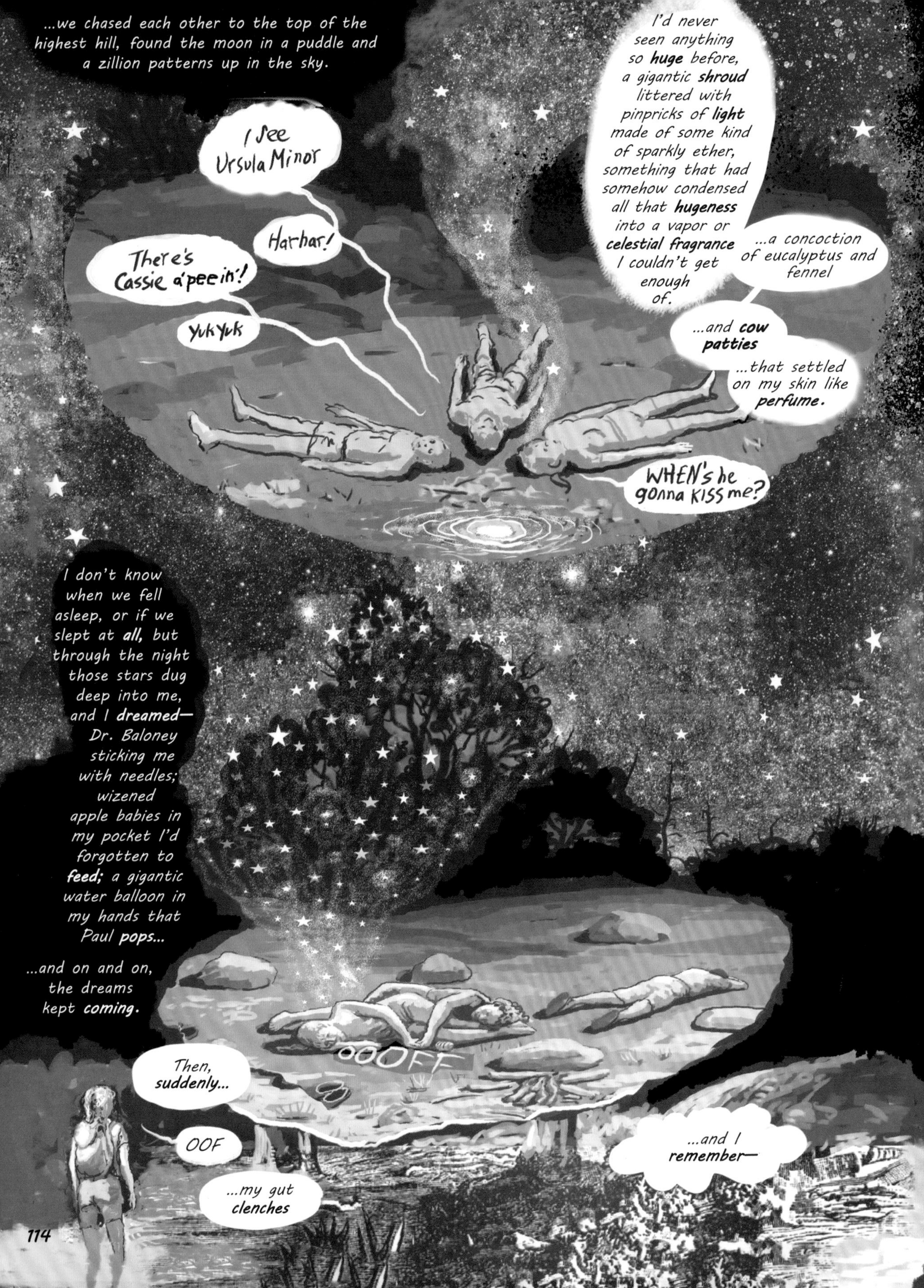
...we chased each other to the top of the highest hill, found the moon in a puddle and a zillion patterns up in the sky.
I'd never seen anything so **huge** before, a gigantic **shroud** littered with pinpricks of **light** made of some kind of sparkly ether, something that had somehow condensed all that **hugeness** into a vapor or **celestial fragrance** I couldn't get enough of.
I see Ursula Minor
Harhar!
There's Cassie a'peein'!
YukYuk
...a concoction of eucalyptus and fennel
...and **cow patties**
...that settled on my skin like **perfume**.
WHEN's he gonna KISS me?
I don't know when we fell asleep, or if we slept at **all**, but through the night those stars dug deep into me, and I **dreamed**— Dr. Baloney sticking me with needles; wizened apple babies in my pocket I'd forgotten to **feed**; a gigantic water balloon in my hands that Paul **pops**...
...and on and on, the dreams kept **coming**.
OOOFF
Then, **suddenly**...
OOF
...my gut **clenches**
...and I **remember**—

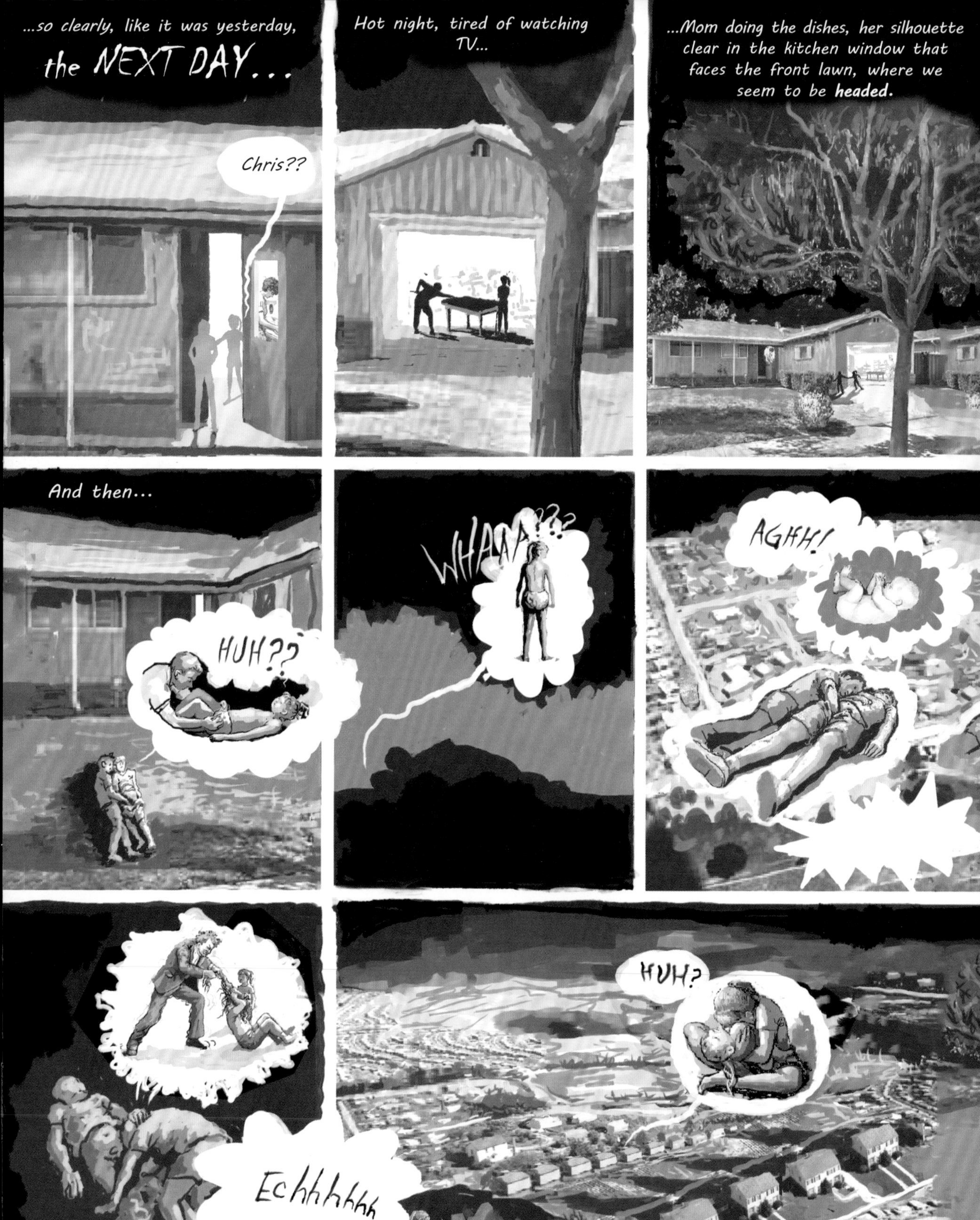
...so clearly, like it was yesterday,
the NEXT DAY...
Chris??
Hot night, tired of watching TV...
...Mom doing the dishes, her silhouette clear in the kitchen window that faces the front lawn, where we seem to be **headed.**
And then...
HUH??
WHAAA???
AGHH!
HUH?
Echhhhhh
I lay in bed that night, hugging my pillow like a **dead** body, proto-words forming a **question** it'll take years for me to **ask...**

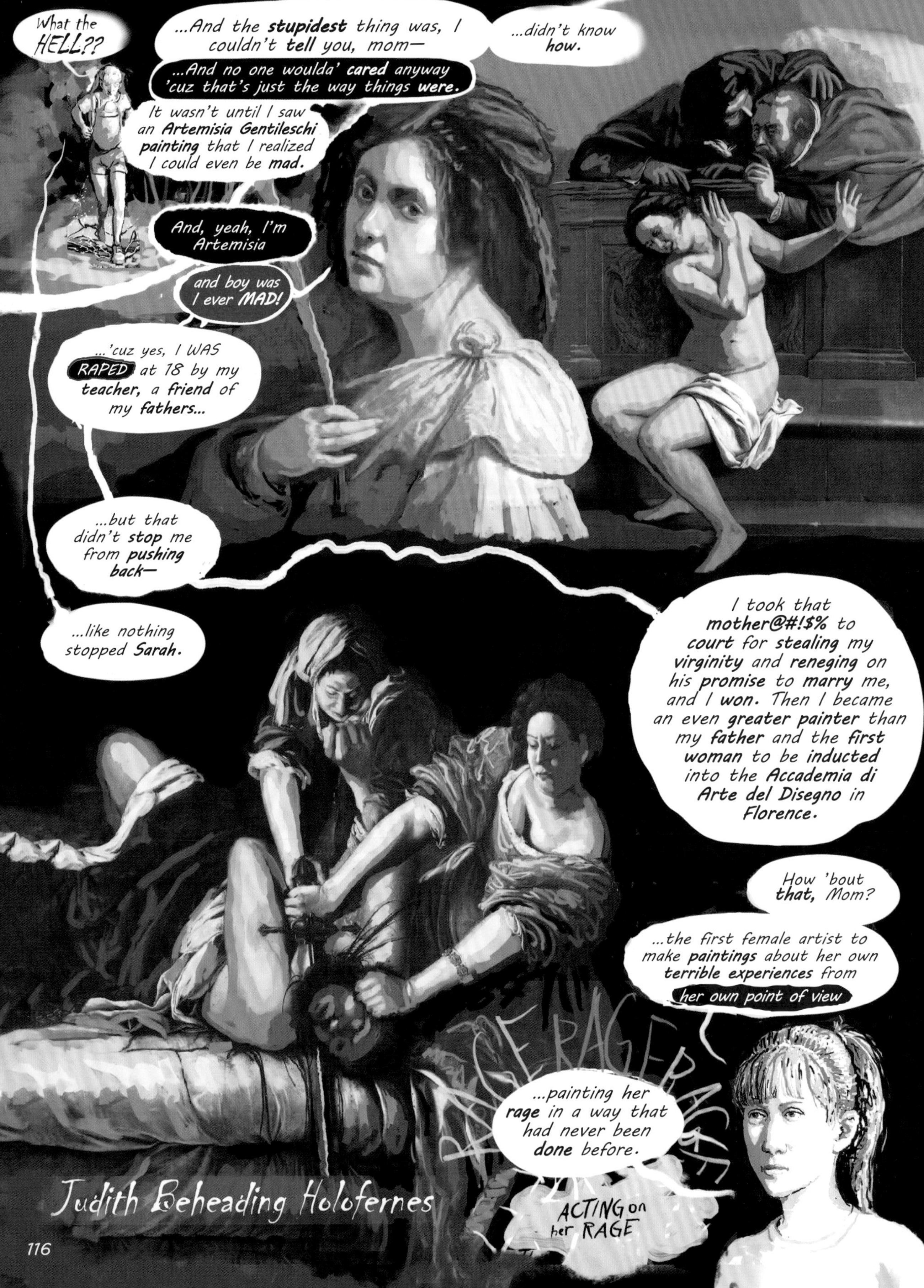
What the HELL??
...And the stupidest thing was, I couldn't tell you, mom—
...didn't know how.
...And no one woulda' cared anyway 'cuz that's just the way things were.
It wasn't until I saw an Artemisia Gentileschi painting that I realized I could even be mad.
And, yeah, I'm Artemisia
and boy was I ever MAD!
...'cuz yes, I WAS RAPED at 18 by my teacher, a friend of my fathers...
...but that didn't stop me from pushing back—
...like nothing stopped Sarah.
I took that mother@#!$% to court for stealing my virginity and reneging on his promise to marry me, and I won. Then I became an even greater painter than my father and the first woman to be inducted into the Accademia di Arte del Disegno in Florence.
How 'bout that, Mom?
...the first female artist to make paintings about her own terrible experiences from her own point of view
...painting her rage in a way that had never been done before.
ACTING on her RAGE
Judith Beheading Holofernes

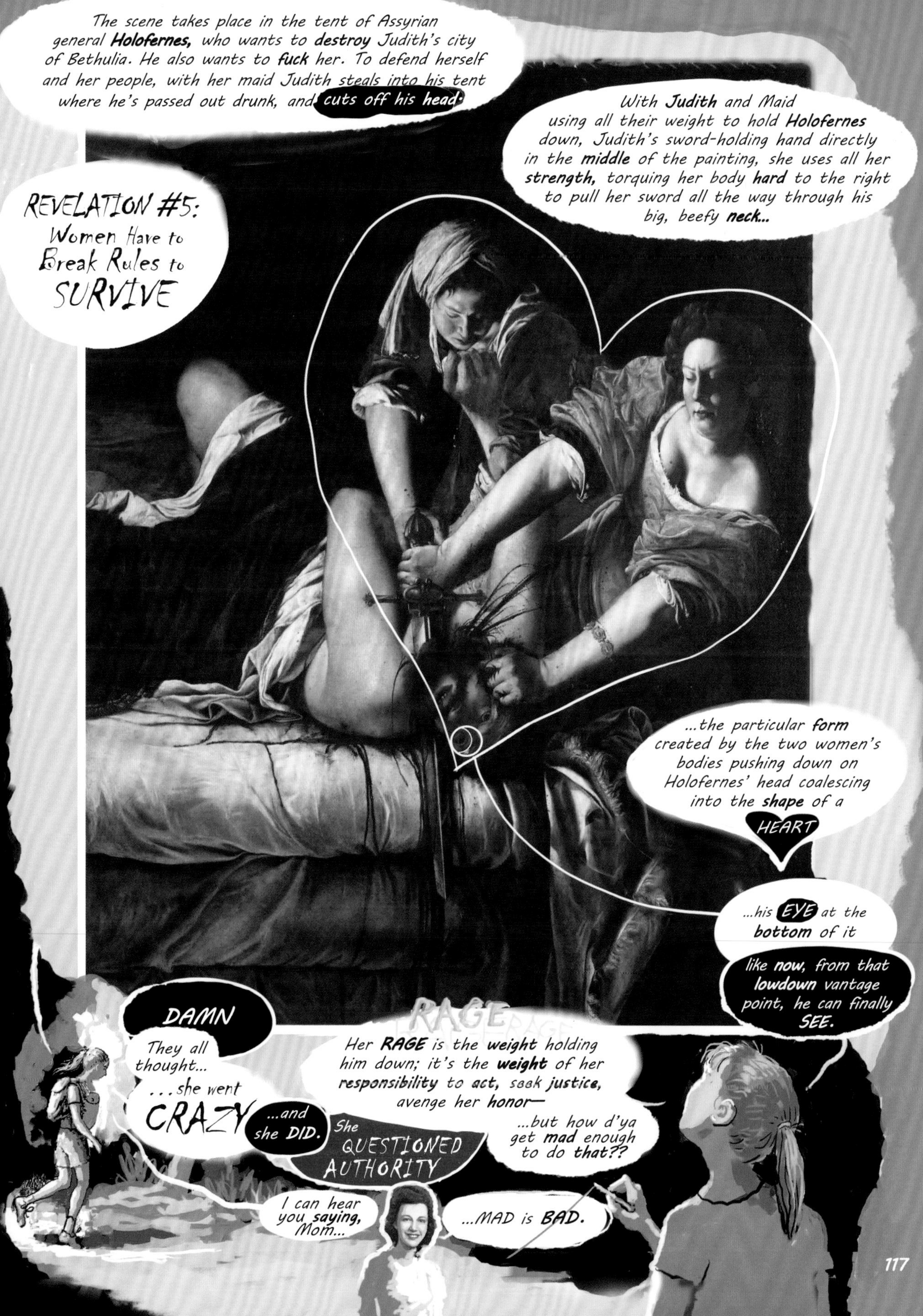
The scene takes place in the tent of Assyrian general **Holofernes,** who wants to **destroy** Judith's city of Bethulia. He also wants to **fuck** her. To defend herself and her people, with her maid Judith steals into his tent where he's passed out drunk, and cuts off his **head**.
With **Judith** and Maid using all their weight to hold **Holofernes** down, Judith's sword-holding hand directly in the **middle** of the painting, she uses all her **strength,** torquing her body **hard** to the right to pull her sword all the way through his big, beefy **neck...**
REVELATION #5: Women Have to Break Rules to SURVIVE
...the particular **form** created by the two women's bodies pushing down on Holofernes' head coalescing into the **shape** of a
HEART
...his EYE at the **bottom** of it
like **now**, from that **lowdown** vantage point, he can finally **SEE.**
DAMN
They all thought...
...she went
CRAZY
...and she **DID.**
RAGE
Her **RAGE** is the **weight** holding him down; it's the **weight** of her **responsibility** to **act,** seek **justice,** avenge her **honor**—
She QUESTIONED AUTHORITY
...but how d'ya get **mad** enough to do **that??**
I can hear you **saying,** Mom...
...MAD is **BAD.**

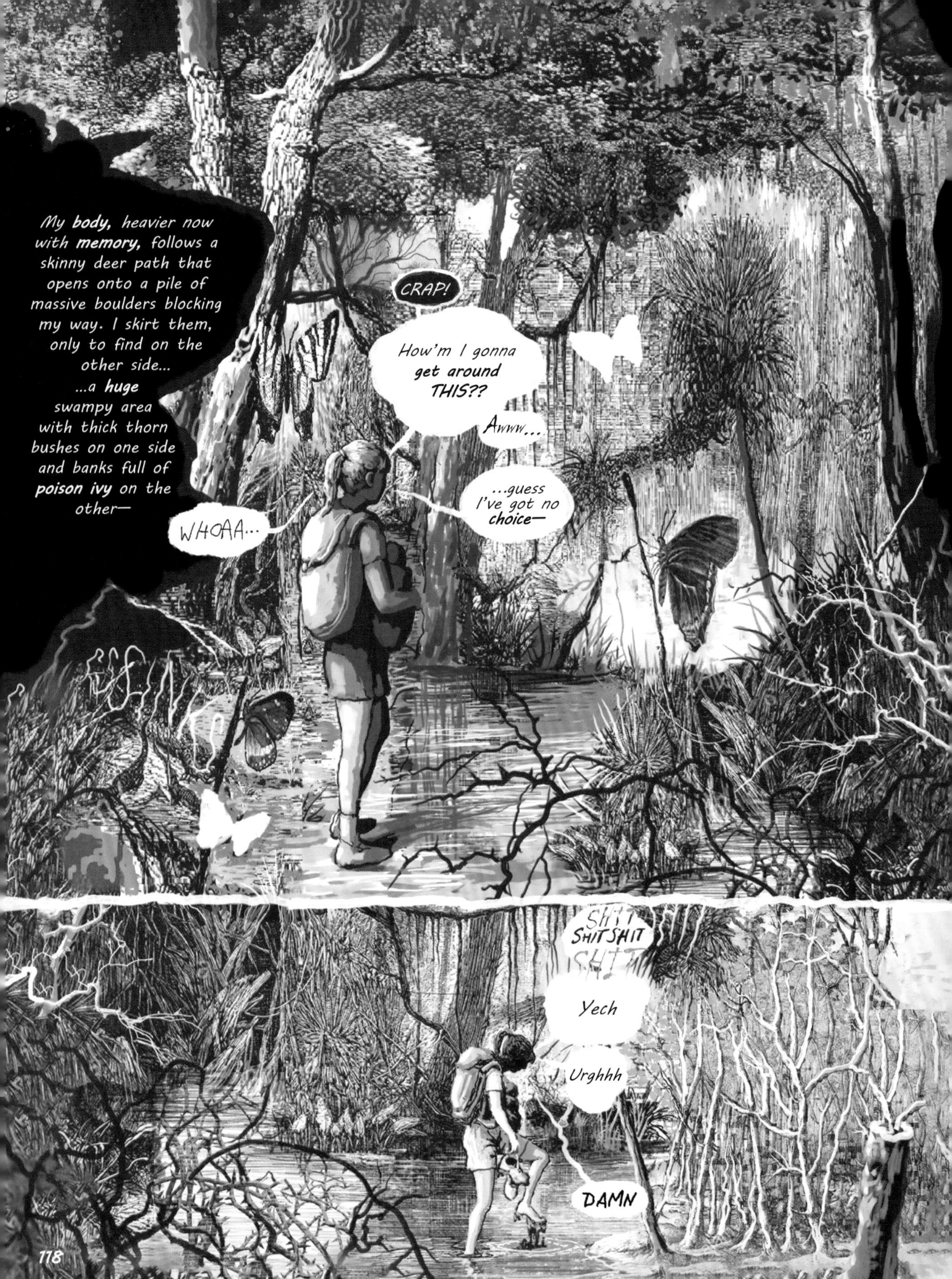
My **body,** heavier now with **memory,** follows a skinny deer path that opens onto a pile of massive boulders blocking my way. I skirt them, only to find on the other side...
...a **huge** swampy area with thick thorn bushes on one side and banks full of **poison ivy** on the other—
CRAP!
How'm I gonna **get around THIS??**
Awww...
WHOAA...
...guess I've got no **choice—**
SHIT
SHITSHIT
Yech
Urghhh
DAMN

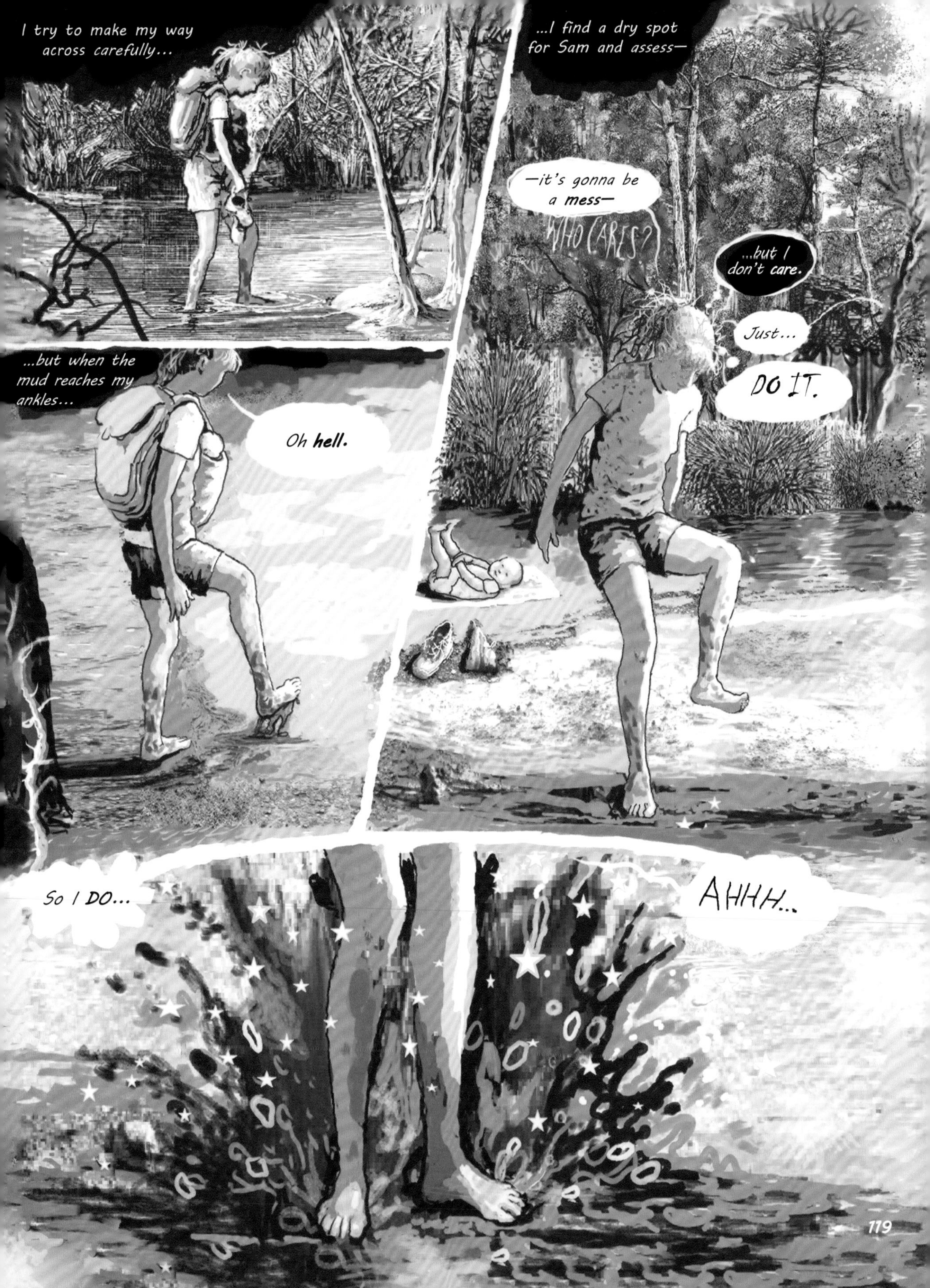
I try to make my way across carefully...
...but when the mud reaches my ankles...
Oh hell.
...I find a dry spot for Sam and assess—
—it's gonna be a mess—
WHO CARES?
...but I don't care.
Just...
DO IT.
So I DO...
AHHH...

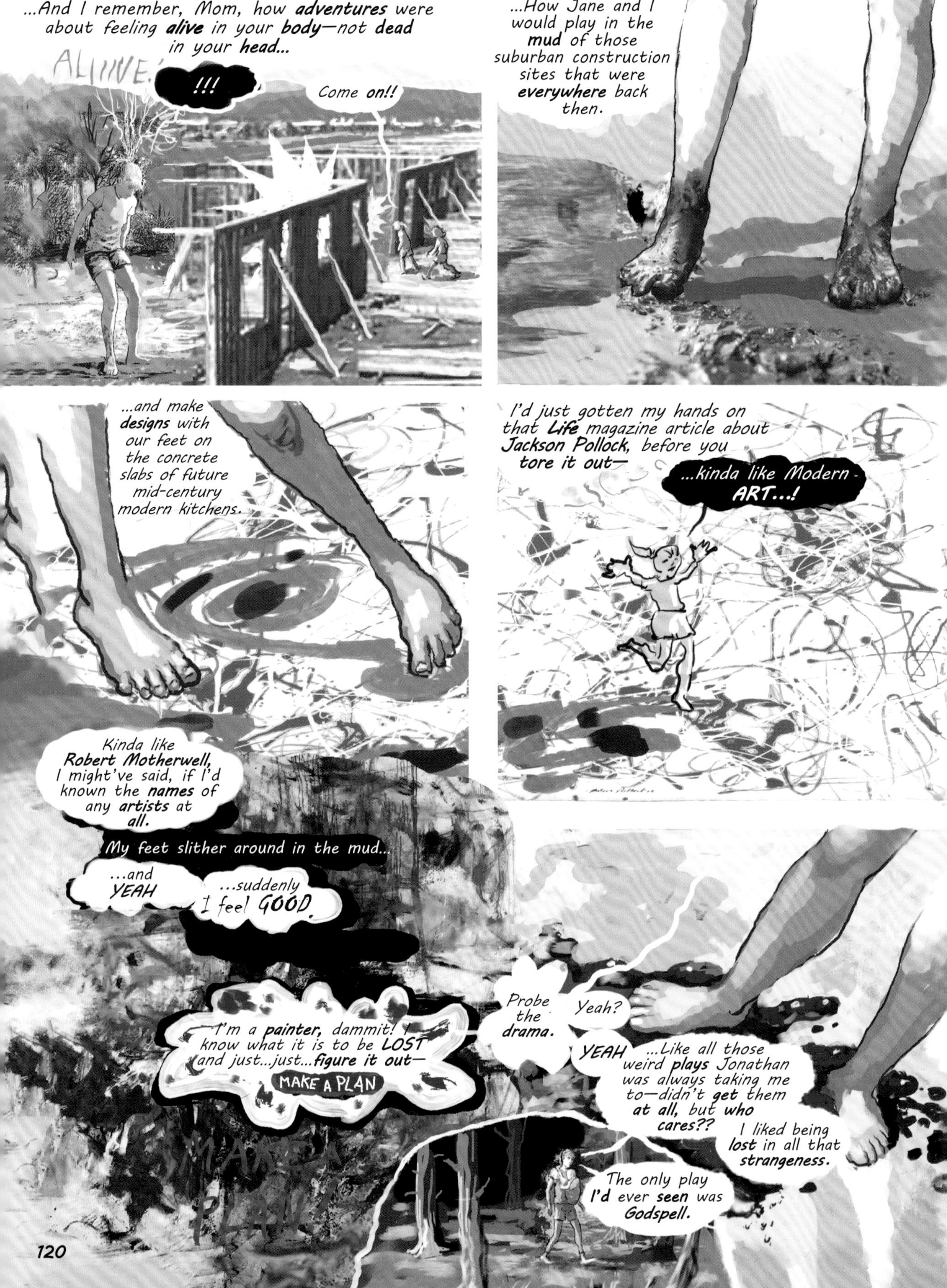

...And I remember, Mom, how adventures were about feeling alive in your body—not dead in your head...
ALIIIVE!
!!!
Come on!!
...How Jane and I would play in the mud of those suburban construction sites that were everywhere back then.
...and make designs with our feet on the concrete slabs of future mid-century modern kitchens.
I'd just gotten my hands on that Life magazine article about Jackson Pollock, before you tore it out—
...kinda like Modern ART...!
Kinda like Robert Motherwell, I might've said, if I'd known the names of any artists at all.
My feet slither around in the mud...
...and YEAH
...suddenly I feel GOOD.
I'm a painter, dammit! I know what it is to be LOST and just...just...figure it out—
MAKE A PLAN
Probe the drama.
Yeah?
YEAH
...Like all those weird plays Jonathan was always taking me to—didn't get them at all, but who cares??
I liked being lost in all that strangeness.
The only play I'd ever seen was Godspell.

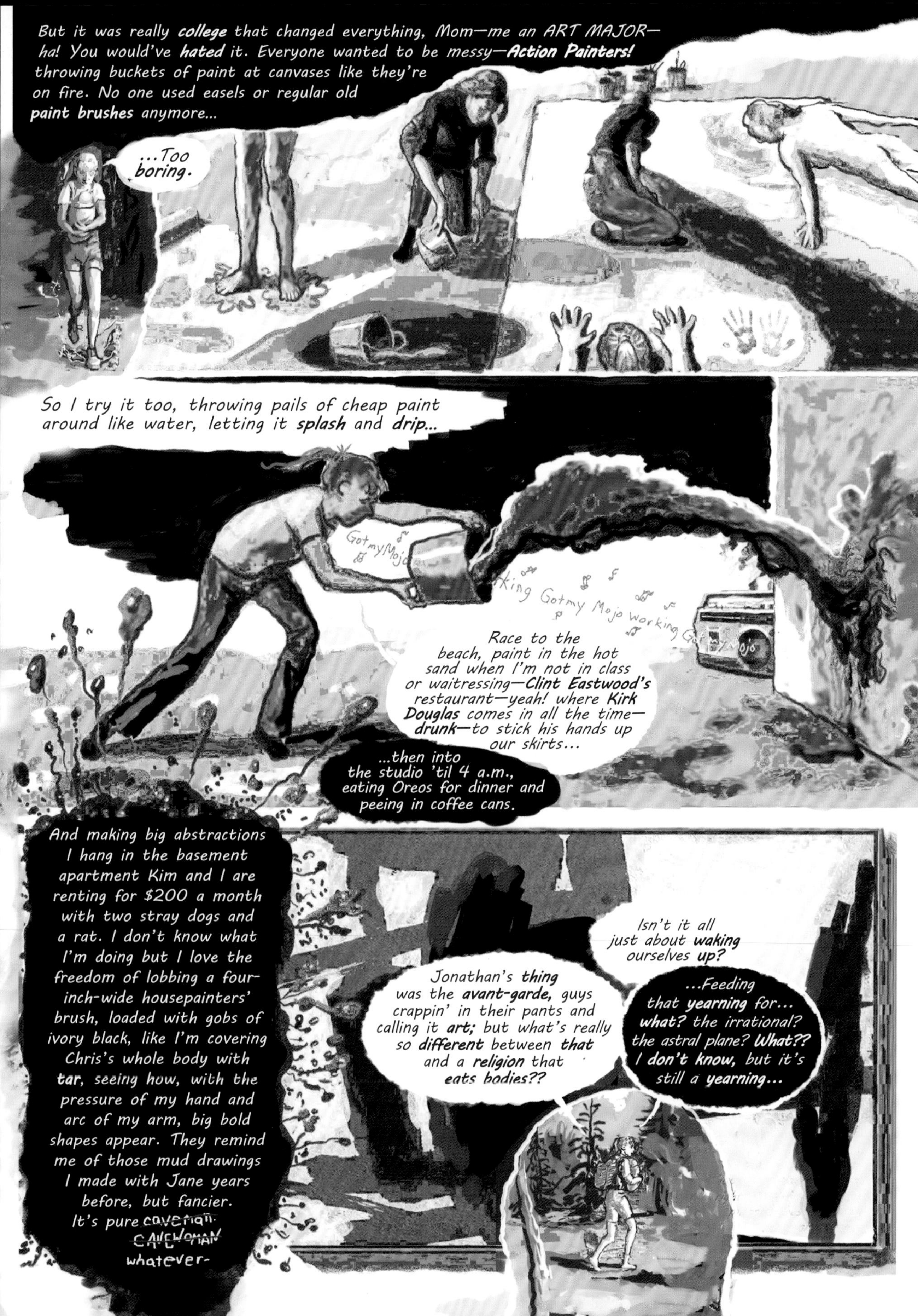

But it was really **college** that changed everything, Mom—me an ART MAJOR—ha! You would've **hated** it. Everyone wanted to be messy—**Action Painters!** throwing buckets of paint at canvases like they're on fire. No one used easels or regular old **paint brushes** anymore...
...Too **boring**.
So I try it too, throwing pails of cheap paint around like water, letting it **splash** and **drip**...
Got my Mojo
Got my Mojo working Got my Mojo
Race to the beach, paint in the hot sand when I'm not in class or waitressing—**Clint Eastwood's** restaurant—yeah! where **Kirk Douglas** comes in all the time—**drunk**—to stick his hands up our skirts...
...then into the studio 'til 4 a.m., eating Oreos for dinner and peeing in coffee cans.
And making big abstractions I hang in the basement apartment Kim and I are renting for $200 a month with two stray dogs and a rat. I don't know what I'm doing but I love the freedom of lobbing a four-inch-wide housepainters' brush, loaded with gobs of ivory black, like I'm covering Chris's whole body with **tar**, seeing how, with the pressure of my hand and arc of my arm, big bold shapes appear. They remind me of those mud drawings I made with Jane years before, but fancier. It's pure ~~caveman~~ CAVEWOMAN whatever-
Isn't it all just about **waking** ourselves **up**?
Jonathan's **thing** was the **avant-garde**, guys crappin' in their pants and calling it **art**; but what's really so **different** between **that** and a **religion** that **eats bodies??**
...Feeding that **yearning** for... **what?** the irrational? the astral plane? **What??** I **don't know,** but it's still a **yearning**...

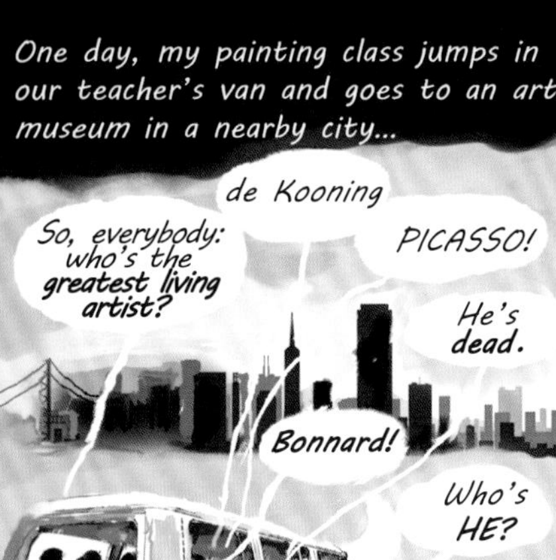

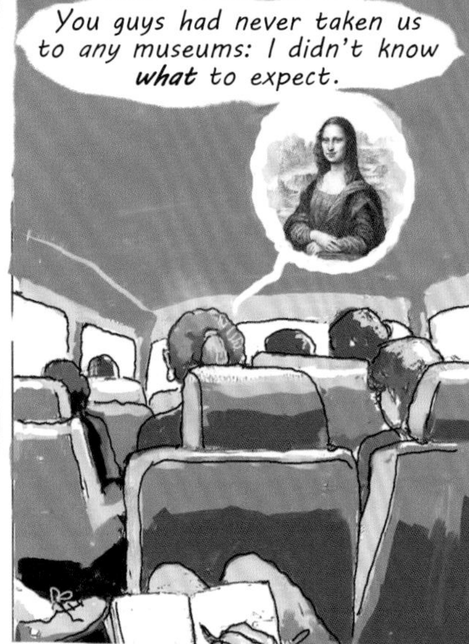

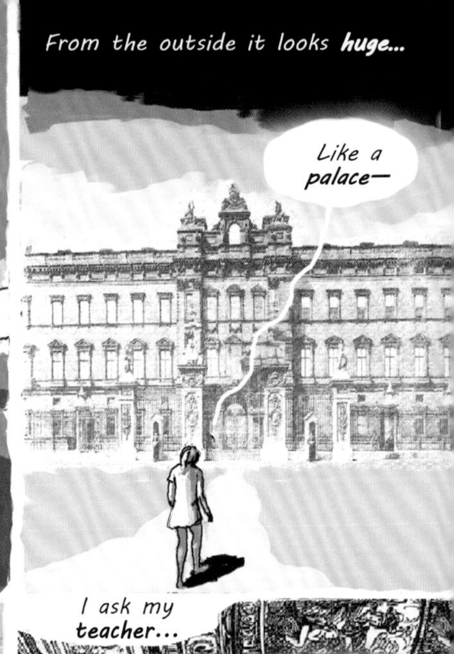

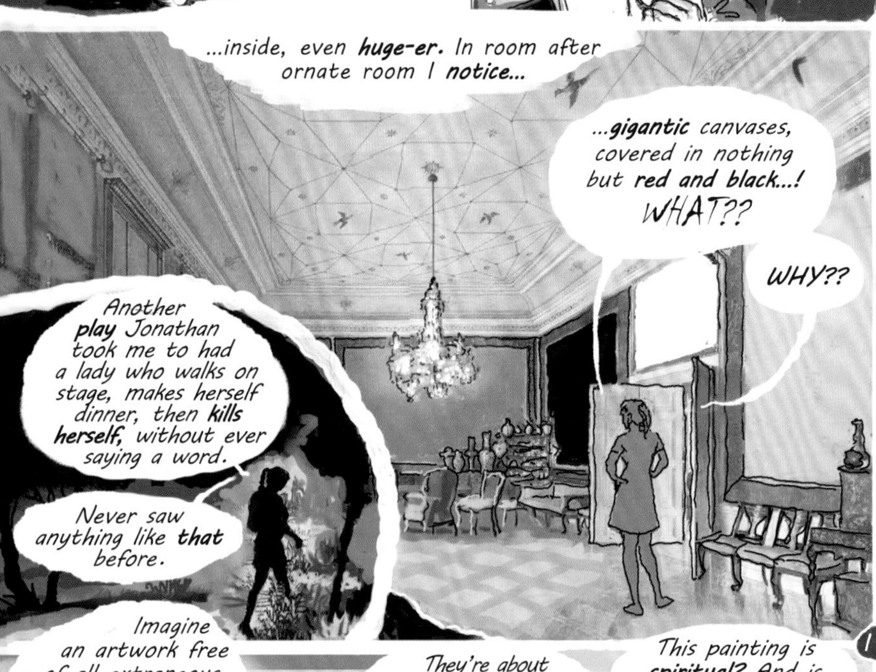

I ask my **teacher...**
Is this **ART??**
Why would anyone want to **do... that??**
Well, y'see, this is **MINIMALISM**
Veeery important movement, started in the '60s in reaction to Abstract Expressionism...
The artists wanted to expose the **essence** of their subject matter
...by reducing everything to **line, shape,** and **color.**
But **WHY?** Isn't **imagination** essential too??

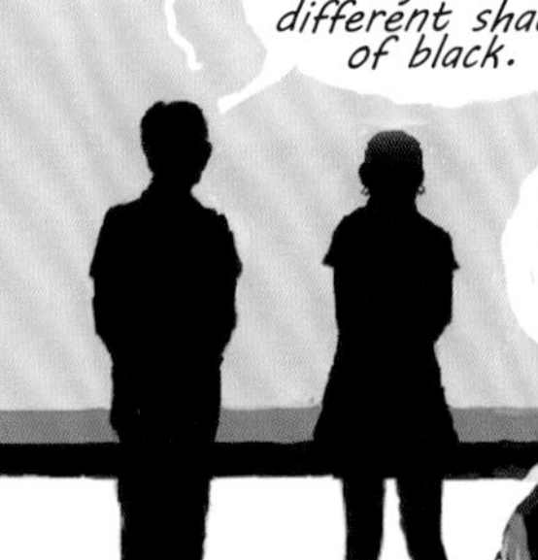

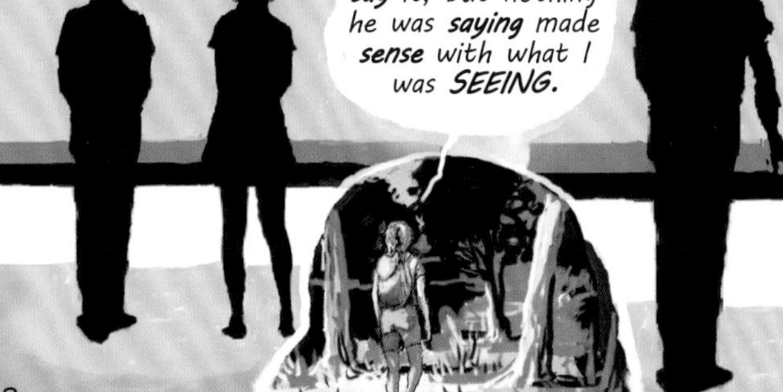

I want to say...
Gad!! Everything you say sounds like it comes from a **book!!**
Don't you ever just **trust** your **EYES??**
???
There'reSO manyamazingartists outtherewhogivetheir heartandsoultotheir work,whoarevisionary andpassionatebut nobodyeverpays **attention**to them—
...Sarah Winchester was one!

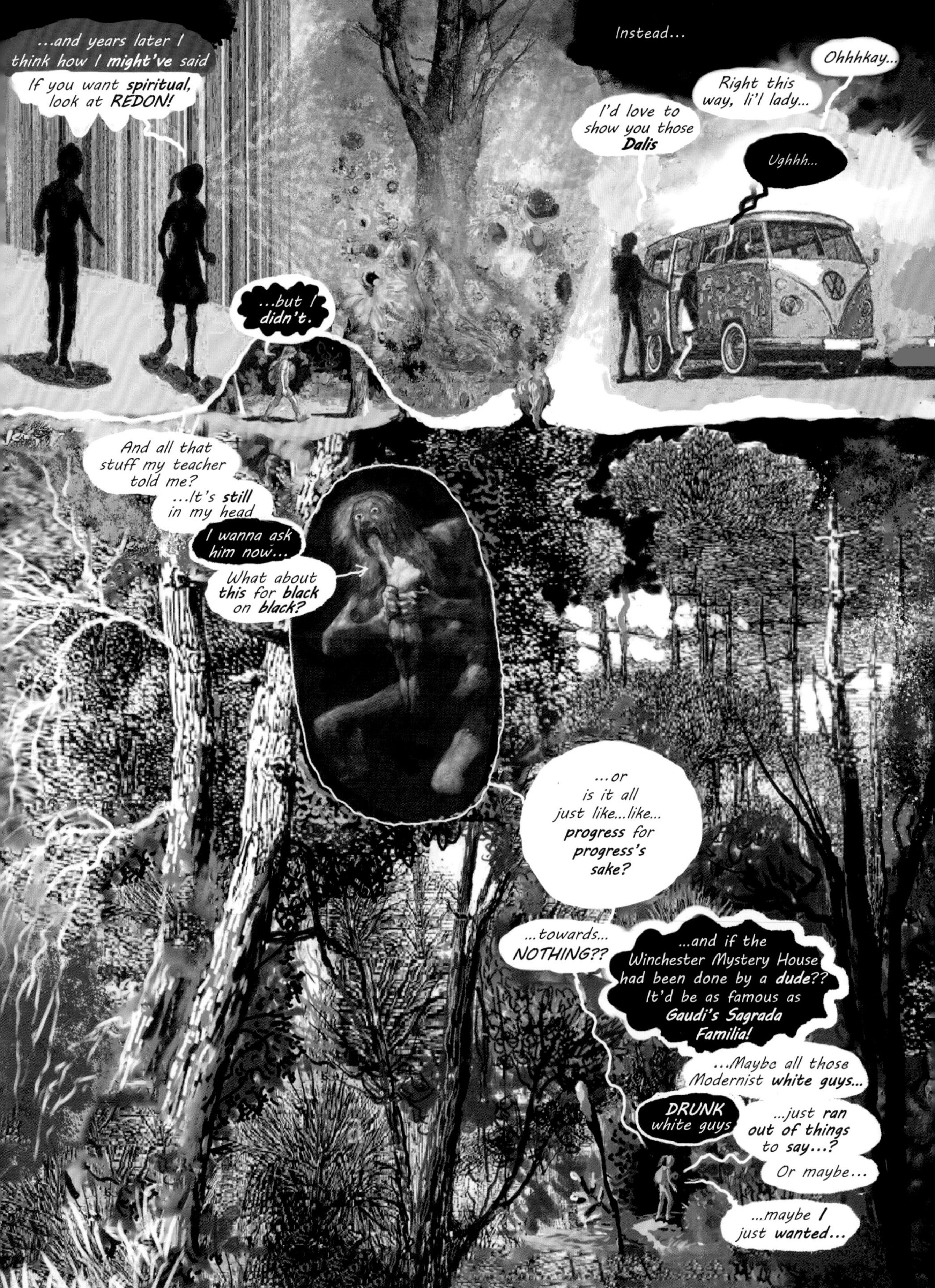
...and years later I think how I might've said
If you want spiritual, look at REDON!
...but I didn't.
Instead...
I'd love to show you those Dalis
Right this way, li'l lady...
Ohhhkay...
Ughhh...
And all that stuff my teacher told me?
...It's still in my head
I wanna ask him now...
What about this for black on black?
...or is it all just like...like... progress for progress's sake?
...towards... NOTHING??
...and if the Winchester Mystery House had been done by a dude?? It'd be as famous as Gaudi's Sagrada Familia!
...Maybe all those Modernist white guys...
DRUNK white guys
...just ran out of things to say...?
Or maybe...
...maybe I just wanted...

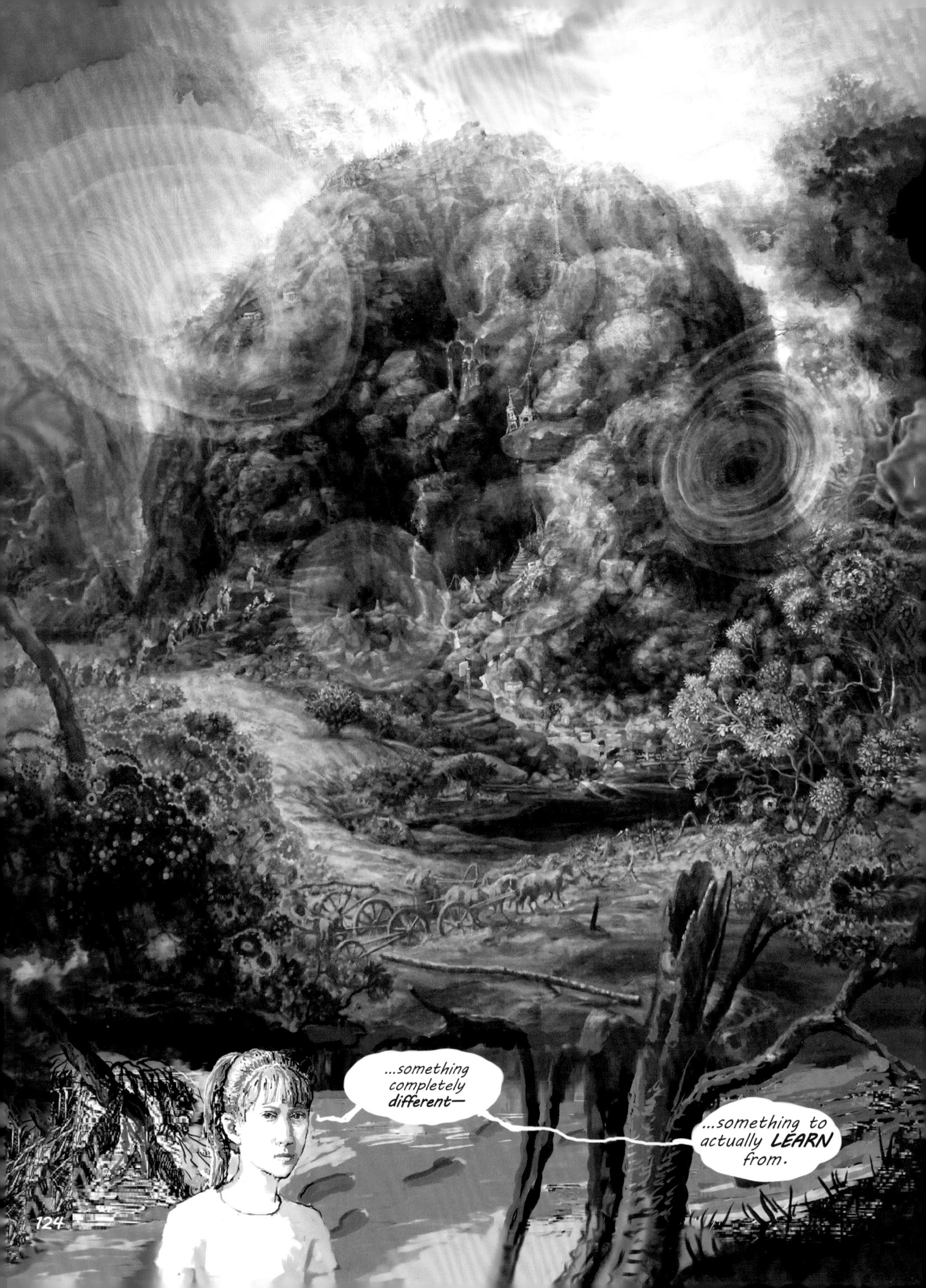
...something completely different—
...something to actually LEARN from.

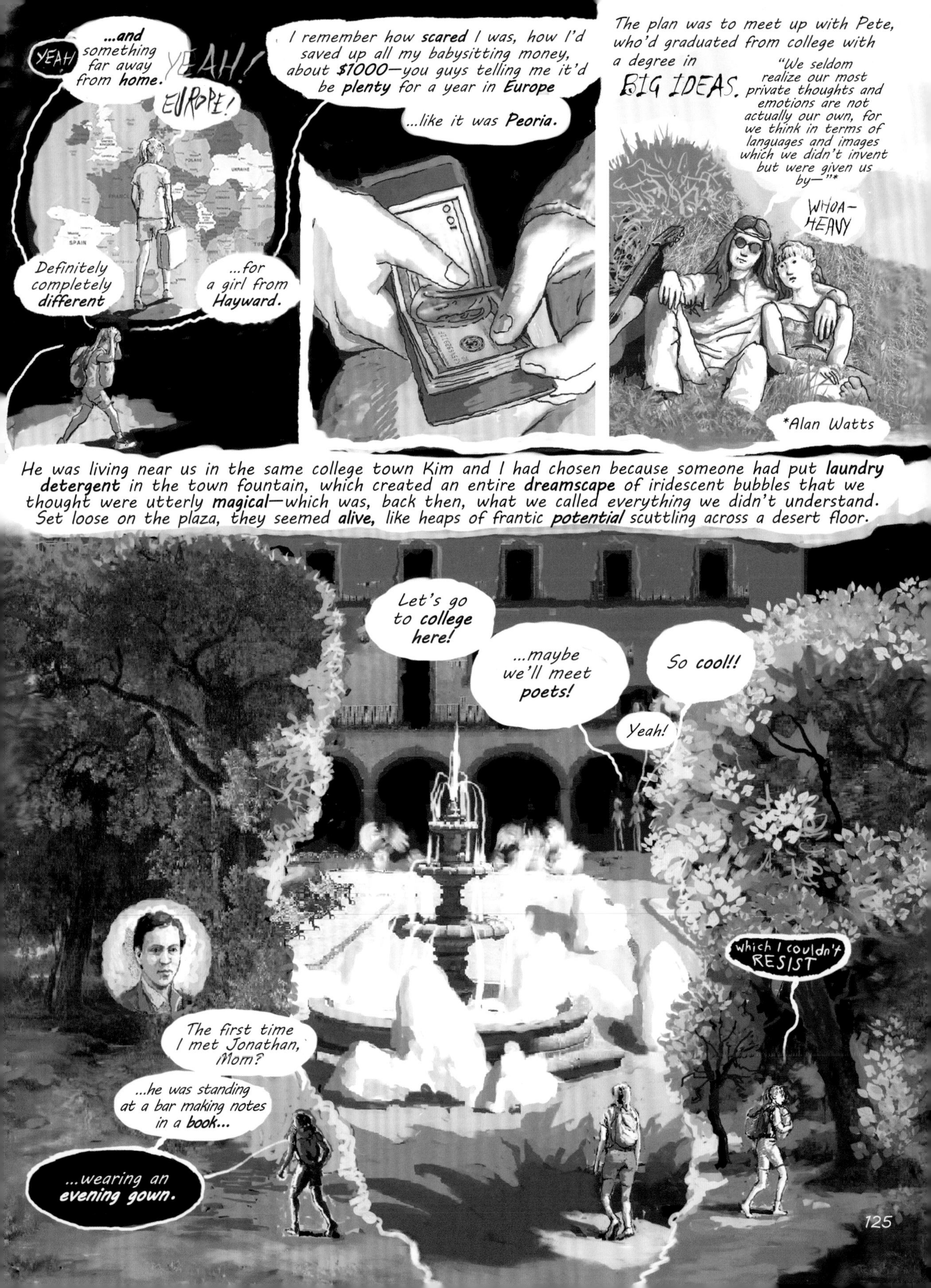

YEAH!

...**and** something far away from **home**.

YEAH!

EUROPE!

Definitely completely **different**

...for a girl from **Hayward**.

I remember how **scared** I was, how I'd saved up all my babysitting money, about **$1000**—you guys telling me it'd be **plenty** for a year in **Europe**

...like it was **Peoria**.

The plan was to meet up with Pete, who'd graduated from college with a degree in

BIG IDEAS.

"We seldom realize our most private thoughts and emotions are not actually our own, for we think in terms of languages and images which we didn't invent but were given us by—"*

WHOA—HEAVY

*Alan Watts

He was living near us in the same college town Kim and I had chosen because someone had put **laundry detergent** in the town fountain, which created an entire **dreamscape** of iridescent bubbles that we thought were utterly **magical**—which was, back then, what we called everything we didn't understand. Set loose on the plaza, they seemed **alive,** like heaps of frantic ***potential*** scuttling across a desert floor.

Let's go to **college here!**

...maybe we'll meet **poets!**

So **cool!!**

Yeah!

which I couldn't RESIST

The first time I met Jonathan, Mom?

...he was standing at a bar making notes in a **book**...

...wearing an **evening gown**.

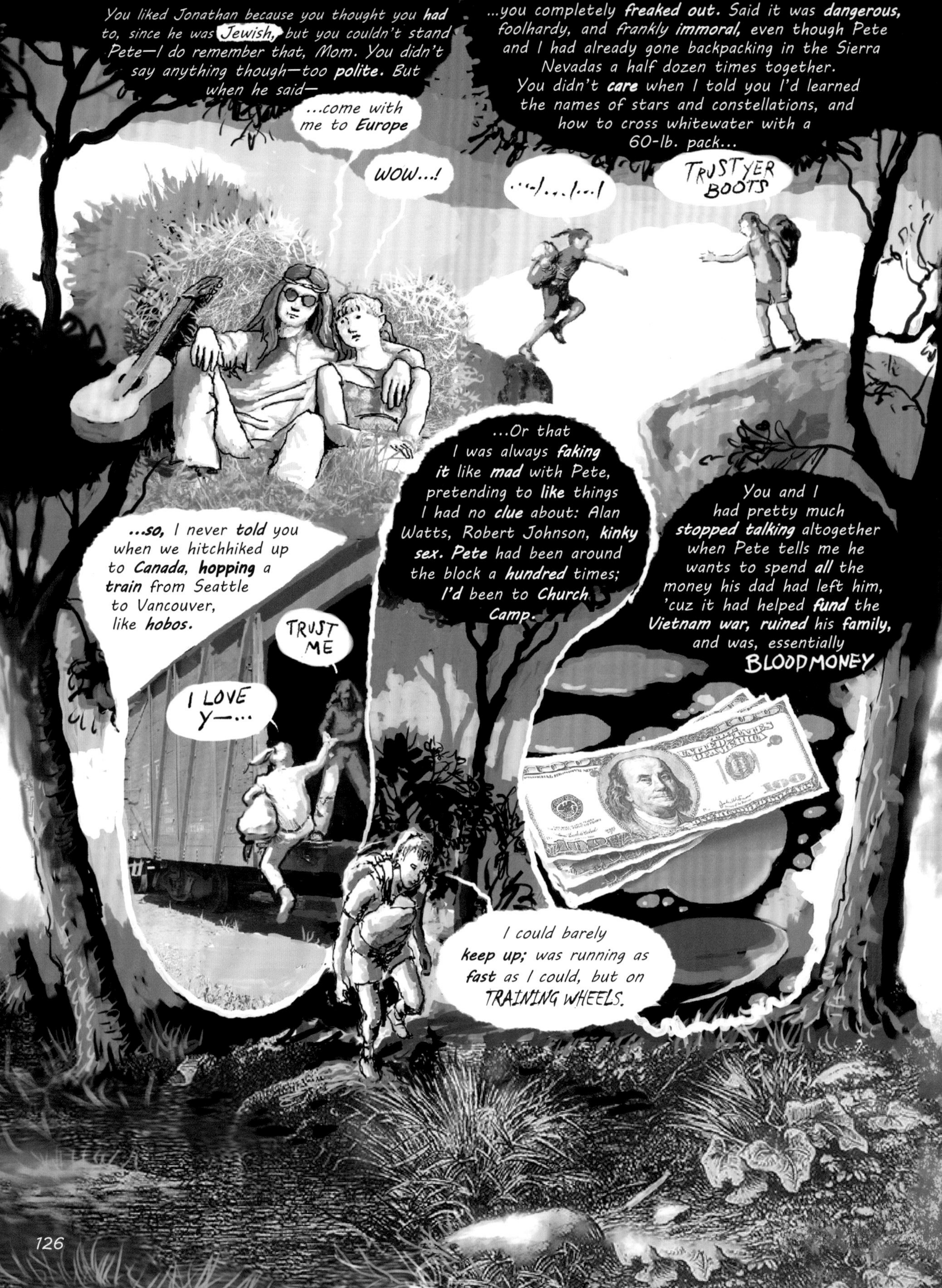
You liked Jonathan because you thought you had to, since he was Jewish, but you couldn't stand Pete—I do remember that, Mom. You didn't say anything though—too polite. But when he said—
...come with me to Europe
WOW...!
...you completely freaked out. Said it was dangerous, foolhardy, and frankly immoral, even though Pete and I had already gone backpacking in the Sierra Nevadas a half dozen times together. You didn't care when I told you I'd learned the names of stars and constellations, and how to cross whitewater with a 60-lb. pack...
...!...!...!
TRUST YER BOOTS
...so, I never told you when we hitchhiked up to Canada, hopping a train from Seattle to Vancouver, like hobos.
TRUST ME
I LOVE Y—...
...Or that I was always faking it like mad with Pete, pretending to like things I had no clue about: Alan Watts, Robert Johnson, kinky sex. Pete had been around the block a hundred times; I'd been to Church Camp.
You and I had pretty much stopped talking altogether when Pete tells me he wants to spend all the money his dad had left him, 'cuz it had helped fund the Vietnam war, ruined his family, and was, essentially BLOODMONEY
I could barely keep up; was running as fast as I could, but on TRAINING WHEELS.

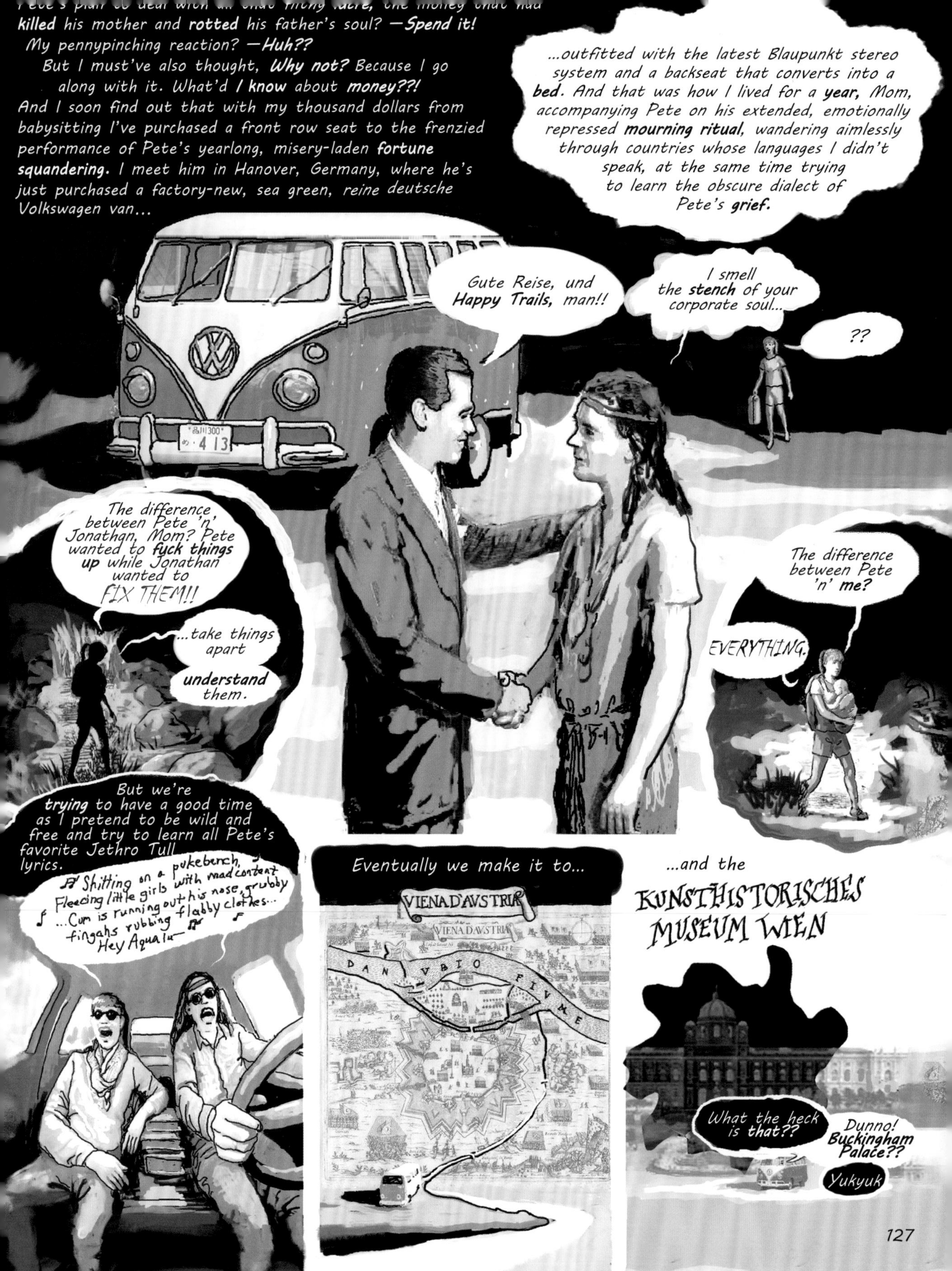

Pete's plan to deal with all that filthy lucre, the money that had **killed** his mother and **rotted** his father's soul? —***Spend it!***

My pennypinching reaction? —***Huh??***

But I must've also thought, ***Why not?*** Because I go along with it. What'd **I know** about ***money??!*** And I soon find out that with my thousand dollars from babysitting I've purchased a front row seat to the frenzied performance of Pete's yearlong, misery-laden **fortune squandering.** I meet him in Hanover, Germany, where he's just purchased a factory-new, sea green, reine deutsche Volkswagen van...

...outfitted with the latest Blaupunkt stereo system and a backseat that converts into a **bed**. And that was how I lived for a **year,** Mom, accompanying Pete on his extended, emotionally repressed **mourning ritual**, wandering aimlessly through countries whose languages I didn't speak, at the same time trying to learn the obscure dialect of Pete's **grief.**

Gute Reise, und **Happy Trails,** man!!

I smell the **stench** of your corporate soul...

??

The difference between Pete 'n' Jonathan, Mom? Pete wanted to **fuck things up** while Jonathan wanted to FIX THEM!!

...take things apart

understand them.

The difference between Pete 'n' **me?**

EVERYTHING.

But we're **trying** to have a good time as I pretend to be wild and free and try to learn all Pete's favorite Jethro Tull lyrics.

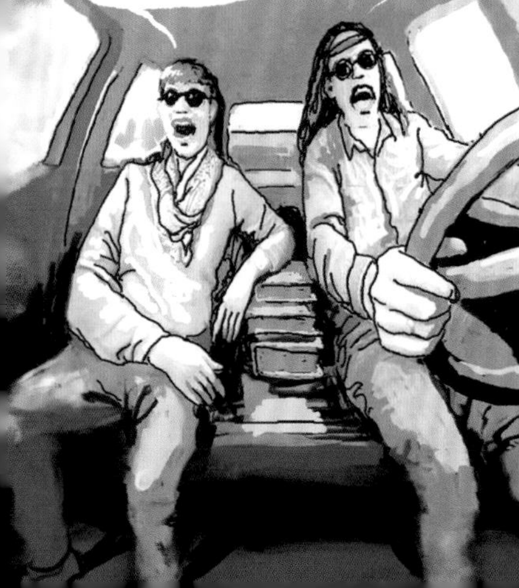

Eventually we make it to...

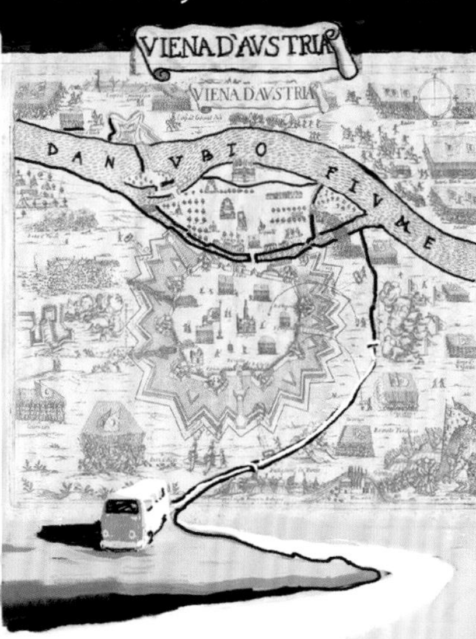

...and the

KUNSTHISTORISCHES MUSEUM WIEN

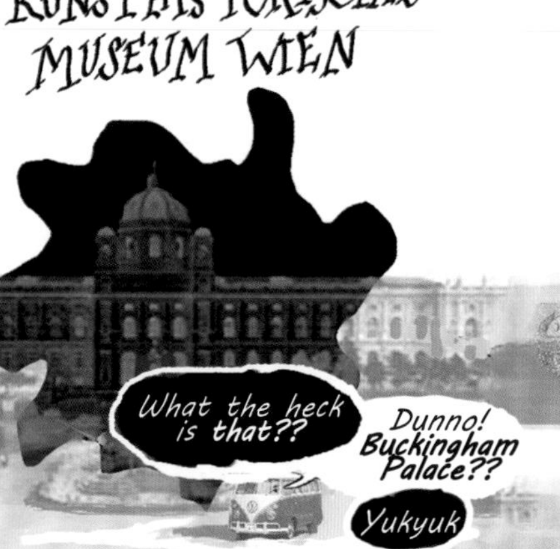

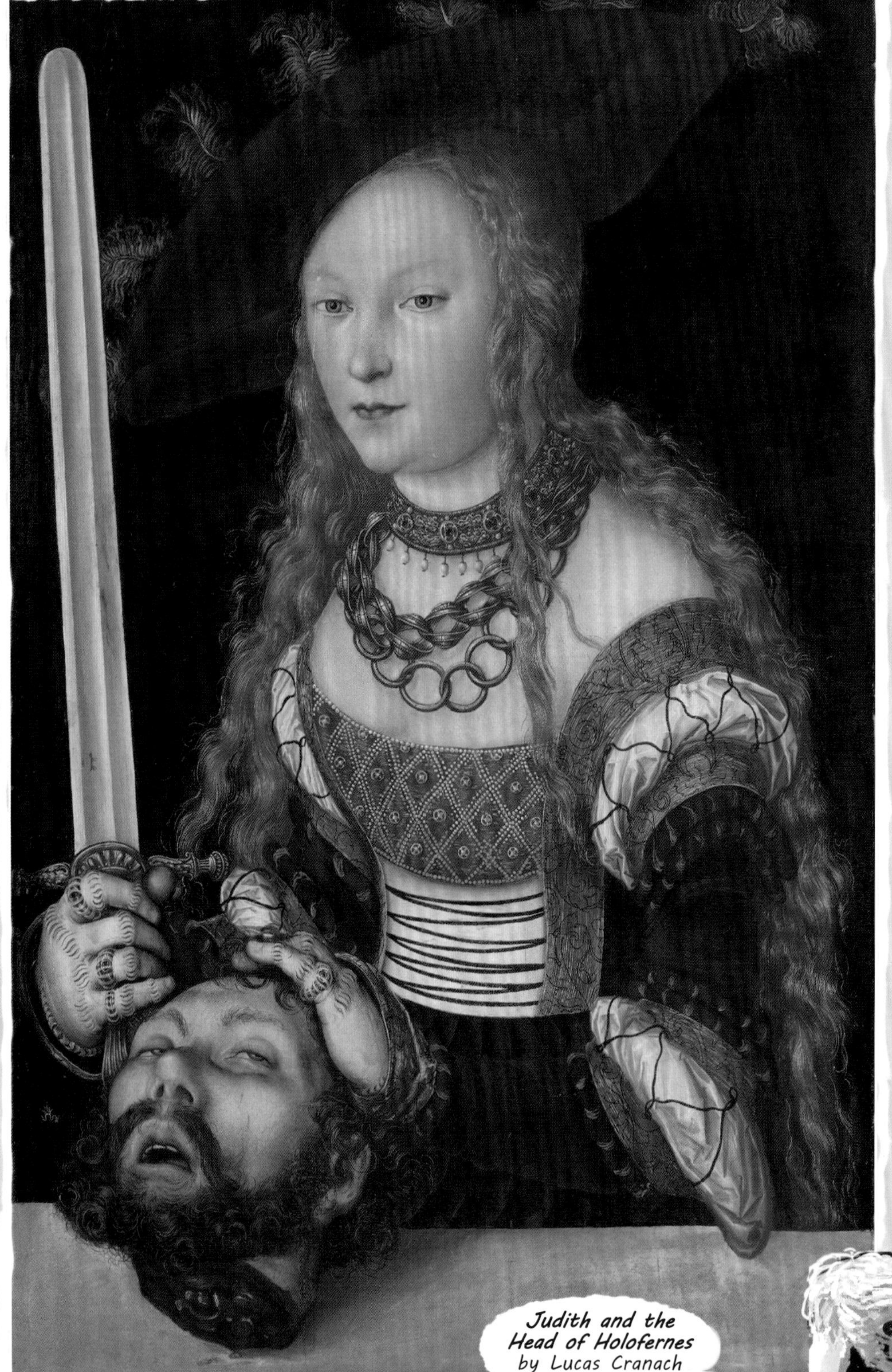
...with things inside it like **this**...
Judith and the Head of Holofernes by Lucas Cranach
...things that blow a **hole** open in my head...
...that show me stuff I'd never **dreamed** of
You can do... THAT?

...things I'm guessing you wouldn't **like,** mom
...things the **Church** wouldn't like...

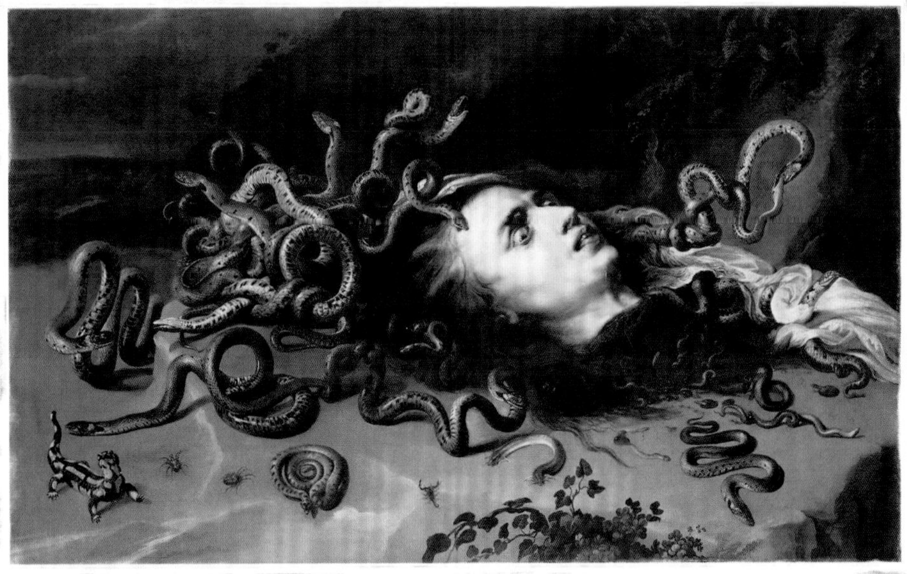

Ruben's **Medusa**...

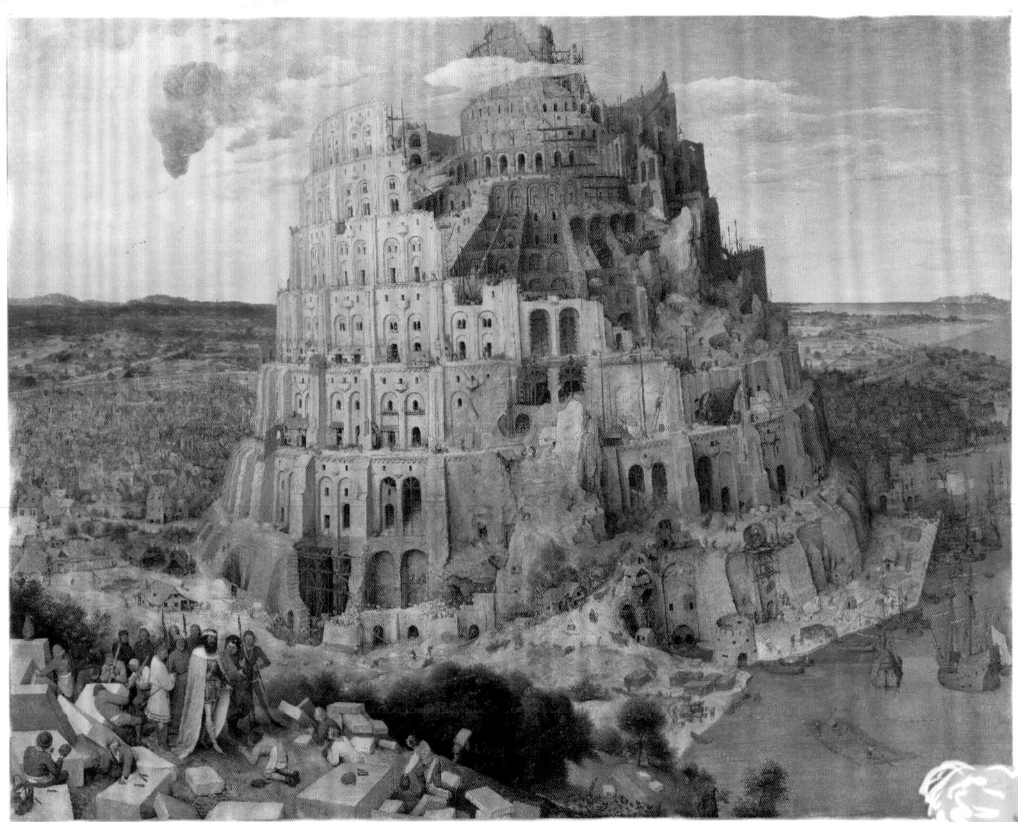

Brueghel's **The Tower of Babel...**
...stuff that could completely change your BRAIN
...**reshape** it, BLOW UP a tiny little world.

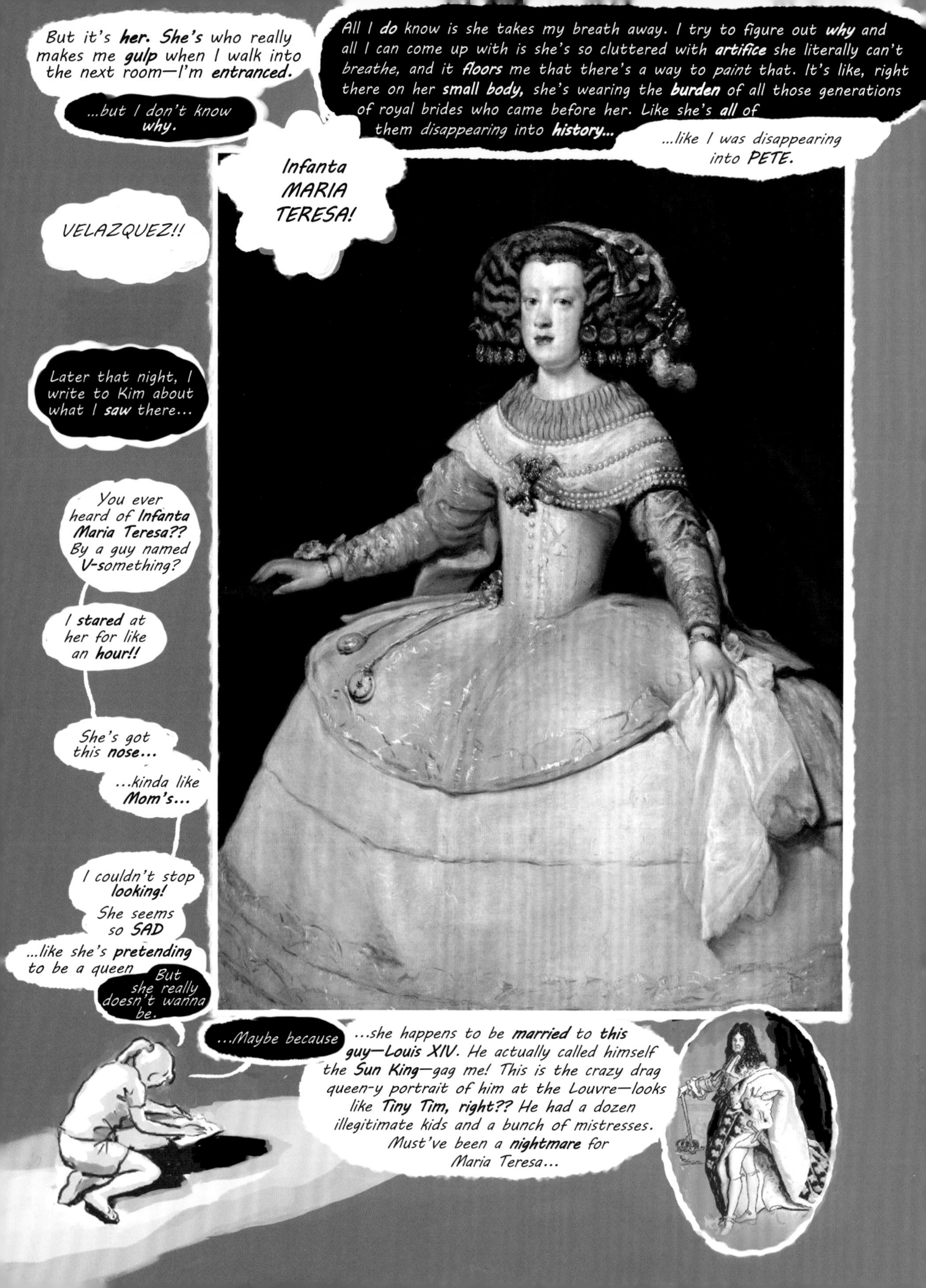

But it's **her**. **She's** who really makes me **gulp** when I walk into the next room—I'm **entranced.**

...but I don't know **why**.

All I **do** know is she takes my breath away. I try to figure out **why** and all I can come up with is she's so cluttered with **artifice** she literally can't breathe, and it **floors** me that there's a way to paint that. It's like, right there on her **small body**, she's wearing the **burden** of all those generations of royal brides who came before her. Like she's **all** of them disappearing into **history...**

...like I was disappearing into **PETE**.

Infanta MARIA TERESA!

VELAZQUEZ!!

Later that night, I write to Kim about what I **saw** there...

You ever heard of **Infanta Maria Teresa??** By a guy named **V-something?**

I **stared** at her for like an **hour!!**

She's got this **nose...**

...kinda like **Mom's...**

I couldn't stop **looking!**

She seems so **SAD**

...like she's **pretending** to be a queen

But she really doesn't wanna be.

...Maybe because

...she happens to be **married** to **this guy—Louis XIV**. He actually called himself the **Sun King**—gag me! This is the crazy drag queen-y portrait of him at the Louvre—looks like **Tiny Tim, right??** He had a dozen illegitimate kids and a bunch of mistresses. Must've been a **nightmare** for Maria Teresa...

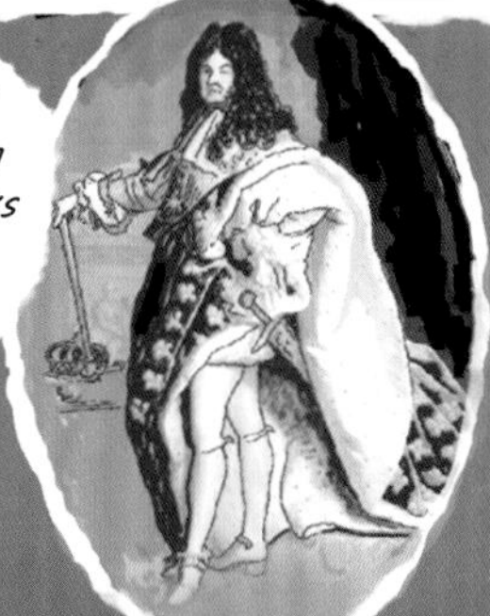

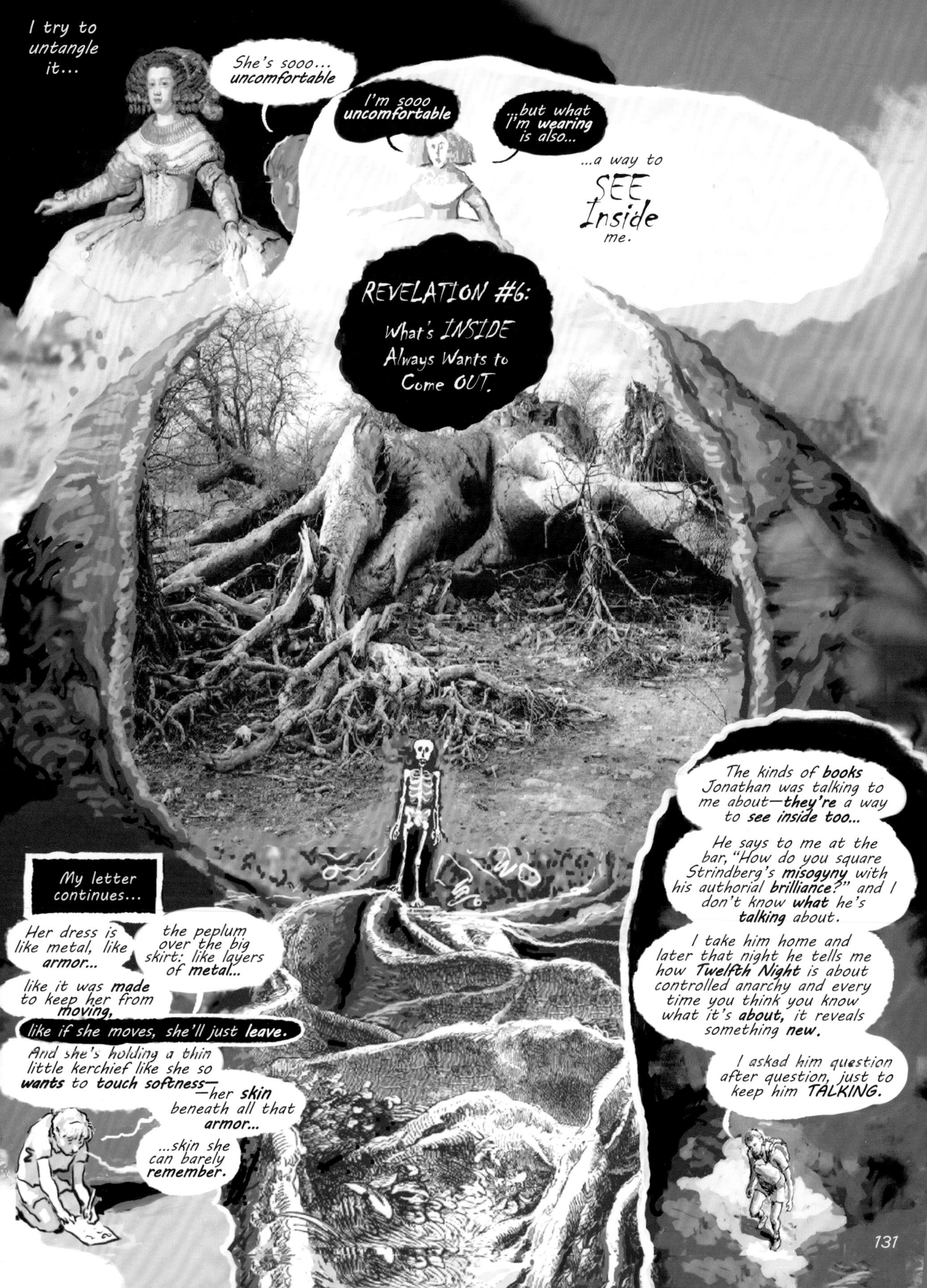
I try to untangle it...
She's sooo... uncomfortable
I'm sooo uncomfortable
...but what I'm wearing is also...
...a way to SEE Inside me.
REVELATION #6: What's INSIDE Always Wants to Come OUT.
My letter continues...
Her dress is like metal, like armor...
the peplum over the big skirt: like layers of metal...
like it was made to keep her from moving,
like if she moves, she'll just leave.
And she's holding a thin little kerchief like she so wants to touch softness—
—her skin beneath all that armor...
...skin she can barely remember.
The kinds of books Jonathan was talking to me about—they're a way to see inside too...
He says to me at the bar, "How do you square Strindberg's misogyny with his authorial brilliance?" and I don't know what he's talking about.
I take him home and later that night he tells me how Twelfth Night is about controlled anarchy and every time you think you know what it's about, it reveals something new.
I asked him question after question, just to keep him TALKING.

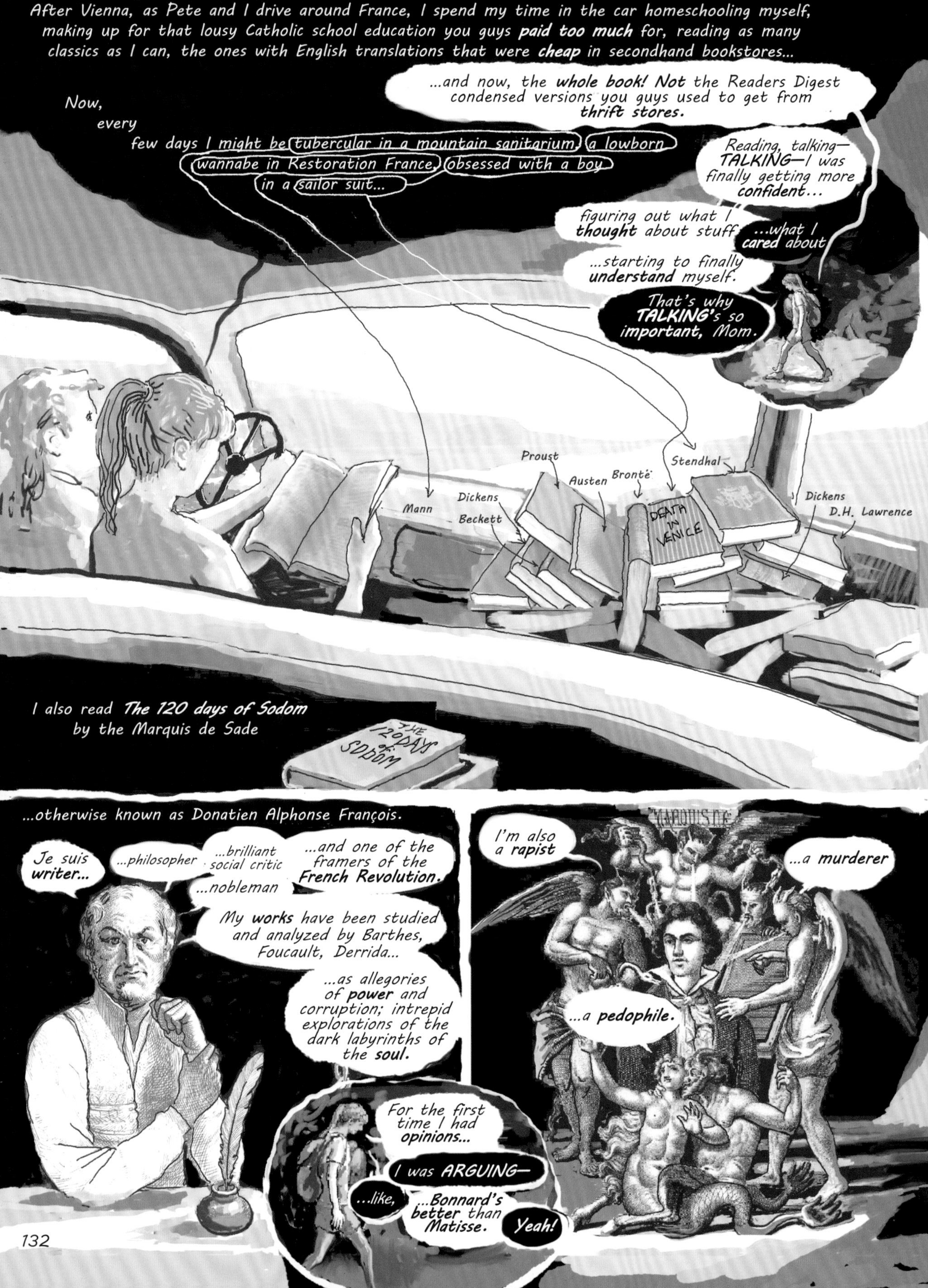
After Vienna, as Pete and I drive around France, I spend my time in the car homeschooling myself, making up for that lousy Catholic school education you guys **paid too much** for, reading as many classics as I can, the ones with English translations that were **cheap** in secondhand bookstores...
...and now, the **whole book! Not** the Readers Digest condensed versions you guys used to get from **thrift stores.**
Now, every few days I might be tubercular in a mountain sanitarium, a lowborn wannabe in Restoration France, obsessed with a boy in a sailor suit...
Reading, talking— **TALKING**—I was finally getting more **confident**...
figuring out what I **thought** about stuff
...what I **cared** about
...starting to finally **understand** myself.
That's why **TALKING's** so **important,** Mom.
Proust
Stendhal
Austen
Brontë
Dickens
Mann
Beckett
Dickens
D.H. Lawrence
DEATH IN VENICE
I also read ***The 120 days of Sodom*** by the Marquis de Sade
THE 120 DAYS of SODOM
...otherwise known as Donatien Alphonse François.
Je suis **writer...**
...philosopher
...brilliant social critic
...and one of the framers of the **French Revolution.**
...nobleman
My **works** have been studied and analyzed by Barthes, Foucault, Derrida...
...as allegories of **power** and corruption; intrepid explorations of the dark labyrinths of the **soul.**
For the first time I had **opinions...**
I was **ARGUING—**
...like,
...Bonnard's **better** than Matisse.
Yeah!
I'm also a **rapist**
...a **murderer**
...a **pedophile.**

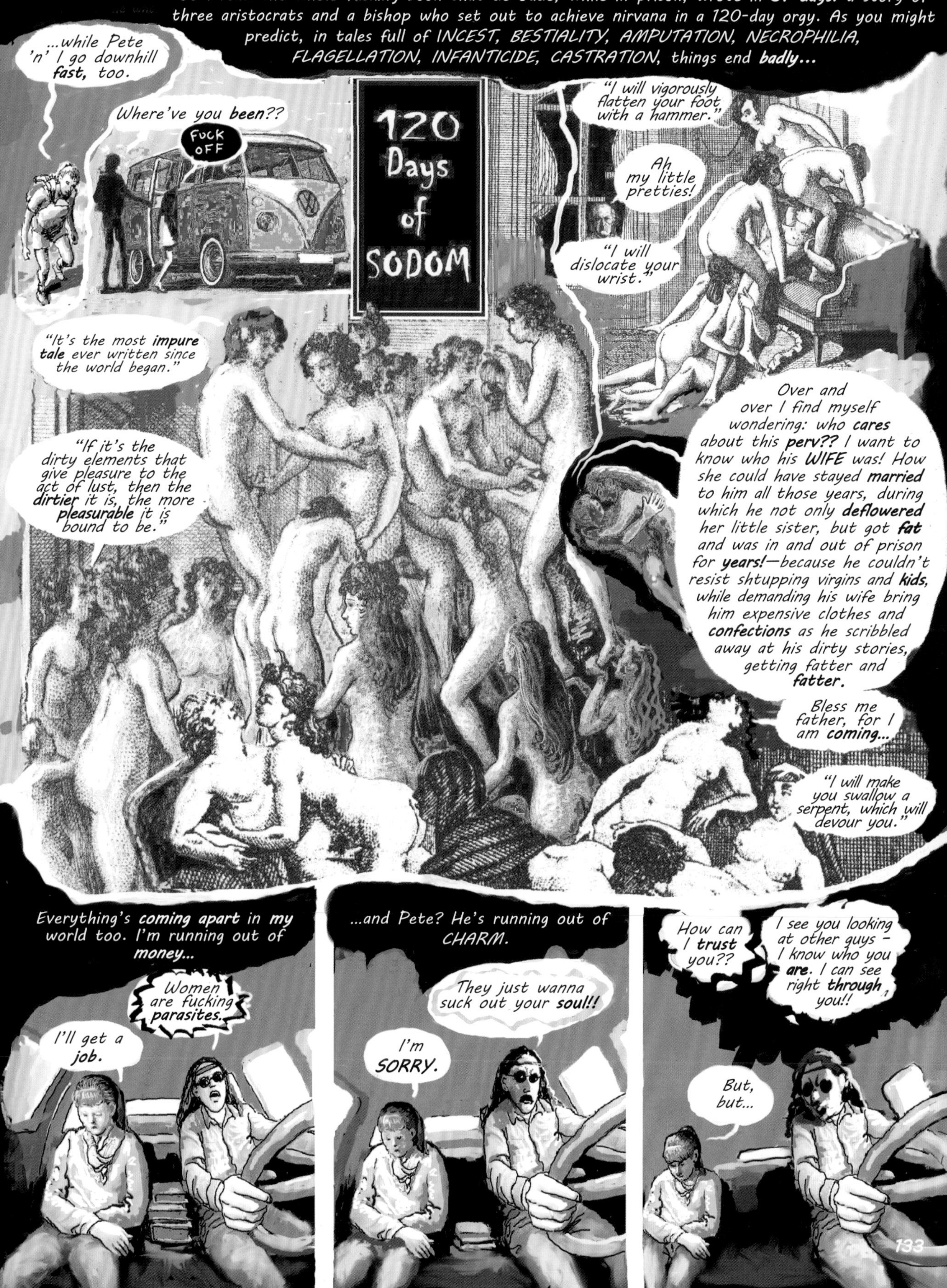
three aristocrats and a bishop who set out to achieve nirvana in a 120-day orgy. As you might predict, in tales full of INCEST, BESTIALITY, AMPUTATION, NECROPHILIA, FLAGELLATION, INFANTICIDE, CASTRATION, things end badly...
...while Pete 'n' I go downhill fast, too.
Where've you been??
FUCK OFF
120 Days of SODOM
"I will vigorously flatten your foot with a hammer."
Ah my little pretties!
"I will dislocate your wrist."
"It's the most impure tale ever written since the world began."
"If it's the dirty elements that give pleasure to the act of lust, then the dirtier it is, the more pleasurable it is bound to be."
Over and over I find myself wondering: who cares about this perv?? I want to know who his WIFE was! How she could have stayed married to him all those years, during which he not only deflowered her little sister, but got fat and was in and out of prison for years!—because he couldn't resist shtupping virgins and kids, while demanding his wife bring him expensive clothes and confections as he scribbled away at his dirty stories, getting fatter and fatter.
Bless me father, for I am coming...
"I will make you swallow a serpent, which will devour you."
Everything's coming apart in my world too. I'm running out of money...
Women are fucking parasites.
I'll get a job.
...and Pete? He's running out of CHARM.
They just wanna suck out your soul!!
I'm SORRY.
How can I trust you??
I see you looking at other guys – I know who you are. I can see right through you!!
But, but...

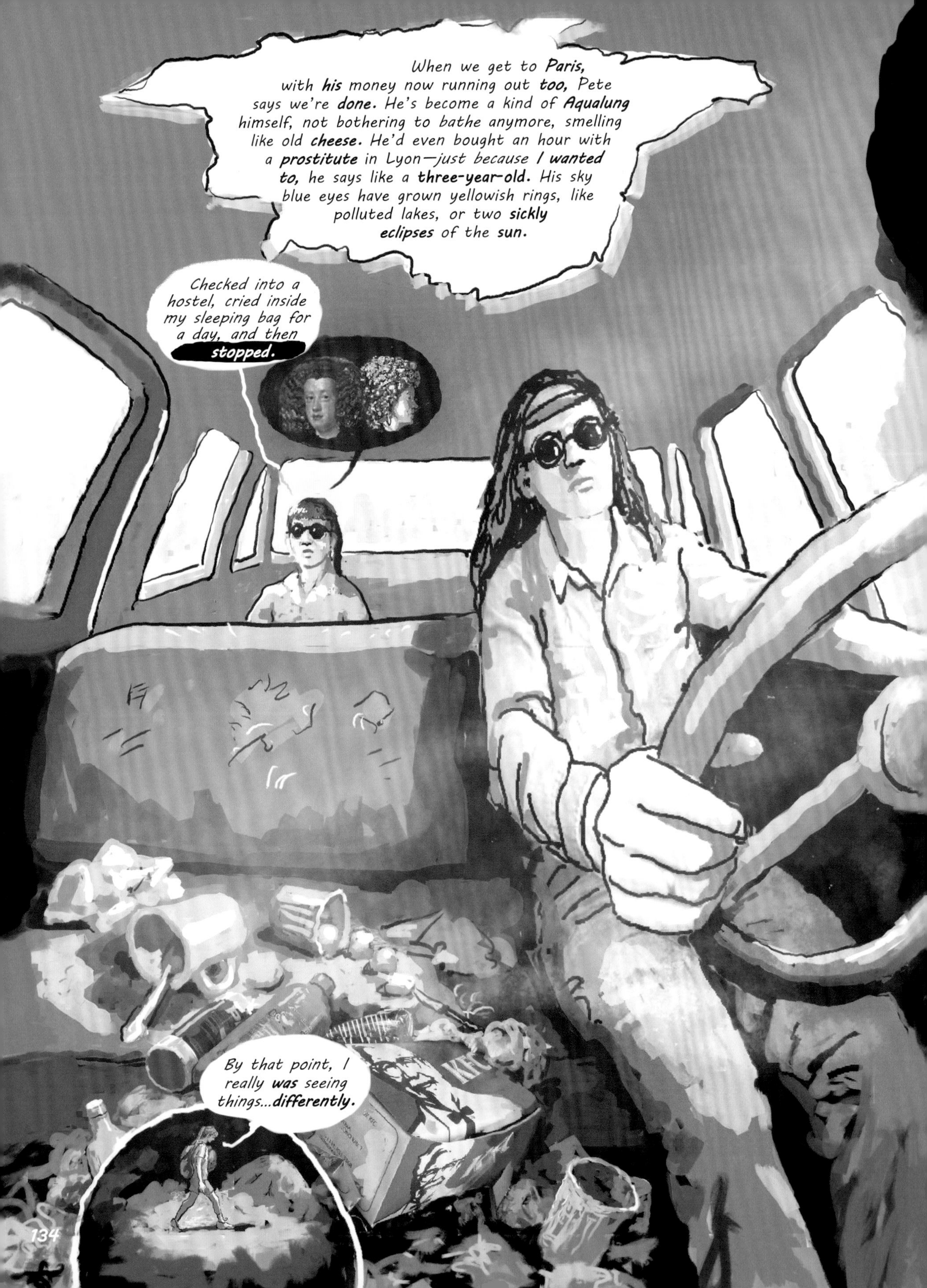
When we get to Paris, with his money now running out too, Pete says we're done. He's become a kind of Aqualung himself, not bothering to bathe anymore, smelling like old cheese. He'd even bought an hour with a prostitute in Lyon—just because I wanted to, he says like a three-year-old. His sky blue eyes have grown yellowish rings, like polluted lakes, or two sickly eclipses of the sun.
Checked into a hostel, cried inside my sleeping bag for a day, and then stopped.
By that point, I really was seeing things...differently.

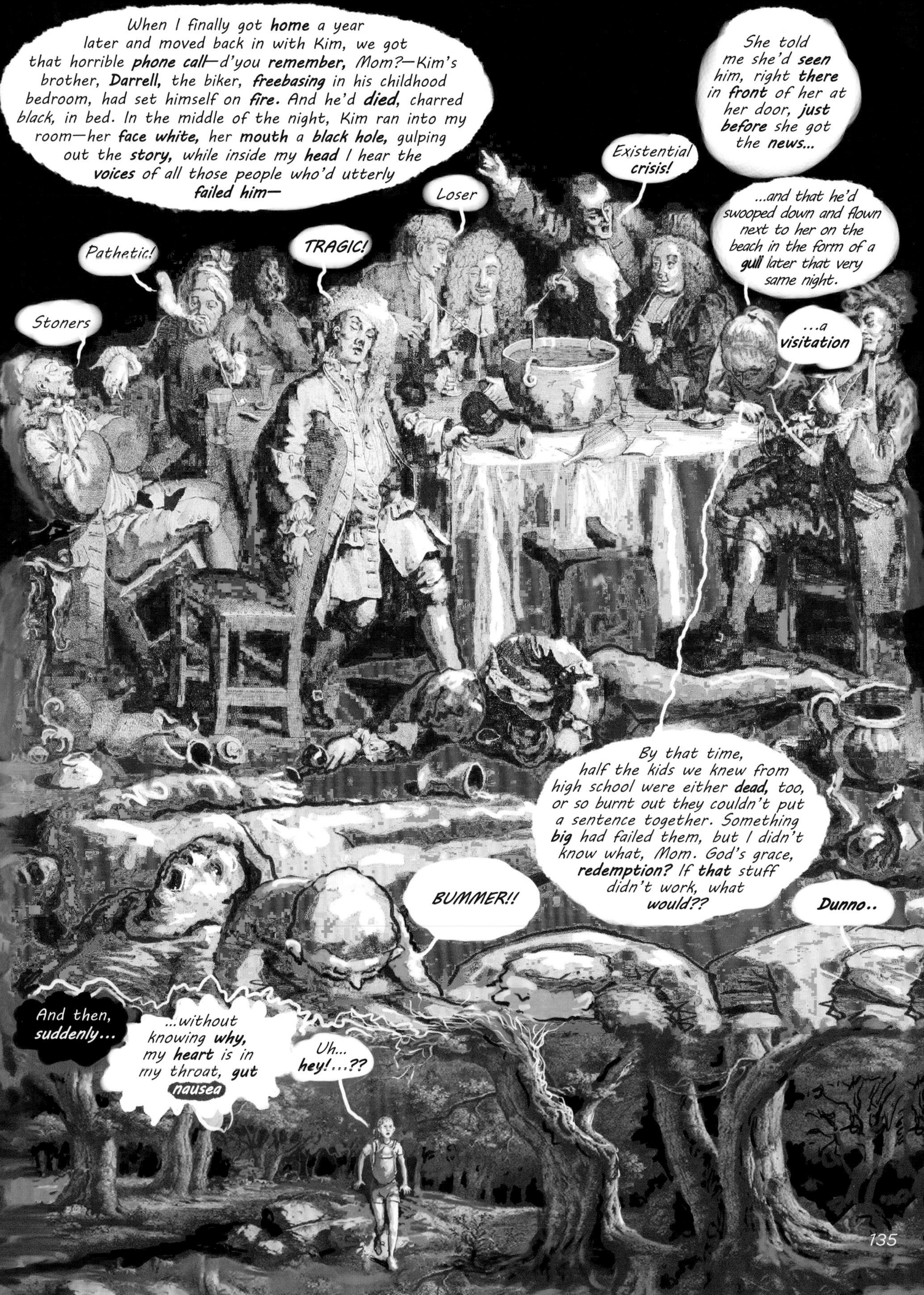
When I finally got home a year later and moved back in with Kim, we got that horrible phone call—d'you remember, Mom?—Kim's brother, Darrell, the biker, freebasing in his childhood bedroom, had set himself on fire. And he'd died, charred black, in bed. In the middle of the night, Kim ran into my room—her face white, her mouth a black hole, gulping out the story, while inside my head I hear the voices of all those people who'd utterly failed him—
Stoners
Pathetic!
TRAGIC!
Loser
Existential crisis!
She told me she'd seen him, right there in front of her at her door, just before she got the news...
...and that he'd swooped down and flown next to her on the beach in the form of a gull later that very same night.
...a visitation
By that time, half the kids we knew from high school were either dead, too, or so burnt out they couldn't put a sentence together. Something big had failed them, but I didn't know what, Mom. God's grace, redemption? If that stuff didn't work, what would??
BUMMER!!
Dunno..
And then, suddenly...
...without knowing why, my heart is in my throat, gut nausea
Uh... hey!...??

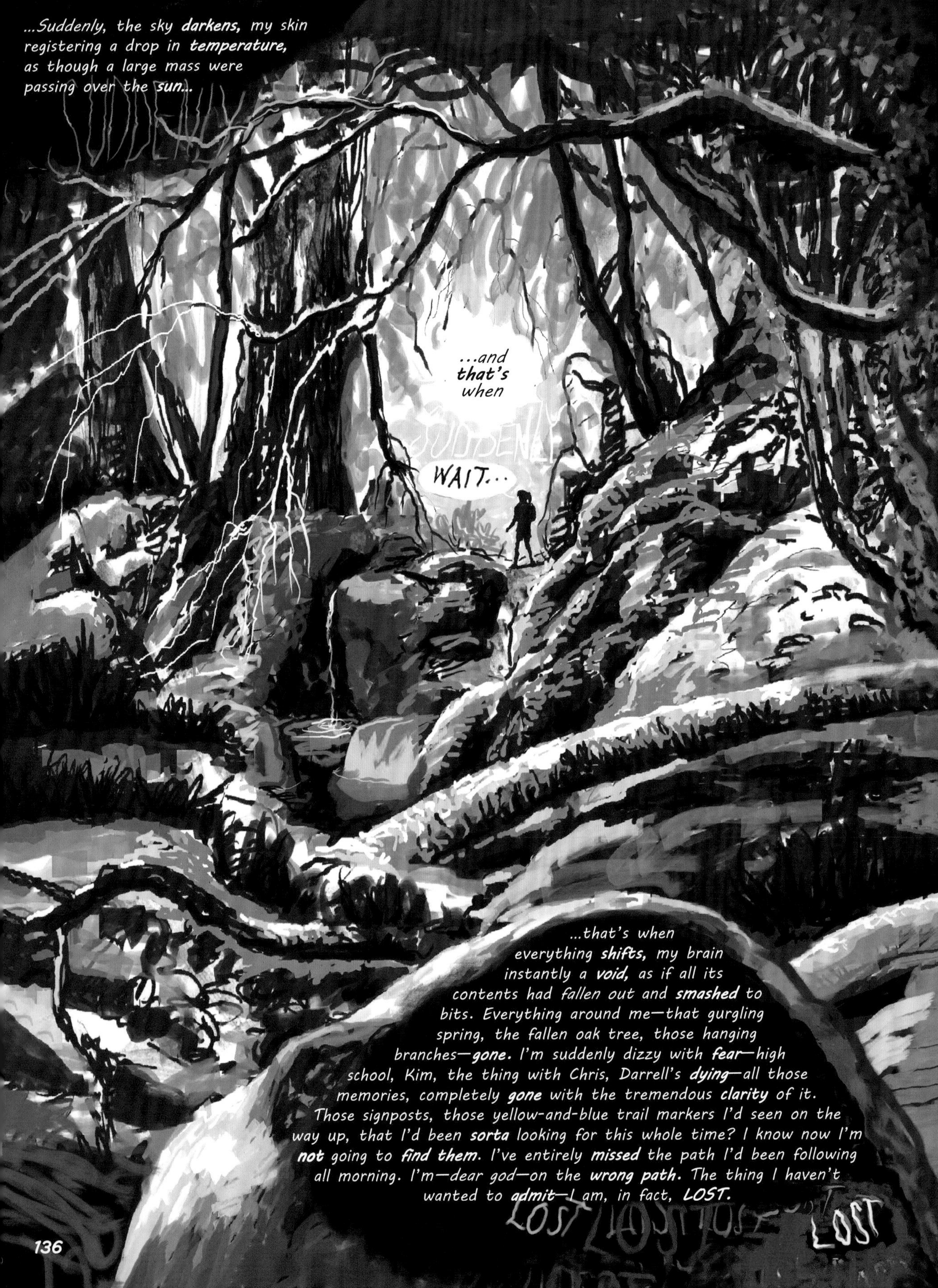
...*Suddenly*, the sky **darkens**, my skin registering a drop in **temperature**, as though a large mass were passing over the **sun**...
...and **that's** when
WAIT...
...that's when everything **shifts**, my brain instantly a **void**, as if all its contents had fallen out and **smashed** to bits. Everything around me—that gurgling spring, the fallen oak tree, those hanging branches—**gone**. I'm suddenly dizzy with **fear**—high school, Kim, the thing with Chris, Darrell's **dying**—all those memories, completely **gone** with the tremendous **clarity** of it. Those signposts, those yellow-and-blue trail markers I'd seen on the way up, that I'd been **sorta** looking for this whole time? I know now I'm **not** going to **find them**. I've entirely **missed** the path I'd been following all morning. I'm—dear god—on the **wrong path**. The thing I haven't wanted to **admit**—I am, in fact, **LOST**.
LOST

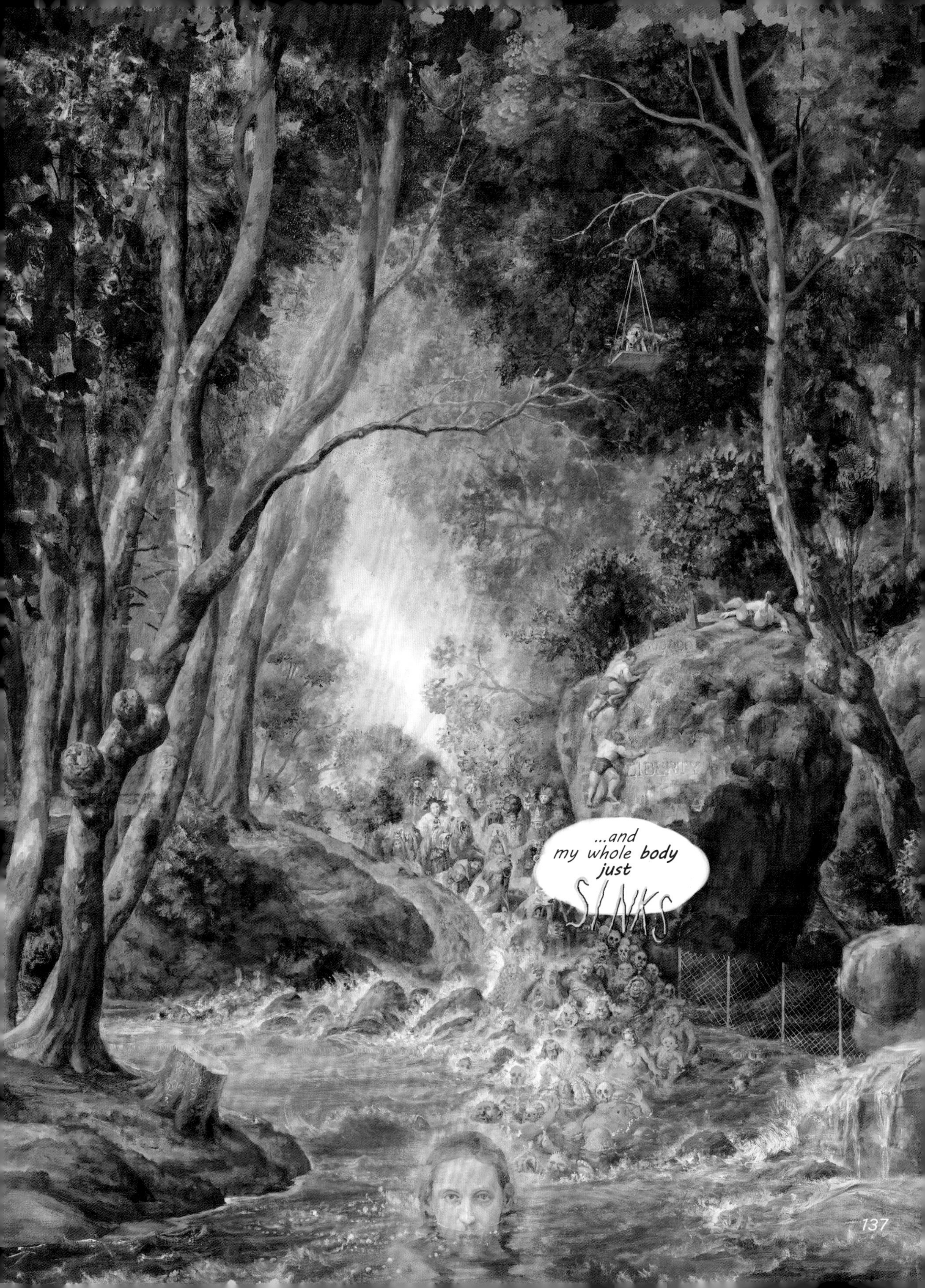
...and my whole **body** just
SINKS

Chapter SEVEN

...**ELECTRICITY** shimmering through my body like a **virus**, deep within me, I can **hear** a hard voice, **repeating...**

YOU have done the UNTHINKable you have ENDANGERed your BABY– an innocent VICTIM of your heedless, utterly UNNECESary desire for ESCAPE from a life full of RICHES more plentiful than ever before in HISTORY How could you be SO so STUPID?

BAD MOTHER

OHHHHH

I'M SORRY

WHAT KINDA PERSON TAKES A BABY INTO THE WOODS?

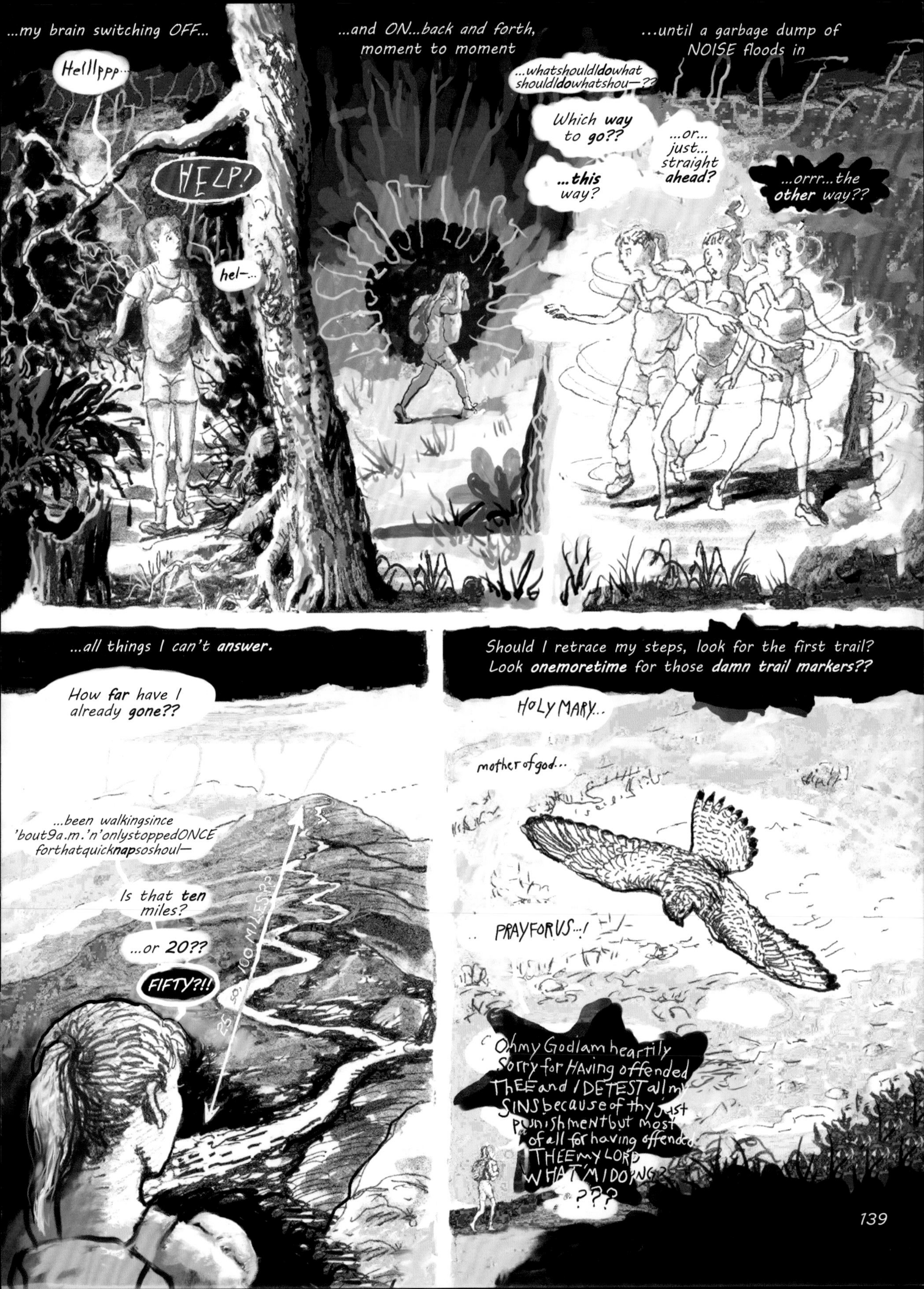

...my brain switching OFF...

Helllppp...

HELP!

hel-...

...and ON...back and forth, moment to moment

...until a garbage dump of NOISE floods in

...whatshouldIdowhat shouldIdowhatshou—??

Which **way** to **go??**

...this way?

...or... just... straight **ahead?**

...orrr...the **other** way??

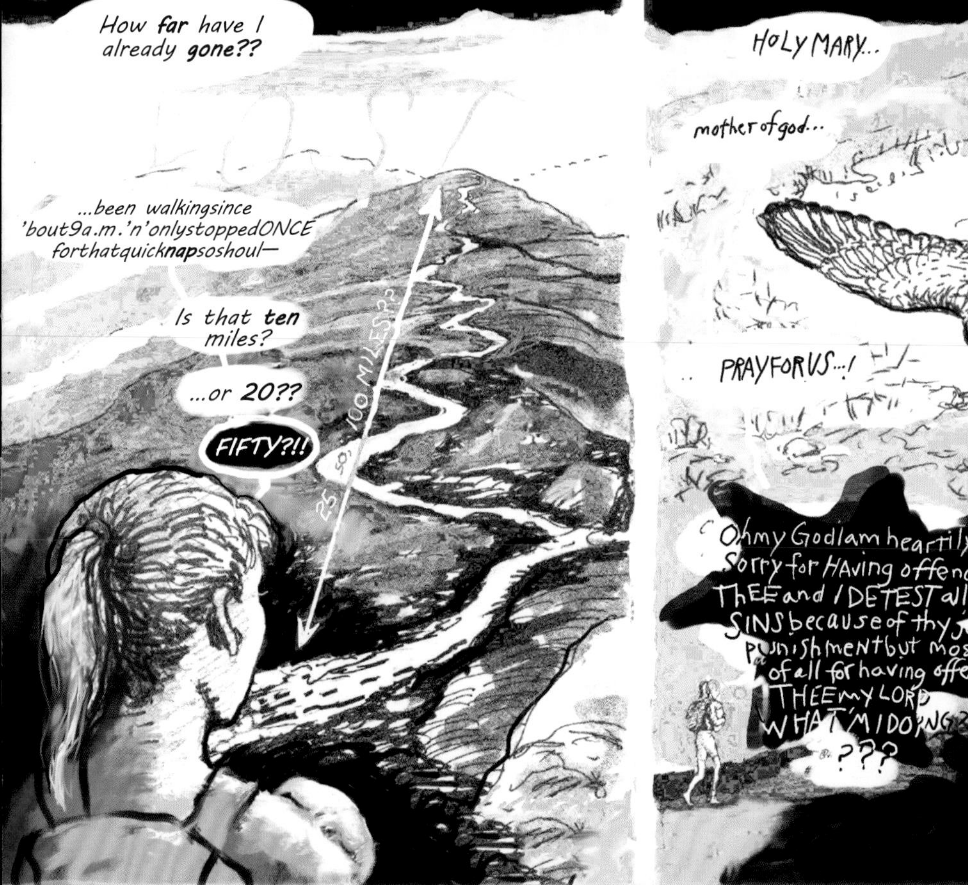

Should I retrace my steps, look for the first trail? Look **onemoretime** for those **damn trail markers??**

HOLY MARY...

mother of god...

PRAYFORUS...!

OhmyGodIamheartily SorryforHAVINGoffended THEEand I DETEST allmy SINSbecauseofthyjust punishmentbut most ofall for having offended THEEmyLORD WHAT'MIDOING? ???

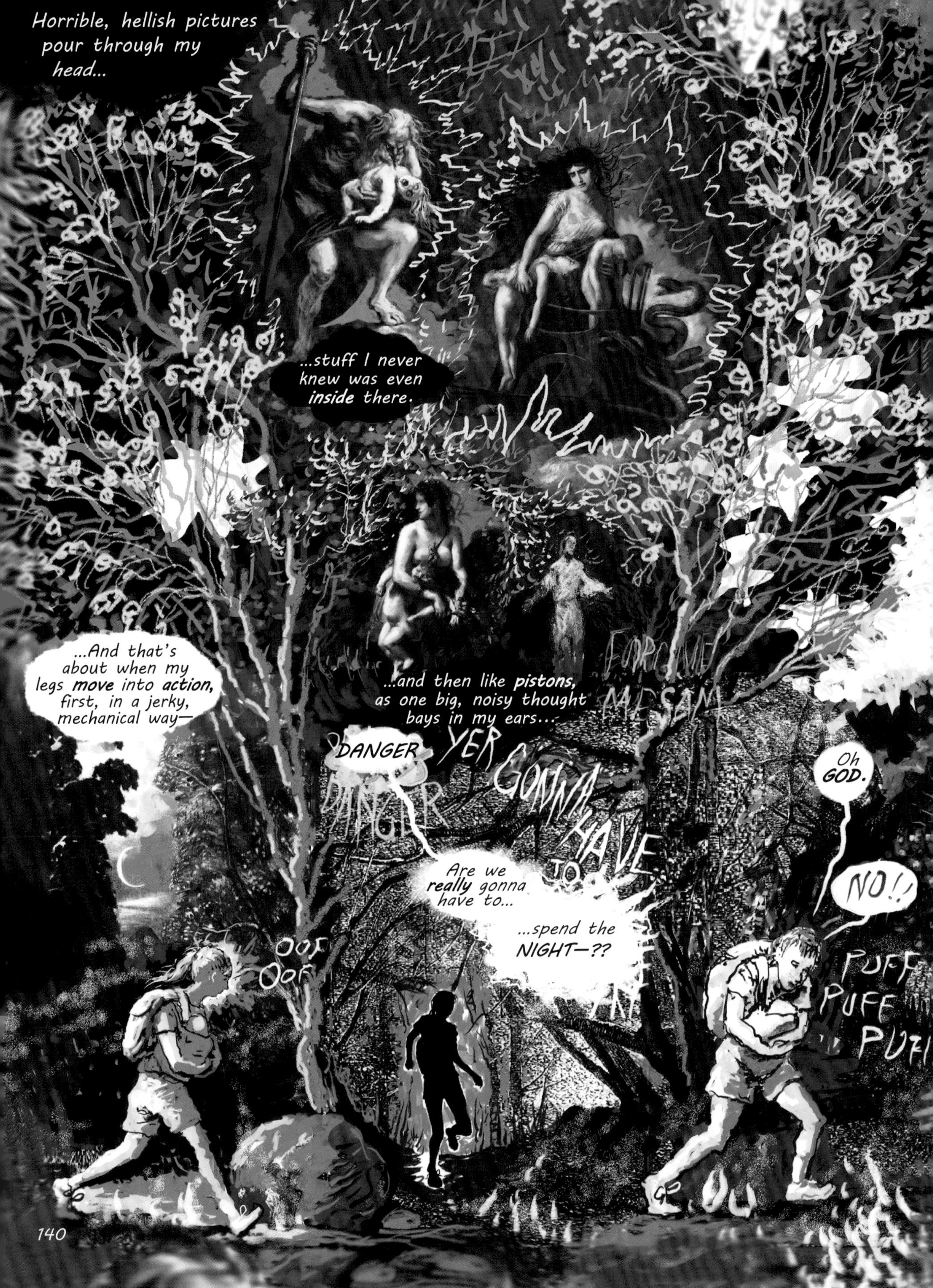

Horrible, hellish pictures pour through my head...
...stuff I never knew was even *inside* there.
...And that's about when my legs **move** into **action,** first, in a jerky, mechanical way—
...and then like **pistons,** as one big, noisy thought bays in my ears...
DANGER
YER GONNA HAVE TO
DANGER
OOF
OOF
Are we **really** gonna have to...
...spend the NIGHT—??
Oh **GOD.**
NO!!
PUFF
PUFF

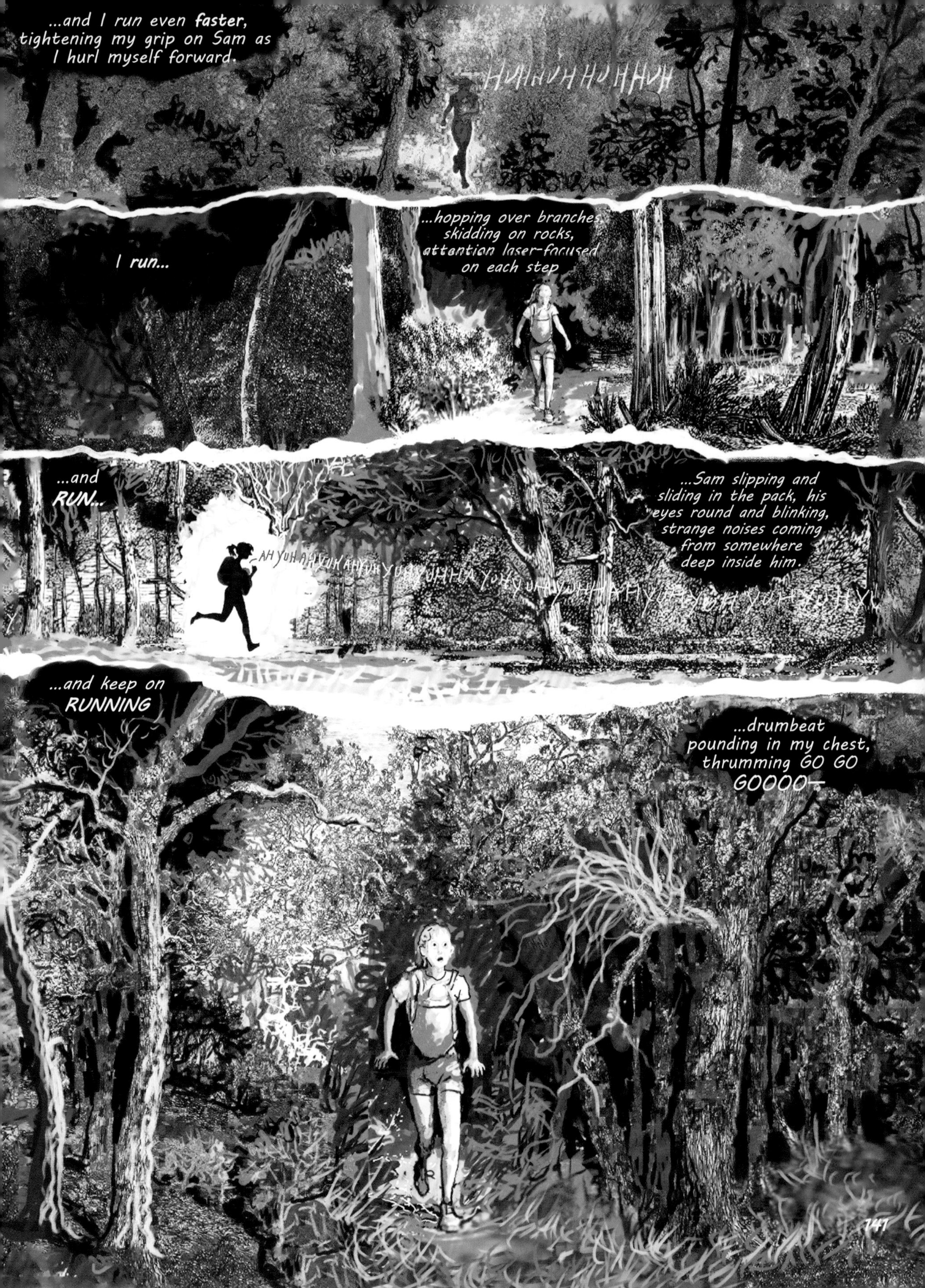
...and I run even faster, tightening my grip on Sam as I hurl myself forward.
HUHHUH HUHHUH
I run...
...hopping over branches, skidding on rocks, attention laser-focused on each step
...and RUN...
AH YUH AH YUH AH YUH
...Sam slipping and sliding in the pack, his eyes round and blinking, strange noises coming from somewhere deep inside him.
...and keep on RUNNING
...drumbeat pounding in my chest, thrumming GO GO GOOOO—

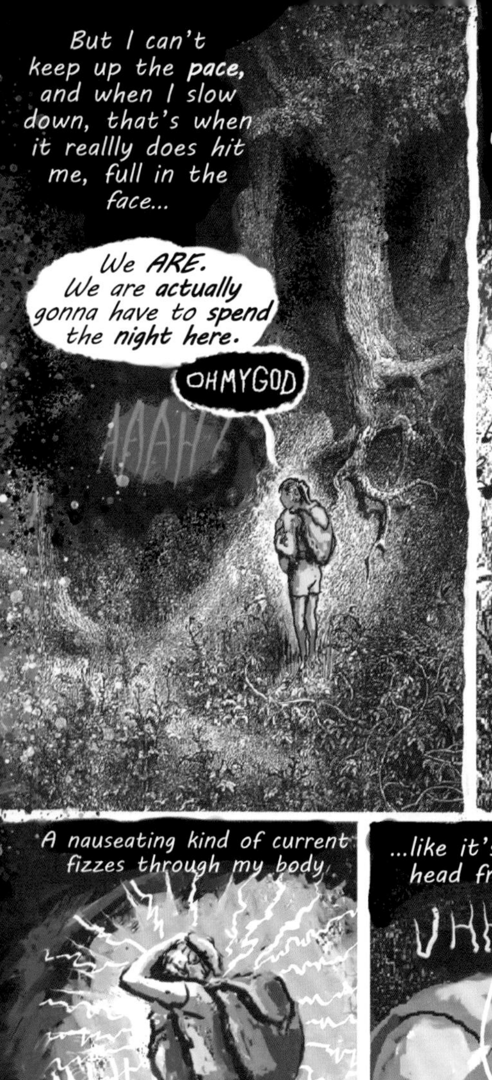

But I can't keep up the pace, and when I slow down, that's when it reallly does hit me, full in the face...
We ARE. We are actually gonna have to spend the night here.
OHMYGOD
AAAH!

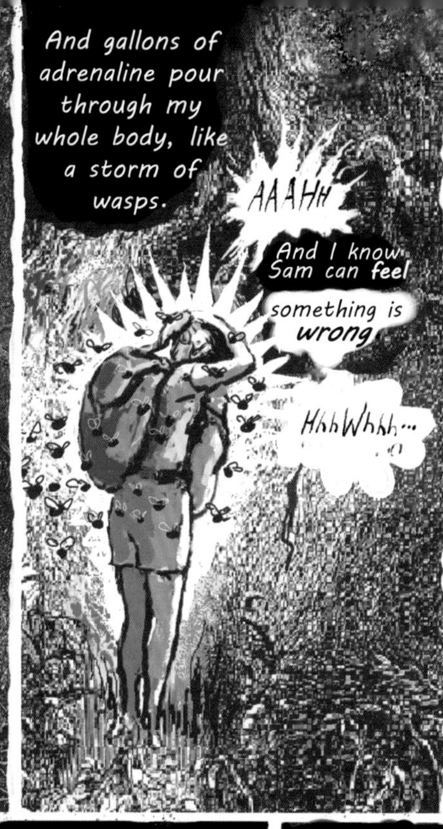

And gallons of adrenaline pour through my whole body, like a storm of wasps.
AAAHH
And I know Sam can feel something is wrong
HhhWhhh...

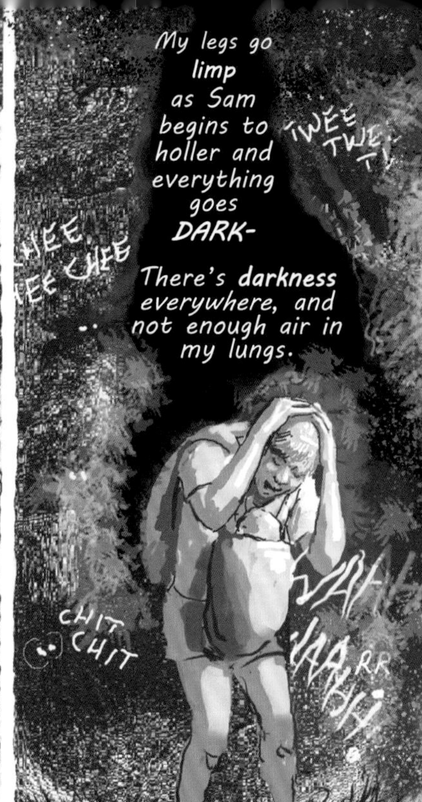

My legs go limp as Sam begins to holler and everything goes DARK-
There's darkness everywhere, and not enough air in my lungs.
TWEE TWEE
CHIT CHIT

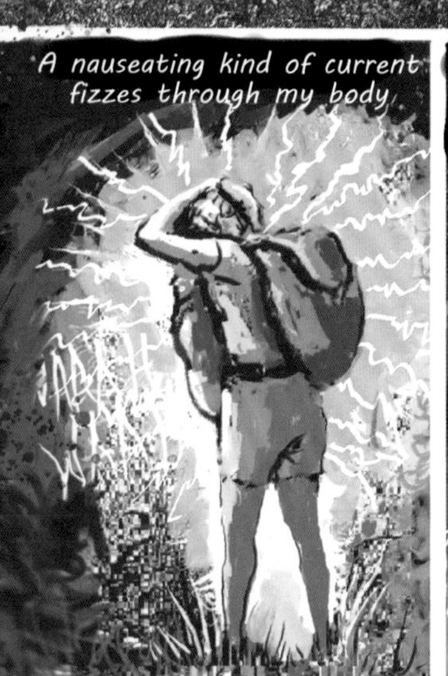

A nauseating kind of current fizzes through my body

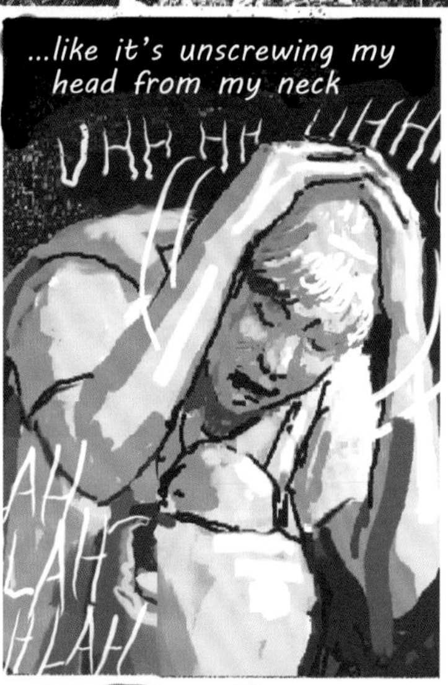

...like it's unscrewing my head from my neck
AH LAH LAH

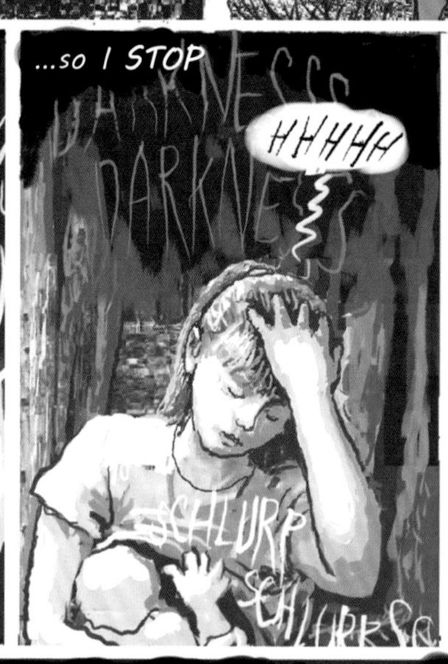

...so I STOP
DARKNESS DARKNESS
HHHHH
SCHLURP

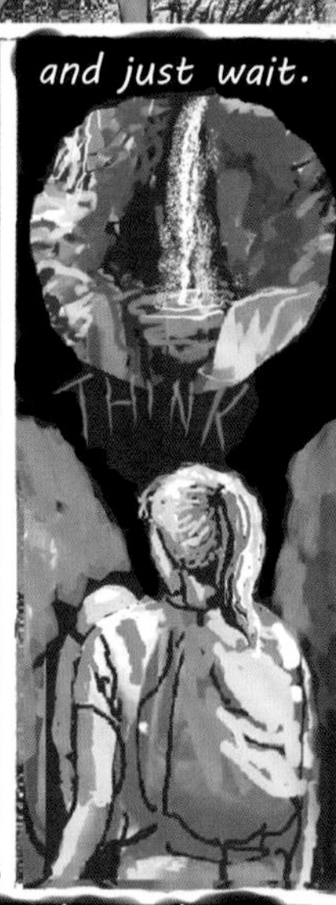

and just wait.
THINK

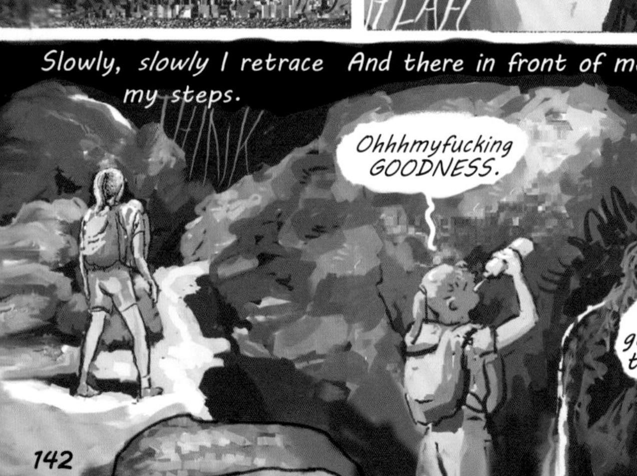

Slowly, slowly I retrace my steps.
And there in front of me ...is the spring I'd seen, but not seen
...gushing, clear, cold WATER
Ohhhmyfucking GOODNESS.
HALLELUJAH
Clean enough!
Please don't kill me, please
You're gonna like this, Sam
I think I remember reading... ...germs and bacteria in water are filtered out of breast milk
I don't care if it kills me!

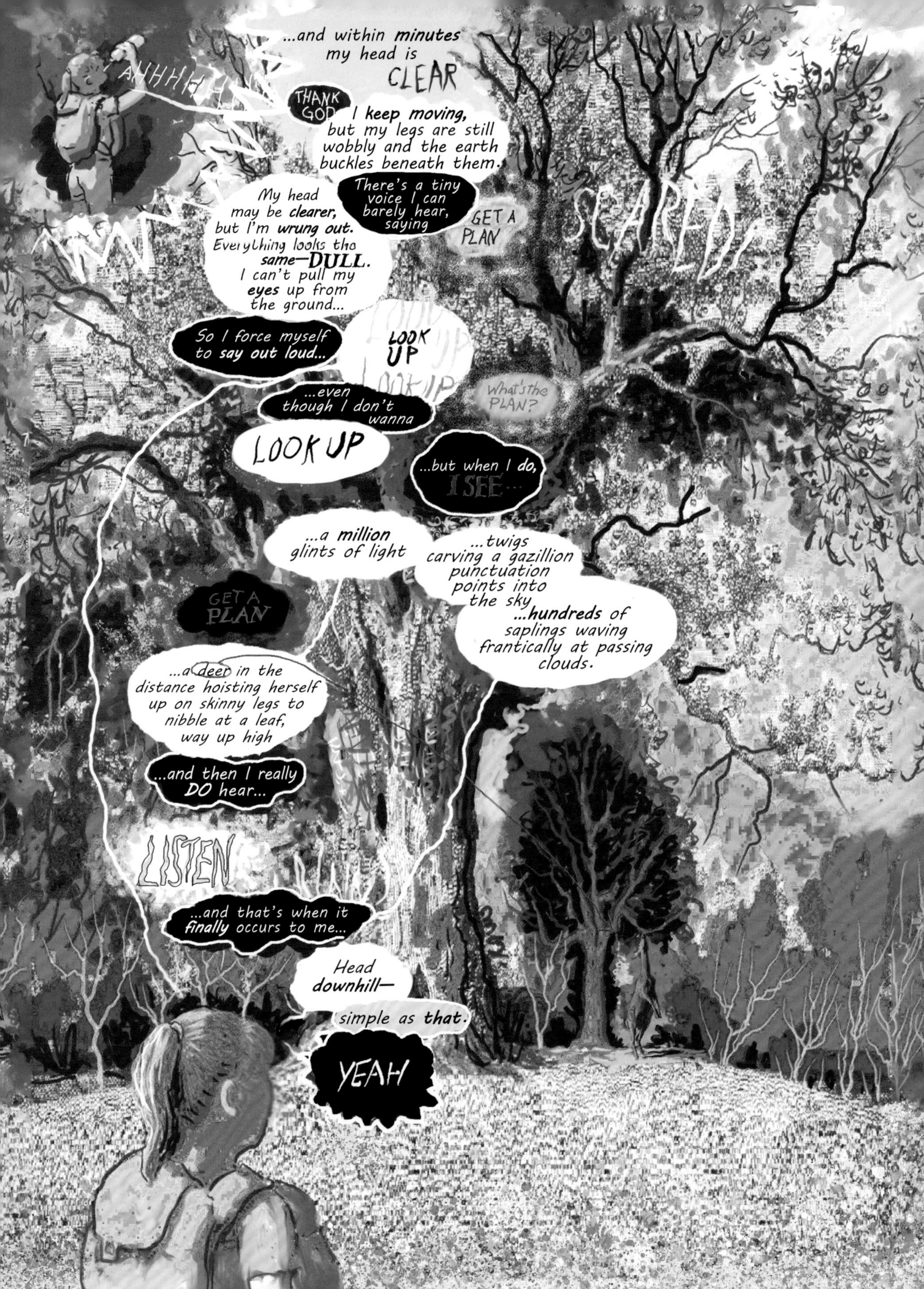
AHHHHHHHH
...and within minutes my head is CLEAR
THANK GOD
I keep moving, but my legs are still wobbly and the earth buckles beneath them.
SCARED
My head may be clearer, but I'm wrung out. Everything looks the same—DULL. I can't pull my eyes up from the ground...
There's a tiny voice I can barely hear, saying
GET A PLAN
So I force myself to say out loud...
LOOK UP
What's the PLAN?
...even though I don't wanna
LOOK UP
...but when I do, I SEE...
...a million glints of light
...twigs carving a gazillion punctuation points into the sky
...hundreds of saplings waving frantically at passing clouds.
GET A PLAN
...a deer in the distance hoisting herself up on skinny legs to nibble at a leaf, way up high
...and then I really DO hear...
LISTEN
...and that's when it finally occurs to me...
Head downhill—
simple as that.
YEAH

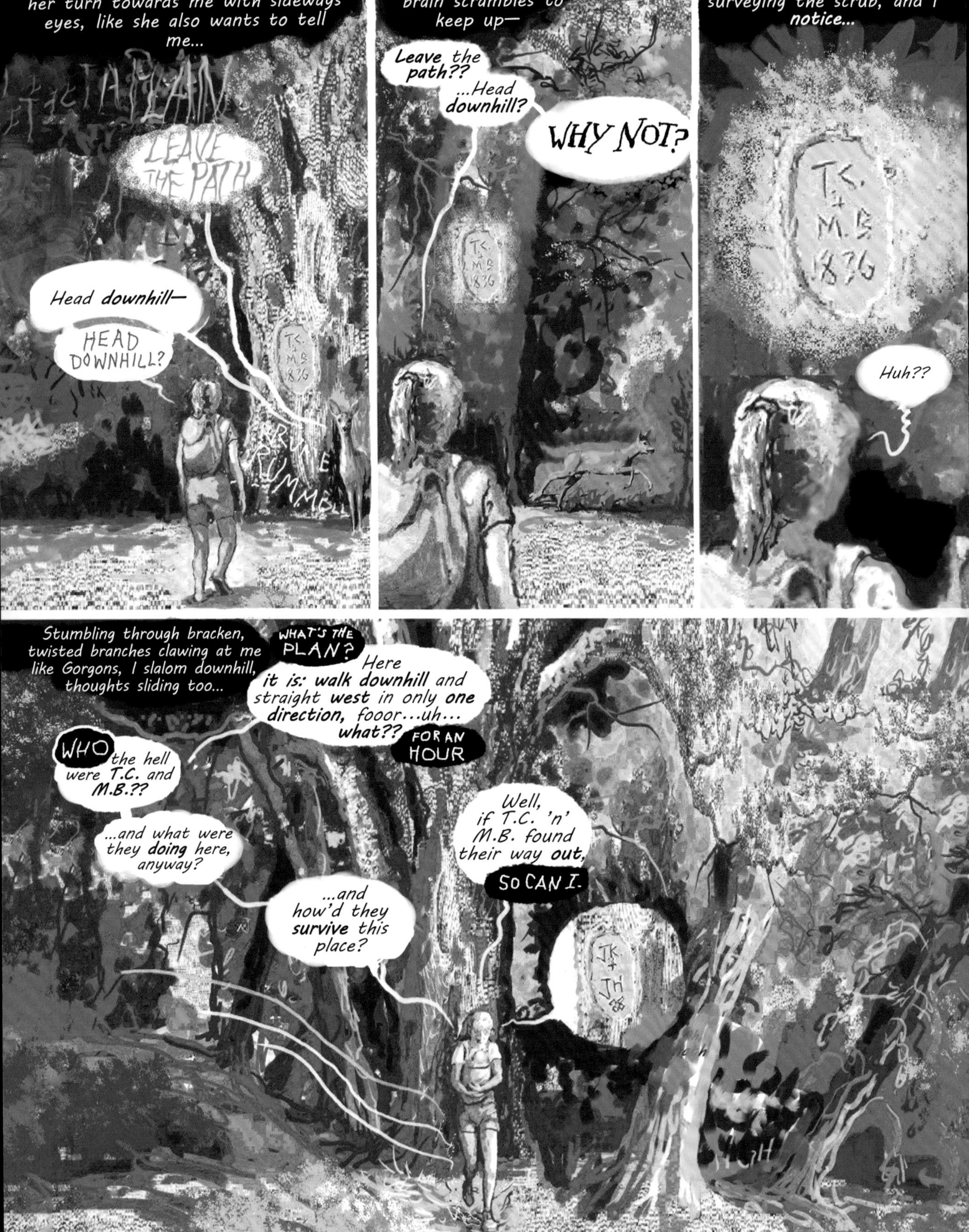
That deer in front of me? I watch her turn towards me with sideways eyes, like she also wants to tell me...
LEAVE THE PATH
Head downhill—
HEAD DOWNHILL?
T.C. + M.B 1836
As she leaps away, my brain scrambles to keep up—
Leave the path??
...Head downhill?
WHY NOT?
T.C. + M.B 1836
My eye sweeps around, surveying the scrub, and I notice...
T.C. + M.B 1836
Huh??
Stumbling through bracken, twisted branches clawing at me like Gorgons, I slalom downhill, thoughts sliding too...
WHAT'S THE PLAN?
Here it is: walk downhill and straight west in only one direction, fooor...uh... what??
FOR AN HOUR
WHO the hell were T.C. and M.B.??
...and what were they doing here, anyway?
...and how'd they survive this place?
Well, if T.C. 'n' M.B. found their way out,
SO CAN I.
JK + JH

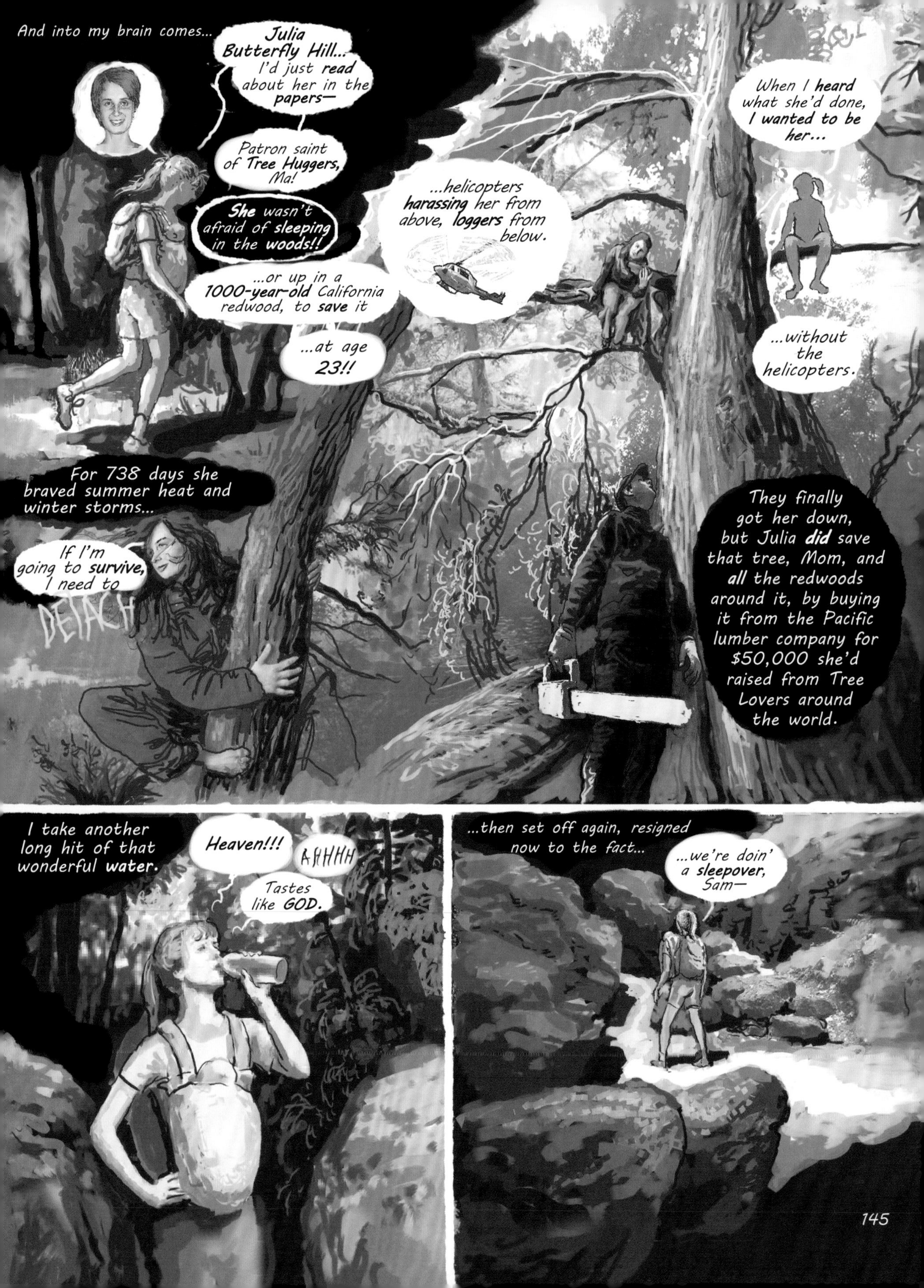

And into my brain comes...

Julia Butterfly Hill... I'd just **read** about her in the **papers—**

Patron saint of **Tree Huggers,** Ma!

She wasn't afraid of **sleeping** in the **woods!!**

...or up in a **1000-year-old** California redwood, to **save** it

...at age **23!!**

...helicopters **harassing** her from above, **loggers** from below.

When I **heard** what she'd done, **I wanted to be her...**

...without the helicopters.

For 738 days she braved summer heat and winter storms...

If I'm going to **survive,** I need to

DETACH

They finally got her down, but Julia **did** save that tree, Mom, and **all** the redwoods around it, by buying it from the Pacific lumber company for $50,000 she'd raised from Tree Lovers around the world.

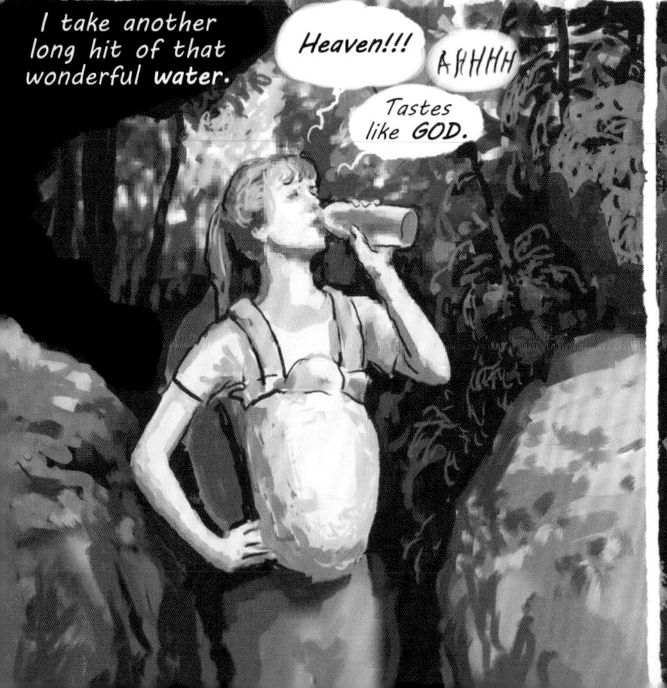

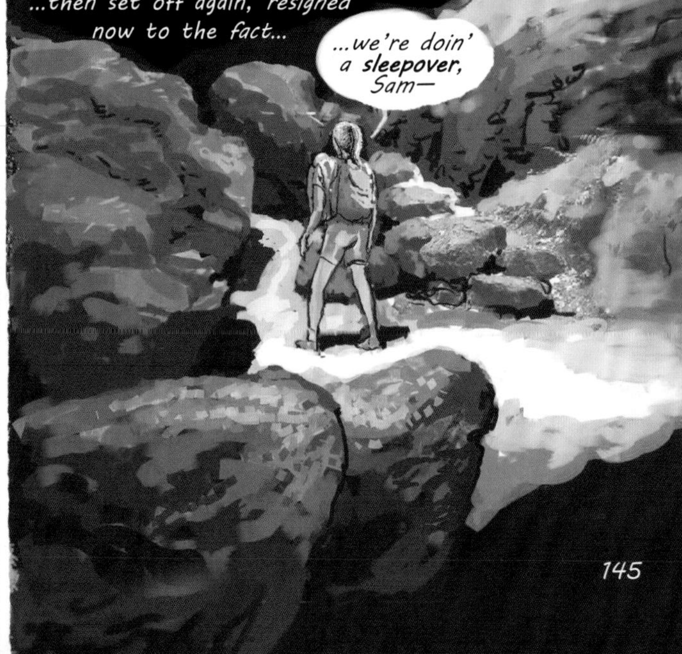

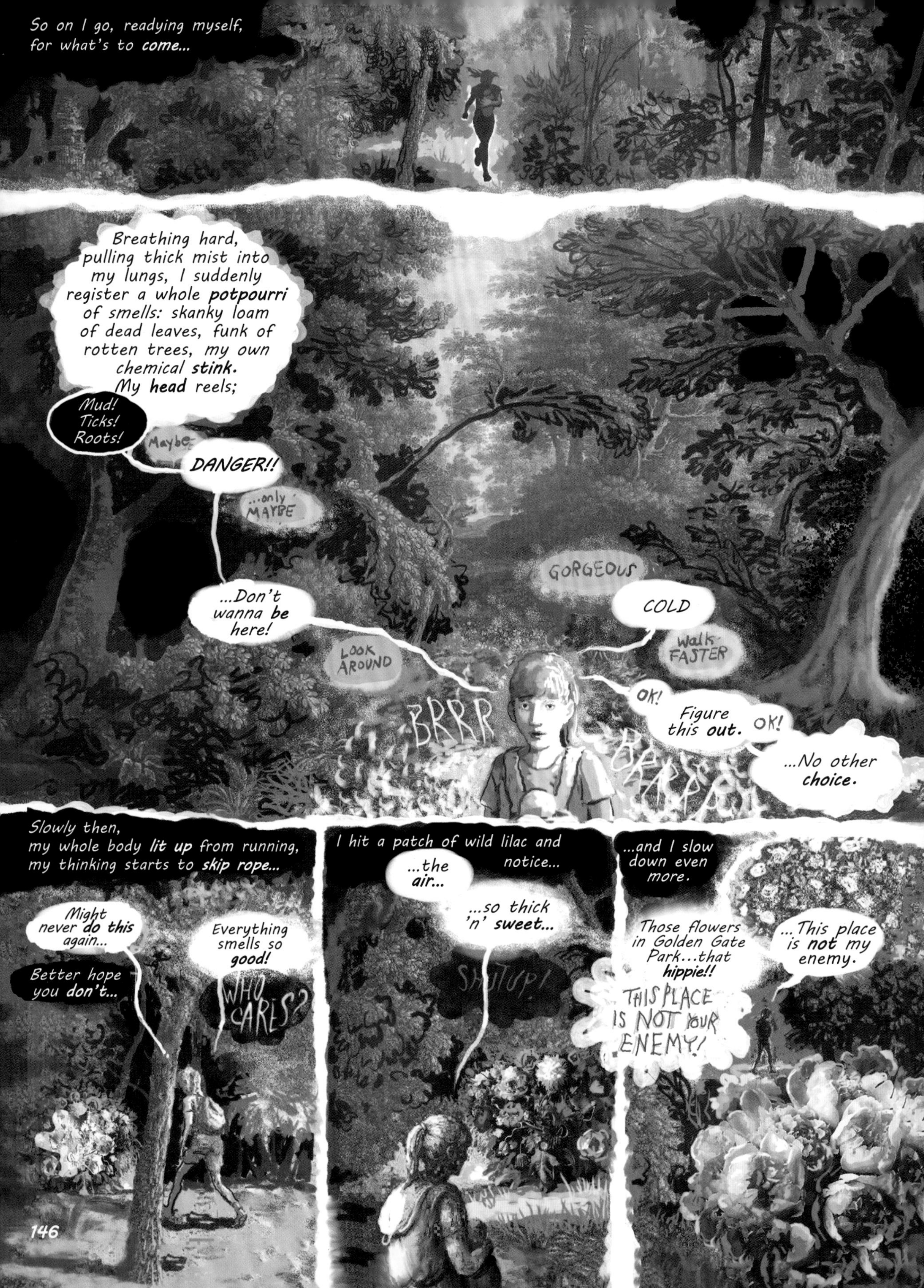
So on I go, readying myself, for what's to come...
Breathing hard, pulling thick mist into my lungs, I suddenly register a whole potpourri of smells: skanky loam of dead leaves, funk of rotten trees, my own chemical stink. My head reels;
Mud! Ticks! Roots!
Maybe
DANGER!!
...only MAYBE
...Don't wanna be here!
GORGEOUS
COLD
LOOK AROUND
Walk FASTER
BRRR
OK!
Figure this out.
OK!
...No other choice.
Slowly then, my whole body lit up from running, my thinking starts to skip rope...
Might never do this again...
Everything smells so good!
Better hope you don't...
WHO CARES?
I hit a patch of wild lilac and notice...
...the air...
...so thick 'n' sweet...
SHUTUP!
...and I slow down even more.
Those flowers in Golden Gate Park...that hippie!!
...This place is not my enemy.
THIS PLACE IS NOT YOUR ENEMY!

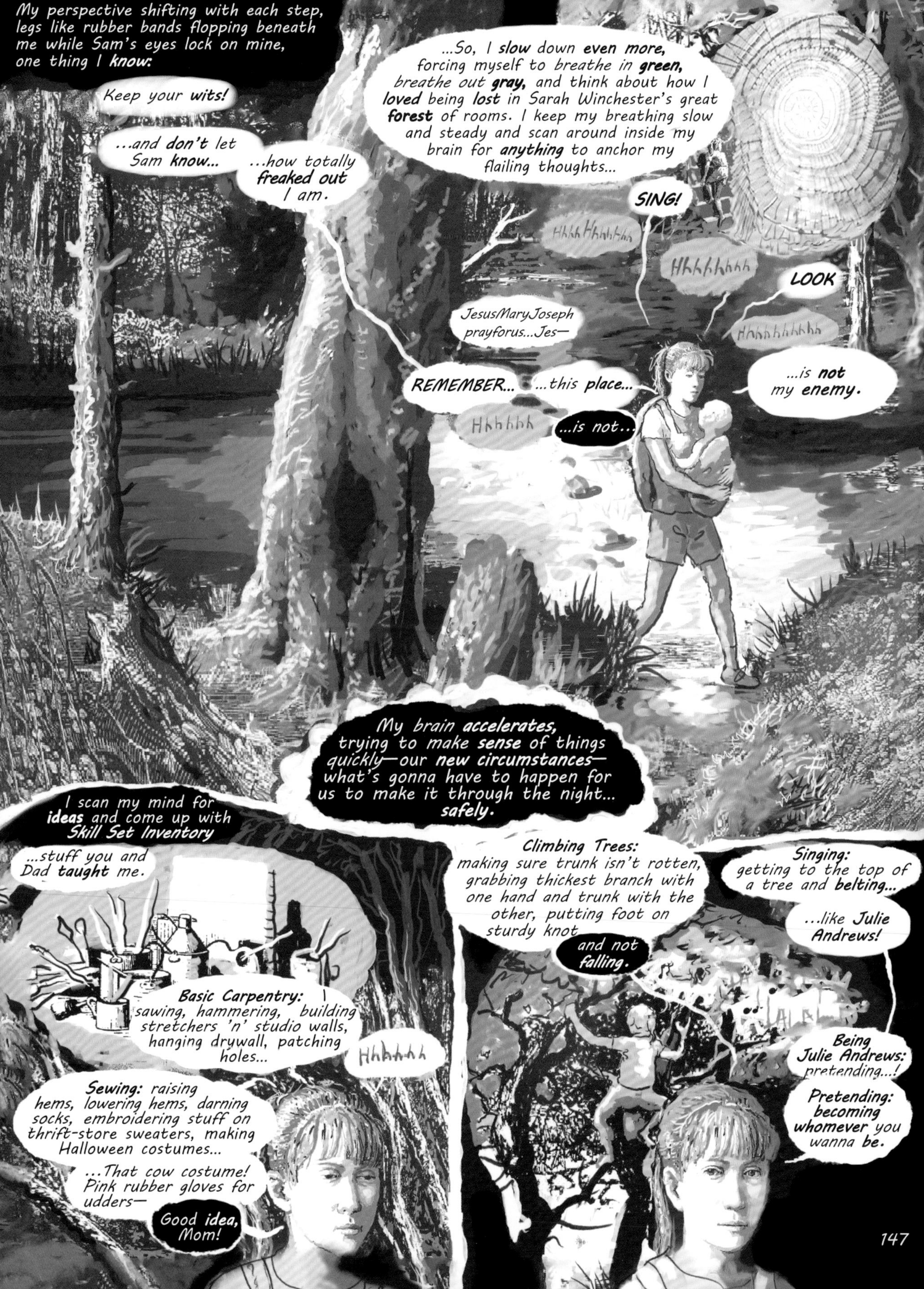
My perspective shifting with each step, legs like rubber bands flopping beneath me while Sam's eyes lock on mine, one thing I know:
Keep your wits!
...and don't let Sam know...
...how totally freaked out I am.
...So, I slow down even more, forcing myself to breathe in green, breathe out gray, and think about how I loved being lost in Sarah Winchester's great forest of rooms. I keep my breathing slow and steady and scan around inside my brain for anything to anchor my flailing thoughts...
Hhhhhhhhhh
SING!
Hhhhhhhh
LOOK
Hhhhhhhhh
JesusMaryJoseph prayforus...Jes—
REMEMBER...
...this place...
Hhhhhh
...is not...
...is not my enemy.
My brain accelerates, trying to make sense of things quickly—our new circumstances—what's gonna have to happen for us to make it through the night... safely.
I scan my mind for ideas and come up with Skill Set Inventory
...stuff you and Dad taught me.
Basic Carpentry: sawing, hammering, building stretchers 'n' studio walls, hanging drywall, patching holes...
Hhhhhh
Sewing: raising hems, lowering hems, darning socks, embroidering stuff on thrift-store sweaters, making Halloween costumes...
...That cow costume! Pink rubber gloves for udders—
Good idea, Mom!
Climbing Trees: making sure trunk isn't rotten, grabbing thickest branch with one hand and trunk with the other, putting foot on sturdy knot
and not falling.
Singing: getting to the top of a tree and belting...
...like Julie Andrews!
Being Julie Andrews: pretending...!
Pretending: becoming whomever you wanna be.

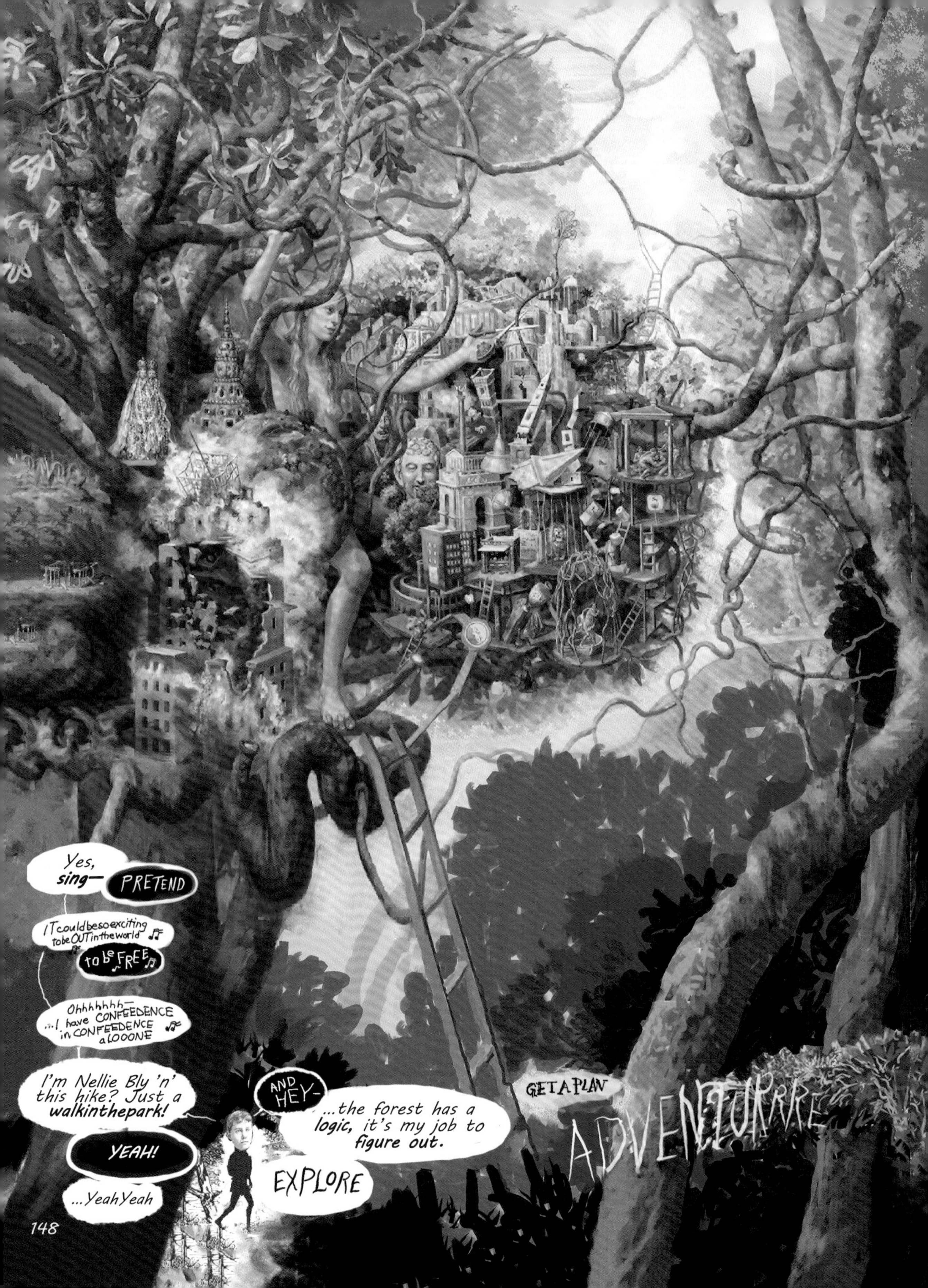

Yes, sing—
PRETEND
ITcouldbesoexciting tobeOUTintheworld
to be FREE
Ohhhhhhh— ...I have CONFEEDENCE in CONFEEDENCE aLOOONE
I'm Nellie Bly 'n' this hike? Just a walkinthepark!
YEAH!
...YeahYeah
AND HEY-
...the forest has a logic, it's my job to figure out.
EXPLORE
GETAPLAN
ADVENTURRRE

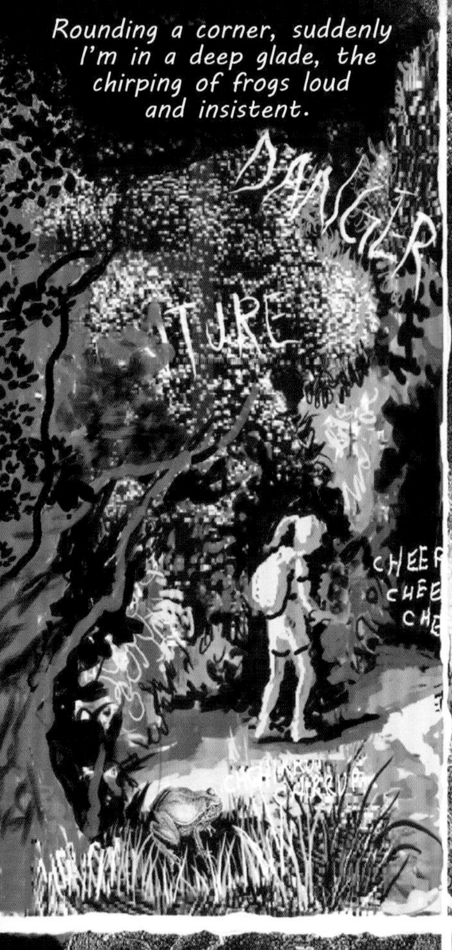
Rounding a corner, suddenly I'm in a deep glade, the chirping of frogs loud and insistent.
DANGER

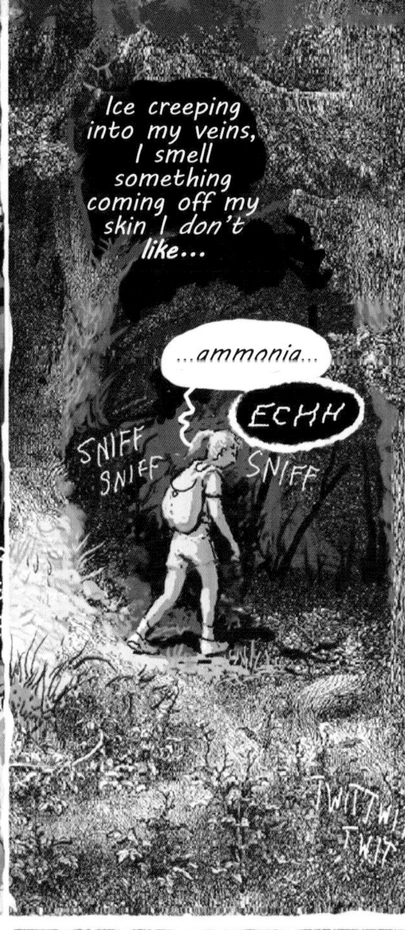
Ice creeping into my veins, I smell something coming off my skin I don't **like**...
...ammonia...
ECHH
SNIFF SNIFF
SNIFF

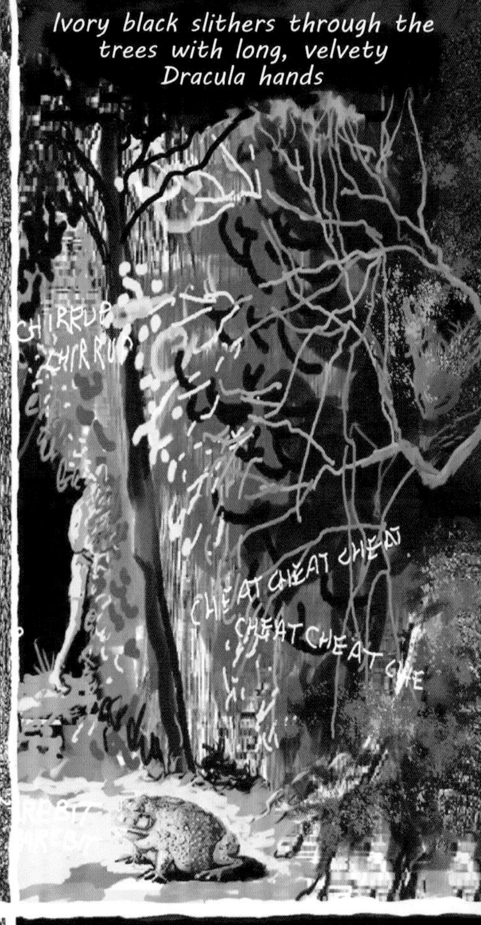
Ivory black slithers through the trees with long, velvety Dracula hands
CHEAT CHEAT CHEAT
CHEAT CHEAT CHEAT CHE

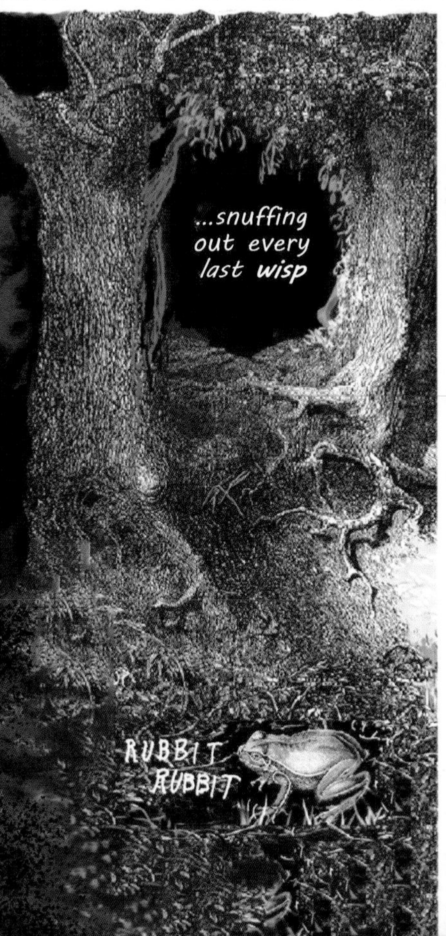
...snuffing out every last **wisp**
RUBBIT RUBBIT

...of **LIGHT**.

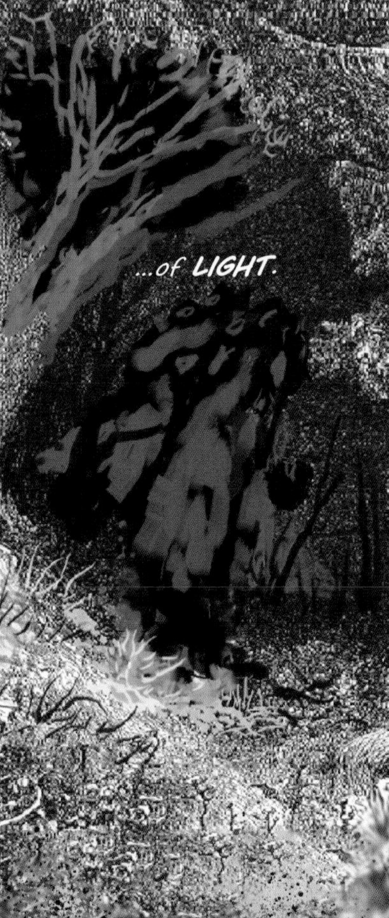

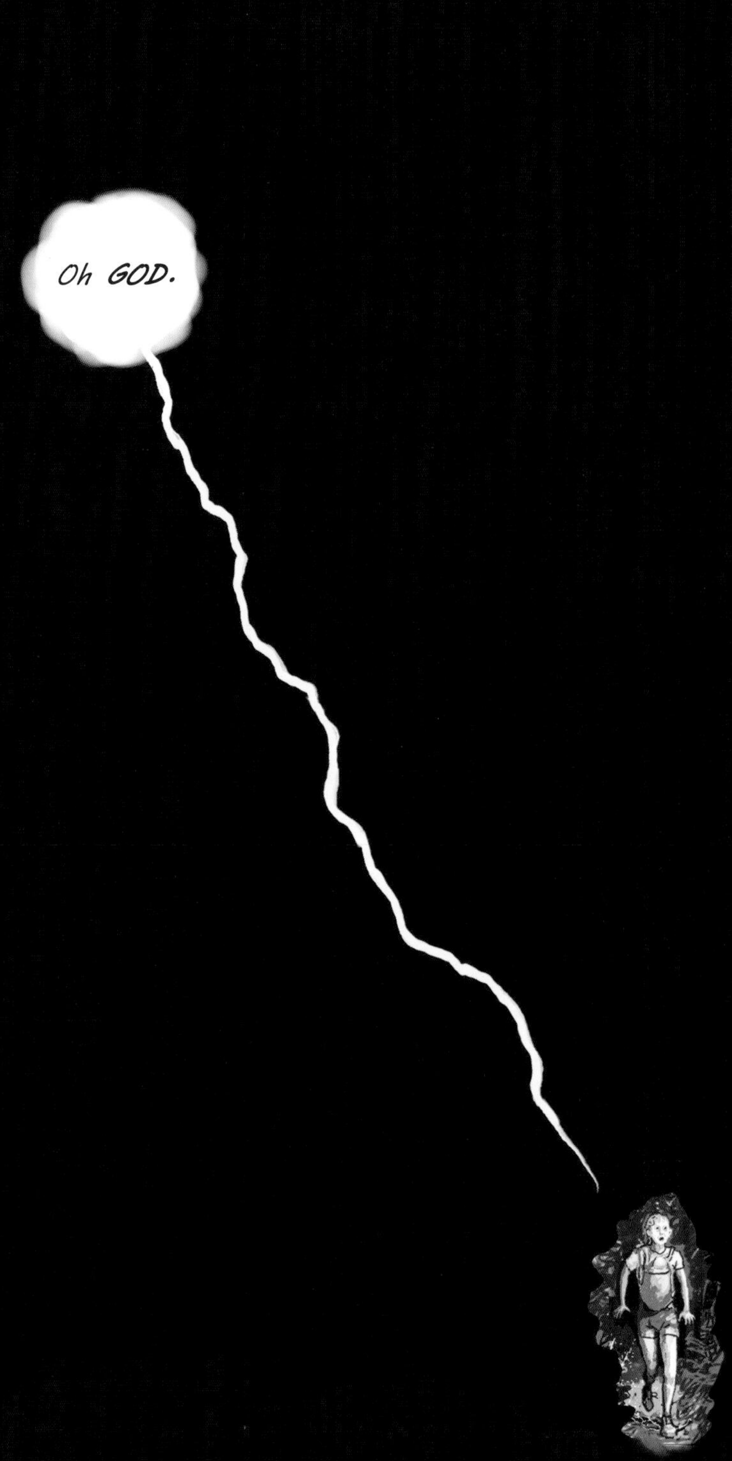
Oh GOD.

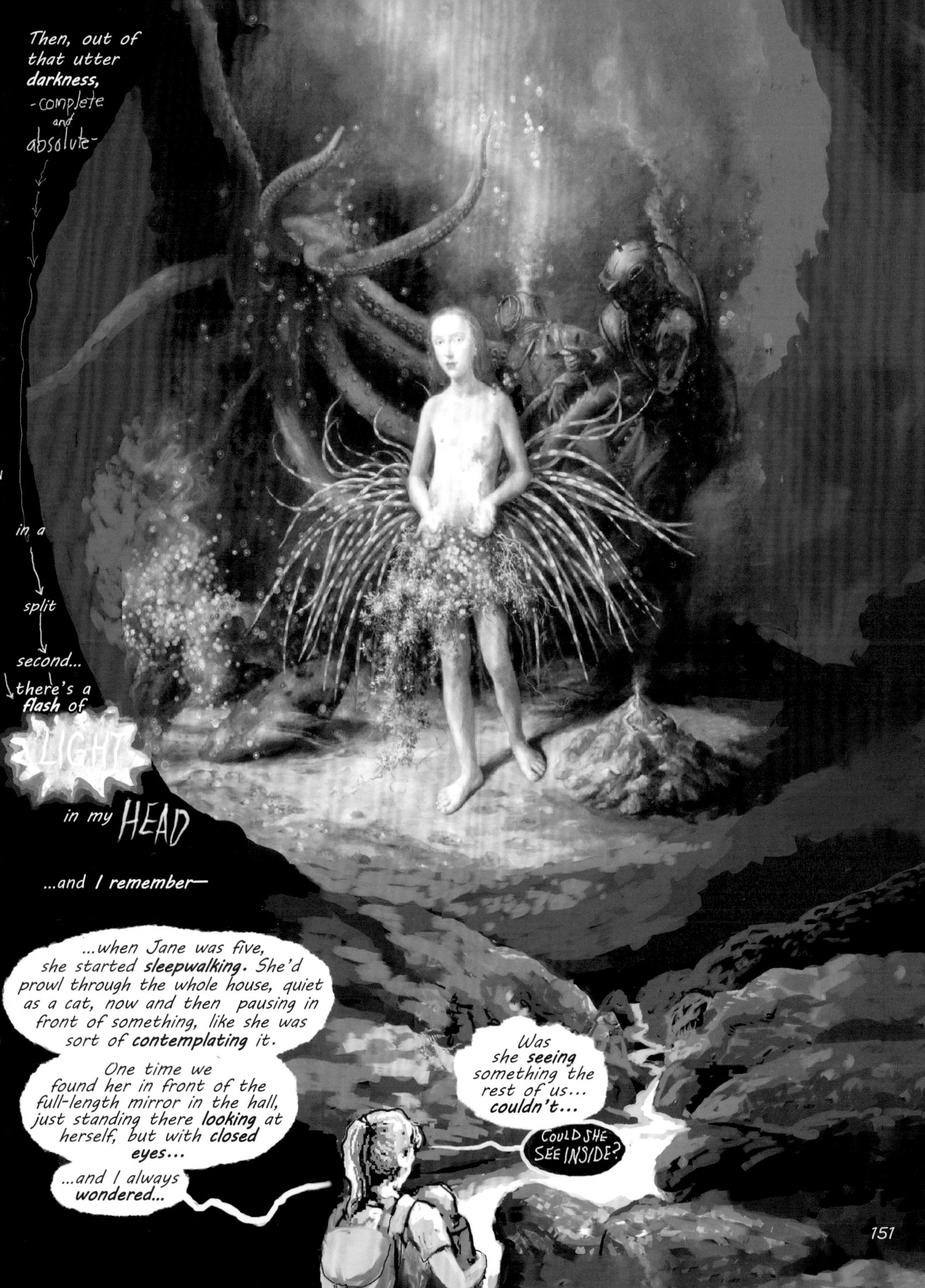
Then, out of that utter darkness,
-complete and absolute-
in a
split
second...
there's a flash of
LIGHT
in my HEAD
...and I remember—
...when Jane was five, she started sleepwalking. She'd prowl through the whole house, quiet as a cat, now and then pausing in front of something, like she was sort of contemplating it.
One time we found her in front of the full-length mirror in the hall, just standing there looking at herself, but with closed eyes...
...and I always wondered...
Was she seeing something the rest of us... couldn't...
COULD SHE SEE INSIDE?

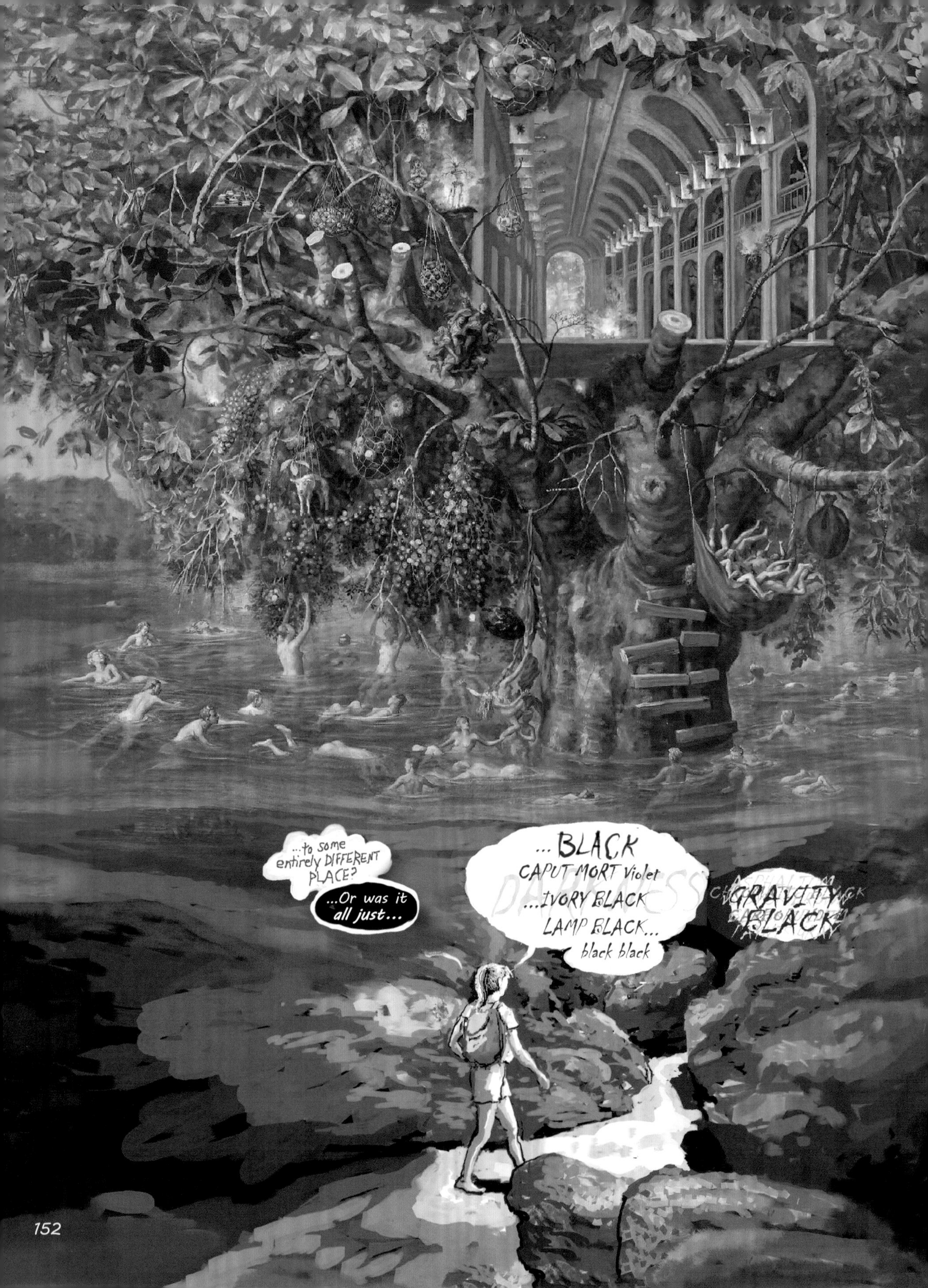
...to some entirely DIFFERENT PLACE?
...Or was it all just...
...BLACK
CAPUT MORT Violet
DARKNESS
...IVORY BLACK
LAMP BLACK...
black black
ASPHALTUM
GRAVITY BLACK

Chapter EIGHT

Feet *aching*, saying

we're DONE

—finished, *finito*—I stumble my way through DARKNESS, following the silhouette of the tree canopy against a silver sky, mapping a path through the *void* in front of me.

I'm trying hard to stay calm,

but it's not *working*.

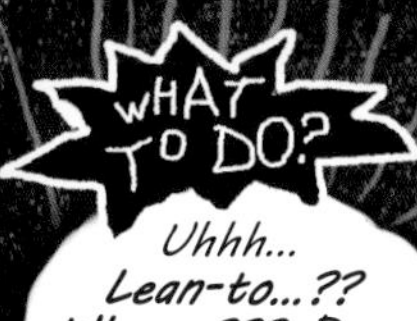

Uhhh... **Lean-to...??** ***Whaa—???*** Prop some sticks up...? That's ***it***? What ***else??***

I don't KNOW

so TIRED

fucking HOPELESS

GROANNN

huff huff huff YAWN

OH SAM

I'M SORRY

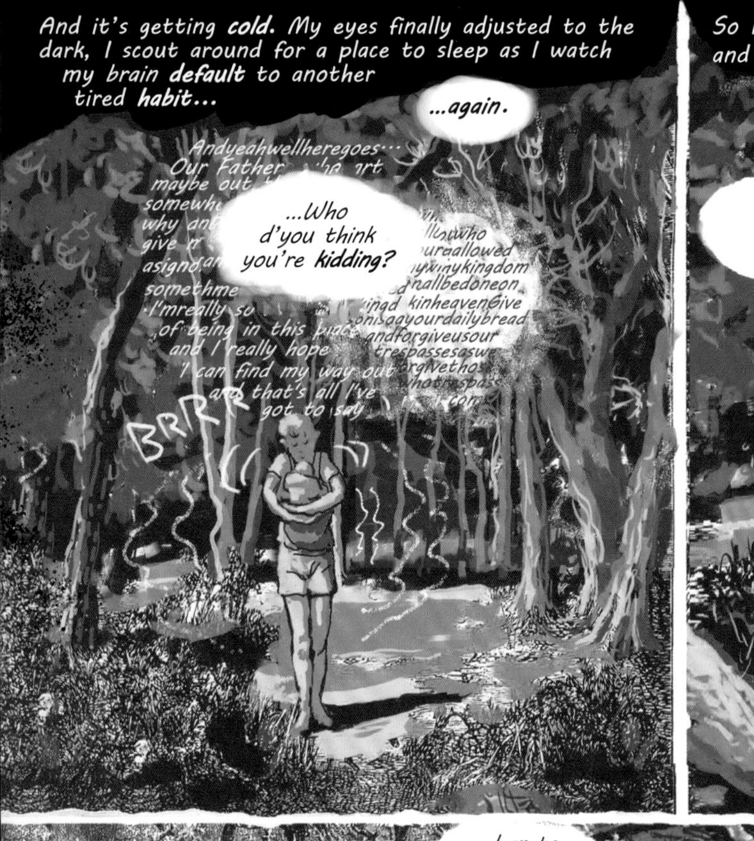

And it's getting **cold**. My eyes finally adjusted to the dark, I scout around for a place to sleep as I watch my brain **default** to another tired **habit**...
...again.
Andyeahwellheregoes...
...Who d'you think you're **kidding?**
and I really hope I can find my way out and that's all I've got to say
BRRR

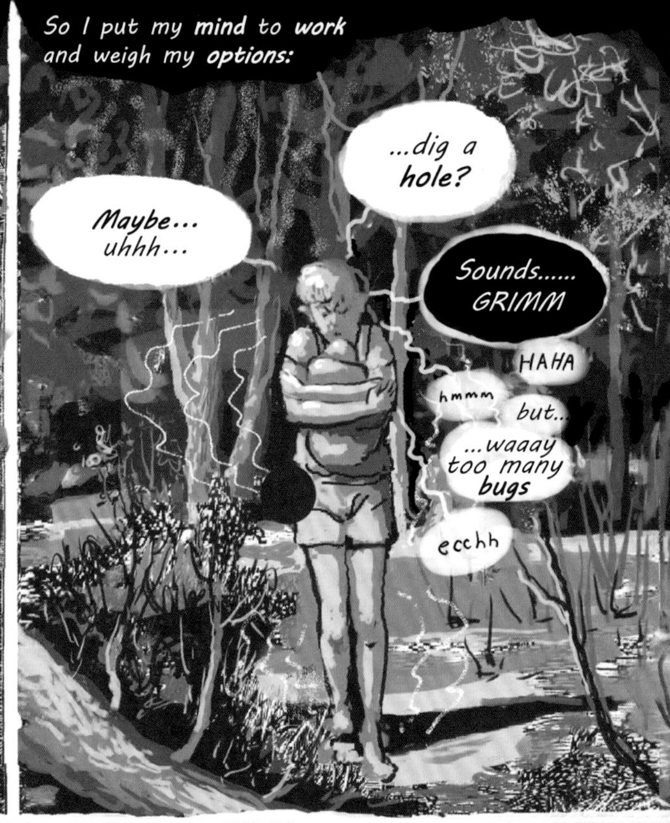

So I put my **mind** to **work** and weigh my **options:**
Maybe... uhhh...
...dig a **hole?**
Sounds...... GRIMM
HAHA
hmmm
but...
...waaay too many **bugs**
ecchh

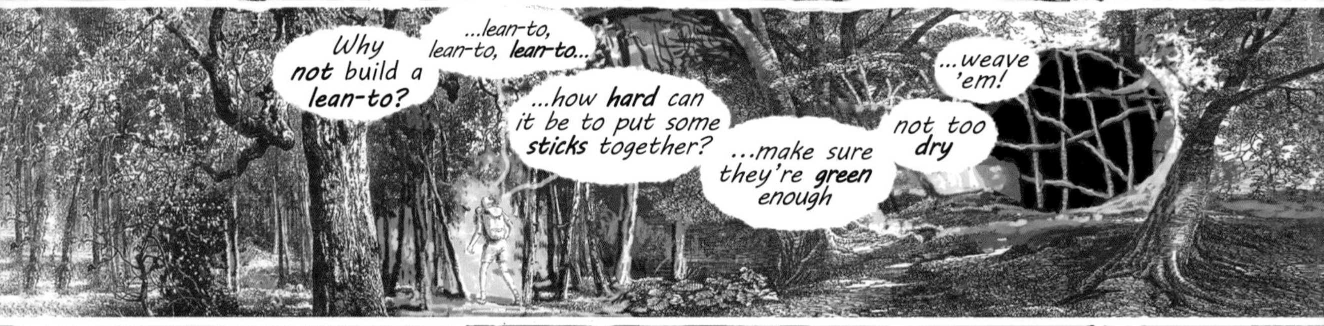

Why **not** build a **lean-to?**
...lean-to, lean-to, **lean-to...**
...how **hard** can it be to put some **sticks** together?
...make sure they're **green** enough
not too **dry**
...weave 'em!

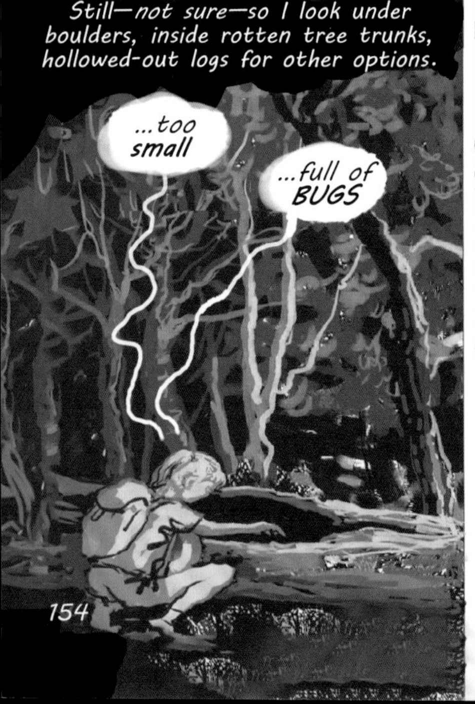

Still—*not sure*—so I look under boulders, inside rotten tree trunks, hollowed-out logs for other options.
...too **small**
...full of **BUGS**

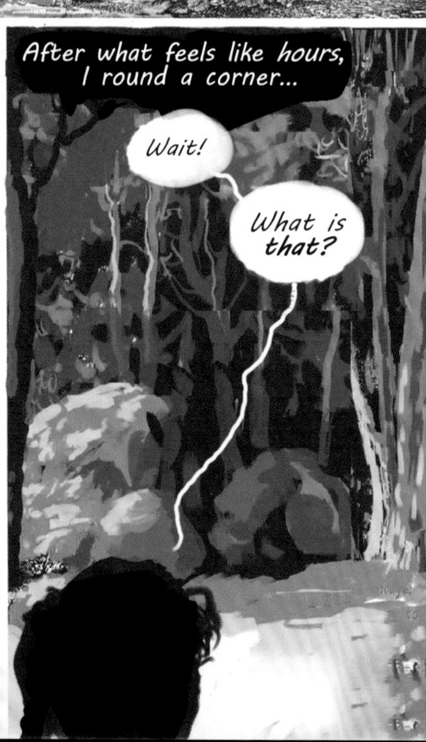

After what feels like hours, I round a corner...
Wait!
What is **that?**

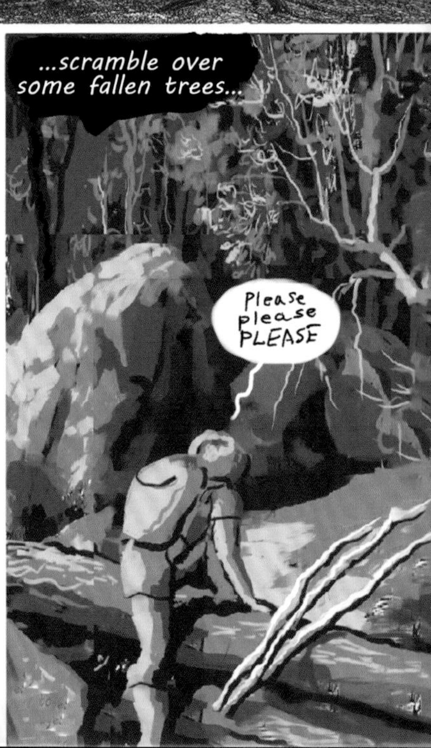

...scramble over some fallen trees...
Please please PLEASE

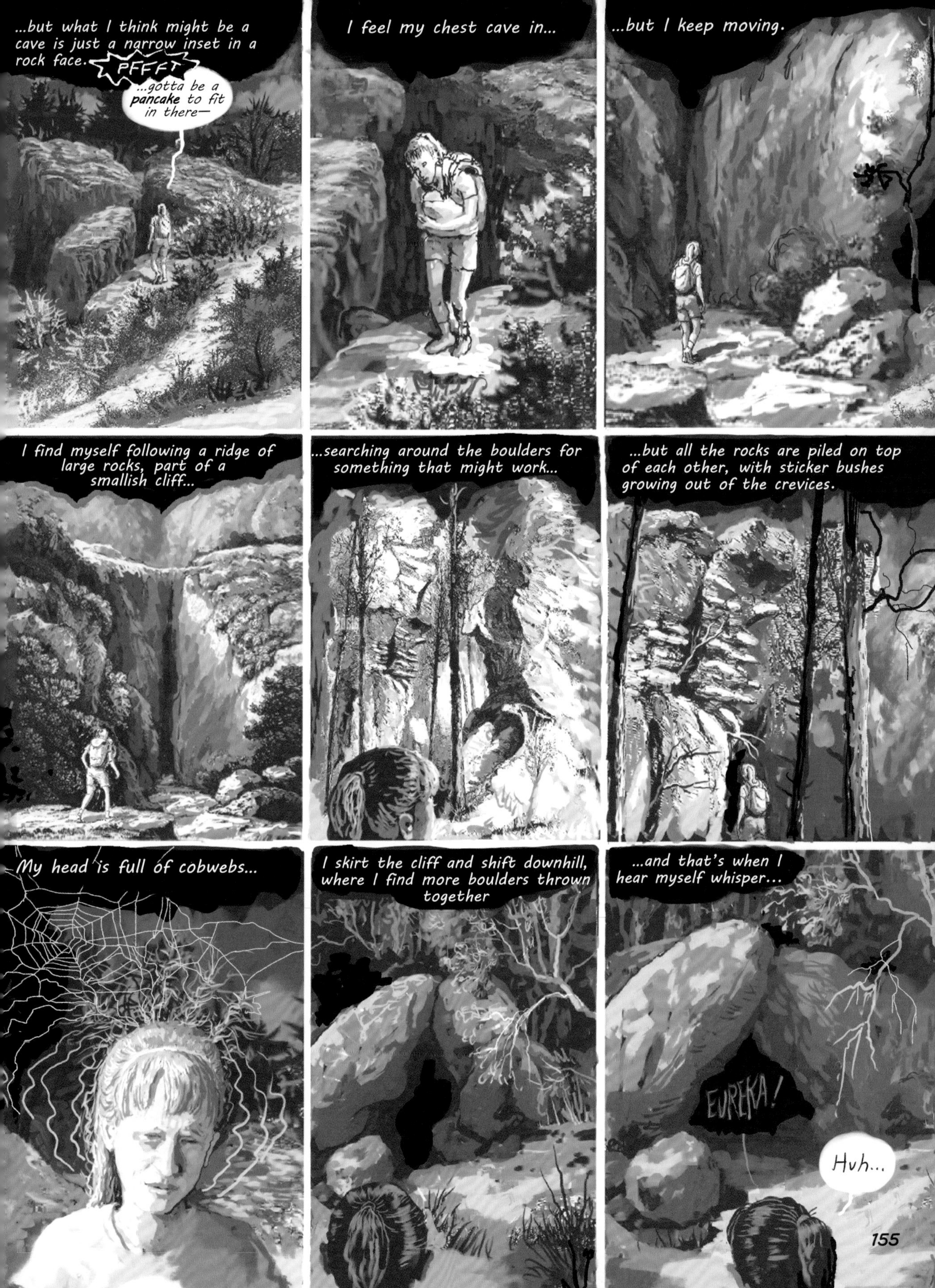

...but what I think might be a cave is just a narrow inset in a rock face.
PFFFT
...gotta be a pancake to fit in there—
I feel my chest cave in...
...but I keep moving.
I find myself following a ridge of large rocks, part of a smallish cliff...
...searching around the boulders for something that might work...
...but all the rocks are piled on top of each other, with sticker bushes growing out of the crevices.
My head is full of cobwebs...
I skirt the cliff and shift downhill, where I find more boulders thrown together
...and that's when I hear myself whisper...
EUREKA!
Huh...

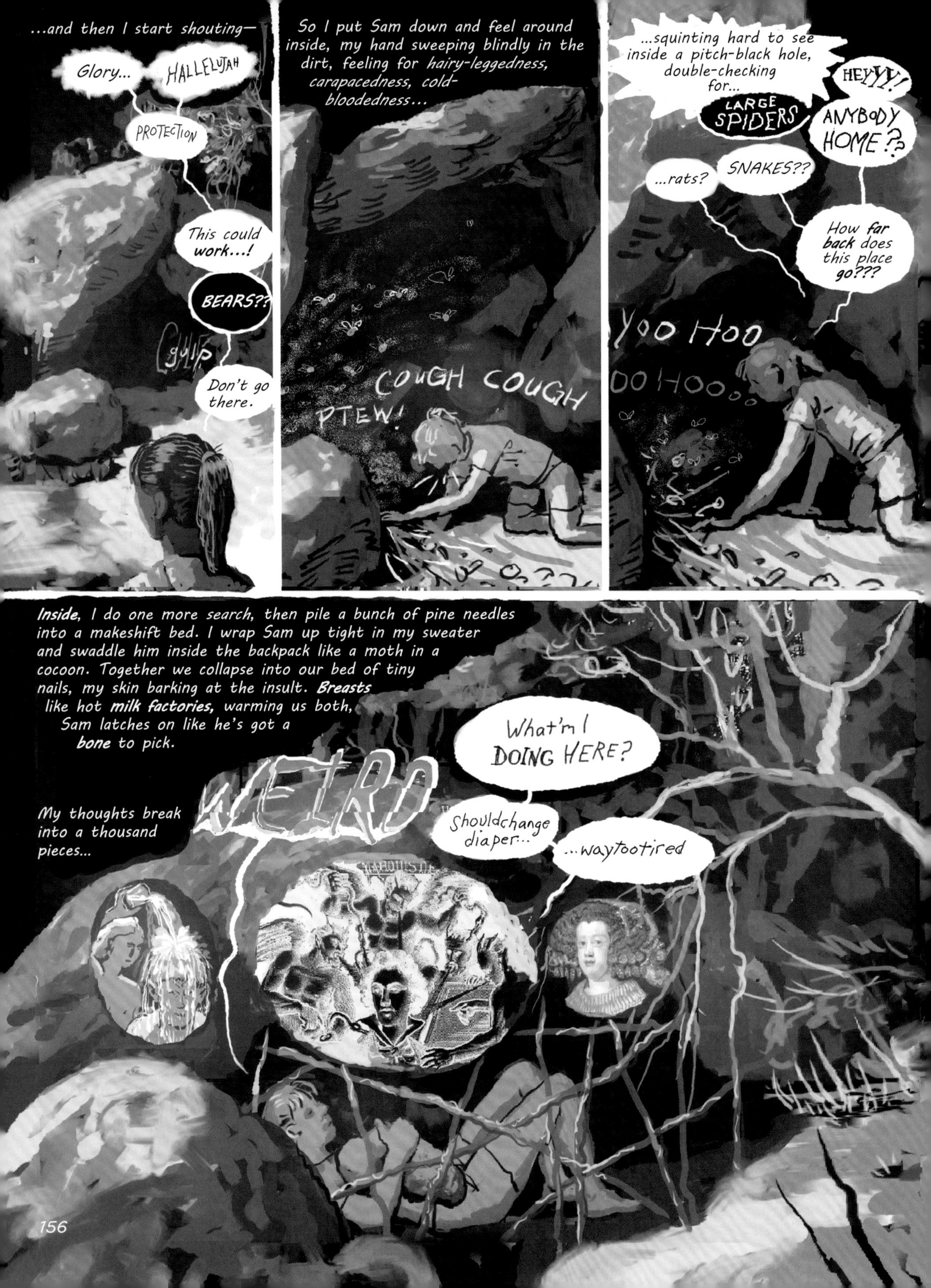

...and then I start shouting—

Glory...

HALLELUJAH

PROTECTION

This could **work...!**

BEARS??

gulp

Don't go there.

So I put Sam down and feel around inside, my hand sweeping blindly in the dirt, feeling for hairy-leggedness, carapacedness, cold-bloodedness...

COUGH COUGH

PTEW!

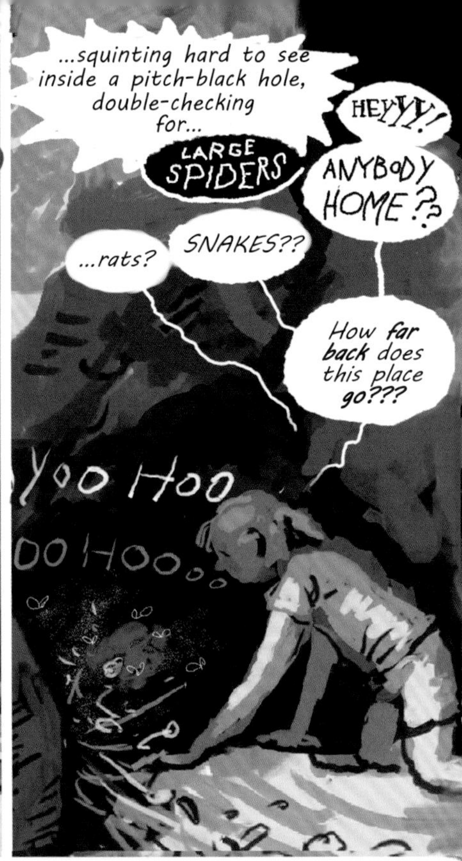

Inside, I do one more search, then pile a bunch of pine needles into a makeshift bed. I wrap Sam up tight in my sweater and swaddle him inside the backpack like a moth in a cocoon. Together we collapse into our bed of tiny nails, my skin barking at the insult. ***Breasts*** like hot ***milk factories,*** warming us both, Sam latches on like he's got a ***bone*** to pick.

What'm I DOING HERE?

WEIRD

My thoughts break into a thousand pieces...

Shouldchange diaper...

...waytootired

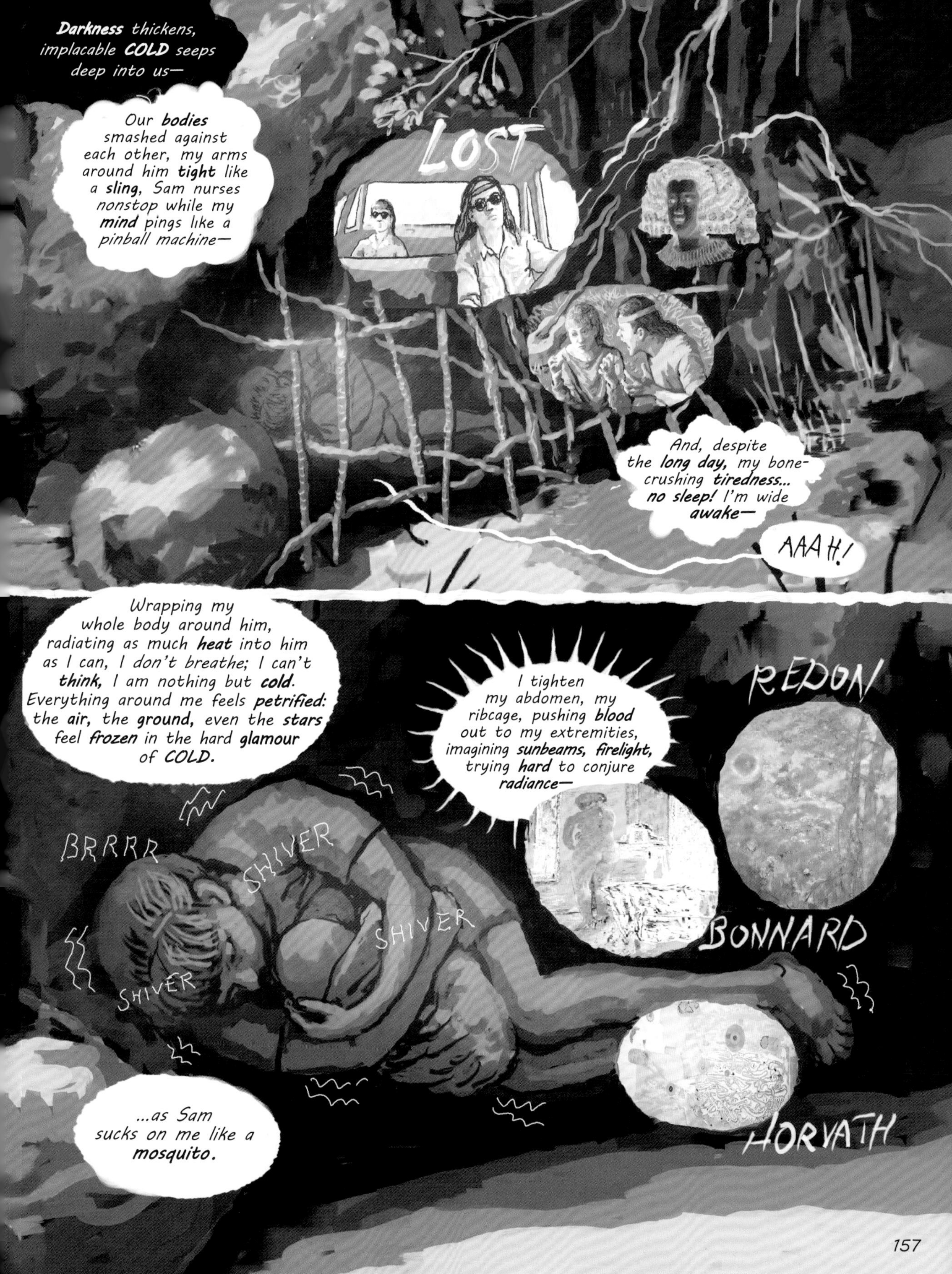
Darkness thickens, implacable COLD seeps deep into us—
Our bodies smashed against each other, my arms around him tight like a sling, Sam nurses nonstop while my mind pings like a pinball machine—
LOST
And, despite the long day, my bone-crushing tiredness... no sleep! I'm wide awake—
AAAH!
Wrapping my whole body around him, radiating as much heat into him as I can, I don't breathe; I can't think, I am nothing but cold. Everything around me feels petrified: the air, the ground, even the stars feel frozen in the hard glamour of COLD.
I tighten my abdomen, my ribcage, pushing blood out to my extremities, imagining sunbeams, firelight, trying hard to conjure radiance—
REDON
BRRRR
SHIVER
SHIVER
SHIVER
BONNARD
...as Sam sucks on me like a mosquito.
HORVATH

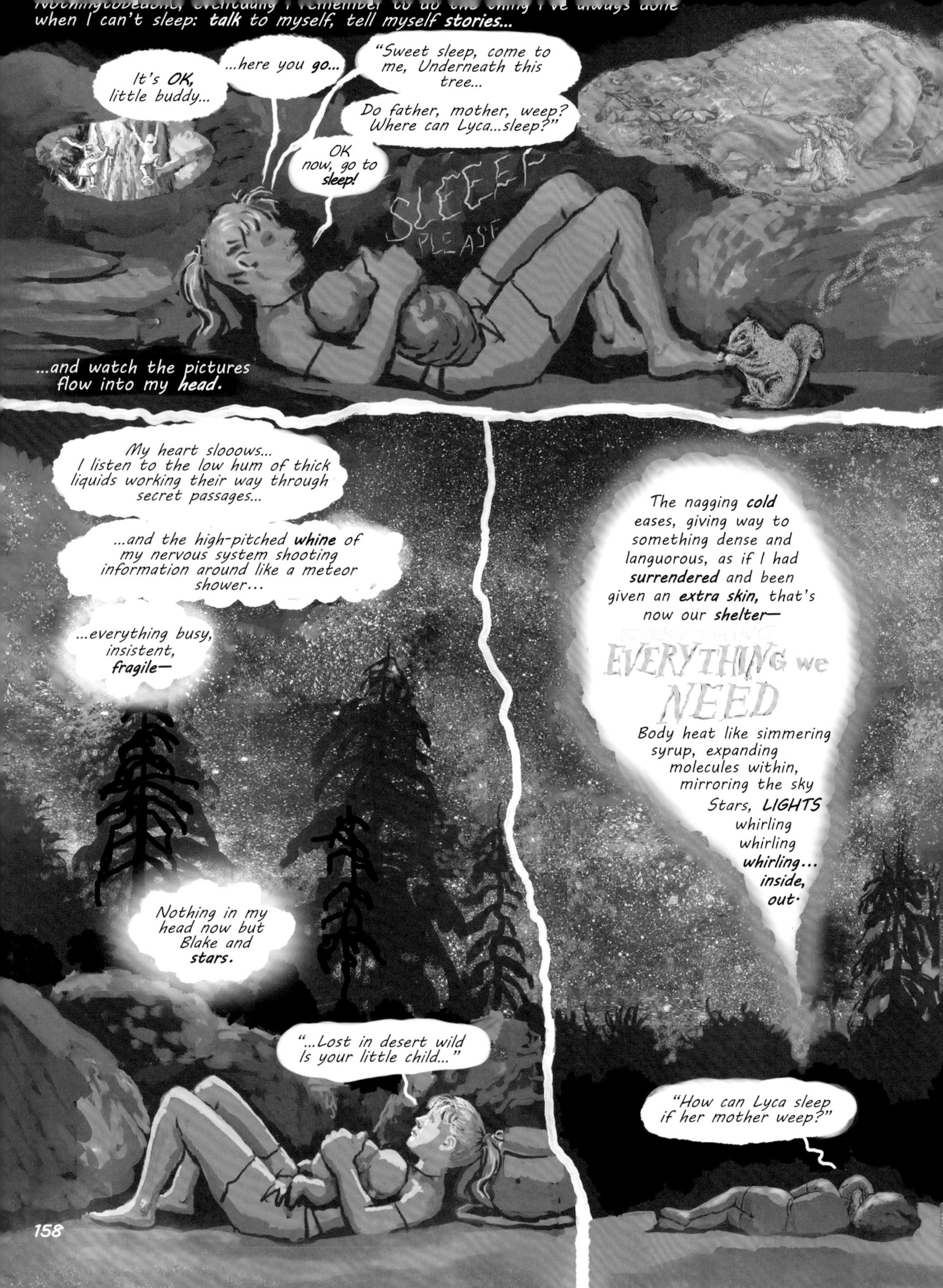
when I can't sleep: **talk** to myself, tell myself **stories...**
It's **OK,** little buddy...
...here you **go...**
"Sweet sleep, come to me, Underneath this tree...
Do father, mother, weep? Where can Lyca...sleep?"
OK now, go to **sleep!**
SLEEEP
PLEASE
...and watch the pictures flow into my **head.**
My heart slooows... I listen to the low hum of thick liquids working their way through secret passages...
...and the high-pitched **whine** of my nervous system shooting information around like a meteor shower...
...everything busy, insistent, **fragile—**
The nagging **cold** eases, giving way to something dense and languorous, as if I had **surrendered** and been given an **extra skin,** that's now our **shelter—**
EVERYTHING we NEED
Body heat like simmering syrup, expanding molecules within, mirroring the sky
Stars, **LIGHTS** whirling whirling **whirling... inside, out.**
Nothing in my head now but Blake and **stars.**
"...Lost in desert wild Is your little child..."
"How can Lyca sleep if her mother weep?"

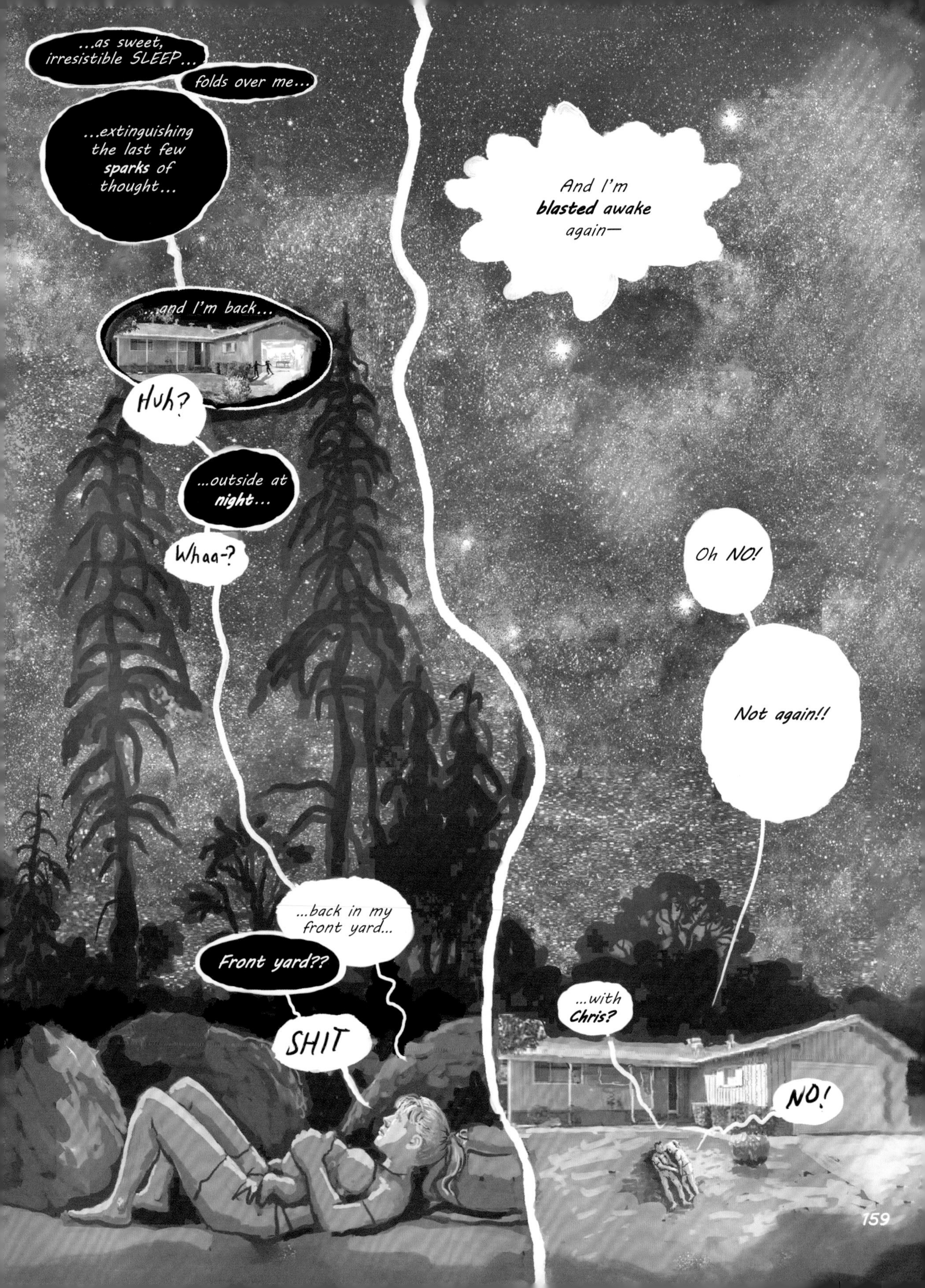

...as sweet, irresistible SLEEP...

folds over me...

...extinguishing the last few **sparks** of thought...

...and I'm back...

Huh?

...outside at **night**...

Whaa-?

...back in my front yard...

Front yard??

SHIT

And I'm **blasted awake** again—

Oh NO!

Not again!!

...with **Chris?**

NO!

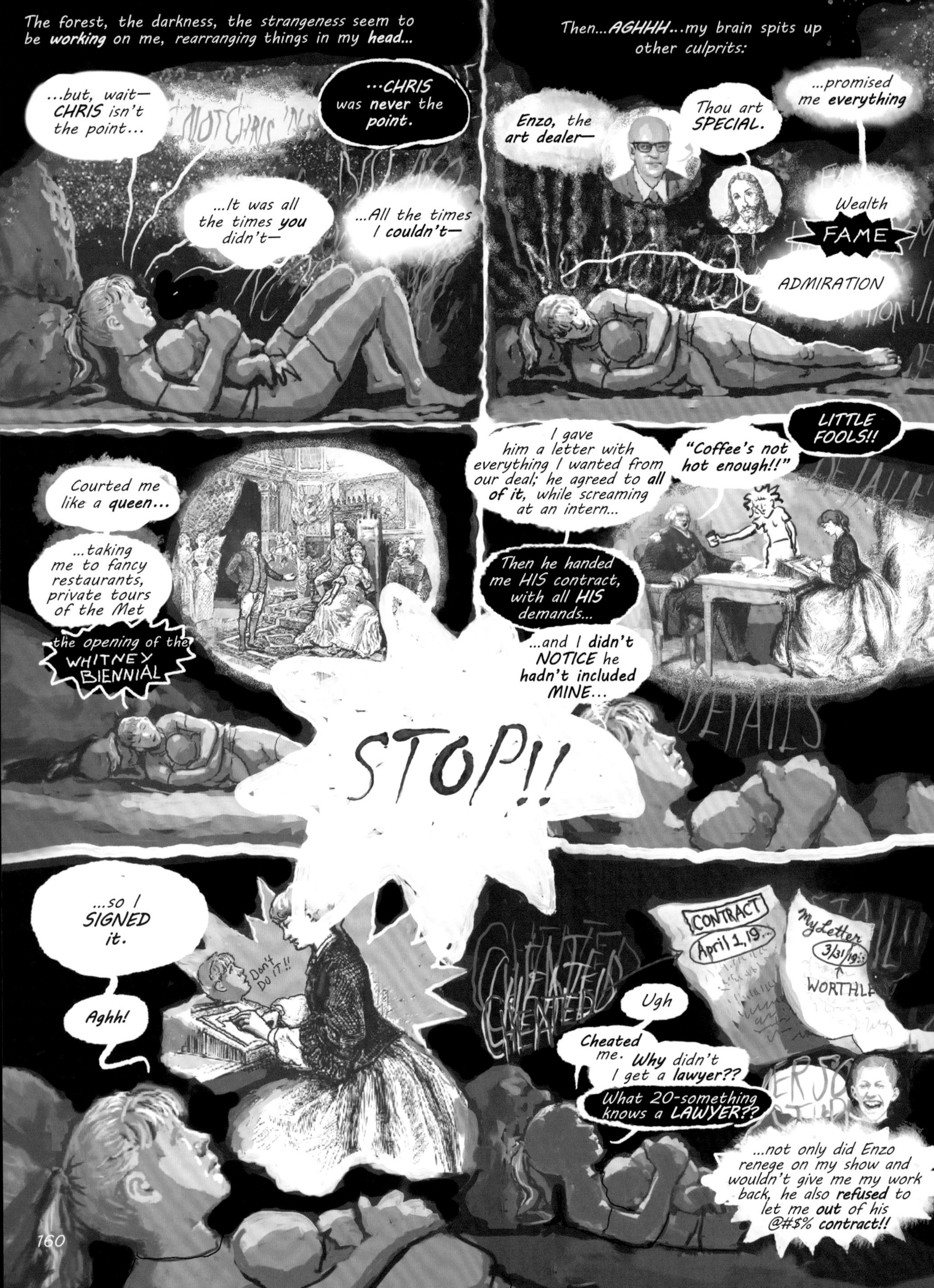
The forest, the darkness, the strangeness seem to be **working** on me, rearranging things in my **head**...
...but, wait— **CHRIS** isn't the point...
...**CHRIS** was **never** the **point.**
...It was all the times **you** didn't—
...All the times I **couldn't**—
Then...**AGHHH**...my brain spits up other culprits:
Enzo, the **art dealer**—
Thou art **SPECIAL.**
...promised me **everything**
Wealth
FAME
ADMIRATION
Courted me like a **queen**...
...taking me to fancy restaurants, private tours of the Met
the opening of the WHITNEY BIENNIAL
I gave him a letter with everything I wanted from our deal; he agreed to **all of it,** while screaming at an intern...
"Coffee's not hot enough!!"
LITTLE FOOLS!!
Then he handed me HIS contract, with all **HIS** demands...
...and I **didn't NOTICE** he **hadn't included MINE**...
STOP!!
...so I **SIGNED it.**
Don't DO IT!!
Aghh!
CONTRACT
April 1, 19...
My Letter
3/31/19...
WORTHLE
Ugh
Cheated me. **Why** didn't I get a **lawyer??**
What 20-something knows a **LAWYER??**
...not only did Enzo renege on my show and wouldn't give me my work back, he also **refused** to let me **out** of his @#$% **contract!!**

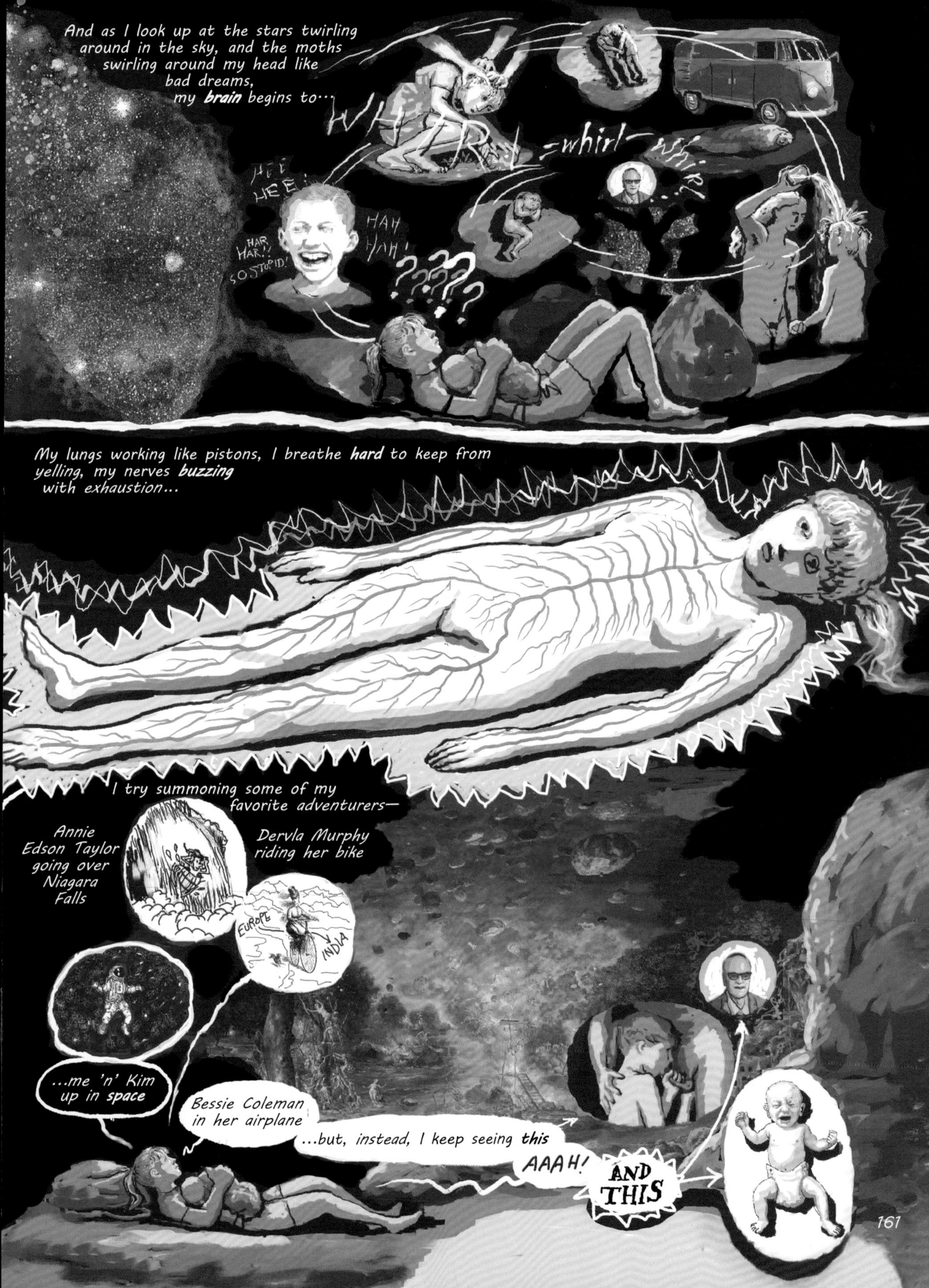

And as I look up at the stars twirling around in the sky, and the moths swirling around my head like bad dreams, my **brain** begins to…
WHIRL
whirl
HEE HEE!
HAR HAR!! SO STUPID!
HAH HAH!
My lungs working like pistons, I breathe **hard** to keep from yelling, my nerves **buzzing** with exhaustion…
I try summoning some of my favorite adventurers—
Annie Edson Taylor going over Niagara Falls
Dervla Murphy riding her bike
EUROPE
INDIA
…me 'n' Kim up in **space**
Bessie Coleman in her airplane
…but, instead, I keep seeing **this**
AAAH!
AND THIS

I can't **stand** it anymore so I sit up, rebundling Sam in the sweater he's wriggled out of...

...and crawl outside.

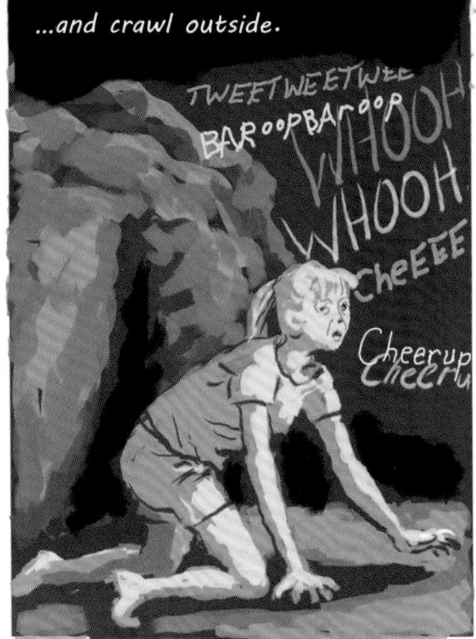

It's warmer than I expect—our shelter closer to the temperature of a **cave**—and I begin to **pace**.

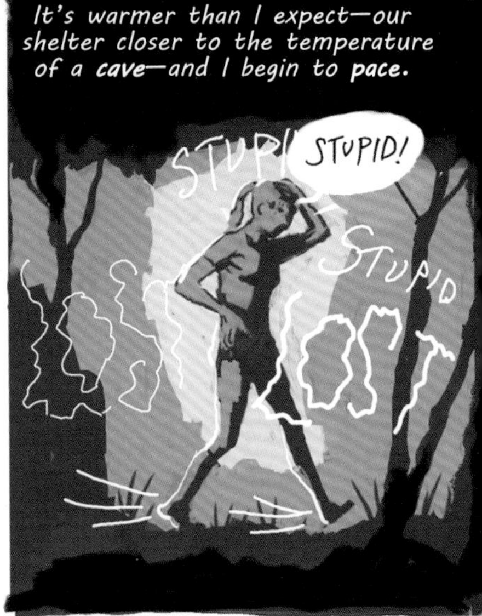

'Round and 'round I go, skirting roots and dead branches, my heart beating faster and faster...

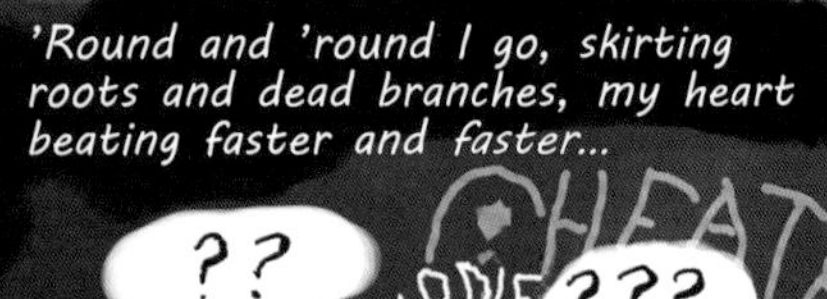

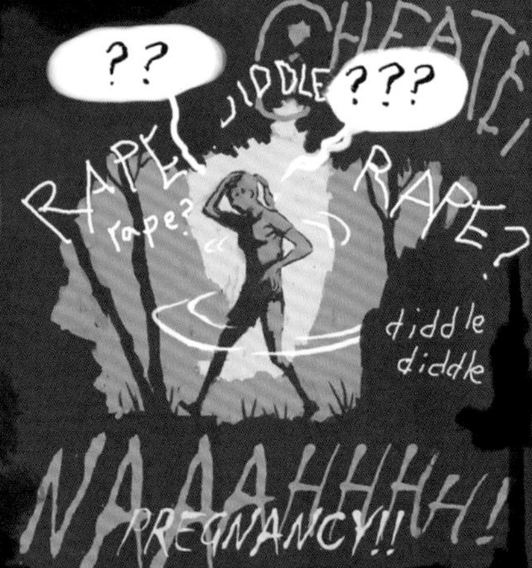

Then, I find myself...

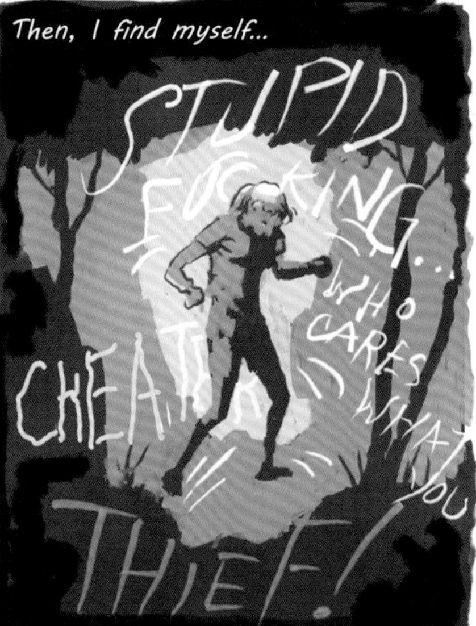

...just kinda... **freaking out.**

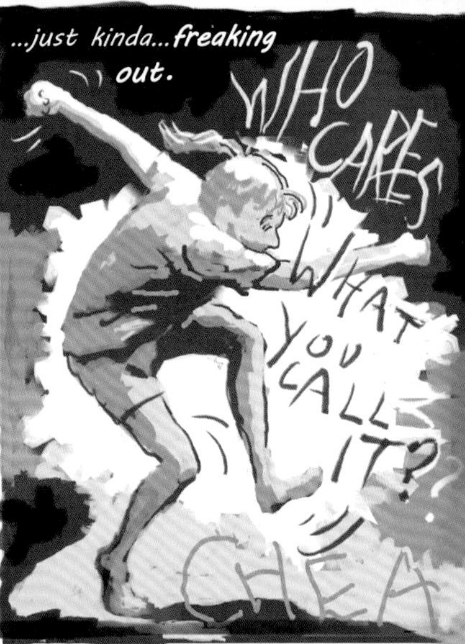

My arms pumping up and down, I pound the dirt...

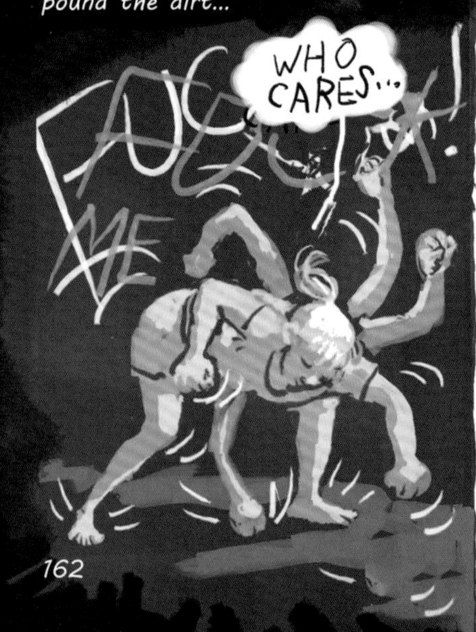

...swooping, panting, like a **mad dog**

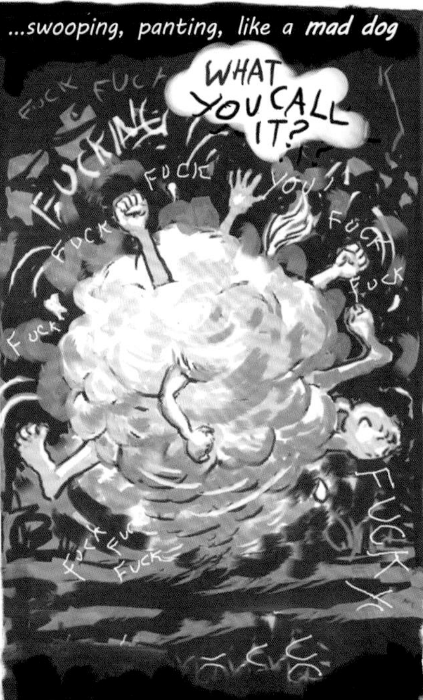

...on and on until I wear myself out.

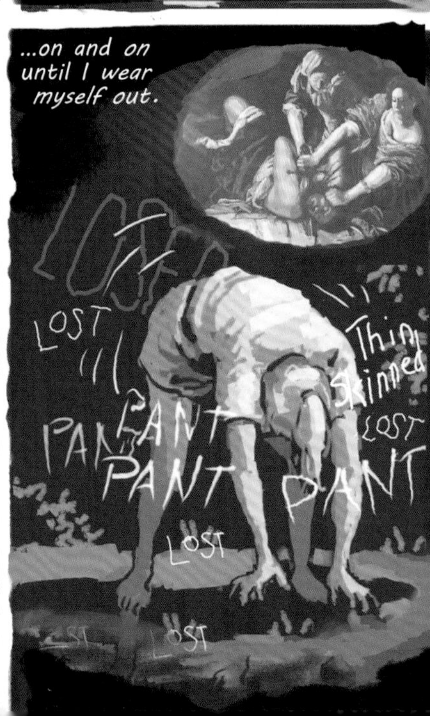

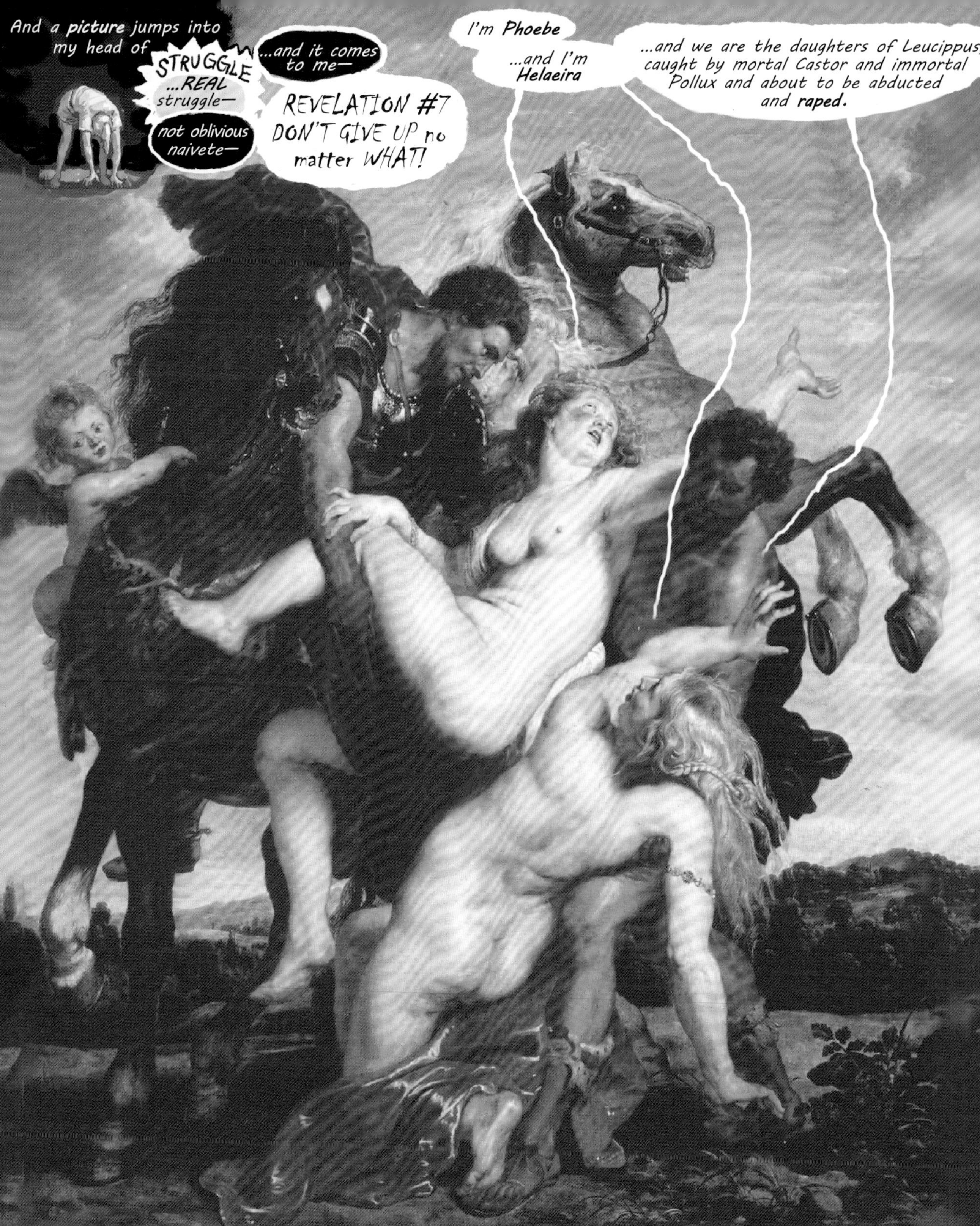

RAPE of the DAUGHTERS of LEUCIPPUS

by Peter Paul Rubens and Jan Wildens

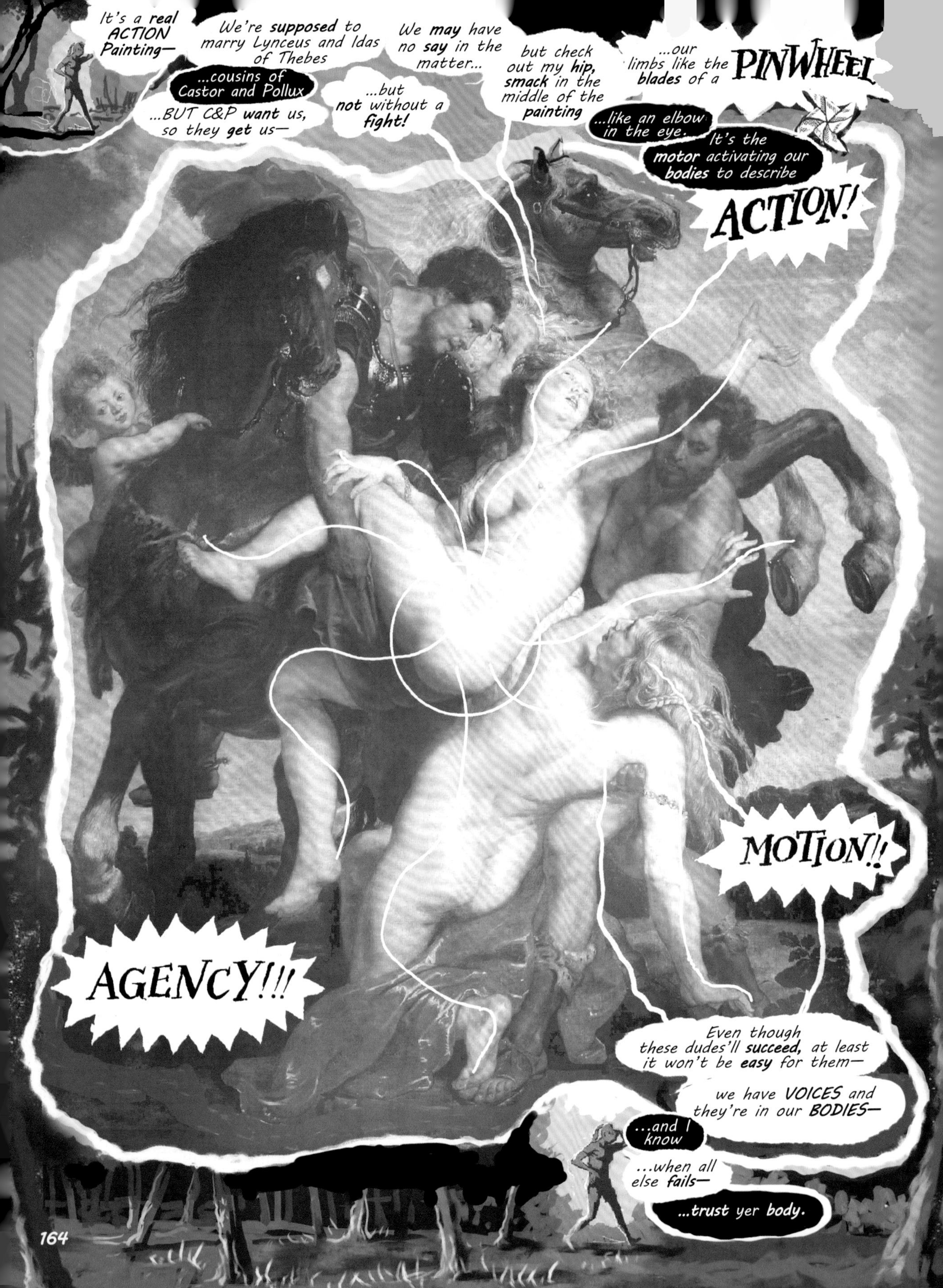

It's a real ACTION Painting—
We're supposed to marry Lynceus and Idas of Thebes
...cousins of Castor and Pollux
...BUT C&P want us, so they get us—
We may have no say in the matter...
...but not without a fight!
but check out my hip, smack in the middle of the painting
...our limbs like the blades of a PINWHEEL
...like an elbow in the eye.
It's the motor activating our bodies to describe
ACTION!
MOTION!!
AGENCY!!!
Even though these dudes'll succeed, at least it won't be easy for them—
we have VOICES and they're in our BODIES—
...and I know
...when all else fails—
...trust yer body.

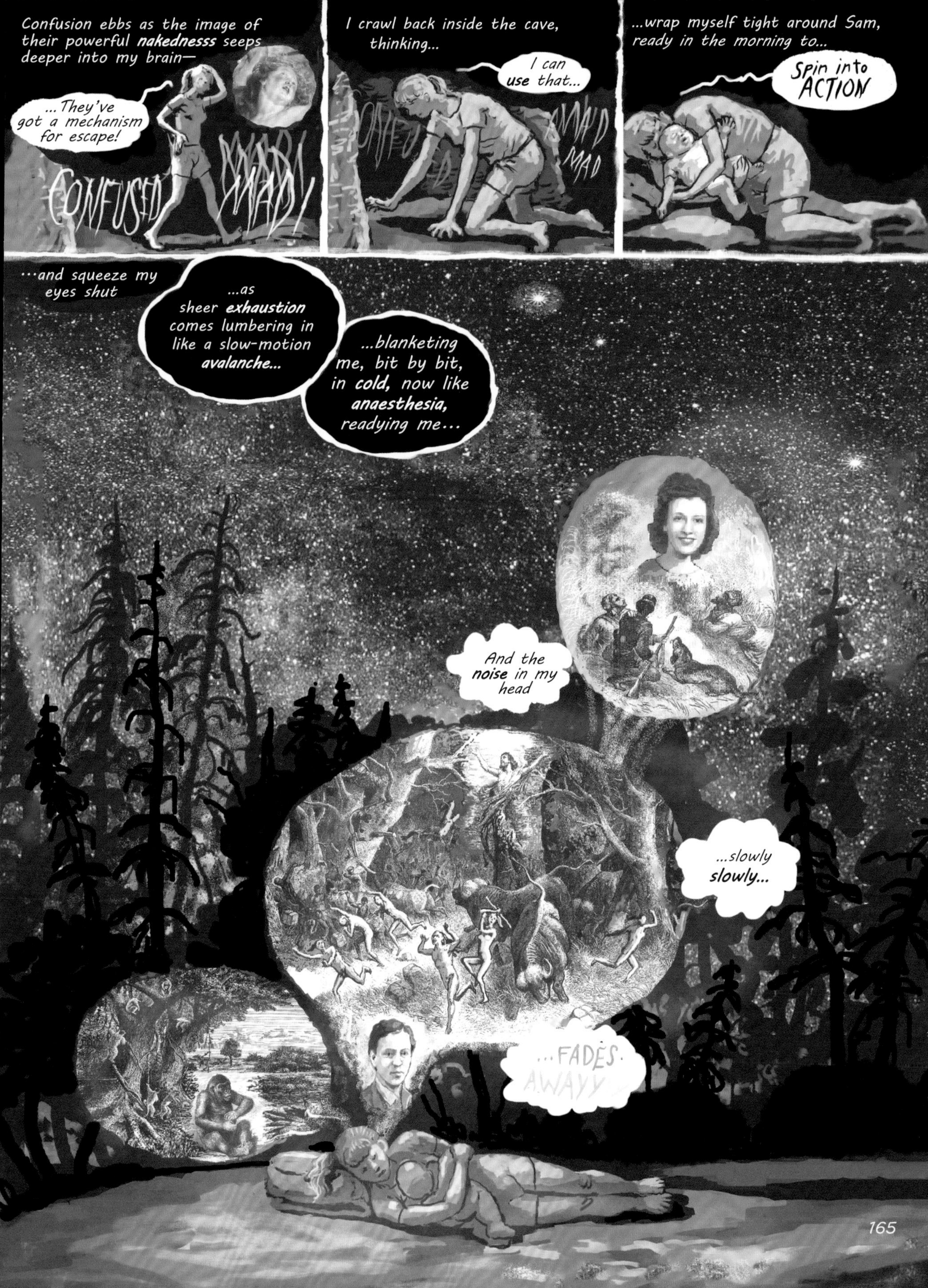
Confusion ebbs as the image of their powerful **nakednesss** seeps deeper into my brain—
...They've got a mechanism for escape!
CONFUSED
MAD
I crawl back inside the cave, thinking...
I can **use** that...
...wrap myself tight around Sam, ready in the morning to...
Spin into ACTION
...and squeeze my eyes shut
...as sheer **exhaustion** comes lumbering in like a slow-motion **avalanche...**
...blanketing me, bit by bit, in **cold,** now like **anaesthesia,** readying me...
And the **noise** in my head
...slowly **slowly...**
...FADES AWAYY

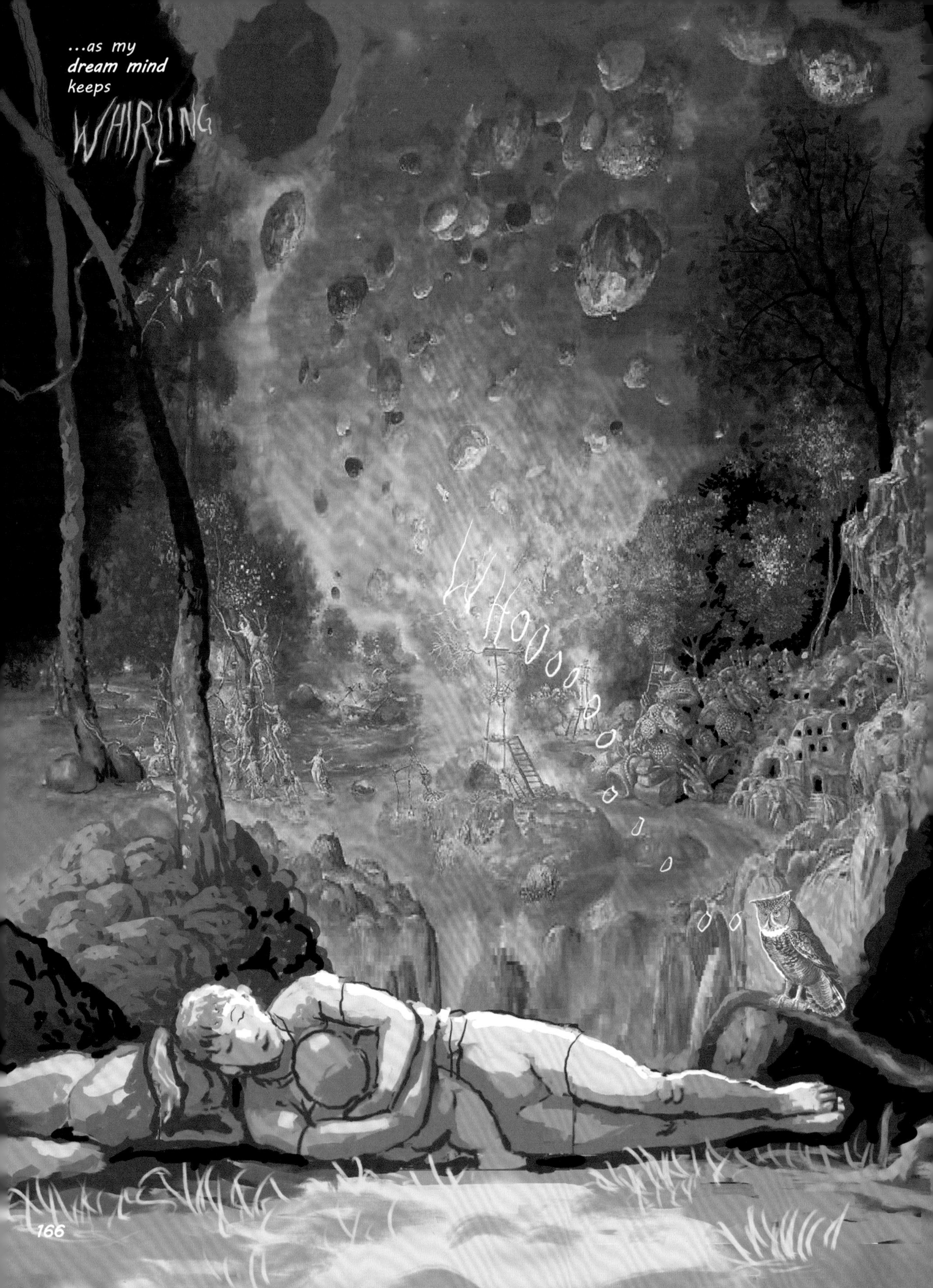
...as my
dream mind
keeps
WHIRLING
WHOOOOOOOOOOO

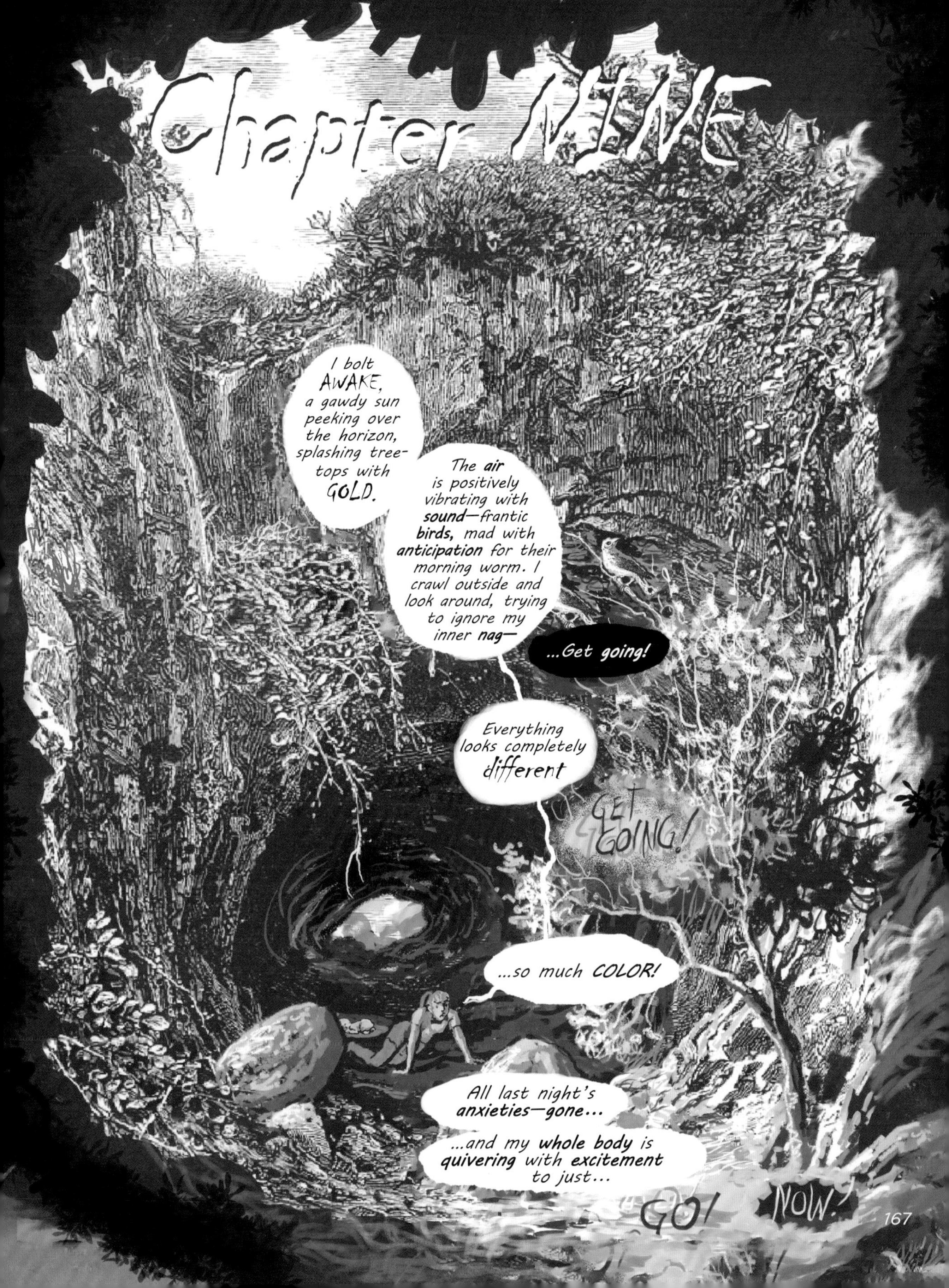

Chapter NINE

I bolt AWAKE, a gawdy sun peeking over the horizon, splashing tree-tops with GOLD.

The **air** is positively vibrating with **sound**—frantic **birds,** mad with **anticipation** for their morning worm. I crawl outside and look around, trying to ignore my inner **nag**—

...Get **going!**

Everything looks completely different

GET GOING!

...so much **COLOR!**

All last night's **anxieties—gone...**

...and my **whole body** is **quivering** with **excitement** to just...

GO! NOW!

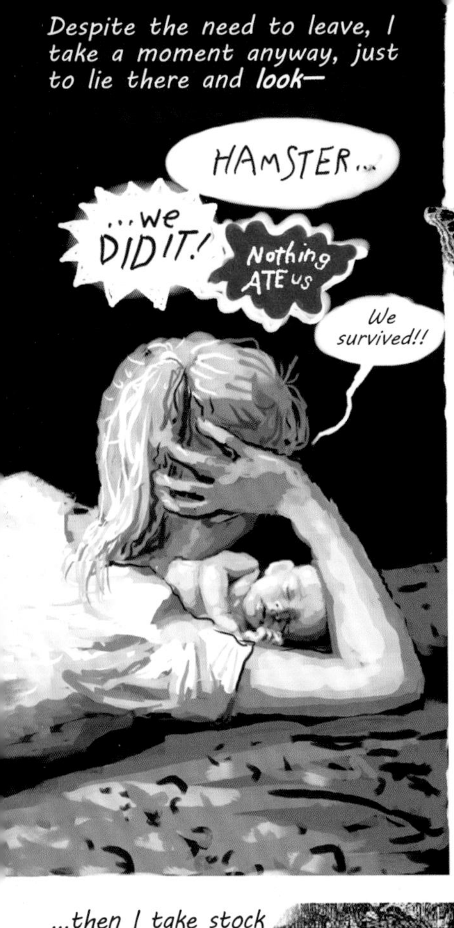
Despite the need to leave, I take a moment anyway, just to lie there and **look**—
HAMSTER...
...we DID IT!
Nothing ATE us
We survived!!

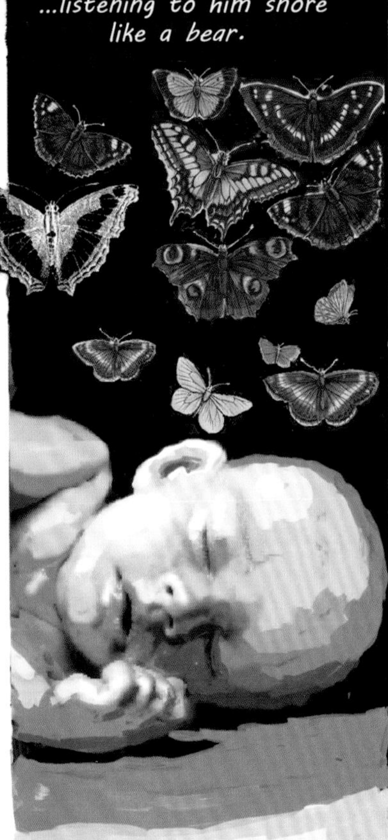
...listening to him snore like a bear.

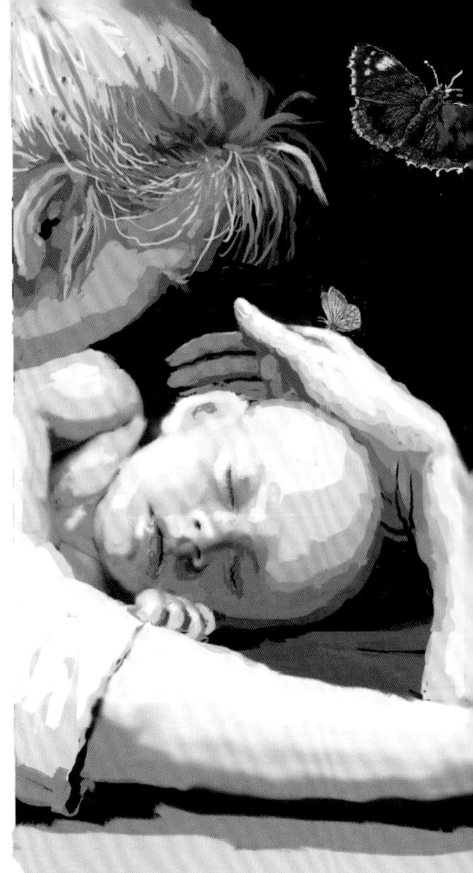

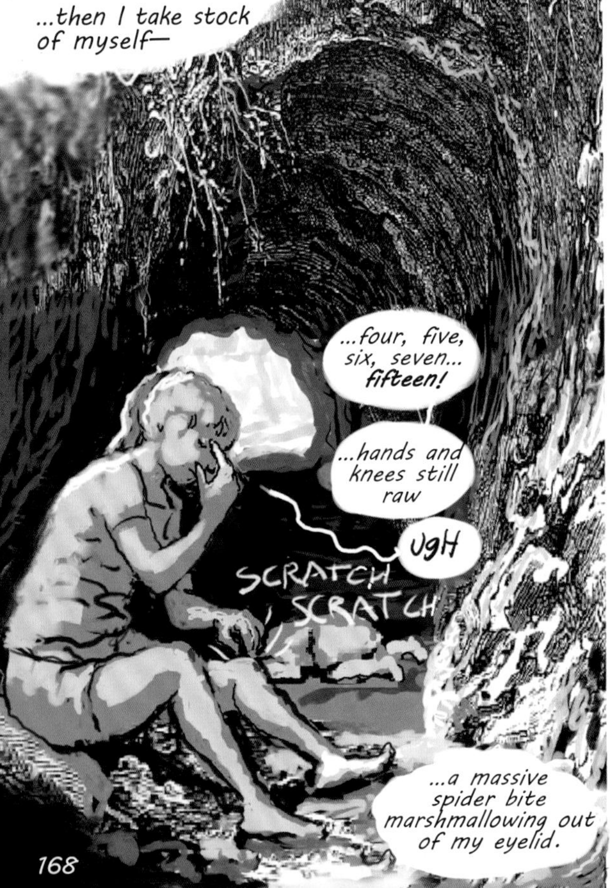
...then I take stock of myself—
...four, five, six, seven... **fifteen!**
...hands and knees still raw
UgH
SCRATCH SCRATCH
...a massive spider bite marshmallowing out of my eyelid.

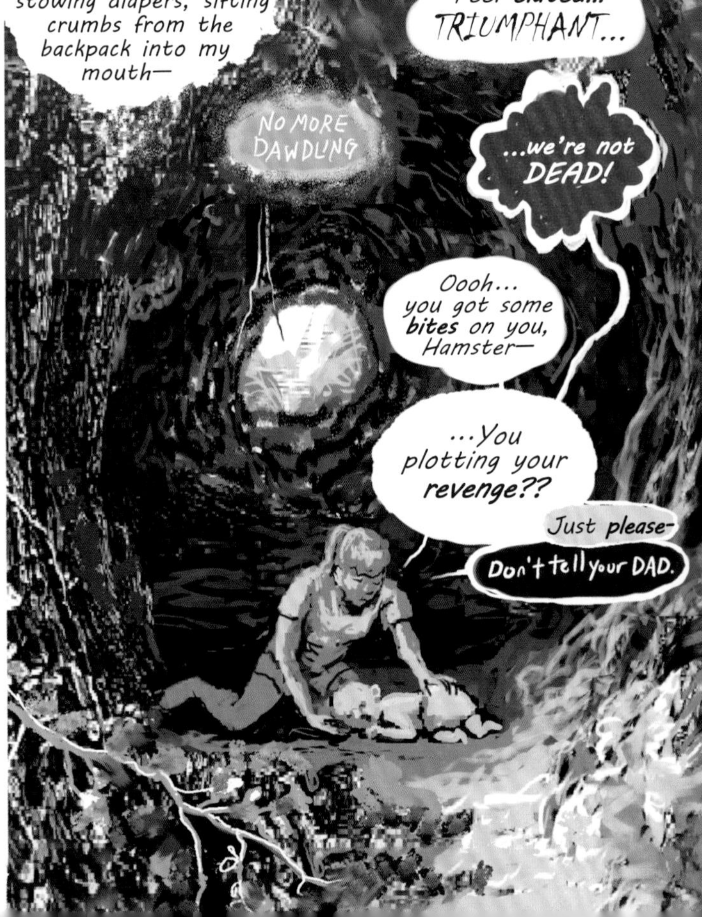
I gather up our things, stowing diapers, sifting crumbs from the backpack into my mouth—
Feel **elated...** TRIUMPHANT...
NO MORE DAWDLING
...we're not DEAD!
Oooh... you got some **bites** on you, Hamster—
...You plotting your **revenge??**
Just **please**-
Don't tell your DAD.

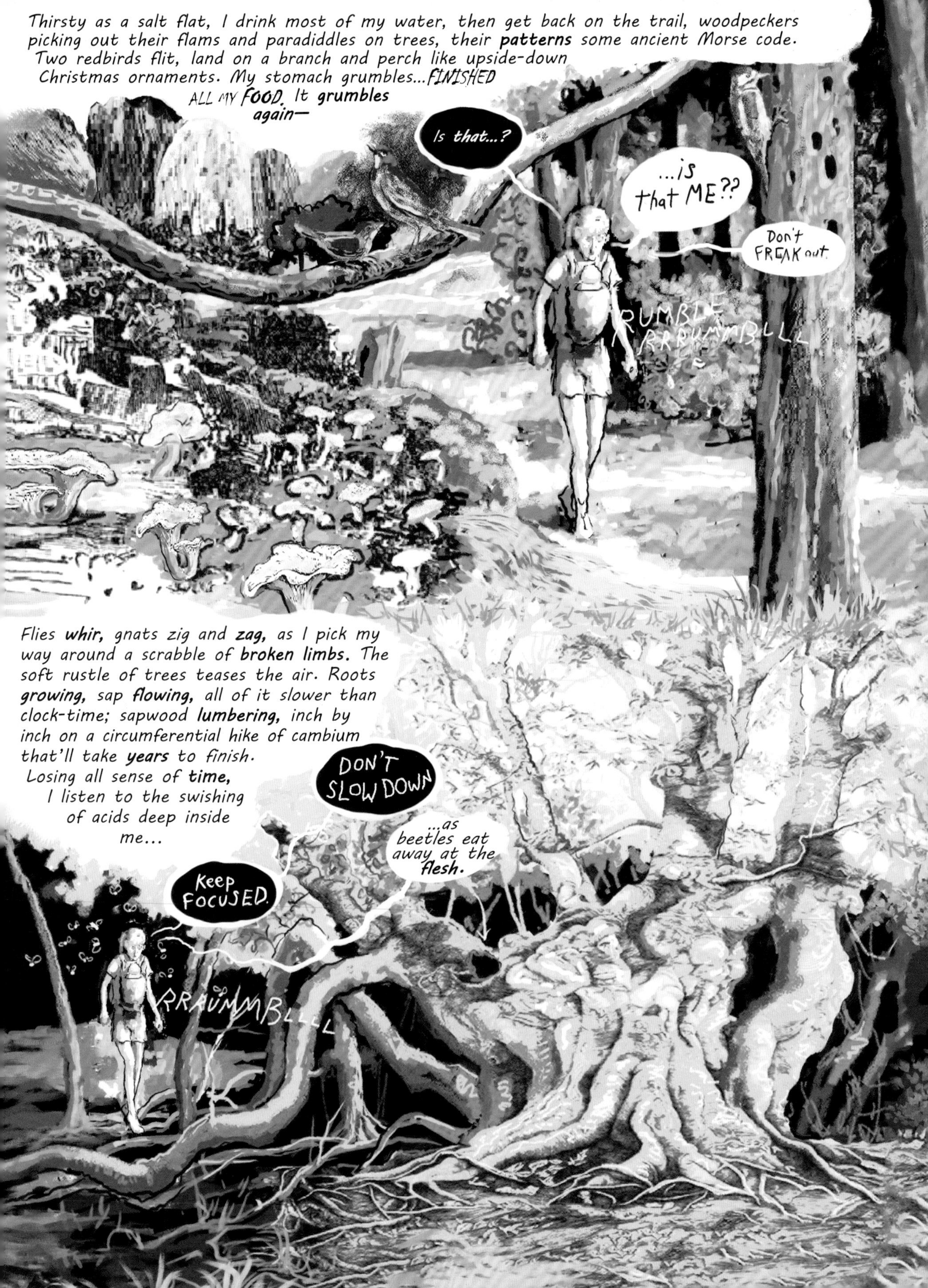

Thirsty as a salt flat, I drink most of my water, then get back on the trail, woodpeckers picking out their flams and paradiddles on trees, their **patterns** some ancient Morse code. Two redbirds flit, land on a branch and perch like upside-down Christmas ornaments. My stomach grumbles...FINISHED ALL MY **FOOD.** It **grumbles** again—
Is that...?
...is that ME??
Don't FREAK out.
RUMBLE RRRUMMBLLL
Flies **whir,** gnats zig and **zag,** as I pick my way around a scrabble of **broken limbs.** The soft rustle of trees teases the air. Roots **growing,** sap **flowing,** all of it slower than clock-time; sapwood **lumbering,** inch by inch on a circumferential hike of cambium that'll take **years** to finish. Losing all sense of **time,** I listen to the swishing of acids deep inside me...
DON'T SLOW DOWN
...as beetles eat away at the **flesh.**
Keep FOCUSED.
RRAUMMBLLL

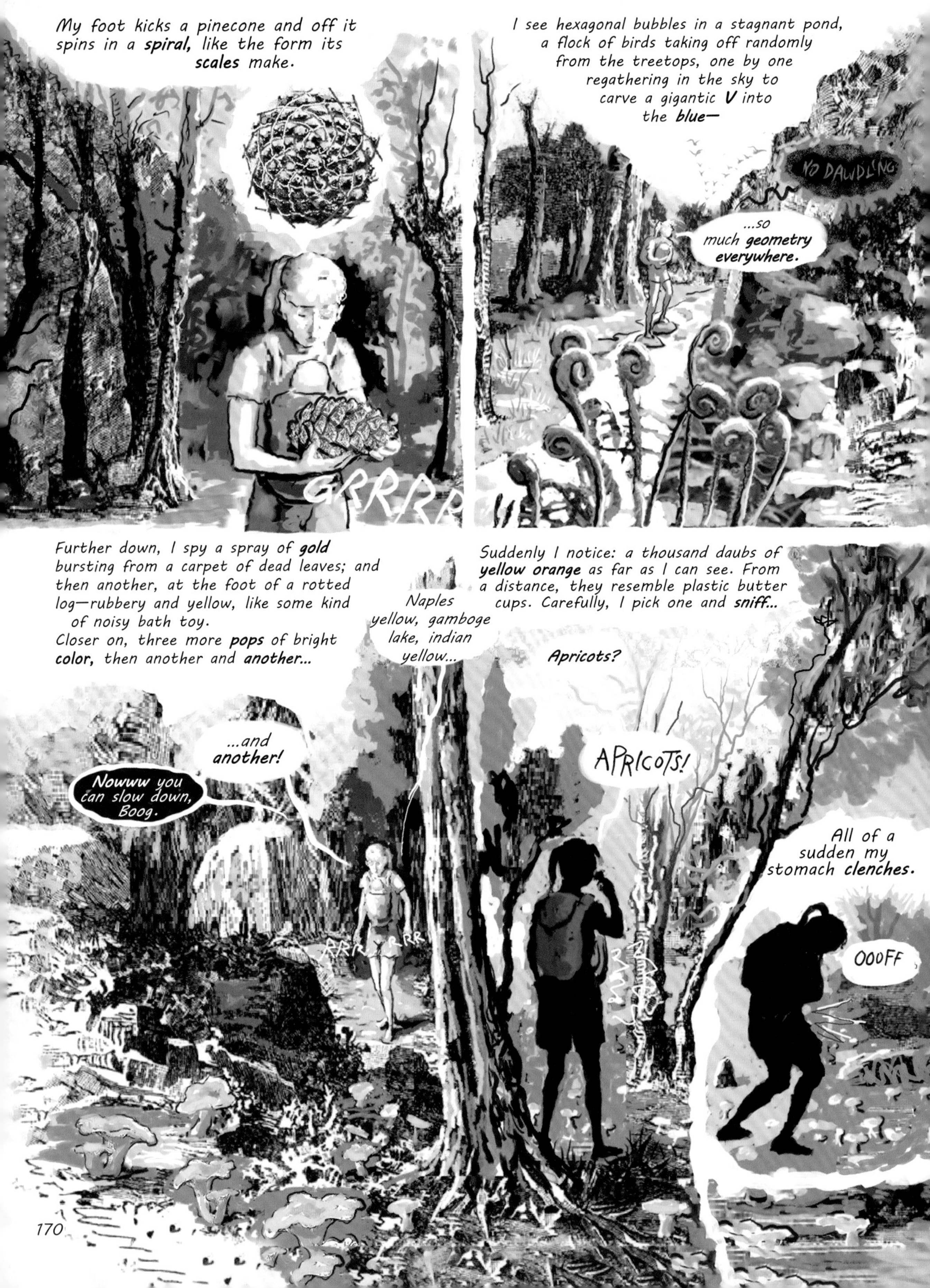
My foot kicks a pinecone and off it spins in a **spiral,** like the form its **scales** make.
GRRRRR
I see hexagonal bubbles in a stagnant pond, a flock of birds taking off randomly from the treetops, one by one regathering in the sky to carve a gigantic **V** into the **blue**—
NO DAWDLING
...so much **geometry everywhere.**
Further down, I spy a spray of **gold** bursting from a carpet of dead leaves; and then another, at the foot of a rotted log—rubbery and yellow, like some kind of noisy bath toy.
Closer on, three more **pops** of bright **color,** then another and **another...**
Naples yellow, gamboge lake, indian yellow...
...and **another!**
Nowww you can slow down, Boog.
RRR RRR
Suddenly I notice: a thousand daubs of **yellow orange** as far as I can see. From a distance, they resemble plastic butter cups. Carefully, I pick one and **sniff...**
Apricots?
APRICOTS!
All of a sudden my stomach **clenches.**
OOOFF

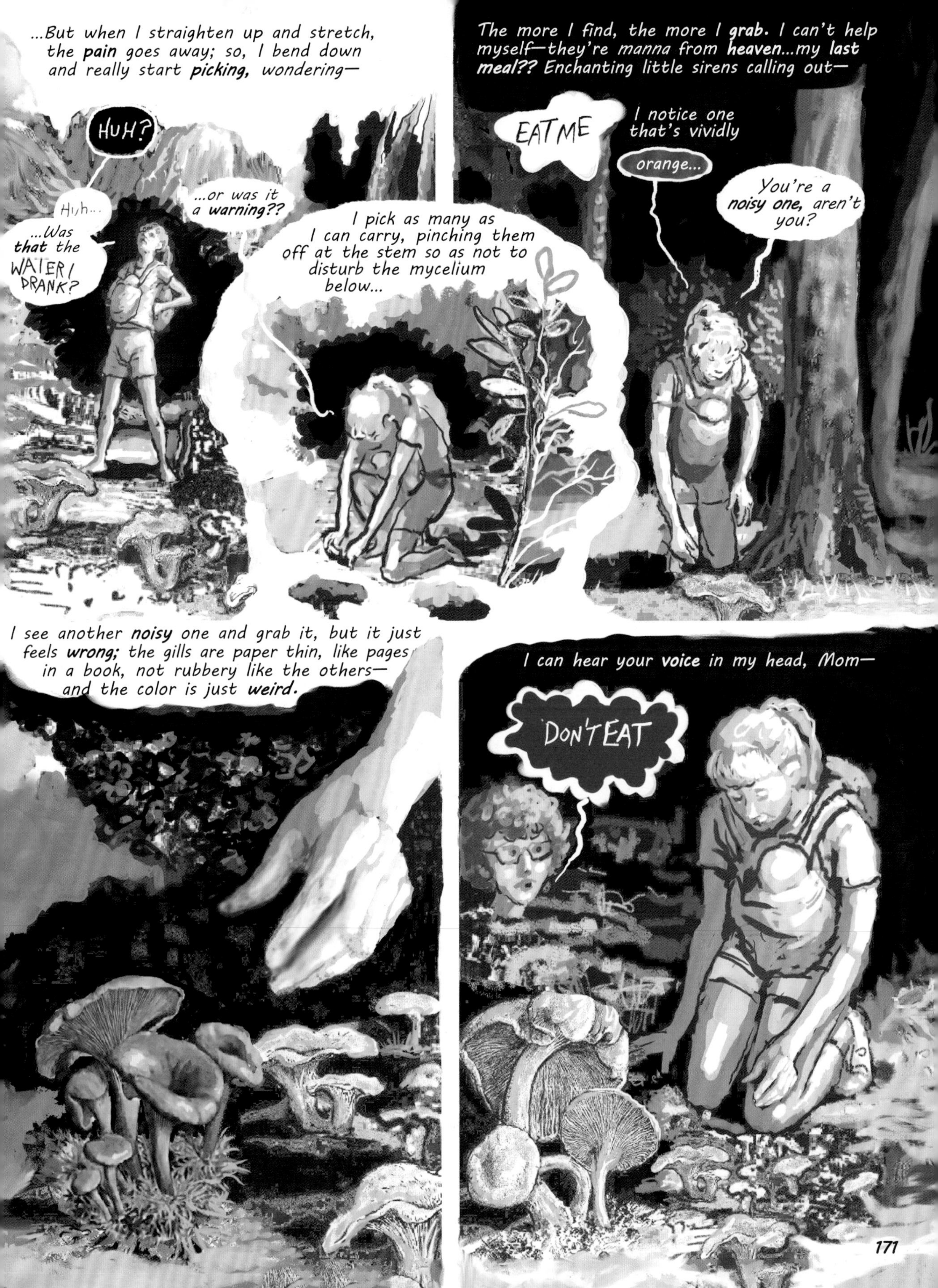

...But when I straighten up and stretch, the **pain** goes away; so, I bend down and really start **picking,** wondering—

HUH?

Huh...

...Was **that** the WATER I DRANK?

...or was it a **warning??**

I pick as many as I can carry, pinching them off at the stem so as not to disturb the mycelium below...

The more I find, the more I **grab.** I can't help myself—they're *manna* from **heaven**...my **last meal??** Enchanting little sirens calling out—

EAT ME

I notice one that's vividly

orange...

You're a **noisy one,** aren't you?

I see another **noisy** one and grab it, but it just feels **wrong;** the gills are paper thin, like pages in a book, not rubbery like the others—and the color is just **weird.**

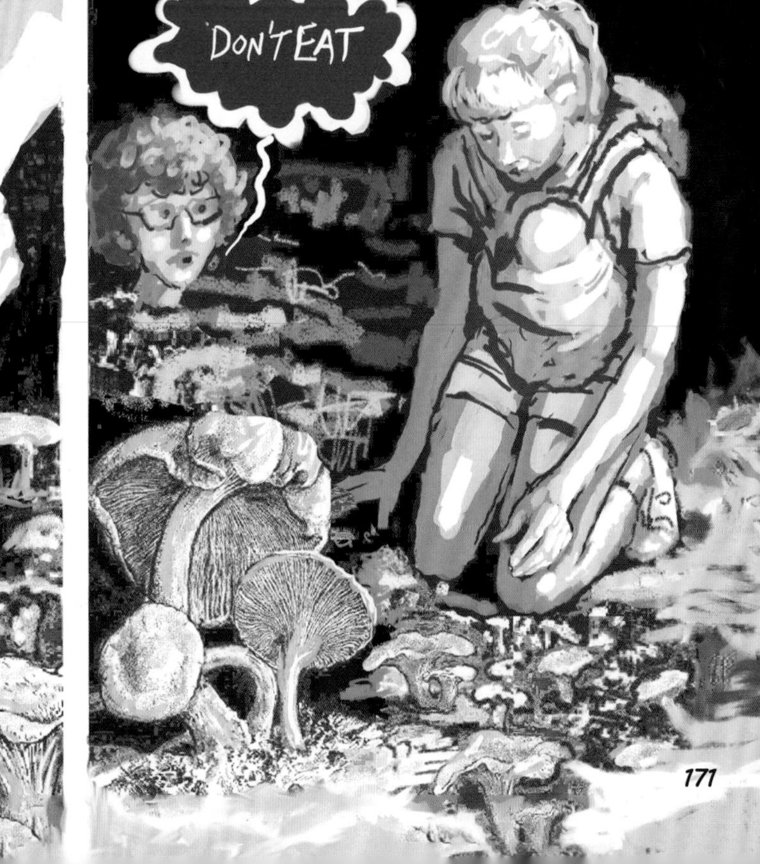

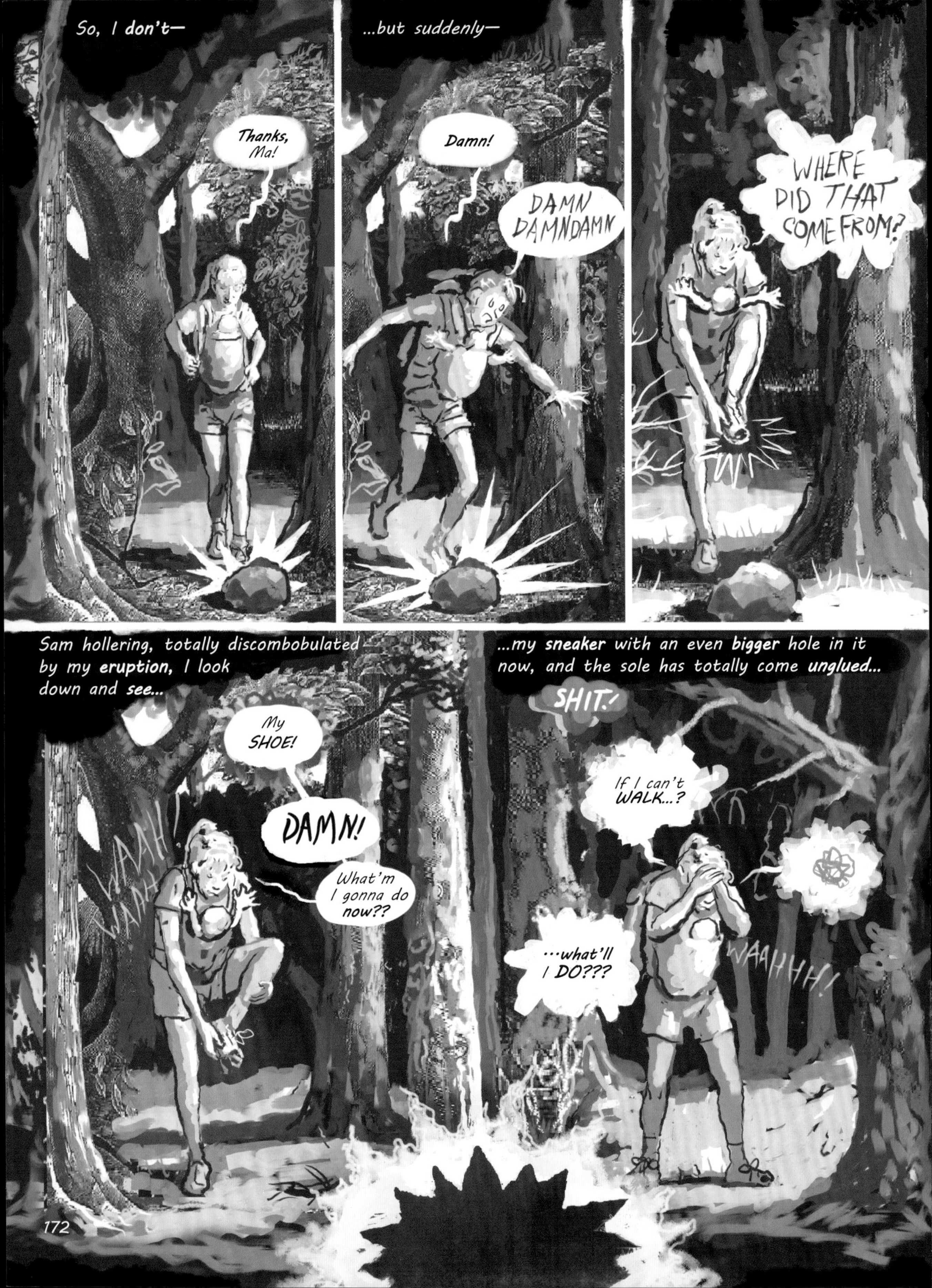

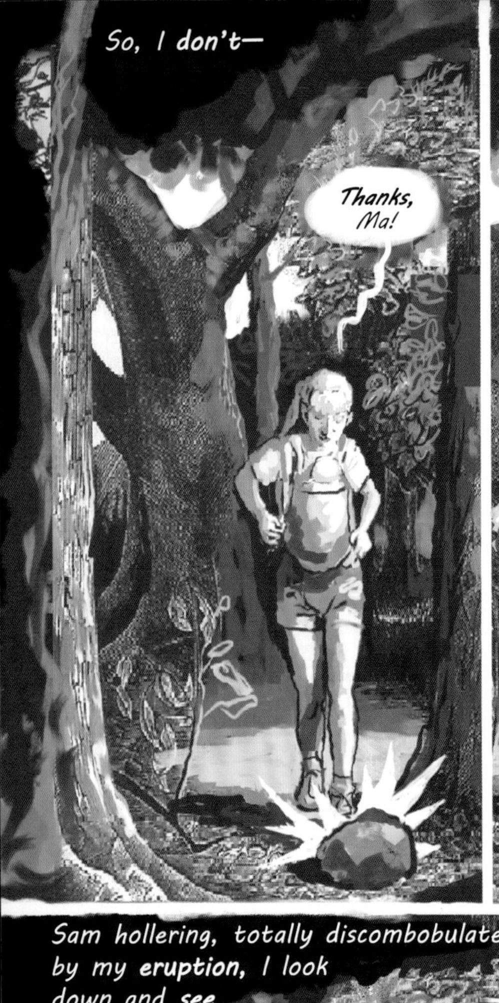

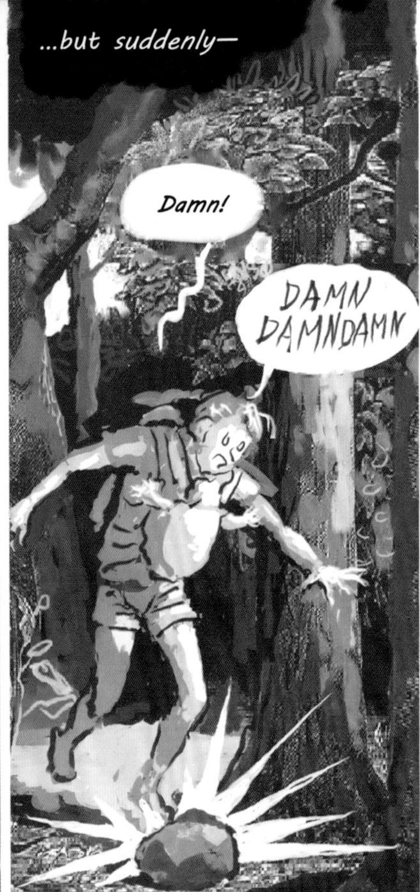

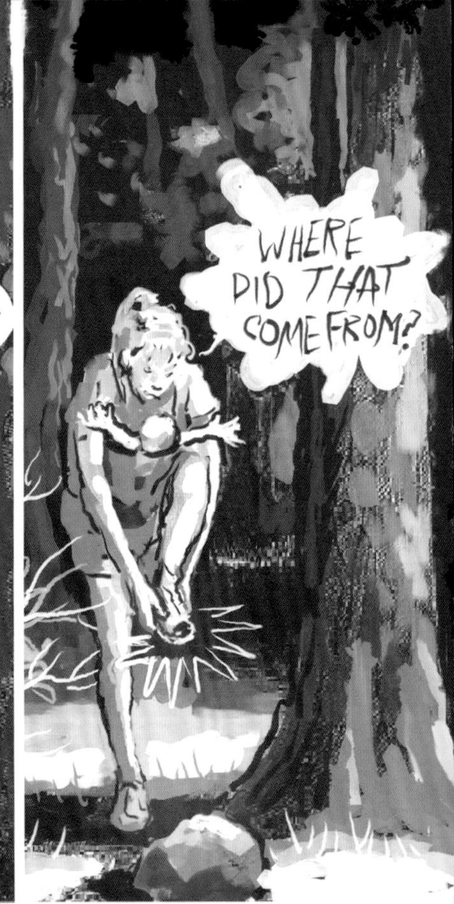

Sam hollering, totally discombobulated by my **eruption,** I look down and **see...**

WAAH! WAAH!

My SHOE!

DAMN!

What'm I gonna do **now??**

...my **sneaker** with an even **bigger** hole in it now, and the sole has totally come **unglued...**

SHIT!

If I can't **WALK...?**

...what'll I **DO???**

WAAHHH!

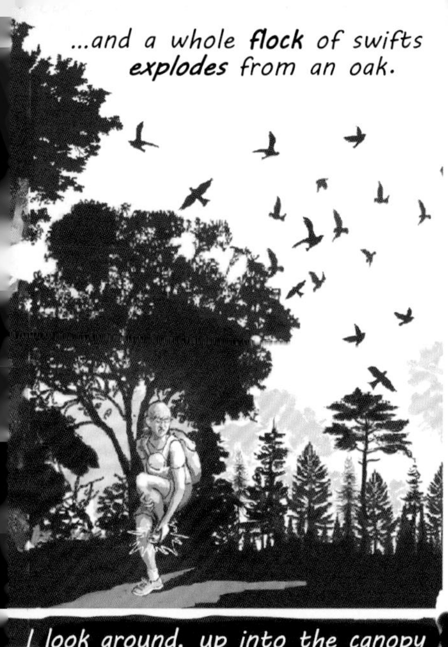
...and a whole flock of swifts explodes from an oak.

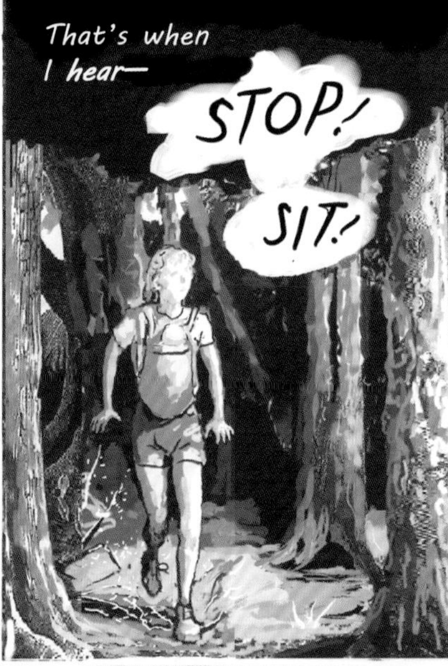
That's when I hear—
STOP!
SIT!

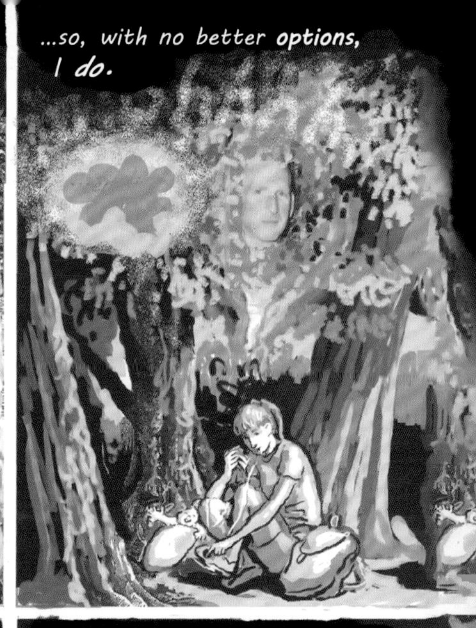
...so, with no better options, I do.

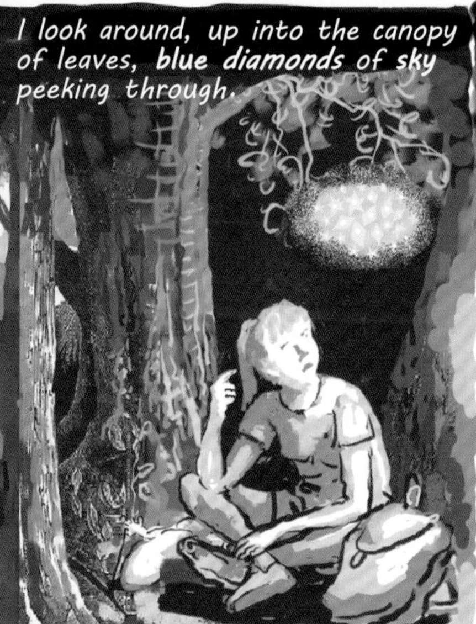
I look around, up into the canopy of leaves, blue diamonds of sky peeking through...

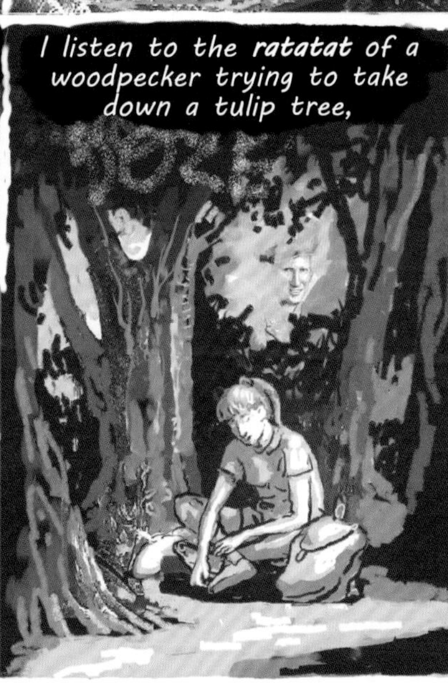
I listen to the ratatat of a woodpecker trying to take down a tulip tree,

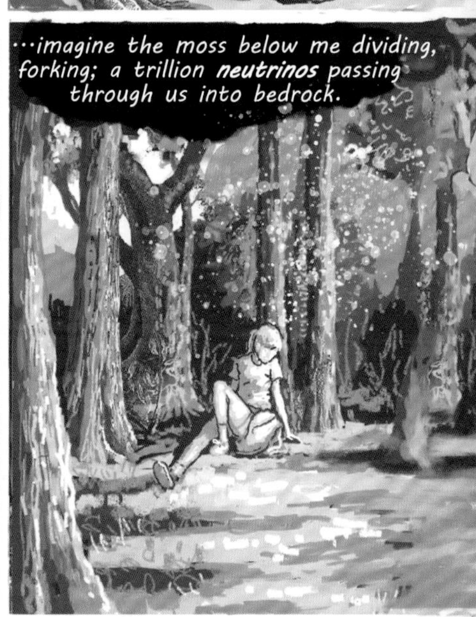
...imagine the moss below me dividing, forking; a trillion neutrinos passing through us into bedrock.

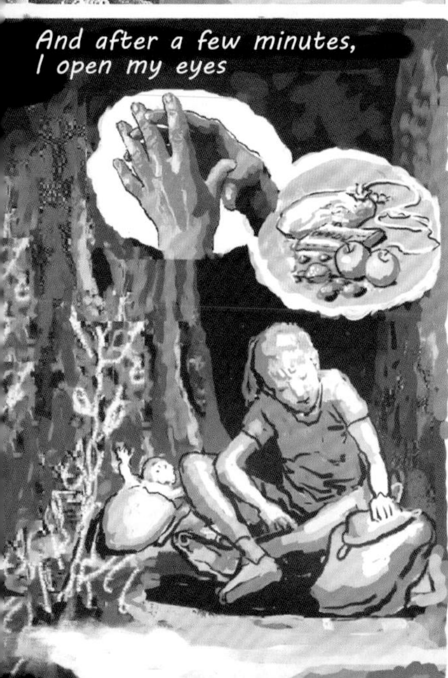
And after a few minutes, I open my eyes

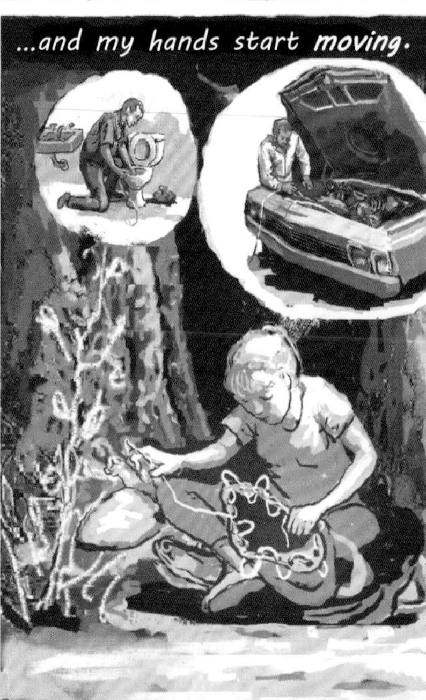
...and my hands start moving.

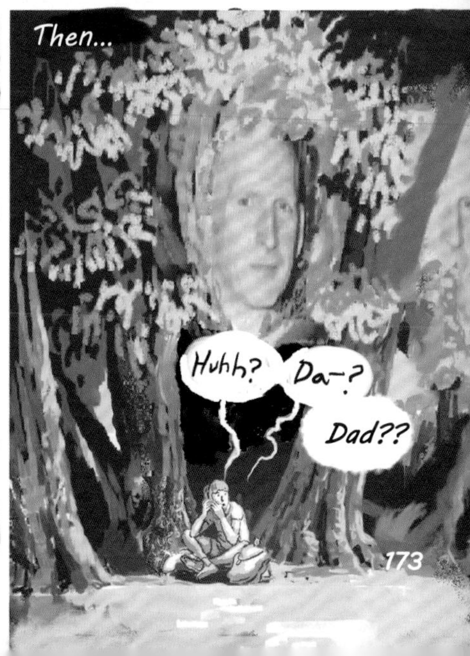
Then...
Huhh?
Da-?
Dad??

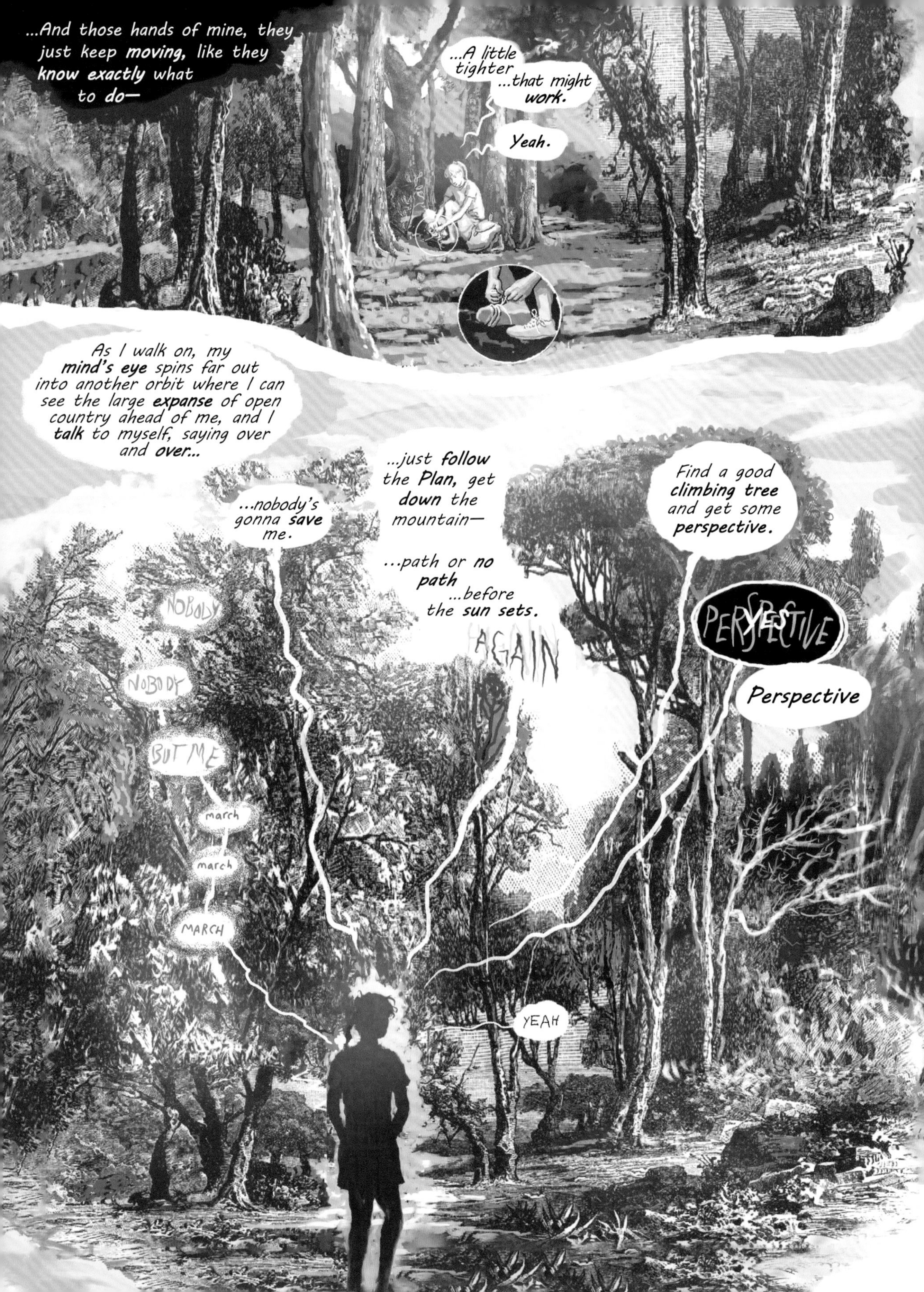

...And those hands of mine, they just keep moving, like they know exactly what to do—
...A little tighter ...that might work.
Yeah.
As I walk on, my mind's eye spins far out into another orbit where I can see the large expanse of open country ahead of me, and I talk to myself, saying over and over...
...nobody's gonna save me.
...just follow the Plan, get down the mountain—
...path or no path ...before the sun sets.
Find a good climbing tree and get some perspective.
NOBODY
NOBODY
BUT ME
march
march
MARCH
AGAIN
PERSPECTIVE
YES
Perspective
YEAH

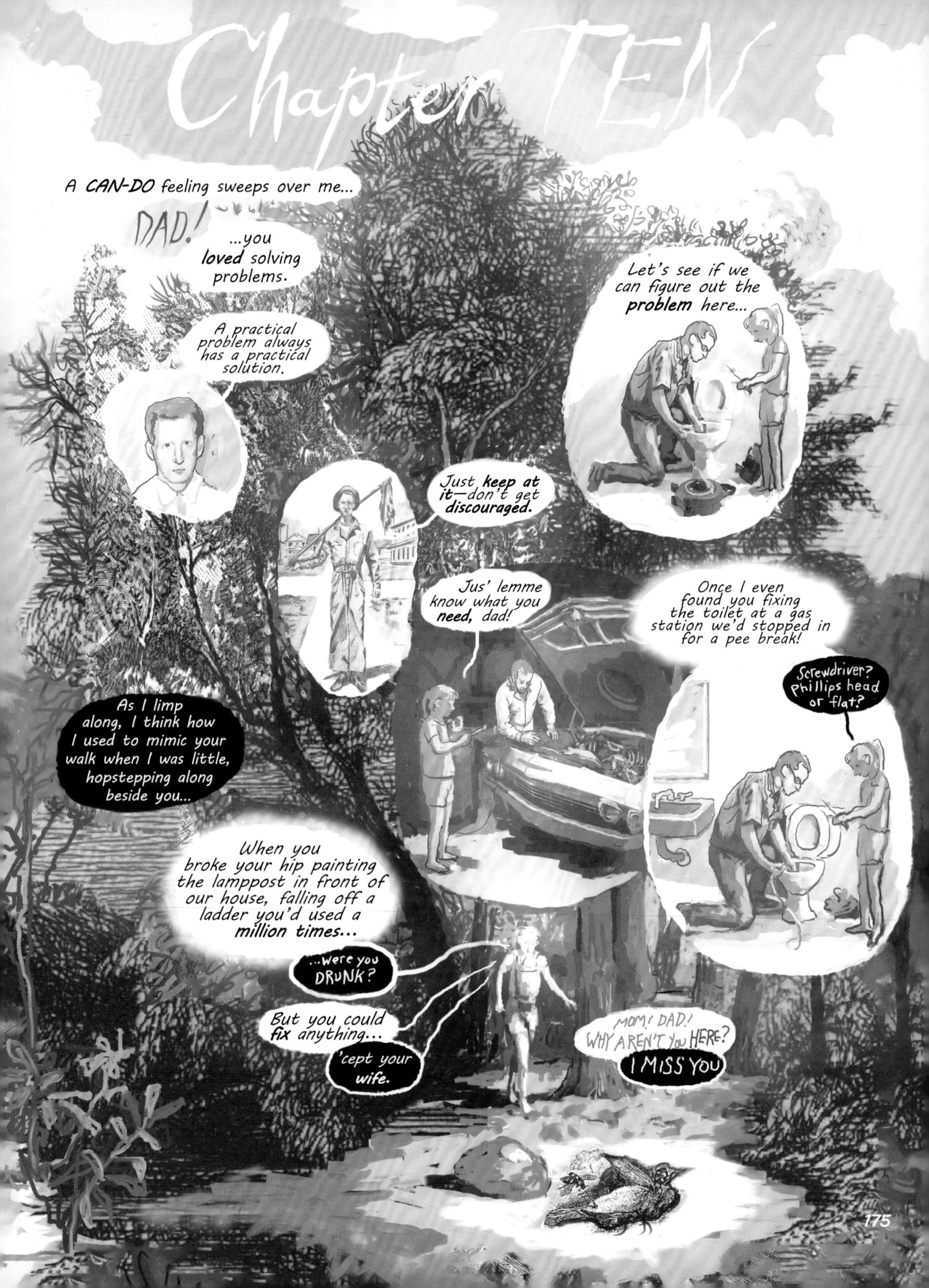

Chapter TEN

A **CAN-DO** feeling sweeps over me...

DAD!

...you **loved** solving problems.

A practical problem always has a practical solution.

Just **keep at it**—don't get **discouraged.**

Let's see if we can figure out the **problem** here...

Jus' lemme know what you **need,** dad!

Once I even found you fixing the toilet at a gas station we'd stopped in for a pee break!

Screwdriver? Phillips head or flat?

As I limp along, I think how I used to mimic your walk when I was little, hopstepping along beside you...

When you broke your hip painting the lamppost in front of our house, falling off a ladder you'd used a **million times...**

...were you DRUNK?

But you could **fix** anything...

'cept your **wife.**

MOM! DAD! WHY AREN'T YOU HERE?

I MISS YOU

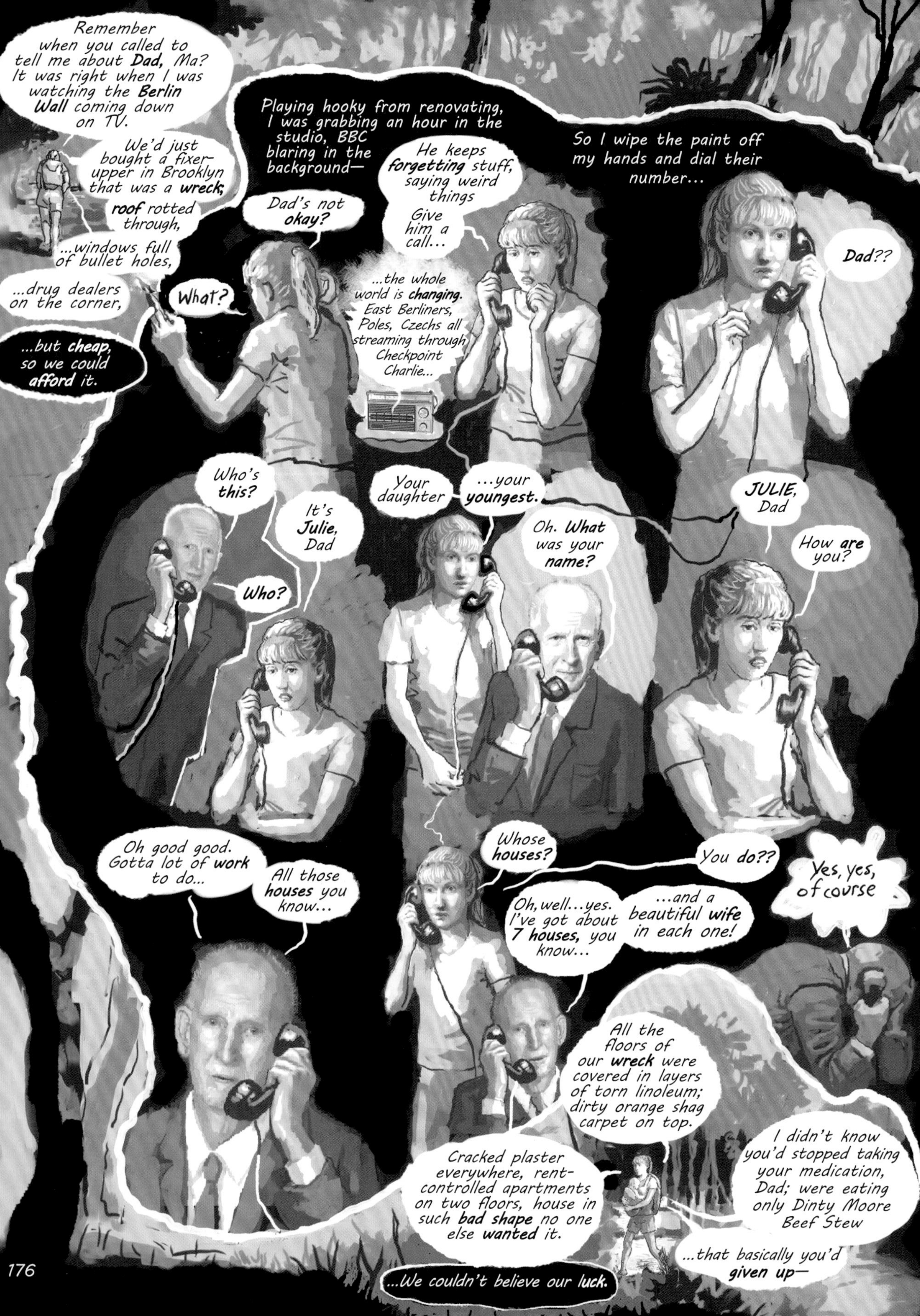
Remember when you called to tell me about **Dad**, Ma? It was right when I was watching the **Berlin Wall** coming down on TV.
We'd just bought a fixer-upper in Brooklyn that was a **wreck**;
roof rotted through,
...windows full of bullet holes,
...drug dealers on the corner,
...but **cheap**, so we could **afford** it.
Playing hooky from renovating, I was grabbing an hour in the studio, BBC blaring in the background—
Dad's not **okay?**
What?
He keeps **forgetting** stuff, saying weird things
Give him a call...
...the whole world is **changing**. East Berliners, Poles, Czechs all streaming through Checkpoint Charlie...
So I wipe the paint off my hands and dial their number...
Dad??
Who's **this?**
It's **Julie**, Dad
Who?
Your daughter
...your **youngest**.
Oh. **What** was your **name?**
JULIE, Dad
How **are** you?
Oh good good. Gotta lot of **work** to do...
All those **houses** you know...
Whose **houses?**
You **do??**
Oh, well...yes. I've got about **7 houses**, you know...
...and a beautiful **wife** in each one!
Yes, yes, of course
All the floors of our **wreck** were covered in layers of torn linoleum; dirty orange shag carpet on top.
Cracked plaster everywhere, rent-controlled apartments on two floors, house in such **bad shape** no one else **wanted** it.
I didn't know you'd stopped taking your medication, Dad; were eating only Dinty Moore Beef Stew
...that basically you'd **given up**—
...We couldn't believe our **luck**.

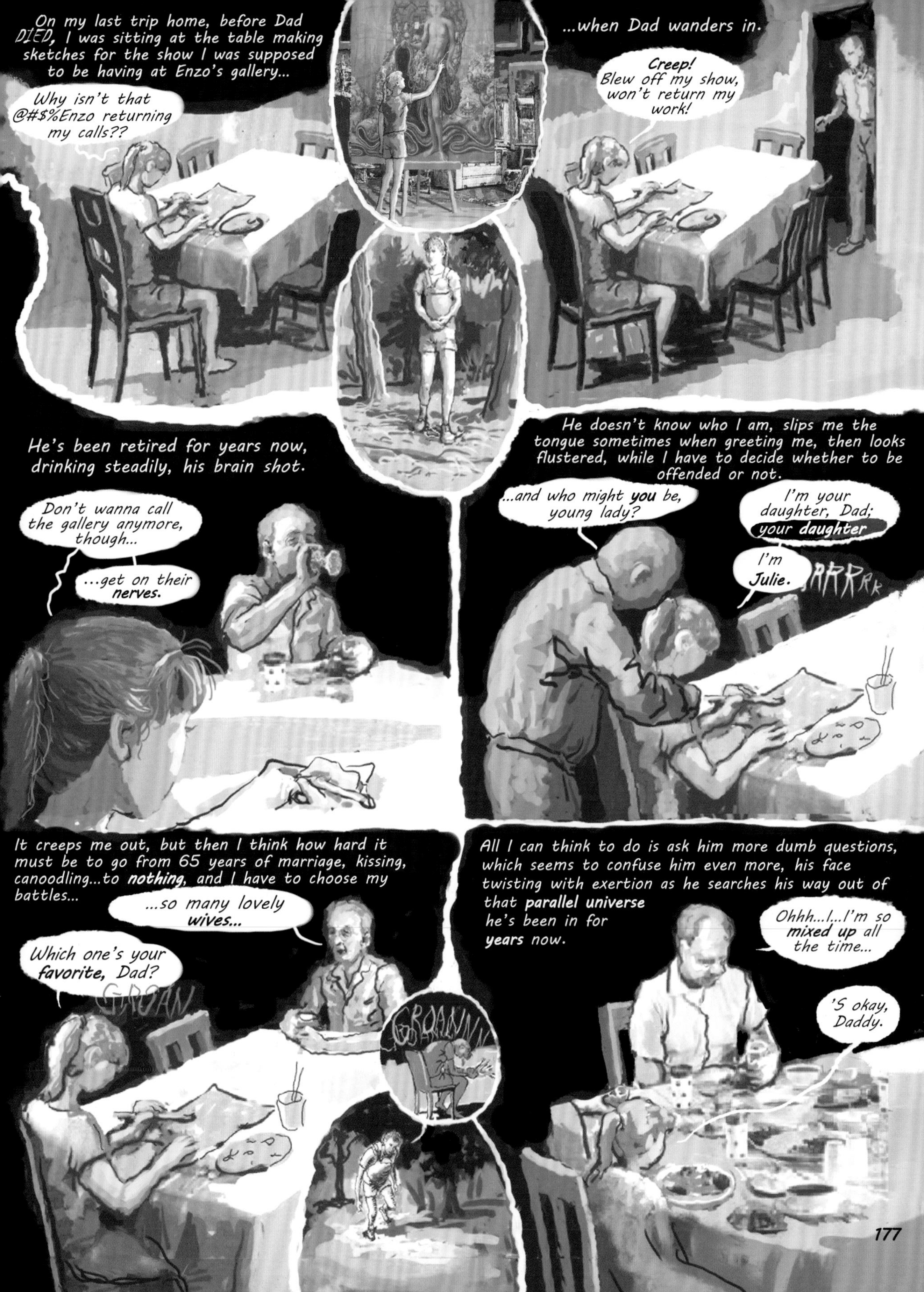
On my last trip home, before Dad DIED, I was sitting at the table making sketches for the show I was supposed to be having at Enzo's gallery...
Why isn't that @#$%Enzo returning my calls??
...when Dad wanders in.
Creep! Blew off my show, won't return my work!
He's been retired for years now, drinking steadily, his brain shot.
Don't wanna call the gallery anymore, though...
...get on their **nerves.**
He doesn't know who I am, slips me the tongue sometimes when greeting me, then looks flustered, while I have to decide whether to be offended or not.
...and who might **you** be, young lady?
I'm your daughter, Dad; your **daughter**
I'm **Julie.**
RRRRrk
It creeps me out, but then I think how hard it must be to go from 65 years of marriage, kissing, canoodling...to **nothing**, and I have to choose my battles...
...so many lovely **wives...**
Which one's your **favorite,** Dad?
GROAN
GROANNN
All I can think to do is ask him more dumb questions, which seems to confuse him even more, his face twisting with exertion as he searches his way out of that **parallel universe** he's been in for **years** now.
Ohhh...I...I'm so **mixed up** all the time...
'S okay, Daddy.

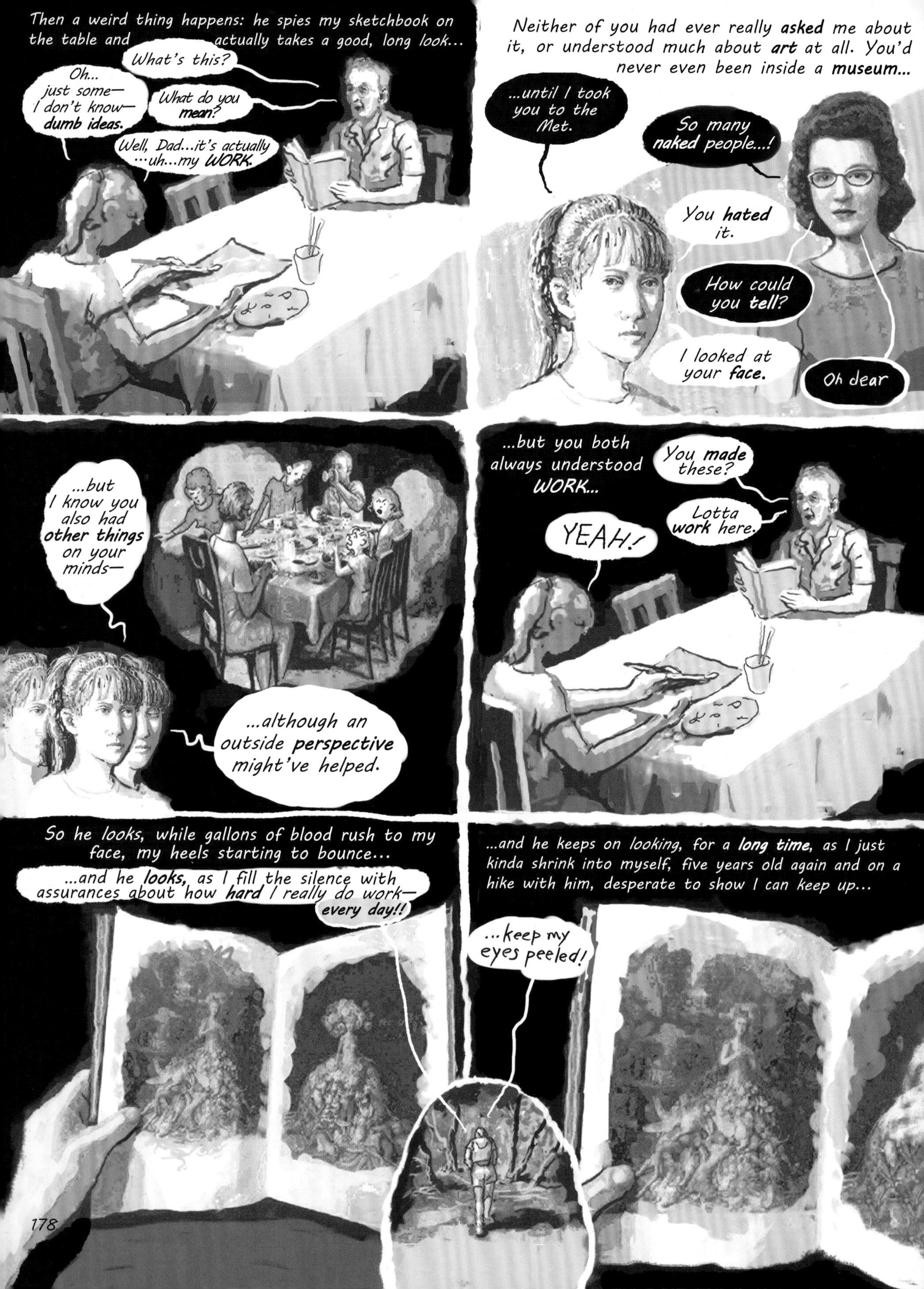
Then a weird thing happens: he spies my sketchbook on the table and actually takes a good, long look...
What's this?
Oh... just some— I don't know— dumb ideas.
What do you mean?
Well, Dad...it's actually ...uh...my WORK.
Neither of you had ever really asked me about it, or understood much about art at all. You'd never even been inside a museum...
...until I took you to the Met.
So many naked people...!
You hated it.
How could you tell?
I looked at your face.
Oh dear
...but I know you also had other things on your minds—
...although an outside perspective might've helped.
...but you both always understood WORK...
You made these?
Lotta work here.
YEAH!
So he looks, while gallons of blood rush to my face, my heels starting to bounce...
...and he looks, as I fill the silence with assurances about how hard I really do work— every day!!
...and he keeps on looking, for a long time, as I just kinda shrink into myself, five years old again and on a hike with him, desperate to show I can keep up...
...keep my eyes peeled!

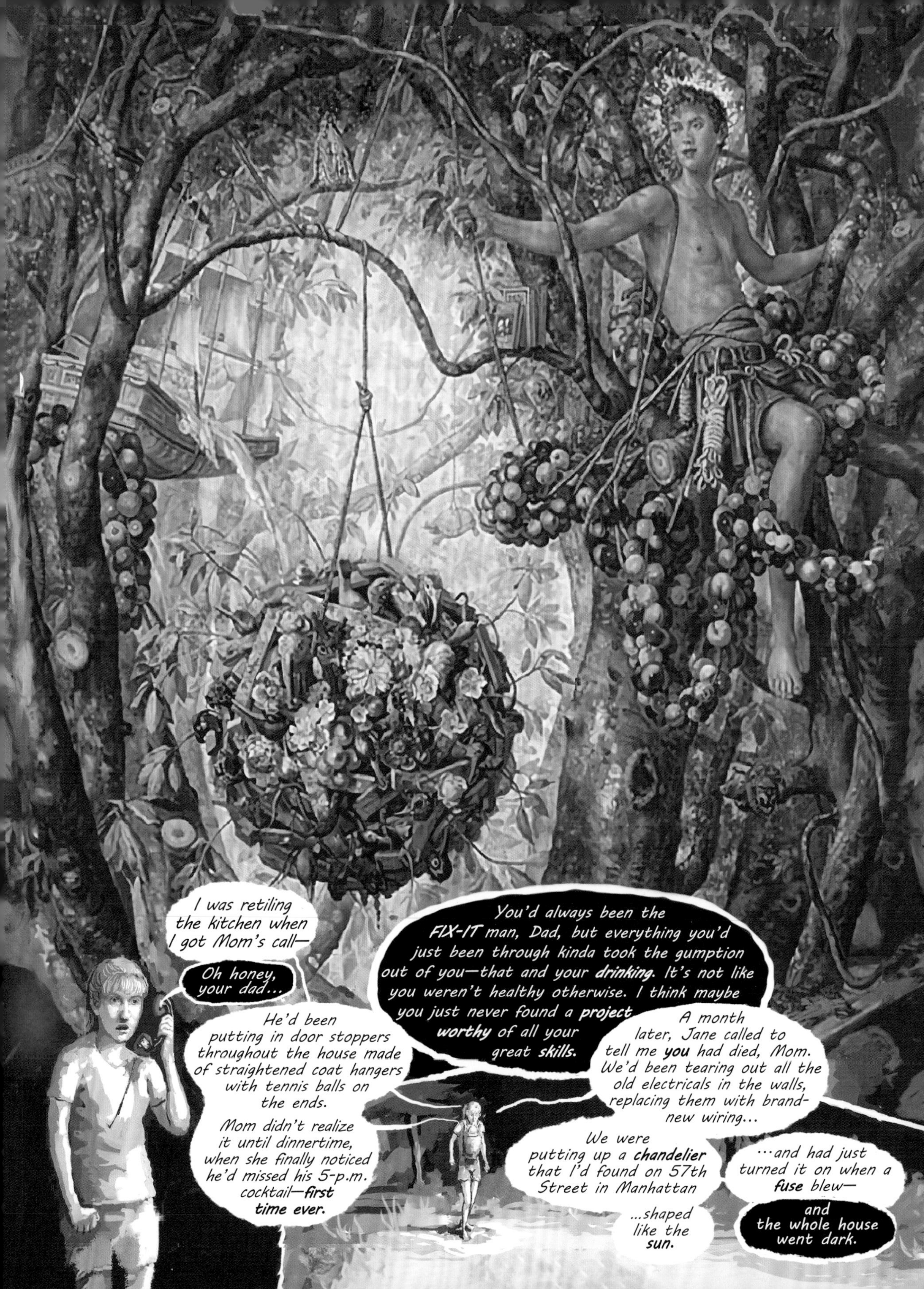

I was retiling the kitchen when I got Mom's call—
Oh honey, your dad...
He'd been putting in door stoppers throughout the house made of straightened coat hangers with tennis balls on the ends.
Mom didn't realize it until dinnertime, when she finally noticed he'd missed his 5-p.m. cocktail—**first time ever.**
You'd always been the **FIX-IT** man, Dad, but everything you'd just been through kinda took the gumption out of you—that and your **drinking**. It's not like you weren't healthy otherwise. I think maybe you just never found a **project worthy** of all your great **skills.**
A month later, Jane called to tell me **you** had died, Mom. We'd been tearing out all the old electricals in the walls, replacing them with brand-new wiring...
We were putting up a **chandelier** that I'd found on 57th Street in Manhattan
...shaped like the **sun.**
...and had just turned it on when a **fuse** blew—
and the whole house went dark.

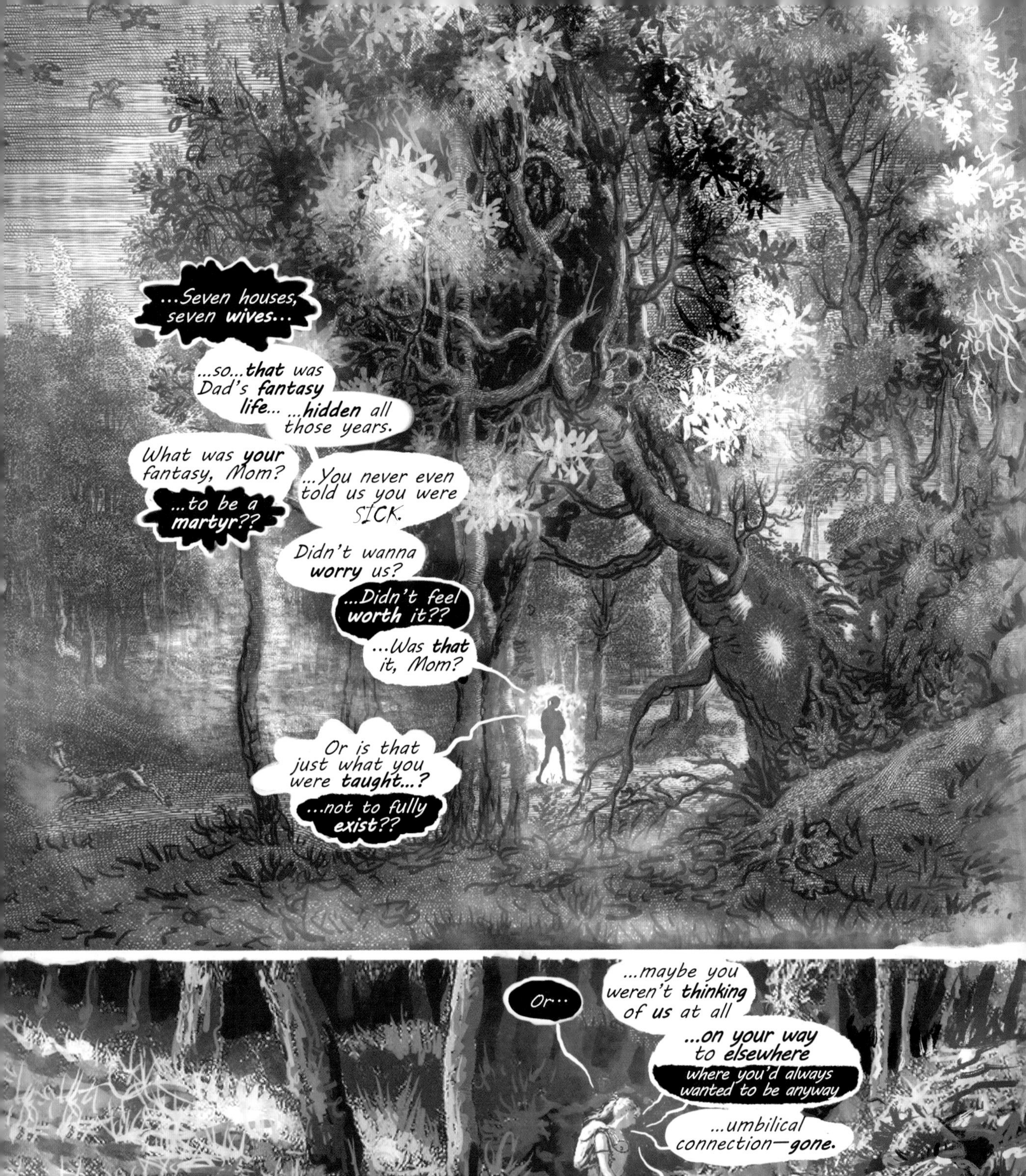
...Seven houses, seven **wives**...
...so...**that** was Dad's **fantasy life**... ...**hidden** all those years.
What was **your** fantasy, Mom?
...to be a **martyr??**
...You never even told us you were SICK.
Didn't wanna **worry** us?
...Didn't feel **worth** it??
...Was **that** it, Mom?
Or is that just what you were **taught**...?
...not to fully **exist??**
Or..
...maybe you weren't **thinking** of **us** at all
...on your way to elsewhere
where you'd always wanted to be anyway
...umbilical connection—**gone.**
DAMN
WHY'm I so **MAD** at You, Mom??!

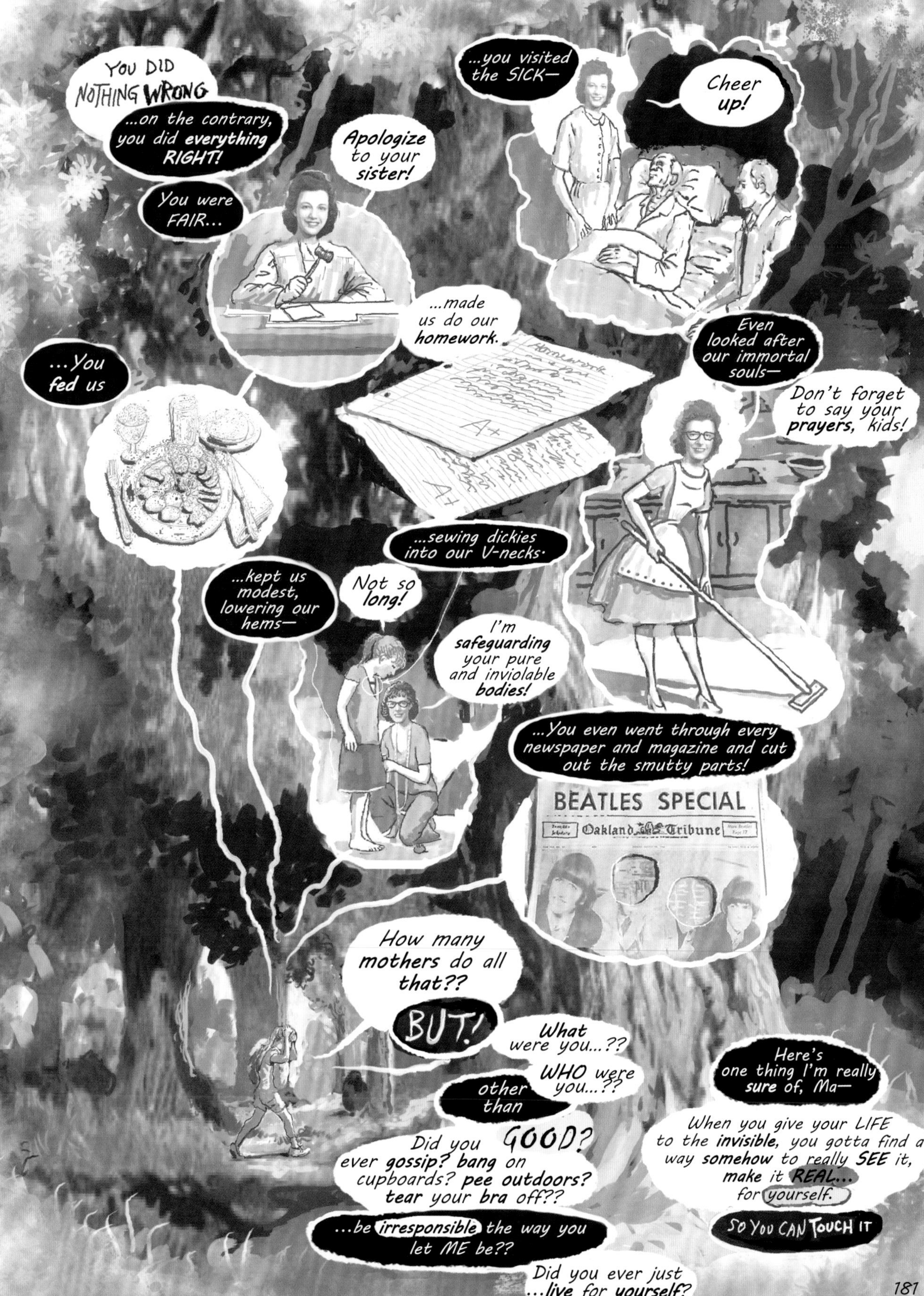

YOU DID NOTHING WRONG
...on the contrary, you did everything RIGHT!
You were FAIR...
Apologize to your sister!
...you visited the SICK—
Cheer up!
...made us do our homework.
...You fed us
Even looked after our immortal souls—
Don't forget to say your prayers, kids!
...sewing dickies into our V-necks.
...kept us modest, lowering our hems—
Not so long!
I'm safeguarding your pure and inviolable bodies!
...You even went through every newspaper and magazine and cut out the smutty parts!
BEATLES SPECIAL
Oakland Tribune
How many mothers do all that??
BUT!
What were you...??
WHO were you...??
other than GOOD?
Did you ever gossip? bang on cupboards? pee outdoors? tear your bra off??
...be irresponsible the way you let ME be??
Did you ever just ...live for yourself?
Here's one thing I'm really sure of, Ma—
When you give your LIFE to the invisible, you gotta find a way somehow to really SEE it, make it REAL... for yourself.
SO YOU CAN TOUCH IT

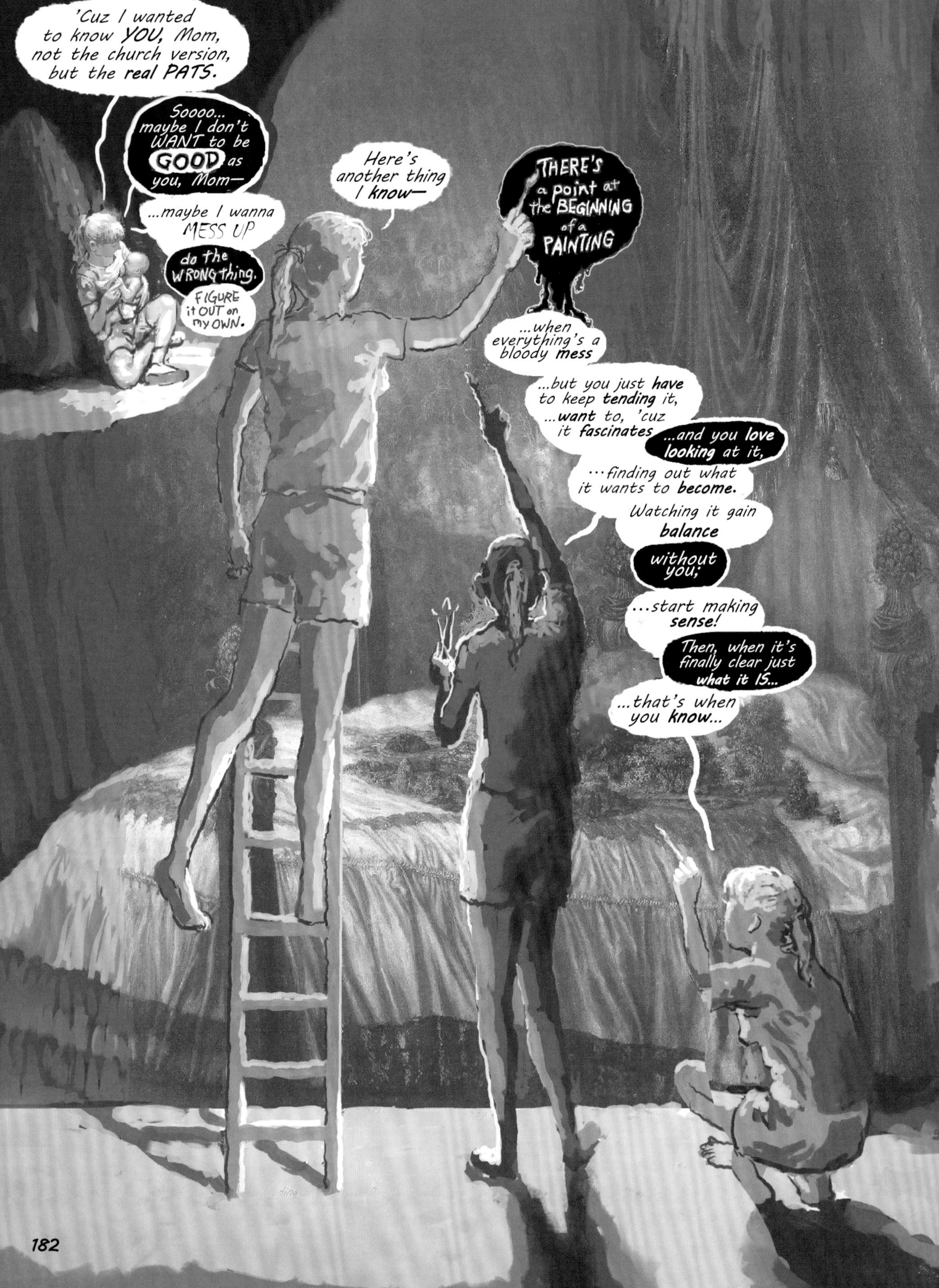
'Cuz I wanted to know YOU, Mom, not the church version, but the real PATS.
Soooo... maybe I don't WANT to be GOOD as you, Mom—
...maybe I wanna MESS UP
do the WRONG thing.
FIGURE it OUT on my OWN.
Here's another thing I know—
THERE'S a point at the BEGINNING of a PAINTING
...when everything's a bloody mess
...but you just have to keep tending it, ...want to, 'cuz it fascinates
...and you love looking at it,
...finding out what it wants to become.
Watching it gain balance
without you;
...start making sense!
Then, when it's finally clear just what it IS...
...that's when you know...

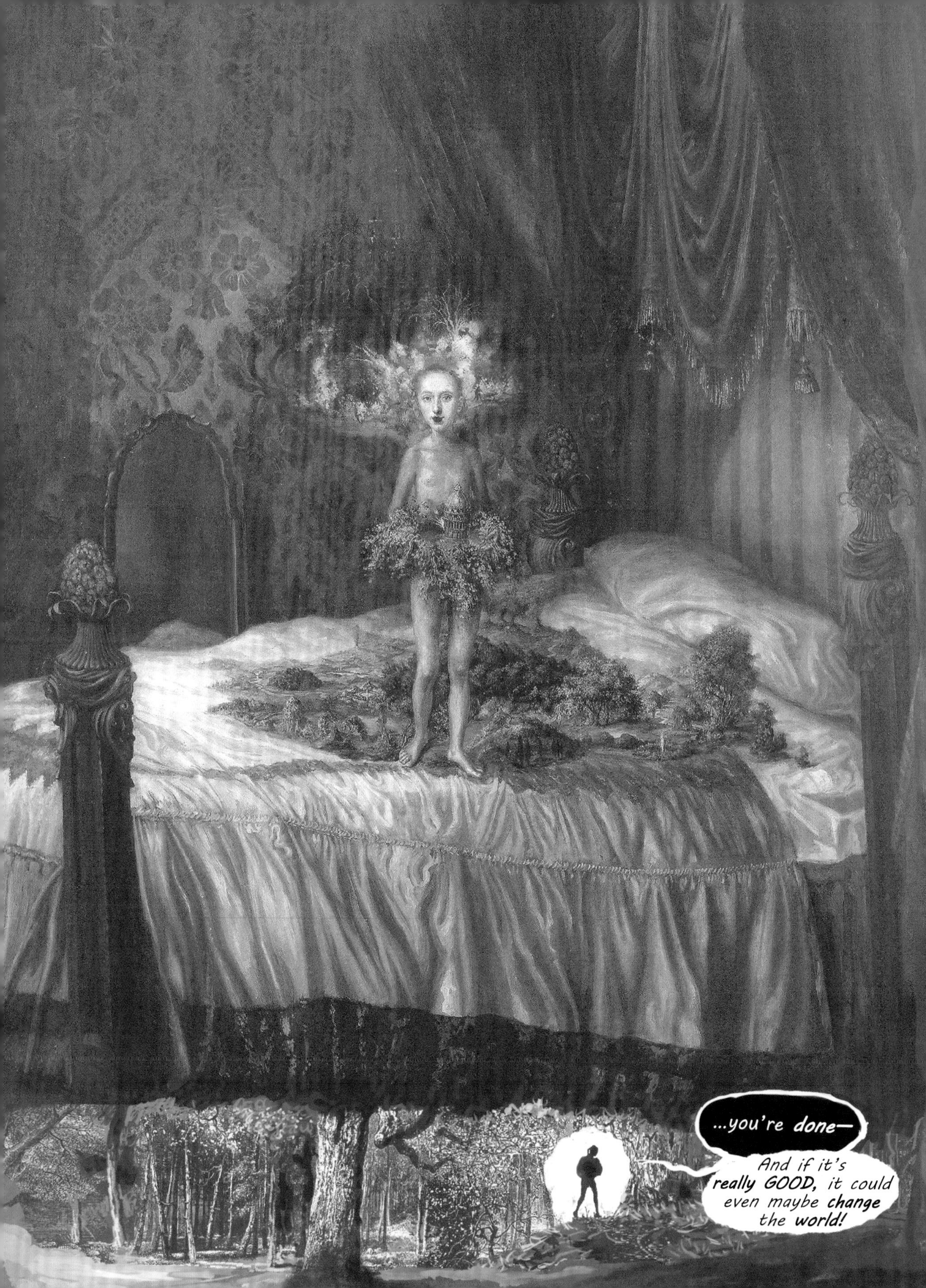
...you're done—
And if it's really GOOD, it could even maybe change the world!

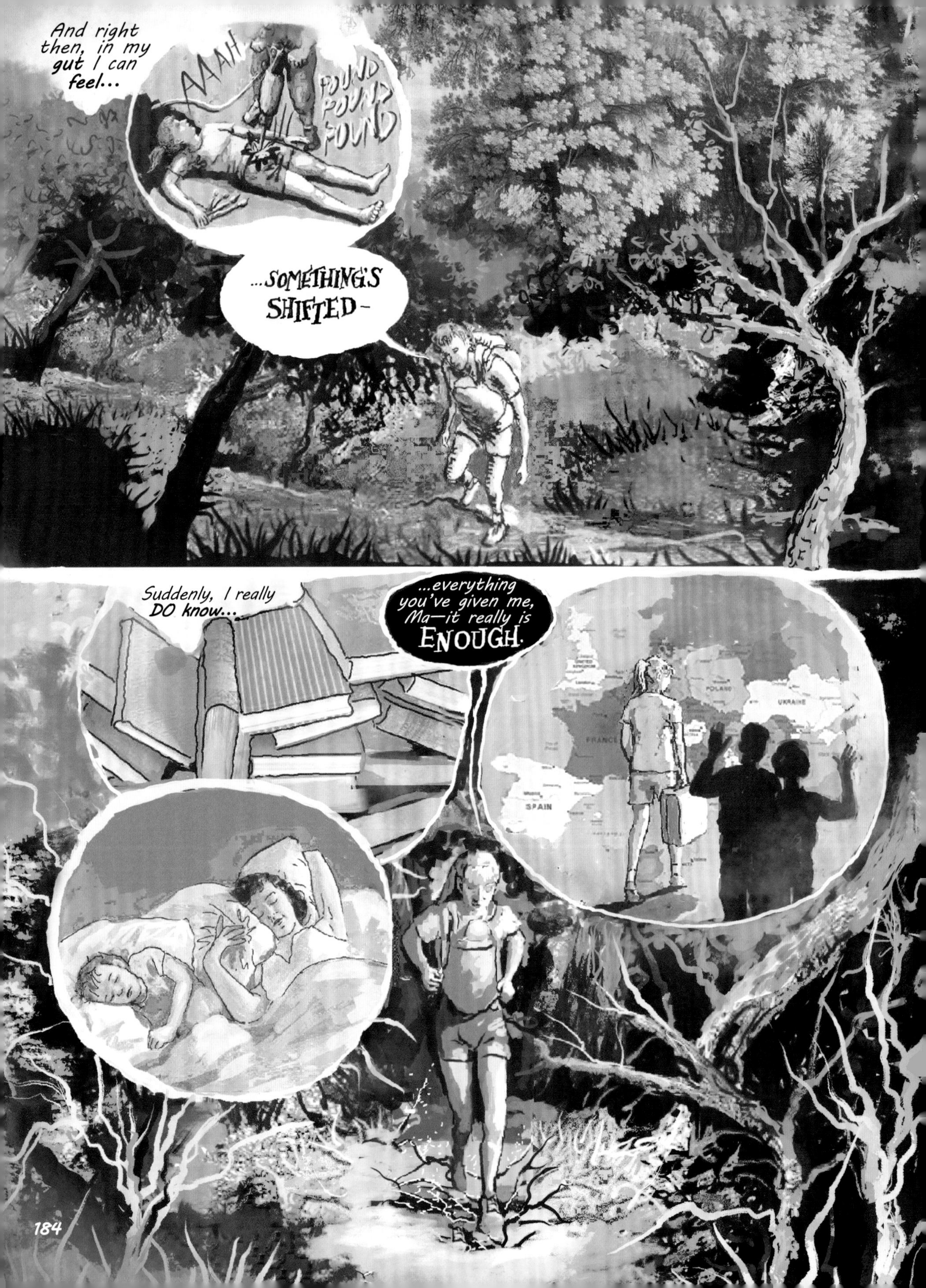

And right then, in my *gut* I can *feel*...

AAAH

POUND POUND POUND

...SOMETHING'S SHIFTED–

Suddenly, I really **DO know**...

...everything you've given me, Ma—it really is ENOUGH.

POLAND

UKRAINE

FRANCE

SPAIN

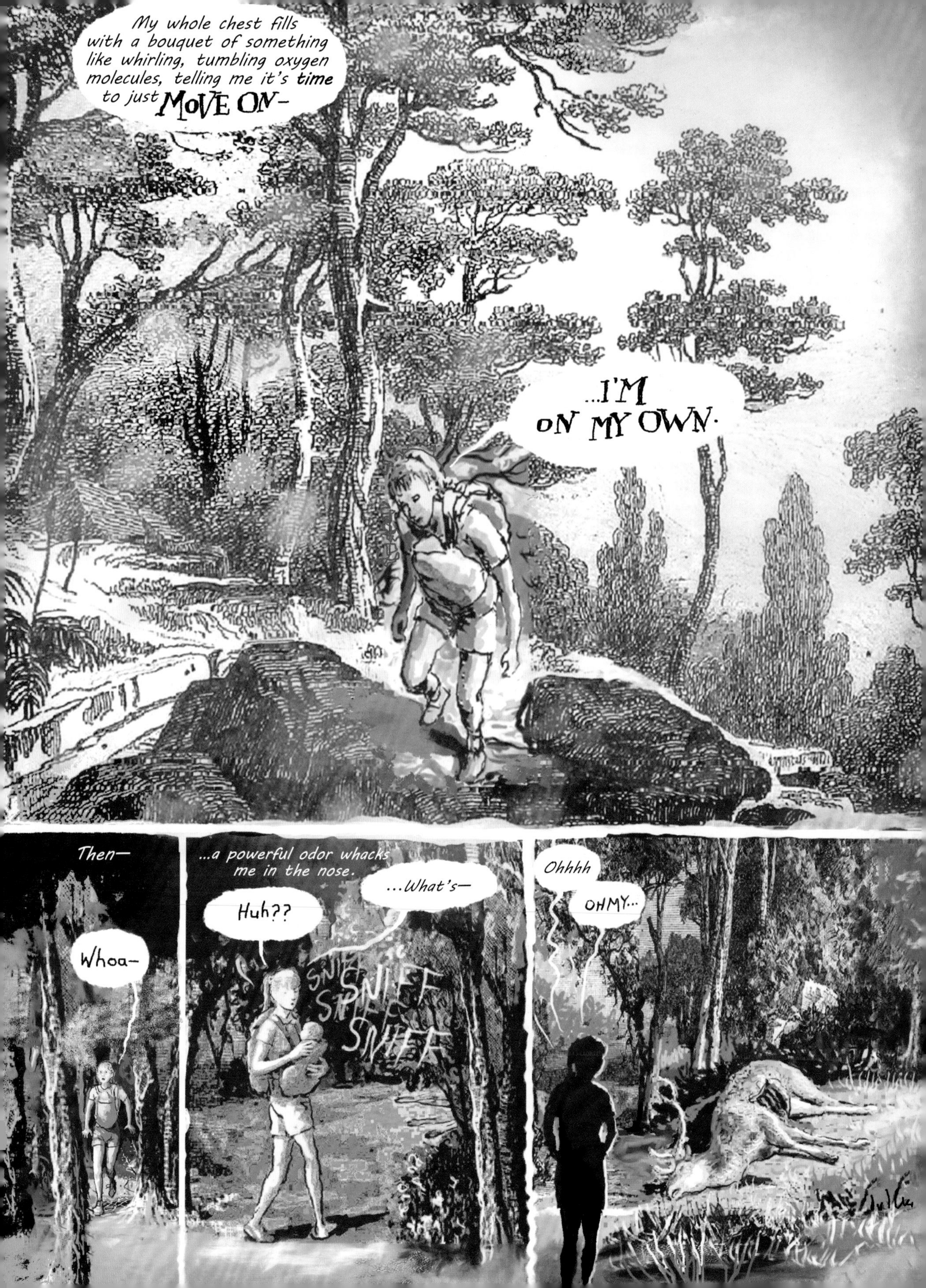

My whole chest fills with a bouquet of something like whirling, tumbling oxygen molecules, telling me it's **time** to just MOVE ON–

...I'M ON MY OWN.

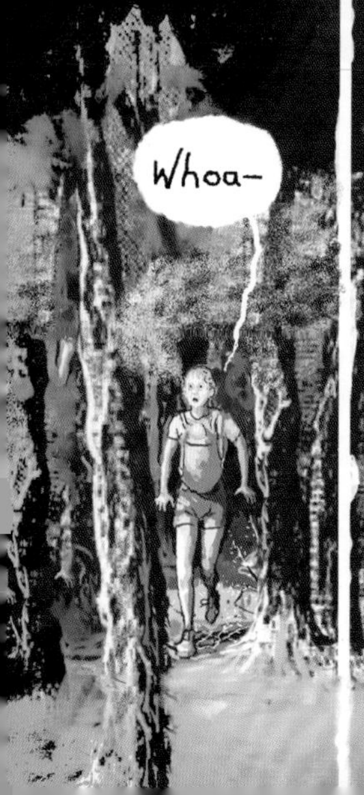

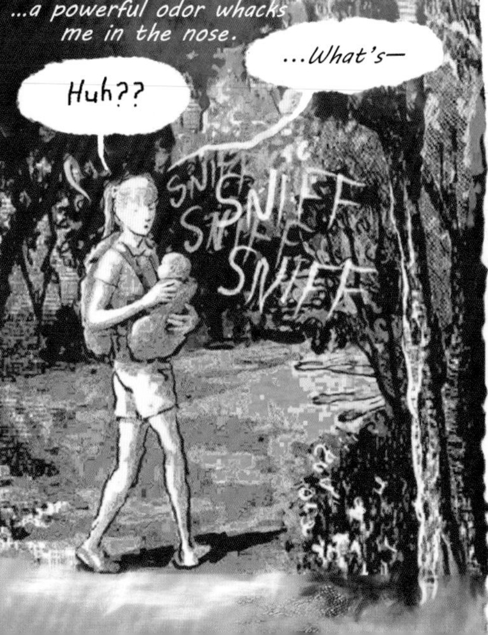

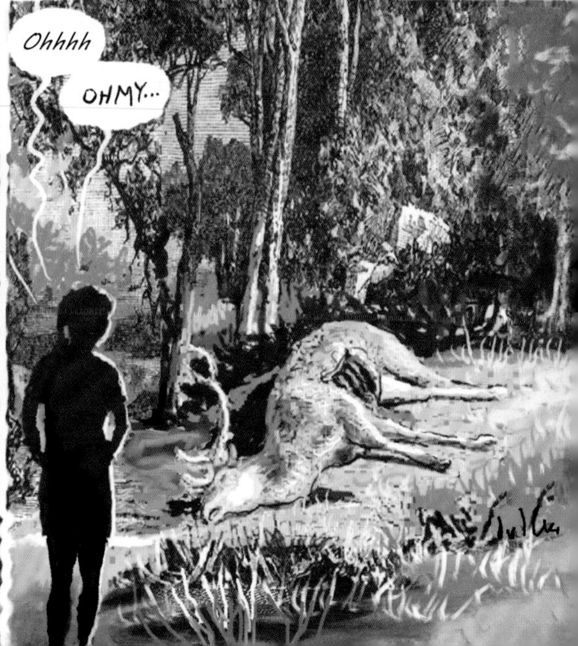

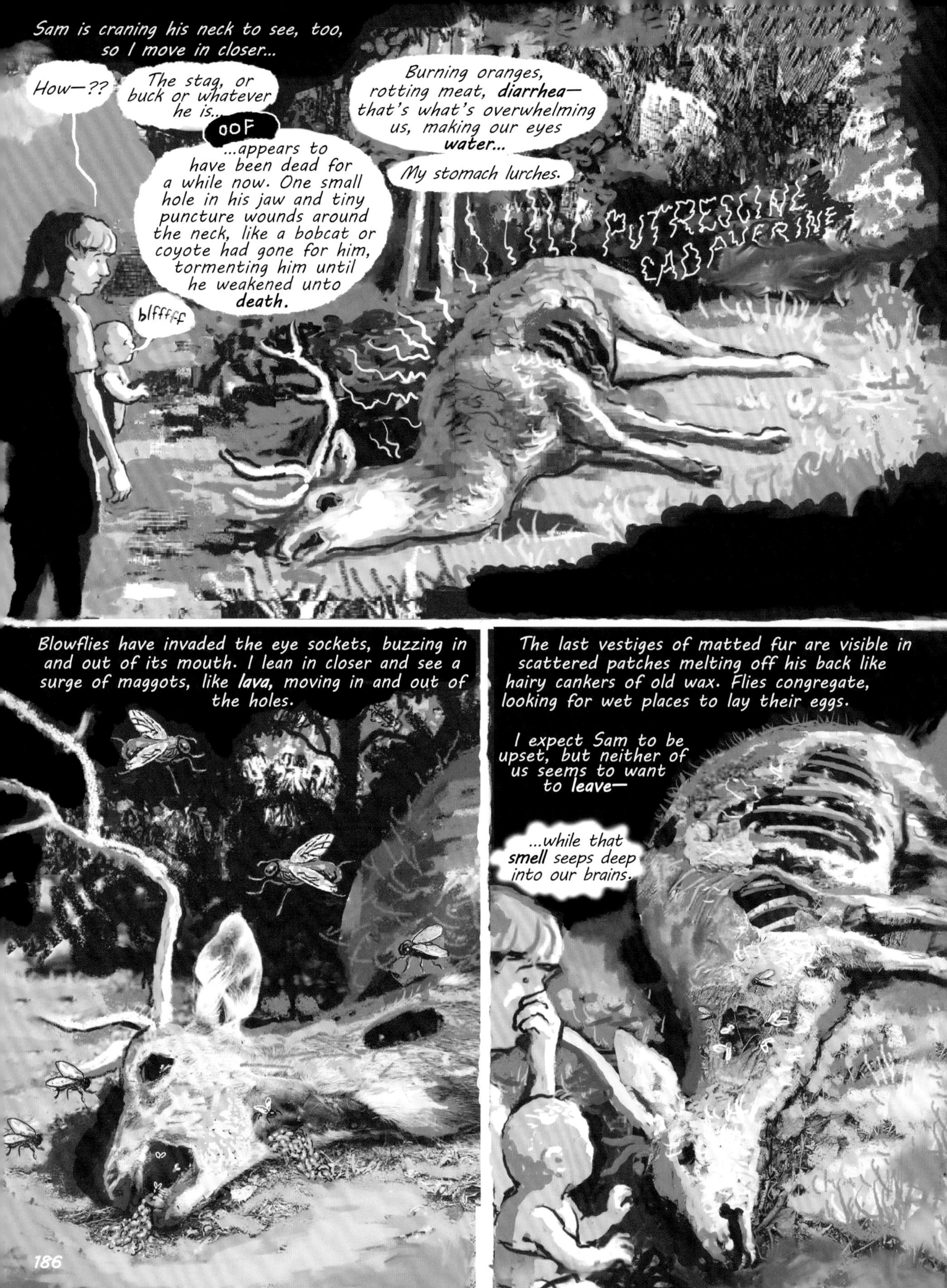

Sam is craning his neck to see, too, so I move in closer...
How—??
The stag, or buck or whatever he is...
OOF
...appears to have been dead for a while now. One small hole in his jaw and tiny puncture wounds around the neck, like a bobcat or coyote had gone for him, tormenting him until he weakened unto **death.**
blffff
Burning oranges, rotting meat, **diarrhea**—that's what's overwhelming us, making our eyes **water...**
My stomach lurches.
PUTRESCINE
CADAVERINE
Blowflies have invaded the eye sockets, buzzing in and out of its mouth. I lean in closer and see a surge of maggots, like **lava,** moving in and out of the holes.
The last vestiges of matted fur are visible in scattered patches melting off his back like hairy cankers of old wax. Flies congregate, looking for wet places to lay their eggs.
I expect Sam to be upset, but neither of us seems to want to **leave**—
...while that **smell** seeps deep into our brains.

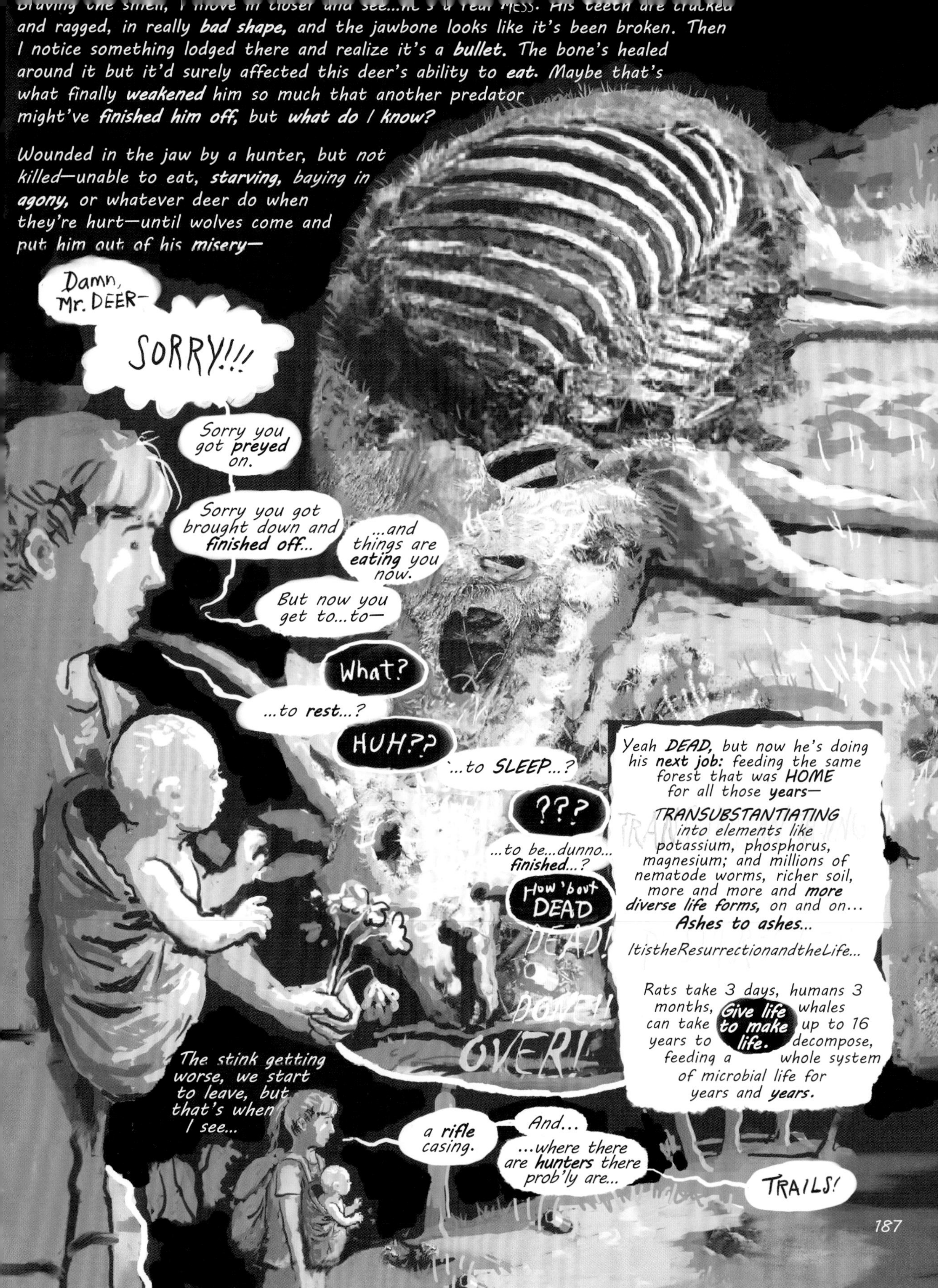

Braving the smell, I move in closer and see...it's a real MESS. His teeth are cracked and ragged, in really bad shape, and the jawbone looks like it's been broken. Then I notice something lodged there and realize it's a bullet. The bone's healed around it but it'd surely affected this deer's ability to eat. Maybe that's what finally weakened him so much that another predator might've finished him off, but what do I know?
Wounded in the jaw by a hunter, but not killed—unable to eat, starving, baying in agony, or whatever deer do when they're hurt—until wolves come and put him out of his misery—
Damn, Mr. DEER—
SORRY!!!
Sorry you got preyed on.
Sorry you got brought down and finished off...
...and things are eating you now.
But now you get to...to—
What?
...to rest...?
HUH??
...to SLEEP...?
???
...to be...dunno... finished...?
How 'bout DEAD
DEAD!
DONE!
OVER!
Yeah DEAD, but now he's doing his next job: feeding the same forest that was HOME for all those years—
TRANSUBSTANTIATING into elements like potassium, phosphorus, magnesium; and millions of nematode worms, richer soil, more and more and more diverse life forms, on and on...
Ashes to ashes...
ItistheResurrectionandtheLife...
Rats take 3 days, humans 3 months, whales can take up to 16 years to decompose, feeding a whole system of microbial life for years and years.
Give life to make life.
The stink getting worse, we start to leave, but that's when I see...
a rifle casing.
And...
...where there are hunters there prob'ly are...
TRAILS!

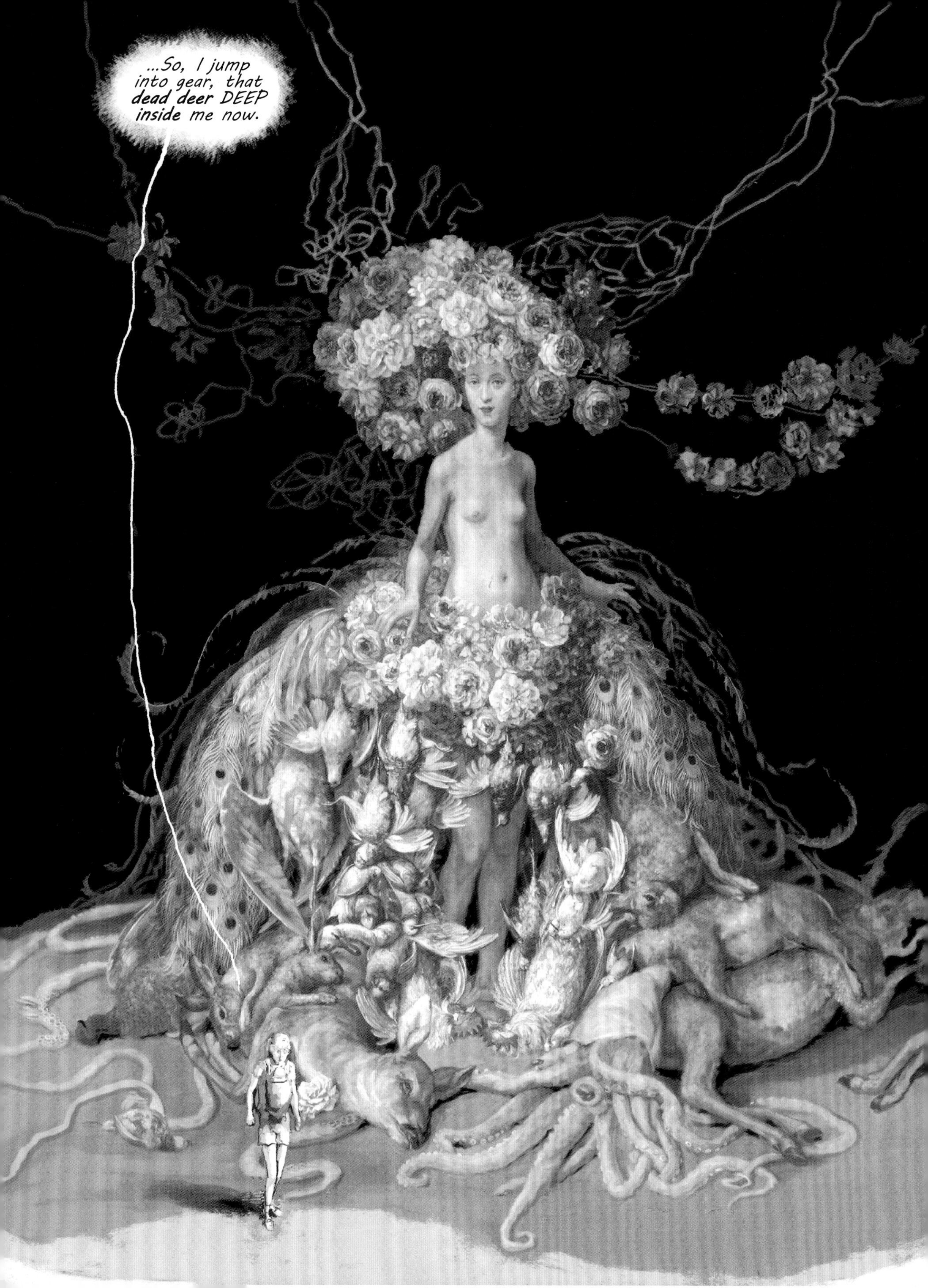
...So, I jump into gear, that **dead deer DEEP inside** me now.

Chapter ELEVEN

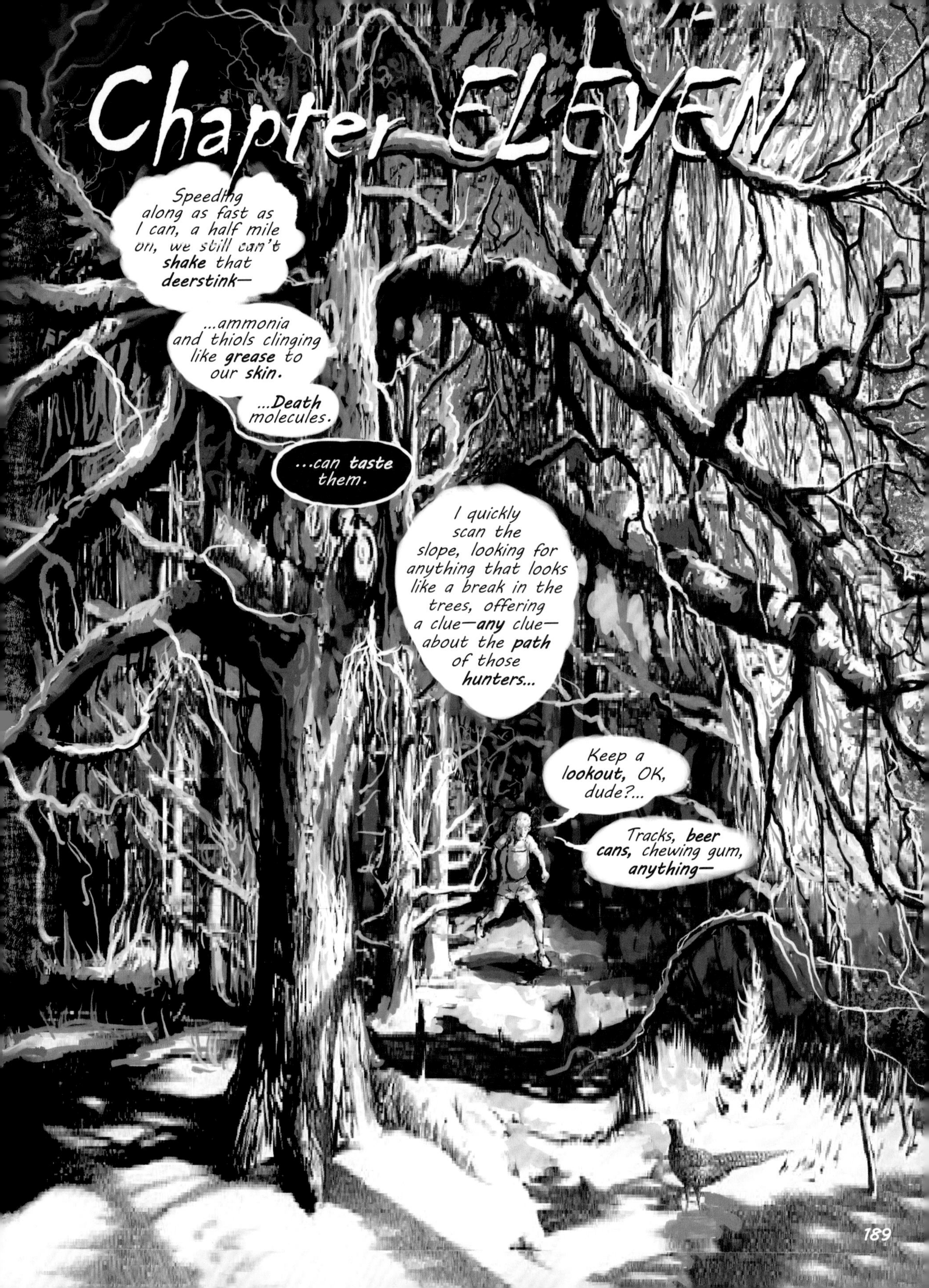

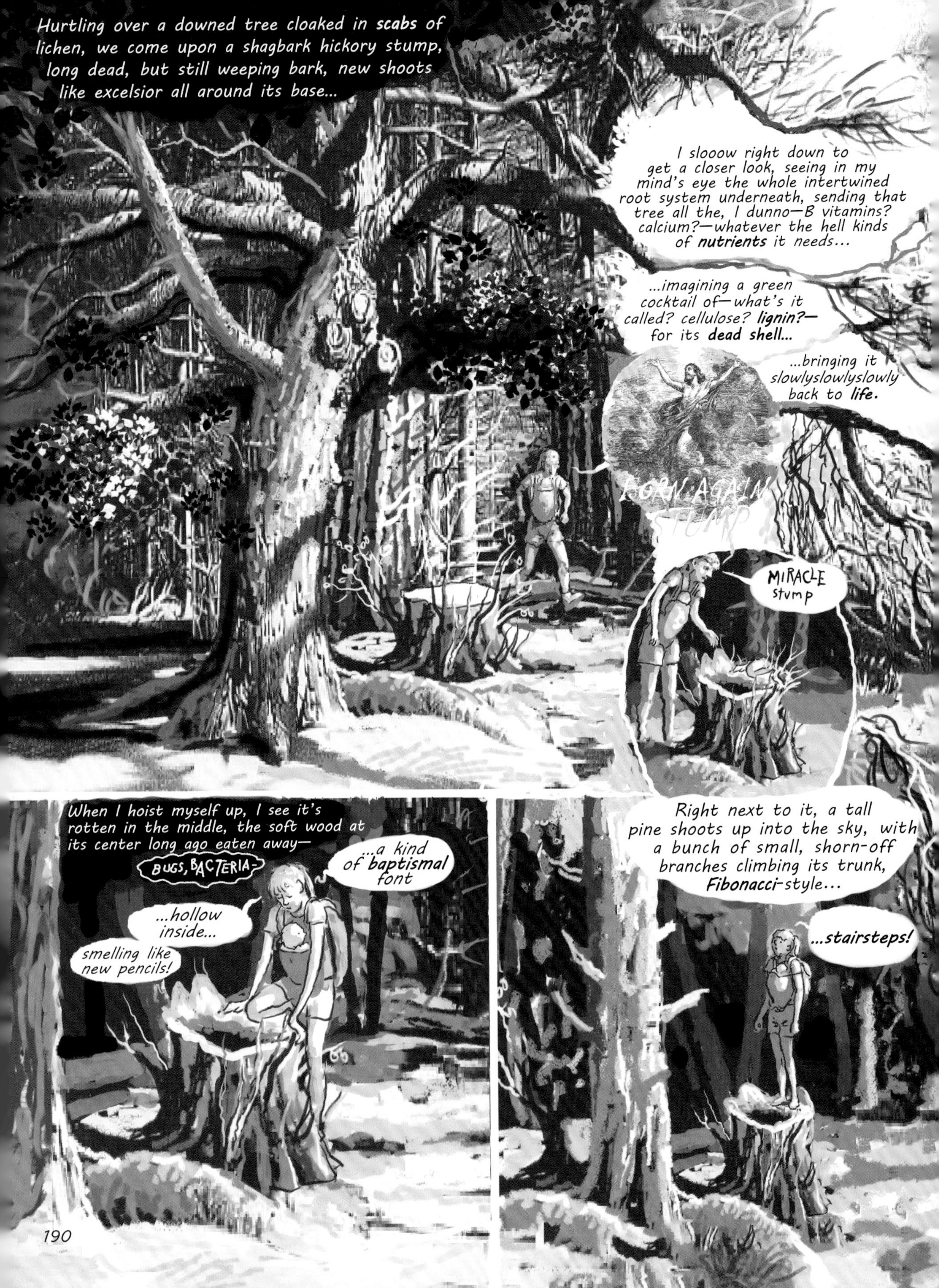
Hurtling over a downed tree cloaked in **scabs** of lichen, we come upon a shagbark hickory stump, long dead, but still weeping bark, new shoots like excelsior all around its base...
I slooow right down to get a closer look, seeing in my mind's eye the whole intertwined root system underneath, sending that tree all the, I dunno—B vitamins? calcium?—whatever the hell kinds of **nutrients** it needs...
...imagining a green cocktail of—what's it called? cellulose? **lignin?**—for its **dead shell...**
...bringing it slowlyslowlyslowly back to **life.**
BORN AGAIN STUMP
MIRACLE stump
When I hoist myself up, I see it's rotten in the middle, the soft wood at its center long ago eaten away—
BUGS, BACTERIA—
...a kind of **baptismal** font
...hollow inside...
smelling like new pencils!
Right next to it, a tall pine shoots up into the sky, with a bunch of small, shorn-off branches climbing its trunk, **Fibonacci**-style...
...stairsteps!

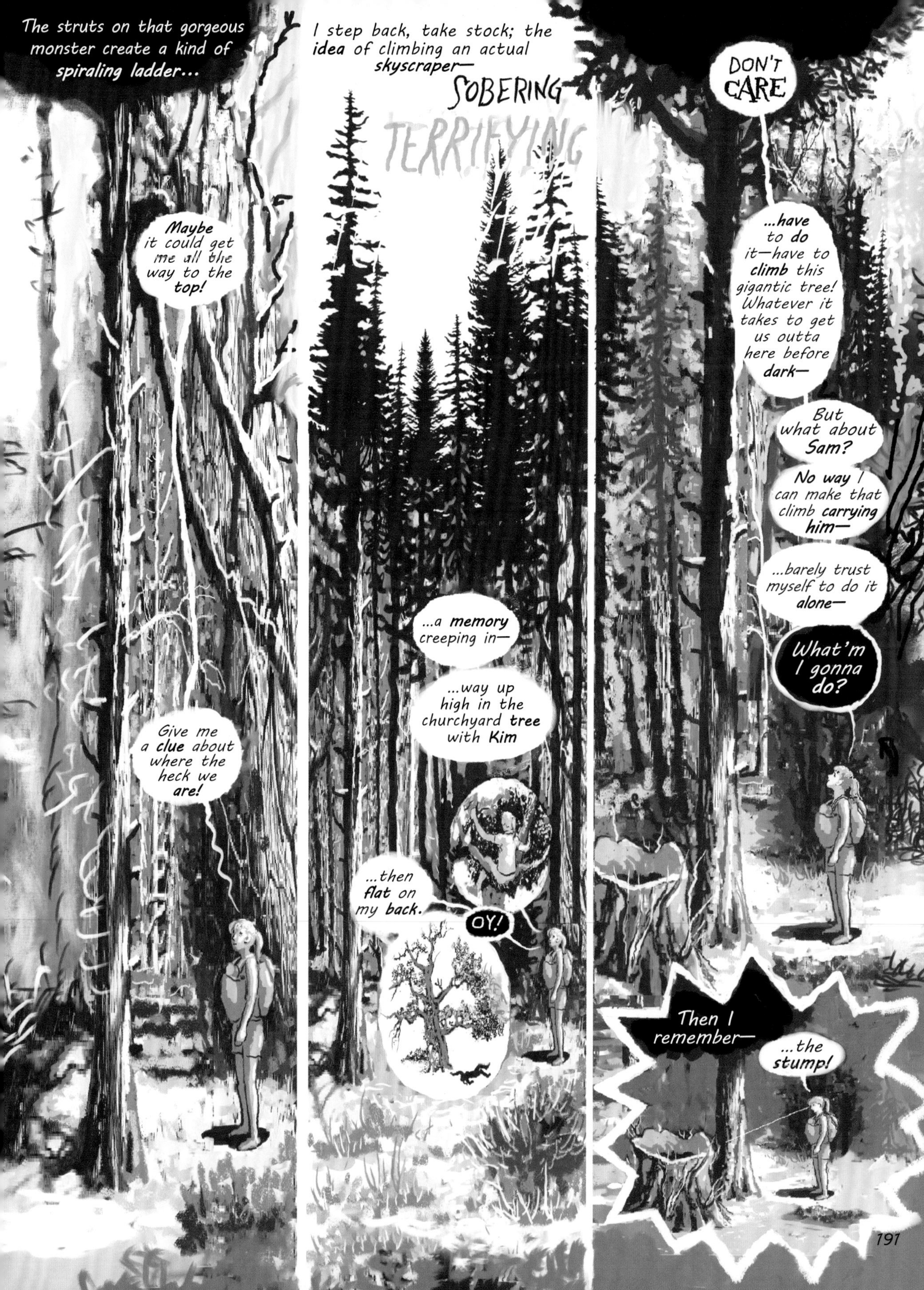
The struts on that gorgeous monster create a kind of spiraling ladder...
Maybe it could get me all the way to the top!
Give me a clue about where the heck we are!
I step back, take stock; the idea of climbing an actual skyscraper—
SOBERING
TERRIFYING
...a memory creeping in—
...way up high in the churchyard tree with Kim
...then flat on my back.
OY!
DON'T CARE
...have to do it—have to climb this gigantic tree! Whatever it takes to get us outta here before dark—
But what about Sam?
No way I can make that climb carrying him—
...barely trust myself to do it alone—
What'm I gonna do?
Then I remember—
...the stump!

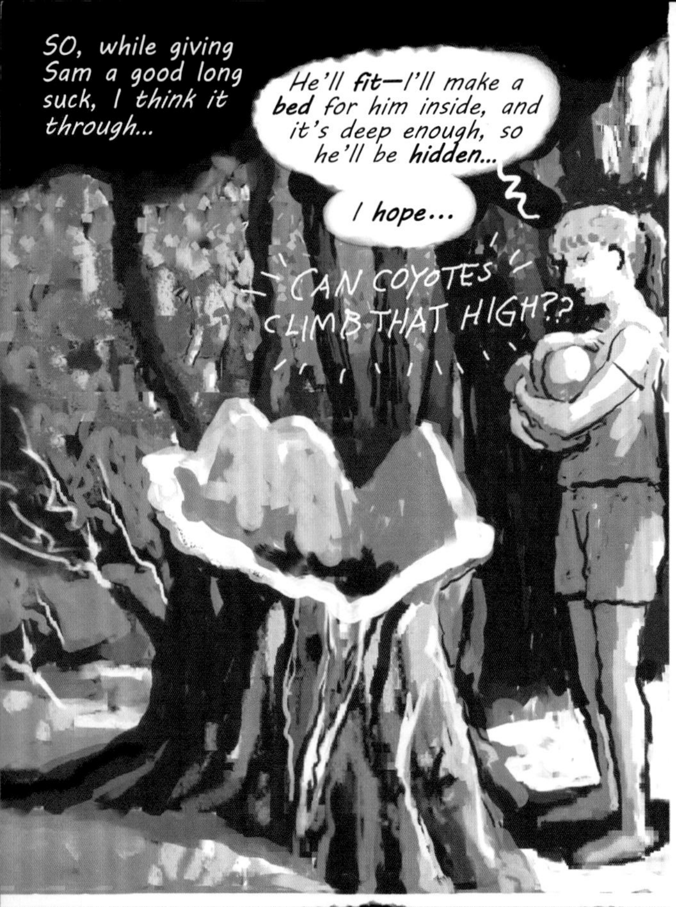
SO, while giving Sam a good long suck, I think it through...
He'll **fit**—I'll make a **bed** for him inside, and it's deep enough, so he'll be **hidden**...
I hope...
CAN COYOTES CLIMB THAT HIGH??

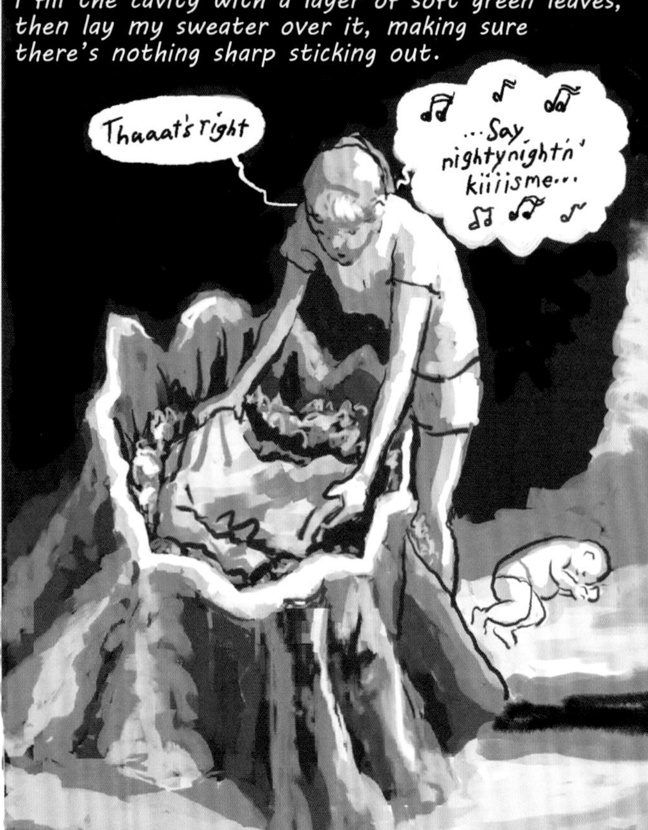
I fill the cavity with a layer of soft green leaves, then lay my sweater over it, making sure there's nothing sharp sticking out.
Thaaat's right
...Say nightynight'n' kiiiisme...

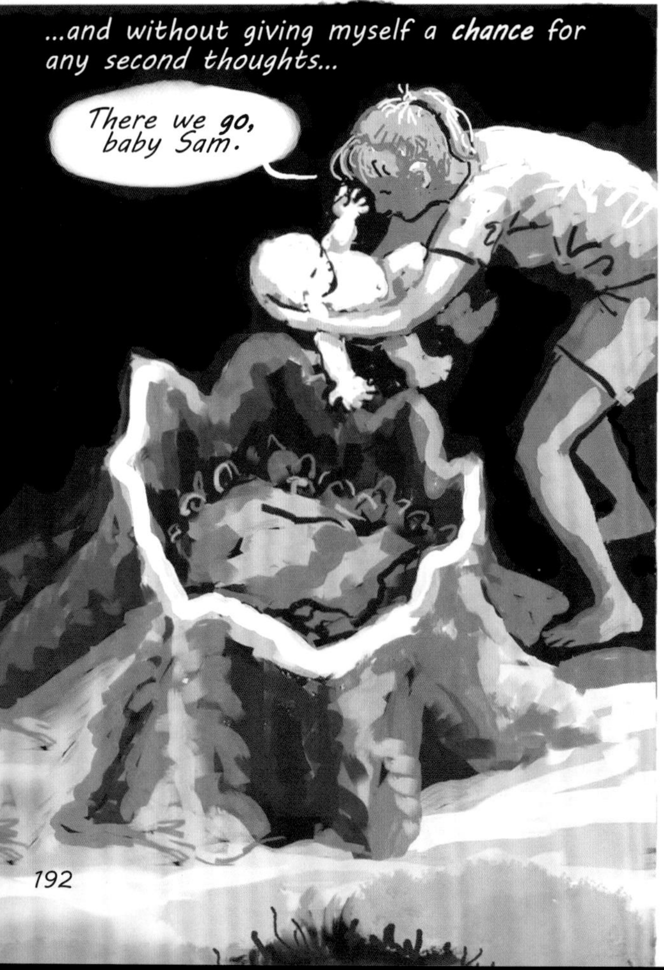
...and without giving myself a **chance** for any second thoughts...
There we **go,** baby Sam.

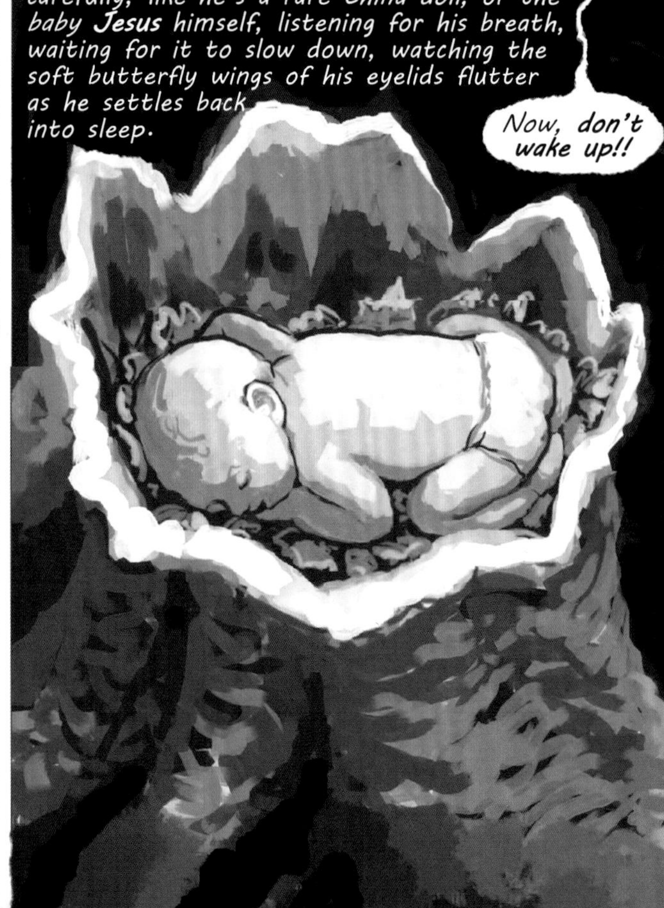
I lay him down inside his stump manger sooooo carefully, like he's a rare China doll, or the baby **Jesus** himself, listening for his breath, waiting for it to slow down, watching the soft butterfly wings of his eyelids flutter as he settles back into sleep.
Now, **don't wake up!!**

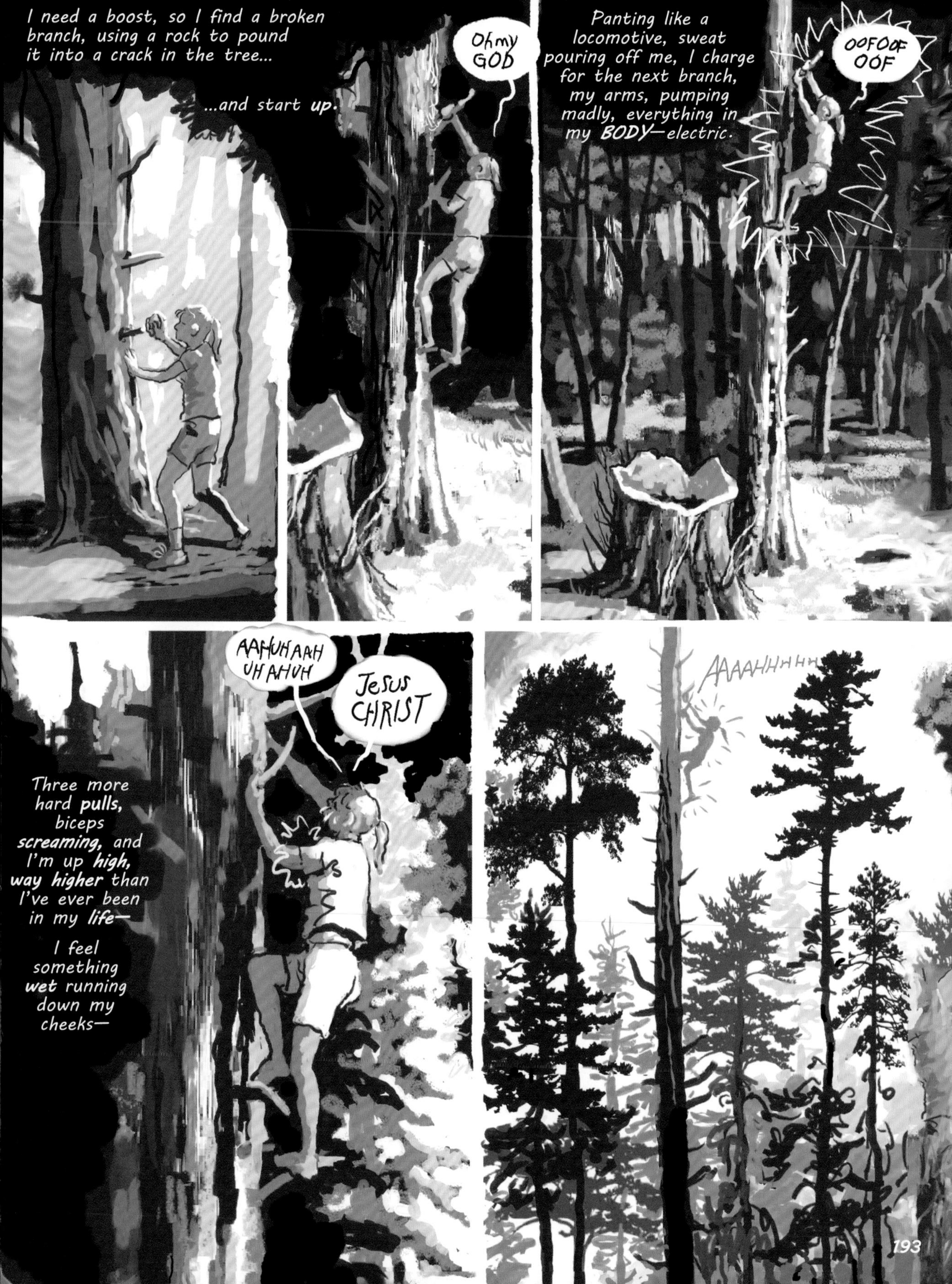
I need a boost, so I find a broken branch, using a rock to pound it into a crack in the tree...
...and start up.
Oh my GOD
Panting like a locomotive, sweat pouring off me, I charge for the next branch, my arms, pumping madly, everything in my BODY—electric.
OOFOOF OOF
AAHUHAAH UHAHUH
JESUS CHRIST
Three more hard pulls, biceps screaming, and I'm up high, way higher than I've ever been in my life—
I feel something wet running down my cheeks—
AAAAHHHHHH

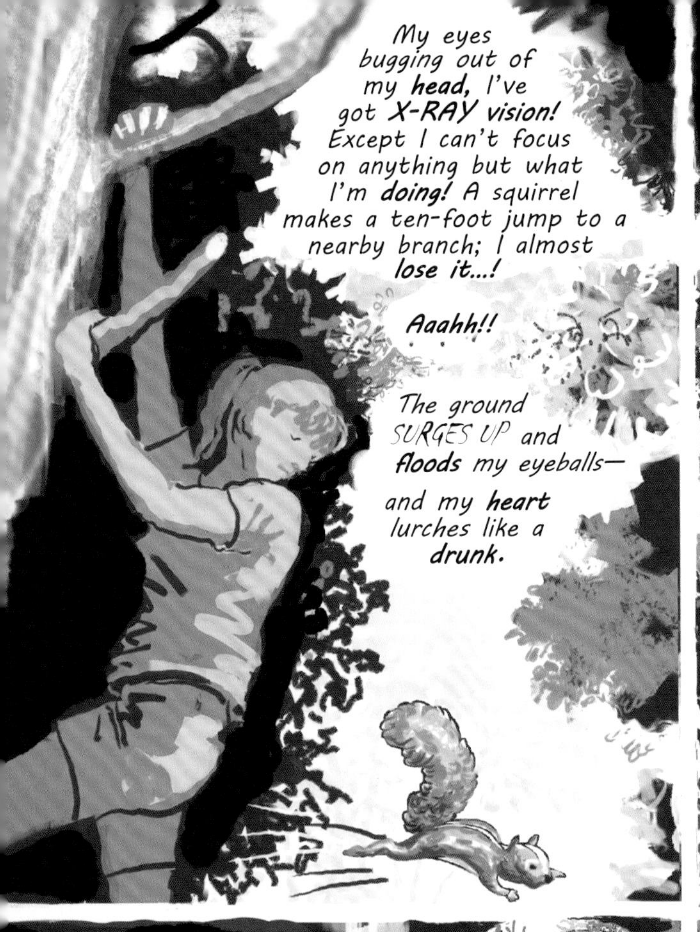

My eyes bugging out of my head, I've got X-RAY vision! Except I can't focus on anything but what I'm doing! A squirrel makes a ten-foot jump to a nearby branch; I almost lose it...!
Aaahh!!
The ground SURGES UP and floods my eyeballs—
and my heart lurches like a drunk.

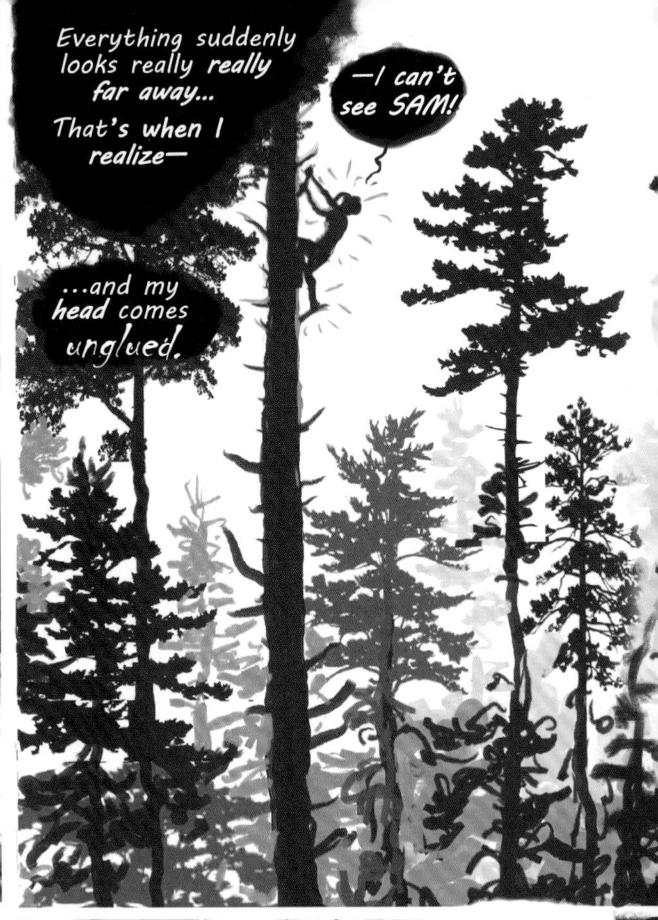

Everything suddenly looks really really far away...
That's when I realize—
—I can't see SAM!
...and my head comes unglued.

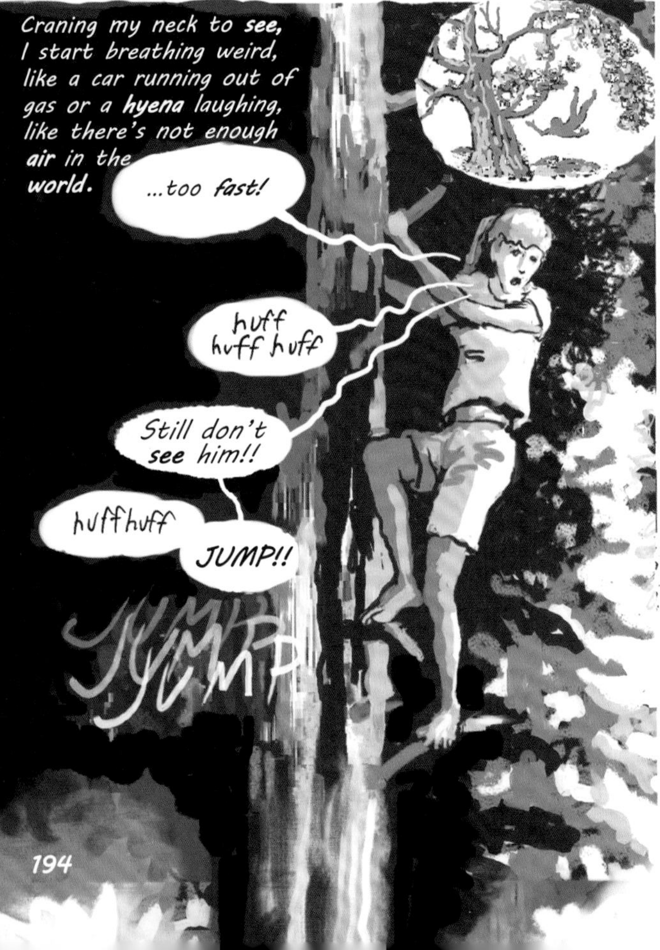

Craning my neck to see, I start breathing weird, like a car running out of gas or a hyena laughing, like there's not enough air in the world.
...too fast!
huff huff huff
Still don't see him!!
huffhuff
JUMP!!
JUMP

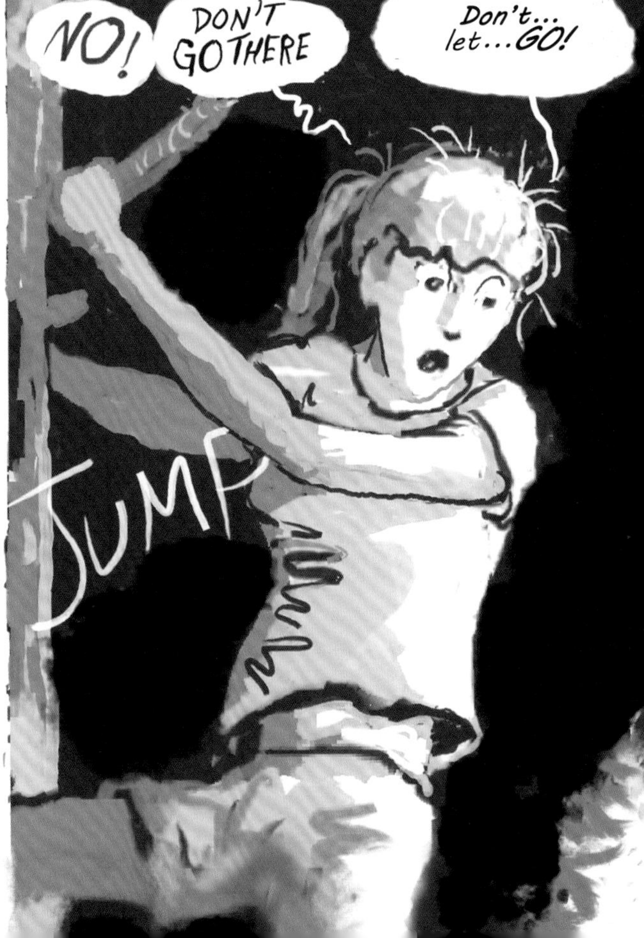

NO!
DON'T GO THERE
Don't... let... GO!
JUMP

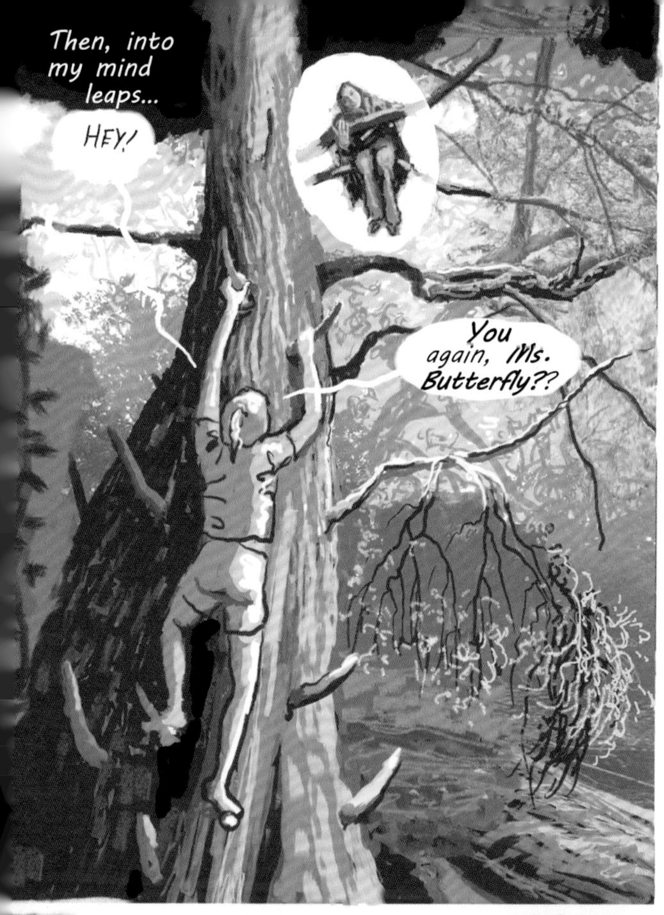
Then, into my mind leaps...
HEY!
You again, Ms. Butterfly??

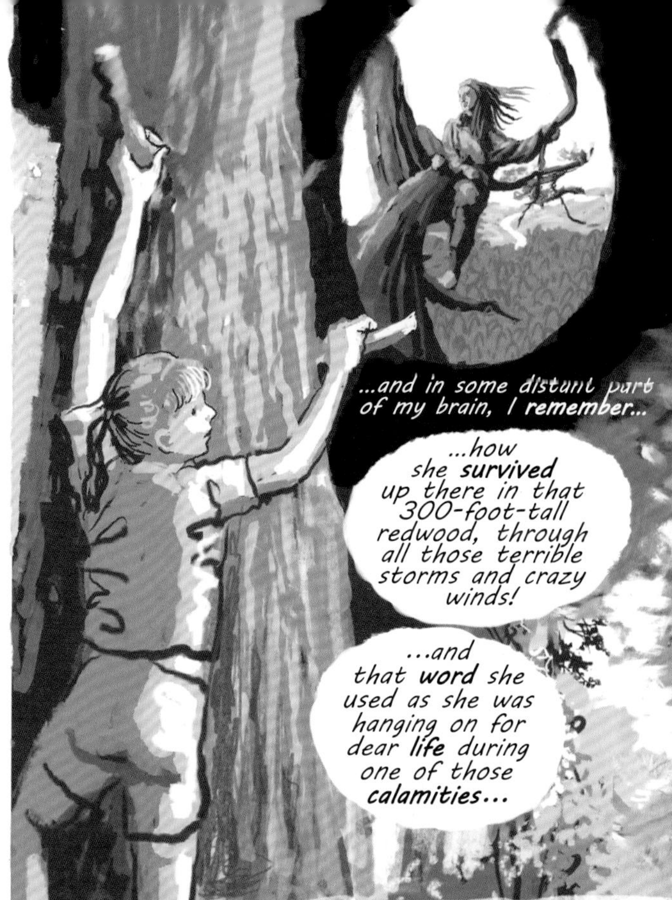
...and in some distant part of my brain, I remember...
...how she survived up there in that 300-foot-tall redwood, through all those terrible storms and crazy winds!
...and that word she used as she was hanging on for dear life during one of those calamities...

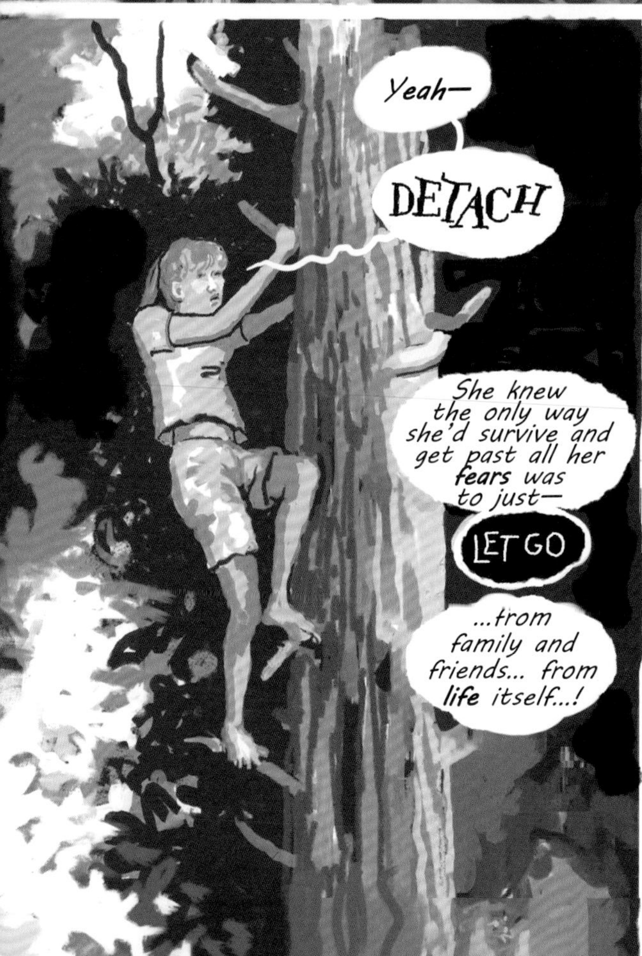
Yeah—
DETACH
She knew the only way she'd survive and get past all her fears was to just—
LET GO
...from family and friends... from life itself...!

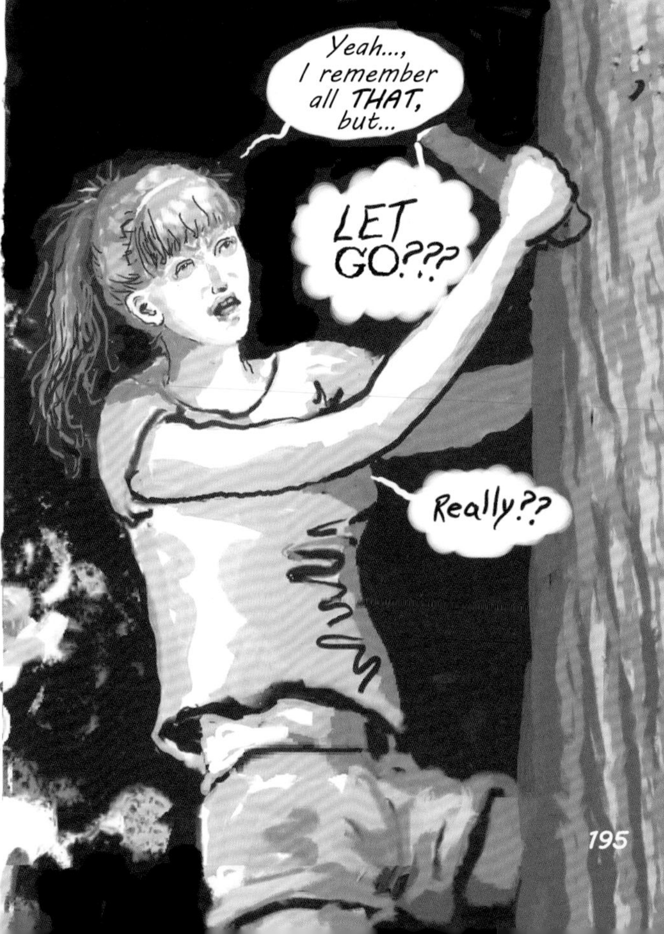
Yeah..., I remember all THAT, but...
LET GO???
Really??

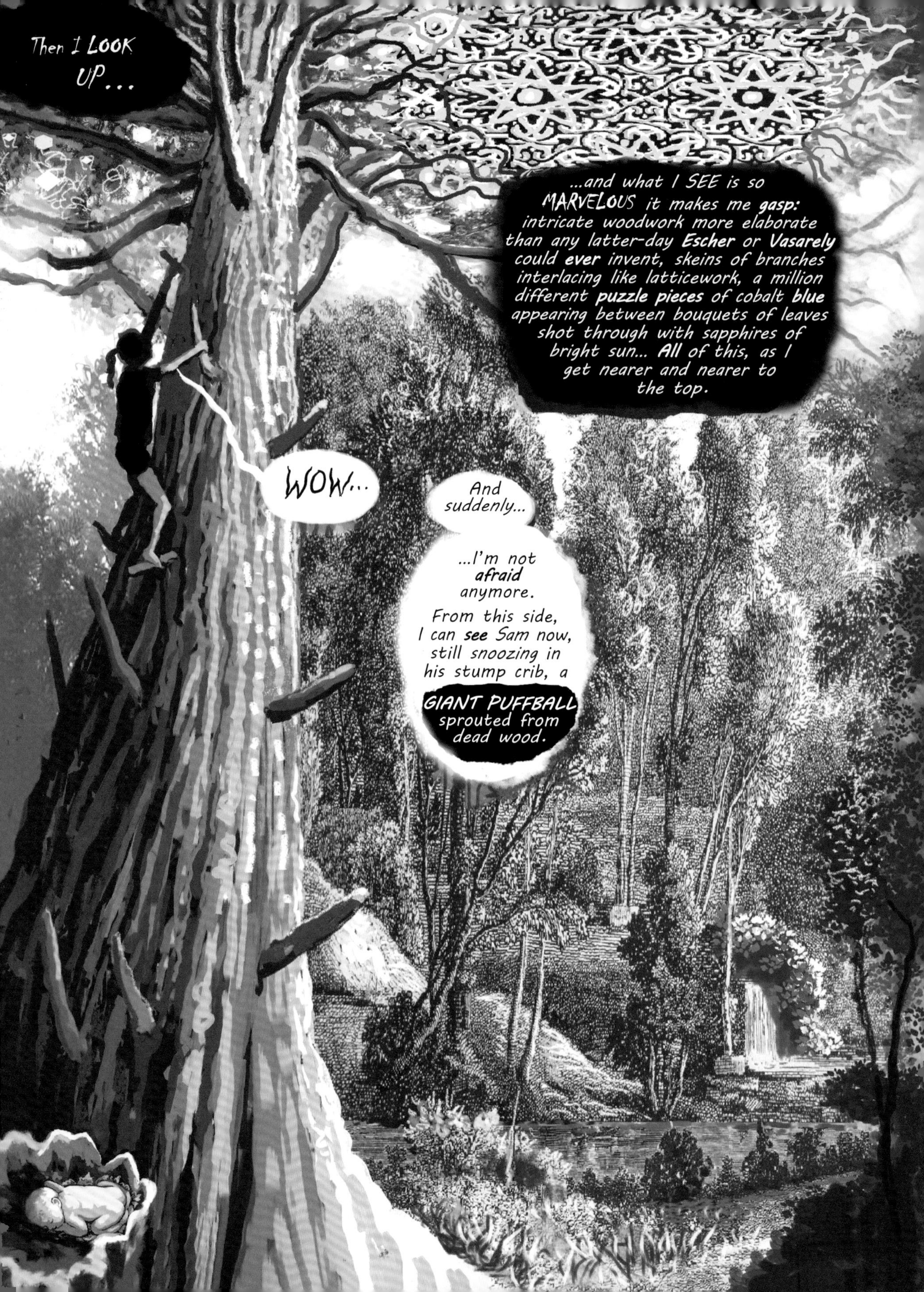
Then I LOOK UP...
...and what I SEE is so MARVELOUS it makes me gasp: intricate woodwork more elaborate than any latter-day Escher or Vasarely could ever invent, skeins of branches interlacing like latticework, a million different puzzle pieces of cobalt blue appearing between bouquets of leaves shot through with sapphires of bright sun... All of this, as I get nearer and nearer to the top.
WOW...
And suddenly...
...I'm not afraid anymore.
From this side, I can see Sam now, still snoozing in his stump crib, a
GIANT PUFFBALL sprouted from dead wood.

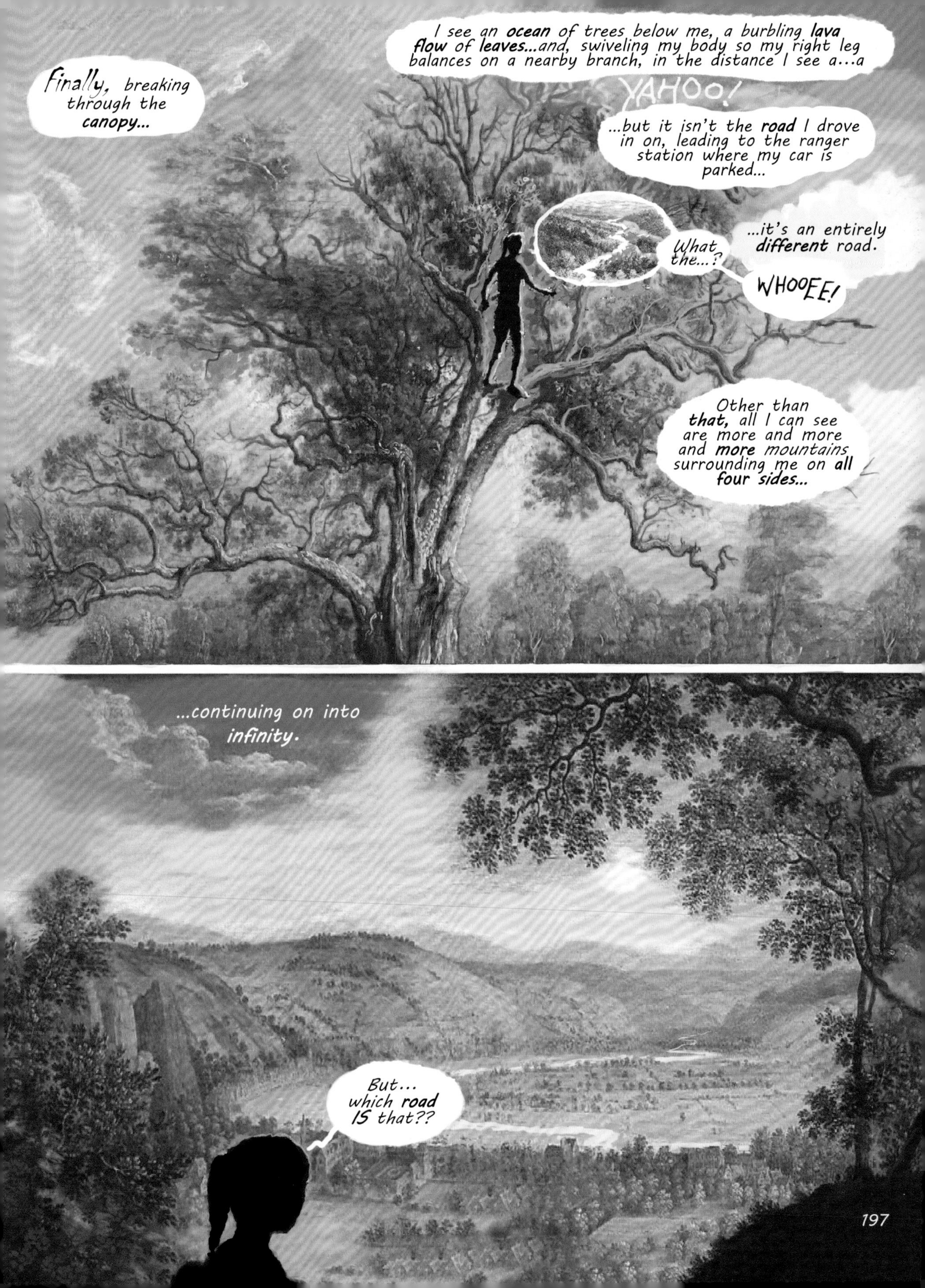

Finally, breaking through the canopy...

I see an ocean of trees below me, a burbling lava flow of leaves...and, swiveling my body so my right leg balances on a nearby branch, in the distance I see a...a

YAHOO!

...but it isn't the road I drove in on, leading to the ranger station where my car is parked...

What the...?

...it's an entirely different road.

WHOOEE!

Other than that, all I can see are more and more and more mountains surrounding me on all four sides...

...continuing on into infinity.

But... which road IS that??

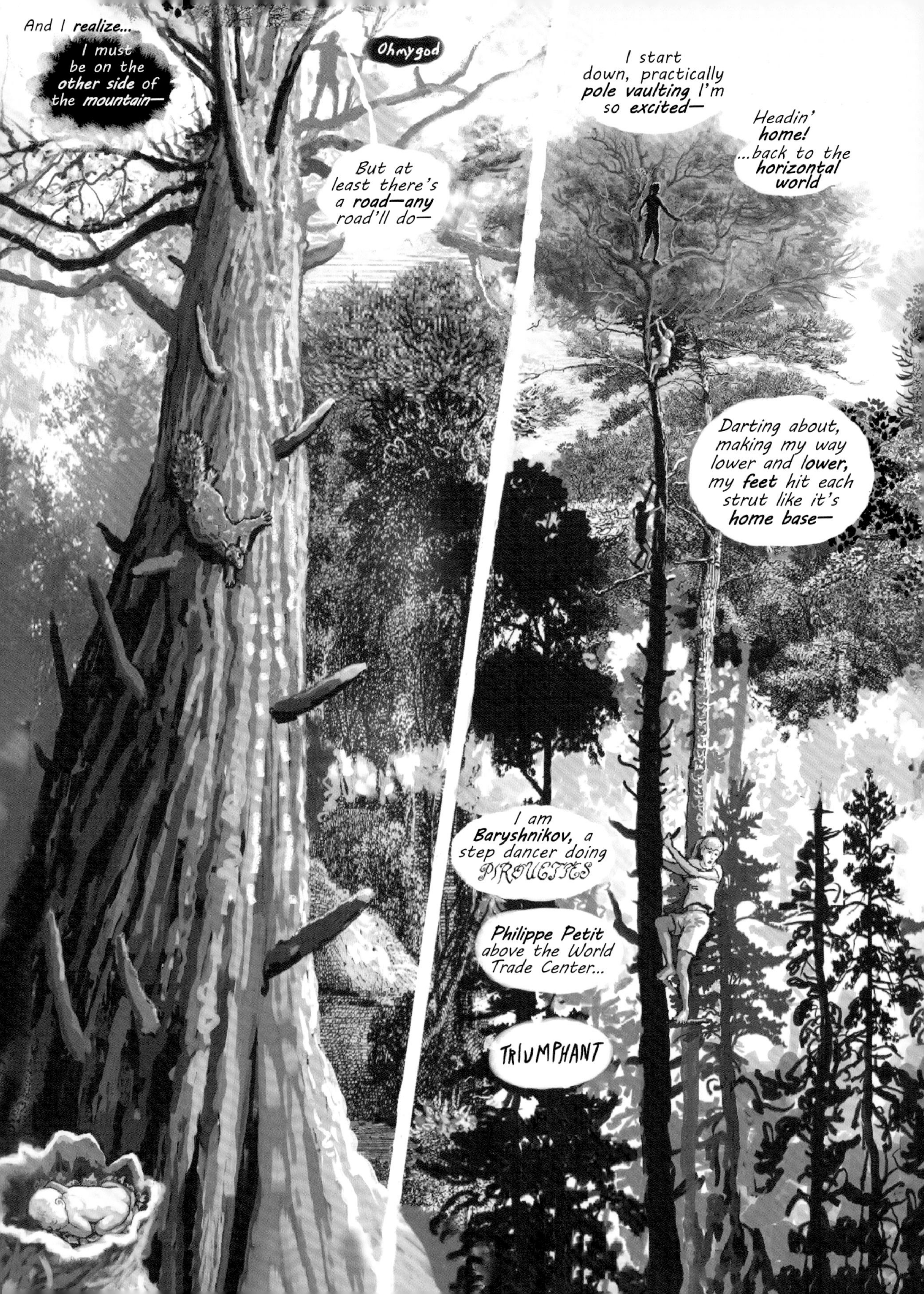
And I realize...
I must be on the other side of the mountain—
Ohmygod
But at least there's a road—any road'll do—
I start down, practically pole vaulting I'm so excited—
Headin' home! ...back to the horizontal world
Darting about, making my way lower and lower, my feet hit each strut like it's home base—
I am Baryshnikov, a step dancer doing PIROUETTES
Philippe Petit above the World Trade Center...
TRIUMPHANT

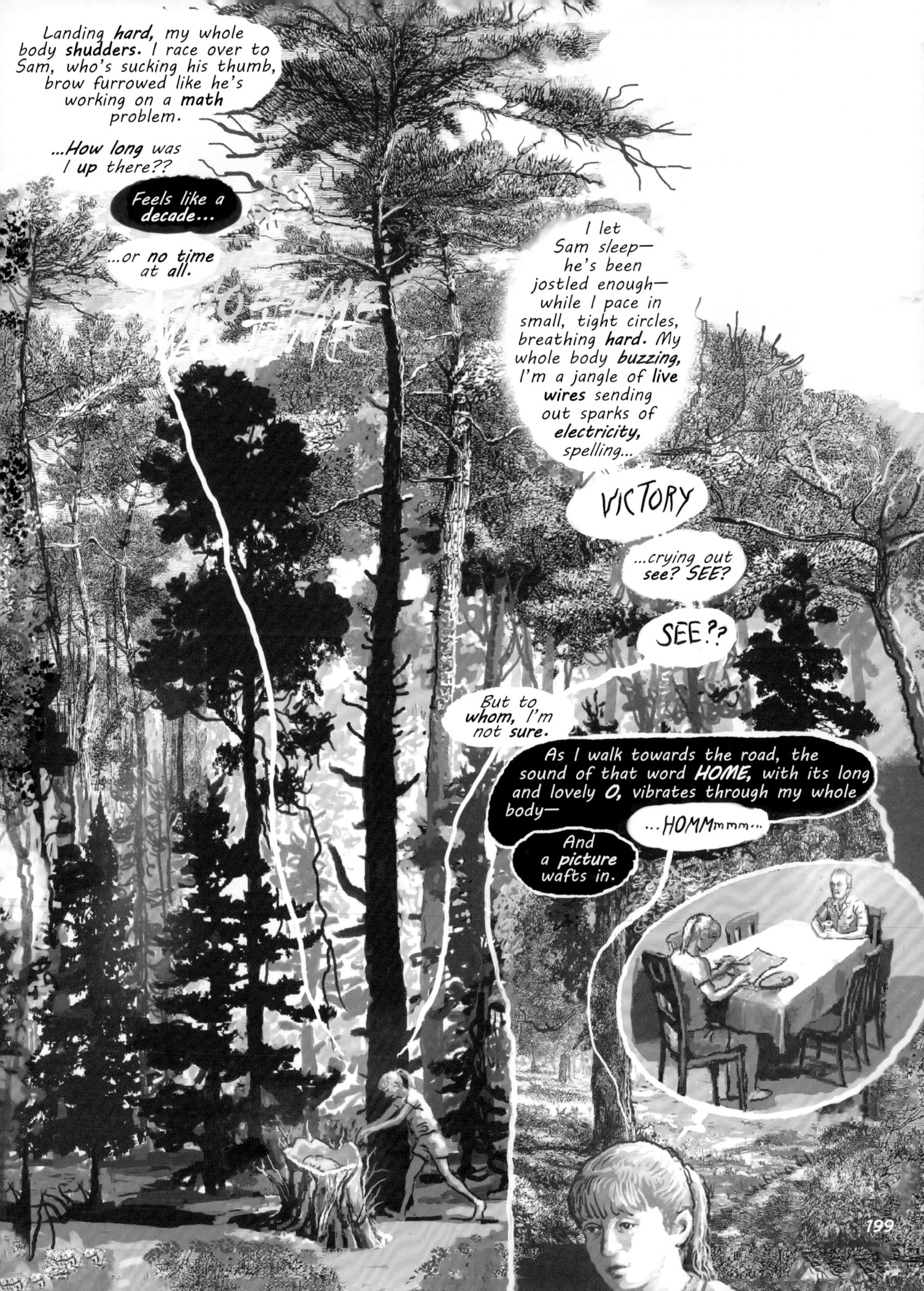
Landing hard, my whole body shudders. I race over to Sam, who's sucking his thumb, brow furrowed like he's working on a math problem.
...How long was I up there??
Feels like a decade...
...or no time at all.
I let Sam sleep— he's been jostled enough— while I pace in small, tight circles, breathing hard. My whole body buzzing, I'm a jangle of live wires sending out sparks of electricity, spelling...
VICTORY
...crying out see? SEE?
SEE??
But to whom, I'm not sure.
As I walk towards the road, the sound of that word HOME, with its long and lovely O, vibrates through my whole body—
...HOMMmmm...
And a picture wafts in.

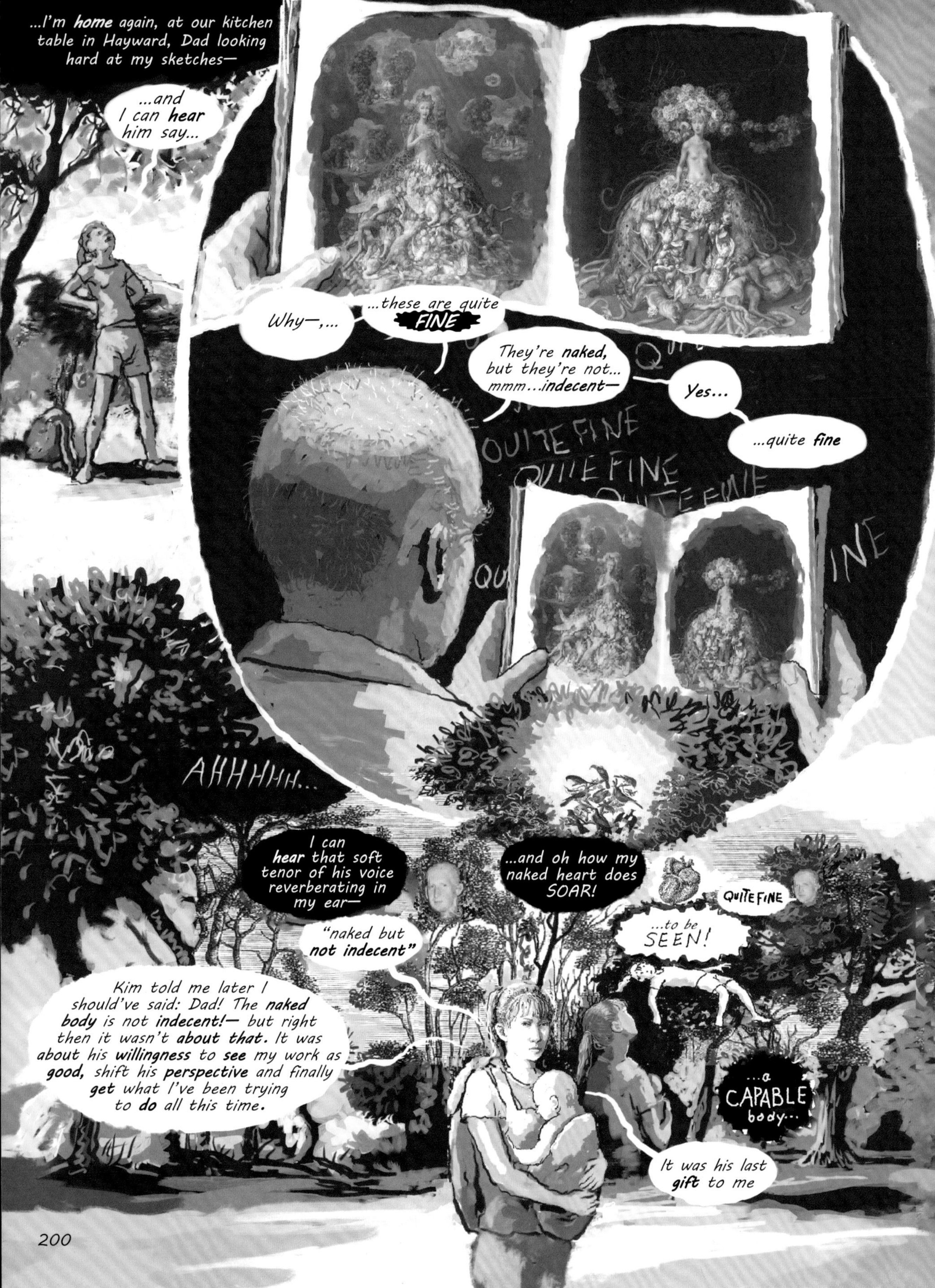

...I'm home again, at our kitchen table in Hayward, Dad looking hard at my sketches—
...and I can hear him say...
Why—,...
...these are quite FINE
They're naked, but they're not... mmm...indecent—
Yes...
...quite fine
QUITE FINE
QUITE FINE
AHHHHH...
I can hear that soft tenor of his voice reverberating in my ear—
...and oh how my naked heart does SOAR!
QUITE FINE
"naked but not indecent"
...to be SEEN!
Kim told me later I should've said: Dad! The naked body is not indecent!— but right then it wasn't about that. It was about his willingness to see my work as good, shift his perspective and finally get what I've been trying to do all this time.
...a CAPABLE body...
It was his last gift to me

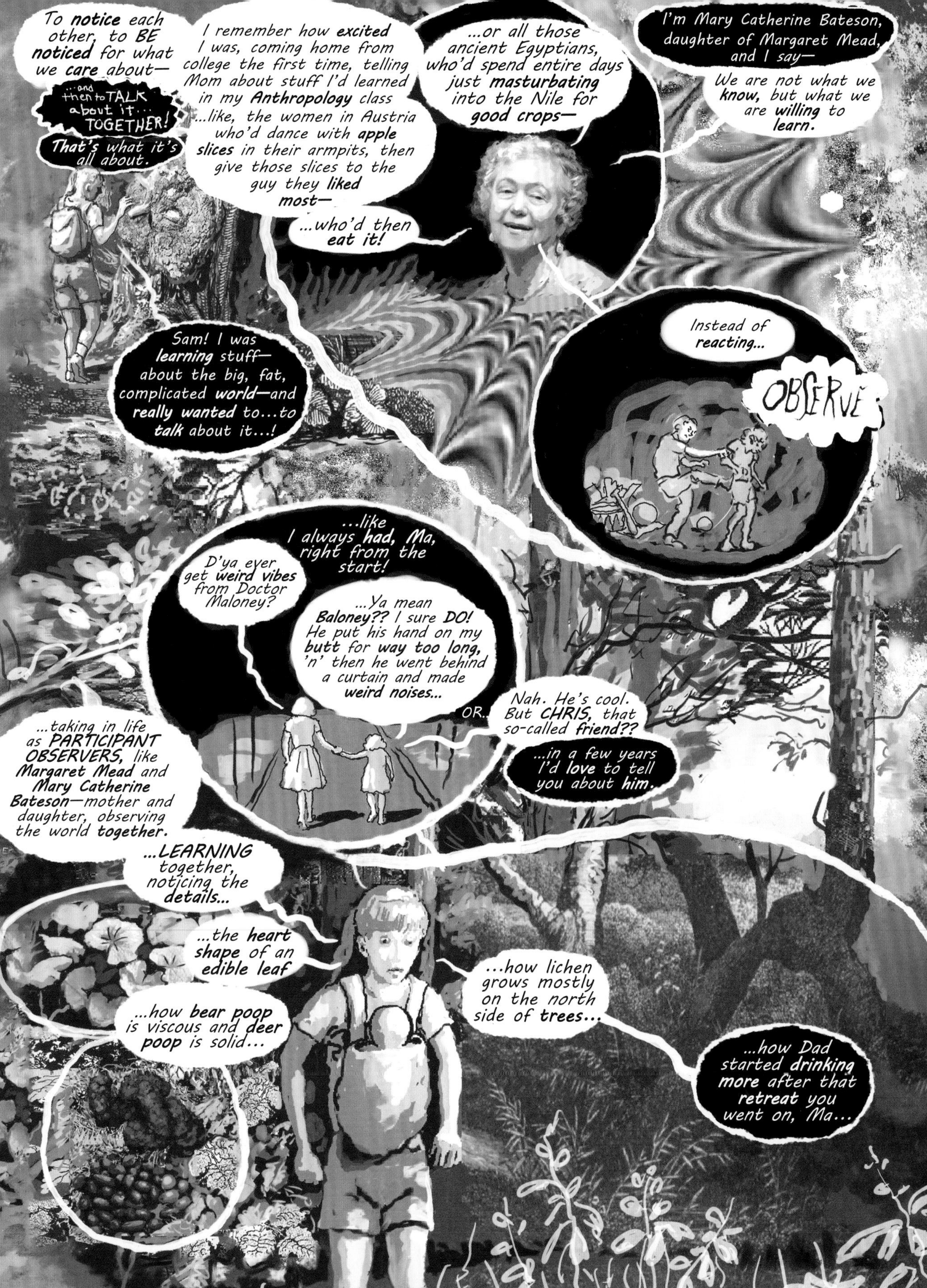
To notice each other, to BE noticed for what we care about—
...and then to TALK about it... TOGETHER!
That's what it's all about.
I remember how excited I was, coming home from college the first time, telling Mom about stuff I'd learned in my Anthropology class ...like, the women in Austria who'd dance with apple slices in their armpits, then give those slices to the guy they liked most—
...who'd then eat it!
...or all those ancient Egyptians, who'd spend entire days just masturbating into the Nile for good crops—
I'm Mary Catherine Bateson, daughter of Margaret Mead, and I say—
We are not what we know, but what we are willing to learn.
Sam! I was learning stuff—about the big, fat, complicated world—and really wanted to...to talk about it...!
Instead of reacting...
OBSERVE
...like I always had, Ma, right from the start!
D'ya ever get weird vibes from Doctor Maloney?
...Ya mean Baloney?? I sure DO! He put his hand on my butt for way too long, 'n' then he went behind a curtain and made weird noises...
OR...
Nah. He's cool. But CHRIS, that so-called friend??
...in a few years I'd love to tell you about him.
...taking in life as PARTICIPANT OBSERVERS, like Margaret Mead and Mary Catherine Bateson—mother and daughter, observing the world together.
...LEARNING together, noticing the details...
...the heart shape of an edible leaf
...how bear poop is viscous and deer poop is solid...
...how lichen grows mostly on the north side of trees...
...how Dad started drinking more after that retreat you went on, Ma...

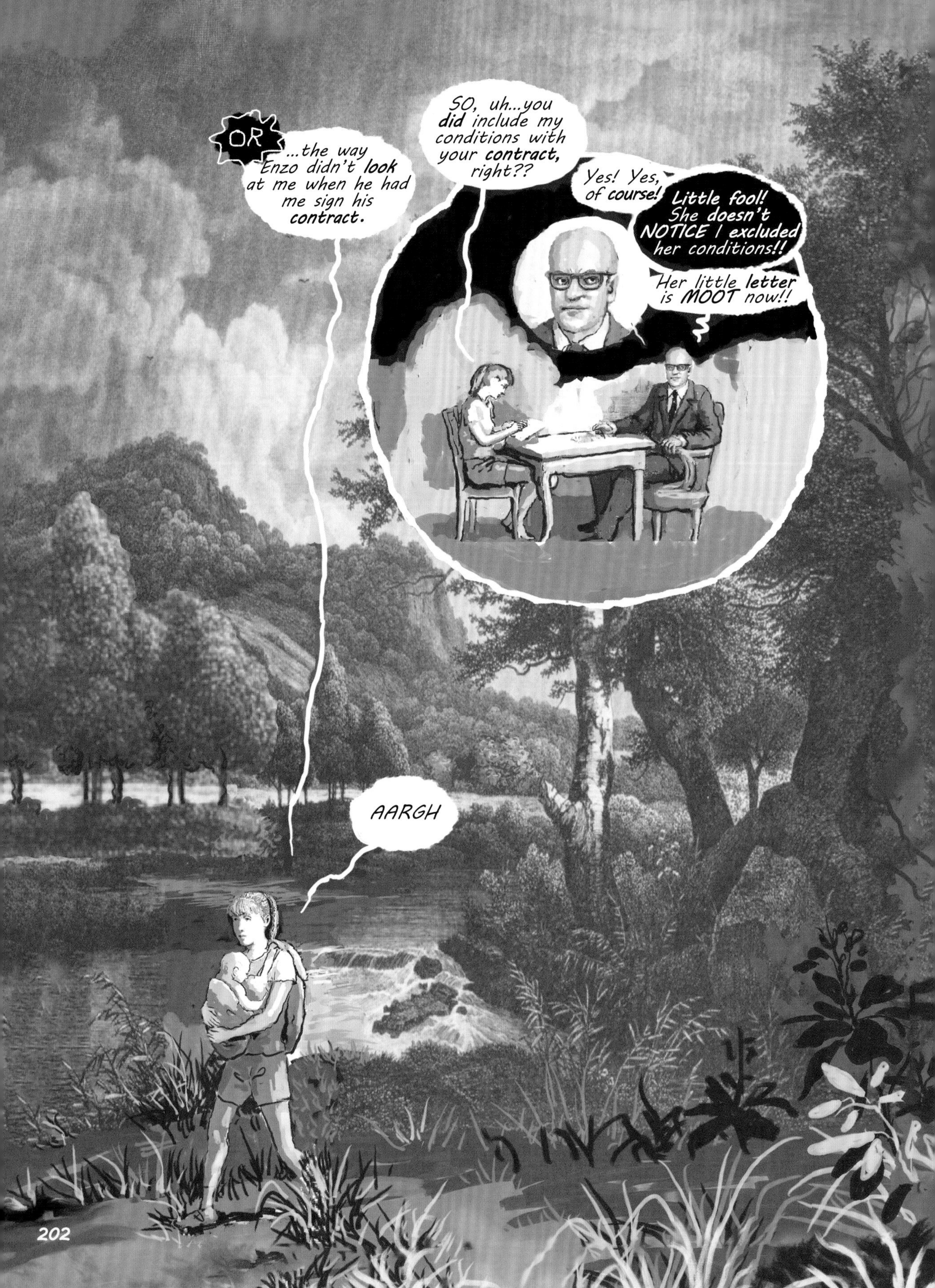
OR
...the way Enzo didn't look at me when he had me sign his contract.
SO, uh...you did include my conditions with your contract, right??
Yes! Yes, of course!
Little fool! She doesn't NOTICE I excluded her conditions!!
Her little letter is MOOT now!!
AARGH

Artists like **Artemisia noticed** the **details...**
...made herself a **witness.**
Look at these **sickos** spying on Bathsheba—
They're both the famous **King David**—
...more like **Peeping Tom.**
RAPIST
We're both **Bathsheba,** wife of Uriah, one of King David's top commanders. That creep **killed** my husband to get to me even though he already had six wives.
And if you haven't already figured it out...
David, King of the United Monarchy of Israel and Judah...
Yeah, he's a king, but he's also a **molester,** lurking around Bathsheba as she's taking her bath, **leering** at her from his parapet or behind a tree while she's simply trying to **wash** herself.
He's got the whole **power** of the **palace** around him
...while she's utterly **vulnerable:** her only supports are the **women** around her.
the *WOMEN!*
And that's when I think...
Hey!
Wait a **minute...**
the INTERN!
I'm the one who brought him coffee, remember?
I was right there, **watching everything!**
Yeah!
She's my **witness!**
With her **help,** I can **confront Enzo**
...**SUE** him??!
YEAH, RIGHT-
THANK YOU INTERN!!

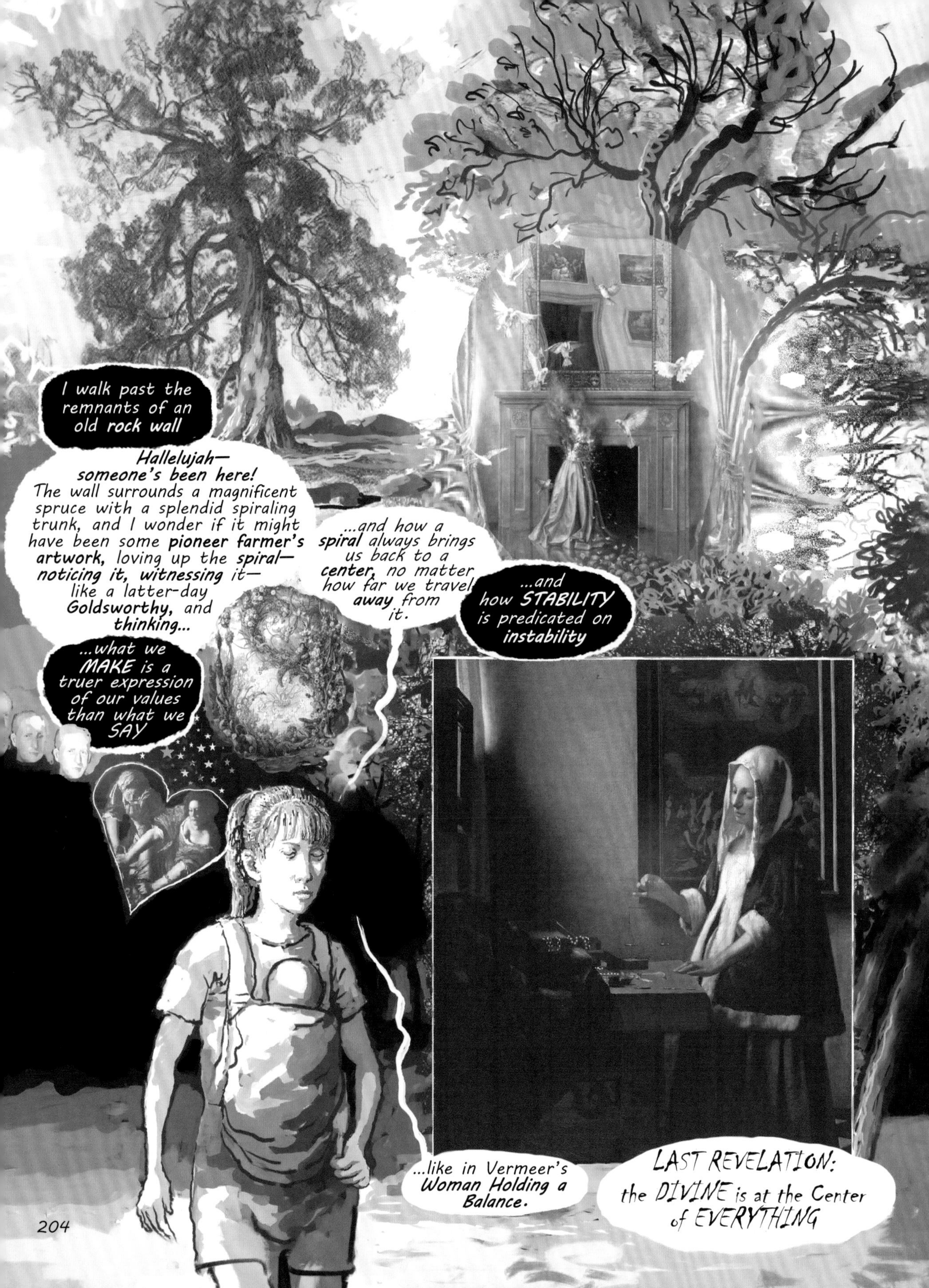
I walk past the remnants of an old **rock wall**
Hallelujah— someone's been here! The wall surrounds a magnificent spruce with a splendid spiraling trunk, and I wonder if it might have been some **pioneer farmer's artwork,** loving up the **spiral— noticing it, witnessing** it— like a latter-day **Goldsworthy,** and **thinking...**
...what we *MAKE* is a truer expression of our values than what we *SAY*
...and how a **spiral** always brings us back to a **center,** no matter how far we travel **away** from it.
...and how **STABILITY** is predicated on **instability**
...like in Vermeer's **Woman Holding a Balance.**
LAST REVELATION: the DIVINE is at the Center of EVERYTHING

...and I don't mean churchy DIVINE but **real divine**–the kind that tingles in your spine to the top of your **head.** The question **Vermeer explores** here is: how do we find **balance** and **fulfillment** in **life?** From **earthly treasures** or **spiritual?** From this life or an afterlife? That question is distilled in everything from the bifurcated back wall—one side illuminated by white light signifying ***grace,*** the other by a dark Ascension, Christ leaving the Earth...

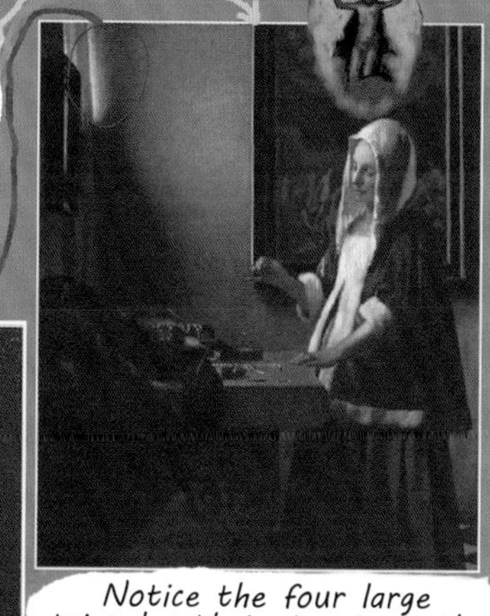

Notice the four large triangles that structure the entire composition, how **all** are in ***BALANCE***

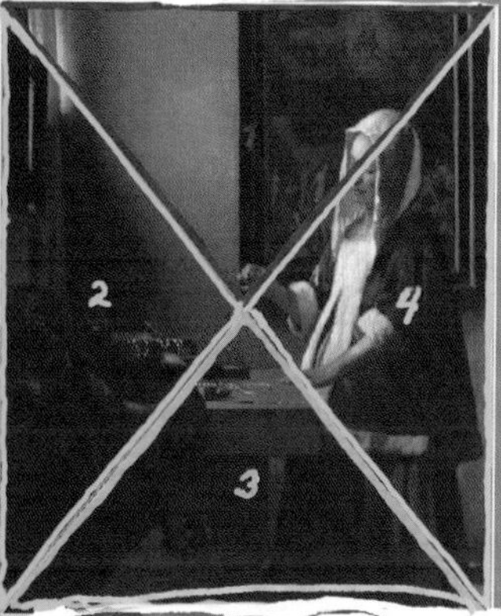

...and how her hand is just above the midpoint, but the scales are just below...

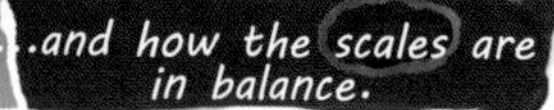

...and how the scales are in balance.

And look at how a spiral originates at the triangle made by her fingers holding the scale, then moves around her hand, and down through the scales, then back around through the slit in her robe revealing that protuberance, and finalizes in the space of that divine white light.

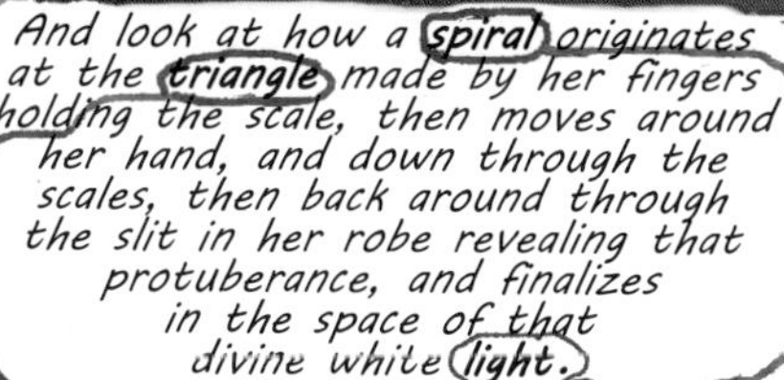

Remember: an upward pointing triangle means ***DIVINE*** because it also means the ***Trinity:*** God the Father, God the Son, and God the Holy Spirit (the ***genderless*** one)

Lotsa **men** but no **women in that Godhead...**

But just ***wait!*** All those tiny details together ***seem*** to turn this painting of a woman engaged in the banal task of weighing her wealth into a profound ***meditation*** on human values, whether to seek ***wealth*** or ***grace.*** Vermeer seems to be advocating for a ***balance*** between them, but it's her ***hand,*** right smack in the ***middle*** of the painting, that's the ***clue*** to what ***Vermeer*** really ***thinks...***

as transcendence leaps from her head!

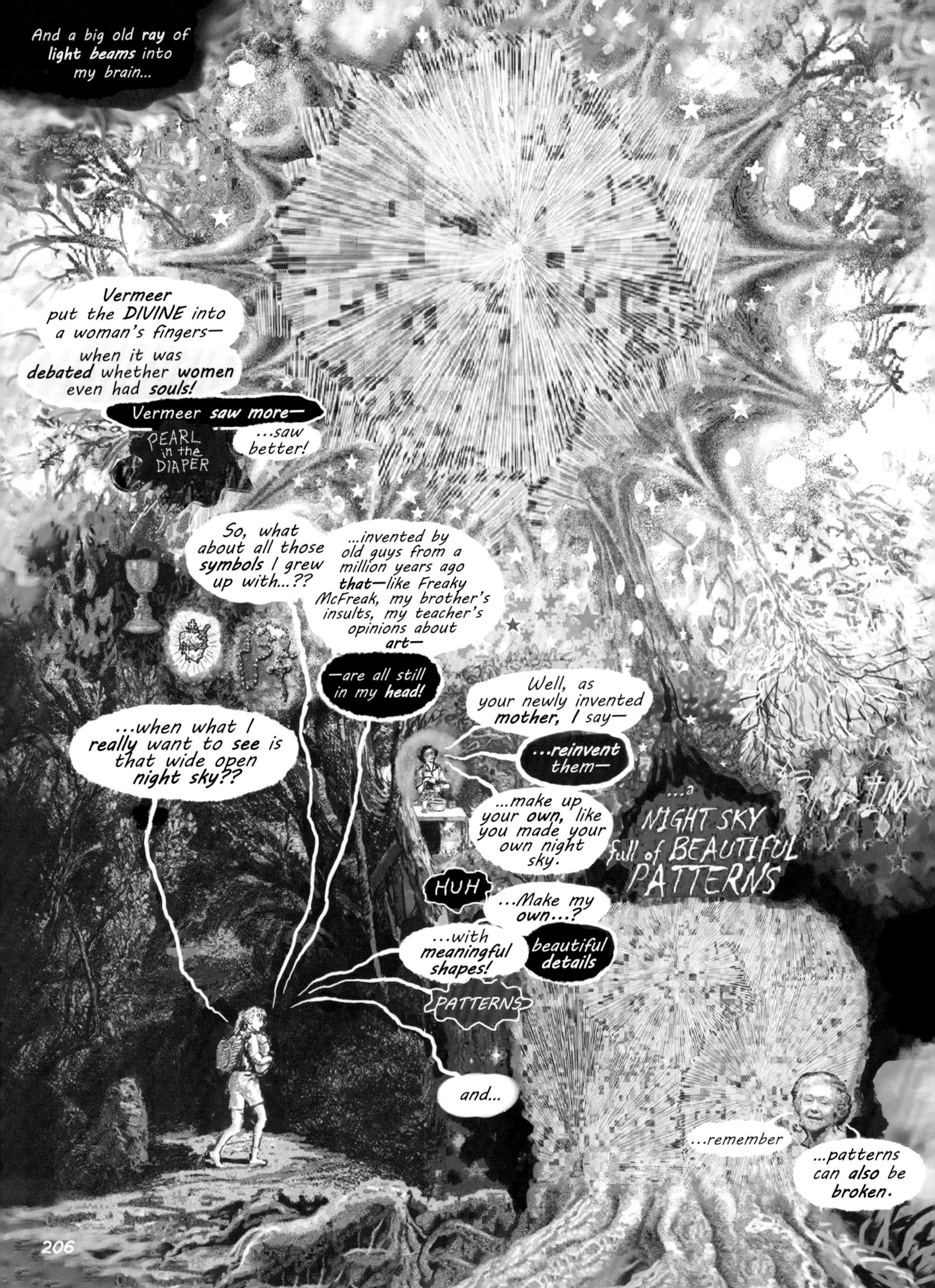

And a big old ray of light beams into my brain...
Vermeer put the DIVINE into a woman's fingers— when it was debated whether women even had souls!
Vermeer saw more—
...saw better!
PEARL in the DIAPER
So, what about all those symbols I grew up with...??
...invented by old guys from a million years ago that—like Freaky McFreak, my brother's insults, my teacher's opinions about art—
—are all still in my head!
...when what I really want to see is that wide open night sky??
Well, as your newly invented mother, I say—
...reinvent them—
...make up your own, like you made your own night sky.
...a NIGHT SKY full of BEAUTIFUL PATTERNS
HUH
...Make my own...?
...with meaningful shapes!
beautiful details
PATTERNS
and...
...remember
...patterns can also be broken.

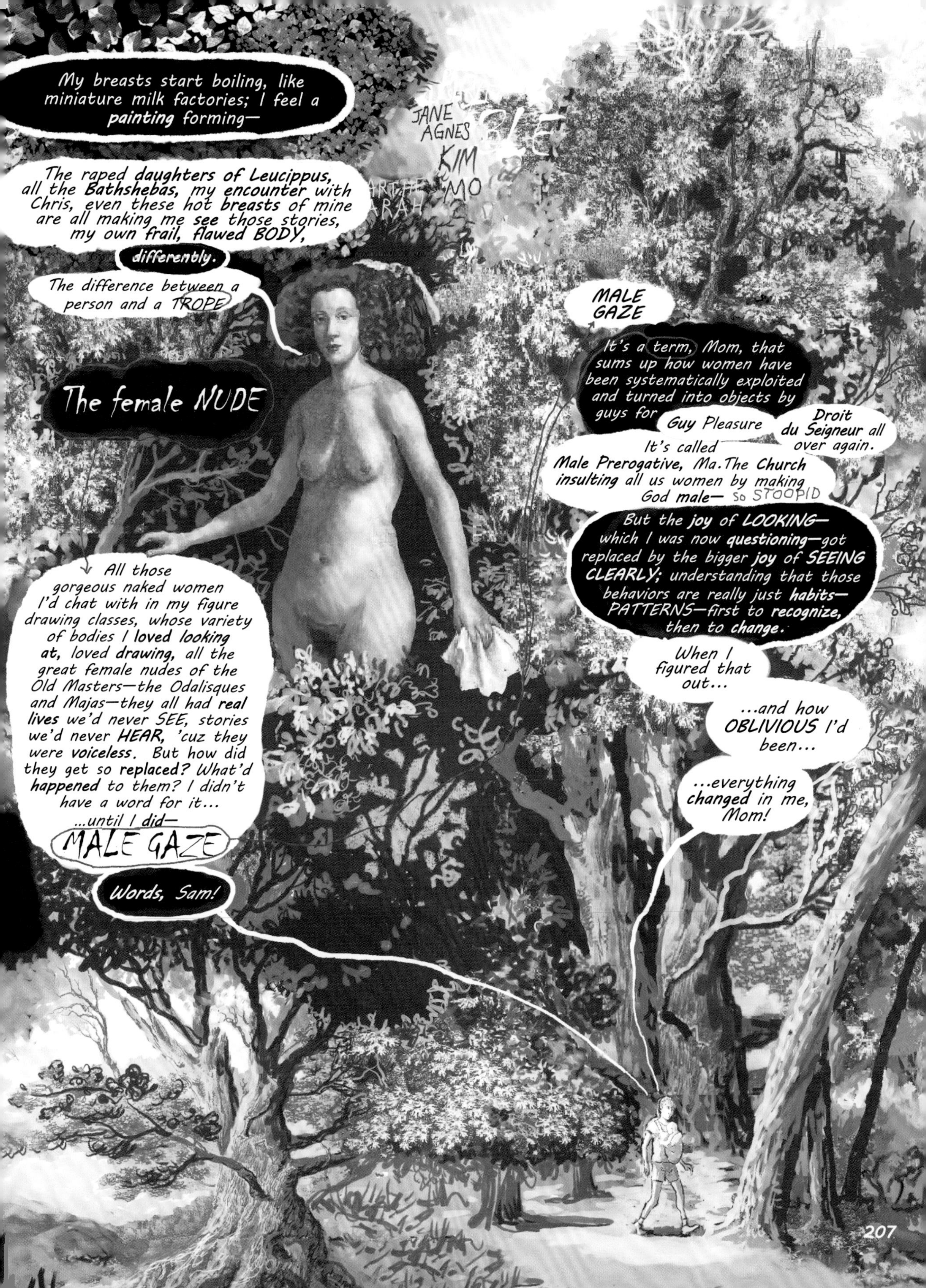

My breasts start boiling, like miniature milk factories; I feel a painting forming—
JANE
AGNES
KIM
MO
The raped daughters of Leucippus, all the Bathshebas, my encounter with Chris, even these hot breasts of mine are all making me see those stories, my own frail, flawed BODY,
differently.
The difference between a person and a TROPE
The female NUDE
All those gorgeous naked women I'd chat with in my figure drawing classes, whose variety of bodies I loved looking at, loved drawing, all the great female nudes of the Old Masters—the Odalisques and Majas—they all had real lives we'd never SEE, stories we'd never HEAR, 'cuz they were voiceless. But how did they get so replaced? What'd happened to them? I didn't have a word for it... ...until I did—
MALE GAZE
Words, Sam!
MALE GAZE
It's a term, Mom, that sums up how women have been systematically exploited and turned into objects by guys for
Guy Pleasure
Droit du Seigneur all over again.
It's called Male Prerogative, Ma. The Church insulting all us women by making God male— so STOOPID
But the joy of LOOKING—which I was now questioning—got replaced by the bigger joy of SEEING CLEARLY; understanding that those behaviors are really just habits—PATTERNS—first to recognize, then to change.
When I figured that out...
...and how OBLIVIOUS I'd been...
...everything changed in me, Mom!

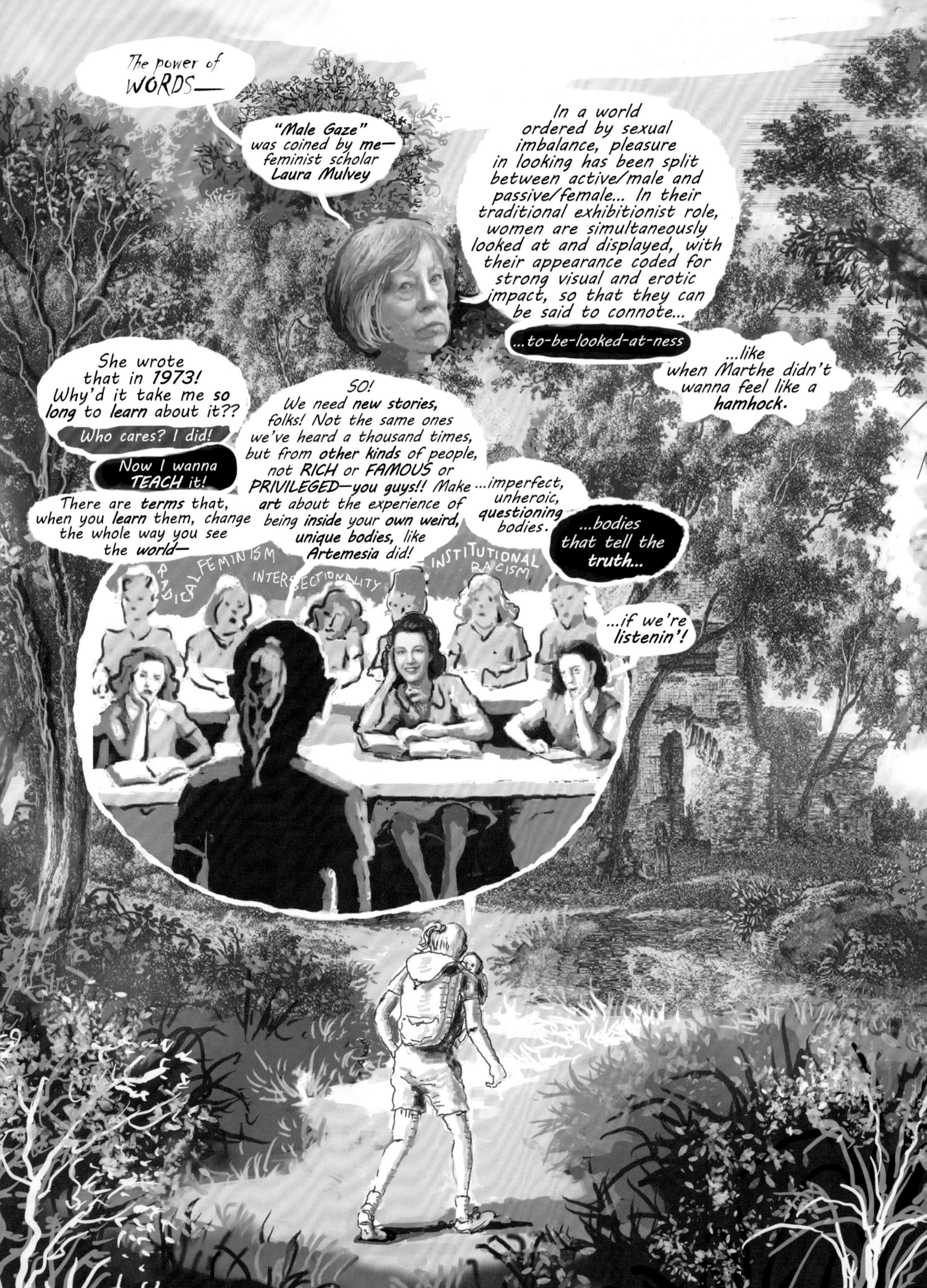
The power of WORDS—
"Male Gaze" was coined by me— feminist scholar Laura Mulvey
In a world ordered by sexual imbalance, pleasure in looking has been split between active/male and passive/female... In their traditional exhibitionist role, women are simultaneously looked at and displayed, with their appearance coded for strong visual and erotic impact, so that they can be said to connote...
...to-be-looked-at-ness
...like when Marthe didn't wanna feel like a hamhock.
She wrote that in 1973! Why'd it take me so long to learn about it??
Who cares? I did!
Now I wanna TEACH it!
There are terms that, when you learn them, change the whole way you see the world—
SO! We need new stories, folks! Not the same ones we've heard a thousand times, but from other kinds of people, not RICH or FAMOUS or PRIVILEGED—you guys!! Make art about the experience of being inside your own weird, unique bodies, like Artemesia did!
...imperfect, unheroic, questioning bodies.
...bodies that tell the truth...
...if we're listenin'!
RADICAL FEMINISM
INTERSECTIONALITY
INSTITUTIONAL RACISM

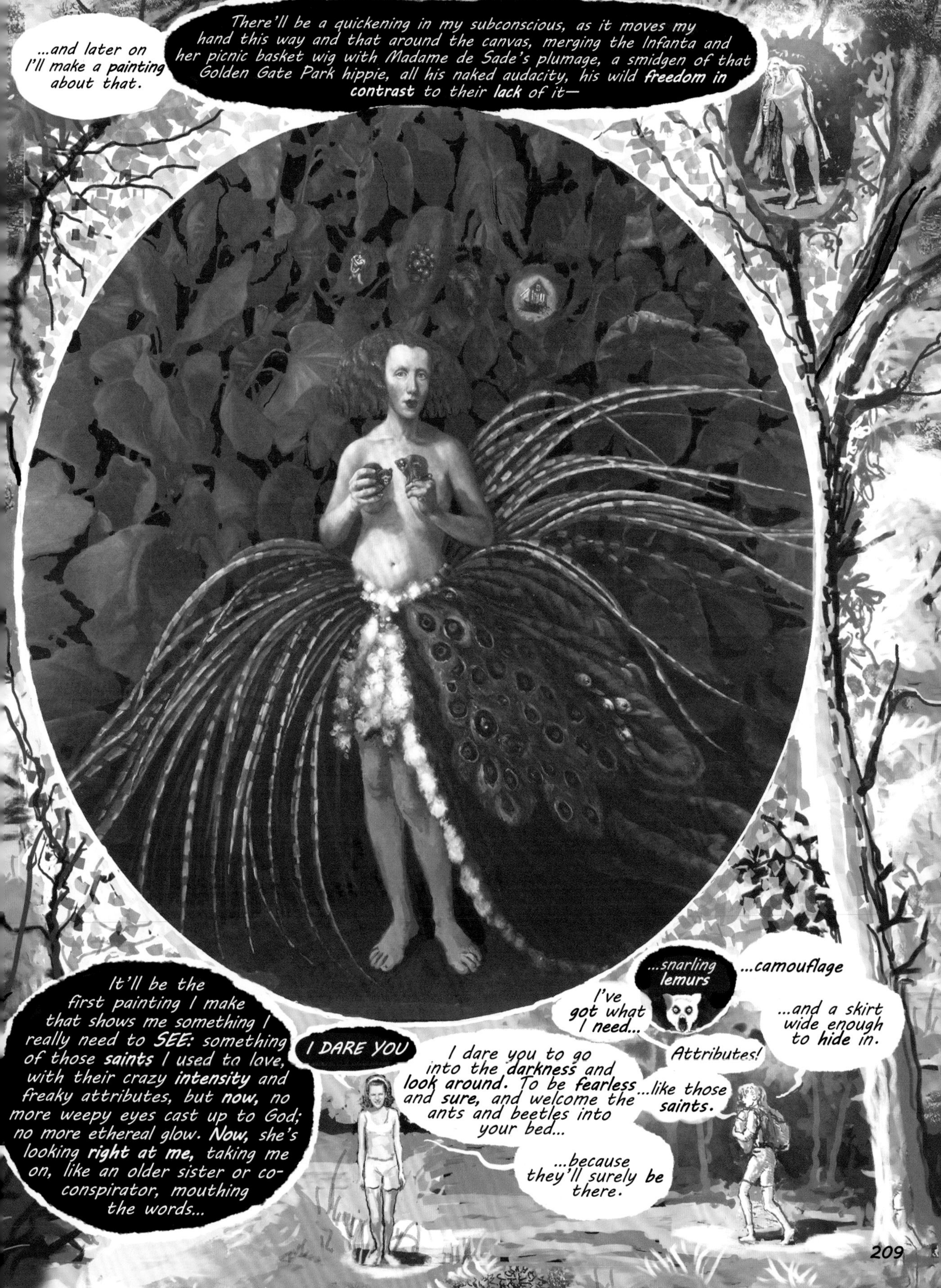

...and later on I'll make a painting about that.
There'll be a quickening in my subconscious, as it moves my hand this way and that around the canvas, merging the Infanta and her picnic basket wig with Madame de Sade's plumage, a smidgen of that Golden Gate Park hippie, all his naked audacity, his wild freedom in contrast to their lack of it—
It'll be the first painting I make that shows me something I really need to SEE: something of those saints I used to love, with their crazy intensity and freaky attributes, but now, no more weepy eyes cast up to God; no more ethereal glow. Now, she's looking right at me, taking me on, like an older sister or co-conspirator, mouthing the words...
I DARE YOU
I dare you to go into the darkness and look around. To be fearless and sure, and welcome the ants and beetles into your bed...
...because they'll surely be there.
...like those saints.
Attributes!
I've got what I need...
...snarling lemurs
...camouflage
...and a skirt wide enough to hide in.

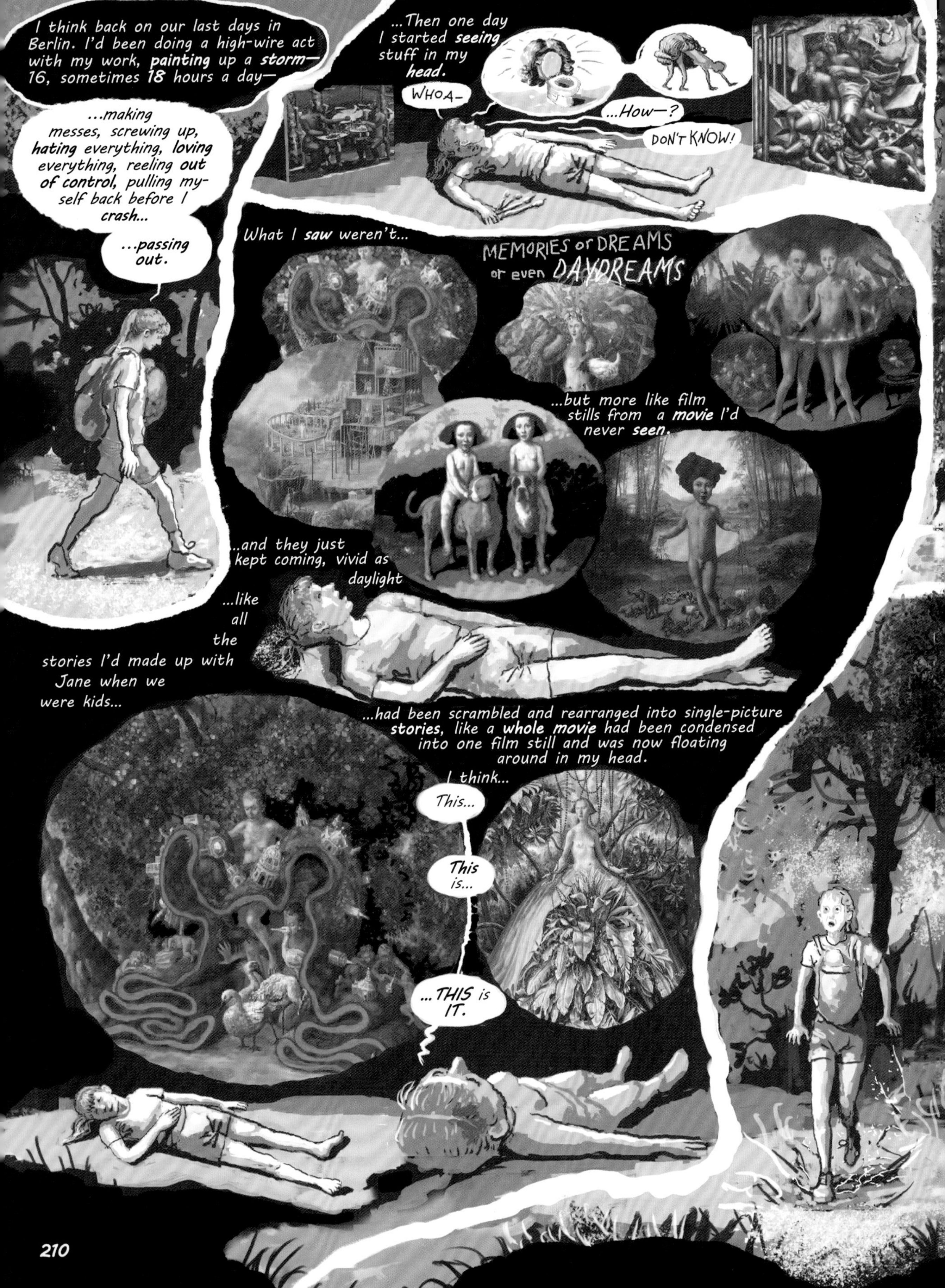
I think back on our last days in Berlin. I'd been doing a high-wire act with my work, painting up a storm— 16, sometimes 18 hours a day—
...making messes, screwing up, hating everything, loving everything, reeling out of control, pulling myself back before I crash...
...passing out.
...Then one day I started seeing stuff in my head.
WHOA-
...How—?
DON'T KNOW!
What I saw weren't...
MEMORIES or DREAMS or even DAYDREAMS
...but more like film stills from a movie I'd never seen.
...and they just kept coming, vivid as daylight
...like all the stories I'd made up with Jane when we were kids...
...had been scrambled and rearranged into single-picture stories, like a whole movie had been condensed into one film still and was now floating around in my head.
I think...
This...
This is...
...THIS is IT.

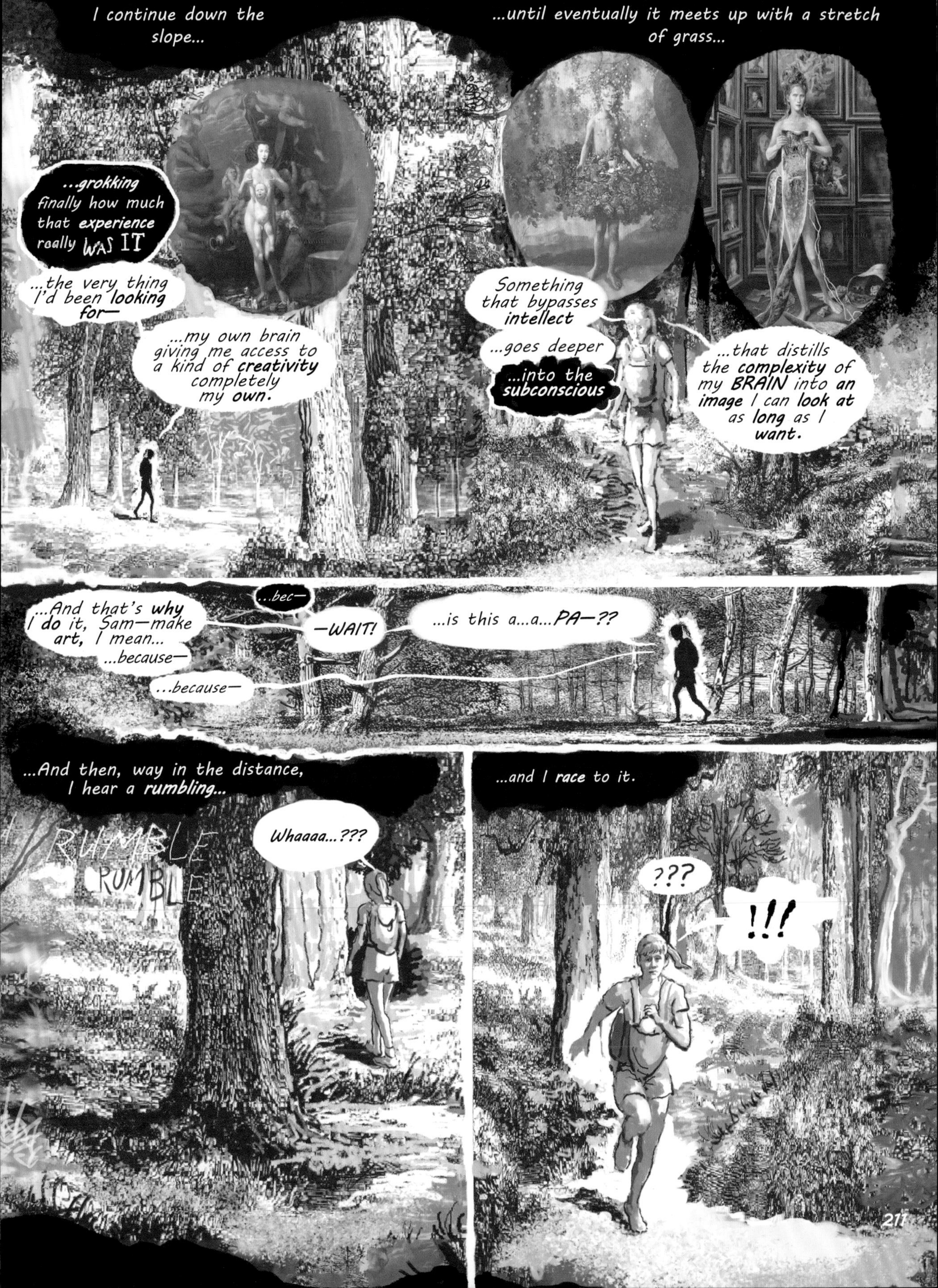

I continue down the slope...

...grokking finally how much that **experience** really WAS IT

...the very thing I'd been **looking for**—

...my own brain giving me access to a kind of **creativity** completely my **own**.

...until eventually it meets up with a stretch of grass...

Something that bypasses **intellect**

...goes deeper

...into the **subconscious**

...that distills the **complexity** of my **BRAIN** into **an image** I can **look at** as **long** as I **want**.

...And that's **why** I **do** it, Sam—make **art**, I mean...

...because—

...because—

...bec—

—WAIT!

...is this a...a...PA—??

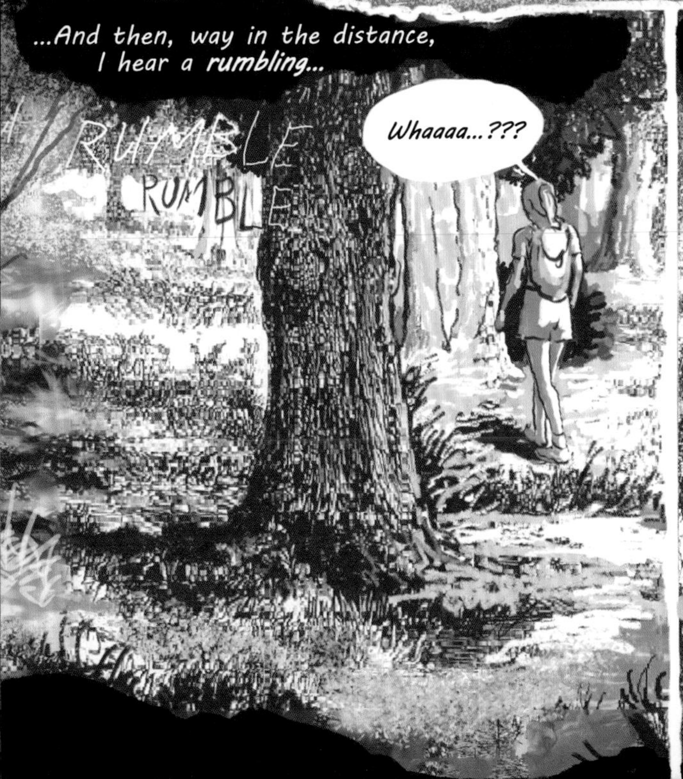

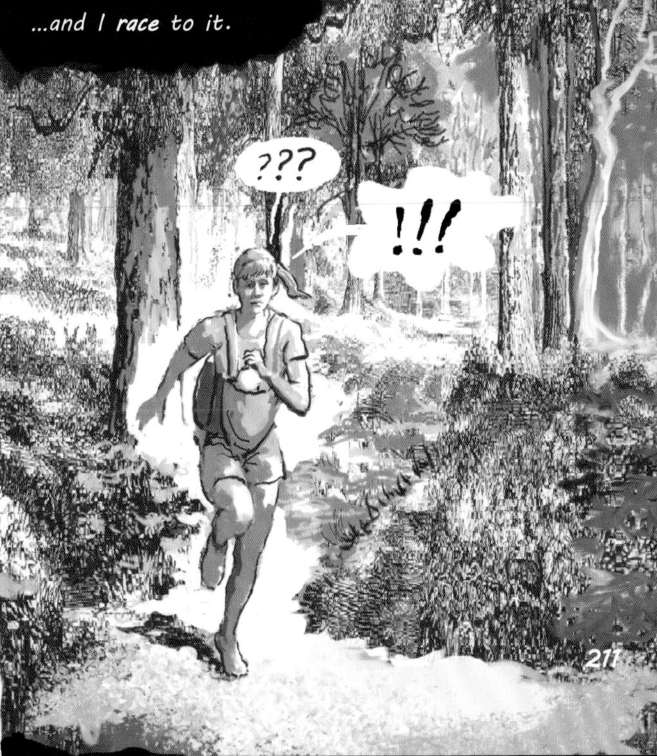

Chapter TWELVE

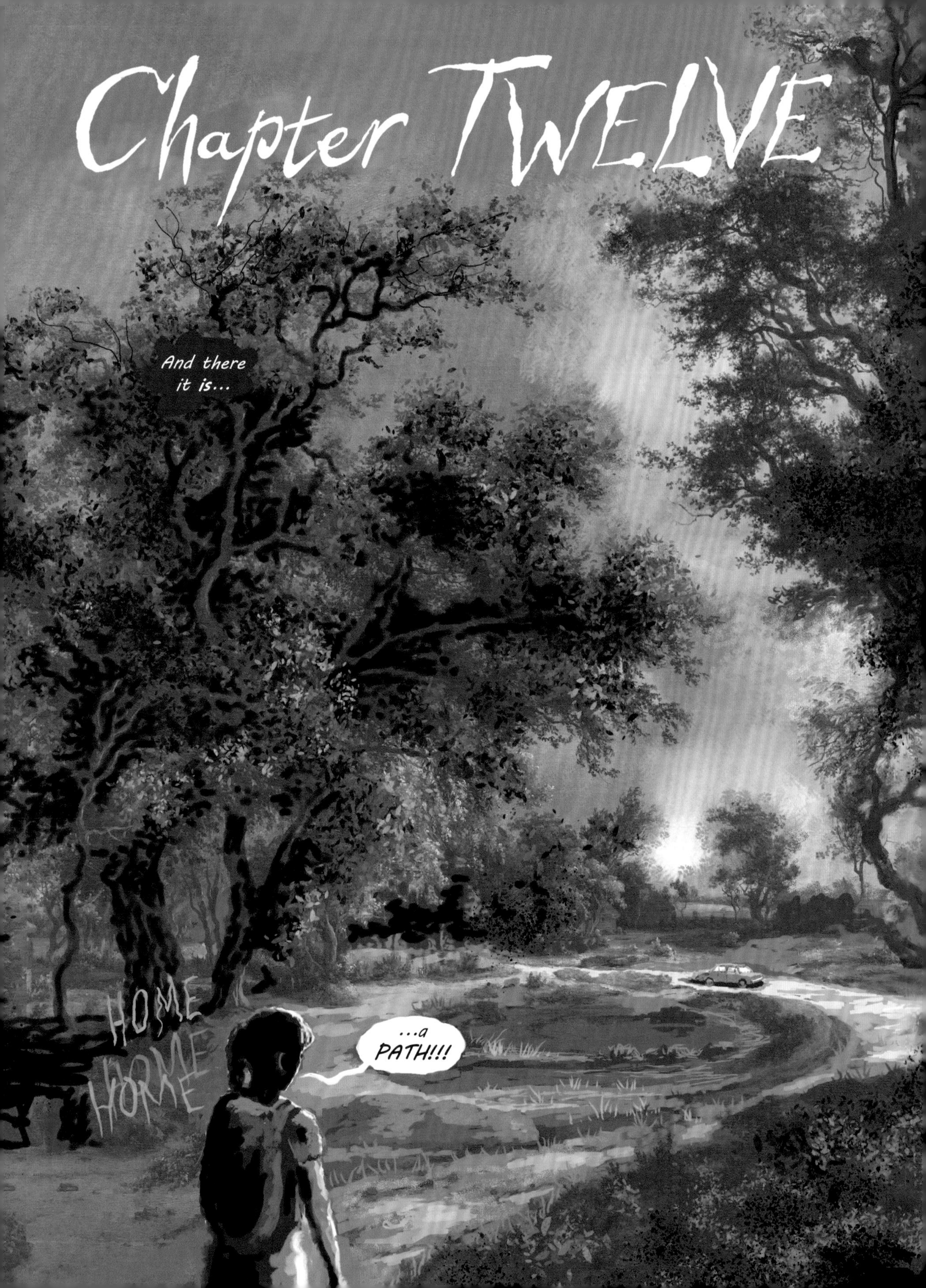

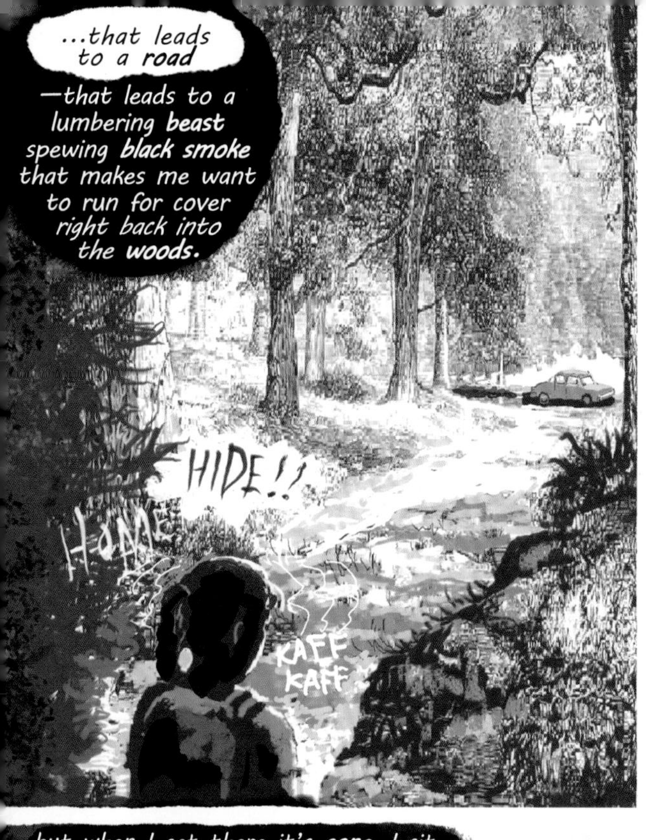
...that leads to a **road**
—that leads to a lumbering **beast** spewing **black smoke** that makes me want to run for cover right back into the **woods.**
HIDE!!
HOME
KAFF KAFF

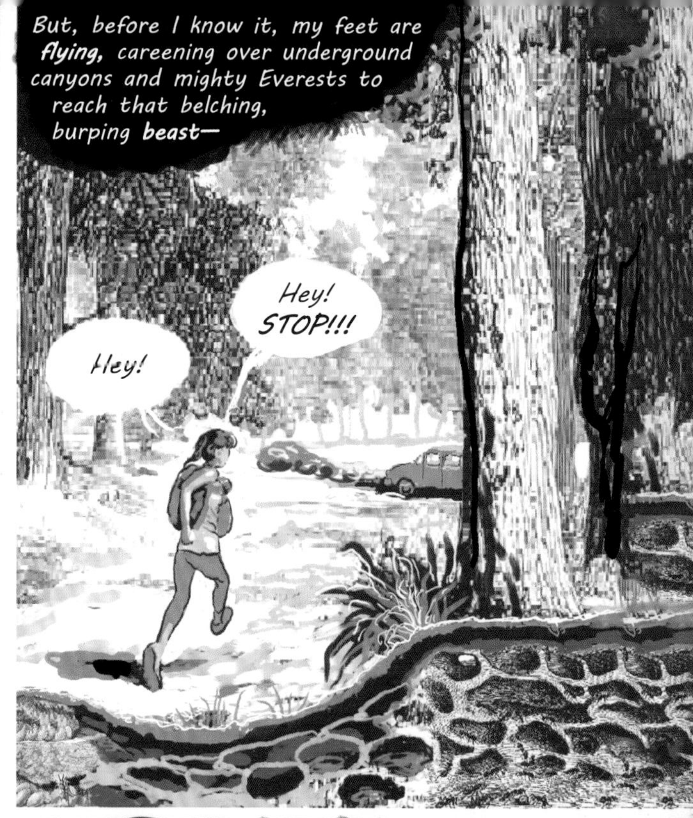
But, before I know it, my feet are ***flying,*** careening over underground canyons and mighty Everests to reach that belching, burping **beast—**
Hey!
Hey! STOP!!!

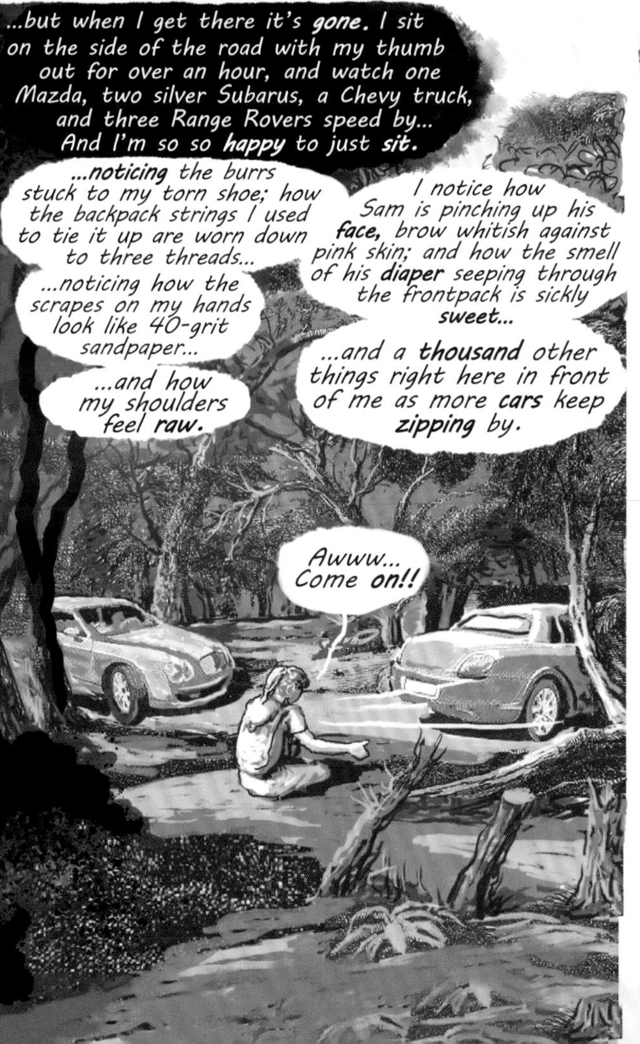
...but when I get there it's **gone.** I sit on the side of the road with my thumb out for over an hour, and watch one Mazda, two silver Subarus, a Chevy truck, and three Range Rovers speed by... And I'm so so **happy** to just **sit.**
...noticing the burrs stuck to my torn shoe; how the backpack strings I used to tie it up are worn down to three threads...
...noticing how the scrapes on my hands look like 40-grit sandpaper...
...and how my shoulders feel **raw.**
I notice how Sam is pinching up his **face,** brow whitish against pink skin; and how the smell of his **diaper** seeping through the frontpack is sickly **sweet...**
...and a **thousand** other things right here in front of me as more **cars** keep **zipping** by.
Awww... Come **on!!**

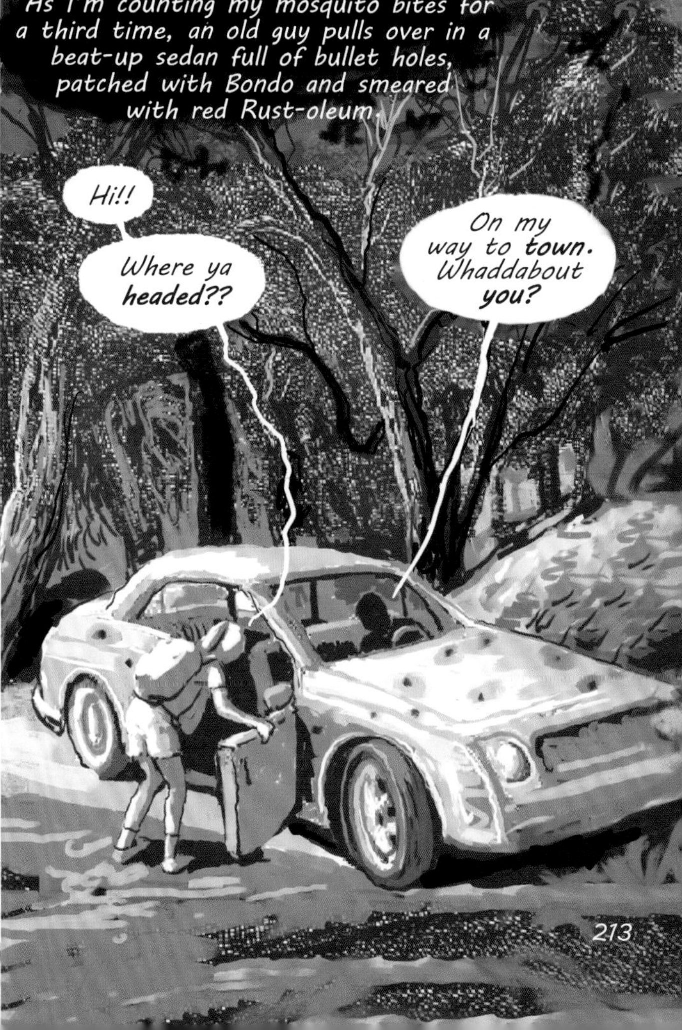
As I'm counting my mosquito bites for a third time, an old guy pulls over in a beat-up sedan full of bullet holes, patched with Bondo and smeared with red Rust-oleum.
Hi!!
Where ya **headed??**
On my way to **town.** Whaddabout **you?**

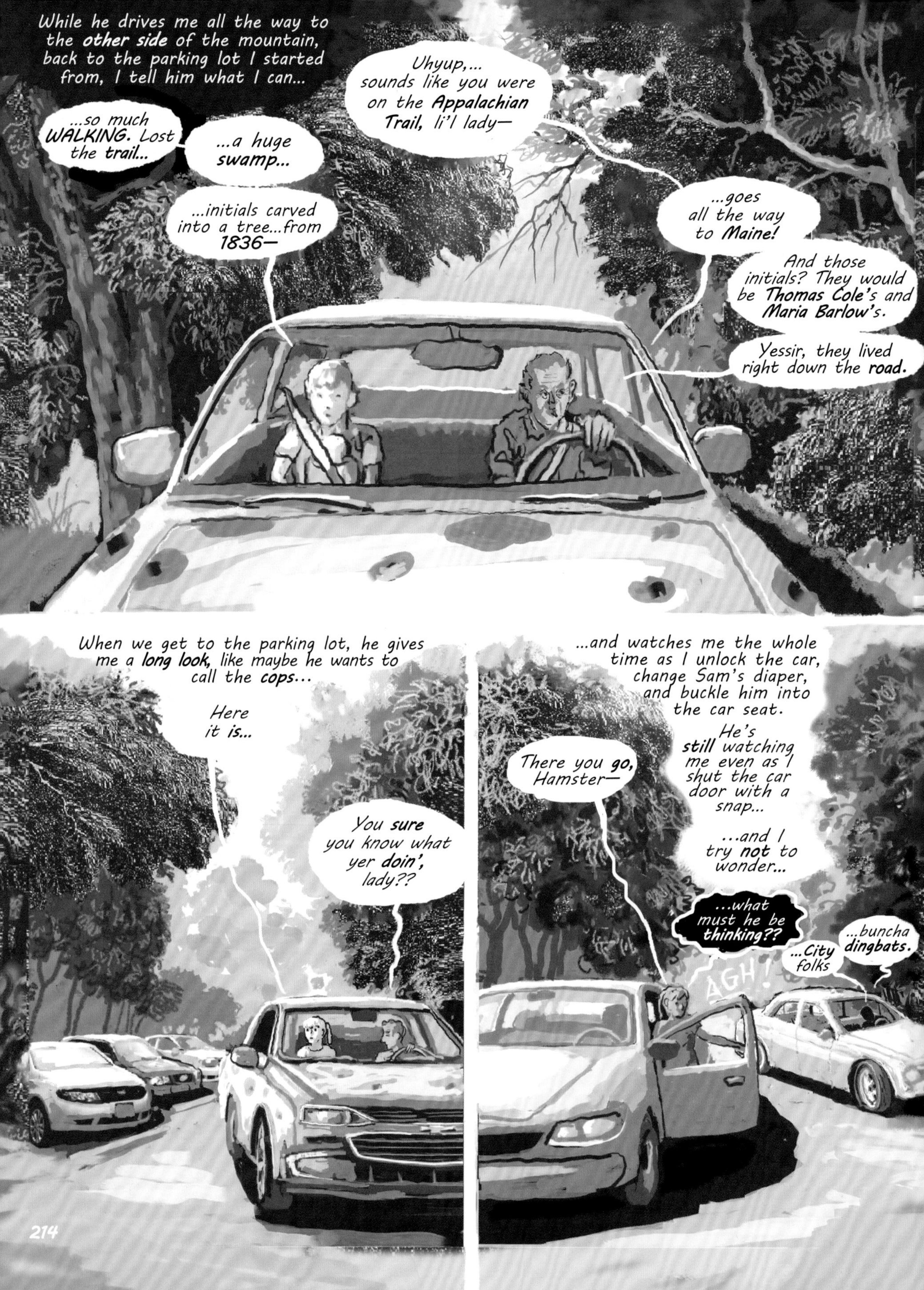

While he drives me all the way to the **other side** of the mountain, back to the parking lot I started from, I tell him what I can...

...so much **WALKING.** Lost the **trail...**

...a huge **swamp...**

...initials carved into a tree...from **1836**—

Uhyup,... sounds like you were on the **Appalachian Trail,** li'l lady—

...goes all the way to **Maine!**

And those initials? They would be **Thomas Cole's** and **Maria Barlow's.**

Yessir, they lived right down the **road.**

When we get to the parking lot, he gives me a **long look,** like maybe he wants to call the **cops...**

Here it **is...**

You **sure** you know what yer **doin',** lady??

...and watches me the whole time as I unlock the car, change Sam's diaper, and buckle him into the car seat.

He's **still** watching me even as I shut the car door with a snap...

There you **go,** Hamster—

...and I try **not** to wonder...

...what must he be **thinking??**

AGH!

...**City** folks

...buncha **dingbats.**

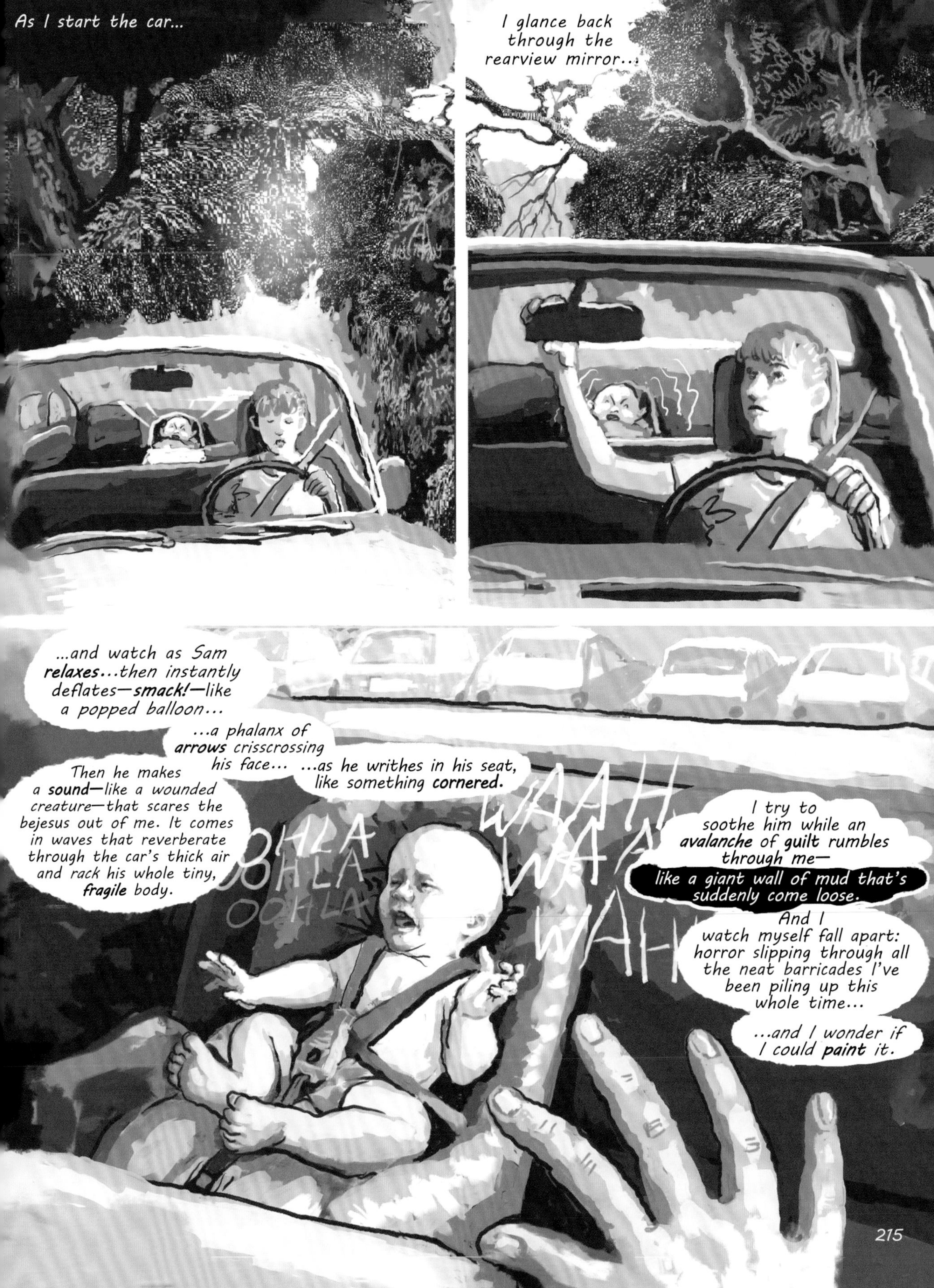
As I start the car...
I glance back through the rearview mirror...
...and watch as Sam relaxes...then instantly deflates—smack!—like a popped balloon...
...a phalanx of arrows crisscrossing his face...
...as he writhes in his seat, like something cornered.
Then he makes a sound—like a wounded creature—that scares the bejesus out of me. It comes in waves that reverberate through the car's thick air and rack his whole tiny, fragile body.
OOHLA
OOHLA
OOHLA
WAAH
WAA
WA
WAH
I try to soothe him while an avalanche of guilt rumbles through me—
like a giant wall of mud that's suddenly come loose.
And I watch myself fall apart: horror slipping through all the neat barricades I've been piling up this whole time...
...and I wonder if I could paint it.

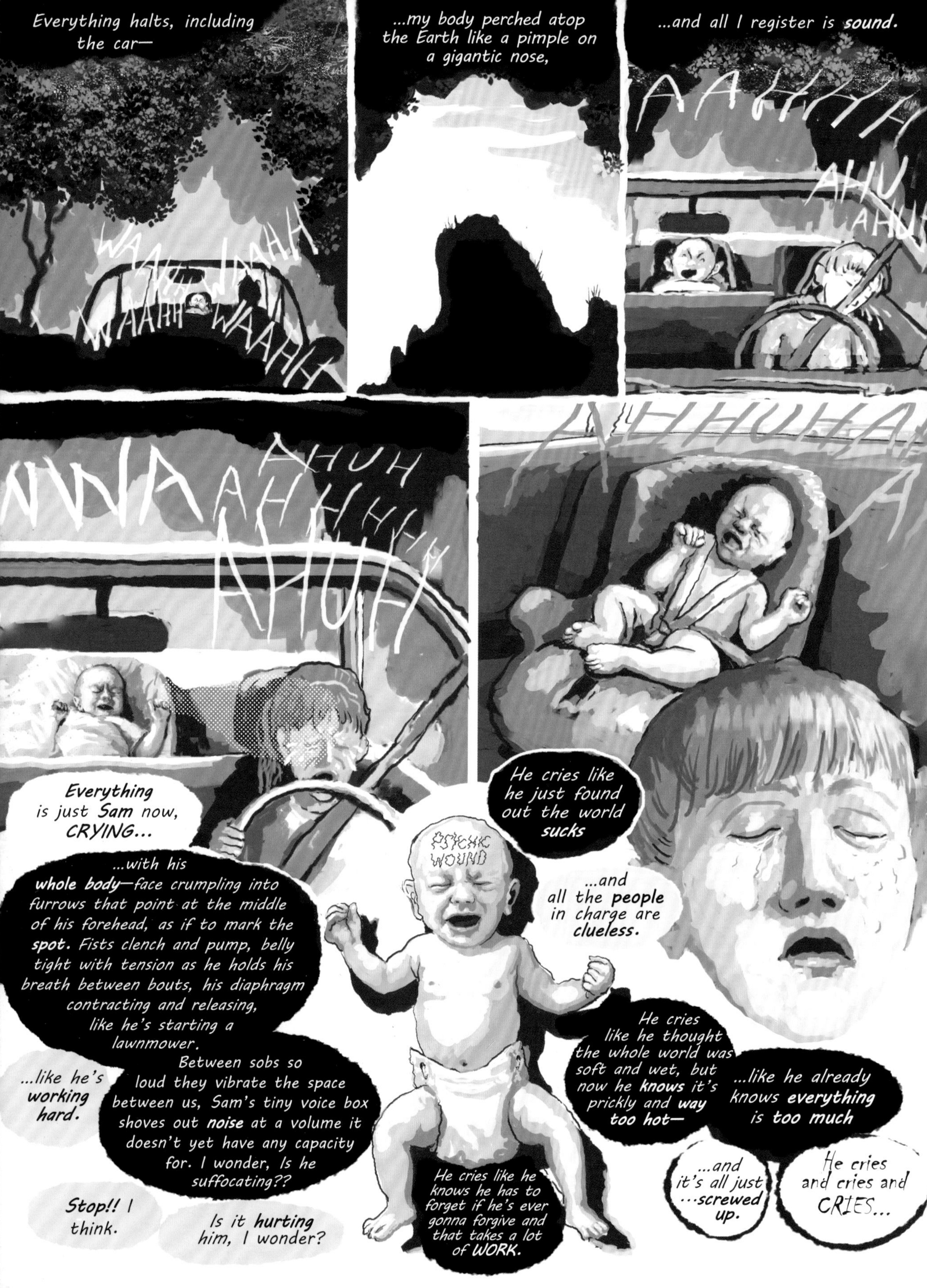
Everything halts, including the car—
WAAHH WAAHH WAAHH WAAHH
...my body perched atop the Earth like a pimple on a gigantic nose,
...and all I register is sound.
AAHHH
AHU AHU
WWA AHUH AHHHH AHUH
Everything is just Sam now, CRYING...
...with his whole body—face crumpling into furrows that point at the middle of his forehead, as if to mark the spot. Fists clench and pump, belly tight with tension as he holds his breath between bouts, his diaphragm contracting and releasing, like he's starting a lawnmower.
Between sobs so loud they vibrate the space between us, Sam's tiny voice box shoves out noise at a volume it doesn't yet have any capacity for. I wonder, Is he suffocating??
...like he's working hard.
Stop!! I think.
Is it hurting him, I wonder?
He cries like he just found out the world sucks
...and all the people in charge are clueless.
PSYCHIC WOUND
He cries like he knows he has to forget if he's ever gonna forgive and that takes a lot of WORK.
He cries like he thought the whole world was soft and wet, but now he knows it's prickly and way too hot—
...like he already knows everything is too much
...and it's all just ...screwed up.
He cries and cries and CRIES...

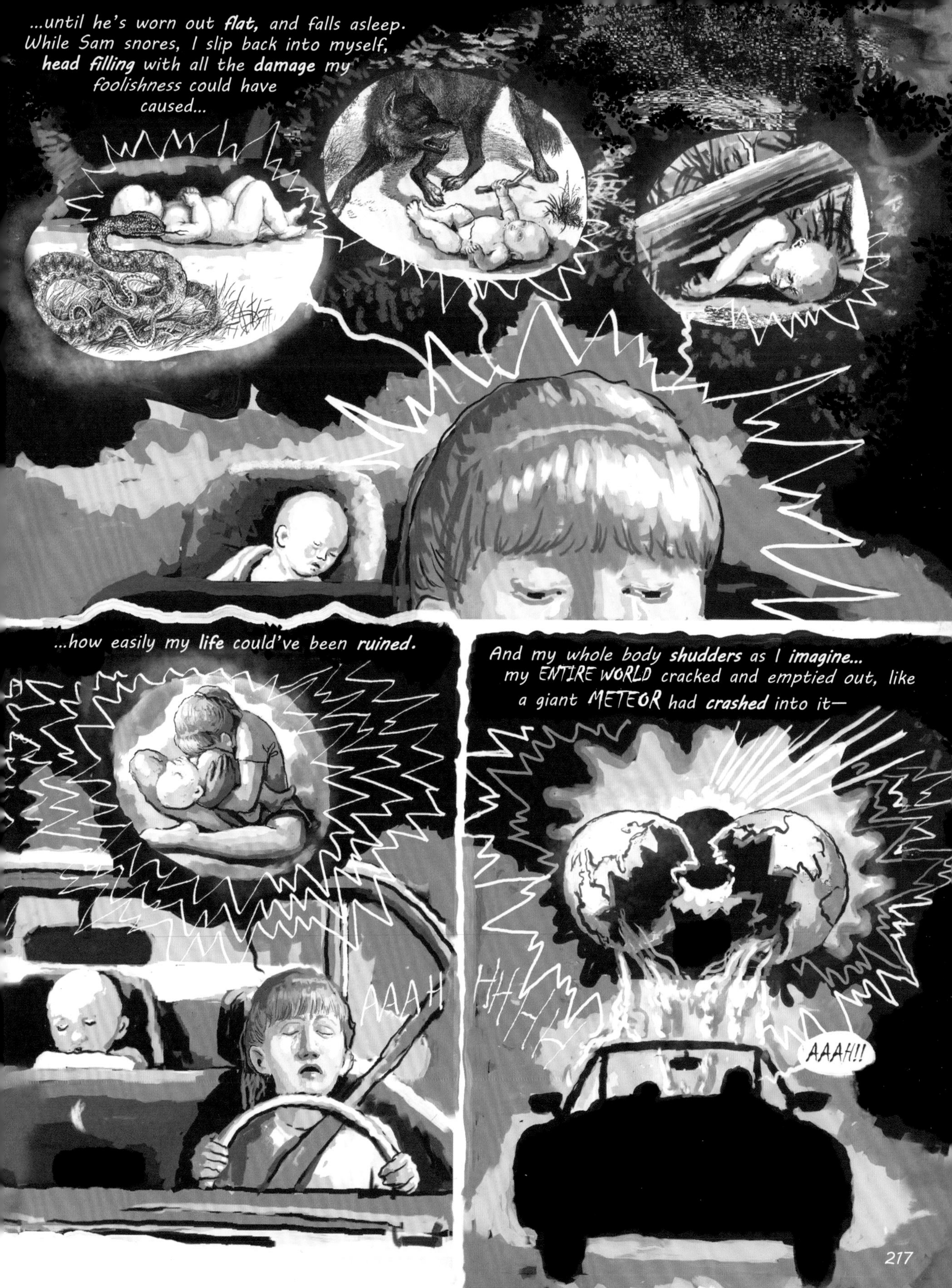
...until he's worn out flat, and falls asleep. While Sam snores, I slip back into myself, head filling with all the damage my foolishness could have caused...
...how easily my life could've been ruined.
AAAH
And my whole body shudders as I imagine... my ENTIRE WORLD cracked and emptied out, like a giant METEOR had crashed into it—
HHH
AAAH!!

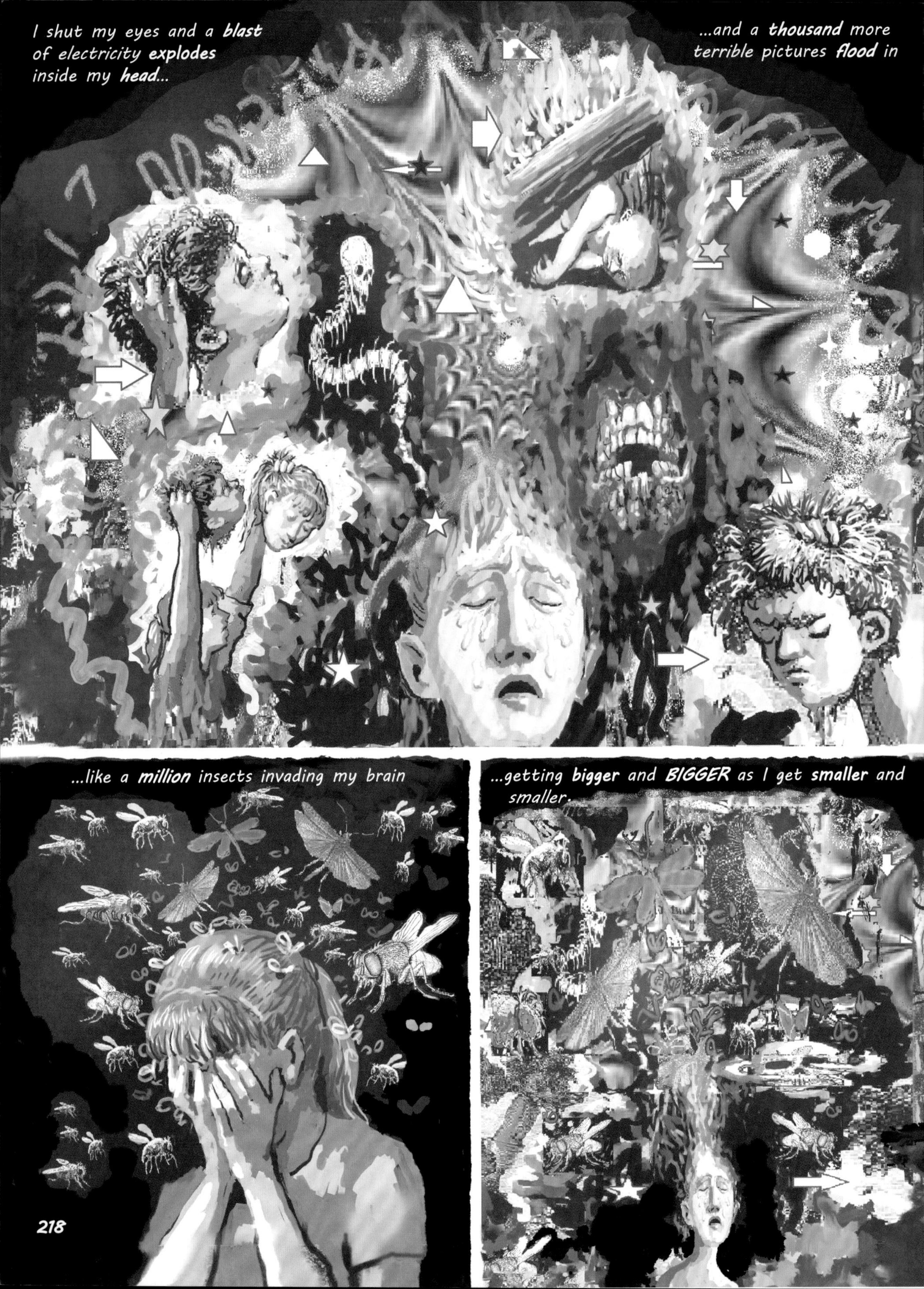

*I shut my eyes and a **blast** of electricity **explodes** inside my **head**...*

*...and a **thousand** more terrible pictures **flood** in*

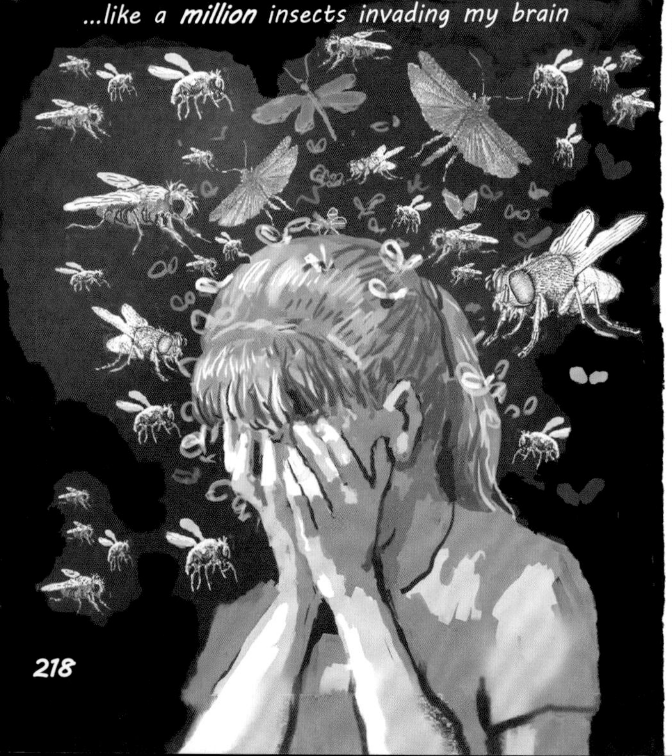

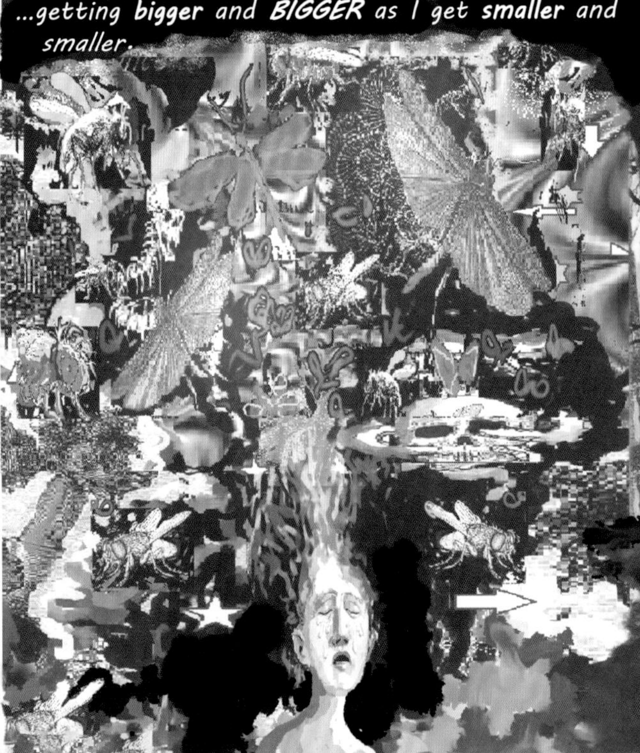

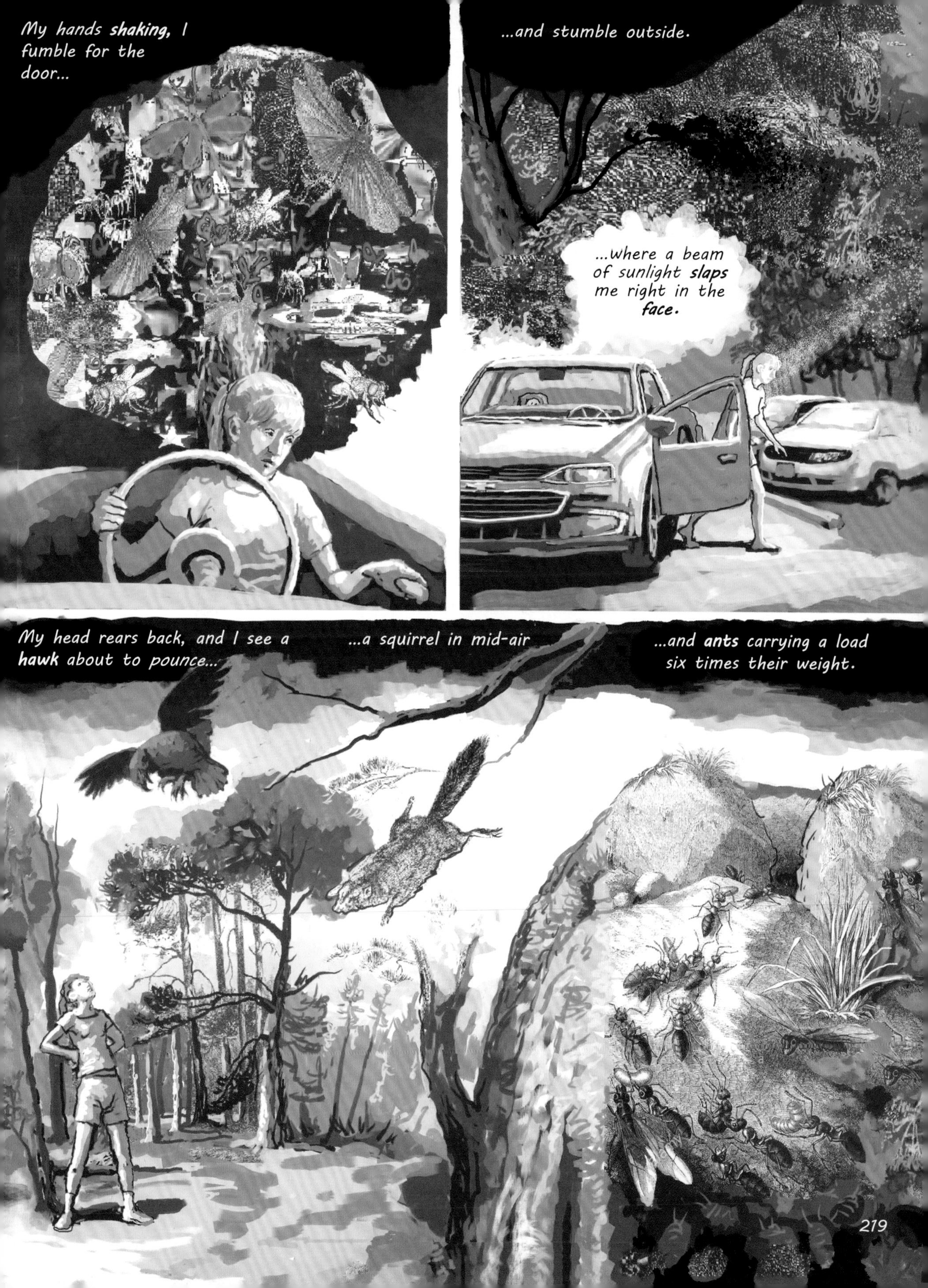

My hands **shaking,** I fumble for the door...
...and stumble outside.
...where a beam of sunlight **slaps** me right in the **face.**
My head rears back, and I see a **hawk** about to pounce...
...a squirrel in mid-air
...and **ants** carrying a load six times their weight.

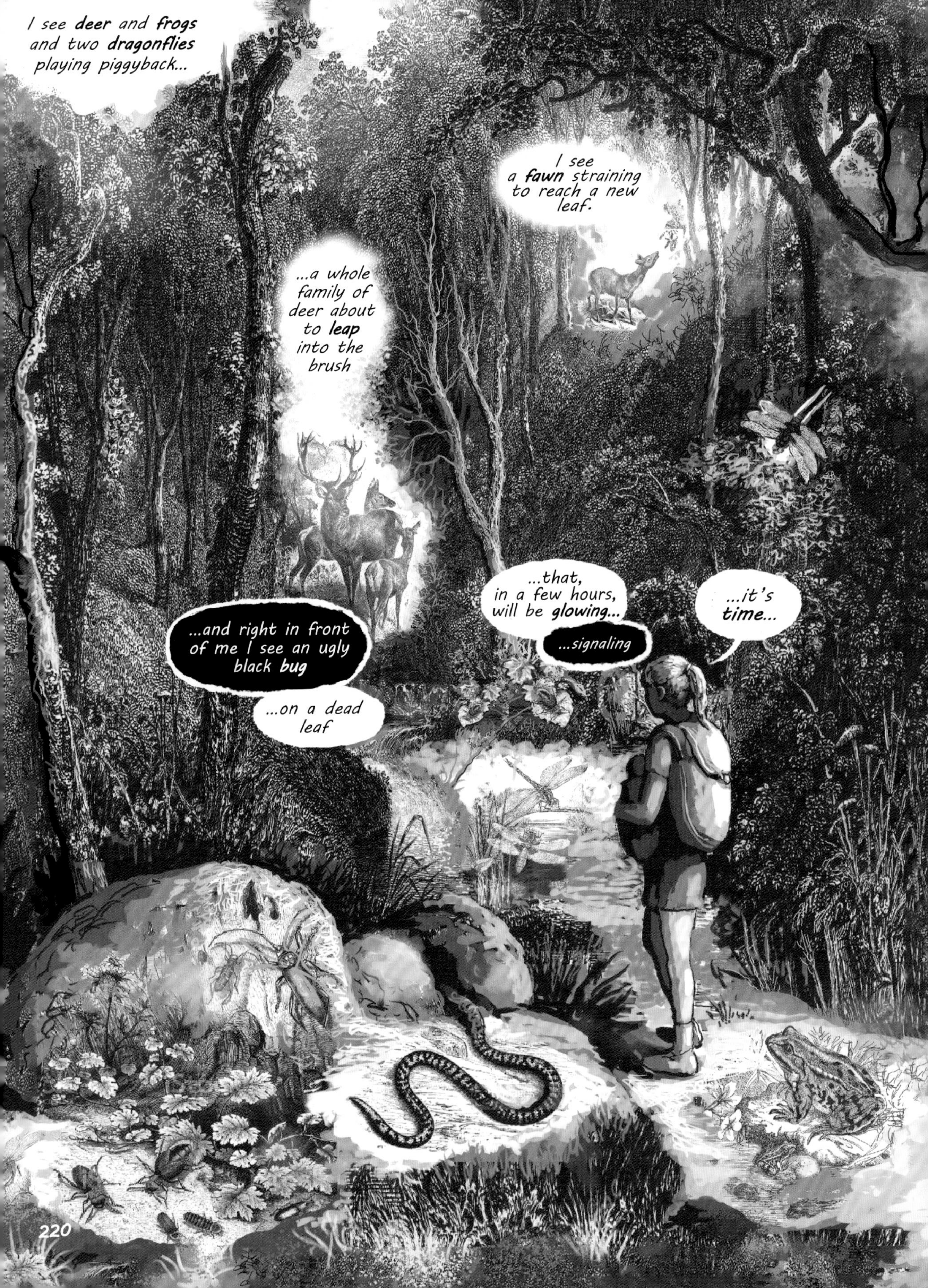
I see deer and frogs and two dragonflies playing piggyback...
I see a fawn straining to reach a new leaf.
...a whole family of deer about to leap into the brush
...and right in front of me I see an ugly black bug
...on a dead leaf
...that, in a few hours, will be glowing...
...signaling
...it's time...

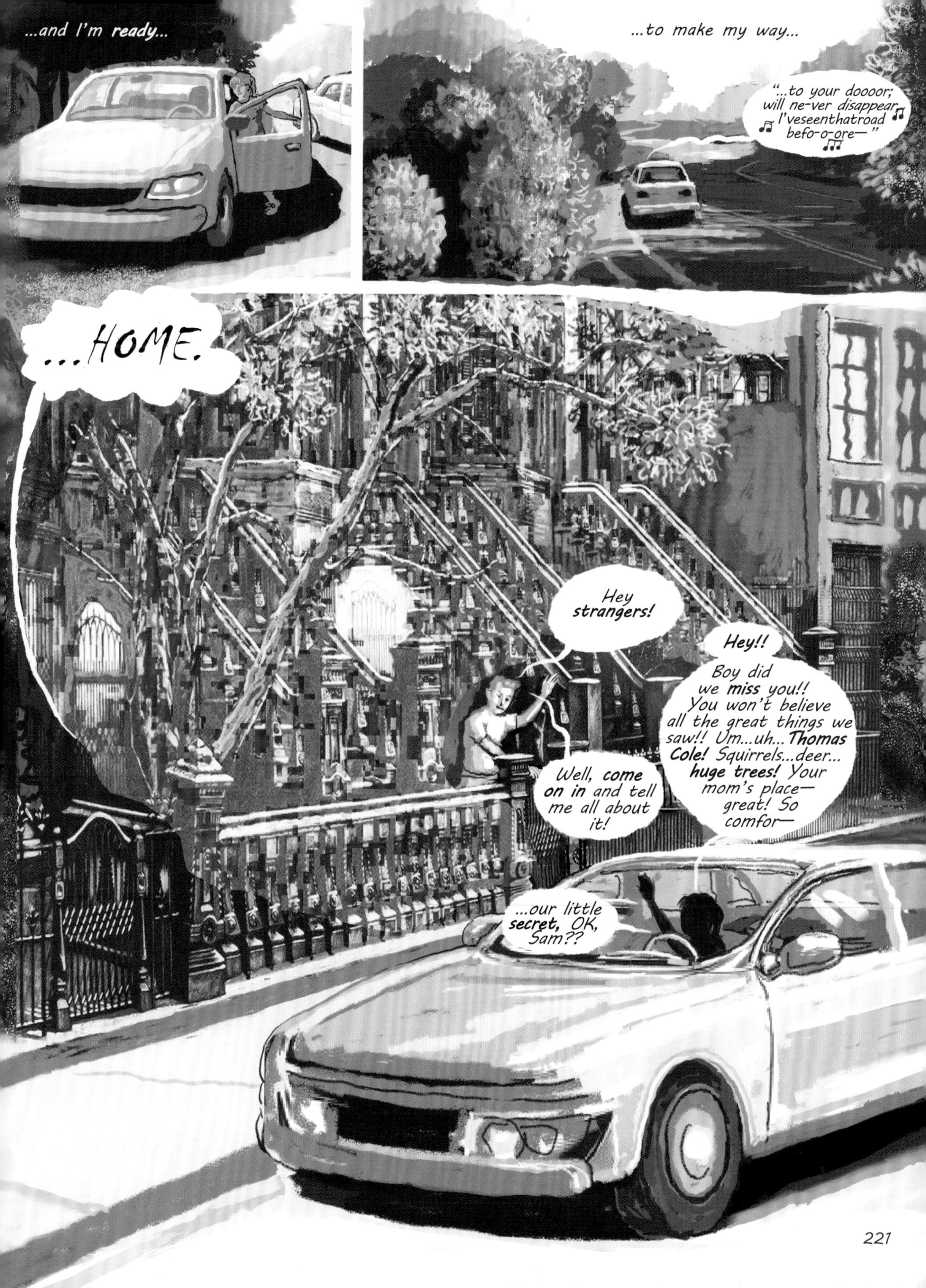

...and I'm **ready**...
...to make my way...
"...to your doooor; will ne-ver disappear I'veseenthatroad befo-o-ore— "
...HOME.
Hey **strangers!**
Well, **come on in** and tell me all about it!
Hey!!
Boy did we **miss** you!! You won't believe all the great things we saw!! Um...uh... **Thomas Cole!** Squirrels...deer... **huge trees!** Your mom's place— great! So comfor—
...our little **secret,** OK, Sam??

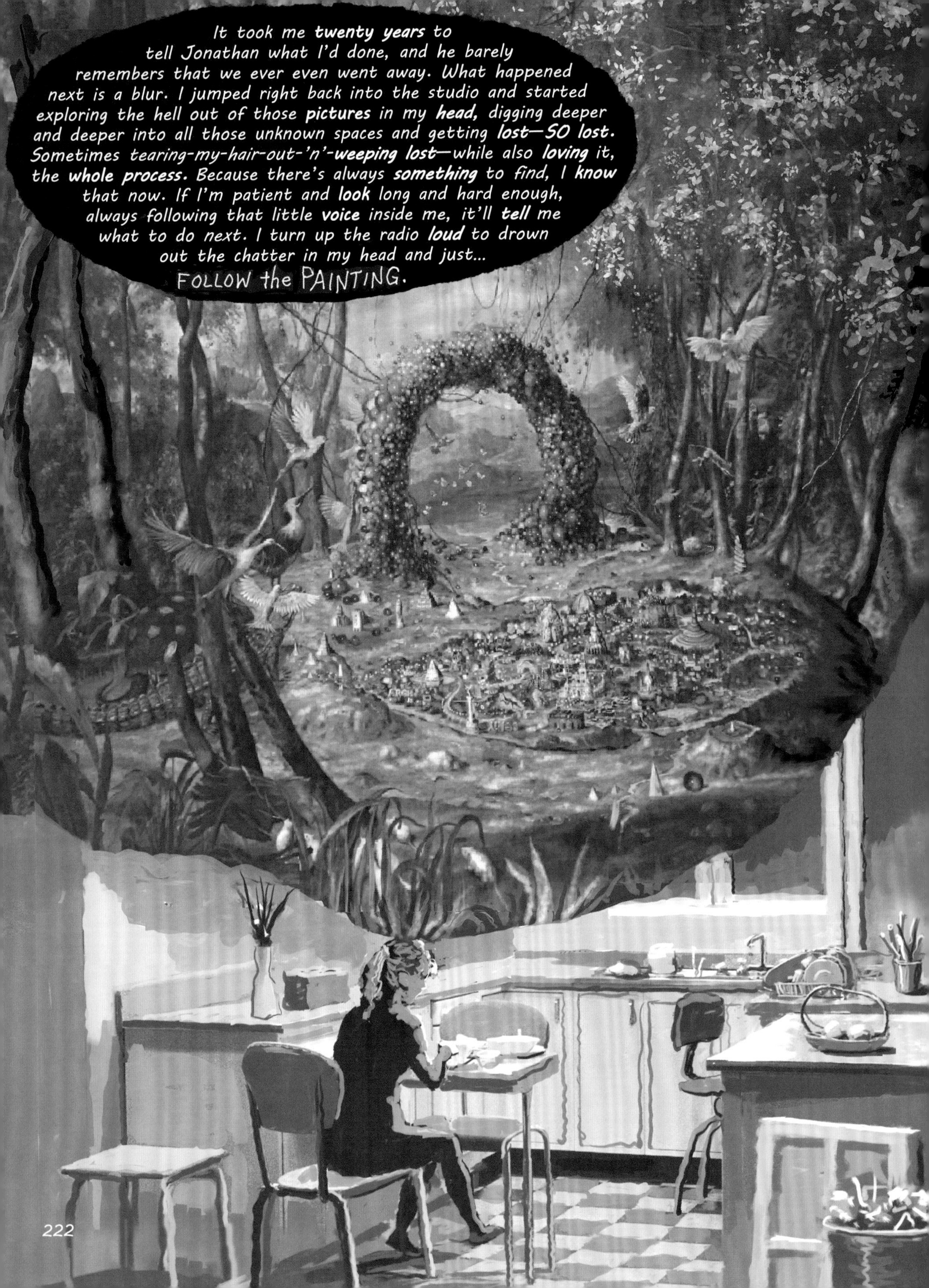
It took me twenty years to tell Jonathan what I'd done, and he barely remembers that we ever even went away. What happened next is a blur. I jumped right back into the studio and started exploring the hell out of those pictures in my head, digging deeper and deeper into all those unknown spaces and getting lost—SO lost. Sometimes tearing-my-hair-out-'n'-weeping lost—while also loving it, the whole process. Because there's always something to find, I know that now. If I'm patient and look long and hard enough, always following that little voice inside me, it'll tell me what to do next. I turn up the radio loud to drown out the chatter in my head and just...
FOLLOW the PAINTING.

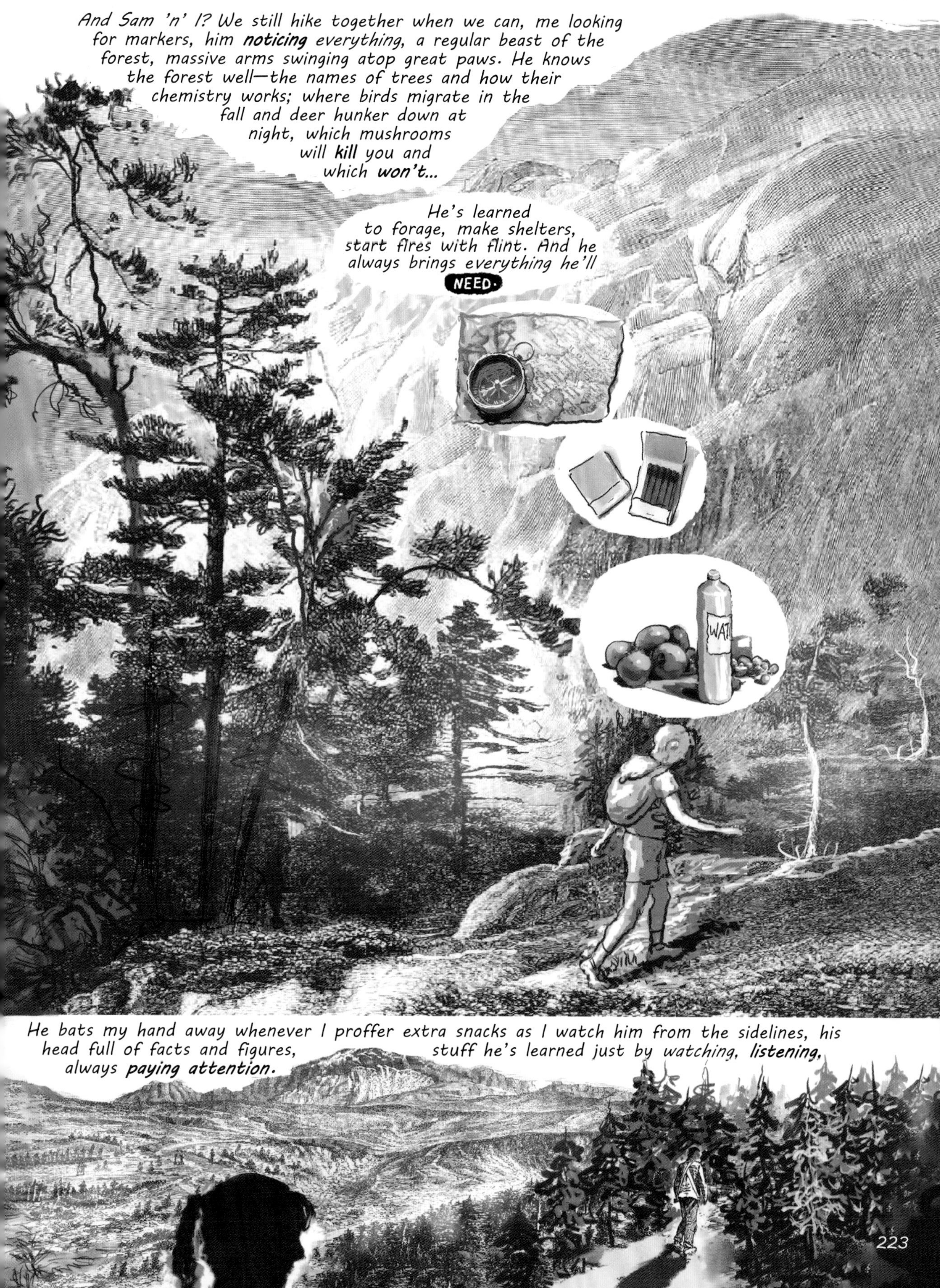
And Sam 'n' I? We still hike together when we can, me looking for markers, him **noticing** everything, a regular beast of the forest, massive arms swinging atop great paws. He knows the forest well—the names of trees and how their chemistry works; where birds migrate in the fall and deer hunker down at night, which mushrooms will **kill** you and which **won't...**
He's learned to forage, make shelters, start fires with flint. And he always brings everything he'll **NEED.**
He bats my hand away whenever I proffer extra snacks as I watch him from the sidelines, his head full of facts and figures, stuff he's learned just by watching, **listening,** always **paying attention.**

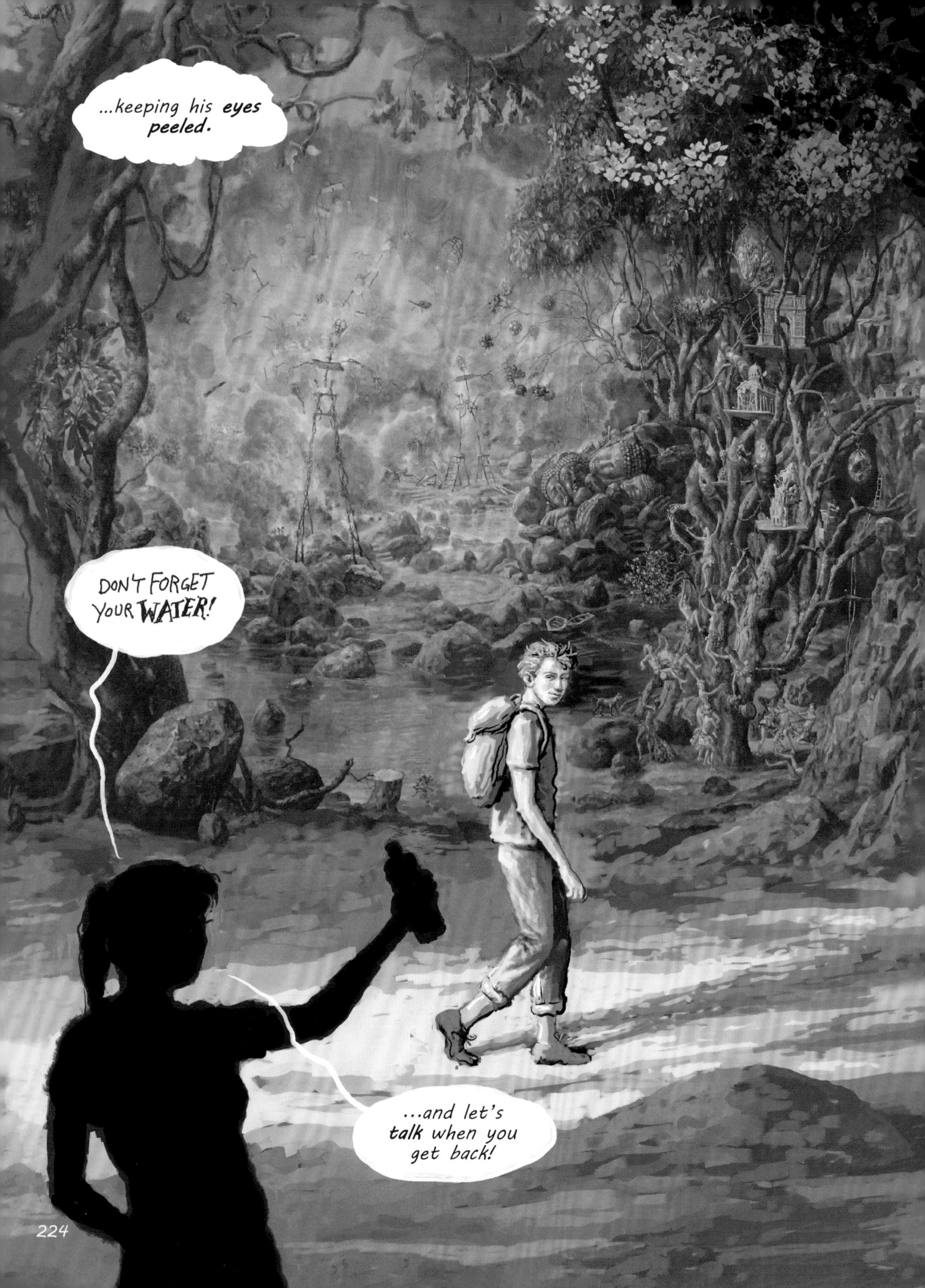
...keeping his eyes peeled.
DON'T FORGET YOUR WATER!
...and let's talk when you get back!

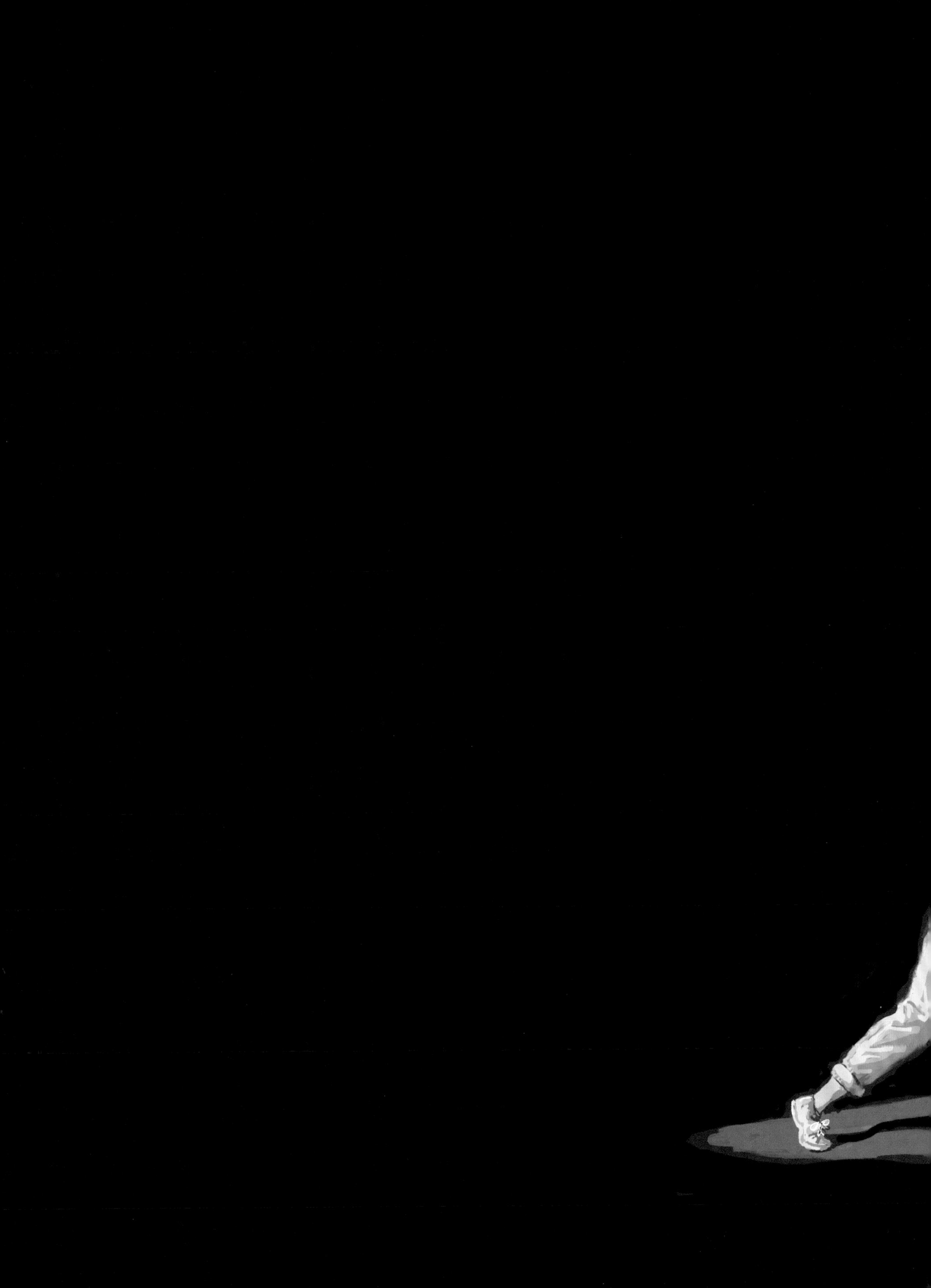

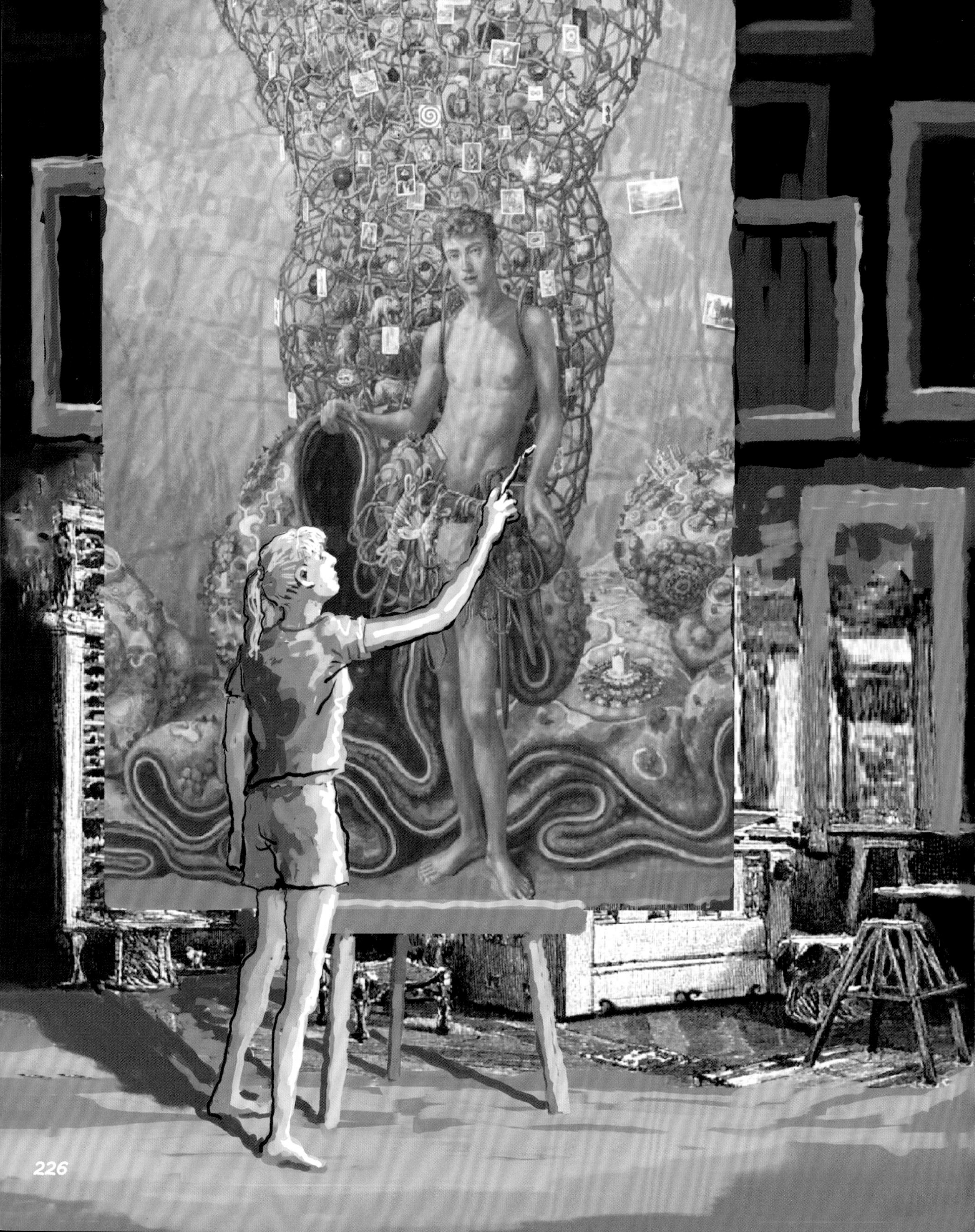

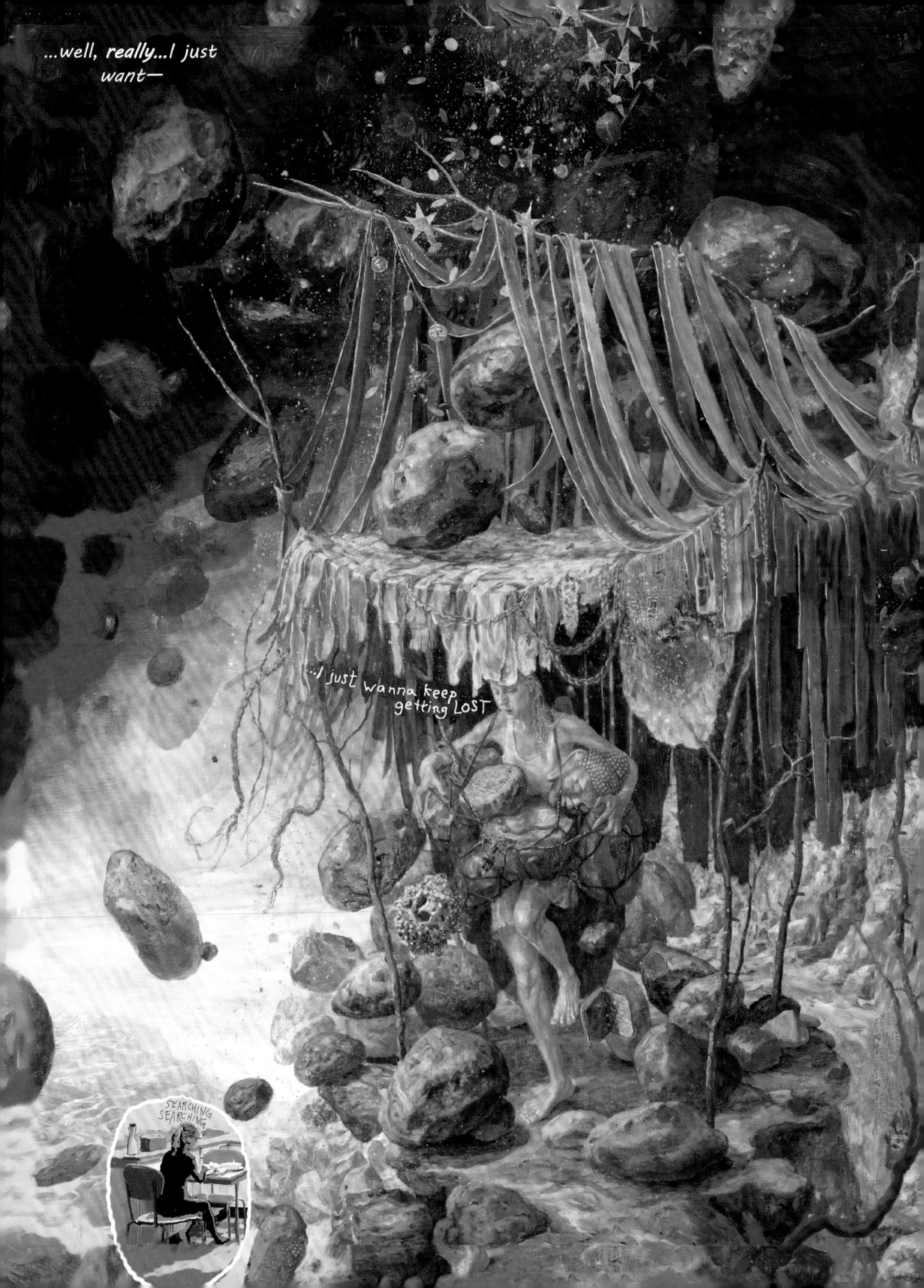
...well, really...I just want—
...I just wanna keep getting LOST
SEARCHING
SEARCHING

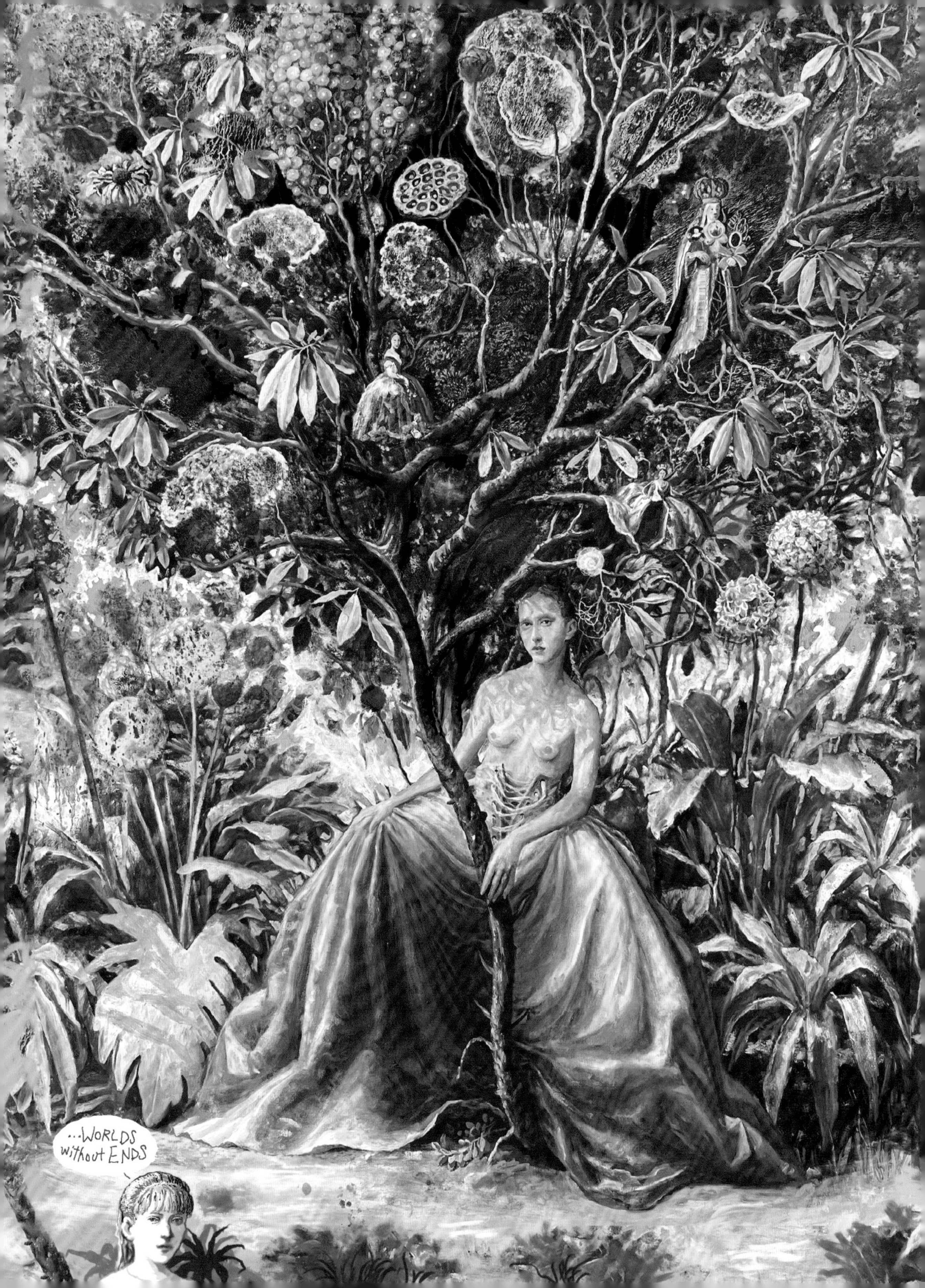
...WORLDS without ENDS

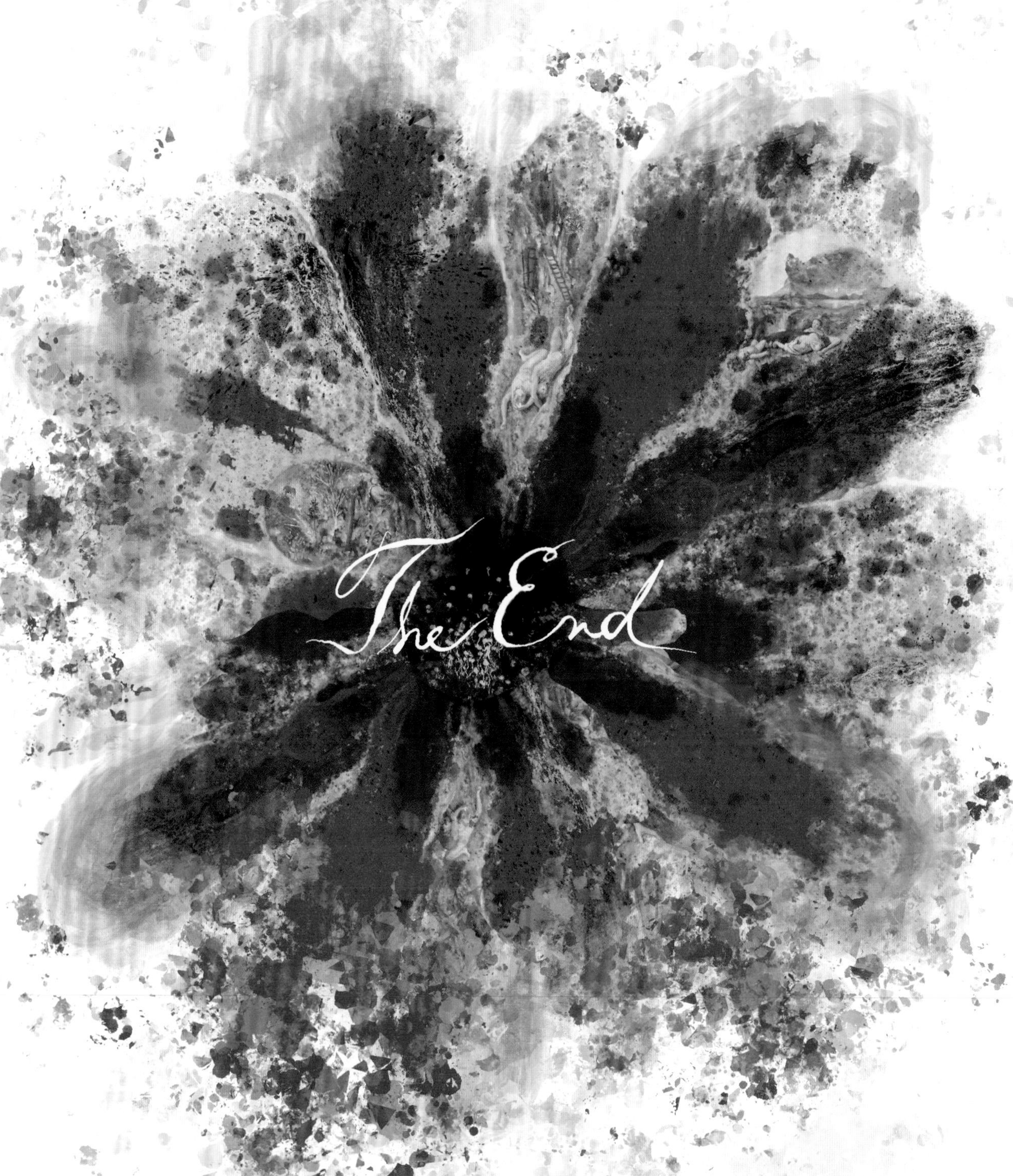
The End

NOTES ON PAINTINGS

Note: All paintings are by the author unless otherwise indicated.

Chapter 1

page 8 detail, *Last Resort* (2013), oil on canvas, 34 x 54 in., Private Collection
page 12 details, *Birth Painting* (1999), oil on canvas, 62 x 68 in., Private Collection; *Self-Portrait as Astyanax* (1999), oil on canvas, 66 x 90 in., Private Collection; *Self-Portrait as Mother/Child* (1999), oil on canvas, 74 x 60 in., Private Collection
page 13 detail, *Self-Portrait with Places to Go* (2009), oil on canvas, 70 x 68 in., Private Collection
page 17 detail, *Self-Portrait as Mad Queen* (2022), oil on canvas, 96 x 75 in., Courtesy of the artist
page 18 detail, *Great Acceleration* (2016), oil on canvas, 67 x 60 in., Courtesy of the artist
page 22 Albrecht Dürer, *Self-Portrait at the Age of Twenty Eight* (1500), oil on panel, 67.1 x 48.9 cm., Alte Pinakothek Bayerische Gemäldesammlungen, Munich, Germany
pages 26-27 Rogier van der Weyden, *Portrait of a Lady* (c. 1460), oil on panel, 33 ⅜ x 10 1/16 in., Andrew W. Mellon Collection
page 34 detail, *Self-Portrait as Snake Charmer* (2002), oil on canvas, 52 x 68 in., Private Collection
page 35 detail, *Self-Portrait as Floating Market* (1999), oil on canvas, 50 x 68 in., Private Collection

Chapter 2

page 45 detail, *Self-Portrait as Random Perfect Being* (1999), oil on canvas, 74 x 60 in., Private Collection
page 46 detail, *Self-Portrait as Shanty Town* (2014), oil on canvas, 67 x 44 in., Private Collection
page 51 detail, *Self-Portrait with Fabulous Droppings* (2005), oil on canvas, 72 x 60 in., Private Collection
page 53 detail, *Self-Portrait with Several Tiny Homes* (2009), oil on canvas, 68 x 54 in., Private Collection

Chapter 3

pages 58-59 Giotto di Bondone, *Massacre of the Innocents* (c. 1305), fresco, 200 x 185 cm., Scrovegni (Arena) Chapel, Veneto, Italy
page 64 Eugène Delacroix, *The Duc d'Orleans Showing His Mistress to the Duc de Bourgogne* (1825–1826), oil on canvas, 13.9 x 10 in., Thyssen-Bornemisza National Museum, Madrid, Spain
page 65 detail, *Self-Portrait as Big World* (2008), oil on canvas, 65 x 68 in., Private Collection
page 70 *Self-Portrait as Big World* (2008), oil on canvas, 65 x 68 in., Private Collection

Chapter 4

page 76 detail, *Self-Portrait as Tree House* (2010), oil on canvas, 68 x 65 in., Private Collection
page 77 *Self-Portrait as Tree House* (2010), oil on canvas, 68 x 65 in., Private Collection
page 79 *Self-Portrait as Broken Home* (2008), oil on canvas, 67 x 57 in., Private Collection
page 83 *Self-Portrait as Thing in the Forest II* (2002), oil on canvas, 80 x 78 in., Private Collection
page 86 detail, *Self-Portrait with Many Heads* (2020), oil on canvas, 24 x 18 in., Courtesy of the artist
page 87 detail, *Self-Portrait as Boy in Flight* (2010), oil on canvas, 52 x 68 in., Private Collection
page 88 *Self-Portrait as Wunderkabinett* (2003), oil on canvas, 78 x 60 in., Private Collection

Chapter 5

page 93 detail, *Self-Portrait as Gorgeous Tumor* (2005), oil on canvas, 68 x 56 in., Private Collection
pages 94-96 Pierre Bonnard, *Large Yellow Nude* (1931), oil on canvas, 107 x 107.3 cm., Private Collection; Pierre Bonnard: details, *Nude in Bathtub* (c. 1941–1946), 48 ¼ x 59 ¼ in., Carnegie Museum of Art, Pittsburgh, Penn.; *White Interior* (1932), 109.5 x 155.8 cm., Musée de Grenoble, France
page 102 *Self-Portrait as Luminous Body* (2004), oil on canvas, 61 x 57 in., Private Collection
pages 103-4 El Greco, *Portrait of Fray Hortensio Felix Paravicino* (1609), oil on canvas, 44.1 x 33.9 in., Museum of Fine Arts, Boston
page 105 *Self-Portrait as Radiant Host* (1999), oil on canvas, 83 x 82 in., Private Collection
page 106 detail and modified: *Self-Portrait as Tap Root* (2009), oil on canvas, 82 x 56 in., Private Collection
page 107 *Self-Portrait as Arms and the Men* (2006), oil on canvas, 82 x 60 in., Private Collection

Chapter 6

pages 116-17 Artemisia Gentileschi, *Judith Slaying Holofernes* (c. 1612–1630), oil on canvas, 78.33 x 64.13 in., Museo di Capodimonte, Naples, Italy
page 123 detail, Odilon Redon, *Buddha in His Youth* (1904), distemper on canvas, 159.8 x 121.1 cm., Van Gogh Museum, Amsterdam, the Netherlands; Francisco Goya, *Saturn Devouring His Son* (1820–1823), mixed media and mural transferred to canvas, 56.5 x 32 in., Museo Nacional del Prado, Madrid
page 124 *Great Acceleration* (2016), oil on canvas, 67 x 60 in., Private Collection
page 128 Lucas Cranach the Elder, *Judith with the Head of Holofernes* (c. 1530), oil on lime, 34.5 x 22.8 in., Kunsthistorisches Museum, Vienna, Austria
page 129 Peter Paul Rubens and attributed to Frans Snyders, *The Head of Medusa* (c. 1617), oil on canvas, 26.9 x 46.4 in., Kunsthistorisches Museum, Vienna, Austria; Pieter Brueghel the Elder, *The (Great) Tower of Babel* (c. 1563), oil on wood panel, 45 x 61 in., Kunsthistorisches Museum, Vienna, Austria
page 130 Diego Velázquez, *The Infanta Maria Theresa of Spain* or *The Infanta Maria Theresa aged 14* (1652–1653), oil on canvas, 50 x 38.8 in.; Kunsthistorisches Museum, Vienna, Austria
page 137 *Feast of Fools* (2019), oil on canvas, 68 x 66 in., Courtesy of the artist

Chapter 7

page 148 detail and modified: *Self-Portrait Cleaning House* (2012), oil on canvas, 60 x 68 in., Private Collection
page 151 *Self-Portrait in a Fiery Sea* (2002), oil on canvas, 60 x 52 in., Private Collection
page 152 *Study for Self-Portrait as Refuge* (2011), oil on canvas, 54 x 50 in., Private Collection

Chapter 8

pages 163-64 Peter Paul Rubens, *Rape of the Daughters of Leucippus* (c. 1618), oil on canvas, 88 x 82 in., Alte Pinakothek, Bayerische Gemäldesammlungen, Munich, Germany
page 166 *Self-Portrait as Thief who was Saved* (2011), oil on canvas, 84 x 112 in., Private Collection

Chapter 10

page 179 *Tender Trapper* (2010), oil on canvas, 66 x 60 in., Private Collection
page 183 *Self-Portrait in the Bedroom* (2003), oil on canvas, 67 x 60 in., Private Collection
page 188 *Self-Portrait as Postscript* (2007), oil on canvas, 67 x 56 in., Private Collection

Chapter 11

page 203 details, Artemisia Gentileschi, *Susanna and the Elders* (1610), oil on canvas, 67 x 47 in., Schloss Weissenstein, Pommersfelden, Germany
page 204 details, *Self-Portrait as Agnostic* (2003), oil on canvas, 68 x 58 in.; Private Collection; *Self-Portrait as Arms and the Men* (2006), oil on canvas, 82 x 60 in., Private Collection
pages 204-5 Johannes Vermeer, *Woman Holding a Balance* (c. 1664), oil on canvas, 16.7 x 15 in., National Gallery of Art, Washington, DC
page 209 *Self-Portrait as Infanta Maria Teresa Dreaming Madame de Sade* (1999), oil on canvas, 60 x 60 in., Private Collection

Chapter 12

page 222 detail, *Great Leap* (2010), oil on canvas, 68 x 72 in., Private Collection
page 224 detail, *Self-Portrait as Other Thief* (2013), oil on canvas, 76 x 96 in., Private Collection
page 226 detail, *Self-Portrait as Great Scout Leader* (2010), oil on canvas, 72 x 54 in., Private Collection
page 227 detail, *Self-Portrait with Sanctuary* (2021), oil on canvas, 102 x 76 in., Courtesy of the artist
page 228 *Spill (Victoria)* (2022), oil on canvas, 72 x 54 in., Courtesy of the artist

ACKNOWLEDGMENTS

There is some fact to this fiction and the other way around. Resemblances to anyone living or dead are purely coincidental.

THANK YOU to all my dear ones for your wisdom and insights: to Jonathan Kalb who helped me birth this manuscript from beginning to end, and to those who helped enormously with their multiple close readings—Oliver Kalb, Annice Jacoby, Virginia Pye, Lynne Buschman and Liz Budnitz. Much gratitude goes out to Ruth Marten for her unwavering encouragement and holy hand, and Virginia Wagner for helping me through so many technical meltdowns. Big thanks to those who offered comments and support along the way—Sam Kalb, John Ravenal, Lydia Stryk, Sarah Brooks, Loren Segan, Kyle Staver, Patty Horing, Rebecca Chace, Livia Alexander, Zachary Keeting, Chris Joy, Brian Fielding, and Anne Landsman; and especially to Kim Barker, for your strength and resilience and our long, ongoing, amazing friendship.

Thanks to my parents and siblings, who helped me see things more clearly.

To Sharon Horvath and James Siena, for the use of your beautiful artwork; and to Daniel Mason, for use of his flams and paradiddles.

And to all the great painters and their "Images of Wisdom," as well as those nineteenth-century landscape artists who loved the woods into everlastingness in their drawings, paintings, prints, and woodcuts, and whose visions helped me bring this manuscript to life.

Thank you to my agents, Lyn DelliQuadri and Jane Lahr, who saw promise in the manuscript; and the team at Algonquin, including Christopher Moisan and Jovanna Brinck.

My great thanks to Montclair State University and Dean Daniel Gurskis for supporting this project from the very outset.

And for believing in my story and willing it into life, a special thank you with ribbons and festoonery goes out to Algonguin editor and publisher, Betsy Gleick.

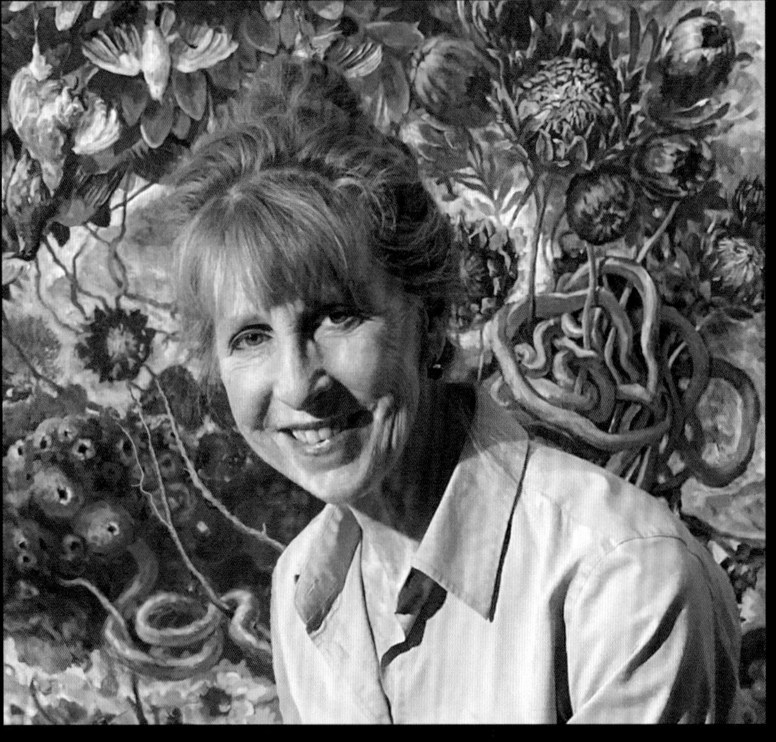

JULIE HEFFERNAN is a Professor of Fine Arts at Montclair State University and is represented by Hirschl & Adler Modern in New York and Catharine Clark Gallery in San Francisco. Heffernan has had over fifty solo exhibitions nationally and internationally and is the recipient of numerous grants, including an NEA, NYFA, and Fullbright Fellowship. Her work has been reviewed by major publications, including the *New York Times*, *Art in America*, and *Artforum*, and is in the collections of the Brooklyn Museum and VMFA, among others. She lives and works in Brooklyn, New York.